Lecture Notes in Computer Science 15722

Founding Editors

Gerhard Goos
Juris Hartmanis

AF148196

Series Editors

Elisa Bertino, *Purdue University, West Lafayette, IN, USA*
Wen Gao, *Peking University, Beijing, China*
Bernhard Steffen , *TU Dortmund University, Dortmund, Germany*
Moti Yung , *Columbia University, New York, NY, USA*

The series Lecture Notes in Computer Science (LNCS), including its subseries Lecture Notes in Artificial Intelligence (LNAI) and Lecture Notes in Bioinformatics (LNBI), has established itself as a medium for the publication of new developments in computer science and information technology research, teaching, and education.

LNCS enjoys close cooperation with the computer science R & D community, the series counts many renowned academics among its volume editors and paper authors, and collaborates with prestigious societies. Its mission is to serve this international community by providing an invaluable service, mainly focused on the publication of conference and workshop proceedings and postproceedings. LNCS commenced publication in 1973.

Sokratis Katsikas · Basit Shafiq
Editors

Data and Applications Security and Privacy XXXIX

39th IFIP WG 11.3 Annual Conference
on Data and Applications Security and Privacy, DBSec 2025
Gjøvik, Norway, June 23–24, 2025
Proceedings

 Springer

Editors
Sokratis Katsikas (iD)
Norwegian University of Science
and Technology
Gjøvik, Norway

Basit Shafiq (iD)
Lahore University of Management Sciences
Lahore, Pakistan

ISSN 0302-9743   ISSN 1611-3349 (electronic)
Lecture Notes in Computer Science
ISBN 978-3-031-96589-0   ISBN 978-3-031-96590-6 (eBook)
https://doi.org/10.1007/978-3-031-96590-6

This Springer imprint is published by the registered company Springer Nature Switzerland AG
The registered company address is: Gewerbestrasse 11, 6330 Cham, Switzerland

Preface

This book contains revised versions of the papers presented at the 39th edition of the Annual IFIP WG 11.3 Conference on Data and Applications urity and Privacy (DBSec 2025). The conference was held in Gjøvik, Norway, on June 23–24, 2025.

DBSec 2025 brought together researchers, practitioners, and experts from academia, industry, and government to share their cutting-edge findings and insights in all theoretical and practical aspects of data protection, privacy, and applications urity. DBSec 2025 attracted 59 high-quality submissions, each of which was assigned to 3 referees for single-blind review; the review process resulted in 19 full and 5 short papers accepted to be presented and included in the proceedings. The chairs and members of the Program Committee were neither involved with nor had visibility of the reviewing process of submissions authored or co-authored by them or with which conflict of interest existed. The accepted papers cover topics related to many aspects of information urity and privacy, ranging from AI applications in urity and privacy, to user and data privacy, to database and storage urity, to differential privacy, to attackers and attack detection, to access control & internal controls and audit process, to cryptography for urity and privacy. The conference program also included two keynote talks by Jaideep Vaidya (Rutgers University, USA) and Spyros Kokolakis (University of the Aegean, Greece).

We would like to express our thanks to all those who assisted us in organizing the event and putting together the program. We are very grateful to the members of the Program Committee and to the external reviewers for their timely and rigorous reviews. We also thank everyone who provided assistance and ensured a smooth organization process, particularly Günther Pernul and Vasileios Gkioulos for their efforts as General Chairs. Additionally, we acknowledge Sara Foresti (IFIP WG 11.3 chair) and Jaideep Vaidya for their guidance and support, Hafiz Asif (Publicity Chair) for his assistance with publicity, Lama Amro (Web Chair) for managing the conference web page, Linda Derawi (local organization chair) and Anne Hilde Ruen Nymoen for contributing to other conference arrangements. Last, but by no means least, we would like to thank all the authors who submitted their work to the conference and contributed to an interesting set of proceedings.

June 2025
Sokratis Katsikas
Basit Shafiq

Organization

General Chairs

Vasileios Gkioulos	Norwegian University of Science and Technology, Norway
Günther Pernul	Universität Regensburg, Germany

Program Chairs

Sokratis Katsikas	Norwegian University of Science and Technology, Norway
Basit Shafiq	Lahore University of Management Sciences, Pakistan

Publicity Chair

Hafiz Asif	Hofstra University, USA

Web Chair

Lama Amro	Norwegian University of Science and Technology, Norway

Local Organization Chair

Linda Derawi	Norwegian University of Science and Technology, Norway

Program Committee

Aida Akbarzadeh	Norwegian University of Science and Technology, Norway
Massimiliano Albanese	George Mason University, USA

Sandeep Pirbhulal	Norwegian Computing Center, Norway
Nikolaos Pitropakis	Edinburgh Napier University, UK
Indrajit Ray	Colorado State University, USA
Rodrigo Roman	University of Málaga, Spain
Pierangela Samarati	Università degli studi di Milano, Italy
Andreas Schaad	WIBU-Systems, Germany
Anoop Singhal	NIST, USA
Scott Stoller	Stony Brook University, USA
Shamik Sural	Indian Institute of Technology Kharagpur, India
Jaideep Vaidya	Rutgers University, USA
Lingyu Wang	Concordia University, Canada
Edgar Weippl	University of Vienna, Austria
Nicola Zannone	Eindhoven University of Technology, The Netherlands
Fei Zuo	University of Central Oklahoma, USA

External Reviewers

Cristina Alcaraz	University of Málaga, Spain
Thomas Baumer	University of Regensburg, Germany
Shir Buchner	Ben-Gurion University of the Negev, Israel
Thrasyvoulos Giannakopoulos	University of Piraeus, Greece
Dimitrios Kasimatis	Edinburgh Napier University, UK
Sascha Kern	University of Regensburg, Germany
Vasileios Kouliaridis	University of the Aegean, Greece
Zhuohang Li	Vanderbilt University, USA
Andreas Menegatos	University of the Aegean, Greece
Raphael Neudert	University of Regensburg, Germany
Ruben Rios	University of Málaga, Spain
Christos Smiliotopoulos	University of the Aegean, Greece

Contents

Attackers and Attack Detection

Access Control and Internal Controls and Audit Process

Cryptography for Security and Privacy

AI Applications in Security and Privacy

Jibber-Jabber!: Encoding the (Un-)Natural Language of Network Devices and Applications

Maxwel Bar-on[1], Kiley Krosky[1], Federico Larrieu[1],
Bruhadeshwar Bezawada[2(✉)], Indrakshi Ray[1], and Indrajit Ray[1]

[1] Colorado State University, Fort Collins, CO, USA
[2] Southern Arkansas University, Magnolia, AR, USA
bez.bru@gmail.com

Abstract. Modern networks are composed of a diverse group of devices and applications, all of which speak different protocols and exhibit varied network behaviors. Understanding these communication patterns is a critical requirement for a network security analyst to enforce effective access control against malicious behavior. The heterogeneity of devices, the diverse communication patterns and the lack of detailed documentation makes it harder to detect malicious behavior.

Towards this end, we model the network communication patterns akin to natural language and design a custom transformer architecture to provide the necessary comprehension. We use natural language processing (NLP) transformers for the analysis of network traffic flows, especially for those flows exhibiting high spatial contextualization and temporal correlation. Through extensive experiments, we demonstrate that our model provides a reasonably generic understanding of network flows when applied to solve critical network problems such as application identification, device-type fingerprinting and threat identification. We tested our approach on three diverse data sets with the following results: (a) IoT device-type fingerprinting, an average recall of 97%, (b) application identification, an average recall of 99.6% and (c) threat detection, an average recall of 97%.

Keywords: Network traffic modeling · Transformers · IoT fingerprinting · Application identification · Threat Detection

1 Introduction

1.1 Motivation

Modern organizational networks have become increasingly complex with a diverse set of connected computing devices and a large number of network appli-

This work was partially supported by NSF under Grant No. CNS 1822118 and CNS 2226232, Award Numbers DMS 2123761, the member partners of the NSF IUCRC Center for Cyber Security Analytics and Automation – AMI, NewPush, Cyber Risk Research, NIST and ARL, and also the State of Colorado Cybersecurity Center (#SB 18-086) and NIST Grant no. 60NANB23D152.

S. Katsikas and B. Shafiq (Eds.): DBSec 2025, LNCS 15722, pp. 3–22, 2025.
https://doi.org/10.1007/978-3-031-96590-6_1

cations. Managing the security of such complex networks is a major challenge for the network administrators as they need to be aware of the types of devices and applications present in the network. Accurate identification of the applications and devices helps to identify misbehaving devices and applications, and enforce necessary network access controls to protect the network. This task is challenging since the networks are composed of general computing devices and a significant ratio of Internet-of-Things (IoT) devices and smart devices running different types of applications and protocols.

One approach to identify the devices and applications is by generating a *"fingerprint"*, which is a meaningful representation of their communication patterns, from the network traffic traces they generate. However, the vast diversity in the networking protocols used by these devices and the complex communication patterns[1] of the applications make this a non-trivial task. We propose a solution to this problem and help network security administrators in their goal of securing their networks against internal and external threats.

1.2   Problem Statement

Our problem statement can be stated as the design of two algorithms: A_f, a fingerprinting algorithm and M, a matching algorithm described below. Without loss of generality, we use the terms *device* and *application* interchangeably.

System Definitions.   Formally, let $T_t : \{\rho_1, \rho_2, \cdots, \rho_n\}$ denote a fixed size network packet traffic trace captured at a time snapshot Δ_t, ρ_i denotes the ith packet in the trace, and $PROT$ is the set of protocols in the trace. A protocol element $prot \in PROT$ defines a relation R_i on the data and control fields of a packet in T_t. Therefore, $PROT$ is a collection of all such relations: $PROT : R_1 \times R_2 \times \cdots \times R_{|PROT|}$. By extension, packet ρ_i can be viewed as a subset of $PROT$ as each packet contains various protocols and their field values. A fingerprint F_s, of a device or application, is a concise representation that is generated out of a given network trace T_s captured at some random time snapshot s.

The fingerprinting problem is to design an algorithm A_f that generates a fingerprint F_s by taking as input a traffic trace $T_{\{s \in \Delta\}}$ and $PROT$ where Δ is the time duration of network trace collection. Now, if the same device generates another trace T_x, which is different from T_s, at another time-snapshot x, A_f can compute the fingerprint F_x of T_x. The fingerprint matching problem is to design a matching algorithm M that accurately compares the two fingerprints F_s and F_x, to confirm the identification of the same device.

1.3   Limitations of Prior Art

Several existing works [9,10,20] have addressed the extraction of grammar rules for network protocols and applied the results for classifying traffic, and identifying applications. Network traffic classification [2,3,12,15,16,23,27] is the task of

---

[1] *Jibber-Jabber* or Gibberish refers to incomprehensible speech patterns like speaking too fast or too slow and/or using strange vocabulary.

assigning sequences of packets to different categories based on their characteristics. Although the problem of network traffic classification is well studied, we focus only on solutions that proposed deep learning models and identify their shortcomings.

– *Bi-directional flow semantics and shortage of data.* Existing literature has focused on using IP flow-based semantics, especially bi-directional flows, i.e., incoming and outgoing packets of the same flow. However, from our observations and experiments, we found that many IoT devices and smart applications do not generate sufficient bi-directional data, which makes it difficult to apply many existing results in practice.
– *Related flow semantics.* We observed that a particular device or application typically generates several uni-directional flows to perform a specific task. We note that existing literature has not explored the relational semantics of such uni-directional flows, as most such flows would be considered independent and processed as such.
– *Lack of multi-class network classifiers.* We note that many existing methods perform poorly when classifying network data into multiple classes due to the constraints of the chosen deep learning model to learning the conversational features of the network traffic.

1.4   System and Threat Model

System Model. Our system consists of a group of IoT devices and smart applications running over an organizational network. The inward and outward traffic flows from these devices are subject to monitoring by the network administrator. The network administrator can perform deep analysis and enforce necessary access controls.

Threat Model. We consider the threats that cause devices and applications to exhibit significant deviation from their normally acceptable or understood behavior. For instance, if a device is compromised and is generating high amounts of traffic in contrast to its original specification, such a device needs to be detected and isolated. We also consider active threats into the network from external and internal actors who might be performing scanning, reconnaissance or malware injection via the network.

1.5   Proposed Approach

In our approach, to overcome the limitations in prior art, we model the network traffic packets as natural language data. For NLP, input samples are sequences of language "words"; whereas, for network traffic, input samples are sequences of packets. Compared to multi-variate time-series problems, such as weather forecasting, network traffic has a closer resemblance to natural language because each time step represents a single event instead of multiple interrelated events.

To address the first limitation of lack of bi-directional flow data, we consider packets within a specified window of view and process all flows within this window. This ensures that our method is not limited by the requirement of sufficient bi-directional flows from a device. To address the second limitation of relative flow semantics, we design *relative features*, which capture the relations among the various packets and flows within the same window. This ensures that we cover the case where a device uses several, seemingly unrelated, uni-directional flows for performing a certain task. Finally, to address the third limitation of multi-class classification, we choose the NLP transformer as our classification architecture because of its ability to encode relationships between words in a sentence. The transformer was originally developed for natural language translation [26], but has since been applied to other NLP tasks [6], including classification [21].

1.6 Key Contributions

Our contributions are summarized as follows:

– We describe a window based data model to create the analogy to natural language sentences and NLP transformers to solve the problem of network traffic analysis.
– We describe relative features for capturing the inter-dependencies of correlated uni-directional communications originating from a device.
– We describe a multi-class classification technique based on our approach and use it to address a few network security problems such as IoT device-type fingerprinting, application identification, and threat identification.
– We provide a comprehensive evaluation of our approach on real-world data sets.

Organization. The paper is organized as follows. Section 2 outlines background and related work. Section 3 describes our proposed approach and Sect. 4 describes our classification architecture. Section 5 discusses the performance on various tasks. Finally, Sect. 6 outlines our conclusions and future work.

2 Related Work

2.1 NLP Methods for Networking Problems

Bar et al. [2] use NLP techniques to distinguish between malicious and benign network traffic, and to identify the use of VPNs (Virtual Private Networks). They use a SimCSE-based model to extract vector representations of packets, then classify the vector embeddings using SVMs and Random Forests. Meng at al. [16] propose an architecture for producing high-quality latent representations of network packets to improve the performance of traffic classification tasks. The drawback of these approaches is their use of traffic features, such as IP addresses and encrypted payloads, which results in overfitting the deep-learning model. For example, a classification model may learn to associate IP addresses of packets with a particular class; however, the IP addresses in the training data will likely differ from unseen samples as they are assigned dynamically. In our work represents each packet as a single event, similar to words in a sentence.

2.2   IoT Fingerprinting

IoT-Portrait is a transformer-based architecture, proposed by Wang et al. [27], for identifying the types of IoT devices based on sequences of traffic generated by the devices. This architecture consists of a transformer encoder followed by a linear multinomial classifier. We use a similar approach to [27]; however, we introduce more meaningful features to increase the amount of useful information contained in packet-feature vectors.

Alioghli et al. [1] address the challenge of detecting anomalies in multivariate time-series data generated by IoT devices. The authors evaluate different positional encoding (PE) mechanisms in transformer networks, including Absolute PE, Rotary PE, and two modifications of Relative PE: Representative attention and Global attention. Msadek et al. [18] explore a machine learning approach to identify IoT devices based on encrypted traffic patterns. Their approach includes a segmentation technique using an adaptive sliding window, feature extraction from packet headers, and the evaluation of multiple machine learning classifiers such as k-Nearest Neighbors (KNN), Support Vector Machine (SVM), Random Forest (RF), AdaBoost, and Extra-Trees.

The IoTTFID [8] approach focuses on identifying new IoT devices by analyzing their network traffic fingerprints. It involves extracting device traffic fingerprints, converting them into feature vectors, and updating the original model to recognize new devices. Luo et al. [14] developed a novel IoT device-type identification framework based on transformer models to handle heterogeneous IoT traffic. In the first stage, they use a transformer-based traffic diagnosis model to classify traffic into normal and abnormal types. In the second stage, they employ another transformer-based model to identify the device type from the normal traffic, and improve accuracy with a results-ensemble algorithm.

Yin et al. [30] introduce GraphIoT, a method for IoT device detection that uses graph classifiers to analyze lightweight flow information like packet length, direction, and timestamp. This data is transformed into an IoT Device Traffic Graph Representation (IoT-DTGR), which is then classified using a Graph Neural Network (GNN) that considers node and edge features and subgraph structures.

2.3   Application Identification

A study done by Yamansavascilar et al. [29] focuses on identifying individual applications, such as Facebook, Twitter, and Skype, through network traffic classification using machine learning methods. Unlike previous studies, which classified applications into broad categories such as FTP, HTTP, VoIP, Instant Messaging (IM) or Streaming (Video, Music, or Gaming), this research aims to identify specific applications. The authors used the UNB ISCX Network Traffic dataset and their internal dataset to evaluate four classification algorithms: J48, Random Forest, k-Nearest Neighbors (k-NN), and Bayes Net.

Miskovic et al. [17] propose AppPrint, a system for automatically fingerprinting mobile applications. Traditional methods typically rely on app identifiers like

User-Agent fields or analytics services, but AppPrint can determine app identities from generic HTTP traffic, even when identifiers are not included.

The APPSNIFFER framework [19] addresses the limitations of existing mobile app fingerprinting systems referenced above like FlowPrint and AppScanner, when Virtual Private Networks (VPNs) are used. It uses a two-stage classification process: the first stage distinguishes VPN traffic from normal traffic, while the second stage identifies specific mobile apps using a stacked ensemble model combining Light Gradient Boosting Machine (LightGBM) and a FastAI library-based neural network.

AppScanner is a framework designed to fingerprint and recognize Android apps solely from encrypted network traffic [24]. By running apps on physical devices, AppScanner collects network traces, pre-processes them to separate individual app flows, and applies supervised learning for classification. Taylor et al. [25] extended this to develop a technique for recognizing smartphone apps through encrypted network traffic. The main enhancement is that it introduces ambiguity detection using reinforcement learning to handle common traffic from shared libraries like ads or analytics services.

The Fine-Grained Open-World Android App Fingerprinting (FOAP) approach [11] aims to identify method-level fine-grained user actions of Android apps when the apps are unknown to the system. It involves open-world app recognition by filtering out irrelevant traffic segments and uses a novel metric called structural similarity to focus on the necessary parts.

2.4   Threat Detection

Shaukat et al. [22] evaluates the performance of three primary classifiers - deep belief network (DBN), decision tree, and support vector machine (SVM), assessed on benchmark datasets such as KDD CUP 99, NSL-KDD, Spambase and Twitter dataset. The study found that DBN performs best for detecting spam, decision trees are most effective for intrusion detection, and SVM achieves the highest accuracy for malware classification.

Sarhan et al. [4] presents a machine learning-based approach for insider threat detection using the CERT insider threat dataset. It utilizes Deep Feature Synthesis (DFS) that automates feature engineering, resulting in 69,738 features, and then used PCA to mitigate dimensionality issues and determine the most important characteristics in the dataset.

3   Proposed Approach

3.1   Sliding Window Network Data Model

In our data model for network traffic, the network traces are divided into overlapping sequences of packets where each sequence is a *"sentence"* and each packet is a *"word"*. Our network datasets consist of .pcap files containing network traffic collected by recording packets transmitted over the relevant network interface. Input samples are generated by sliding a window of size w over the collected traffic and extracting 17 features, *standard* and *relative*, from each sub-sequence of w packets. For each packet ρ_t where $w < t \leq n$ is the index in a traffic trace of length n, this will yield an input sample $X \in \mathbb{R}^{w \times 17} = [\rho_{t-w}, \rho_{t-w+1}, \ldots, \rho_t]$. Each input sample is tagged with a corresponding label T_t, specifying the class of the sample. For most network datasets [3,5,13], we annotate samples using the labels of their corresponding .pcap files since each file is associated with a single class. Conversely, for the UNSW IoT dataset [23], we annotate samples using the known MAC addresses of IoT device-types connected to the UNSW network. We filter packets by their MAC address prior to applying the sliding-window approach to ensure that all packets in a window will be from the same device-type.

Our feature set includes 13 standard network features, as well as 4 relative features that are extracted through our novel relative encoding technique.

3.2 Standard Features

Standard features are extracted from each packet in a window. These features encode basic information about the protocol and payload of the packet and include a mixture of binary and continuous features as shown in Table 1. Payload Length and Payload Entropy are statistics describing the payload of a packet, while the remaining features are extracted from header fields.

Table 1. Packet Features

Feature	Explanation
Subnet Src	1 if source IP is in subnet else 0
Subnet Dst	1 if destination IP is in subnet else 0
Broadcast Dst	1 if destination IP is broadcast else 0
TLS	1 if packet includes TLS handshake header else 0
TCP	1 if packet includes TCP header else 0
UDP	1 if packet includes UDP header else 0
HTTP	1 if packet uses HTTP port else 0
SSL	1 if packet uses SSL port else 0
Common Src	1 if packet uses common source port else 0
Common Dst	1 if packet uses common dst port else 0
Header Length	length of transport-layer header (bytes)
Payload Length	length of payload (bytes)
Payload Entropy	information entropy of payload

3.3 Relative Features

Relative features are encoded representations of the endpoints of packets and are useful for capturing relationships among packets and flows within the window. To generate these features, we use a relative encoding scheme that maps

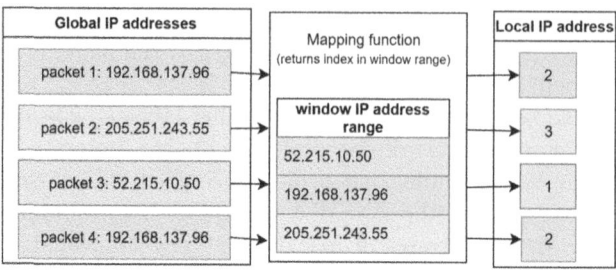

Fig. 1. Deriving relative feature values for an example endpoint-identifier (IP source address) in a window with 4 packets.

each endpoint-identifier field from a global scale to a local scale. Using a local scale preserves relationship information while reducing the dimensionality of our model and preventing overfitting. We interpret these as categorical features to avoid imposing any arbitrary ordering on the values within a local scale. Relative features include localized representations for each of the following four endpoint-identifier fields:
<source IP address, destination IP address, source port, destination port>.

These four fields act as a "flow-label" for each packet. Unlike the common approach of manually filtering packets based on flows prior to classification, flow-labels allow the model to identify relationships between packets within multi-flows. This is useful for understanding complex network behaviors that involve multiple overlapping flows.

As shown in Fig. 1, we use a mapping function to convert global endpoint-identifier values to a local scale. Let $S = \{P^{(1)}, P^{(2)}, \ldots, P^{(n)}\}$ be a window of n packets where each packet $P^{(j)} : (src\text{-}IP, dst\text{-}IP, src\text{-}prt, dst\text{-}prt)$ is defined as a four-tuple containing the packet's endpoint-identifiers. To obtain the relative features for a packet, we use the mapping function $R(P^{(j)}, S) \rightarrow \mathbb{Z}^4$. We define the mapping function for endpoint-identifier field i of packet $P^{(j)}$ as follows:

$$R(P^{(j)}, S)_i = \left| \{k \leq P_i^{(j)} \mid k \in \pi_i(S)\} \right| \tag{1}$$

where $P_i^{(j)}$ is the global value of the ith endpoint-identifier field for packet $P^{(j)}$ and $\pi_i(S)$ is the set of unique values for the field i found in window S. Essentially, the mapping function counts the number of unique values for field i in window S that are less than or equal to $P_i^{(j)}$.

Justification of Relative Features. Relative encoding preserves semantic properties that allow a deep-learning model to identify relationships between packets in a sequence. These relationships enhance the model's understanding of multi-packet behaviors contained in a traffic trace, which improves its decision making. Due to the size of the global scales for endpoint-identifiers, there is minimal overlap between the unique sets of values associated with different classes of traffic in the available training data. As a result, using global values will cause the model to become reliant on endpoint-identifiers for assigning labels to traffic samples. This is undesirable because unseen samples of traffic won't necessarily use the exact same global endpoint-identifiers observed in the training data, causing the model to misclassify them. Relative features are less rigid, which prevents the model from memorizing correlations between endpoint-identifiers and traffic labels. By mapping values to a local scale, we ensure that classes in the training data cannot be uniquely identified by their endpoint-identifiers. This teaches the model to use flow-labels for finding relationships between packets.

Illustrative Example. To illustrate how relative features can reveal relationships, we use an example window S of five packets ($|S| = 5$) with the following endpoint-identifiers and relative features:

- $R\left(P^{(1)} : (192.168.137.96, \ 205.251.243.55, \ 42000, \ 443), \ S\right) = [1, 2, 3, 2]$
- $R\left(P^{(2)} : (205.251.243.55, \ 192.168.137.96, \ 443, \ 42000), \ S\right) = [2, 1, 1, 3]$
- $R\left(P^{(3)} : (192.168.137.96, \ 205.251.243.55, \ 45000, \ 137), \ S\right) = [1, 2, 4, 1]$
- $R\left(P^{(4)} : (192.168.137.96, \ 205.251.243.55, \ 42000, \ 443), \ S\right) = [1, 2, 3, 2]$
- $R\left(P^{(5)} : (192.168.137.96, \ 205.255.4.123, \ 40000, \ 137), \ S\right) = [1, 3, 2, 1]$

Based on these features, we can see that $P^{(1)}$ and $P^{(4)}$ belong to the same unidirectional network flow, $P^{(2)}$ is the only incoming packet, $P^{(3)}$ is communicating with the same host machine as $P^{(1)}$ and $P^{(4)}$ but is part of a separate flow, and $P^{(5)}$ is using the same type of service as $P^{(3)}$ (audio/video streaming) but on a different host machine. We can estimate the relationships between packets in this example by calculating the attention, as described in the transformer architecture in [26], between indicator-variable representations of relative features for each packet, a common machine-learning technique for representing categorical values. We note that, we only use indicator-variables for illustrating how the attention mechanism identifies relationships between packets. In our architecture, we implement relative features as lookup-table indices instead to reduce storage and computational overhead.

Let $\delta(P^{(j)}, S) \in \{0, 1\}^{4*|S|}$ be a vector containing the indicator-variable representations for each relative feature of a packet $P^{(j)} \in S$ defined as:

$$\delta(P^{(j)}, S) = \left[\mathbb{I}\left(R(P^{(j)}, S)_1\right) \| \ldots \| \mathbb{I}\left(R(P^{(j)}, S)_4\right)\right] \qquad (2)$$

where $\mathbb{R}^m \| \mathbb{R}^n \to \mathbb{R}^{m+n}$ is the element-wise concatenation of vectors and $\mathbb{I}(v) \to \{0, 1\}^{|S|}$ returns the indicator-variable representation for an endpoint-identifier value v as follows:

$$\mathbb{I}(v)_i = \begin{cases} 1 & \text{if } i = v \\ 0 & \text{else} \end{cases} \qquad (3)$$

Using these representations, we calculate an attention matrix M for S using the attention operation [26] as follows:

$$M_{i,j} = \frac{e^{\left(\sum_k^{4\,|S|} \delta(P^{(i)},S)_k * \delta(P^{(j)},S)_k\right)}}{\sum_h^{|S|} e^{\left(\sum_k^{4\,|S|} \delta(P^{(i)},S)_k * \delta(P^{(h)},S)_k\right)}} \tag{4}$$

We show the attention matrix M for this example in Table 2. This matrix shows that the attention scores between packets is higher when the packets are related. $P^{(2)}$ has a high attention score with itself because it is the only incoming packet. The attention values along the diagonal are smaller for outgoing packets because there are more of them in the window. The attention values between $P^{(1)}$ and $P^{(4)}$ are relatively high, reflecting the strong relationship between packets in the same uni-directional flow.

Table 2. Attention matrix.

	$P^{(1)}$	$P^{(2)}$	$P^{(3)}$	$P^{(4)}$	$P^{(5)}$
$P^{(1)}$	0.4538	0.0083	0.0614	0.4538	0.0226
$P^{(2)}$	0.0171	0.9317	0.0171	0.0171	0.0171
$P^{(3)}$	0.0950	0.0129	0.7021	0.0950	0.0950
$P^{(4)}$	0.4538	0.0083	0.0614	0.4538	0.0226
$P^{(5)}$	0.0397	0.0146	0.1080	0.0397	0.7979

4   Transformer Architecture for Traffic Classification

Our architecture consists of three modules: an embedding layer, a Transformer encoder, and a fully-connected neural network classifier as shown in Fig. 2.

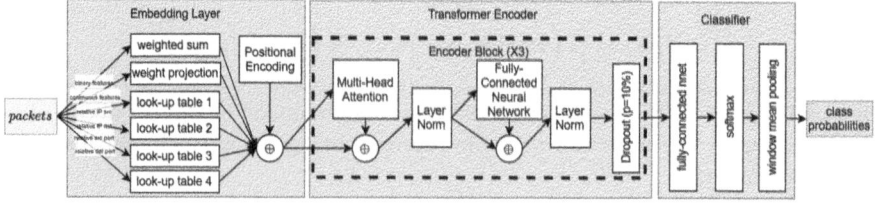

Fig. 2. Classification Architecture.

4.1   Embedding Layer

The purpose of the embedding layer is to produce representations of input samples in a lower-dimensional continuous vector space [26] that encodes desired semantic properties. This layer is responsible for handling the heterogeneous packet features, allowing the encoder and classifier to operate on homogeneous representations.

Given a packet feature vector $X \in \mathbb{R}^{17}$, where $X_{1 \leq j \leq 10} \in \{0,1\}^{10}$ are binary standard features, $X_{11 \leq j \leq 13} \in \mathbb{R}^3$ are continuous standard features, and $X_{14 \leq j \leq 17} \in \mathbb{Z}^4$ are relative features, this layer will produce a vector $E \in \mathbb{R}^d$, where d is the embedding dimensionality of the model.

The embedding layer is configured to handle each subspace of X according to the type of features in that region. The layer produces a d-dimensional embedding vector for each region, which are combined through element-wise addition.

For binary features $(X_{1 \leq j \leq 10})$, the embedding layer uses a learnable weight matrix $\mathbb{W}^{(b)} \in \mathbb{R}^{10 \times d}$ and produces an embedding vector $E^{(b)} \in \mathbb{R}^d$ as follows:

$$E_i^{(b)} = \sum_{j=1}^{10} \begin{cases} \mathbb{W}_{j,i}^{(b)} & \text{if } X_j = 1 \\ 0 & \text{if } X_j = 0 \end{cases} \tag{5}$$

For continuous features $(X_{11 \leq j \leq 13})$, the embedding layer uses a learnable weight matrix $\mathbb{W}^{(c)} \in \mathbb{R}^{3 \times d}$ and produces an embedding vector $E^{(c)} \in \mathbb{R}^d$ as:

$$E_i^{(c)} = \sum_{j=11}^{13} \mathbb{W}_{j,i}^{(c)} * X_j \tag{6}$$

Finally, the categorical relative features $(X_{14 \leq j \leq 17})$ are handled using a set of 4 lookup-tables implemented as a tensor $\mathbb{W}^{(r)} \in \mathbb{R}^{4 \times w \times d}$ with one weight matrix per relative feature where the number of rows is equivalent to the number of categories for the corresponding feature and the number of columns is equal to d. Finally, the categorical relative features $(X_{14 \leq j \leq 17})$ are handled using a set of 4 lookup-tables implemented as a tensor $\mathbb{W}^{(r)} \in \mathbb{R}^{4 \times w \times d}$, where each slice $\mathbb{W}_i^{(r)}$ is a weight matrix corresponding to a relative feature i. The number of rows in $\mathbb{W}_i^{(r)}$ is equivalent to the number of values in the local range for i and the number of columns is equal to d. Lookup-tables are used by returning the row corresponding to a relative feature value. The selected row vectors from each table are combined through element-wise addition. We set the number of rows to the window size (w) for all lookup-tables since this is the maximum possible number of unique values for a particular endpoint-identifier that may be observed in a window of w packets. Therefore, each relative feature will be in the range $[1, w]$. For the relative features, the embedding layer will produce a vector $E^{(r)} \in \mathbb{R}^d$ as follows:

$$E_i^{(r)} = \sum_{j=14}^{17} \mathbb{W}_{j-13,X_j,i}^{(r)} \tag{7}$$

Putting it all together, the output of the embedding layer is defined as:

$$E = E^{(r)} \oplus E^{(c)} \oplus E^{(b)} \oplus PE_t \tag{8}$$

where $\oplus$ denotes the element-wise addition of two vectors, $PE \in \mathbb{R}^{w \times d}$ is a fixed positional encoding [26], and t is the index of packet X in its associated window.

Lookup-tables allow us to store categorical variables as integers instead of one-hot-vectors while maintaining orthogonal separation of categories. Let v be a relative feature value with corresponding lookup-table $\mathbb{W} \in \mathbb{R}^{w \times d}$. The indicator-variable representation $\mathbb{I}(v) \in \{0,1\}^d$ of v is defined according to Eq. 3. Our lookup-table approach will represent v as the row-vector $\mathbb{W}_v \in \mathbb{R}^d$, which is equivalent to taking the dot-product of $\mathbb{I}(v)$ and $\mathbb{W}$:

$$\mathbb{W}_{v,i} = \sum_j^w \mathbb{W}_{j,i} \mathbb{I}(v)_i \tag{9}$$

Therefore, this representation preserves the following orthogonality property of the categorical variables: $\sum_j^w \mathbb{I}(a)_j \mathbb{I}(b)_j = 0$ if $a \neq b$ where a and b are examples of a relative feature with w categories.

We note that, although $d > 17$, we consider the embedding space to be lower-dimensional because each relative feature carries the same amount of information as a $[w]$-dimensional one-hot vector. The true feature dimensionality is $13 + 4w$; consequently, the total number of learnable parameters in the embedding layer is $d(13 + 4w)$, which represents the number of parameters used to map packets from a $[13 + 4w]$-dimensional heterogeneous representation to a $[d]$-dimensional continuous representation. Given an input window $X \in \mathbb{R}^{w \times 17}$, this layer will produce an embedding sequence $E \in \mathbb{R}^{w \times d}$, which is input to the Transformer encoder module. Please see Appendix 1 for details of encoding and Appendix 2 for details of the classifier.

4.2 Training

We jointly train all components of our architecture to minimize the negative-log-likelihood loss between the classifier's predictions and the true labels of our training samples. Let C be the set of classes, $X \in \mathbb{R}^{n \times w \times 17}$ be a batch of n samples with labels $T \in \{0,1\}^{n \times |C|}$ defined as:

$$T_{i,j} = \begin{cases} 1 & \text{if } class(X_i) = C_j \\ 0 & otherwise \end{cases} \tag{10}$$

Now let $f(X; \theta) \to P$ be a model parameterized by θ, that, when given X, will produce probabilities $P \in [0,1]^{n \times |C|}$ over C. We define our loss function $\mathcal{L}(P, T)$ as:

$$\mathcal{L}(P, T) = \frac{-1}{n|C|} \sum_i^n \sum_j^{|C|} T_{i,j} \ln(P_{i,j}) \tag{11}$$

Using this, we train our model by approximating the optimization problem:

$$\theta \approx \min_{\theta} (\ \mathcal{L}\left(f(X;\theta),T\right)\ ) : \forall (X,T) \in D_{tr} \tag{12}$$

where $D_{tr} \subset D$ is the set of all window-label pairs in the training data and D is the set of collected data.

We train our model using *Adam* on the training data with an initial learning rate of 0.01 for a maximum of $10,000$ epochs and evaluate $\mathcal{L}$ on a validation set $(D_{val} \subset D)$ after every epoch, saving the model's parameters if the loss is lower than the previous lowest validation loss. If the validation loss does not improve for 15 epochs, we decay the learning rate by a factor of $3\times$ and halt the training if the learning rate decays below the threshold 0.0001. After training, we evaluate the model on the test set $(D_{te} \subset D)$ using the parameters that achieved the lowest validation loss. Our data-partitioning process ensures that these subsets of D will have no overlap $(D_{val} \cap D_{tr} \cap D_{te} = \{\emptyset\})$ to ensure a fair evaluation of trained models and prevent overfitting through validation-set guided training.

5   Performance Evaluation

We evaluate our approach for network traffic classification on three tasks:

1. IoT fingerprinting: identifying the type of an unknown IoT device
2. Application identification: determining the identity of an application
3. Threat detection: determining whether a process is malicious or benign

For each task, we evaluate our approach by training and testing our model using 5-fold cross validation and report the average classification metrics over all folds. We use a 7:1:2 (train : validation : test) ratio for data partitioning.

5.1   Task and Architecture Details

Table 3. Sizes of datasets for each task.

Task	IoT	Application	Threat
Data Size(MB)	0.67	1.38	1.38
# samples	$302,451$	$191,979$	$191,979$
# classes	19	9	2

In Table 3, we show the size of the datasets used for each task. For IoT fingerprinting, our dataset consists of $302,451$ total windows from 19 unique IoT device-types, combining data from 3 sources: Colorado State University [3] (2 device-types), Canadian Institute of Cybersecurity [5] (5 device-types), and University of New South Wales [23] (12 device-types). we only include device-types with at least $10,000$ packets from each source. For the Application Identification task, we use $191,979$ windows from 9 different applications extracted from the public USTC-TFC dataset [13]. In this dataset, 6 applications are benign while 3 are compromised by malware. We also use the USTC-TFC dataset for the threat detection task; however, we treat this as a binary classification problem, rather than a multinomial classification problem. For threat detection, we label samples from the 6 benign applications as 'benign' and samples from the 3 compromised applications as 'malicious'.

Table 4. Architecture Hyperparameter configurations for each task

	Task	IoT	Application	Threat
Hyperparameter	Window Size	32	100	100
	Heads	4	4	4
	attention dim	16	32	16
	embedding dim	40	40	40
	$\alpha^{(h)}$ Dropout	10%	0.0%	10.0%

We explore a variety of different hyperparameter values to discover the optimal configurations of our architecture for each task. In Table 4, we show the window size, number of heads (H), attention dimensionality (u), embedding dimensionality (d), and dropout rate applied to the outputs of each head during training. We also apply dropout with a rate of 10% to the output of each encoder block for all tasks.

5.2 Performance

Table 5. Average Recall, Precision, Accuracy on each task with all features vs. standard features

	Features	IoT		Application		Threat	
		all	standard	all	standard	all	standard
Metric	Recall	97.11	96.0	99.64	97.84	97.32	96.77
	Precision	97.13	96.06	99.38	97.71	96.93	96.14
	Accuracy	97.07	95.95	99.6	97.85	96.74	96.07

In this section, we evaluate the performance of our approach on our selected network classification tasks. For each task, we evaluate our architecture with and without relative features to outline the benefits of including relative features for identifying relationships between packets (Table 5).

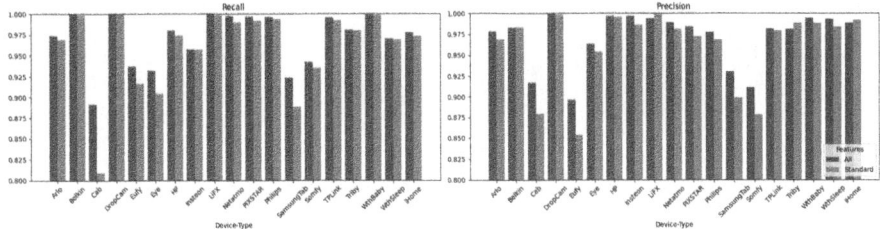

Fig. 3. Performance on IoT fingerprinting task. The blue bars show the performance with all 13 features and the orange bars with standard features. (Color figure online)

IoT Fingerprinting Results. Our architecture achieves a strong performance on the IoT fingerprinting task. As shown in Table 6, we achieve an average device identification rate (recall) over 97%, which demonstrates that our model is able to correctly identify the majority of IoT traffic samples. If a fingerprinting model is used for security profiling, it is important to maintain a high recall score to ensure correct identification of insecure device-types on a network. Meanwhile, we achieve a precision of 0.9713 which shows that the model's predictions are reliable. If a fingerprinting model is used for access control, it is important to maintain a high precision score because, otherwise, it may impose incorrect access-control policies on device-types. Without relative features, the average precision is reduced by 1.1% while the recall is reduced by 1.14%. The performance improvement from using relative features is particularly evident in complex device-types such as "Cab" and "Eufy" as shown in Fig. 3. With relative features, the model is able to understand the complex network behaviors of these device-types. These results demonstrate the potential of relative features for improving the performance and reliability of IoT fingerprinting models.

Application Identification. Our model performs well for application identification for the nine (9) applications considered with an average recall of 99.6%. These results also show the importance of relative features as the difference in performance is over 5% for some applications. Since applications have more complex communication patterns, it stands to reason that relative features have a higher bearing on the results (Fig. 4).

Threat Detection. Our approach performs well for threat detection as shown in Table 6. Our model is capable of identifying threats with over 99% recall. For threat detection, the inclusion of relative features does show improvement on average, increasing F1 scores for both classes. We note that, a detailed empirical or experimental comparison to existing approaches is not provided in the interest of space.

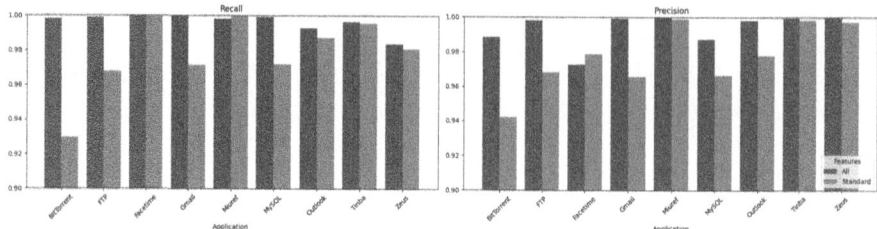

Fig. 4. Performance on the Application Identification task. The blue bars show the performance with all 13 features and the orange bars with standard features. (Color figure online)

Table 6. Performance on the Threat Detection task with all features vs. only standard features.

	Features	Benign		Malicious	
		all	standard	all	standard
Metric	Recall	0.95	0.94	0.996	0.995
	Precision	0.998	0.997	0.941	0.926
	F1	0.973	0.968	0.968	0.959

6 Conclusion and Future Work

In this work, we focused on the problem of network traffic classification using NLP style data modeling and techniques. Leveraging the NLP data model, we described relative encoding of packets found within a window of observation, enabling us to capture flow semantics more effectively. We used a transformer architecture to experiment on three diverse applications: IoT device-type fingerprinting, application identification and threat detection, and achieved high performance across various metrics of importance. Relative features resulted in significant improvement in results, between 2–6% across several classes of traffic. We were able to demonstrate that relative features capture some general characteristics of network traffic flows. In the future, we envisage that our data model and features will result in more applications within the network traffic analysis domain. Development of different types of transformer models, for diverse data sets, may also be an active area for exploration.

Appendix 1   Transformer Encoder

We use a Transformer encoder similar to the encoder described in the machine translation architecture described by Vaswani *et al.* [26]. This module receives the output of the embedding layer and applies a series of alternating attention and fully-connected neural network sub-layers, surrounded by residual connections and layer normalizations. Each of these sub-layers is contained in an encoder block and the encoder component includes 3 of these blocks. The attention sub-layers capture temporal relationships between packets, fully-connected sub-layers prevent embeddings in a window from converging [7], residual connections increase the strength of gradient signals to deeper layers and normalization [28] ensures the stability of gradients during training. We use the superscript notation $E^{(n)}$ to refer to embedding sequences where the superscript (n) denotes the position of the embedding in the stack of encoder blocks. For example, the input to the first block is the output of the embedding layer $E^{(1)}$, while the output of the first block and input to the second block is $E^{(2)}$.

In each block, the attention sub-layer has learnable weights $\mathbb{W}^{(Q)}, \mathbb{W}^{(K)}$, $\mathbb{W}^{(V)} \in \mathbb{R}^{d \times u}$, $\mathbb{W}^{(m)} \in \mathbb{R}^{u \times d}$ and biases $\mathbb{B}^{(Q)}, \mathbb{B}^{(K)}, \mathbb{B}^{(V)} \in \mathbb{R}^{u}$, $\mathbb{B}^{(m)} \in \mathbb{R}^{d}$ where u is the total dimensionality of all attention heads. Let $E^{(n)} \in \mathbb{W}^{w \times d}$ be the input to encoder block n. The attention sub-layer first applies three affine transformations (Query, Key, Value) to the input, which are then split into H $\left[\frac{u}{H}\right]$-dimensional subspaces where H is the number of attention heads. Using multiple heads allows the attention layer to identify multiple separate relationship patterns for each packet which improves the modeling capabilities of the transformer. Let $Q^{(h)}, K^{(h)}, V^{(h)} \in \mathbb{R}^{w \times \frac{u}{H}}$ be the Query, Key, and Value transformations respectively obtained using the attention sub-layer's learnable parameters as follows:

$$Q^{(h)} = E^{(n)} \mathbb{W}^{(Q)}_{*,(\frac{hu}{H} < i < \frac{(h+1)u}{H})} + \mathbb{B}^{(Q)}$$
$$K^{(h)} = E^{(n)} \mathbb{W}^{(K)}_{*,(\frac{hu}{H} < i < \frac{(h+1)u}{H})} + \mathbb{B}^{(K)} \qquad (13)$$
$$V^{(h)} = E^{(n)} \mathbb{W}^{(V)}_{*,(\frac{hu}{H} < i < \frac{(h+1)u}{H})} + \mathbb{B}^{(V)}$$

where $M_{*,(\frac{hu}{H} < i < \frac{(h+1)u}{H})}$ is an indexing operation that returns all rows of a matrix M and columns $\frac{hu}{H}$ through $\frac{(h+1)u}{H}$. The attention operation is then applied over each head as follows:

$$\alpha^{(h)} = softmax(\frac{Q^{(h)} K^{(h)T}}{\sqrt{\frac{u}{H}}}) V^{(h)} \qquad (14)$$

The attention values for all heads are concatenated and combined through a fourth affine transformation as follows:

$$Z = [\alpha^{(1)} \| \alpha^{(2)} \| \dots \| \alpha^{(H)}] \mathbb{W}^{(m)} + \mathbb{B}^{(m)} \qquad (15)$$

Finally, the combined value is added to the input and normalized to produce the output of the attention sub-layer $A \in \mathbb{R}^{w \times d}$ as:

$$A = LayerNorm(Z \oplus E^{(n)}) \qquad (16)$$

where $LayerNorm$ is defined as:

$$LayerNorm(X)_{i,j} = \frac{X_{i,j} - \mu(X_{*,j})}{\sigma(X_{*,j})} \qquad (17)$$

and $\mu(X_{*,j})$ and $\sigma(X_{*,j})$ return the mean and standard deviation of the jth feature of X respectively.

The fully-connected layer of each block has learnable weights $\mathbb{W}^{(h)}, \mathbb{W}^{(o)} \in \mathbb{R}^{d \times d}$ and biases $\mathbb{B}^{(h)}, \mathbb{B}^{(o)} \in \mathbb{R}^d$. This sub-layer receives the output of the attention sub-layer and produces the value $Z \in \mathbb{R}^{w \times d}$ defined as:

$$Z = max(0, A\mathbb{W}^{(h)} + \mathbb{B}^{(h)})\mathbb{W}^{(o)} + \mathbb{B}^{(o)} \tag{18}$$

This is followed by an additional residual connection and normalization to produce the output of the nth encoder block $E^{(n+1)} \in \mathbb{R}^{w \times d}$ as follows:

$$E^{(n+1)} = LayerNorm(Z \oplus A) \tag{19}$$

This becomes the input to the subsequent encoder block $n+1$ unless n is the final block in the stack ($n = 3$), in which case, it becomes the input to the classifier module $E^{(4)}$.

Appendix 2   Classifier

The classifier module is a fully-connected neural network that receives the output of the Transformer encoder ($E^{(4)}$) and predicts the corresponding class. For each element in an input sequence, it produces a probability distribution over the set of all classes C. We then take the average over the elements of this sequence and use the average probability distribution to identify the class.

This component uses its neural network with learnable weights $\mathbb{W}^{(h)} \in \mathbb{R}^{d \times 80}$, $\mathbb{W}^{(o)} \in \mathbb{R}^{80 \times |C|}$ and biases $\mathbb{B}^{(h)} \in \mathbb{R}^{80}$, $\mathbb{B}^{(o)} \in \mathbb{R}^{|C|}$ to produce a latent value $Z \in \mathbb{R}^{w \times |C|}$ as follows:

$$Z = max(0, E^{(4)}\mathbb{W}^{(h)} + \mathbb{B}^{(h)})\mathbb{W}^{(o)} + \mathbb{B}^{(o)} \tag{20}$$

Using this latent value, the classifier will produce an average probability distribution $P \in [0, 1]^{|C|}$ as follows:

$$P_j = \frac{1}{w} \sum_i^w \frac{e^{Z_{i,j}}}{\sum_k^{|C|} e^{Z_{i,k}}} \tag{21}$$

During inference, the classifier will return the most likely class as the member of C with the highest corresponding value in P: $C_{argmax(P)}$. During training, the classifier returns P which we use to evaluate the loss over the network.

References

1. Alioghli, A.A., Yıldırım Okay, F.: Enhancing multivariate time-series anomaly detection with positional encoding mechanisms in transformers. J. Supercomput. **81**, 282 (2025)
2. Bar, R., Hajaj, C.: Simcse for encrypted traffic detection and zero-day attack detection. IEEE Access **10**, 56952–56960 (2022)

3. Bar-on, M., Bezawada, B., Ray, I., Ray, I.: A small world-privacy preserving IoT device-type fingerprinting with small datasets. In: Mosbah, M., S, F., Tawbi, N., Ahmed, T., Boulahia-Cuppens, N., Garcia-Alfaro, J. (eds.) Foundations and Practice of Security, pp. 104–122. Springer Nature Switzerland, Cham (2024)

4. Bin Sarhan, B., Altwaijry, N.: Insider threat detection using machine learning approach. Appl. Sci. **13**(1) (2023)

5. Dadkhah, S., Mahdikhani, H., Danso, P.K., Zohourian, A., Truong, K.A., Ghorbani, A.A.: Towards the development of a realistic multidimensional IoT profiling dataset. In: Proceedings of 19th Annual International Conference on Privacy, Security & Trust (PST 2022), 22–24 August 2022

6. Devlin, J., Chang, M.W., Lee, K., Toutanova, K.: Bert: Pre-training of deep bidirectional transformers for language understanding. In: Proceedings of the 2019 Conference of the North American Chapter of the Association for Computational Linguistics: Human Language Technologies, vol. 1 (long and short papers), pp. 4171–4186 (2019)

7. Dong, Y., Cordonnier, J.B., Loukas, A.: Attention is not all you need: pure attention loses rank doubly exponentially with depth. In: Proceedings of International Conference on Machine Learning, pp. 2793–2803. PMLR (2021)

8. Hao, Q., Rong, Z.: Iottfid: an incremental iot device identification model based on traffic fingerprint. IEEE Access **11**, 58679–58691 (2023)

9. Jero, S., Pacheco, M.L., Goldwasser, D., Nita-Rotaru, C.: Leveraging textual specifications for grammar-based fuzzing of network protocols. In: Proceedings of the AAAI Conference on Artificial Intelligence, vol. 33, no. 01, pp. 9478–9483 (2019)

10. Li, H., et al.: A novel network protocol syntax extracting method for grammar-based fuzzing. Appl. Sci. **14**(6) (2024)

11. Li, J., et al.: FOAP: Fine-Grained Open-World android app fingerprinting. In: 31st USENIX Security Symposium (USENIX Security 22), pp. 1579–1596. USENIX Association, Boston, MA (August 2022)

12. Lopez-Martin, M., Carro, B., Sanchez-Esguevillas, A., Lloret, J.: Network traffic classifier with convolutional and recurrent neural networks for internet of things. IEEE Access **5**, 18042–18050 (2017)

13. Lu., D.: Ustc-tfc2016 (2016). https://github.com/yungshenglu/USTC-TFC2016

14. Luo, Y., Chen, X., Ge, N., Feng, W., Lu, J.: Transformer-based device-type identification in heterogeneous iot traffic. IEEE Internet Things J. **10**(6), 5050–5062 (2023)

15. Meng, X., Lin, C., Wang, Y., Zhang, Y.: NetGPT: generative pretrained transformer for network traffic. arXiv:2304.09513v2 (2023)

16. Meng, X., Wang, Y., Ma, R., Luo, H., Li, X., Zhang, Y.: Packet representation learning for traffic classification. In: Proceedings of the 28th ACM SIGKDD Conference on Knowledge Discovery and Data Mining, pp. 3546–3554. KDD '22, Association for Computing Machinery, New York, NY, USA (2022)

17. Miskovic, S., Lee, G.M., Liao, Y., Baldi, M.: AppPrint: automatic fingerprinting of mobile applications in network traffic, In: Proceedings 16th International Conference on Passive and Active Measurements. LNCS 8995, pp. 57–69. New York, NY, USA, March 19–20 2015 (2015)

18. Msadek, N., Soua, R., Engel, T.: IoT device fingerprinting: machine learning based encrypted traffic analysis. In: 2019 IEEE Wireless Communications and Networking Conference (WCNC), pp. 1–8 (2019)

19. Oh, S., Lee, M., Lee, H., Bertino, E., Kim, H.: Appsniffer: towards robust mobile app fingerprinting against vpn. In: Proceedings of the ACM Web Conference 2023,

pp. 2318–2328. WWW '23, Association for Computing Machinery, New York, NY, USA (2023)

20. Pacheco, M.L., Hippel, M.V., Weintraub, B., Goldwasser, D., Nita-Rotaru, C.: Automated attack synthesis by extracting finite state machines from protocol specification documents. In: Proceedings 2022 IEEE Symposium on Security and Privacy (SP), pp. 51–68 (2022)

21. Rodrawangpai, B., Daungjaiboon, W.: Improving text classification with transformers and layer normalization. Mach. Learn. Appl. **10**, 100403 (2022)

22. Shaukat, K., Luo, S., Chen, S., Liu, D.: Cyber threat detection using machine learning techniques: a performance evaluation perspective. In: Proceedings 2020 International Conference on Cyber Warfare and Security (ICCWS), pp. 1–6 (2020)

23. Sivanathan, A., et al.: Classifying IoT devices in smart environments using network traffic characteristics. IEEE Trans. Mob. Comput. **18**(8), 1745–1759 (2019)

24. Taylor, V.F., Spolaor, R., Conti, M., Martinovic, I.: AppScanner: automatic fingerprinting of smartphone apps from encrypted network traffic. In: Proceedings 2016 IEEE European Symposium on Security and Privacy (EuroS&P), pp. 439–454 (2016)

25. Taylor, V.F., Spolaor, R., Conti, M., Martinovic, I.: Robust smartphone app identification via encrypted network traffic analysis. IEEE Trans. Inf. Forensics Secur. **13**(1), 63–78 (2018)

26. Vaswani, A., et al.: Attention is all you need. In: Proceedings of the 31st International Conference on Neural Information Processing Systems, pp. 6000–6010. NIPS'17, Curran Associates Inc., Red Hook, NY, USA (2017)

27. Wang, J., Zhong, J., Li, J.: IoT-portrait: automatically identifying IoT devices via transformer with incremental learning. Future Internet **15**(3) (2023)

28. Xu, J., Sun, X., Zhang, Z., Zhao, G., Lin, J.: Understanding and improving layer normalization. In: Wallach, H., Larochelle, H., Beygelzimer, A., d'Alché-Buc, F., Fox, E., Garnett, R. (eds.) Advances in Neural Information Processing Systems, vol. 32. Curran Associates, Inc. (2019)

29. Yamansavascilar, B., Guvensan, M.A., Yavuz, A.G., Karsligil, M.E.: Application identification via network traffic classification. In: Proceedings 2017 International Conference on Computing, Networking and Communications (ICNC), pp. 843–848 (2017)

30. Yin, Y., et al.: Graphiot: lightweight IoT device detection based on graph classifiers and incremental learning. IEEE Trans. Serv. Comput. 17(6), 3758–3772 (2024)

Automated Privacy Policy Analysis Using Large Language Models

Mian Yang[1], Vijayalakshmi Atluri[1(✉)], Shamik Sural[2], and Ashish Kundu[3]

[1] Rutgers university, Newark, USA
{mian.yang,atluri}@rutgers.edu
[2] Indian Institute of Technology Kharagpur, Kharagpur, India
shamik@cse.iitkgp.ac.in
[3] Cisco Research, San Jose, USA
ashkundu@cisco.com

Abstract. Privacy policies play a critical role in disclosing the collection and sharing of personal information. However, due to their complex and lengthy nature, users often find it difficult to comprehend and therefore tend to simply ignore them. This paper presents a novel approach that leverages the capabilities of large language models to aid users with automatic tools that enable them to discern the policies and assess the privacy risks while minimizing the reliance on human-labeled data. In particular, our approach automatically maps each paragraph of a privacy policy to predefined categories and extract the privacy attributes and their relationships with the first party collection and third party sharing. These attributes and relationships are represented as a graph, enabling the use of readily available graph databases such as Neo4j. This lends itself to answer privacy questions as Cypher queries and to identify inconsistent privacy statements.

1 Introduction

Privacy policies are commonly encountered when users navigate websites, yet they are frequently overlooked due to their lengthy and tedious natural language text, which often includes complex legal language that can be difficult to understand. Despite this, 81% of U.S. adults report being asked to agree to a company's privacy policy terms at least monthly. However, only 22% of U.S. adults consistently read privacy policies thoroughly before agreeing to them, while 38% say they sometimes read them. Of the 60% of U.S. adults who at least occasionally review privacy policies, just 22% read them completely [3]. This trend highlights a significant problem: while privacy policies are designed to inform consumers about how their personal data is collected, used, shared and protected, the actual understanding and usage of the documents is relatively low. Additionally, privacy policies may contain contradictions; for example, an analysis of 11,430 apps by PolicyLint [1] revealed that 14.2% of their privacy policies had conflicting statements. This highlights the critical importance of privacy policy analysis.

© IFIP International Federation for Information Processing 2025
Published by Springer Nature Switzerland AG 2025
S. Katsikas and B. Shafiq (Eds.): DBSec 2025, LNCS 15722, pp. 23–43, 2025.
https://doi.org/10.1007/978-3-031-96590-6_2

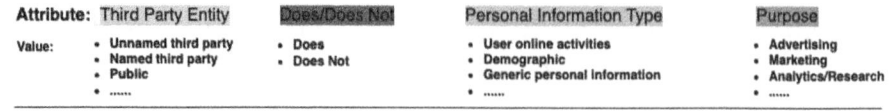

Attribute:	Third Party Entity	Does/Does Not	Personal Information Type	Purpose
Value:	• Unnamed third party • Named third party • Public •	• Does • Does Not	• User online activities • Demographic • Generic personal information •	• Advertising • Marketing • Analytics/Research • ......

Example from Atlantic.com Privacy Policy:
The Atlantic and that service may share certain information about you and your activities. With your consent, we also may share information about your activities, including what you view on the Sites, with that social networks users.

Fig. 1. Privacy Policy Attribute Annotation Example

The poor readability makes privacy policies difficult for the average user to comprehend [8]. To address this challenge, structured annotation and information extraction techniques have been proposed to enhance users' ability to quickly grasp key information from privacy policies. Annotation helps categorize privacy policy statements into predefined classes, making it easier to extract structured insights about data collection, sharing, and purpose. A common manual approach to privacy policy annotation involves labeling key statements with predefined attributes. As illustrated in Fig. 1, privacy policy statements can be annotated with attributes such as *Third Party Entity*, *Does/Does Not*, *Personal Information Type*, and *Purpose* to determine whether a user's personal information is shared with third parties and for what reasons. In the figure, *"Third Party Entity"* denotes the companies or platforms that receive shared data, while *"Does/Does Not"* indicates whether the data is shared. *"Personal Information Type"* specifies the type of personal data involved, such as user online activities, location, or email address, while *"Purpose"* describes the reason for data collection or sharing. If an attribute is missing, it implies that the website does not explicitly state it. In manual annotation methods, certain tools highlight these attributes within the privacy policy text and map each attribute to one or more corresponding values to create a structured representation of the extracted information. For example, in Fig. 1, the annotated data indicates that the user's online activities are shared with an unnamed third-party entity and the public, but the purpose of sharing is not explicitly stated. However, manual annotation is labor-intensive and impractical for analyzing large volumes of privacy policies at scale. Although automated machine learning-based techniques have been developed, these methods still rely on large amounts of annotated data for training.

To mitigate the need for extensive human annotation, large language models (LLMs), such as GPT-4o, offer a viable solution. By utilizing GPT-4o, we can automate the annotation process and significantly reduce the reliance on manually labeled datasets, enabling efficient extraction of key attributes from privacy policies. However, while GPT-4o offers powerful capabilities, relying solely on it presents certain challenges, including proprietary access constraints, computational costs, and the potential for hallucinations—where the model may generate inaccurate or misleading annotations. These issues can affect the reliability of extracted information and introduce inconsistencies in downstream tasks.

Furthermore, simply generating textual summaries and presenting them to users may still leave out key aspects of the policy, such as how their personal information flows from first-party to third-party or where contradictions and inconsistencies exist within the policy. A text-based summary alone may not effectively capture these relationships; however, a graph-based representation naturally models and visualizes these connections. Additionally, by leveraging a graph database, users can later query specific aspects of the privacy policy, such as which third parties receive their data, what types of personal information are collected, or whether conflicting statements exist.

To enable practical deployment while maintaining the benefits of GPT-4o-powered annotation, we employ knowledge distillation to transfer its advanced capabilities to open-source models, such as BERT [6]. This approach reduces dependency on proprietary models while enabling fine-tuning of the distilled model specifically for privacy policy analysis. By combining graph-based representations and fine-tuned open-source models, we provide a scalable and interpretable solution for privacy policy understanding, allowing users to efficiently extract, query, and analyze privacy terms. This paper aims to streamline privacy policy analysis using LLMs with minimal human-labeled data, enabling end users to quickly understand what data is collected, how it is used, with whom it is shared, and whether conflicts or inconsistencies exist. The framework begins by segmenting the privacy policy into paragraph-length sections, which are then subjected to *Privacy Label Mapping* to classify each segment into predefined privacy categories, such as *First Party Collection/Use* and *Third Party Sharing/Collection*. Next, the identified paragraphs are further decomposed into individual sentences, and *Privacy Attribute Mapping* is applied to extract relevant text spans corresponding to specific attribute types, such as *First Party Entity*, *Third Party Entity*, and *Personal Information Type*, as well as relationships, including *Action* and *Purpose*, from each sentences and their values are predicted accordingly. Finally, the extracted attribute-value pairs are used to construct a graph-based representation of the privacy policy. This structured graph enables advanced query-answering capabilities, allowing users to obtain clear and precise answers to privacy-related questions, such as *"What personal information is collected by the first party?"*, *"What personal information is shared with third parties?"*, and *"Do conflicting or contradictory statements exist within the policy?"*

This paper is organized as follows. Section 2 introduces the key background concepts and the dataset used in this study. Section 7 reviews previous work on analyzing privacy policies. Section 3 presents the overall framework of our proposed approach, which consists of three main steps. The first step, detailed in Sect. 4, involves privacy label mapping, where we apply LLM knowledge distillation to significantly reduce training data requirements. Our approach achieves comparable results to previous methods while using only 20% of the dataset, whereas prior methods rely on over half of the available data for training. The second step, discussed in Sect. 5, focuses on mapping attribute and relationship values. In this step, we distill and fine-tune a separate student LLM model for each attribute to enhance prediction accuracy. Finally, the third step, described in Sect. 6, focuses on the construction of a privacy policy graph, where privacy policies are modeled as graphs and implemented in Neo4j. Finally, Sect. 8 offers the conclusions and directions to future research.

2   Background

This section provides an overview of the core concepts and tools employed in our privacy policy analysis.

2.1   Large Language Models (LLMs)

LLMs mark a significant advancement in artificial intelligence, particularly in natural language processing. As stated in Yang et al. [17], LLMs are pre-trained on vast datasets, enabling them to develop a broad understanding of language. LLMs can be categorized into three primary architectural types: Encoder-Decoder models, Encoder-only models, and Decoder-only models. Decoder-only models, such as GPT [12], have become the dominant architecture in LLM development, excelling in text generation and contextual reasoning. These models rely on a massive number of parameters to support their learning and predictive capabilities. For example, GPT-4o contain approximately over a trillion parameters. On the other hand, Encoder-only models, such as BERT, specialize in deep contextual understanding and token-level representations, making them suitable for tasks requiring precise text comprehension, such as privacy policy analysis, named entity recognition, and sentence classification. Unlike GPT models, which generate text auto-regressively, BERT-style models process input bidirectionally, capturing richer semantic relationships within text.

2.2   LLMs Knowledge Distillation

LLMs Knowledge Distillation is a critical method for transferring advanced capabilities from leading proprietary LLMs, such as GPT-4, to open-source counterparts like BERT. This process not only bridges the gap between cutting-edge proprietary models and accessible open-source alternatives but also enables smaller, more efficient models to inherit the knowledge and performance of their larger counterparts [18]. The proprietary LLM is called teacher, and the open-source LLM is called student.

The process of distilling knowledge from a teacher model to a student model involves four key steps. In the first step, the teacher LLM is guided toward a specific target skill or domain through steering instructions. Once the target area is defined, the second step entails providing the teacher LLM with seed knowledge. This seed knowledge typically consists of a small dataset or specific data cues relevant to the desired skill or domain knowledge. For example, in *Privacy Label Mapping*, a seed dataset includes manually labeled examples of privacy statements categorized into *First Party Collection/Use* and *Third Party*

Sharing/Collection. In the third step, the teacher LLM generates knowledge examples based on the seed knowledge and steering instructions. Finally, in the fourth step, these generated knowledge examples are used to train the student model, enabling it to acquire the targeted skill or domain expertise. The knowledge elicitation capabilities of teacher LLMs can be applied in various ways, including labeling, data expansion, data curation, and more. In our approach, we leverage data expansion to enhance privacy policy analysis.

2.3   OPP 115

Wilson et al. [16] introduced OPP-115, a corpus consisting of 115 annotated website privacy policies written in natural language. This corpus consists of 3,792 segmented paragraphs and over 23,000 fine-grained data practices, making it a valuable resource for privacy policy analysis. Each policies were carefully reviewed and annotated by three graduate law students, ensuring a high level of annotation accuracy and consistency. Their annotations focused on identifying and categorizing specific data practices across ten predefined categories, which include: (1) First Party Collection/Use, (2) Third Party Sharing/Collection, (3) User Choice/Control, (4) User Access Edit & Deletion, (5) Data Retention, (6) Data Security, (7) Policy Change, (8) Do Not Track, (9) International & Specific Audiences, and (10) Other. And Each category is further detailed through a category-specific set of attributes. In this work, we utilize OPP-115 as our dataset for privacy policy analysis. However, rather than considering all ten predefined categories, we focus specifically on *First Party Collection/Use* and *Third Party Sharing/Collection*, as these categories are most relevant to our objective of analyzing how data is collected, used, and shared across entities.

3   Overall Framework

The goal of our work is to efficiently structure privacy policy statements into a graph database using LLMs while minimizing the need for human-labeled data. Our approach enables end users to quickly understand what data is collected, how it is used, with whom it is shared, and whether conflicts or inconsistencies exist within the policy. For example, one section of a policy may state that a particular piece of personal information is collected, while another claims it is not, or a policy might indicate that certain data is shared with third parties, whereas another section denies this. Additionally, users can freely query these aspects, allowing for interactive and flexible exploration of privacy-related concerns. Figure 2 illustrates the entire workflow of our approach for analyzing privacy policies, which is a three step process. In the following, we provide a brief description of each of these steps. **Privacy Label Mapping:** In the first step, the privacy policy is segmented into distinct sections, and each section is assigned labels. To enable a direct comparison with previous methods, we first segment the text into paragraph-length sections. The dataset we utilize, OPP-115, provides privacy policies in HTML format, where paragraphs boundaries are marked by |||. We leverage these markers to segment the policy into distinct paragraphs, ensuring consistency with prior research. Each paragraph is then processed by the LLM, which assigns one or more predefined labels based on its content. These labels help identify and categorize specific types of privacy-related information within each paragraph. By applying this labeling step, we can filter out paragraphs that do not contain relevant information and focus on processing only those that align with our analysis objectives.

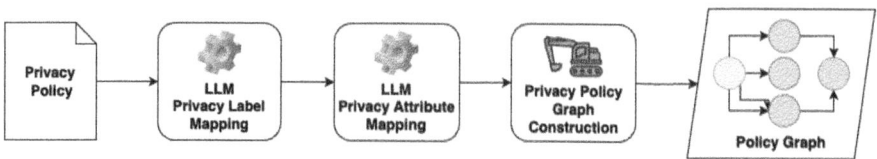

Fig. 2. Overall Framework

Privacy Attribute Mapping: This step focuses on extracting and mapping values associated with specific privacy attributes and relationships using the LLM. While Privacy Label Mapping assigns high-level categories to paragraph, Privacy Attribute Mapping operates at a finer granularity by identifying and extracting specific attributes within these categorized paragraphs. In this process, we transition from paragraph-level to sentence-level processing to improve attribute extraction accuracy. Privacy policies often contain complex and dense information, with multiple attributes embedded within a single paragraph. Processing text at the sentence level reduces potential information loss by allowing the model to analyze each sentence independently, ensuring that all relevant attributes are accurately identified and extracted. The analysis is limited to the labels *First Party Collection/Use* and *Third Party Sharing/Collection*, with separate processing for each category. All other labels are discarded at this stage. For each category, the LLM identifies relevant text spans and maps them to corresponding attribute and relationship values, which are then organized into structured sets.

Privacy Policy Graph Construction: In the final step, the structured attribute sets generated in the previous stage are used to construct a graph, which is a representation of the privacy policy. In this graph, the extracted attribute values are represented as nodes, while their relationships are depicted as edges. To enable efficient data retrieval, the graph is implemented using Neo4j, a graph database platform. This implementation allows users to query the graph using Cypher, Neo4j's specialized query language, enabling effective exploration and analysis of privacy policies.

The next three sections provide a detailed discussion of our approaches for these three distinct steps, along with the corresponding experimental results.

4   Privacy Label Mapping

This section describes the process of mapping privacy policy paragraphs to predefined categories using an LLM with limited human-labeled data. Existing methods rely heavily on human annotations, whereas we leverage the LLM to reduce this dependency. Furthermore, by employing LLM knowledge distillation, we enable a smaller student LLM to handle this task efficiently.

The key elements of the Privacy Label Mapping process are defined as follows:
Document (D): Refers to the privacy policy documents. Each document is segmented into n paragraphs, represented as $D = \{p_0, p_1, \cdots, p_n\}$, where p_i denotes the i-th paragraph in D.
Label (L): Refers to the set of predefined privacy labels, as described in Sect. 2.3. Each label l_m in the set corresponds to a specific category, with $1 \leq m \leq 10$.

During the *Privacy Label Mapping* process, each paragraph p_i is analyzed by the trained student LLM, which is assigned one or more relevant privacy labels. To formalize this, a mapping function f is defined:

$$f : p_i \rightarrow \{\{l_1 \cdots l_m\} | \{l_1 \cdots l_m\} \subseteq L\} \tag{1}$$

Here, the function f associates a paragraph p_i with a subset of labels of L.

4.1   LLMs Knowledge Distillation of Privacy Label Mapping Process

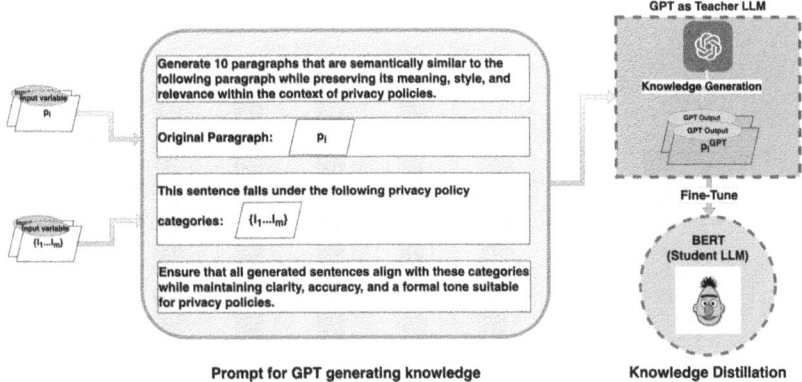

Fig. 3. Knowledge Distillation of Privacy Label Mapping Process

Previous methods rely heavily on human annotations, often requiring more than half of the dataset for training. For instance, Wilson et al. [16] use 75 out of 115 policies as training data, while Harkous et al. [10] use 65 out of 115. This reliance on human-labeled data limits scalability and increases annotation costs.

To mitigate this limitation, our approach leverages knowledge distillation, enabling us to train the model using only 23 out of 115 human-labeled policies. By utilizing a teacher-student learning framework, we distill knowledge from a large-scale LLM (GPT-4o) into a smaller, more efficient model (BERT). This approach significantly reduces the dependency on extensive manual annotations while maintaining high classification performance.

Figure 3 illustrates the knowledge distillation process used for privacy label mapping. The process begins by randomly selecting 23 human-labeled policies from OPP-115 as the seed knowledge base, where each of these policies contains manually annotated paragraphs categorized into predefined privacy-related labels. To expand the dataset, we employ GPT-4o as the teacher LLM to generate additional labeled text. Specifically, for each paragraph p_i and its corresponding labels $\{l_1, \ldots, l_m\}$, GPT-4o generates 10 semantically similar variations using a structured prompt while preserving the original category labels. To balance diversity and consistency in the generated text, we set the temperature parameter to 0.7. This data augmentation strategy enhances the model's ability to generalize while preserving label consistency. Once the augmented dataset is generated, we use it to fine-tune a student model, BERT, which is later employed to map privacy labels for each paragraph p_i.

Example 1. Table 1 shows three representative paragraphs (p_0, p_6 and p_9) from the Atlantic.com privacy policy. After fine-tuning BERT using knowledge distilled from GPT, we use the trained model to predict labels for each paragraph. In the next step of privacy attribute mapping, we retain only paragraphs containing at least one relevant label. For example, in Table 1, p_0 is discarded as it is labeled solely as "Other", while p_6 and p_9 are retained for the next step.

4.2   Experimental Results of Student LLM

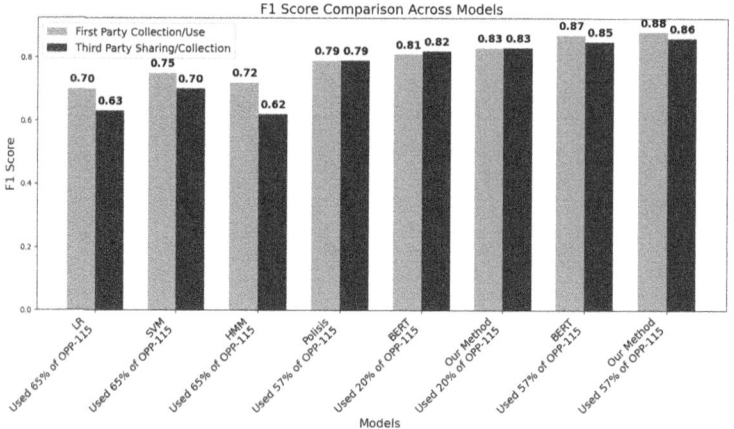

Note: The percentages indicate the proportion of the OPP-115 dataset used for training. Models LR, SVM, and HMM were trained on 75 policies (65% of OPP-115). Polisis used 65 policies (57% of OPP-115), while our method was tested with both 23 policies (20%) and 65 policies (57%).

Fig. 4. F1 Score Comparison Across Models

After the knowledge distillation process, we obtain a fine-tuned BERT model, which we evaluate on the remaining 92 privacy policies from the OPP-115 dataset to assess its performance.

Figure 4 presents the F1-score comparison of different models for the tasks of First Party Collection/Use and Third Party Sharing/Collection. Our knowledge-distilled model, trained on only 20% of the dataset (23 policies), outperforms traditional machine learning methods, including Logistic Regression (LR), Support Vector Machine (SVM), and Hidden Markov Model (HMM), which were trained on 75 privacy policies. Additionally, our model surpasses Polisis, which was trained on 65 policies, achieving a 4% improvement in F1-score over Polisis, the previous best-performing model in both categories. We also evaluate a directly fine-tuned BERT model, using the same parameters but without knowledge distillation from a teacher LLM. This model was tested under both 23 and 65 policies, yet it remained slightly below our method in both cases. This result highlights the effectiveness of domain adaptation, demonstrating that even with significantly fewer parameters (millions in BERT vs. trillions in GPT-4), our task-specific knowledge-distilled training achieves superior performance. Furthermore, we conduct an experiment where our model is trained on the same 65-policy dataset used in Polisis. The findings reveal a substantial improvement, with our model achieving a 9% higher F1-score for *First Party Collection/Use* and a 7% increase for *Third Party Sharing/Collection* compared to Polisis. This substantial performance gain underscores the advantages of knowledge distillation, demonstrating that our approach can enhance privacy policy classification accuracy, even when constrained to the same number of human-labeled policies.

5   Privacy Attribute Mapping

Building on the foundation established by the *Privacy Label Mapping* process, the next step focuses on extracting and mapping privacy attributes from relevant paragraphs to predefined attribute values. While *Privacy Label Mapping* assigns high-level categories to paragraphs, *Privacy Attribute Mapping* aims to capture fine-grained details within these categorized paragraphs by identifying and extracting specific attribute values. To simulate human annotation, we adopt a structured extraction approach. Given a predefined attribute, we first identify the most relevant text span within the paragraph. Once this span is determined, the model predicts the corresponding attribute value from a predefined set of possible values.

Previously, our BERT model operated at the paragraph level, where the input was an entire paragraph, and the output was the predicted privacy category associated with that paragraph. However, we observed that paragraphs are often lengthy and contain multiple sentences, each addressing different aspects of data collection and sharing. This structure caused the model to focus primarily on the beginning of the paragraph, sometimes overlooking important details in later sentences. To address this issue, we adopt a sentence-level processing approach, where the BERT model now takes an individual sentence as input and outputs its corresponding predicted category as shown in Table 2.

5.1   Privacy Attributes

We first define the attributes and relationships that need to be extracted from the privacy policy in order to answer our questions. These include three attribute types and two relationship types.

- **First Party Entity**: An attribute type that represents the organization involved, typically the website itself. The value corresponding to this attribute is denoted as v_{fp}.
- **Third Party Entity**: An attribute type that refers to an external party involved, such as a service provider or partner. The value corresponding to this attribute is denoted as v_{tp}.
- **Personal Information Type**: An attribute type that categorizes the information collected or shared, such as an email address or IP address. The value corresponding to this attribute is denoted as v_{pi}.
- **Action**: A relationship type that defines the specific action associated with the data (e.g., does collect, share, does not collect, etc.). The value corresponding to this attribute is denoted as v_a.
- **Purpose**: A relationship type that defines the intended use of the information (e.g., analytics, marketing). The value corresponding to this attribute is denoted as v_{pp}.

Let AT represent the entire set of all output attribute sets, with subsets AT_F and AT_T corresponding to the output extracted from *First Party Collection/Use* and *Third Party Sharing/Collection*, respectively, such that $AT = AT_F \cup AT_T$

For sentences labeled as *First Party Collection/Use*, the extracted attribute sets are denoted by at_{f_i}, where $1 \leq i \leq |AT_F|$. Each at_{f_i} is represented in the following format, with specific positions corresponding to predefined attributes: $at_{f_i} = (v_{fp}, v_a, v_{pi}, v_{pp})$. In this representation, $v_{fp}(at_{f_i})$ refers to the value of the first party entity, $v_a(at_{f_i})$ denotes the value of action, $v_{pi}(at_{f_i})$ represents the value of personal information type, and $v_{pp}(at_{f_i})$ indicates the value of purpose.

For sentences labeled as *Third Party Sharing/Collection*, the extracted attribute sets are denoted by at_{t_i}, where $1 \leq i \leq |AT_T|$. Each at_{t_i} is represented in the following format, with specific positions corresponding to predefined attributes: $at_{t_i} = (v_{pi}, v_a, v_{tp}, v_{pp})$, and $v_{pi}(at_{t_i})$ represents the value of personal information type, $v_a(at_{t_i})$ denotes the value of action, $v_{tp}(at_{t_i})$ refers to the value of the third party entity, and $v_{pp}(at_{t_i})$ indicates the value of purpose.

Privacy Attribute Mapping Function. The Privacy Attribute Mapping process consists of two sequential steps: text span identification and attribute value prediction. Given a sentence s_i^j from paragraph p_i, which has been assigned a label l from the Privacy Label Mapping step, the goal is to extract specific privacy attributes by first identifying the relevant text span and then predicting its corresponding value.

In the first step, a text span identification model, denoted as g_1, takes as input a labeled sentence s_i^j and a predefined attribute a. The model outputs the text span t within the sentence that best represents the given attribute. This process can be formalized as:

$$g_1 : (s_i^j, l, a) \to t \tag{2}$$

Once the text span has been identified, a second model, the attribute value prediction model, denotes as g_2, takes t and the attribute a as input and produces the predicted attribute value v. This process is represented as:

$$g_2 : (t, a) \to v \tag{3}$$

Following this two-step process, the extracted attribute values are grouped into structured sets based on the assigned label l. If the label corresponds to *First Party Collection/Use*, the resulting attribute set is represented as $at_{f_i} = (v_{\text{fp}}, v_{\text{a}}, v_{\text{pi}}, v_{\text{pp}})$. While if the label corresponds to *Third Party Sharing/Collection*, the extracted set follows the format $at_{t_i} = (v_{\text{pi}}, v_{\text{a}}, v_{\text{tp}}, v_{\text{pp}})$.

Predefined Attribute Values. To ensure consistency and enable direct comparison with results from the OPP-115 dataset, we restrict the possible values for the *Third Party Entity, Personal Information Type*, and *Purpose* attributes to predefined sets, as listed in Tables 4, 5, and 6 in the Appendix. These predefined values were derived by iterating through the OPP-115 dataset to identify all values associated with these attributes. Additionally, the Action attribute is treated as a binary variable, taking one of two values: "does" or "does not". Since OPP-115 does not contain the *First Party Entity* attribute, its values are extracted directly from the text span within the privacy policy.

Example 2. Consider paragraph p_6 from Atlantic.com, as shown in Table 1. In Table 2, this paragraph is segmented into four sentences (p_6^1 to p_6^4), each assigned a predicted label. To extract attributes from these sentences, we apply a two-step process. First, the text span model g_1 identifies relevant spans for each attribute under the predicted labels. The extracted spans are recorded in the Span Text column of Table 2. Next, for each extracted span, we use the attribute value prediction model g_2 to determine the corresponding attribute values. After processing, the extracted attribute set for sentence p_6^1 consists of (Atlantic, does collect, Social media data, Unspecified). Similarly, for p_6^2, the extracted attributes are (we, does collect, Social media data, Unspecified). For p_6^3, the extracted attributes include (User online activities, does share, Unnamed third party, Additional service/feature), while for p_6^4, the set consists of (User online activities, does share, Unnamed third party, Unspecified).

5.2   Knowledge Distillation of Privacy Attribute Mapping Process

Similar to Sect. 4.1, we use the same 23 human-labeled policies from OPP-115 as seed knowledge for training. In this process, GPT, serving as the teacher LLM, rewrites privacy policy sentence while preserving their original meaning.

Given an input sentence s_i^j, attribute a, and corresponding label l from the Privacy Label Mapping step, GPT generates a semantically equivalent variation of the sentence. Additionally, GPT identifies and extracts the text span t in the rewritten sentence that corresponds to the predefined text span in the original sentence. The knowledge distilled from GPT - consisting of rewritten sentences, extracted spans, and their corresponding predefined labels - is then used to train the student LLM, BERT. During training, BERT learns to perform the two key sub-tasks defined in the Privacy Attribute Mapping Process as described in Sect. 5.1. Additionally, we train separate BERT models for each attribute a to optimize performance for individual attribute extraction tasks.

5.3   Experimental Results

We evaluate the performance of the Privacy Attribute Mapping process across two key tasks: text span identification and attribute value prediction.

To assess text span identification, we compare BERT-predicted spans with the corresponding ground-truth spans from OPP-115 for each attribute. A partial match is considered a successful match under our evaluation criteria. Using this metric, our model achieves a span identification accuracy of 82.5%, demonstrating its ability to effectively locate relevant attribute spans within privacy policies. The model's performance in predicting attribute values for Third Party Entity, Personal Information Type, and Purpose is presented in Tables 4, 5, and 6. These results include Precision, Recall, and F1-Score for each attribute category, providing a comprehensive assessment of the model's effectiveness in structured privacy attribute extraction.

Third Party Entity Prediction. Table 4 presents the model's performance in classifying third-party entities. The highest F1-score is achieved for the Public category (0.8395), followed by Unnamed third party (0.7914). However, performance varies across different entity types, with lower F1-scores observed for Unspecified (0.2500) and Other users (0.5349). These variations suggest that certain third-party categories are more challenging to classify, likely due to ambiguous or inconsistent mentions in privacy policies.

Personal Information Type Prediction. Table 5 compares our method with Polisis, a prior benchmark model trained on 65 human-labeled policies, whereas our model is trained on only 23 policies. Despite using significantly fewer labeled examples, our method outperforms Polisis in multiple categories. For instance, Cookies and tracking elements achieves an F1-score of 0.9584, surpassing Polisis (0.9), while Health data extraction achieves 0.8387, significantly outperforming Polisis (0.61). Additionally, our method performs comparably to Polisis in several categories, such as Financial (0.8945 vs. 0.87) and Survey data (0.7027 vs. 0.81), demonstrating strong generalization capabilities.

Purpose. Table 6 presents the results for purpose classification, comparing our model against Polisis. Our method achieves the highest F1-scores in Merger/Acquisition (0.97), outperforming Polisis (0.95), as well as in Advertising (0.92) and Legal requirement (0.91), matching Polisis (0.92 and 0.91 respectively). However, our model underperforms in certain categories, such as Personalization/Customization, where Polisis achieves an F1-score of 0.80, compared to our 0.64. This suggests that additional labeled data or refined training approaches may be needed to enhance performance in lower-frequency purpose attributes.

6   Graph Construction

This section describe the method for constructing a directed graph $G = (V, E)$, where V is the set of nodes and E is the set of directed edges. This graph is constructed based on the extracted attributes collection AT from Sect. 5.

6.1   Modeling Privacy Policy as Graph

Given the output set of AT_F and AT_T, we construct a graph representation of the privacy policy.

– for each $v_{fp}(at_{f_i})$, there exists a vertex $v_{fp} \in V$.
– for each $v_{tp}(at_{t_i})$, there exists a vertex $v_{tp} \in V$.
– for each $v_{pi}(at_{f_i})$ and $v_{pi}(at_{t_i})$, there exists a vertex $v_{pi} \in V$.
– for each $v_{fp}(at_{f_i})$ and $v_{pi}(at_{f_i})$:
  - If $v_a(at_{f_i}) = $ 'does': there exist an edge $(v_{fp}(at_{f_i}) \xrightarrow{v_{pp}(at_{f_i})} v_{pi}(at_{f_i})) \in E$
  - If $v_a(at_{f_i}) = $ 'does not': there exist an edge $(v_{fp}(at_{f_i}) \xrightarrow{DN} v_{pi}(at_{f_i})) \in E$, where DN is the abbreviation for *Does Not*.
– for each $v_{tp}(at_{t_i})$ and $v_{pi}(at_{t_i})$:
  - If $v_a(at_{t_i}) = $ 'does': there exist an edge $(v_{pi}(at_{t_i}) \xrightarrow{v_{pp}(at_{t_i})} v_{tp}(at_{t_i})) \in E$
  - If $v_a(at_{t_i}) = $ 'does not': there exist an edge $(v_{pi}(at_{t_i}) \xrightarrow{DN} v_{tp}(at_{t_i})) \in E$

Nodes in the graph represent the attribute entities, while edges capture the relationships between these entities, as described in Sect. 5.1. Each node consists of an attribute name and its corresponding value, with nodes of the same attribute type containing distinct values. Edges define how information flows between entities and the conditions under which these actions occur, ensuring the graph accurately models the relationships extracted from privacy policies.

Example 3. Consider Example 2. In the result (Atlantic, does, Social media data, Unspecified), "Atlantic" represents the *First Party Entity*, mapped as the yellow node in Fig. 5, while "Social media data" represents the *Personal Information Type*, mapped as the blue node. The *Action* "does collect" establishes a relationship between these nodes, with "Unspecified" as the corresponding *Purpose*.

For the result of (User online activities, does, Unnamed third party, Additional service/feature), "User online activities" is mapped as a blue node representing the *Personal Information Type*, and "Unnamed third party" as a green node representing the *Third Party Entity*. The relationship "does share" links these nodes, with "Additional service/feature" assigned as the *Purpose*.

6.2   Implementation in Neo4j

The constructed graph is implemented in Neo4j, a native graph database designed to store and query data as vertices (nodes) and edges (relationships). Neo4j's Cypher query language offers a straightforward mechanism to build, analyze, and explore the privacy policy graph. Each entity in the graph is represented as a node in Neo4j, with the node containing an entity name and its associated value. For example, in the more complex privacy policy graph shown in Fig. 5, entities such as "We," "The First Party," and "The Atlantic" belong to the *First Party Entity* category. These nodes can be created in Cypher as:

```
CREATE (fp:FirstPartyEntity {name: "We"});
CREATE (fp:FirstPartyEntity {name: "The First Party"});
CREATE (fp:FirstPartyEntity {name: "The Atlantic"});
```

Similarly, nodes for other entities, such as *Third Party Entity* (depicted as green nodes in Fig. 5) and *Personal Information Type* (depicted as blue nodes), can be created using analogous Cypher commands.

The relationship "Unspecified" between "The First Party" and "Generic personal information" in Fig. 5 is represented in Neo4j by creating an edge between these nodes. This can be achieved using the following Cypher query:

```
MATCH (fp:FirstPartyEntity {name: "The First Party"}),
(pi:PersonalInformationType {type: "Generic personal
information"})
CREATE (fp)-[:COLLECTS {purpose: "Unspecified"}]->(pi);
```

Similarly, the relationship "Does Not" between "The First Party" and "Generic personal information" in Fig. 5 can be represented as:

```
MATCH (fp:FirstPartyEntity {name: "The First Party"}),
(pi:PersonalInformationType {type: "Generic personal
information"})
CREATE (pi)-[:DOES_NOT]->(tp);
```

Once the graph is constructed, Cypher queries can be used to answer the following questions of interest:

1. Identify Personal Information Collected for a Given Purpose: Suppose we want to find all types of personal information that the first party collects for "Unspecified" purposes. We can run:

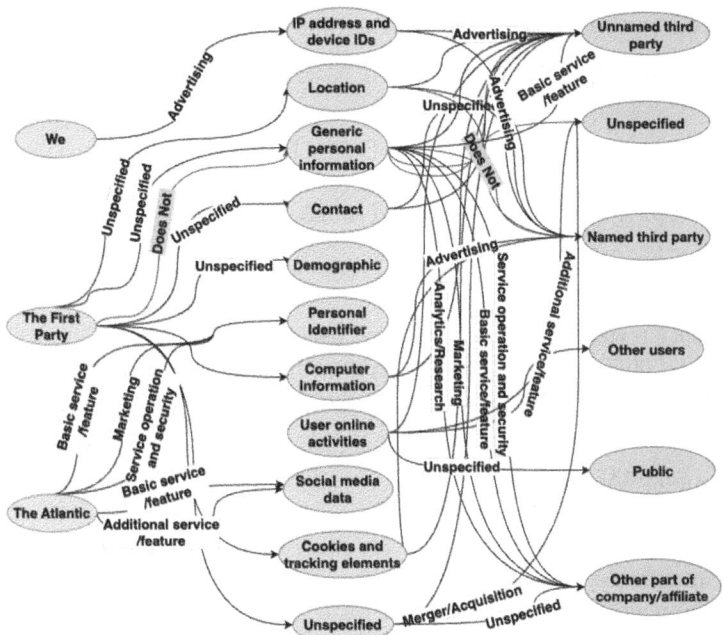

Fig. 5. Partial Graph Representation of Atlantic.com

```
MATCH (fp:FirstPartyEntity)-[r:COLLECTS {purpose:
"Unspecified"}]->(pi:PersonalInformation)
RETURN fp.name AS FirstParty, pi.name AS PersonalIn-
formation
```

This query matches nodes labeled `FirstPartyEntity` connected via a `COLLECTS` relationship to nodes labeled `Personal InformationType`, filtering by the `Purpose` property.

2. Tracing Information Flow to Third Parties: To see how information reaches external entities, we might look for paths that start at a first party entity and lead to a third party entity. For example:

```
MATCH (fp:FirstPartyEntity)-[:COLLECTS|:DOES_NOT*]
->(pi:PersonalInformationType)-[:SHARED_FOR|:DOES_
NOT*]->(tp:ThirdPartyEntity)
RETURN fp.name AS FirstParty, pi.name AS PersonalIn-
formation, tp.name AS ThirdParty
```

This pattern considers any chain of relationships from the `FirstPartyEntity` to `PersonalInformationType` (including those with `COLLECTS` or `DOES_NOT`, followed by a `SHARED_` `FOR` or `DOES_NOT` relationship to a third party.

3. Detecting Conflicting Privacy Statements: If the privacy policy is internally inconsistent—for instance, if it both states that the first party collects and does not collect the same type of personal information for the same or overlapping conditions—we can detect these conflicts by querying for nodes connected by contradictory relationships:

```
MATCH p1=(fp1:FirstPartyEntity)-[:COLLECTS]-(pi: PersonalInformati-
onType)
MATCH p2=(fp2:FirstPartyEntity)-[:DOES_NOT]-(pi: PersonalInformati-
onType)
RETURN p1,p2
```

This query returns any first party and personal information pairs where both COLLECTS and DOES_NOT relationships exist simultaneously, indicating a potential conflict or ambiguity in the policy.

7   Related Work

Many studies have been conducted to analyze privacy policies, employing a range of methodologies and tools. Breaux et al. [4] focused on formalizing privacy requirements using a description logic language called Eddy. Their work enabled automated detection of conflicting privacy requirements and tracing of data flows, ensuring consistency between privacy policies and actual data practices. Wilson et al. [16] and Harkous et al. [10] utilized the OPP-115 corpus, applying machine learning techniques to predict data practice categories. Similarly, Mathieu d'Aquin et al. [7] introduced a semantic framework based on an ontology to represent annotated practices. Their approach allowed for SPARQL queries, facilitating the structured extraction of privacy-relevant information and moving beyond traditional text processing methods. Story et al. [14] introduced a three-tiered classification framework to identify privacy practice statements within privacy policies based on data types, parties, and modalities. Andow et al. [1] addressed the critical issue of internal contradictions within a single privacy policy. Meanwhile, Andow et al. [2] tackled the challenge of aligning actual data flows with the stated practices in privacy policies. Jain et al. [11] used an ensemble-based NLP classifier to predict privacy labels from privacy policies and detected discrepancies between privacy policies and labels. Expanding further, Cui et al. [5] modeled entire policies as knowledge graphs, offering a more structured approach to privacy policy analysis. Despite their contributions, these approaches required extensive labeled datasets, manually defined rules, or regular expressions for extracting privacy-related information. Recent advancement in LLMs have demonstrated their potential in privacy policy analysis. Studies by Rodriguez et al. [13], Tang et al. [15], and Goknil et al. [9] highlight the effectiveness of LLMs in identifying, categorizing, and analyzing practices with high accuracy and minimal manual effort. However, these works primarily focus on label prediction and lack in-depth exploration of fine-grained attribute and relationship mapping and construction.

Our work builds on these advancements by utilizing the pre-trained capabilities of LLMs to predict labels, extract attributes, and map relationships from privacy policies. By structuring the extracted information into graph representations and implementing them in a graph database, such as Neo4j, we enable users to query and analyze privacy practices more effectively, providing a robust framework for detailed privacy policy analysis.

8   Conclusions and Future Work

In this paper, we propose a three-step approach for analyzing and assessing privacy policies written in natural language while reducing the need for human-labeled training data. The approach begins with privacy label mapping, where an LLM identifies relevant parts of the privacy policy and their privacy labels. In the second step, privacy attribute mapping, the LLM extracts detailed attributes and relationships from these labeled sections. Through knowledge distillation, we achieve comparable results to previous methods while using less than half of the training data. The final step constructs a structured graph representation of the extracted information by encoding entities and relationships. This graph-based model, implemented in Neo4j, enables efficient storage, querying, and exploration of privacy policies.

Future work will focus on several key issues to expand the applicability of this approach. First, the current graph is constructed individually for each privacy policy, limiting its ability to compare privacy practices across different companies. A unified graph structure could enable cross-policy comparisons, highlighting similarities and discrepancies between policies. Second, we aim to extend the framework by adding more entity types to capture a broader range of privacy practices, such as data retention periods or consent mechanisms. We plan to enhance the graph's query capabilities to answer more complex questions about data flows and potential conflicts within or across policies, further supporting the analysis of privacy practices. Lastly, we plan to implement a tool that enables users to assess the privacy risk by analyzing the privacy policies published by organizations, and make it publicly available.

Acknowledgments. The work was supported in part by a grant from CISCO Research.

A   Attribute Value Prediction Results

Table 1. Example Privacy Policy Segments from Atlantic.com with True Labels and Student BERT Predictions

Index	Paragraph	True Label	Predicted Label
p_0	Privacy Policy Effective: January 1, 2015 At the Atlantic Monthly Group, Inc. ("The Atlantic") ...	Other	Other
p_6	Collection of Personally Identifiable Information From or Through Social Media Sites. In addition, when you interact with any The Atlantic property page or account on a social media platform ...	First Party Collection/Use; Third Party Sharing/Collection	First Party Collection/Use; Other; Third Party Sharing/-Collection
p_9	We may also use web beacons and web storage technologies. A web beacon (also known as an action tag, tracer tag, or single-pixel gif) is an invisible graphic on a web page ...	First Party Collection/Use; Third Party Sharing/Collection	First Party Collection/Use; Third Party Sharing/Collection

Table 2. Predicted Labels for Sentence-Level Segmentation from Paragraph p_6 in Atlantic.com Privacy Policy

P_Index	S_Index	Sentence	Predicted Label
p_6	p_6^1	Collection of Personally Identifiable Information From or Through Social Media Sites. In addition, when you interact with any The Atlantic property page or account on a social media platform, such as Facebook, Twitter, Tumblr, or LinkedIn, we may collect the personally identifiable information that you make available to us on that page or account including your social media account ID.	First Party Collection/Use
p_6	p_6^2	However, we will comply with the privacy policies of the corresponding social media platform and we will only collect and store such personally identifiable information that we are permitted to collect by those social media platforms.	First Party Collection/Use, Other
p_6	p_6^3	If you choose to link or login to your The Atlantic account with or through a social networking service, The Atlantic and that service may share certain information about you and your activities.	Third Party Sharing/Collection
p_6	p_6^4	With your consent, we also may share information about your activities, including what you view on the Sites, with that social network's users.	Third Party Sharing/Collection

(See Table 3).

Table 3. Extracted Attribute Values from Sentence-Level Spans in Paragraph p_6

P_Index	S_Index	Span Text	Extracted Attribute with Value
p_6	p_6^1	First Party Entity: Atlantic; Action: may collect; Personal Information Type: collect the personally identifiable information that you make available to us on that page or account including your social media account ID; Purpose: NA	First Party Entity: Atlantic; Action: Does; Personal Information Type: Social media data; Purpose: Unspecified
p_6	p_6^2	First Party Entity: we; Action: collect; Personal Information Type: such personally identifiable information that we are permitted to collect by those social media platforms.; Purpose: NA	First Party Entity: we; Action: Does; Personal Information Type: Social media data; Purpose: Unspecified
p_6	p_6^3	Third Party Entity: share information about your activities; Action: share; Personal Information Type: you and your activities; Purpose: If you choose to link or login to your The Atlantic account with or through a social networking service	Third Party Entity: Unnamed third party; Action: Does; Personal Information Type: User online activities; Purpose: Additional service/feature
p_6	p_6^4	Third Party Entity: may share information; Action: share; Personal Information Type: your activities; Purpose: NA	Third Party Entity: Unnamed third party; Action: Does; Personal Information Type: User online activities; Purpose: Unspecified

Table 4. Attribute Value Prediction for Third Party Entity

Attribute Value	Precision	Recall	F1-Score
Unnamed third party	0.74	0.86	0.80
Unspecified	0.25	0.25	0.25
Named third party	0.6944	0.64	0.67
Other users	0.59	0.49	0.53
Public	1.00	0.72	0.84
Other part of company/affiliate	0.83	0.39	0.53

Table 5. Attribute Value Prediction for Personal Information Type and comparison with Polisis

Attribute Value	Our Method (with 23 human labeled data)			Polisis (with 65 human labeled data)		
	Precision	Recall	F1-Score	Precision	Recall	F1-Score
Unspecified	0.76	0.85	**0.80**	0.71	0.7	0.71
Cookies and tracking elements	0.95	0.97	**0.96**	0.95	0.89	0.9
Financial	0.96	0.84	**0.89**	0.89	0.86	0.87
Contact	0.73	0.96	0.83	0.9	0.89	**0.9**
User Profile	0.82	0.54	0.65	0.79	0.68	**0.72**
Generic personal information	0.86	0.79	**0.82**	0.82	0.79	0.8
User online activities	0.79	0.85	**0.82**	0.8	0.82	0.81
Personal identifier	0.17	0.04	0.06	0.67	0.61	**0.63**
Survey data	0.68	0.72	0.70	0.77	0.86	**0.81**
Demographic	0.87	0.81	0.84	0.93	0.9	**0.92**
Location	0.94	0.79	0.86	0.88	0.88	**0.88**
IP address and device IDs	0.9	0.81	0.85	0.93	0.93	**0.93**
Computer information	0.94	0.68	0.78	0.84	0.8	0.82
Health	0.76	0.93	**0.84**	1	0.56	0.61

Table 6. Attribute Value Prediction for Purpose and comparison with Polisis

Attribute Value	Our Method (with 23 human labeled data)			Polisis (with 65 human labeled data)		
	Precision	Recall	F1-Score	Precision	Recall	F1-Score
Unspecified	0.69	0.70	**0.70**	0.72	0.68	**0.70**
Basic service/feature	0.52	0.67	0.59	0.76	0.73	**0.74**
Marketing	0.82	0.78	0.80	0.86	0.83	**0.84**
Additional service/feature	0.53	0.56	0.54	0.75	0.76	**0.75**
Advertising	0.96	0.88	**0.92**	0.92	0.91	**0.92**
Analytics/Research	0.85	0.83	0.84	0.88	0.86	**0.87**
Service operation and security	0.82	0.54	0.65	0.81	0.77	**0.79**
Merger/Acquisition	0.95	0.99	**0.97**	0.95	0.96	0.95
Legal requirement	0.86	0.96	**0.91**	0.92	0.91	**0.91**
Personalization/Customization	0.65	0.63	0.64	0.79	0.80	**0.80**

References

1. Andow, B., et al.: Policylint: investigating internal privacy policy contradictions on google play. In: Proceedings of the 28th USENIX Conference on Security Symposium, pp. 585–602. SEC'19 (2019)
2. Andow, B., et al.: Actions speak louder than words: entity-sensitive privacy policy and data flow analysis with policheck. In: Proceedings of the 29th USENIX Conference on Security Symposium. SEC'20 (2020)
3. Auxier, B., Rainie, L., Anderson, M., Perrin, A., Kumar, M., Turner, E.: Americans and privacy: concerned, confused and feeling lack of control over their personal information. Technical report, Pew Research Center (November 2019)

4. Breaux, T.D., Hibshi, H., Rao, A.E.: Eddy, a formal language for specifying and analyzing data flow specifications for conflicting privacy requirements. Requir. Eng. **19**(3), 281–307 (2014)
5. Cui, H., Trimananda, R., Markopoulou, A., Jordan, S.: Poligraph: automated privacy policy analysis using knowledge graphs. In: Proceedings of the 32nd USENIX Conference on Security Symposium. SEC '23 (2023)
6. Devlin, J., Chang, M.W., Lee, K., Toutanova, K.: Bert: pre-training of deep bidirectional transformers for language understanding (2019)
7. d'Aquin, M., et al.: Privonto: a semantic framework for the analysis of privacy policies. Semant. Web **9**(2), 185–203 (2018)
8. Ermakova, T., Baumann, A., Fabian, B., Krasnova, H.: Privacy policies and users' trust: does readability matter? In: Proceedings of the 20th Americas Conference on Information Systems (2014)
9. Goknil, A., Gelderblom, F.B., Tverdal, S., Tokas, S., Song, H.: Privacy policy analysis through prompt engineering for llms (2024)
10. Harkous, H., Fawaz, K., Lebret, R., Schaub, F., Shin, K.G., Aberer, K.: Polisis: automated analysis and presentation of privacy policies using deep learning. In: Proceedings of the 27th USENIX Conference on Security Symposium, pp. 531–548. SEC'18, USENIX Association, USA (2018)
11. Jain, A., Rodriguez, D., del Alamo, J.M., Sadeh, N.: ATLAS: automatically detecting discrepancies between privacy policies and privacy labels. In: Proceedings of the International Workshop on Privacy Engineering (2023)
12. Radford, A., Narasimhan, K., Salimans, T., Sutskever, I.: Improving language understanding by generative pre-training (2019)
13. Rodriguez, D., Yang, I., Del Alamo, J.M., et al.: Large language models: a new approach for privacy policy analysis at scale. Computing **106**, 3879–3903 (2024)
14. Story, P., et al.: Natural language processing for mobile app privacy compliance. In: AAAI Spring Symposium on Privacy Enhancing AI and Language Technologies (2019)
15. Tang, C., et al.: Policygpt: automated analysis of privacy policies with large language models (2023)
16. Wilson, S., et al.: The creation and analysis of a website privacy policy corpus. In: Proceedings of the 54th Annual Meeting of the Association for Computational Linguistics (Volume 1: Long Papers), pp. 1330–1340. Berlin, Germany (2016)
17. Yang, J., et al.: Harnessing the power of llms in practice: a survey on chatgpt and beyond. ACM Trans. Knowl. Discov. Data **18**(6) (2024)
18. Zhang, C., Cai, H., Li, Y., Wu, Y., Hou, L., Abdul-Mageed, M.: Distilling text style transfer with self-explanation from LLMs. In: Proceedings of the 2024 Conference of the North American Chapter of the ACLs: Human Language Technologies (Volume 4: Student Research Workshop), pp. 200–211 (June 2024)

Data Chameleon: A Self-adaptive Synthetic Data Management System

Qianying Liao[1]([✉]), Maarten Kesters[1], Dimitri Van Landuyt[1,2],
and Wouter Joosen[1]

[1] DistriNet, Department of Computer Science, KU Leuven, 3001 Leuven, Belgium
{qianying.liao,maarten.kesters,dimitri.landuyt,wouter.joosen}@kuleuven.be
[2] LIRIS, Faculty of Economics and Business, KU Leuven, 3000 Leuven, Belgium

Abstract. The data economy thrives on data-centric collaboration between organizations. However, open data sharing remains a pipe dream without addressing pragmatic, regulatory, and strategic concerns – which include data protection and confidentiality. Generative artificial intelligence supports the production of realistic synthetic datasets on demand, and is a promising technology to alleviate such concerns. However, the replacement of an original dataset with a synthetic dataset incurs a specific trade-off between utility and privacy, and the appropriateness of this trade-off is highly context- and application-dependent. Manually establishing and managing different synthetic generators that have diverging properties is error-prone and time-consuming, lacks flexibility, and thus is costly and impractical.

This paper introduces Data Chameleon, a novel self-adaptive data management architecture for different synthetic data generators. Data Chameleon adaptively samples from different synthetic data generators in function of the data request at hand. Furthermore, in a longer-term adaptation loop, Data Chameleon monitors and evaluates the overall suitability of the available generators, to monitor evolutions in data demand, or possible concept drifts. Based on this, the Chameleon autonomously decides to re-train existing generators, or instantiate additional ones in a self-adaptive manner. The Data Chameleon architecture enhances the practical applicability of synthetic data generation, enabling more efficient and secure data sharing in real-world scenarios.

Keywords: data protection · synthetic data generation · data privacy · adaptive data management · privacy-utility trade-off · MLOps

1 Introduction

Data analytics have become common practice in contemporary information systems. However, data records in their original form are often prohibited from being shared due to legal regulations such as GDPR and HIPAA, and as they often contain sensitive or exploitable information. As a result, the privacy-preserving

S. Katsikas and B. Shafiq (Eds.): DBSec 2025, LNCS 15722, pp. 44–56, 2025.
https://doi.org/10.1007/978-3-031-96590-6_3

tactic of replacing original data with synthetic data has gained traction. Examples of the industrial usage of synthetic data sets include: (i) the Toyota Research Institute, where photo-realistic synthetic datasets with different street driving scenarios are used to train autonomous driving algorithms, in a variety of conditions that are otherwise costly to replicate in the real world [5], and (ii) IBM Research, where synthetic transaction data are used for developing and testing fraud detection algorithms [3].

Compared to traditional data privacy-enhancement approaches such as data de-identification [11]—which typically generalizes or suppresses values in the original dataset—synthetic data preserves some of the characteristics of the original dataset, making it more versatile for various use cases [19]. In addition to fulfilling the requirement of *fidelity*—i.e., preserving statistical properties of the original data—synthetic data should also meet the requirements of *utility* (meaning it should perform comparably to the original data on analytical tasks) and *privacy* (minimizing the risk of disclosing sensitive attribute information, as well as the risks of linking to additional information and re-identifying individuals). However, synthetic data surrogacy is subject to privacy-utility trade-offs, meaning that it is impossible to simultaneously optimize these requirements.

We argue that a practical industrial privacy-preserving data sharing system which incorporates synthetic data generators should consider adaptability from three different angles. Firstly, different use cases of the same problem require different synthetic datasets, as utility, fidelity, and privacy requirements may vary. Hence, the production of synthetic data should adapt to the varying requirements of different use cases. Secondly, the attributes and authorized original records involved in synthetic data generation evolve over time. These changes may arise not only from the emergence of unanticipated use cases, but also from requests to withdraw or update personal data from the data subjects involved. Therefore, the synthetic data system must adapt to these evolutions and updates. Thirdly, the presence of concept drifts in the original data—meaning that the distribution and relationships among attributes in the original data change over time [15]—can lead to different outcomes even with the same set of privacy and utility requirements. This implies that old data generators may become obsolete and need to be updated over time. Continuously monitoring performance changes in use cases and adapting accordingly is therefore considered essential.

A static approach to creating synthetic data generators tailored to use cases, specific data protection demands, and major changes in data context requires significant manual effort, maintenance, and monitoring. We argue that more comprehensive Machine Learning Operations (MLOps) methods are needed for a managing different synthetic data generators, that are each tailored to specific analytical use cases. Adaptability to changing demands and contexts with varying privacy and utility requirements is a key requirement for such methods.

Although adaptability is essential for the practical application of synthetic data generators, surprisingly little research has been devoted to this area. Previous studies on synthetic data generation and usage have either focused on fundamental designs of generative models to create private synthetic data based on specific data requirements [18] or applied existing models to specific use cases, assuming static requirements [2]. These studies ignore the practical and dynamic aspects of synthetic data generation and usage. There is a current gap in adaptive architectural approaches for the practical and industrial application of generative models, particularly in the MLOps domain. Additionally, there is a gap in the literature on private data sharing, as the literature often overlooks the need to accommodate multiple data recipients with different privacy and utility needs.

Contribution. This short paper presents the architectural design of a novel data management system called Data Chameleon. Data Chameleon (i) has the ability to dynamically respond to the varying requirements of different use cases with minimal delay by sampling data from the most appropriate generator(s) at run-time; (ii) is extensible and adaptable to the longer-term changes in demands and contexts of original data, new generative models, and new privacy and utility metrics, ensuring compliance with evolving data context, privacy standards and technological advancements. (iii) performs these adaptations in a self-adaptive manner. Its design is based on the well-known Monitor, Analyze, Plan, Execute, and Knowledge (MAPE-k) architecture [10] for self-adaptive systems.

Outline. The rest of the paper is organized as follows: Sect. 2 introduces the background of generative models and privacy-utility trade-offs. Section 3 details the motivation and challenges of incorporating generative models in real-world settings. Section 4 presents the architecture design of `Data Chameleon`. The related work is discussed in Sect. 5. Finally, Sect. 6 concludes the paper and outlines the validation plan.

2   Background

This section provides a broader background on synthetic tabular data and discusses its inherent utility-privacy trade-offs.

2.1   Synthetic Data Generation

The generation of synthetic tabular data is usually conducted in two phases: (i) in the **training phase**, a statistical model or machine learning (ML) model is created which approximates the properties of the original data, (ii) in the **operation phase**, synthetic data records can be sampled upon demand from the resulting model. Existing tools and enablers such as Synthcity [21], SDV [19], and DataSynthesizer [20] provide practitioners with practical means to train a synthetic data generators and introduce these capabilities in production systems.

However, the training phase itself is affected by a large number of factors and practitioners are exposed to an extensive and complex parameter and hyperparameter space, including the choice of algorithm, the number of epochs, the learning rate, batch sizes, but also the comparison or fitness function, data type-specific constraints, and constraints for generation. Depending on these specific choices, the instantiation of a new generator becomes expensive in resources.

2.2 Privacy-Utility Trade-Offs

Evaluation metrics provide the means to quantitatively assess how well synthetic data meets the requirements of privacy, utility, and fidelity.

Privacy. Synthetic data that closely approximate the original data result in residual privacy risks. Privacy metrics assess the extent of privacy risks, ensuring that the synthetic variant does not allow the re-identification of individuals or the disclosure of confidential information. There are two types of privacy metrics: non-adversarial metrics and adversarial metrics. Non-adversarial metrics are similarity-based. One example is the *nearest neighbor distance*, which measures the average distance from real data to the closest neighbor in the synthetic data [21]. A shorter distance implies higher privacy risks. Adversarial metrics, on the other hand, involve conducting privacy attacks on the synthetic datasets and measuring their success rates. These privacy attacks exploit the generative model's tendency to memorize real data due to overfitting during training. For instance, a *membership inference attack* involves an attacker trying to determine whether a specific data point was part of the training dataset [4]. Another example is an *attribute inference attack*, where the attacker attempts to infer missing information about a data point using synthetic data and partial information [25].

Utility. Maintaining data utility is crucial for ensuring the effectiveness of synthetic data in analytical tasks [6]. Utility metrics assess the usefulness of synthetic data by measuring its suitability for downstream applications, such as ML tasks. Quantifying utility can be challenging, as it often depends on the specific analytical task or a set of tasks relevant to the use case.

Fidelity. Fidelity metrics quantify how well generative models capture the statistical properties and patterns of the original dataset within the synthetic data [1]. These metrics involve directly comparing the synthetic dataset with the real dataset using statistical measures such as the *inverse KL-divergence*. This metric measures how similar the distribution of the synthetic data is to that of the real data. A low value indicates different distributions, while a value near one suggests the datasets are similar. A synthetic dataset with high fidelity is generally considered useful, as its similarity to the original data enables it to be employed for analytical tasks in a comparable manner.

The Privacy-Utility Trade-off. The above objectives are competing: it is mathematically impossible to preserve all characteristics of the original data without risking privacy leakage. A fundamental trade-off exists between privacy and utility[1]. As privacy is increased, synthetic data deviates further from the original data, generally resulting in a loss of utility. Conversely, data sets with

---

[1] Much of the literature on synthetic data emphasizes the two-dimensional trade-off between utility and privacy, often treating fidelity as a component of utility.

the highest possible utility are identical to the original data, thus incur a privacy loss. Moreover, independent of the use case, a baseline requirement for privacy is essential to prevent the re-identification of individuals from the original data within the synthetic data and to ensure no inferences can be made about them [13].

3 Motivational E-Commerce Use Case

This section motivates self-adaptive MLOps solutions for a data generation system through a case study.

3.1 Adapting for Downstream Use Cases

The data economy assumes that a single dataset must support multiple use cases, each with different privacy-utility trade-offs. To illustrate this, we use an e-commerce scenario. Online retail stores generate large volumes of transaction data that reveal customer behavior and market trends. A notable example is the Online Retail dataset from the UCI Repository [7]. The 2013 Target breach [14], which exposed over 40 million credit card records, highlights the importance of strong privacy measures. The e-commerce ecosystem includes diverse stakeholders with varying needs. We define four key use cases, each with distinct privacy risks and utility demands, summarized in Table 1.

Table 1. Different privacy-utility trade-offs in use cases on e-commerce data.

Use Case	Privacy	Utility	Reason
Fraud detection	Low	High	Detailed transaction records are essential for training ML models to detect fraud
Personalized marketing	Moderately Low	Moderately High	Purchase histories and product relationships are key to building a recommendation system
Inventory management	Moderately High	Moderately Low	Product demand forecasting relies on aggregated data, not individual transactions
Trend analysis	High	Low	Identifying market trends requires only high-level information

3.2 Adapting to Changing Data Privacy Concept

Data privacy is a dynamic concept, as what is considered private today may not be regarded as private tomorrow. There are two reasons behind the temporary nature of decisions about data privacy: (i) beliefs about the privacy of the dataset in question need to be constantly re-evaluated and updated with new information and analytical techniques, and (ii) the available data may change as individuals withdraw their consent for its use. The dynamic nature of data privacy can be explained, first, by the evolving and unbounded nature of personal identifiers—i.e., information that can uniquely identify an individual or allow another person to deduce their identity. Thus, the interpretation of, and subsequently the belief in, what is deemed private may change as new data is released and collected, and as advancements in privacy attack techniques emerge. A well-known example of the unbounded nature of data privacy is that of the Netflix Prize competition, where only minimal structured— <user-id, movie, date of grade, grade>—was released by Netflix in a public crowdsourcing challenge to optimize recommendation algorithms. Although no explicit private information was disclosed, Narayanan and Shmatikov [17] later showed that individuals could be re-identified by linking this data with records from the Internet Movie Database (IMDB).

Second, previously-available data entries may become inaccessible later. Individuals may restrict the use of certain data attributes, limiting access to specific information. Alternatively, they may revoke their consent for data usage entirely by exercising their 'right to be forgotten and to erasure,' as defined by HIPAA and GDPR. Under this right, individuals have the freedom and authority to request the correction, deletion, or updating of information about themselves.

Hence, the ongoing arms race in de-identifying personal identifiers, along with potential updates or modifications to data subjects' agreements on data usage, impacts the accessibility and availability of original data. This is also evident in the provision of synthetic data in our e-commerce example. For applications such as fraud detection, personalized marketing, inventory management, and trend analysis, outdated data that no longer complies with data protection regulations must be discarded, and new synthetic data must be re-generated and shared.

3.3   Adapting to Concept Drifts in Original Data

A prominent challenge in adaptive, data-driven analytics is the occurrence of changes in data [15]. These changes can occur suddenly, as in the case of black swan events, or in the emergence of hotspot objects [9]. For example, during the global Covid-19 pandemic, the sales of previously niche products such as masks, and disinfectant sprays surged dramatically, altering the outcomes of personalized marketing, inventory management, and trend analysis. Changes can also occur gradually, as seen in the sales of peer-to-peer communication devices, with a shift from landlines to smartphone texting over recent decades. Additionally, changes may happen incrementally, as observed in the growing preference for online shopping over physical stores. Finally, changes can be recurrent, as exemplified by seasonal purchasing behaviors, such as increased bikini sales in summer in the e-commerce example.

This overall phenomenon, where the underlying distribution of the original data changes over time, is called Concept Drift [15]. Concept drift mandates the regeneration of synthetic data; otherwise, the synthetic data risks becoming obsolete. Effectively addressing concept drift requires continuous monitoring and detection, thorough analysis and understanding, and timely adaptation. Model re-training can be employed to adapt to sudden, gradual, or incremental drifts, while ensembles of models are suitable for addressing recurrent drifts.

3.4 Requirements for an Adaptive Architecture

Our research objective is to design a self-adaptive data management system that adjusts to evolving data contexts while balancing privacy and utility. To achieve this, the proposed solution must meet the following two requirements:

R1. Self-adaptive: The solution should be self-adaptive, i.e. capable of adjusting to changes in data context and use case needs while balancing privacy and utility requirements.

R2. Extensible: The solution should be extensible, allowing for the future integration of new generative models but also metrics. This ensures that the system can be effectively utilized in industrial applications.

4   System Design

We present the design of an MLOps system for synthetic data generation and sharing that is capable of managing multiple generators and adapting them over time. We refer to this system as the `Data Chameleon` architecture, highlighting its adaptive nature, akin to a chameleon.

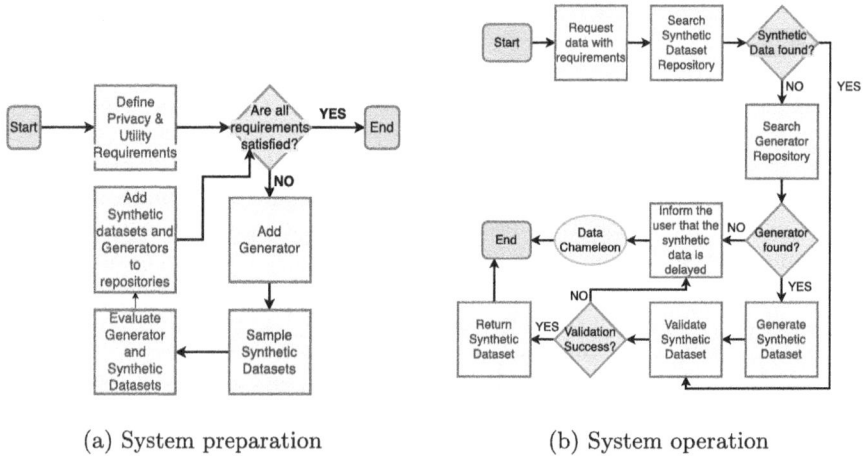

(a) System preparation   (b) System operation

Fig. 1. Flow-chart of the system preparation and operation phases of the Data Chameleon.

The Data Chameleon comprises of three complementary processes:

1. System Preparation: In the Data Chameleon, the System Preparation serves as a pivotal step towards getting the system ready to respond to data requests (System Operation). Different synthetic data generators are instantiated and trained at the basis the anticipated utility and privacy requirements. A selection of generators is made to ensure maximum coverage of anticipated requests during the System Operation. The process of the System Preparation is depicted as a flow-chart in Fig. 1a. There are two options for adding generators to prepare the system for a given use case: (i) create a new generator or (ii) merge synthetic data generated by existing generators in the system. To create a new generator, the generative model can be configured manually or the system can automatically try to find the right configuration for the given privacy/utility requirement.

2. System Operation: The operation of the Data Chameleon system marks the stage where requests for data from data consumers are processed and answered. Figure 1b presents a flow-chart of the System Operation. This process handles data consumer requests for synthetic datasets, which are submitted alongside an expression of the privacy and utility requirements[2]. It processes these requests by either sampling from a suited generator, or by sampling data from multiple generators and returning a merged dataset.

3. System Self-adaptation: By performing longer-term monitoring, detection, and analysis, the Data Chameleon takes longer term-adaptation actions, such as deciding to train new generators, to change the sampling and recombination strategy. Taking such a broader perspective allows evaluating overall compliance with privacy regulations, but also to adapt to concept drift.

4.1   Data Chameleon Adaptation Scenarios

In the Data Chameleon, if the system has no cached synthetic data or generator in the repository capable of satisfying the user's requests, or if the original data has drifted to the point of becoming obsolete, the self-adaptive nature of the system is activated (**R1**). The System Adaptation process is based on a well-known model for self-adaptive systems, the MAPE-k model [10], introduced by IBM. The MAPE-k model consists of an adaptation loop that includes four processes (Monitor, Analyse, Plan and Execute) and a shared knowledge base.

Figure 2 illustrates the MAPE-k-based self-adaptive data generation process, which monitors context changes and handles requests for synthetic data. This process is managed by the self-adaptive controller, the core component of the MLOps system. In the Monitor process, drifts in the original data are monitored, and incoming requests for synthetic data are processed. The system examines the Knowledge base for evidence of concept drifts and new adaptive requests. The Analyze process is triggered once any of the following are detected: i) significant drifts in the original data, ii) unanswered requests due to the emergence of new requirements, iii) requests for the removal or modification of personal data.

---

[2] Two tuples, referring to a privacy metric and a threshold value, and a utility metric and a threshold value.

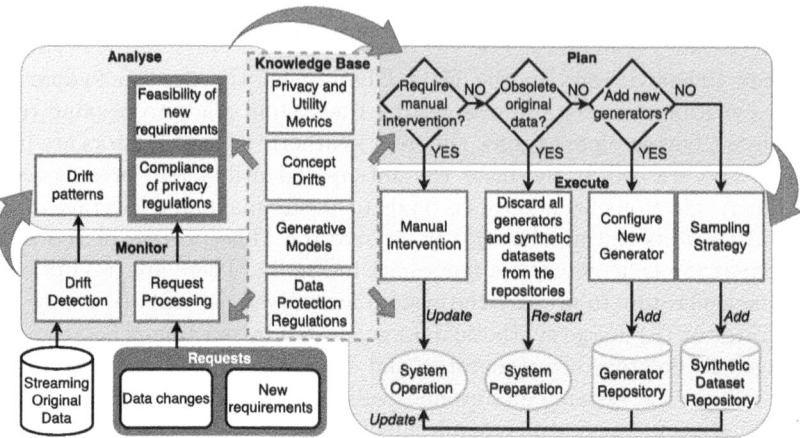

Fig. 2. MAPE-k Diagram of the `System Adaptation` process, which involves the longer-term reconfigurations of the Data Chameleon.

A change in data context or an unanswered request initiates an adaptation request for the `Plan` process. At this stage, the system determines whether to proceed with a manual adaptation plan or an automatic adaptation plan. These plans then provide instructions to automatically assess the current data context, add a new generator, or notify the system operator with an intervention request for manual configuration of additional generators and investigation of data. In the `Execute` process, the system implements changes by discarding and archiving existing generators and synthetic datasets, creating new generators, or merging synthetic datasets. It is important to note that the `Knowledge base` must be continuously updated to maintain up-to-date information on privacy and utility metrics, concept drifts, generative models, and data protection regulations. The following subsections outline the corresponding strategies for addressing different types of changes.

Adaptation to Concept Drifts. `Data Chameleon` employs different strategies to address various types of drift. In the case of sudden and permanent drift, where the current operational context becomes obsolete, all generators and cached synthetic datasets are archived and discarded. The `System Preparation` process is then triggered. For recurrent drift, new generators must be added, and the cached data and existing generators should be updated according to the drift pattern. In our motivating e-commerce example, this involves seasonally swapping generators and clearing cached synthetic datasets. For gradual changes, which typically occur over a longer time span and are more challenging to handle with automated adaptation strategies, manual intervention is required.

Adaptation to Data Changes. In the event of a data change in the original data (e.g., data subjects enacting the right to be forgotten or requesting to correct data, or new data incrementally being collected), the synthetic data generative models in the repository must be retrained or incrementally trained. If possible, techniques such as *machine unlearning* [23] can be adopted to completely remove the use of sensitive entries without having to train a generator from scratch. This involves triggering the `System Preparation` process.

Adaptation to New Use Cases. New requirements are identified when user requests arrive with privacy or utility requirements that the Data Chameleon is currently not equipped for. As a result, a new synthetic dataset should be generated, or a new generator should be trained to meet these previously-unseen requirements defined by the new metrics and their corresponding trade-off values. Again, this involves triggering the `System Preparation` process[3].

5 Related Work

We discuss related work in the context of data management layers (governing data storage, data access, data placement, etc.) that similarly adopt self-adaptation to attain (i) privacy objectives, (ii) security objectives or (iii) other non-functional properties.

Self-adaptation for Data Protection and Privacy Goals. Chennareddy et al. [8] propose an adaptive data minimization method for AI training datasets, using Reservoir Sampling and a utility-focused test suite. Experiments show it achieves similar accuracy with significantly less data.

Self-adaptation for Security and Confidentiality. CryptDICE [22] is an adaptive data management layer for honest-but-curious clouds, selecting suitable encryption schemes based on specific requirements and making trade-offs across data granularity levels. Verreydt et al. [24] propose a dynamic digital twin threat model to assess risks in real time. A self-adaptive security system uses these insights to guide access control and trigger mitigations when needed.

Self-adaptation for Other Non-functional Properties. Zhou et al. [26] present an adaptive data transmission and synchronization approach between vehicles that communicate in a peer-to-peer fashion, and which takes into account the bandwidth costs, the ecological impact (energy consumption) and overall stability. Lujic et al. [16] presented SEA-Leaf, a locality-aware edge analytics approach. This approach involves identifying the most optimal location to perform specific analytics tasks, taking into account available resources and data locality. The results indicate that adopting an adaptive approach leads to a reduction in overall analytics requests execution time.

---

[3] Alternatively, the system should notify the operator with an intervention request to manually add a new generator or assess the feasibility of the new requirements.

6 Conclusions and Future Work

Collaborative data sharing operations such as the ones emerging in the context of Data Spaces—which are part of the EU's strategic agenda—are gaining in importance and relevance. Instead of resorting to binary access decisions, deriving value from datasets that would otherwise not be processed or shared is a compelling enabler for realizing such data market ecosystems. This can be accomplished via synthetic dataset representations, and by taking on a more self-adaptive risk-aware approach.

This paper presents Data Chameleon, a self-adaptive MLOps system architecture for synthetic data generation which adapts data responses to different use cases with varying privacy and utility requirements. To the best our knowledge, this is the first work to introduce the MLOps principles of self-adaptation in the training, operation and access to different synthetic data generators.

We are currently prototyping the Data Chameleon and equipping it with state-of-the-art generative models and metrics from open-source libraries such as Synthcity [21] and Anonymeter [12]. In future work, we will set up simulation-based evaluations to experimentally validate the system's adaptability. This overall evaluation plan consists of three phases. In the first phase, the preparation is conducted, bootstrapping the system with a range of generative models that should meet the utility and privacy requirements anticipated and known at design time. Next, the operation phase will be tested by executing an artificial workload of incoming data requests. Here, we can evaluate the privacy and utility of the obtained system responses, but also measure system metrics such as response time, throughput, latency, memory cost, etc. Finally, long-term adaptations will be evaluated by artificially modifying data distributions, attributes, and entries in the original data.

Acknowledgements. This research is partially funded by the Research Fund KU Leuven, and by the Cybersecurity Research Program Flanders.

References

1. Alaa, A., Van Breugel, B., Saveliev, E.S., van der Schaar, M.: How faithful is your synthetic data? Sample-level metrics for evaluating and auditing generative models. In: International Conference on Machine Learning, pp. 290–306 (2022)
2. Alabdulwahab, S., Kim, Y.T., Seo, A., Son, Y.: Generating synthetic dataset for ML-Based IDS using CTGAN and feature selection to protect smart IoT environments. Appl. Sci. **13**(19), 10951 (2023)
3. Altman, E.: Synthesizing credit card transactions. In: Proceedings of the Second ACM International Conference on AI in Finance, pp. 1–9 (2021)
4. Backes, M., Berrang, P., Humbert, M., Manoharan, P.: Membership privacy in MicroRNA-based studies. In: Proceedings of the 2016 ACM SIGSAC Conference on Computer and Communications Security, pp. 319–330 (2016)
5. Bao, Z., Tokmakov, P., Jabri, A., Wang, Y.X., Gaidon, A., Hebert, M.: Discovering objects that can move. In: Proceedings of the IEEE/CVF Conference on Computer Vision and Pattern Recognition, pp. 11789–11798 (2022)

6. Bhattarai, B., Baek, S., Bodur, R., Kim, T.K.: Sampling strategies for GAN synthetic data. In: ICASSP 2020-2020 IEEE International Conference on Acoustics, Speech and Signal Processing (ICASSP), pp. 2303–2307. IEEE (2020)
7. Chen, D.: Online Retail. UCI Machine Learning Repository (2015). https://doi.org/10.24432/C5BW33
8. Chennareddy, V., Koppula, R.C.: Enhancing AI data management: combining reservoir sampling and self-adaptive testing for efficiency. In: 2024 International Conference on Intelligent Systems for Cybersecurity (ISCS), pp. 1–5 (2024). https://doi.org/10.1109/ISCS61804.2024.10581365
9. Claesen, C., Rafique, A., Van Landuyt, D., Joosen, W.: A YCSB workload for benchmarking hotspot object behaviour in NoSQL databases. In: Nambiar, R., Poess, M. (eds.) TPCTC 2021. LNCS, vol. 13169, pp. 1–16. Springer, Cham (2022). https://doi.org/10.1007/978-3-030-94437-7_1
10. Computing, A., et al.: An architectural blueprint for autonomic computing. IBM White Paper **31**(2006), 1–6 (2006)
11. Garfinkel, S., Garfinkel, S., Near, J., Dajani, A., Singer, P., Guttman, B.: De-Identifying Government Datasets: Techniques and Governance. US Department of Commerce, National Institute of Standards and Technology (2023)
12. Giomi, M., Boenisch, F., Wehmeyer, C., Tasnádi, B.: A unified framework for quantifying privacy risk in synthetic data. arXiv preprint arXiv:2211.10459 (2022)
13. James, S., Harbron, C., Branson, J., Sundler, M.: Synthetic data use: exploring use cases to optimise data utility. Disc. Artif. Intell. **1**(1), 1–13 (2021). https://doi.org/10.1007/s44163-021-00016-y
14. Kitten, T.: Target breach: What happened? Bank info security (2013). https://www.bankinfosecurity.com/target-breach-what-happened-a-6312
15. Lu, J., Liu, A., Dong, F., Gu, F., Gama, J., Zhang, G.: Learning under concept drift: a review. IEEE Trans. Knowl. Data Eng. **31**(12), 2346–2363 (2018)
16. Lujic, I., De Maio, V., Venugopal, S., Brandic, I.: SEA-LEAP: self-adaptive and locality-aware edge analytics placement. IEEE Trans. Serv. Comput. **15**(2), 602–613 (2022). https://doi.org/10.1109/TSC.2021.3104458
17. Narayanan, A., Shmatikov, V.: How to break anonymity of the Netflix prize dataset. arXiv preprint cs/0610105 (2006)
18. Papernot, N., Song, S., Mironov, I., Raghunathan, A., Talwar, K., Erlingsson, Ú.: Scalable private learning with PATE. arXiv preprint arXiv:1802.08908 (2018)
19. Patki, N., Wedge, R., Veeramachaneni, K.: The synthetic data vault. In: 2016 IEEE International Conference on Data Science and Advanced Analytics (DSAA), pp. 399–410. IEEE (2016)
20. Ping, H., Stoyanovich, J., Howe, B.: Datasynthesizer: privacy-preserving synthetic datasets. In: Proceedings of the 29th International Conference on Scientific and Statistical Database Management, pp. 1–5 (2017)
21. Qian, Z., Cebere, B.C., van der Schaar, M.: Synthcity: facilitating innovative use cases of synthetic data in different data modalities (2023). https://doi.org/10.48550/ARXIV.2301.07573. https://arxiv.org/abs/2301.07573
22. Rafique, A., Van Landuyt, D., Beni, E.H., Lagaisse, B., Joosen, W.: CryptDICE: distributed data protection system for secure cloud data storage and computation. Inf. Syst. **96**, 101671 (2021)
23. Shaik, T., Tao, X., Xie, H., Li, L., Zhu, X., Li, Q.: Exploring the landscape of machine unlearning: a comprehensive survey and taxonomy. IEEE Trans. Neural Netw. Learn. Syst. (2024)
24. Verreydt, S., Van Landuyt, D., Joosen, W.: Run-time threat models for systematic and continuous risk assessment. Softw. Syst. Model., 1–24 (2024)

25. Yeom, S., Giacomelli, I., Fredrikson, M., Jha, S.: Privacy risk in machine learning: analyzing the connection to overfitting. In: 2018 IEEE 31st Computer Security Foundations Symposium (CSF), pp. 268–282. IEEE (2018)
26. Zhou, Y., Yu, F.R., Ren, M., Chen, J.: Adaptive data transmission and computing for vehicles in the Internet-of-Intelligence. IEEE Trans. Veh. Technol. (2023)

Operating Under Constraints: Identifying Requirements for Enhanced Cyber Resilience Management

Francis Wanko Naa[(✉)], Nora Boulahiacuppens, and Frederic Cuppens

Polytechnique Montreal, Montreal, QC H3T 0A3, Canada
{francis.wanko-naa,nora.boulahiacuppens,
frederic.cuppens}@polymtl.ca

Abstract. Organizations operate in a constantly changing environment. They face many disruptions that can affect their sustainability. Cyber resilience is a de facto concept on which they can rely on to ensure their sustainability. It is defined as the ability of a nation, organization, or mission or business process to anticipate, withstand, recover from, and evolve to improve capabilities in the face of adverse conditions, stresses, or attacks on the supporting cyber resources it needs to function. It is influenced by several disciplines. From these disciplines, it is necessary to extract the requirements that the organization must comply with to be able to be cyber resilient. Once the requirements have been extracted, they need to be cleaned up to eliminate duplicates, so that only a single set of requirements applicable to the organization remains. Manual extraction is tedious. We propose an approach integrating Machine Learning to automate the extraction of cyber resilience requirements from documents written in natural language. This extraction is followed by the identification of duplicates to retain single set of requirements that will be implemented for cyber resilience enhancement.

Keywords: Cyber resilience · NLP · Requirements · text classification · semantic similarity

1 Introduction

Organizations evolves in environments with perpetual changes, forcing them to constantly readapt to maintain a competitive edge and ensure their long-term existence. Cyber resilience can be a relevant concept that organizations can draw on to ensure their long-term success. It is defined by [1] as "the ability to anticipate, withstand, recover from, and adapt to adverse conditions, stresses, attacks, or compromises on systems that use or are enabled by cyber resources". It can also be defined as "the ability of a nation, organization, mission or business process to anticipate, resist, recover and evolve to improve its capabilities in the face of adverse conditions, stresses or attacks on the cyber resources it needs to function" [2]. In other words, it's the ability of a nation, organization,

© IFIP International Federation for Information Processing 2026
Published by Springer Nature Switzerland AG 2025
S. Katsikas and B. Shafiq (Eds.): DBSec 2025, LNCS 15722, pp. 57–72, 2025.
https://doi.org/10.1007/978-3-031-96590-6_4

mission or business process to anticipate, resist, recover and evolve to improve its capabilities in the face of adverse conditions, tensions, or attacks on its cyber-resources. To achieve this, organizations must constantly assess their level of cyber resilience, propose and implement improvement strategies to ensure that the resulting enterprise architecture can adequately support business needs despite disruptions. It's a question of organizations truly taking charge of their operational resilience management which is for [3] the ability of the organization to achieve its mission even under degraded circumstances. This is achieved by establishing cyber resilience requirements that help define the processes by which the organization designs, develops, implements, manages and improves strategies for protecting and maintaining high-value services and associated assets such as people, information, technologies and facilities [3]. Business practices are influenced by requirements derived from various frameworks (e.g. DORA [4]) or best practices (e.g. ISO/AWI 223162, NIST-SP800–1603, CERT Resilience management model, etc. [3, 5, 6] and [7]). These frameworks document the set of processes and procedures that need to be put in place to support a business practice. Cyber resilience is a concept that is realized through the implementation of requirements that originate from several areas of activity. These include cyber security, business continuity and IT operations [3]. Consequently, the requirements to be followed to be cyber resilient are drawn from different domains, and only their consistent implementation can ensure a level of cyber resilience for the organization. Extracting requirements from frameworks is a tedious exercise when done manually. According to [8], this is an enormous time-consuming task which requires a lot of effort from analysts since every requirement document must be read and manually classified. For [9], "This [...] manual process involves data collection and decision-making by experts [...] and usually costs a lot of money and time". Automating requirements extraction can be very cost effective in terms of time and money. This is done today with techniques derived from the field of artificial intelligence, such as natural language processing (NLP). In this work, our Text Classification (TC) approach provides an automated method for extracting sentences from documents and classifying them as requirements for cyber-resilience requirements engineering purposes. To achieve this, we propose an approach in 3 main steps. The first step aims to identify and create an inventory of reference frameworks and laws that define cyber resilience requirements for organizations. The second step, subdivided into 3 sub-steps, allows preprocessing of the documents from the inventory to extract the candidate sentences to be requirements and to train a ML model to effectively classify each sentence according to the predefined category and finally identify within the extracted requirement the duplicates. The third step allows validation of the results obtained from the ML model. The rest of this paper is organized as follows: Section 2 presents the scope and motivation of our work. Section 3 the state of art regarding requirement extraction. Section 4 presents our proposed approach for cyber resilience requirement extraction. Section 5 presents results and evaluation. In Sect. 6 we discuss about some of the challenges faced and Sect. 7 conclude our paper and present future potential work.

2 Scope and Motivation

2.1 Scope: An Organizational Capability

Cyber resilience focuses on the resilience of the cyber resources on which the mission, business processes and organization depend to deliver value. Cyber resource is defined by [2] and [6] as an information resource which creates, stores, processes, manages, transmits, or disposes of information in electronic form and which can be accessed via a network or using networking methods. According to [10], cyber resilience is about enabling the achievement of mission and business objectives that depend on cyber resources in an environment disrupted by events such as errors, infrastructure failures, cyber-attacks, etc. Cyber resilience is a property of an organization that can be desirable at several levels, as shown in the Fig. 1 from [2] below.

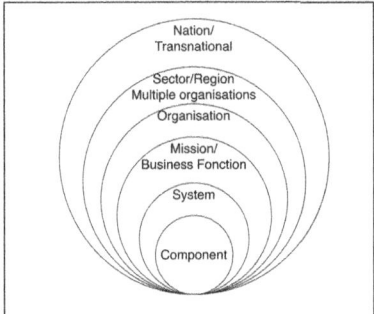

Fig. 1. Scope and scale at which cyber resilience can be assessed

The scope chosen for this article covers the cyber resilience of the capabilities which the organization relies on to deliver value. A capability referred to the power or ability to do something according to the Oxford dictionary. It translates into an organization as the integration of a set of elements designed to be combined to achieve a specific result [11]. It is made up of at least one of the following six elements: business function, business processes, organizational units, know-how, information assets, technological assets, brand and physical resources [11]. According to [11] and [12], these concepts are defined as follows: a business function is a kind of work done by the organization. A business process is a set of activities, methods, and practices that transforms a set of inputs into a set of products and services. An organization unit is a team of people with a common goal that is headed by a manager. Know-how comprises skills and expertise and information assets are fact provided or learned about something or someone. Technology asset is a tangible or intangible asset that is the result of the application of scientific knowledge for practical purpose. Brand is a name and/or logo associated with the number of products and/or services to distinguish them from other similar products and/or services, and to convey that these products and/or services share important customer value proposition attributes. Natural resources include such thing as parcels of land, natural oil, etc. From an enterprise architecture point of view, a capability is a set of components, systems, business functions and organization. According to [2], a component is defined as a part of a system that can be replaced or managed separately from other parts of the system. Examples include infrastructure, embedded devices, servers, applications and so on. A system or system of systems, on the other hand, brings together a set of systems to perform a task that none of the systems can accomplish on its own. Finally, business functions are activities, processes or sets of related activities or processes designed to achieve a business mission or objective. More specifically, according to [13] the modelling approach derived from The Open Group Architecture Framework (TOGAF), which structures enterprise architecture in three major views, a capability can be seen as a vertical cross-section of the enterprise, comprising the business architecture (business processes and functions), the information systems architecture, which supports the data and the technological architecture, which presents all the technological infrastructure. In this article, we propose an approach to automatically extract cyber resilience requirements from the reference frameworks for an organization's capabilities. In this way, we address requirements related to business architecture, technology architecture and systems architecture in connection with disruptions caused by cyber-attacks. These requirements are derived from frameworks for domains that contribute to the cyber resilience of capabilities such as cyber security, business continuity and IT. The Fig. 2 below presents a conceptual view of the relation between enterprise architecture and cyber resilience domain as addressed in this article.

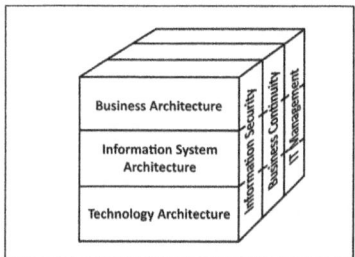

Fig. 2. Enterprise architecture and cyber resilience domain

Figure 2 illustrates the fact that cyber resilience is a cross-functional concept in organizations. It draws on areas such as cyber security, business continuity and information technology management. It must be considered when defining business needs (business architecture), when implementing technological systems (technological architecture), and when defining, acquiring and operating information systems and the data that the organization produces, processes and stores. Each level of this enterprise architecture is subject to different types of requirements that will enable the organization to ensure its cyber resilience.

2.2 Motivation and Contribution

Identifying the requirements placed on a system has always been an essential activity in the development of organizations. Very few authors have addressed this exercise at the level of an organization itself. Defining these requirements and extracting them is done as part of the development of a new technology/software solution. An organization as an independent legal entity is also subject to a set of requirements that it must obey to ensure its perennity. Our contribution is essentially to demonstrate the applicability of a cyber resilience requirements extraction approach defined for the scope of an organizational capability.

3   State of the Art

In this section we present approaches that have been used to automatically extract requirements from texts written in natural language. Those approaches could originally be developed for software but can be adapted to the organization level requirements. As mentioned in [8], informal textual descriptions written in natural language are a common means for specifying requirements in early phases of software projects. In [14], the authors propose an approach to requirements identification based on machine learning and more specifically NLP, to differentiate between requirements and non-requirements in a standard. To achieve this, they propose a 4-step approach. The first step is to analyze the requirements document. This stage extracts all the sentences from the document and removes irrelevant information such as annotations. The second step consists in extracting the relevant features for training a learning model. Step 3 involves using the trained model to predict the requirement or non-requirement status of each sentence. This step makes it possible to identify many requirements, which facilitates step 4 (post-processing), when analysts refine the results obtained. The authors propose a tool based on the 4-step approach for extracting and differentiating requirements from nonrequirements. It should be noted that the model training process follows a supervised approach, in which an annotator has been selected to manually identify requirements and nonrequirements in a document. This prior identification served as the basis for training the AI model with the labels provided by the annotator. The authors in [15] propose an NLP-based text classification approach to classify requirements and nonrequirement in PDF documents. They propose a ML-based approach that identifies the different sections existing in a PDF document, labels them using a predefined set of labels and automatically classifies them based on the model trained with the extracted features. The authors in [16] propose an approach using machine learning (ML) to automatically extract cybersecurity requirements from natural language documents. These requirements are then linked to control objectives either explicitly or implicitly formulated in the requirements. The main control objectives identified by the authors include confidentiality, integrity, identification and authentication, availability, accountability and privacy. The authors in [8] propose a semi-supervised text classification approach for the extraction of non-functional requirements. To this end, they use the Naive Bayesian approach to identify non-functional requirements and classify them according to the category to which they belong (security, etc.). Their approach comprises 3 stages: pre-processing, semi-supervised learning and classification. In the pre-processing phase, sentences are extracted. Then, in a supervised learning approach, a classifier automatically recognizes different types of non-functional requirements in a set of documents, each one describing a requirement for the system written in natural language and presents them to analysts for review. The classifier has first been trained with data on which labels have been applied to facilitate its training. In [17], the authors propose a ML-based technique for automating the detection and classification of non-functional requirements related to properties such as security, performance, and usability. Their article introduces and describes a nonfunctional requirement classifier, for retrieving and classifying nonfunctional requirements (NFR) scattered across both structured and unstructured documents. Their approach is composed of 3 main steps: training, classification and applications. During the training phase indicator terms are mined from existing requirements. These terms are then used during the retrieval phase to detect and classify other NFRs. In the application phase, the classified requirements are used to support more advanced software engineering activities such as requirements negotiation or architectural design. Like these authors, we use a machine-learning approach to identify requirements. In our approach, however, the scope is that of an organization capability. In addition, requirements are extracted from frameworks whose structure and writing approach are very different. What's more, once the requirements have been extracted, we compare them to identify duplicates.

4 Methodology

A requirement defines a customer's need or objective or specifies a condition or capability that an entity must have to meet that need or achieve that objective. It can be defined at multiple level as mentioned in Fig. 1. Several challenges arise when it comes to extracting cyber resilience requirements from documents. The requirements are written in natural language, cyber resilience covers several domains. This implies that requirements come from different business domains. The structure and content of requirements texts may vary according to the approaches used to document them. Our proposed approach for extracting cyber resilience requirements from reference documents is presented in the Fig. 3 below:

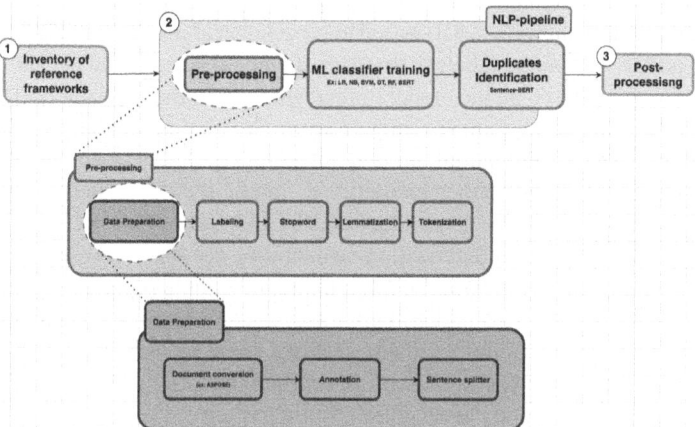

Fig. 3. Automated cyber resilience requirement process

This approach is composed of three main steps:

1. **Inventory of reference frameworks:** To extract the cyber resilience requirements that apply to a particular organization, it is first necessary to identify the frameworks that govern cyber resilience practices in the context of that organization. Once the frameworks have been identified, a multi-compliance framework can be established. There are many frameworks that organizations need to comply with, such as the Digital Operational Resilience Act (DORA), ISO22316, NIST, CERT RMM, etc. They are often initiated by industry bodies, organizations and governments [9] and have both legal and reputational implications [18].
2. **NLP Pipeline:** Frameworks are mainly written in text documents intended to be read by humans [19]. The aim of the NLP step is to take raw text from frameworks and regulatory texts and extract requirements from each of them. The NLP approach proposed in this article is text classification (TC). Text classification has witnessed a booming interest in the last years, due to the increased availability of documents in digital form and the ensuing need to organize them [20]. According to [21], it is the process of assigning predefined category labels to new documents based on the classifier learnt from training examples. The input to a classifier is a training set of records, each of which is tagged with a class label [22]. The text classification goal is according to [22], induce a model or description for each class in terms of the attributes. The model is then used to classify future records whose classes are unknown. Many text classification models exist in the literature [23]. Within the NLP Pipeline, we have a pre-processing step and the ML classifier training.

– *Pre-processing:* The pre-processing step we use in this article is based on the methodology proposed by [24] and can be broken down as follows:

a) Data preparation: after conversion into an easily exploitable format, the document is broken down to extract a set of requirements with all the unvaluable information being removed (e.g.: page number, table of contents, etc.).
b) Labelling: It consists of classifying text units (sentences, paragraphs or entire documents) into categories and, assigning them labels [24].
c) Stop words: Meaningless words that have low discrimination power should be removed [25] [26].
d) emmatization: Here, we replace the suffix of a word with a different one or removes the suffix of a word completely to get the basic word form (lemma) [19]. It is the process of finding the normalized form of a word [27].
e) Tokenization: This stage is used to cut text into pieces, called tokens, and removing certain characters, such as punctuation [28]. At the syntactic level, statements are segmented into words, punctuation (i.e. tokens) and each token is assigned a tag in the form of a noun, verb, adjective, adverb and so on (Part of Speech Tagging) [29]. It is essential for text classification, as the text must be represented as a feature vector for the classifier to perform statistical analysis [24].
f) Feature Selection: It is the process of selecting a subset of features to represent the text [24]. The aim here is to improve NLP model performance by removing irrelevant or redundant features, thus reducing the number of total features.

g) Word embedding: It is a feature learning technique in which each word or phrase from the vocabulary is mapped to an N dimension vector of real numbers [23]. It is one of the most useful deep learning methods used for constructing vector representations of words and documents [30]. The NLP pipeline stage identifies candidate phrases that may be cyber resilience requirements. The next step is to train the ML classifier to adequately distinguish between requirement and non-requirement candidates.

– *ML Classifier Training*

a) ML models for requirement classification: Several classifiers have been trained separately to predict the categories (requirements or non-requirements) of texts to them. According to [31], Naive Bayes (NB) is one of the most favored and commonly deployed methods. Other algorithms such as decision trees (DT) and have also been reported to be effective for text classification based on [32]. Random Forest according to [15] is also part of a well-known ML algorithm that can be used for text classification. [22] identifies logistic regression also as one of the most popular text classification algorithms. The output of the ML Classification phase is the text classification results that form the input for the next step.

b) ML models for duplicate identification: Duplicates are requirements from one or more documents that have the same semantic meaning. Several approaches [33–37] have been proposed in the literature to identify phrases or words with the same meaning. In this sense, similarity can be defined as the commonness between two text snippets [38]. To properly identify duplicates, we need to determine the semantic similarity between the different candidate requirements. It is defined as the measure of semantic equivalence between two blocks of text [39]. The semantic approach focuses on meaning of the words and hidden semantic connections between words and consequently between documents [34]. Techniques for determining semantic similarity can be grouped into three broad categories. The knowledge-based, corpus-based and deep neural network-based semantic similarity methods are proposed in [34, 39]. Knowledge-based semantic similarity methods calculate semantic similarity between two terms based on the information derived from one or more underlying knowledge sources like ontologies/lexical databases, thesauri, dictionaries [39] for example the WorldNet lexical database. Corpus-based semantic similarity methods measure semantic similarity between terms using the information retrieved from large corpora example word2vec, Glove and BERT [39]. Deep neural networks can be considered as a separate group, even though they use word embeddings built from large corpora examples CNN, LSTM and Sentence BERT. According to [36, 39] "Knowledge-based methods consider the actual meaning of the text but are not adaptable across domains and languages. Corpus-based implemented across languages, but they do not consider the actual meaning of the text. Deep neural network-based methods show better performance but require high computational resources and lack interpretability".

3. **Post-processing:** The post-processing stage consists of reviewing the extracted requirements to validate that they have been properly categorized. This phase is carried out by an analyst. In our context, the cost of misclassifying a nonrequirement

as a requirement (false positive) is considerably less than that of misclassifying a requirement as a non-requirement (false negative). The rationale here is that, if false positives are not too many, the effort of manually discarding them is an interesting trade-off [40].

5 Application and Evaluation

In our work, we experimented with the proposed theoretical approach using documents from various sources (NIST, ISO, etc.). Our aim being to automatically extract cyber resilience requirements from these various documents, we opted for an approach based on ML techniques. To achieve this, we first annotated four selected frameworks documents to facilitate the subsequent training of the model. The selection of documents to be annotated was based on criteria such as:

- The document must belong to one of the domains of cyber resilience as mentioned by [3] and must constitute a recognized reference framework.
- The requirements of the document must be adapted to the scale of the organization.
- The document must be available in English to train the machine learning model.
- The document must be available in PDF or Word format.

5.1 Experimental Settings

1. **Inventory of Reference Frameworks:**Cyber resilience is a concept that is influenced by several fields with diverse frameworks (NIST, ISO, COBIT, ITIL and others). This multitude of frameworks, which are written in natural language, does not necessarily follow the same structures for specifying requirements. For our experiment, we used the NIST SP800-53 [41], which deals with security and privacy controls for information systems and organizations. For business continuity, we have the ISO22301 standard [43], which deals with security and resilience (business continuity management system). For IT service management, we used the COBIT 5 [44] reference framework which is a business and management framework for governance and management of enterprise IT. Figure 4 shows an extract from the ISO and NIST frameworks, in which the structure of the documents and the way in which the requirements are formulated are different. The wording used in ISO 22301 uses expressions such as 'shall', which are recommendations of good practice according to [45, 46].
2. **NLP Pipeline:**As mentioned in the Fig. 1, the NLP pipeline has two main steps: the pre-processing and the ML classifier training.
    1) Pre-processing: Once the frameworks have been identified according to the criteria defined in section IV, each of them was annotated by a professional.
        a. Data preparation: We converted PDF document into Word files using ASPOSE to facilitate further processing. Once converted, a sentence splitter approach is applied to extract all sentences which are considered as requirement candidate.
        b. Labelling: Once extracted, manual analysis was conducted to annotate sentences. This annotation was carried out using predefined labels as presented in table 1.
        c. Stop words: The stop-word step removes words such as {'a', 'after', 'again'}.

Table 1. Example of labels used for the annotation

Label	Description	Family
Document_title	Document title	Non_requirement
Req_ID	A requirement ID number	Non_requirement
Req_text	A requirement text	Requirement
Table	A table caption	Non_requirement
Title	Section or subsection title	Non_requirement
Figure	An image caption	Non_requirement

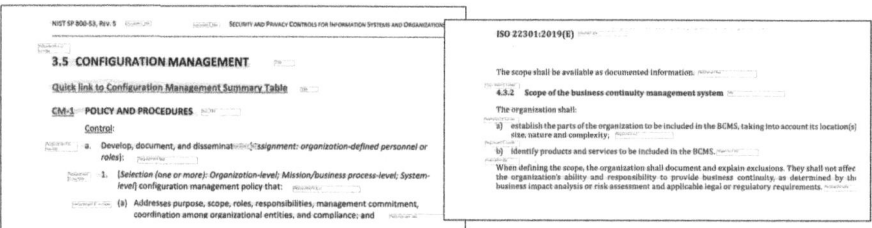

Fig. 4. Example from a manually annotated extract from NIST SP800–53 and ISO 22301

    d. Lemmatization: This stage brings words back to their root for each of the words contained in the sentences extracted in the previous phases.

    e. Tokenization: by applying the definition in Sect. 4 by [47] and [48] to a requirement from [41] *"Baseline configurations are documented"* we will have a result like {*'baseline' 'configurations' 'are' 'documented'*}.

ML Classifier Training

1. Text Classification technique: It can be performed using several techniques like Naïve Bayes (NB), logistic regression (LR), decision trees (DT), Random Forest (RF), Support vector machine (SVM) and BERT. Number of authors [23, 31, 49–54] have identified these techniques as being widely used approaches for this purpose. We have selected these models because of their popularity in the field of text classification, but also because of the advantages they offer for example, simplicity of implementation, low training requirements, high speed, efficient operation with text data and low computational resources consumption [23, 49].

2. Evaluation metrics for ML classifier training: After training, each classifier was evaluated according to metrics, enabling us to compare their effectiveness in extracting requirements. Each method was evaluated using the criteria of precision, accuracy and recall. For [10, 13], Accuracy is the fraction of correct predictions over all predictions [19]; Precision is the ratio of requirement candidates correctly classified as a requirement to all requirement candidates classified as requirements and Recall is the fraction of all requirements correctly demarcated. We define TP and TN as the number of true positives and true negatives, i.e., correctly classified cases of requirements and

non-requirements. FP is the number of false positives, i.e. non-requirements predicted as requirements, and FN is the number of false negatives, i.e. requirements classified as non-requirements. Model valuation metrics are calculated as follows as proposed by [17, 19] and [15]: Accuracy = (TP + TN)/ (TP + TN + FP + FN); Precision = TP/ (TP + FP); Recall = TP/ (TP + FN)

3. Experimental results: Several ML approaches were tested to identify the one with the best performance. Table 2 below shows the accuracy, precision, and recall results for the seven classifiers (LR, DT, RF, NB, SVM, RNN and pre-trained BERT).

Table 2. Result of the text classifiers

ML classifier	Accuracy metric (%)	Precision metric (%)	Recall metric (%)
Decision tree	0,87	0,89	0,87
Random forest	0,91	0,91	0,91
Naive's Bayes	0,86	0,86	0,86
Support vector machine	0,85	0,85	0,85
Logistic regression	0,88	0,88	0,87
BERT	0,95	0,98	0,97

We found that the approach using the pre-trained BERT model performed best, with an accuracy of 95%, precision of 98% and recall of 97%.

Duplicates Identification: The previous stage ends with the production of a list of sentences that the model has classified as cyber resilience requirements. Having been derived from multiple sources, there is a real risk that duplicates will appear, both from a syntactic and semantic point of view. For this reason, the set of classified requirements needs to be further processed to identify duplicate. As mentioned in section IV, we have used an approach based on the deep neural network, as this seems to offer the most promising results. To this end, we chose the Sentence-BERT model for experimentation. To determine the semantic similarity between the sentences of the different requirements, we used cosine similarity. Cosine-similarity is the cosine of the angle between two vectors and similarity in "cosine similarity" refers to the fact that larger values in distance metrics indicate closer proximity [55]. By identifying duplicates, only unique requirements can be retained and duplicate remove if needed. Experimentation with the ISO 22301 and NIST SP800–53 produced the following results in Table 3:

Table 3 shows the percentage of requirements extracted from the documents, the Number of sentences per document, the percentage of intra-document duplicates. Table 4 below shows examples of extracted requirements identified as duplicates.

Table 3. Results of duplicate identification

Reference framework	N. of Requirement candidates	% of sentence classified as requirements	% of duplicates within a framework
NST SP800–53	8804	18,8%	9,8%
ISO_22301_2019	242	46,3%	10,7%

Table 4. Example of duplicates requirements

Sentence	Candidate duplicates	Cosine similarity
The organization shall evaluate the BCMS performance and the effectiveness of the BCMS	10.2 Continual improvement The organization shall continually improve the suitability, adequacy and effectiveness of the BCMS, based on qualitative and quantitative measures	0,85
Establishing the following **system -level** metrics to be monitored: [Assignment: organization - defined system -level metrics];	Establishing the following **organization -wide metrics** to be monitored: [Assignment: organization- defined metrics];	0,87

6 Discussion

In this work, we focused on the automated extraction of cyber resilience requirements from frameworks to facilitate their implementation within organizations and achieve the desired level of cyber resilience. The diversity of requirement sources and formats (PDF, Word, etc.) makes initial pre-processing operations complex. Converting a PDF document into a Word document, for example, often changes the structure of sentences, requiring additional checking to ensure sentence consistency. Even using more advanced technologies, the coherence of the sentences still needs to be validated before the training. Figure 5 below shows an example of an inconsistent requirement after converting the NIST PDF document into a Word document.

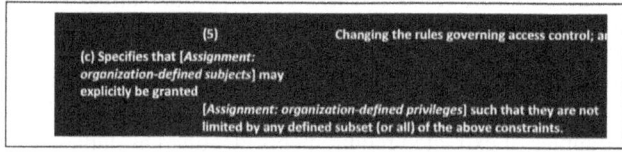

Fig. 5. Example of NIST requirement extract after conversion form PDF to word

Another problem is language. The documents submitted to our BERT model for requirements extraction are written in the same language (English). It would be interesting to repeat the exercise with documents written in different languages, which could be beneficial for organizations represented in countries with different languages. Once the sentences are well structured, the model can be trained to distinguish requirements from non-requirements in the light of the performances obtained in Table 2. After identifying duplicates, manual work is still required to validate the extracted requirements. This should be carried out by a subject matter expert. This phase is easier because the effort required to identify misclassified requirements is less, since the number of requirements extracted from the different documents is smaller compared to the total number of sentences in each document. Figure 6 shows an example of cyber resilience requirements extracted form ISO and NIST.

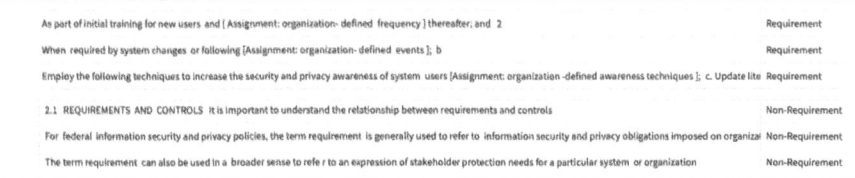

Fig. 6. Extract of requirement classification from NIST and ISO

7   Conclusion and Future Work

In this article, we discuss the concept of cyber resilience. After defining cyber resilience, we identify the scope within which it can be applied in an organization, and the frameworks that organizations can draw on to implement and improve their cyber resilience. Being a multidisciplinary concept, the operationalization of cyber resilience requires the identification and implementation of requirements from various disciplines. Extracting these requirements for an organization can be tedious and costly. We have proposed an NLP-based text classification approach to help organizations automatically extract requirements from frameworks. Experimental results have shown that pre-trained BERT models perform better in document requirement extraction than other basic models such as DT, LR. SVM, NB. After the initial classification, we automatically identified duplicates to group them together and enable each identified requirement to be treated uniquely. To achieve this, we used a pre-trained SBERT model to determine the semantic similarity between requirements from different frameworks. The results of the experiments showed that around 10% of the requirements extracted from the different frameworks (NIST, ISO, etc.) had a high degree of semantic similarity and could, after validation, be grouped together as single requirement. There are many research opportunities that can be derived from cyber resilience. Future work can be about evaluating cyber resilience based on requirements in place in organizations or else about measuring cyber resilience and recommending operational strategies to enhance the posture of organizations.

Acknowledgments. I would like to thank Ms Neda Moghadam and Mr Njike Cedric for their help in training the models used for the experiments in this article.

Disclosure of Interests. The authors have no competing interests to declare that are relevant to the content of this article.

References

1. Ross, R., Graubart, R., Bodeau, D., Mcquaid, R.: Systems Security Engineering. National Institute of Standards and Technology. NIST Special Publication 800-160 vol. 2 (1992)
2. Deborah, J., Bodeau, R.D., Graubart, R.M., McQuaid, J.W.: Cyber Resiliency Metrics, Measures of Effectiveness, and Scoring, p. 119 (2018)
3. Caralli, R.A., Allen, J.H., Curtis, P.D., White, D.W., Young, L.R.: CERT Resilience Management Model, Version 1.0 », Carnegie Mellon University & Software Engineering Institute. TECHNICAL REPORT CMU/SEI-2010-TR-012 ESC-TR-2010-012 (2010)
4. European Union. The Digital Operational Resilience Act (DORA) - Regulation (EU) 2022/2554. Digital Operational Resilience Act (DORA). https://www.digital-operational-res ilience-act.com/
5. ISO. Sécurité et résilience—Résilience organisationnelle—Principes et attributs, 22316:2017 (2017)
6. Ross, R., Pillitteri, V., Graubart, R., Bodeau, D., McQuaid, R.: Developing cyber-resilient systems: a systems security engineering approach. National Institute of Standards and Technology (U.S.), Gaithersburg, MD, NIST SP 800-160v2r1 (2021). https://doi.org/10.6028/NIST.SP.800-160v2r1
7. Caralli, R.A., Allen, J.H., White, D.W., Young, L.R., Mehravari, N., Curtis, P.D.: CERT® Resilience Management Model, Version 1.2. Softw. Eng. Institue, p. 860 (2016)
8. Casamayor, A., Godoy, D., Campo, M.: Identification of non-functional requirements in textual specifications: a semi-supervised learning approach. Inf. Softw. Technol. **52**(4), 436–445 (2010). https://doi.org/10.1016/j.infsof.2009.10.010
9. Ullah, K.W.: Automated Security Compliance Tool for the Cloud (2012)
10. Ross, R., Pillitteri, V., Graubart, R., Bodeau, D., McQuaid, R.: Developing cyber-resilient systems: a systems security engineering approach. National Institute of Standards and Technology, Gaithersburg, MD, NIST SP 800-160v2r1 (2021). https://doi.org/10.6028/NIST.SP.800-160v2r1
11. Hadaya, P., Gagnon, B.: Business Architecture: The missing link in strategy Formulation, Implementation and Execution. ASATE publishing, Montréal (2017)
12. Object Management Group. Business process maturity model (version 1). Object management group (2008)
13. The Open Group, Éd., TOGAF Version 9.1, 1st ed. in TOGAF series. Van Haren Publishing, Zaltbommel (2011)
14. Abualhaija, S., Arora, C., Sabetzadeh, M., Briand, L.C., Vaz, E.: A machine learning-based approach for demarcating requirements in textual specifications. In: 2019 IEEE 27th International Requirements Engineering Conference (RE), pp. 51-62. IEEE, Jeju Island (2019). https://doi.org/10.1109/RE.2019.00017
15. Abdoun, N., Chami, M.: Automatic text classification of PDF documents using NLP techniques. INCOSE Int. Symp. **32**(1), 1320–1331 (2022). https://doi.org/10.1002/iis2.12997
16. Riaz, M., King, J., Slankas, J., Williams, L.: Hidden in plain sight: automatically identifying security requirements from natural language artifacts. In: 2014 IEEE 22nd International Requirements Engineering Conference (RE), pp. 183–192. IEEE, Karlskrona (2014). https://doi.org/10.1109/RE.2014.6912260

17. Cleland-Huang, J., Settimi, R., Zou, X., Solc, P.: Automated classification of non-functional requirements. Requir. Eng. **12**(2), 103–120 (2007). https://doi.org/10.1007/s00766-007-0045-1

18. Wong, A., Yip, F., Ray, P., Paramesh, N.: Towards semantic interoperability for it governance: an ontological approach. Comput. Infrm. **27**, 131–155 (2008)

19. Zhou, Y.C., Zheng, Z., Lin, J.R., Xin-Zheng, L.: Integrating NLP and context-free grammar for complex rule interpretation towards automated compliance checking. Comput. Ind. **142**, 103746 (2022). https://doi.org/10.1016/j.compind.2022.103746

20. Sebastiani, F.: Machine learning in automated text categorization. ACM Comput. Surv. **34**(1), 1–47 (2002). https://doi.org/10.1145/505282.505283

21. Liu, B., Dai, Y., Li, X., Lee, W.S., Yu, P.S.: Building text classifiers using positive and unlabeled examples. In: Third IEEE International Conference on Data Mining, pp. 179-186. IEEE Computer Society, Melbourne (2003). https://doi.org/10.1109/ICDM.2003.1250918

22. X. Zhou et al., « A survey on text classification and its applications », Web Intell., vol. 18, no 3, p. 205-216, sept. 2020, https://doi.org/10.3233/WEB-200442

23. Kowsari, K., Meimandi, K.J., Heidarysafa, M., Mendu, S., Barnes, L., Brown, D.: Text classification algorithms: a survey. Information **10**(4), 150 (2019). https://doi.org/10.3390/info10040150

24. Salama, D.M., El-Gohary, N.M.: Semantic text classification for supporting automated compliance checking in construction. J. Comput. Civil Eng. **30**(1), 04014106 (2016). https://doi.org/10.1061/(ASCE)CP.1943-5487.0000301

25. Lo, R.T.-W., He, B., Ounis, I.: Automatically Building a Stopword List for an Information Retrieval System (2005)

26. Saif, H., Fernandez, M., He, Y., Alani, H.: On stopwords, filtering and data sparsity for sentiment analysis of twitter (2014)

27. Plisson, J., Lavrac, N., Mladenic, D.: A rule based approach to word lemmatization. In: Proceedings of 7th International MultiConference Information Society 2004 (2004)

28. Manning, C., Raghavan, P., Schuetze, H.: Introduction to Information Retrieval. Cambridge University Press, Cambridge (2009)

29. S. Singh, « Natural Language Processing for Information Extraction », 6 juillet 2018, arXiv: arXiv:1807.02383. Consulté le: 6 mai 2023. [En ligne]. Disponible sur: http://arxiv.org/abs/1807.02383

30. Rezaeinia, S.M., Ghodsi, A., Rahmani, R.: Improving the accuracy of pre-trained word embeddings for sentiment analysis (2017). arXiv. https://doi.org/10.48550/ARXIV.1711.08609

31. Occhipinti, A., Rogers, L., Angione, C.: A pipeline and comparative study of 12 machine learning models for text classification. Expert Syst. Appl. **201**, 117193 (2022). https://doi.org/10.1016/j.eswa.2022.117193

32. Trivedi, S.K., Dey, S.: Interplay between probabilistic classifiers and boosting algorithms for detecting complex unsolicited emails. J. Adv. Comput. Netw. **1**(2), 132–136 (2013). https://doi.org/10.7763/JACN.2013.V1.27

33. Majumder, G., Pakray, P., Gelbukh, A., Pinto, D.: Semantic textual similarity methods, tools, and applications: a survey. Computación y Sistemas **20**(4) (2016). https://doi.org/10.13053/cys-20-4-2506

34. Altınel, B., Ganiz, M.C.: Semantic text classification: a survey of past and recent advances. Inf. Process. Manag. **54**(6), 1129–1153 (2018). https://doi.org/10.1016/j.ipm.2018.08.001

35. Ali, A., Alfayez, F., Alquhayz, H.: Semantic similarity measures between words: a brief survey. Sci. Int. (Lahore) **30**(6), 907–914 (2018)

36. Wang, J., Dong, Y.: Measurement of text similarity: a survey. Information **11**(9), 421 (2020). https://doi.org/10.3390/info11090421

37. Hadj Taieb, M.A., Zesch, T., Ben Aouicha, M.: A survey of semantic relatedness evaluation datasets and procedures. Artif. Intell. Rev. **53**(6), 4407–4448 (2020). https://doi.org/10.13140/RG.2.2.17358.69449

38. Lin, D.: An information-theoretic Definition of similarity. In: Proceedings of International Conference on Machine Learning, pp. 296–304 (1998)

39. Chandrasekaran, D., Mago, V.: Evolution of semantic similarity—a survey. ACM Comput. Surv. **54**(2), 1–37 (2022). https://doi.org/10.1145/3440755

40. Berry, D.M.: Evaluation of tools for hairy requirements and software engineering tasks. In: 2017 IEEE 25th International Requirements Engineering Conference Workshops (REW), pp. 284-291. IEEE, Lisbon (2017). https://doi.org/10.1109/REW.2017.25

41. Joint Task Force Interagency Working Group. Security and Privacy Controls for Information Systems and Organizations. National Institute of Standards and Technology (2020). https://doi.org/10.6028/NIST.SP.800-53r5

42. Joint Task Force Interagency Working Group, Security and Privacy Controls for Information Systems and Organizations (2020). https://doi.org/10.6028/NIST.SP.800-53r5

43. Security and resilience. Business continuity management systems. Requirements (2019). https://doi.org/10.3403/30382483

44. Information Systems Audit and Control Association, Éd., COBIT 5: a business framework for the governance and management of enterprise IT: an ISACA® framework. ISACA, Rolling Meadows (2012)

45. Bourque, P.: R. E, Guide to the Software Engineering Body of Knowledge Version 3.0 (SWEBOK Guide V3.0). IEEE Computer Society (2014)

46. Wiegers, K., Joy, B.: Software Requirements, vol. 3. Microsoft Press (2013)

47. Verma, T., Renu, R., Gaur, D.: Tokenization and filtering process in RapidMiner. Int. J. Appl. Inf. Syst. **7**(2), 16–18 (2014). https://doi.org/10.5120/ijais14-451139

48. Gupta, G., Malhotra, S.: Text document tokenization for word frequency count using rapid miner (taking resume as an example). Int. J. Comput. Appl **975**, 8887 (2015)

49. Thangaraj, M., Sivakami, M.: Text classification techniques: a literature review. Interdisc. J. Inf. Knowl. Manag. **13**, 117–135 (2018). https://doi.org/10.28945/4066

50. Gasparetto, A., Marcuzzo, M., Zangari, A., Albarelli, A.: A survey on text classification algorithms: from text to predictions. Information **13**(2), 83 (2022). https://doi.org/10.3390/info13020083

51. Minaee, S., Kalchbrenner, N., Cambria, E., Nikzad, N., Chenaghlu, M., Gao, J.: Deep learning--based text classification: a comprehensive review. ACM Comput. Surv. **54**(3), 1–40 (2022). https://doi.org/10.1145/3439726

52. Tsangaratos, P., Ilia, I.: Comparison of a logistic regression and Naïve Bayes classifier in landslide susceptibility assessments: the influence of models complexity and training dataset size. CATENA **145**, 164–179 (2016). https://doi.org/10.1016/j.catena.2016.06.004

53. Allahyari, M., et al.: A brief survey of text mining: classification, clustering and extraction techniques (2017). arXiv: arXiv:1707.02919. https://doi.org/10.48550/arXiv.1707.02919

54. Devlin, J., Chang, M.-W., Lee, K., Toutanova, K.: BERT: pre-training of deep bidirectional transformers for language understanding (2019). arXiv: arXiv:1810.04805. https://doi.org/10.48550/arXiv.1810.04805

55. Steck, H., Ekanadham, C., Kallus, N.: Is cosine-similarity of embeddings really about similarity?. In: Companion Proceedings of the ACM Web Conference 2024, pp. 887–890 (2024). https://doi.org/10.1145/3589335.3651526

Towards the Identification of Vulnerability-Fixing Code Lines in OSS Security Patches Using Lexical Code Segmentation and LLMs

Reika Nishimura Arakawa$^{(\boxtimes)}$ [ID], Yo Kanemoto [ID], and Mitsuaki Akiyama [ID]

NTT Social Informatics Laboratories, Tokyo 180-8585, Japan
reika.arakawa@ntt.com

Abstract. Reusing open-source software (OSS) code has become standard in software development. When vulnerabilities are discovered in reused code, maintainers typically apply security patches. However, these patches often include non-vulnerability-related changes, such as code refactoring or updating a setting file. Applying a patch without distinguishing these changes can lead to unintended software malfunctions. Existing techniques do not account for non-remediation code lines in security patches. This study aims to mitigate unexpected failures caused by indiscriminate patch application.

We propose a method for identifying the code lines that directly remediate vulnerabilities in security patches. By leveraging lexical preprocessing and Large Language Models (LLMs), our approach semantically classifies code lines within a security patch, distinguishing vulnerability-fixing changes from unrelated changes. In an experimental evaluation using security patches for 25 distinct vulnerability types, the proposed method achieved an F1 score of 0.88, improving 0.22 over the baseline. The results also indicate that classification accuracy decreases for vulnerability types requiring extensive modifications, such as injection and authentication vulnerabilities. Additionally, we revealed that nine out of twenty-five security patches (36% of the patch examined) contained code changes unrelated to vulnerability remediation. Furthermore, we identified key challenges and technical requirements for automating security patch analysis and provided recommendations for the platform providers and the OSS maintainers on best practices for security patches.

1 Introduction

Software is required to have a wide range of functionality, leading to increased complexity in code bases. To improve development efficiency, developers frequently integrate open-source software (OSS) into their products by forking repositories or copying and pasting OSS code. Studies have shown that reused OSS code constitutes over 60% of Android applications [9] and more than 90% of enterprise-developed products [23, 26]. However, OSS code may contain vulnerabilities, potentially introducing security risks to the products to the products

© IFIP International Federation for Information Processing 2025
Published by Springer Nature Switzerland AG 2025
S. Katsikas and B. Shafiq (Eds.): DBSec 2025, LNCS 15722, pp. 73–95, 2025.
https://doi.org/10.1007/978-3-031-96590-6_5

in which it is reused [7,19]. To mitigate these risks, it is crucial to identify and address the vulnerable portions of the code.

There are two primary approaches to fixing vulnerabilities in reused OSS code: (1) updating the codebase to a newer version released by the OSS project that fixes the vulnerability and (2) manually patching only the vulnerable portion of the code using the provided security patch. The first method is generally suitable when the developer unmodified the reused code. However, when developers have made modifications, such as refactoring, to the reused code, a straightforward update may cause issues with the product's functionality. In such cases, fixing the vulnerability by applying patches directly [22,24] is more practical. A study investigating firmware in IoT devices reported that approximately 15.6% of the programs[1] contained independently patched modifications by developers [1]. This finding suggests that fixing vulnerabilities using publicly available security patches rather than version upgrades is also common in OSS-based development. This study focuses on vulnerability remediation using security patches in scenarios where developers reuse third-party OSS. When a vulnerability is found, maintainers must apply public patches, but doing so without fully understanding the reused code and patch changes may introduce unintended malfunctions.

To address this issue, we propose a method for identifying vulnerability fixing code lines within security patches. Our approach focuses on publicly available security patches for known vulnerabilities, aiming to enhance vulnerability remediation and streamline patching. Existing techniques for security patch analysis consider lexical differences between pre-and post-patch code but do not account for the semantic nature of code changes. Therefore, this study presents a novel approach to analyzing the content of code changes in a security patch. We concentrated on large language models (LLMs), which excel at code analysis and generation, and conducted a preliminary experiment. A preliminary experiment prompted an LLM to classify vulnerability-fixing lines from security patches, but the accuracy was significantly lower than expected. Analysis revealed that the LLM struggled to identify modification boundaries and relationships between code segments, highlighting a key challenge for this task.

We introduced improvements to the preliminary experiment methodology. Specifically, we incorporated a preprocessing step for security patches. This step segments the patch based on defined rules and associates each code snippet with its corresponding file path and function name. The preprocessed security patches are provided as input to the LLM. This paper refers to each segmented code snippet of a security patch as a "code block". A code block is a unit that distinguishes the code changes described in the security patch. To evaluate the effectiveness of the proposed method, we experimented with comparing classification accuracy across four conditions, including three conditions that excluded the improvements introduced in our approach. The experiment utilized 25 security patches corresponding to high-risk vulnerability types as defined by MITRE's CWE Top

---

[1] Programs included in IoT firmware that are continuously updated across all firmware versions.

25 Most Dangerous Software Weaknesses [10,11]. The results showed that our proposed method improved the F1-score by approximately 0.22, achieving an F1-score of 0.88 compared to the baseline. Notably, a security patch segmentation significantly impacted identification accuracy, contributing to a 0.23 improvement in the F1 score. Furthermore, our analysis revealed that nine out of twenty-five security patches contained non-vulnerability-fixing code changes to software behavior unrelated to vulnerability fixes (excluding documentation updates). We have identified the challenges and technical requirements for automating security patch analysis. Additionally, we have proposed best practices for committing security patches, providing guidelines to enhance patch clarity and effectiveness. Our study provides the following key contributions:

– We propose a method for identifying vulnerability-fixing code lines within security patches. Existing approaches primarily focus on lexical differences and do not account for the semantic content of changes.
– We address this limitation by integrating a code segmentation process based on predefined lexical rules and a preprocessing step that explicitly associates file and function names. Experimental evaluation demonstrated that the proposed method improved the F1 score by approximately 0.22 compared to the baseline. Additionally, we revealed that nine out of twenty-five security patches contained code changes unrelated to vulnerability remediation.
– We identified key challenges and technical requirements for automating security patch analysis. Based on these findings, we provide practical recommendations for OSS maintainers and platform providers, advocating that commits should include only vulnerability-related modifications to enhance clarity and maintainability.

2   Background

2.1   Software Vulnerability and Security Patch

A software vulnerability is a security weakness caused by design flaws or bugs in IT systems. When exploited, it can lead to data breaches, tampering, malware infections, or unauthorized access. Each vulnerability is tracked using a CVE (Common Vulnerabilities and Exposures) identifier. As of January 22, 2025, a total of 278,452 CVEs have been recorded since 1999, with an average annual growth of approximately 1.15×. Many OSS-related CVEs include links to security patches in advisories, typically pointing to commit-based fixes in public code repositories such as Git.

2.2   Motivating Example

We present a motivating example of a security patch that illustrates the challenges discussed in Sect. 1. This example pertains to CVE-2018-1000867 (CWE-89) [16], a SQL injection vulnerability that could allow unauthorized database

reads. The vulnerability was caused by how SQL variables were handled in
`youractions*.php` and was mitigated by enhancing the validation of variables
obtained from client input. Listing 1.1 shows an excerpt of the code changes
that remediate the SQL injection vulnerability in the security patch. The name
of the modified file is specified in the "`diff -git`" line, and the changed lines
of code are identified by header lines that start with "`@@`", known as "hunk
headers." The hunk header provides context about the code changes made to
the file, and in some cases, the function name may be appended at the end of
the header. For example, in `@@ -99,8 +99,9 @@` from Listing 1.1, the original
file (yourauctions.php) had a block of code starting at line 99, which contained
eight lines before the change. In the modified file, the block still begins at line
99 but now contains nine lines after the change. Lines beginning with "−" indicate removals, while lines beginning with "+" indicate additions introduced to
remediate the vulnerability.

Listing 1.1. Excerpt of the vulnerability-fixing code lines in the security patch for
CVE-2018-1000867

```
...
diff --git a/yourauctions.php b/yourauctions.php
index 53f09125..0a3244bc 100644
--- a/yourauctions.php
+++ b/yourauctions.php
@@ -99,8 +99,9 @@
      $_SESSION['oa_ord'] = 'title';
      $_SESSION['oa_type'] = 'asc';
 } elseif (!empty($_GET['oa_ord'])) {
-      $_SESSION['oa_ord'] = $_GET['oa_ord'];
-      $_SESSION['oa_type'] = $_GET['oa_type'];
+      // check oa_ord && oa_type are valid
+      $_SESSION['oa_ord'] = (in_array($_GET['oa_ord'], array('title', '
        starts', 'ends', 'num_bids', 'current_bid'))) ? $_GET['oa_ord'] :
        'title';
+      $_SESSION['oa_type'] = (in_array($_GET['oa_type'], array('asc', '
        desc'))) ? $_GET['oa_type'] : 'asc';
...
```

When segmenting the security patch based on hunk headers, this patch is
divided into 27 code blocks. Among them, only five code blocks contain changes
directly related to fixing the SQL injection vulnerability. However, the remaining
22 code blocks include unrelated changes, such as changes to image URL generation or loading, HTML template image display, and auction fee calculations.
These changes are not related to mitigating the SQL injection vulnerability. This
issue arises because security patches are applied at the commit level, where vulnerability fixes are often bundled with unrelated code changes. Consequently,
security patches may contain code changes beyond those necessary for vulnerability remediation. If they are not differentiated and selectively applied, these
changes may introduce unintended software malfunctions.

Several techniques [2,29,30] use machine learning to classify security patches
based on commit message context. However, the commit message for CVE-2018-
1000867—"Number of security fixes & fix for setup fee #510"—includes a typo
(("security", presumably intended to be"security")), making it hard to identify

as a security patch. Additionally, these approaches cannot detect that 22 of the 27 modified code blocks are unrelated to the fix. This highlights the need for classification methods that analyze patch source code directly.

Even if one attempts to classify vulnerability-fixing code based on commit messages, such an approach appears to be inherently difficult. This is supported by our lexical analysis of 13,285 security patch commits from 1999 to 2024, which revealed that only 1,690 commits—approximately 12% of the total—contained keywords indicative of the fix location (e.g., "where", "location"). Further details are provided in Appendix A.

3   Proposal Methodology

In this paper, we propose a method for identifying the code lines that directly remediate vulnerabilities in the security patch. We aim to reduce the effort required for vulnerability analysis and mitigate unintended software failures caused by applying patches. Our approach focuses on publicly available security patches associated with vulnerabilities assigned to CVE identifiers (i.e., a security patch for a known vulnerability). The proposed method leverages code segmentation techniques and the inference capabilities of large language models (LLMs) to analyze security patches, classifying code lines into two categories: vulnerability-fixing code lines and non-vulnerability-fixing code lines, such as those related to refactoring or other modifications.

Figure 1 shows the proposed method's workflow overview. This method consists of three main steps: **Step-①**: Retrieval of a security patch, **Step-②**: Code segmentation process, and **Step-③**: Classification of vulnerability-fixing code lines. Further details of each step are provided in the following sections.

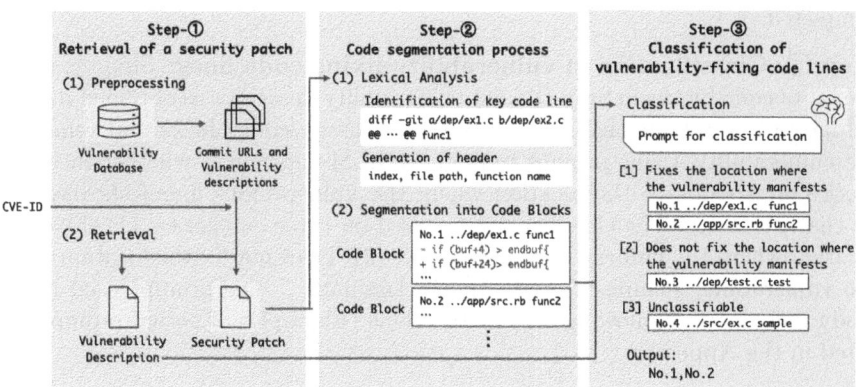

Fig. 1. Overview of the Proposed Method

3.1   Details of Each STEP

Step-①: Retrieval of a security patch: This step retrieves a security patch and vulnerability description corresponding to the CVE-ID provided by the user input. This process references publicly available vulnerability databases to obtain the security patch associated with the input CVE-ID, along with a text that explains the summary characteristics of the vulnerability by utilizing the API request. The security patch in OSS corresponds to committed code that addresses vulnerabilities. Therefore, we extract commit URLs from the reference URL lists provided on vulnerability databases. Specifically, we identify URLs that contain the string `commit` and a domain such as `github.com`. The corresponding security patch is then retrieved by appending `.diff` to the extracted URL and issuing an HTTP request to obtain the response of a commit code.

Step-②: Code segmentation process: The proposed method employs lexical analysis to segment the security patch obtained in Step-①: into structured code snippets. In this process, the line containing `diff -git`, which marks the beginning of a file comparison, is first identified to extract the name of the modified file. Next, the hunk header, which begins with `@@` and defines the specific changes within the file, is detected. If a function name is recorded at the end of the hunk header, it is also extracted. The code changes contained between a line starting with a hunk header and the next hunk header represent a single, cohesive code change. We refer to these code snippets, segmented by hunk headers, as code blocks. The code block constitutes the most minimal unit of code lines subject to classification by the proposed method. Next, we generate header information to associate each code block with the corresponding file and function where the modification occurs. This header is constructed based on the extracted file path and function name. Finally, by assigning an index to each header for code block identification, the segmentation process of security patches into code blocks is completed.

Step-③: Classification of vulnerability-fixing code lines: Step-③: inputs the set of code blocks in Step-②: and vulnerability descriptions obtained in Step-①: into a Large Language Model (LLM) to classify code blocks that remediate the vulnerability. Using prompt tuning, the LLM determines whether each code block corresponds to the location where the vulnerability manifests based on its characteristics. The classification is based on three categories: (1) "Fixes the location where the vulnerability manifests", (2) "Does not fix the location where the vulnerability manifests" and (3) "Unclassifiable." The prompt used in this study includes the following four instructions (Examples of actual prompts are listed in the Appendix C):

Instruction-1: You will act as an expert vulnerability analyst. Please analyze the content of each code block and classify it into one of the three predefined categories.

Instruction-2: Each code block represents a potential remediation for the vulnerability, with the accompanying vulnerability description providing contextual information about its nature and impact. Each code block is prefixed with the corresponding file path and function name.

Instruction-3: Using the vulnerability description as a reference, classify each code block into one of the following three categories: If the modification directly affects the vulnerability trigger point, select (1) "Fixes the location where the vulnerability manifests." If the modification does not alter the vulnerability trigger point, select (2) "Does not fix the location where the vulnerability manifests." If the impact of the modification cannot be determined, select (3) "Unclassifiable."

Instruction-4: For the response format, provide a concise explanation of the classification results for each category, including the rationale behind the assigned classification.

4   Experiment

While existing techniques have proposed methods for classifying whether a commit constitutes a security patch, they do not aim to identify the specific lines of code that fix the vulnerability within such security patches. Since our approach addresses a different problem, a direct comparison with prior studies is not feasible. Therefore, we define our own evaluation conditions for evaluation in Sect. 4.1.

4.1   Comparative Experiment Setup

To assess the effectiveness of each component in the proposed method, we conducted a comparative experiment by defining three additional conditions based on the inclusion or exclusion of specific processes within our approach. The proposed method and the three comparative conditions, including the baseline, are summarized in Table 1.

Table 1. Experimental conditions

	LLM Input Data		Summary
	Vulnerability Description	Segmented Code Blocks	
The proposed method	✓	✓	Classifies segmented code blocks using the vulnerability description
Condition-1	✓	✗	Classifies non-segmented security patches using the vulnerability description
Condition-2	✗	✓	Classifies segmented code blocks without the vulnerability description
Baseline	✗	✗	Classifies non-segmented security patches without a vulnerability description

Condition-1 omits the code segmentation process (Step-②). The LLM receives the complete, unsegmented security patch and vulnerability description in this setting. Classifying the vulnerability-fixing code blocks is instructed based on the expected segmentation units. In other words, Condition-1, which does not perform the code splitting process, has LLM substitute the same splitting as in Step-2.

Condition-2 excludes the use of the vulnerability description (Step-①:). The LLM receives only the segmented code blocks from the security patch and the corresponding CVE ID, classifying the code blocks that address the vulnerability without referencing the vulnerability description.

Baseline Condition excludes both Step-①: and Step-②:. The input to the LLM consists only of the CVE ID and the unsegmented security patch. The LLM must classify the vulnerability-fixing code blocks while being informed of the expected code segmentation units. In summary, LLMs are required to split security patches into expected code blocks and classify code blocks without providing information about vulnerabilities.

4.2   Dataset

To validate the effectiveness of the proposed method, we utilized security patches from open-source software (OSS) that had been publicly disclosed as fixes for known vulnerabilities. This study specifically targeted OSS vulnerabilities that had been assigned CVE identifiers and for which the corresponding security patches were publicly available.

Security Patch and Vulnerability Description. We utilized the National Vulnerability Database(NVD) [14], a comprehensive repository for vulnerability management data maintained by the National Institute of Standards and Technology(NIST) [13]. To construct our dataset, we collected security patches and vulnerability descriptions associated with specified CVE identifiers by referring to the NVD Data Feeds [15], covering vulnerabilities disclosed between 1999 and 2023. Next, we developed a custom JSON parsing program to extract URLs containing the keywords 'commit' and either 'github.com' or 'gitlab.com' from the list of CWEs, CVEs, and reference URLs. For validation, we focused on vulnerabilities classified under the CWE Top 25 Most Dangerous Software Weaknesses [11] in 2023, an annually updated list published by MITRE. To ensure broad coverage, we randomly selected one CVE identifier from each of the 25 CWE categories, choosing CVEs from different years within the 1999–2023 period (Table 2).

Table 2. A list of the types of vulnerabilities utilized in the experiment and the CVE numbers assigned to each. CWEs are vulnerabilities classified under the `CWE Top 25 Most Dangerous Software Weaknesses` in 2023.

CWE	Overview of vulnerability types	CVE id	Programming Language
20	Input data validation flaw	CVE-2016-1000232	Javascript
22	Path Traversal	CVE-2014-10068	Javascript
77	Command Injection	CVE-2023-0315	php
78	OS Command Injection	CVE-2014-0156	Ruby
79	Cross-Site Scripting	CVE-2022-0087	php
89	SQL Injection	CVE-2018-1000867	php
94	Code Injection	CVE-2014-1691	php
119	Improper Buffer Handling	CVE-2015-0206	C
125	Buffer overrun	CVE-2022-0128	C
190	Integer overflow	CVE-2016-10159	C
269	Improper unauthorized access	CVE-2021-39167	Solidity
276	Improper Authorization	CVE-2018-14650	Python
287	Improper Authentication	CVE-2019-1020018	Javascript
306	Improper Authentication in Critical Function	CVE-2023-0919	C#
352	Cross-site request forgery	CVE-2021-21241	Python
362	Improper conflict	CVE-2011-0990	C
416	Improper use after memory release	CVE-2017-1000211	C
434	Dangerous type file upload	CVE-2021-21245	Java
476	NULL pointer reference	CVE-2016-10129	C
502	Untrusted Data Deserialization	CVE-2022-1032	php
787	Buffer Overflow	CVE-2013-7491	Perl
798	Use of Hardcoded Credentials	CVE-2019-14837	Java
862	Missing Authorization Check	CVE-2022-0203	php
863	Incorrect Authorization Check	CVE-2023-0298	php
918	Server-Side Request Forgery	CVE-2016-9752	php

4.3   Implementation

Architecture. We have implemented a prototype for the experiment. The proposed method has the following three modules: a security patch retrieval process, code segmentation process and classification process. Each module was implemented in Python 3.11.7. The proposed method consists of the following three modules We implemented it in Python 3.11.7. The machine specifications used for the experiments are as follows: MacBook Pro with an Intel Core i5 2GHz CPU, 32GB RAM, and a 4TB SSD.

LLM Parameter Configuration. We employed the OpenAI API [17] with the gpt4-turbo model for classification. To ensure deterministic and consistent output while minimizing generative variability, the temperature parameter was set to 0, as recommended for precise classification tasks. A comparison table of classification accuracy using models (gpt-4o, gpt-3.5-turbo) other than gpt4-turbo is provided in Appendix B.

5   Evaluation

We analyzed the results to assess how variations in input data and instruction differences in the prompt impact identification accuracy. Additionally, we evaluated the influence of vulnerability type and the number of code blocks on classification accuracy.

5.1   Evaluation Metrics for Classification Accuracy

We used six metrics to evaluate classification accuracy: True Positive (TP), False Positive (FP), Precision ($\frac{TP}{TP+FP}$), Recall ($\frac{TP}{TP+FN}$), and F1-Score ($\frac{2*(Pr*Re)}{Pr+Re}$). The authors manually assigned the ground truth labels through a visual analysis of each dataset's security patch, examining it block by block. Each code block was labeled as either "fixing the vulnerability activation point" or "not fixing the vulnerability activation point." The FP count was calculated as the sum of (1) the number of code blocks incorrectly classified compared to the ground truth labels and (2) the number of code blocks classified as "unidentifiable." Similarly, the FN count represented the total number of code blocks present in the code block but missing from the output results.

5.2   Evaluation of Accuracy

Table 3 shows the classification accuracy results. The aggregated 25 CWEs results are also shown in the bottom "Average of 25". Condition-1 could classify security patches by segmenting them into partial code blocks; however, the output often contained fewer code blocks than expected, leading to a recall value of approximately 0.36 lower and an F1 score of 0.24 lower than those achieved by the proposed method. These results indicate that pre-segmenting code blocks before inputting them into the LLM is a more practical approach for improving the accuracy of security patch analysis. On the other hand, Condition-2 exhibited only a minor difference compared to the proposed method, with an F1 score decrease of approximately 0.03. Additionally, the comparison between Condition-1 and the baseline showed no significant accuracy reduction, even without a vulnerability description. A likely reason vulnerabilities could still be identified without the provided descriptions is that GPT-4 Turbo, the model used in this experiment, was trained on data up to April 2023. Since the number of CVE identifiers from 2023 included in the experimental dataset was relatively small, these vulnerabilities were probably already present in the model's training data.

Table 3. Experimental results: Accuracy of identification by CWE

CWE	CVE	Code Block	the four comparative conditions											
			Proposed method			Condition-1			Condition-2			Baseline		
			Pr	Re	F1	Pr	Re	F1	Pr	Re	F1	Pr	Re	F1
20	CVE-2016-1000232	5	1.00	1.00	1.00	1.00	0.60	0.75	1.00	1.00	1.00	1.00	0.60	0.75
22	CVE-2014-10068	6	0.67	1.00	0.80	0.50	0.50	0.50	0.67	1.00	0.80	0.67	0.40	0.50
77	CVE-2023-0315	8	0.63	1.00	0.77	0.13	1.00	0.22	0.75	1.00	0.86	0.57	0.80	0.67
78	CVE-2014-0156	5	0.60	1.00	0.75	1.00	0.40	0.57	1.00	1.00	1.00	1.00	0.40	0.57
79	CVE-2022-0087	13	0.77	1.00	0.87	1.00	0.38	0.56	0.84	1.00	0.91	1.00	0.23	0.36
89	CVE-2018-1000867	27	0.78	1.00	0.88	0.60	0.12	0.20	0.78	0.28	0.41	0.67	0.08	0.14
94	CVE-2014-1691	6	0.83	1.00	0.90	0.50	0.20	0.29	0.83	1.00	0.90	0.80	0.80	0.80
119	CVE-2015-0206	8	0.86	0.86	0.86	1.00	0.75	0.86	0.75	1.00	0.86	0.67	0.29	0.40
125	CVE-2022-0128	4	0.75	1.00	0.86	0.75	1.00	0.86	0.75	1.00	0.86	0.75	1.00	0.86
190	CVE-2016-10159	3	1.00	1.00	1.00	1.00	0.67	0.80	1.00	1.00	1.00	1.00	0.67	0.80
269	CVE-2021-39167	5	1.00	1.00	1.00	1.00	0.60	0.75	1.00	1.00	1.00	1.00	0.60	0.75
276	CVE-2018-14650	1	1.00	1.00	1.00	1.00	1.00	1.00	1.00	1.00	1.00	1.00	1.00	1.00
287	CVE-2019-1020018	20	0.53	0.62	0.57	0.57	0.25	0.35	0.57	0.27	0.36	0.57	0.27	0.36
306	CVE-2023-0919	9	0.89	1.00	0.94	0.83	0.63	0.71	1.00	1.00	1.00	0.8	0.5	0.62
352	CVE-2021-21241	9	0.67	1.00	0.80	0.83	0.63	0.71	0.67	1.00	0.80	0.75	0.86	0.80
362	CVE-2011-0990	4	0.75	1.00	0.86	1.00	0.50	0.67	0.75	1.00	0.86	1.00	0.25	0.40
416	CVE-2017-1000211	7	0.86	1.00	0.92	1.00	0.43	0.60	0.86	1.00	0.92	1.00	0.43	0.60
434	CVE-2021-21245	7	0.57	1.00	072	1.00	0.57	0.72	0.57	1.00	0.72	1.00	0.57	0.72
476	CVE-2016-10129	3	1.00	1.00	1.00	1.00	0.67	0.80	1.00	1.00	1.00	1.00	0.67	0.80
502	CVE-2022-1032	4	1.00	1.00	1.00	0.50	1.00	0.67	1.00	1.00	1.00	0.50	1.00	0.67
787	CVE-2013-7491	3	0.67	1.00	0.80	0.50	0.50	0.50	0.67	1.00	0.80	0.67	1.00	0.80
798	CVE-2019-14837	5	0.8	1.00	0.89	0.80	1.00	0.89	0.40	1.00	0.57	0.80	1.00	0.89
862	CVE-2022-0203	5	1.00	1.00	1.00	0.50	0.67	0.57	0.60	1.00	0.75	0.80	1.00	0.89
863	CVE-2023-0298	7	0.86	1.00	0.92	1.00	0.43	0.60	0.86	1.00	0.92	1.00	0.43	0.60
918	CVE-2016-9752	6	0.83	1.00	0.91	0.80	1.00	0.89	0.83	1.00	0.91	0.75	0.75	0.75
	Average	7.2	0.81	0.98	0.88	0.79	0.62	0.64	0.81	0.94	0.85	0.83	0.62	0.66

Case Study of FPs. We analyzed the thirteen CVEs misclassified by the proposed method (i.e., false positives) as shown in Table 4. The incorrectly classified code blocks primarily involved adding test cases and including comments in ChangeLog and NEWS files to indicate that the vulnerability had been addressed (No. 1 and No. 2 in Table 4). These changes do not directly alter the code where the vulnerability manifests. As an improvement, incorporating example-based guidance in the prompt could enhance the classification of such code blocks. For false positives beyond those mentioned above, many were associated with vulnerabilities involving a large number of code blocks. In these cases, the functions responsible for the vulnerability were referenced across multiple functions and files (No. 3,4,5 and 6 in Table 4). Accurately classifying these code blocks requires understanding the calling relationships between the vulnerable functions and their dependencies, making classification inherently complex.

Table 4. A table listing the processing content described in the code block and its frequency of occurrence for the results of the 13 FPs in the proposed method.

No	The contents of the processing described in the code block	Frequency
1	Add a test case	5
2	Add a comment indicating that the vulnerability fix has been completed.	4
3	Add a class for sanitizing processing	1
4	Change in initial login settings	1
5	Change in the process for confirming login acquisition information	1
6	Change in the processing of checking the contents of SQL retrieval	1

Table 5. The table presenting all code blocks for CVE-2021-21245 and the results of the proposed method

ID	Filename	The changes that are described in each code block	Result
1	FilenameUtils.java	Add `sanitizeFilename` method and `FilenameUtils` class	TP
2	InsertUrlPanel.java	Sanitize the name of the file uploaded by the client	TP
3	MarkdownEditor.java	Sanitize the name of the acquired header file	TP
4	ProjectBlobPage.java	Sanitize the name of the file uploaded by the client	TP
5	InsertUrlPanel.java	Import `FilenameUtils` class	FP
6	MarkdownEditor.java	Import `FilenameUtils` class	FP
7	ProjectBlobPage.java	Import `FilenameUtils` class	FP

Table 5 describes a specific security patch example (CVE-2021-21245, CWE = 434, CVSSv3.1 = 9.8) corresponding to entry No. 3 in Table 4. This vulnerability involves improperly handling arbitrary file uploads and was mitigated by sanitizing the requested filename. This security patch is divided into seven code blocks, all of which are changes related to fixing the vulnerability. Specifically, the `FilenameUtils` class and the `sanitizeFilename` method were introduced in `FilenameUtils.java`, while the `FilenameUtils` class was imported in three additional files. The `sanitizeFilename` method is invoked during filename processing to enforce sanitization. The proposed method correctly classified the code block containing the call to the `sanitizeFilename` method as a vulnerability-related fix. However, the other three code blocks changed to import the `FilenameUtils` class were incorrectly classified as unrelated fixes. This misclassification is likely due to the failure to recognize the relationship between the imported class and the methods within the class.

Case Study of FNs. The proposed method caused two False Negatives (FNs) for two security patches (CVE-2015-0206 and CVE-2019-1020018). These were security patches with eight and twenty code blocks, respectively, and the content of the code block changes corresponded to the modification of the point where the vulnerability was triggered. In the security patch for CVE-2015-0206, one of the eight code blocks was an FN. In particular, CVE-2019-1020018 had five of the twentieth code blocks that were not classified, and they were all common to the change that checks the information obtained at the time of login for vulnerabilities in inadequate login authentication.

We also investigated the results for Condition-1 and the baseline. Since these conditions did not have the code segmentation process, they generated many false negatives (FNs). In the two conditions, the FNs were present in 16 of the 21 CVE security patches, and the 16 common security patches had 78% code block matching. These missing code blocks encompassed both vulnerability fixes and non-vulnerability fixes, and no discernible bias was observed in this experiment.

5.3   Evaluation of the Changes Described in the Security Patch

We manually analyzed and classified all code blocks within the 25 security patches used in the experiment. Our analysis revealed that nine out of twenty-five security patches contained non-vulnerability-fixing code changes to software behavior unrelated to vulnerability fixes (excluding documentation updates). Examples include code changes to image URL generation methods, stylesheet updates, the addition of statistical computation libraries, modifications to payment processing logic, and the addition of log output. Additionally, there were seven security patches that had test cases added in addition to the above code changes. There were thirteen cases of updates to documents such as dependency files and CHANGELOGs.

6   Discussion

6.1   Dataset Validity

To evaluate the validity of the security patches used in the experiment, we examined the number of changes in security patches by twenty-five CWEs (`CWE Top 25 Most Dangerous Software Weaknesses` by MITRE). Specifically, we counted the number of code blocks, the average number of functions that had some change, and the average number of files that had some kind of change for all publicly available security patches with the same CWE. We collected and analyzed the security patches published in NVD from 1999 to 2023 for the 25 CWEs used in the experiment (Table 6).

Table 6. Table of analysis result of all known and publicly available security patches for 25 CWEs

CWE	CVE entry	The number of Code block	The number of functions	The number of files
20	455	8.52	2.42	2.57
22	449	9.26	2.99	2.80
77	83	6.58	1.78	2.57
78	179	9.15	3.11	2.73
79	2, 123	25.29	4.01	2.57
89	458	24.38	6.44	8.13
94	166	13.17	4.26	3.79
119	415	4.43	1.73	1.80
125	620	7.34	2.05	1.81
190	222	8.08	3.65	1.93
269	71	9.30	2.46	3.77
276	31	4.29	1.23	1.58
287	172	13.77	3.70	5.05
306	26	7.46	2.46	2.81
352	276	19.89	3.46	10.63
362	131	5.12	2.11	1.10
416	261	4.69	1.57	1.22
434	111	12.98	2.70	5.41
476	405	3.66	1.23	1.08
502	99	17.60	5.84	5.59
787	487	5.85	2.06	1.34
798	24	7.33	2.42	3.21
862	104	7.11	2.27	2.14
863	132	12.45	4.02	3.67
918	145	27.28	7.06	8.74

– the number of CVEs: Total number of CVEs disclosed between 1999 and 2023 assigned to each CWE.
– The number of Code blocks: Average number of code blocks segmented by the code segmentation process in Step-②:.
– The number of Functions: Average number of functions (without duplicates) modified in the security patch.
– The number of Files: Average number of files (without duplicates) modified in the security patch.

To calculate the average number of code blocks that were changed in each security patch, we applied the code segmentation process described in Step-②: of Sect. 3. We calculated the average number of code blocks that were segmented. The method for counting the number of declared functions that have been changed in a security patch is to obtain the function name when the function name exists in the hunk header (i.e., "@@") for each security patch, and to count it by CWE after excluding duplicates. The method used for counting the number of files changed by the patch was to count the file names contained in the line "diff -git" after removing duplicates.

6.2 Challenges and Requirements for Security Patch Analysis

In this section, we analyzed the challenge involved in analyzing security patches, and describe the technical requirements for mitigating these challenges.

Challenges

1. **Mixed Code Changes in Security Patches:** Security patches often include additional modifications, such as code refactoring and processing flow updates, alongside vulnerability fixes. These unrelated modifications complicate the automation of security patch interpretation. As shown in Sect. 5.3, nine out of the twenty-five security patches (36%) used in our experiment contained code changes unrelated to vulnerability remediation.

2. **Lack of a Standardized Patch Structure:** In the OSS ecosystem, there are no standardized guidelines for commits related to vulnerability fixes. As a result, security patches in OSS are often unstructured, making it difficult to apply a universal method to distinguish vulnerability-fixing and non-vulnerability-fixing changes. In our dataset of the twenty-five security patches, we observed that comments or textual indicators were often absent near the modified code addressing vulnerabilities. Furthermore, as highlighted in Sect. 5.2, commit practices varied: some security patches included comments in ChangeLog and SECURITY.md indicating the vulnerability fix, while others only committed the code changes without any accompanying comments.

3. **Impact of Vulnerability Type on Code Modification Scope and Nature:** The distribution of affected code locations varies depending on the nature of the vulnerability, directly influencing the extent and complexity of code modifications required for remediation. In the FP case study in Table 4, the proposed method failed to capture the relationship between class imports and method calls across four different files in seven code blocks. This issue is expected to be particularly severe for vulnerabilities that typically involve a large volume of code modifications, such as CWE-79, CWE-89, and CWE-918. In these cases, the number of modified code segments exceeds 20 on average, and the affected files and functions are often distributed across multiple locations rather than confined to a single module. These vulnerabilities are primarily associated with web applications, where user input handling is frequently implemented across multiple functions and files, contributing to the complexity of security patches.

Technical Requirements

1. **Semantic Analysis of the Entire Codebase Affected by Security Patches:** To effectively analyze security patches, it is essential to develop techniques that can process the entire codebase of the target software and automatically extract relationships between modified and unmodified code. This requires the ability to identify and associate variables and function names involved in the modifications. As shown in Tables 8 and ??, improvements in LLM performance have been found to enhance the accuracy of classifying code modifications in security patches. However, achieving high-precision classification remains challenging. Addressing this issue may contribute to the resolution of Challenges-1 and Challenges-3.
2. **Techniques for Generating Structured Security Patches:** Since security patches often contain code modifications unrelated to vulnerability remediation, it is necessary to develop techniques that automatically annotate each code changes, such as by adding contextual comments. This would enhance the clarity and interpretability of security patch modifications, facilitating more effective analysis and application.

6.3   Recommendation

Recommendations for the OSS Maintainers. Since security patches are published as commit tags and utilized for technical reviews, isolating vulnerability-related changes within commits enhances their interpretability and reliability. To achieve this, OSS maintainers are encouraged to take the following measures:

- Commit vulnerability-fixing code lines separately from unrelated code changes.
- Add comments to the code explaining the mitigation measures applied to the vulnerability-fixing code lines.

Tian et al. [25] specifically proposed recommended rules and guidelines for writing commit messages for general commits, not limited to security patch commits.

Recommendations for Platform Providers. Following automated functionalities provided by platform providers would facilitate the systematic structuring of OSS security patches, improving their clarity and usability.

- Provide standardized documentation to formalize best practices for committing vulnerability fixes.
- Develop automated workflows to structure security patches specifically for vulnerability fixes.

7 Related Work

Many existing techniques related to security patches aim to facilitate vulnerability analysis by either collecting security patch commits to construct datasets or proposing methods for labeling vulnerable code.

Construction a Vulnerability-Related Dataset. Fan et al. [6] provided a dataset of C/C++ code vulnerabilities called Big-Vul. They crawled the CVE database, collected commits from Github repositories, and labeled the differences before and after the commits. Similarly, Georgios et al. [12] constructed a large dataset called CrossVul, collecting code before and after the fixing of vulnerabilities written in 40 programming languages. Their approach was to collect Github commits and label the code before and after applying the patch with `"git -diff"`. Likewise, Bhandari et al. [3] publish a vulnerability dataset called CVEfixes. They obtained repository commits based on vulnerability information obtained from a vulnerability database such as NVD. They also label commits before and after, and provide additional information about each code, such as the type and complexity of the changes made, such as additions and deletions. These studies consider the differences between the pre- and post-commit states; however, they do not specifically label code changes based on the content of security patches. To provide comparative data for machine learning models, Reis et al. [20] collected commits that were unrelated to the vulnerabilities and provided artifacts of the data by collecting them randomly from the repository of the vulnerability. The collection of commits unrelated to vulnerabilities targeted commits that did not contain security keywords in the commit messages. In contrast to the previous studies that primarily relied on diff-based labeling, Zheng et al. [29] provided a dataset called D2A, filtering commits by applying differential analysis and natural language processing (NLP) techniques to commit messages, specifically using keyword identification and semantic similarity analysis. Their approach distinguished security-related commits by checking for specific keywords such as "fix", "bug", and "patch", while filtering out commits that involve documentation updates or refactoring, identified by keywords such as "doc", "refactor", and other non-security-related terms. However, their approach relies solely on commit message filtering and does not perform semantic analysis of the code changes described in security patches. The study investigating commit messages in software development [25] reported that 44% of commit messages lacked information on "What" was changed or "Why" the change was made. Additionally, Dunlap et al. [5] mention that one of the problems with identifying vulnerability fix commits is that the commit messages provided by security advisories often contain incorrect information. Since the code changes in all security patches are not necessarily reflected in the commit messages, filtering based on commit messages alone is insufficient. Focusing on a specific domain, Challande et al. [4] proposed a method for constructing a large-scale vulnerability dataset targeting the Android Open Source Project (AOSP). They provide a vulnerability dataset that associates missing vulnerability information with the fixed commits extracted from AOSP. To further address the issue of missing commit links for security patches in vulnerability databases, Dunlap et al. [5] proposed VFCFinder, which relates security advisories and vulnerability fix commits with high accuracy, to address the issue of missing commit links for security patches in vulnerability databases. They use a machine learning-based approach to identify vulnerability fixing commits using five metrics, including the likelihood of being a vulnerability fixing commit, similarity, and whether the commit message contains a vulnerability identifier.

Labeling for Vulnerability-Related Commit. Alves et al. [2] developed an issue tracking system and identified issue messages that mentioned CVE numbers, labeling the code before and after the commit of the security patch. Building upon similar efforts to track and label vulnerable code, Russell et al. [21] proposed a method for collecting C/C++ function code from open source projects using static analysis tools and labeling the code before and after vulnerability fixes based on whether it has the same code features compared to five CWEs specified by the authors. Focusing on a machine learning-based domain, Zhou et al. [30] a vulnerability detection method called Devign that uses a graph neural network (GNN), and filtered security commits by creating a training data set. They extracted commits from the Github repository that contained security-related keywords (e.g. DoS and Injection), and manually labeled vulnerability fix commits and other commits. Similarly, aiming to automate the labeling process, Raducu et al. [18] proposed SVCP4C, a method for collecting and automatically labeling open source vulnerable code. Specifically, they used a static analysis tool called SonarCloud to detect vulnerable code from OSS repositories, and then identified and labeled functions commonly used in buffer overflows.

Identifying Secret Security Patches. Wang et al. [27] proposed a method for automatically detecting secret security patches that have been applied in secret to OSS, in response to the issue that analyzing security patches for specific OSS can lead to the risk of zero-day attacks on other software. Their approach uses machine learning-based methods to distinguish secret security patches from security patches by identifying specific change features (e.g., conditional statement changes, operator changes). Extending the analysis of software security beyond OSS, Akiyama et al. [1] investigated firmware in IoT devices reported that approximately 15.6% of the programs contained independently patched modifications by developers, as revealed through differential analysis. Similarly, focusing on detecting unpublished security patches, Wu et al. [28] proposed E-SPI, which identifies unpublished security patches in OSS. This identifies patches using a method that combines a model that converts code changes into abstract syntax trees (ASTs) and distinguishes the changes using a machine learning approach, and a model that constructs a dependency graph from the tokens in the commit messages.

Comprehensive Analysis of Security Patches. Li and Paxson [8] conducted a large-scale empirical study of security patch development for open source software, and clarified issues such as patch quality and development. The survey results reported that 5% of the patches examined had a negative impact on the software's operation after patching, and that 7% of the patches did not completely fix the vulnerability. Given the extensive research on security commits, a literature review on source code patch commitment mining has been published [31]. This review consolidates existing studies related to security commits, providing a comprehensive overview of the field.

8   Conclusion

We propose a method to identify vulnerability-fixing code lines, addressing the challenge of unrelated code changes in security patches. Our approach combines code segmentation with LLMs to enhance precision in detecting vulnerability-fixing lines. To evaluate its effectiveness, we conducted experiments on security patches for 25 high-risk software weaknesses. The results showed that code segmentation improved F1 score by 0.22 over the baseline, enabling more comprehensive identification of vulnerability-fixing lines. Additionally, we examined how required fixes vary by vulnerability type and outlined key challenges and requirements for leveraging LLMs in security patch analysis. We provide practical recommendations for OSS maintainers and platform providers.

In future work, we plan to improve the classification accuracy of vulnerability fix locations by explicitly incorporating code relationships via call graphs into the input of large language models (LLMs). Furthermore, we aim to extend this approach to evaluate the applicability of LLMs to vulnerability exploitability assessment.

A   Lexical Analysis Results of Commit Messages in Security Patches

To investigate whether vulnerability-fixing code lines can be identified based on commit messages associated with security patches, we conducted a lexical analysis. Specifically, we collected publicly available OSS security patches and their corresponding commit messages from the period between 1999 and 2024. We analyzed whether these messages explicitly indicated the modified code locations through the presence of specific keywords. The set of location keywords: "where", "location", "function", "class", "method", "module", "variable", and "argument". The results, summarized in Table 7, show that only 1,690 commits—approximately 12.7% of all samples—contained such location-indicative keywords. In addition, the proportion of commits that included vulnerability keywords (i.e., "CVE", "GHSA") was approximately 14.1%. Regarding the word count of commit messages, the average number of words was around 35, with a median of 11 words.

Table 7. Results of lexical analysis for commit messages

Analysis Items	Count or Ratio
Collected security patches	13,285
Security patches with blank commit messages	7
Number of words in commit messages (Average)	35
Number of words in commit messages (Median)	11
Number of security patches containing location keywords	12.7%(1,690/13,285)
Number of Security Patches Containing vulnerability keywords	14.1%(1,867/13,285)

B   The Effect of the Difference of LLM Model on the Accuracy

We analyzed the impact of differences in model performance on classification accuracy. As an additional verification, we limited the analysis to the six CVE numbers for which the proposed method (gpt4-turbo) had a low accuracy of F1-Score of 0.80 or less, and changed the LLM model settings of the proposed method to gpt4-o and gpt3.5-turbo to identify them. The results are shown in Table 8. The results of gpt-4o showed improved accuracy for the three CVEs, and the Recall value was 1.00 for all of them, identifying all of the code blocks without any omissions. gpt-4o correctly identified the test case for CVE-2014-0156, which had been incorrectly identified by gpt-4-turbo, and it also correctly identified the five code blocks that had been missed by gpt-4-turbo for CVE-2019-1020018. On the other hand, when gpt-3.5-turbo was used, identification accuracy decreased, and there was a tendency to output the same code blocks repeatedly, so the accuracy of the output content compared to the prompt content was also inferior to gpt-4-turbo and gpt-4o.

Table 8. Comparison of accuracy when the LLM model is changed using the proposed method

CVE	gpt4-turbo			gpt-4o			gpt-3.5-turbo		
	Pr	Re	F1	Pr	Re	F1	Pr	Re	F1
CVE-2014-10068	0.67	1.00	0.80	1.00	1.00	1.00	0.67	1.00	0.80
CVE-2023-0315	0.63	1.00	0.77	0.75	1.00	0.86	0.38	1.00	0.55
CVE-2014-0156	0.60	1.00	0.75	0.50	1.00	0.67	0.60	1.00	0.75
CVE-2019-1020018	0.53	0.62	0.57	0.50	1.00	0.67	0.60	0.38	0.46
CVE-2021-21245	0.57	1.00	0.73	0.57	1.00	0.73	0.29	1.00	0.44
CVE-2013-7491	0.67	1.00	0.80	0.67	1.00	0.80	0.33	1.00	0.50
Average	0.61	0.94	0.74	0.67	1.00	0.79	0.48	0.89	0.58

As with the proposed method, gpt-4o also showed improved accuracy for three of the six CVEs compared to gpt-4-turbo. gpt-3.5-turbo showed decreased accuracy for three CVEs. From the comparison of Table 8 and Table ??, even when the performance of the model is improved, the Recall and F1-Score are low when the baseline code segmentation process is not used, and vulnerability description information is not given. This shows that the processing of the proposed method is effective.

C Prompt

The following Listing 1.2 is an overview of the LLM prompts used in the experiment (Sect. 4.3). For commercial reasons, we refrain from including specific instructions in the prompts.

Listing 1.2. Overview of the LLM prompts used in the experiment

```
system_prompt=f'''
I want you to act as an expert vulnerability analyst. You must answer
    in JSON format in English.
[Tasks]
1.
2.
...
[Expected_answer]
Code_block_id:,
File_path:,
Function_name:,
Result_of_classification:.
assistant_prompt='''
{"Code_block_id":Integer, "File_path":String,...}'''
prompt = f'''
The "Security patch" is represented as {segmented_security_patch}
The "Vulnerability description" ...
[Constraints]
[Example]
'''
res = Settings().openai_settings.chat.completions.create(
model=Settings().{llm_model},
messages=[
{'role':'system','content':system_prompt},
{'role':'assistant','content':assistant_prompt},
{'role':'user','content':prompt},
],
temperature=Settings().temperature,
response_format={'type':'json_object'}
)
```

References

1. Akiyama, M., Shiraishi, S., Fukumoto, A., Yoshimoto, R., Shioji, E., Yamauchi, T.: Seeing is not always believing: insights on IoT manufacturing from firmware composition analysis and vendor survey. Comput. Secur. **133**, 103389 (2023)

2. Alves, H., Fonseca, B., Antunes, N.: Software metrics and security vulnerabilities: dataset and exploratory study. In: 2016 12th European Dependable Computing Conference (EDCC), pp. 37–44 (2016)
3. Bhandari, G., Naseer, A., Moonen, L.: Cvefixes: automated collection of vulnerabilities and their fixes from open-source software. In: Proceedings of the 17th International Conference on Predictive Models and Data Analytics in Software Engineering, PROMISE 2021, pp. 30–39. Association for Computing Machinery, New York (2021)
4. Challande, A., David, R., Renault, G.: Building a commit-level dataset of real-world vulnerabilities. In: Proceedings of the Twelfth ACM Conference on Data and Application Security and Privacy, CODASPY 2022, pp. 101–106. Association for Computing Machinery, New York (2022)
5. Dunlap, T., Lin, E., Enck, W., Reaves, B.: Vfcfinder: seamlessly pairing security advisories and patches (2023)
6. Fan, J., Li, Y., Wang, S., Nguyen, T.N.: A C/C++ code vulnerability dataset with code changes and CVE summaries. In: 2020 IEEE/ACM 17th International Conference on Mining Software Repositories (MSR), pp. 508–512 (2020)
7. Kim, S., Lee, H.: Software systems at risk: an empirical study of cloned vulnerabilities in practice. Comput. Secur. **77**, 720–736 (2018)
8. Li, F., Paxson, V.: A large-scale empirical study of security patches. In: Proceedings of the 2017 ACM SIGSAC Conference on Computer and Communications Security, CCS 2017, pp. 2201–2215. Association for Computing Machinery, New York (2017)
9. Ma, Z., Wang, H., Guo, Y., Chen, X.: Libradar: fast and accurate detection of third-party libraries in android apps. In: Proceedings of the 38th International Conference on Software Engineering Companion, pp. 653–656 (2016)
10. MITRE. A company unlike any other mission first, people always (2025). https://www.mitre.org/
11. MITRE. CWE top 25 most dangerous software weaknesses (2025). https://cwe.mitre.org/top25/
12. Nikitopoulos, G., Dritsa, K., Louridas, P., Mitropoulos, D.: Crossvul: a cross-language vulnerability dataset with commit data. In: Proceedings of the 29th ACM Joint Meeting on European Software Engineering Conference and Symposium on the Foundations of Software Engineering (2021)
13. NIST. National institute of standards and technology (2025). https://www.nist.gov/
14. NIST. National vulnerability database (2025). https://nvd.nist.gov/
15. NIST. NVD data feeds (2025). https://nvd.nist.gov/vuln/data-feeds
16. NVD. CVE-2018-1000867 (2024)
17. OpenAI. Openai (2025). https://openai.com/
18. Raducu, R., Esteban, G., Rodríguez Lera, F.J., Fernández, C.: Collecting vulnerable source code from open-source repositories for dataset generation. Appl. Sci. **10**(4), 1270 (2020)
19. Reid, D., Jahanshahi, M., Mockus, A.: The extent of orphan vulnerabilities from code reuse in open source software. In: Proceedings of the 44th International Conference on Software Engineering, ICSE 2022, pp. 2104–2115. Association for Computing Machinery, New York (2022)
20. Reis, S., Abreu, R.: A ground-truth dataset of real security patches (2021)
21. Russell, R.L., et al.: Automated vulnerability detection in source code using deep representation learning (2018)
22. snyk. The four steps of the vulnerability correction process (2025). https://snyk.io/jp/learn/vulnerability-remediation-process/

23. Synopsys. Open source security and risk analysis report (2023). https://www.synopsys.com/blogs/software-security/ja-jp/open-source-trends-ossra-report-2/
24. Synopsys. 4 approaches to vulnerability remediation (2024). https://www.synopsys.com/blogs/software-security/vulnerability-remediation-4-options.html
25. Tian, Y., Zhang, Y., Stol, K.-J., Jiang, L., Liu, H.: What makes a good commit message? In: Proceedings of the 44th International Conference on Software Engineering, ICSE 2022, pp. 2389–2401. Association for Computing Machinery, New York (2022)
26. Veracode. Solving your open source risk with sourceclear solving your open source risk with sourceclear by veracode risks associated with open source library use (2018)
27. Wang, X., Sun, K., Batcheller, A., Jajodia, S.: Detecting "0-day" vulnerability: an empirical study of secret security patch in OSS. In: 2019 49th Annual IEEE/IFIP International Conference on Dependable Systems and Networks (DSN), pp. 485–492 (2019)
28. Wu, B., Liu, S., Feng, R., Xie, X., Siow, J., Lin, S.-W.: Enhancing security patch identification by capturing structures in commits. IEEE Trans. Dependable Secure Comput. 1–15 (2022)
29. Zheng, Y., et al.: D2a: a dataset built for AI-based vulnerability detection methods using differential analysis. In: Proceedings of the 43rd International Conference on Software Engineering: Software Engineering in Practice, ICSE-SEIP 2021, pp. 111–120. IEEE Press (2021)
30. Zhou, Y., Liu, S., Siow, J., Du, X., Liu, Y.: Devign: effective vulnerability identification by learning comprehensive program semantics via graph neural networks (2019)
31. Zuo, F., Rhee, J.: Vulnerability discovery based on source code patch commit mining: a systematic literature review. Int. J. Inf. Secur. **23**, 1–14 (2024)

Encrypt What Matters: Selective Model Encryption for More Efficient Secure Federated Learning

Federico Mazzone[1]([✉])[iD], Ahmad Al Badawi[2][iD], Yuriy Polyakov[2][iD], Maarten Everts[1,3][iD], Florian Hahn[1][iD], and Andreas Peter[4][iD]

[1] University of Twente, Enschede, The Netherlands
{f.mazzone,maarten.everts,f.w.hahn}@utwente.nl
[2] Duality Technologies, Hoboken, NJ, USA
{aalbadawi,ypolyakov}@dualitytech.com
[3] Linksight, Utrecht, The Netherlands
[4] Carl von Ossietzky Universität Oldenburg, Oldenburg, Germany
andreas.peter@uni-oldenburg.de

Abstract. The notion that federated learning ensures privacy simply by keeping data local is widely acknowledged to be flawed. Cryptographic techniques such as Multi-Party Computation (MPC) and Fully Homomorphic Encryption (FHE) address this issue by concealing the model during the training procedure, but their extreme computational and communication overhead makes them impractical for real-world deployment.

However, we argue that such strong guarantees are unnecessary. Even with full-model encryption, black-box attacks remain possible during the prediction phase, since model outputs are eventually revealed to the querier. This suggests that instead of enforcing perfect privacy during training, it is sufficient to ensure that the leakage during training is no higher than the leakage during prediction.

To achieve this, we generalize POSEIDON (NDSS 2021), a state-of-the-art FHE-based federated learning approach, by selectively encrypting only the components of the model necessary to match the privacy level of the prediction phase. Our method identifies the parts of the model that contribute most to information leakage and prioritizes their encryption, significantly reducing computational and communication overhead.

Our experiments on dense neural networks show that encrypting only the last layer is often sufficient to hinder white-box attacks, improving efficiency by a linear factor in the number of layers. For deeper models, multiple layers may require encryption, but our approach still achieves a substantial speedup compared to full-model encryption.

Keywords: Federated Learning · Fully Homomorphic Encryption · Privacy Leakage · Privacy-Preserving Machine Learning · Neural Network

This is a significantly reworked version of our preprint on arXiv: arXiv:2409.17283.

S. Katsikas and B. Shafiq (Eds.): DBSec 2025, LNCS 15722, pp. 96–115, 2025.
https://doi.org/10.1007/978-3-031-96590-6_6

1   Introduction

In Federated Learning (FL), multiple parties collaboratively train a shared model by alternating between local training and global aggregation [30]. Each party updates the model using its private data, and these updates are periodically aggregated to refine the global model until convergence. While this approach keeps raw data decentralized, it does not inherently preserve privacy. Model updates can still reveal sensitive information about the underlying datasets, leaving FL vulnerable to various inference attacks [18,26,29,32,37].

To address this issue, cryptographic techniques such as multiparty computation (MPC) [8,11,33,34,50,51] and fully homomorphic encryption (FHE) [16,42] have been proposed to conceal model updates from potential adversaries. These techniques allow multiple parties to train a model jointly while ensuring that intermediate computations remain inaccessible to any individual party. As a result, they provide strong security guarantees by completely blocking the view of a potential adversary.

Despite their strong security guarantees, these techniques introduce significant computational and communication overhead. MPC-based frameworks for FL scale poorly in terms of communication, making them impractical for scenarios with more than four parties unless weaker security models with non-collusion assumptions are used [51]. FHE-based frameworks, in contrast, avoid this communication bottleneck due to the non-interactive nature of homomorphic encryption but suffer from extremely high computational costs. For example, POSEIDON [42], a state-of-the-art FHE-based FL framework, requires approximately 88 h to train a simple three-layer dense network on MNIST. In this work, we focus on FHE-based solutions and propose an approach to reduce their runtime overhead.

A key observation is that the strong security guarantees provided during training may not be necessary for meaningful privacy in FL. While cryptographic techniques can extend to the prediction phase enabling secure queries for ML-as-a-Service (MLaaS), they cannot inherently prevent *black-box attacks* [46], namely privacy attacks that rely solely on model outputs, as opposite to *white-box attacks*, which rely on internal model parameters. Since predictions must eventually be revealed in plaintext to the querier, an adversary can still exploit them to infer sensitive information. Thus, cryptographic approaches just limit the attack surface to black-box attacks, which are less powerful than white-box attacks but still pose privacy risks.[1]

Building on this observation, we propose a more pragmatic approach to secure federated training: rather than enforcing perfect privacy during training, we aim to ensure that the information leaked during training does not exceed what will be exposed during the prediction phase. Instead of fully blocking an adversary's view, we selectively expose parts of the model in plaintext to improve runtime

---

[1] While alternative approaches, such as differential privacy, can protect both training and inference, they typically degrade model accuracy [19,41] and are beyond the scope of this work.

efficiency. FHE is particularly well-suited to this strategy, as it allows us to encrypt only specific layers of the model.

Concretely, we design a generalization of POSEIDON [42], where only a subset of the model layers are encrypted. Our approach encrypts just enough of the model to ensure that the white-box leakage during training is no greater than the black-box leakage during prediction. Given the infeasibility of providing meaningful upper-bounds on attacks' accuracy that hold universally across all models and datasets, our evaluation focuses on a more practical experimental analysis, measuring privacy leakage through concrete attacks [37,46]. Our privacy leakage analysis also aims to identify which layers reveal the most information about the training data. Our selective encryption strategy prioritizes the most privacy-sensitive components of the model while leaving the other components in plaintext (see Fig. 1). Our approach significantly reduces computational and communication overhead compared to full-model encryption.

Experiments on dense neural networks show that encrypting only the final layer is often sufficient to reduce the effectiveness of white-box attacks to match that of black-box attacks, while also leading to a substantial speedup. For an L-layer model, our approach reduces encryption overhead by approximately a factor of L, achieving significant efficiency gains compared to full-model encryption. For instance, we reduce training time by a factor of $2\times$ on the Location dataset, by $3\times$ on MNIST, and by $5\times$ on Purchase-100 and Texas-100 compared to POSEIDON.

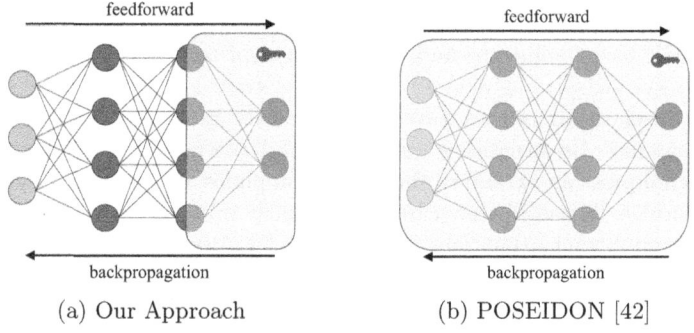

(a) Our Approach   (b) POSEIDON [42]

Fig. 1. Diagram representation of our approach compared to POSEIDON.

2 Background

2.1 Dense Neural Networks

Our work focuses on dense neural networks as they are the most straightforward model to compute under FHE. For a dense network f with L layers, we denote by w_i, b_i, ϕ_i the weights, biases, and activation function of layer i, respectively.

We denote by l_i the output or activation of layer i, that is $l_i = \phi_i(l_{i-1}w_i + b_i)$, where $l_0 := x$ is the input of the model. And we denote the intermediate linear application output as $u_i = l_{i-1}w_i + b_i$. For supervised classification tasks, the loss function is denoted by $L(f(x), y)$, where y is the ground-truth label associated to x, and can be minimized through Gradient Descent (GD) techniques. Figure 2 shows a schematic representation of the computations performed during one step of the training process.

$$
\begin{array}{ccc}
\begin{array}{c} u_1 = l_0 w_1 + b_1 \\ l_1 = \phi_1(u_1) \end{array} & \longrightarrow \cdots \longrightarrow & \begin{array}{c} u_L = l_{L-1} w_L + b_L \\ l_L = \phi_L(u_L) \end{array} \\
\nearrow & & \searrow \\
l_0 = x & & \begin{array}{c} L(l_L, y) \\ e_L = \partial L / \partial l_L \end{array} \\
& & \swarrow \\
\begin{array}{c} \nabla b_1 = e_1 \phi_1'(u_1) \\ \nabla w_1 = e_1 \phi_1'(u_1) l_0^T \\ (e_0 = e_1 \phi_1'(u_1) w_1^T) \end{array} & \longleftarrow \cdots \longleftarrow & \begin{array}{c} \nabla b_L = e_L \phi_L'(u_L) \\ \nabla w_L = e_L \phi_L'(u_L) l_{L-1}^T \\ e_{L-1} = e_L \phi_L'(u_L) w_L^T \end{array}
\end{array}
$$

Fig. 2. One training step for a dense network on input (x, y).

This step is repeated for a batch of examples B, and the resulting gradients are averaged to get a better approximation of the actual loss gradient on the real population. The parameters are then updated by following the negative direction of the gradient, by a step size proportional to a learning rate $\eta > 0$:

$$w_j \leftarrow w_j - \frac{\eta}{|B|} \sum_{(x,y)\in B} \nabla w_j \qquad b_j \leftarrow b_j - \frac{\eta}{|B|} \sum_{(x,y)\in B} \nabla b_j$$

for all $j \in \{1, \ldots, L\}$. This iterative process of feeding the data forward, computing the loss, and updating the model's parameters continues until convergence or for a fixed number of iterations.

2.2 Federated Learning

FL is a collaborative learning approach in which multiple data-owning parties, $P_1, \ldots, P_N$, jointly train a shared model while keeping their data decentralized. A widely adopted FL algorithm is Federated Averaging (FedAvg), introduced by McMahan et al. [30]. FedAvg operates in synchronous training rounds, where each round consists of the following steps:

1. **Local training.** Each party P_i performs a local training step on its local data, updating its model parameters $\{(w_j^i, b_j^i)\}_{j\in\{1,\ldots,L\}}$.

2. **Aggregation.** These locally updated models are sent to a central server (the aggregator), where they are averaged together to form a new global model:

$$w_j \leftarrow \frac{1}{N} \sum_{i=1}^{N} w_j^i \qquad b_j \leftarrow \frac{1}{N} \sum_{i=1}^{N} b_j^i$$

for all $j \in \{1, \ldots, L\}$.

3. **Broadcasting.** The aggregated global model is distributed back to all parties, who use it as the starting point for the next round of local training.

2.3   Fully Homomorphic Encryption

Fully Homomorphic Encryption (FHE) is a public-key cryptosystem that enables the evaluation of arbitrary-depth arithmetic circuits on encrypted data. This is achieved through bootstrapping, a technique that refreshes ciphertexts to mitigate noise accumulation from homomorphic operations.

For neural networks, the most widely used FHE scheme is CKKS [12], which is designed for working with vectors of floating-point values. This makes it particularly well-suited for machine learning tasks. CKKS natively supports componentwise addition and multiplication between ciphertexts, as well as vector rotations. However, it can be extended to encode and operate on matrices, and it allows the evaluation of non-polynomial functions via polynomial approximation [42].

In a multiparty setting such as FL, the secret key is secret-shared among the training parties. This allows the parties to collaboratively generate collective public and evaluation keys without revealing the underlying secret key [35]. These public keys enable any party to encrypt data and perform homomorphic computations in a non-interactive manner. However, operations that depend on the secret key, such as decryption and bootstrapping, require a one-round protocol among the training parties.

2.4   Fully-Encrypted Solutions

We refer to fully-encrypted solutions for FL as those frameworks that utilize multiparty FHE to encrypt an ML model in its entirety, enabling multiple parties to execute federated training on it. One such framework for neural networks is POSEIDON [42], upon which our work builds and improves. The POSEIDON framework operates as follows:

- **FHE Setup.** The training parties generate the secret key shares non-interactively and execute a constant-round protocol to derive the collective public and evaluation keys. These keys, along with the desired model architecture and training hyperparameters, are shared with the aggregator.
- **ML Setup.** The aggregator initializes the model in plaintext, encrypts its parameters (w_j, b_j) using the public key, and distributes the encrypted model to all training parties.

- **Secure Training.** The standard FL protocol is followed, with all computations, including local updates and aggregation, performed on encrypted data. Since the model is never decrypted, a distributed bootstrapping protocol must be periodically executed to refresh ciphertexts and prevent excessive noise accumulation.
- **Secure Prediction.** Once some convergence condition is met, the model can be used for secure predictions in a MLaaS fashion. A querier encrypts their input x with the public key and sends it to one of the training parties. This party performs a feedforward step on the encrypted model and broadcasts the encrypted output. All training parties then generate decryption shares of the output, which are sent to the querier. The querier aggregates these shares to obtain the final plaintext prediction.

Note that, unless threshold secret sharing is employed, all training parties must remain available during the prediction phase to enable the output decryption.

2.5   Privacy Leakage: Membership Inference

In ML, membership inference is a privacy attack aiming to determine whether a given data point was part of a model's training set. These attacks exploit differences in a model's behavior when making predictions on seen versus unseen data. Membership inference provides insight into how much information a model retains from its training data, helping to assess the potential effectiveness of other privacy attacks and for that reason is often used to audit data privacy [9].

Membership inference attacks can operate in a white-box or black-box setting. In the white-box scenario, the attacker has access to internal model parameters, gradients, and activations, whereas in the black-box setting, only the model's predictions are observable. Since white-box attacks leverage more information, they are generally more powerful and yield higher attack accuracy. Below, we describe two well-known implementations of membership inference attacks, which we will use in our assessment.

Nasr et al. [37] *(White-Box).* This attack assumes the attacker has partial knowledge of the private training dataset and trains a supervised attack model to distinguish members from non-members. For each data point known to the attacker, a forward and backward pass is performed, extracting activations, loss values, and gradients. These features are labeled as members and used as inputs to the attack model. Similarly, the attacker extracts features from publicly available data, assumed to be non-members, and labels them accordingly. The attack model is then trained as a binary classifier to differentiate members from non-members using the extracted features.

Shokri et al. [46] *(Black-Box).* This attack relies on training multiple shadow models, which replicate the behavior of the target model and are trained on datasets with similar distributions. Since the attacker knows the membership status of samples used in the shadow model training, they can observe differences in the model's predictions between members and non-members. As in the white-box setting, these observations are then used to train a separate attack model, which learns to infer membership based on the shadow models' predictions.

3   Our Approach: Partially Encrypted Models

3.1   Motivation

Fully-encrypted solutions for FL ensure that all training computations remain encrypted, effectively reducing the attack surface from powerful white-box attacks to weaker black-box attacks. However, black-box attacks, while less effective, still pose privacy risks. This raises the question: do we really need to encrypt the entire model to achieve meaningful privacy guarantees?

Unlike white-box attacks, black-box attacks operate only on model outputs, making them inherently weaker. Given this disparity, we propose that secure federated training should be designed such that the training phase does not expose more information than what will inevitably be leaked during prediction. In other words, if an adversary cannot extract more information during training than they would from querying the model post-training, then the additional encryption effort beyond this threshold provides no returns in terms of privacy.

It is important to note that, while various mitigation strategies exist to limit black-box attacks during prediction such as restricting query access or obfuscating confidence scores, these methods are often ineffective against adversaries with long-term access to the model.

3.2   Layers' Leakage

FHE-based approaches for neural network training typically encrypt model parameters at the granularity of individual layers, ideally encoding each layer's weight matrix and bias vector within individual ciphertexts. This layer-wise encryption leads to a natural way of hiding only part of the network, that is by selecting a subset of layers to encrypt rather than the entire model.

To determine how many and which layers should be encrypted to achieve a given privacy threshold, we analyze the privacy leakage of different layers in a neural network. We conduct this analysis experimentally, exploiting the high flexibility of the attack model's input of Nasr et al. [37]. Specifically, we feed the attack model only the information available from the selected layers (i.e., activations and gradients), simulating a scenario where the remaining layers are encrypted and their information remains hidden.

Prior work on membership inference attacks suggests that earlier layers capture more general, task-agnostic features of the training data, while deeper layers encode task-specific representations that are more privacy-sensitive [37]. Additionally, the parameter capacity of a neural network increases in the later layers, causing the target model to store information about the exact training samples. Therefore, if the last layers of the model are concealed from the attacker, inference attacks tend to be weaker due to the lower degree of information leakage.

Our experimental results in Sect. 4.3 confirm this trend, showing that encrypting layers starting from the output is the most effective approach.

3.3   Protocol Description

For a dense network with L layers, our approach encrypts the final T layers while keeping the first $L - T$ layers in plaintext. The choice of T depends on the specific model architecture and dataset. We propose a method for the training parties to pick and agree on a T in Sect. 5.

Global Training. The protocol follows the standard fully-encrypted training setup described in Sect. 2.4 with a few differences:

- The training parties must agree on the number of layers to encrypt T.
- During model initialization, the aggregator encrypts only the last T layers, leaving the remaining layers in plaintext.
- During aggregation, the parameters from the plaintext layers are averaged in plaintext, while the parameters from the encrypted layers are averaged through homomorphic addition and scalar multiplication by $1/N$.

The training process continues for a fixed number of global iterations, or until a predefined convergence criterion is met.

Local Training. During local training, the forward and backward passes transition between plaintext and encrypted computation.

1. **Plaintext.** The feedforward pass starts in plaintext, processing the first $L-T$ layers without encryption.
2. **Encrypted.** Once layer $L - T + 1$ is reached, computations proceed under encryption. The remaining layers, model output, loss computation, and the initial phase of backpropagation all occur under encryption, with potential bootstrapping to refresh intermediate values.
3. **Plaintext.** When backpropagation reaches layer $L - T$, intermediate results are decrypted, and the remaining weight updates proceed in plaintext.

Protocol 1 outlines one training pass of our approach on input (x, y). Bootstrapping calls are omitted since their frequency depends on the exact FHE parameters. We detail the protocol for dense neural networks trained with the Stochastic Gradient Descent (SGD) optimizer and Mean Squared Error (MSE) loss, but it can be easily generalized to any feed-forward model. Extending the approach to momentum-based optimizers, such as Nesterov Accelerated Gradient, is straightforward and requires only an additional weight update. Adaptive optimizers like AdaGrad [15], RMSProp [48], and Adam [23] require additional care due to the need of performing a homomorphic division by the rescaling coefficient. We can also add L2 regularization at the cost of an additional homomorphic multiplication, by multiplying the weight matrices by $1 - \eta\lambda/B$ during

---

Protocol 1. One Training Pass

1: $l_0 \leftarrow x$
   FEEDFORWARD:
2: **for** $j = 1 \rightarrow L$ **do**
3:     $u_j \leftarrow l_{j-1} w_j + b_j$ (FHE eval. if $j > L - T$)
4:     $l_j \leftarrow \phi_j(u_j)$ (FHE eval. if $j > L - T$)
5: **end for**
   BACKPROPAGATION:
6: $e_L \leftarrow y - l_L$ (FHE eval. if $T > 0$)
7: $\nabla b_L \leftarrow e_L \phi'_L(u_L)$ (FHE eval. if $T > 0$)
8: $\nabla w_L \leftarrow \nabla b_L l_{L-1}^T$ (FHE eval. if $T > 0$)
9: **for** $j = L - 1 \rightarrow 1$ **do**
10:     $e_j \leftarrow \nabla b_{j+1} w_{j+1}^T$ (FHE eval. if $j \geq L - T$)
11:     **if** $j = L - T$ **then**
12:         $e_j \leftarrow \text{Decrypt}(e_j)$
13:     **end if**
14:     $\nabla b_j \leftarrow e_j \phi'_j(u_j)$ (FHE eval. if $j > L - T$)
15:     $\nabla w_j \leftarrow \nabla b_j l_{j-1}^T$ (FHE eval. if $j > L - T$)
16: **end for**

---

the local gradient update, where λ is the weight decay coefficient and B is the local batch size. For adaptations to convolutional layers, we refer to [42].

It is important to note that the parameters (weights and biases) of the first $L - T$ layers will always be in plaintext, while the parameters of the last T layers will always be encrypted and never exposed at any point in time.

Prediction. Extending the protocol to the prediction phase is straightforward, with the following considerations:

– If the querier is one of the training parties, they can locally perform the feedforward step, requesting assistance from others only for bootstrapping and final output decryption.
– If the querier is an external entity, the input will be encrypted. Consequently, even computations in the plaintext layers must be performed under encryption. While matrix multiplication and bias addition remain straightforward, activation functions require approximation for homomorphic evaluation, similarly to the ones in the encrypted layers.

3.4   Security

We provide a security definition that naturally extends the one given in [42].

Lemma 1. *In the semi-honest setting, no party, including the aggregator, can learn more information about the training data of any other party or the model parameters corresponding to any encrypted layer, other than what can be deduced from their own data (including the model output, in case of predictions), and from the parameters and intermediate computations of the layers in plaintext.*

Proof (sketch). We proceed as in [42], but assuming the simulator is also given access to the parameters of the exposed layers at each iteration, and to the output of each decryption call. The idea is to see the overall scheme as a composition of the underlying FHE protocols, which are all simulatable. For the basic protocols like key generation and decryption, we rely on the proofs by Mouchet et al. [35], while for the distributed bootstrapping, we rely on the proof by Sav et al. [42].

Note that the security of our approach does not hold for a malicious adversary, which can use the decryption call in the protocol to decrypt the encrypted layers.

4   Experimental Evaluation

We evaluate our partial-encryption approach by training dense networks on four well-known datasets, assessing the privacy leakage for each layer of the model, and comparing its performance against POSEIDON [42] as a baseline.

4.1   Experimental Setup

We start by training the models in plaintext to assess their privacy leakage as described in Sect. 3.2. This leads to determine the number of layers T that need to be encrypted to ensure the white-box leakage matches the black-box leakage. Next, we assess the training under encryption using T encrypted layers and measuring the computational and communication costs of our approach.

Since the codebase of POSEIDON [42] was not publicly available at the time of writing, we implemented all the machine learning operations under encryption from scratch, building on top of the OpenFHE library[2] for the multiparty FHE functionalities. Our implementation uses CKKS with a 55-bit scaling factor, a multiplicative depth of 8, and a ring dimension of 2^{15}. All parameters are chosen to ensure 128-bit security (see Homomorphic Encryption Standard [3,4]).

We run all experiments within Mininet[3], a network emulator that allows us to configure different network topologies and enforce bandwidth and latency constraints. Multiple virtual hosts are used to simulate the training parties. The virtual hosts are spawned within a machine with an Intel Xeon Platinum 8358 running at 2.60 GHz, with 64 threads on 32 cores, and 512 GB RAM.

For the evaluation, we consider a setup with three training parties and a central server, communicating over TCP in a star topology with the aggregator as center. The network is constrained to 1 Gbps bandwidth and a 10 ms latency.

4.2   Datasets and Models

Datasets. We experiment with four datasets commonly used in PPML and suitable for dense neural networks.

---

[2] https://github.com/openfheorg/openfhe-development.
[3] https://github.com/mininet/mininet.

- MNIST: A handwritten digit dataset with 70,000 grayscale images (10 classes). We downsample images to 8×8^4.
- Purchase-100: A dataset from Kaggle's "Acquire Valued Shoppers" challenge [46], containing 197,324 records with 600 binary features, grouped into 100 purchase behavior classes[5].
- Texas-100: A hospital discharge dataset [46] with 67,330 records, 6,169 binary features related to patient information and medical procedures (100 classes) (See footnote 5).
- Locations: A Foursquare-based dataset [46] with 5,010 records, 446 binary features indicating location visits, and 30 geosocial behavior classes (See footnote 5).

A subset of each dataset is evenly distributed among the training parties.

Models. We employ different dense network architectures depending on the dataset:

- MNIST: A model with two hidden layers of sizes 30 and 20.
- Locations: A model with three hidden layers of sizes 256, 128, and 64.
- Purchase-100 and Texas-100: We adopt the architecture proposed in [37], consisting of four hidden layers with sizes 1024, 512, 256, and 128.

Each layer uses the sigmoid activation function, which, when encrypted, is approximated using a Chebyshev polynomial of degree 13 over the interval $[-10, 10]$. Training is performed using plain SGD while minimizing the MSE loss. For further details on the training settings, we refer to our repository.[6]

4.3   Empirical Results

Privacy Leakage. In Fig. 3, we report the outcome of our privacy leakage assessment on the different models. The bars indicate the accuracy of the white-box attack by Nasr et al. [37], using all available information up to a given layer. For example, attacking layer 2 (L2) means training the attack model with activations and gradients from layers 1 and 2. We ensure an equal number of members and non-members during training and testing, making the attack accuracy baseline 50% (random attacker's choice). The reported values represent the average and maximum attack accuracy over four runs.

Our experimental results confirm the trend that later layers leak more information compared to earlier ones, with the final layer showing the highest privacy leakage. This is especially evident in the cases of Purchase-100 (Fig. 3b) and MNIST (Fig. 3a), where the attack accuracy using layer's activation increases from 55.12% to 90.10% (a 7.8× increase relative to the baseline) and from 50.81% to 64.49% (a 17.8× increase relative to the baseline), respectively, when moving from the second-to-last to the last layer.

---

[4] http://yann.lecun.com/exdb/mnist.
[5] https://github.com/privacytrustlab/datasets.
[6] https://github.com/FedericoMazzone/SmartCryptNN.

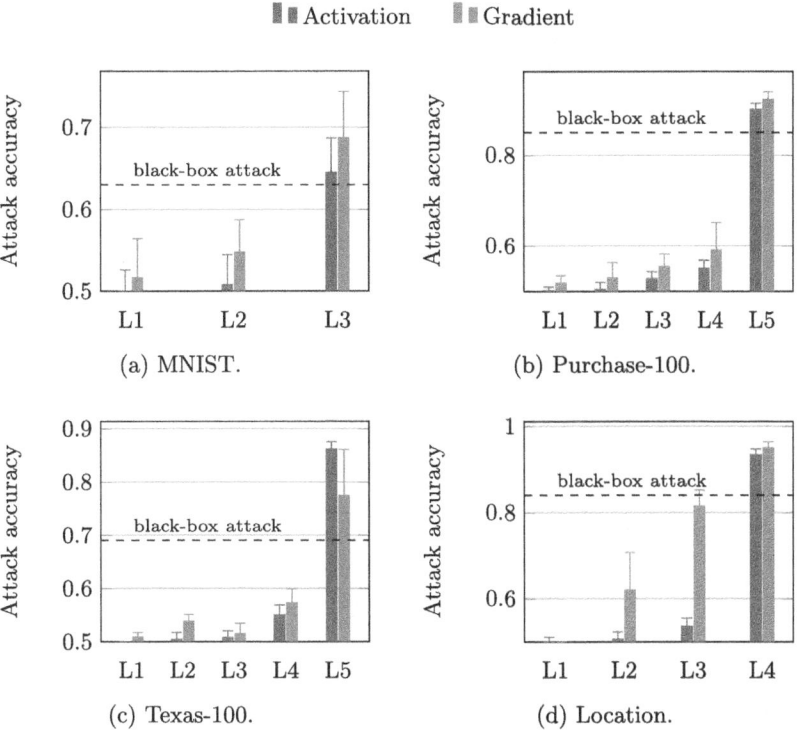

Fig. 3. Layer-wise accuracy of the white-box membership inference attack by Nasr et al. [37] against different datasets and models, exploiting both the layer's activation and gradient.

As a side note, in line with the findings of Nasr et al. [37], our experiments confirm that the availability of gradients contributes to a higher attack accuracy.

We also report the attack accuracy of the black-box attack by Shokri et al. [46] (dashed line), showing that these models can still leak information during the prediction phase. As expected, the amount of information leaked through prediction alone is lower than that available to a white-box attacker. However, in most cases, black-box attacks remain more effective than white-box attacks limited to all but the last layer. This makes the number of layers that need to be encrypted $T = 1$. The only exception in our experiments is with the Location dataset, where encrypting two layers is necessary to ensure that the white-box attack is no stronger than the black-box attack.

Our Approach. To assess the efficiency of our partially-encrypted solution, we evaluate its runtime and communication overhead for different numbers of encrypted layers T. As shown in Fig. 4, both computation time and communication size scale approximately linearly with the number of encrypted layers. In contrast, the contribution of plaintext layers to the overall runtime and communication is negligible compared to that of encrypted layers. Consequently, for our purposes, two dense networks with different number of layers L, but same number of encrypted layers T, achieve the same runtime performance.

Table 1 provides a breakdown of the total training runtime and communication size on the MNIST dataset for different values of T. The case of $T = 3$ corresponds to the baseline POSEIDON approach [42]. We observe that reducing the number of encrypted layers substantially decreases both runtime and communication requirements. For example, decreasing T from 3 to 1 results in an approximately $3\times$ reduction in communication size and training time.

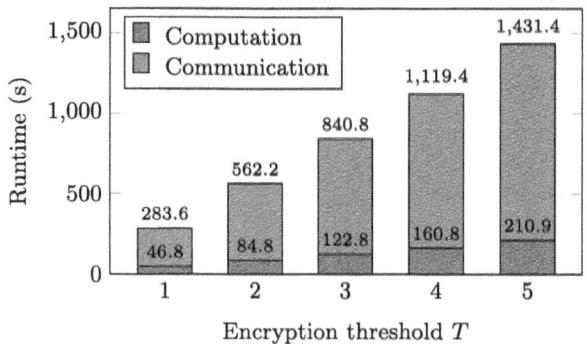

Fig. 4. Computation vs. communication time for one training pass in our approach on a five-layer dense neural network (Purchase-100, Texas-100) for varying number of encrypted layers T.

Table 2 compares our approach against POSEIDON for one training pass across different datasets. We achieve a speed-up of up to $5.05\times$ for datasets such as Purchase-100 and Texas-100 when encrypting only a single layer ($T = 1$). Even in scenarios where $T = 2$, such as the Location dataset, our approach still achieves a nearly $2\times$ improvement. The observed speed-up is approximately L/T, with L the total number of layers in the model.

Our approach maintains the same model accuracy as POSEIDON. However, our implementation is a prototype and lacks many of the runtime optimizations present in the original POSEIDON solution [42]. As a result, our absolute runtime is higher than what reported in their work. Nevertheless, when considering the relative speedup over the baseline, our approach remains more efficient than POSEIDON. The advantage provided by our solution may become even more evident for models with deeper architectures [2,14,24], particularly in settings with constrained communication networks.

Table 1. Runtime and communication size of our approach on the MNIST dataset with varying number of encrypted layers T.

T	Training		Inference	
	Runtime (h)	Comm. (GB)	Runtime (s)	Comm. (MB)
1	726.7	980.8	23.5	10.3
2	1504.1	1988.8	50.0	23.3
3	2232.7	3083.4	76.8	36.3

Table 2. Runtime of our approach vs. POSEIDON [42] for one training step.

Dataset	POSEIDON [42]	Our approach		
	Runtime (s)	Runtime (s)	T	speed-up
MNIST	840.8	283.6	1	2.96×
Purchase-100	1431.4	283.6	1	5.05×
Texas-100	1431.4	283.6	1	5.05×
Location	1119.4	562.2	2	1.99×

5   Procedure to Choose T

Since privacy leakage depends on many factors, including the training dataset, model architecture, training method, and other hyperparameters, there is no general-purpose guideline for determining how many layers to encrypt T. A practical approach to picking this parameter in a distributed fashion is to estimate a lower bound on privacy leakage through an assessment on the local data. Each party can train a dummy model on its private dataset and evaluate its privacy leakage locally. Since each local dataset is a subset of the joint dataset, this assessment provides an empirical worst-case estimate. This follows from the fact that models trained on larger datasets tend to generalize better, and improved generalization is typically associated with lower privacy leakage [46]. Finally, the parties can leverage MPC techniques to collectively agree on the number of layers to encrypt. Depending on the specific setting and requirements, the parties can, for instance, perform a majority vote or a maximum computation.

Limitations. As is common in the literature [36,43], our approach focuses on an experimental analysis of privacy leakage through concrete attacks rather than providing formal privacy guarantees, due to the inherent challenges of computing universal upper-bounds on leakage. Hence, the picture we present in this paper may change if new, stronger attacks emerge. Additionally, our selective encryption strategy assumes that some model components are more sensitive than others, which holds in the models and datasets we tested, but may not always be true in all scenarios.

6   Related Work

PPML literature can be categorized into works that either focus on ensuring privacy during the inference or the training stage.

Privacy-Preserving Inference. In this scenario, an already trained model is typically sent to a cloud server, which provides predictions as a service on behalf of the model's owner. The main goal is to ensure the confidentiality of the user's query input and the corresponding output. This kind of oblivious prediction functionality can be achieved in multiple ways. One approach involves using leveled Homomorphic Encryption to encrypt the query input and perform the inference homomorphically (CryptoNets [17]). Another method involves using MPC among a cluster of non-colluding servers, possibly mixed with Garbled Circuits and HE (Gazelle [22], MiniONN [28], Chameleon [40], CryptFlow [25]). Some of those MPC solutions prevent the cloud servers from accessing or stealing the model by distributing it across multiple servers. This aspect becomes particularly valuable when the model owner lacks trust in the service provider. Some line of work focuses on exploring inference on ML models in Trusted Execution Environments (TEEs), where the main challenges are ensuring performance and resiliency against side-channels attacks (Slalom [49]).

In addition, to protect against users attempting to retrieve information about the training data or reconstruct the model through a smart choice of queries (i.e., black-box attacks), various defense mechanisms have been proposed. General purpose solutions like using differential privacy during model training (Song et al. [47], Abadi et al. [1]) have been widely studied, as well as specific defense strategies against certain attacks. For instance, possible strategies against inference attacks include perturbing the prediction vector with noise (Memguard [20]), masking the output confidence score by only revealing the top-k scores or just the prediction label (Shokri et al. [46], Choquette-Choo et al. [13], Li et al. [27]) employing adversarial regularization by jointly minimizing the classification loss and maximizing a theoretical attack model's loss (Nasr et al. [36]), using knowledge distillation to put distance between the private dataset and the deployed model (PATE [38], Shejwalkar et al. [43]), or simply applying standard regularization techniques (Shokri et al. [46]). Furthermore, other approaches have been developed to prevent model stealing, such as PRADA [21], which checks for structured patterns in user queries, or like PrivDNN [39], which encrypts the individual neurons that contribute the most to the model's utility. It is important to note, however, that while the last two approaches enhance model privacy, they do not inherently safeguard the confidentiality of the training data.

Privacy-Preserving Training. To introduce adversaries during the training stage, we need to consider a collaborative learning setting. In this setting, an adversary may corrupt one or more training parties and potentially the supporting server, making the intermediate model updates vulnerable. Differential privacy can be employed to inject noise during the federated training process, providing privacy guarantees at either data level (Shokri and Shmatikov [45]) or user level (McMahan et al. [31]). Since the supporting server could also be compromised, some lines of work have focused on concealing individual model updates by performing secure aggregation of such values. This is achieved using techniques such as secret sharing (SEPIA [7]), MHE (Shi et al. [44], Chan et al. [10]), or additive masking (Bonawitz et al. [6], Bell et al. [5]). Note that secure aggregation is orthogonal to our approach and can potentially be combined with it to conceal the individual updates corresponding to the exposed layers.

To completely prevent leakage from intermediate (aggregated) models, MPC can be employed, allowing the data owners to jointly execute the training mechanism in a secure manner, usually by exploiting secret sharing schemes. However, a major challenge arises when scaling to a large number of parties, as it leads to impractical communication complexity. To work around such overhead, the data-owners can delegate the computations to a small cluster of non-colluding servers, usually composed of 2 parties (SecureML [34]), 3 parties (ABY^3 [33], Falcon [51], SecureNN [50]), or 4 parties (FLASH [8], Trident [11]). However, this delegation-based approach imposes strong assumptions on the non-collusion of the computing servers, strongly constraining the threat model.

To overcome the limitations of small cluster in MPC solutions to the threat model, a promising research direction has emerged, leveraging FHE schemes to encrypt the model. In this way, the FL process can be conducted entirely under encryption, enabling secure collaboration among a large number of parties (SPINDLE [16] for generalized linear models, POSEIDON [42] for neural networks). Our solution aligns with this trajectory and can be seen as a generalization of these approaches, with the primary aim of enhancing the efficiency of FL under FHE and making its use a bit more feasible in real-world scenarios.

7   Conclusion

In this paper, we propose a selective encryption strategy for secure federated learning that improves the efficiency of FHE-based approaches. Instead of encrypting the entire model, we focus on specific layers, significantly reducing both runtime and communication costs. Our results show that this approach speeds up training while maintaining comparable privacy guarantees to fully encrypted methods. We also examined which layers contribute more to privacy leakage and found that later layers tend to leak the most information, allowing for a more targeted encryption strategy. Our findings suggest that selectively encrypting only the most sensitive layers is a promising direction for making privacy-preserving machine learning more practical.

Future work includes extending this method to other neural network architectures and evaluating privacy under different threat models beyond membership inference attacks. These steps will help further refine the trade-offs between efficiency and security in federated learning.

Acknowledgments. We thank Thijs van Ede for the insightful coffee break discussions. This project has received funding from the European Union's Horizon 2020 research and innovation programme under Grant Agreement No 965315. The results reflect only the authors' view and the European Commission is not responsible for any use that may be made of the information this paper contains. This work was also supported by the Netherlands Organization for Scientific Research under NWO: SHARE project [CS.011].

Disclosure of Interests. The authors have no competing interests to declare that are relevant to the content of this article.

References

1. Abadi, M., et al.: Deep learning with differential privacy. In: Proceedings of the SIGSAC Conference on Computer and Communications Security (2016)
2. Agarap, A.F.: Training deep neural networks for image classification in a homogenous distributed system (2019)
3. Albrecht, M., et al.: Homomorphic encryption security standard. Technical report, HomomorphicEncryption.org, Toronto, Canada (2018)
4. Albrecht, M.R., Player, R., Scott, S.: On the concrete hardness of learning with errors. J. Math. Cryptol. **9**(3), 169–203 (2015)
5. Bell, J.H., Bonawitz, K.A., Gascón, A., Lepoint, T., Raykova, M.: Secure single-server aggregation with (poly) logarithmic overhead. In: Proceedings of the SIGSAC Conference on Computer and Communications Security (2020)
6. Bonawitz, K., et al.: Practical secure aggregation for privacy-preserving machine learning. In: Proceedings of the 2017 ACM SIGSAC Conference on Computer and Communications Security, pp. 1175–1191 (2017)
7. Burkhart, M., Strasser, M., Many, D., Dimitropoulos, X.: SEPIA: privacy-preserving aggregation of multi-domain network events and statistics. In: USENIX Security Symposium (2010)
8. Byali, M., Chaudhari, H., Patra, A., Suresh, A.: Flash: fast and robust framework for privacy-preserving machine learning. Cryptology ePrint Archive (2019)
9. Carlini, N., Chien, S., Nasr, M., Song, S., Terzis, A., Tramer, F.: Membership inference attacks from first principles. In: 2022 IEEE Symposium on Security and Privacy (SP), pp. 1897–1914. IEEE (2022)
10. Chan, T.H.H., Shi, E., Song, D.: Privacy-preserving stream aggregation with fault tolerance. In: Financial Cryptography and Data Security: 16th International Conference, FC 2012, Kralendijk, Bonaire, 27 February-2 March 2012, Revised Selected Papers 16, pp. 200–214. Springer (2012)
11. Chaudhari, H., Rachuri, R., Suresh, A.: Trident: efficient 4PC framework for privacy preserving machine learning. arXiv preprint arXiv:1912.02631 (2019)
12. Cheon, J.H., Kim, A., Kim, M., Song, Y.: Homomorphic encryption for arithmetic of approximate numbers. In: Advances in Cryptology–ASIACRYPT: International Conference on the Theory and Applications of Cryptology and Information Security. Springer (2017)
13. Choquette-Choo, C.A., Tramer, F., Carlini, N., Papernot, N.: Label-only membership inference attacks. In: International Conference on Machine Learning, pp. 1964–1974. PMLR (2021)

14. Dosovitskiy, A., et al.: An image is worth 16x16 words: transformers for image recognition at scale. arXiv preprint arXiv:2010.11929 (2020)
15. Duchi, J., Hazan, E., Singer, Y.: Adaptive subgradient methods for online learning and stochastic optimization. J. Mach. Learn. Res. **12**(7) (2011)
16. Froelicher, D., et al.: Scalable privacy-preserving distributed learning. Proc. Priv. Enhancing Technol. (2021)
17. Gilad-Bachrach, R., Dowlin, N., Laine, K., Lauter, K., Naehrig, M., Wernsing, J.: Cryptonets: applying neural networks to encrypted data with high throughput and accuracy. In: International Conference on Machine Learning, pp. 201–210. PMLR (2016)
18. Gupta, U., Stripelis, D., Lam, P.K., Thompson, P., Ambite, J.L., Ver Steeg, G.: Membership inference attacks on deep regression models for neuroimaging. In: Medical Imaging with Deep Learning, pp. 228–251. PMLR (2021)
19. Huang, X., Ding, Y., Jiang, Z.L., Qi, S., Wang, X., Liao, Q.: DP-FL: a novel differentially private federated learning framework for the unbalanced data. World Wide Web **23**, 2529–2545 (2020)
20. Jia, J., Salem, A., Backes, M., Zhang, Y., Gong, N.Z.: Memguard: defending against black-box membership inference attacks via adversarial examples. In: Proceedings of the 2019 ACM SIGSAC Conference on Computer and Communications Security, pp. 259–274 (2019)
21. Juuti, M., Szyller, S., Marchal, S., Asokan, N.: Prada: protecting against DNN model stealing attacks. In: 2019 IEEE European Symposium on Security and Privacy (EuroS&P), pp. 512–527. IEEE (2019)
22. Juvekar, C., Vaikuntanathan, V., Chandrakasan, A.: {GAZELLE}: a low latency framework for secure neural network inference. In: USENIX Security Symposium (2018)
23. Kingma, D.P., Ba, J.: Adam: a method for stochastic optimization. arXiv preprint arXiv:1412.6980 (2014)
24. Krizhevsky, A., Sutskever, I., Hinton, G.E.: Imagenet classification with deep convolutional neural networks. In: Advances in Neural Information Processing Systems, vol. 25 (2012)
25. Kumar, N., Rathee, M., Chandran, N., Gupta, D., Rastogi, A., Sharma, R.: Cryptflow: secure tensorflow inference. In: 2020 IEEE Symposium on Security and Privacy (SP), pp. 336–353. IEEE (2020)
26. Li, J., Li, N., Ribeiro, B.: Effective passive membership inference attacks in federated learning against overparameterized models. In: The Eleventh International Conference on Learning Representations (2023)
27. Li, Z., Zhang, Y.: Membership leakage in label-only exposures. In: Proceedings of the 2021 ACM SIGSAC Conference on Computer and Communications Security, pp. 880–895 (2021)
28. Liu, J., Juuti, M., Lu, Y., Asokan, N.: Oblivious neural network predictions via minionn transformations. In: Proceedings of the 2017 ACM SIGSAC Conference on Computer and Communications Security, pp. 619–631 (2017)
29. Lu, H., Li, M.J., He, T., Wang, S., Narayanan, V., Chan, K.S.: Robust coreset construction for distributed machine learning. IEEE J. Sel. Areas Commun. **38**(10), 2400–2417 (2020)
30. McMahan, B., Moore, E., Ramage, D., Hampson, S., Arcas, B.A.: Communication-efficient learning of deep networks from decentralized data. In: Artificial Intelligence and Statistics, pp. 1273–1282. PMLR (2017)
31. McMahan, H.B., Ramage, D., Talwar, K., Zhang, L.: Learning differentially private recurrent language models. arXiv preprint arXiv:1710.06963 (2017)

32. Melis, L., Song, C., De Cristofaro, E., Shmatikov, V.: Exploiting unintended feature leakage in collaborative learning. In: Symposium on Security and Privacy (SP). IEEE (2019)
33. Mohassel, P., Rindal, P.: ABY3: a mixed protocol framework for machine learning. In: Proceedings of the SIGSAC Conference on Computer and Communications Security (2018)
34. Mohassel, P., Zhang, Y.: Secureml: a system for scalable privacy-preserving machine learning. In: Symposium on Security and Privacy (SP). IEEE (2017)
35. Mouchet, C., Troncoso-Pastoriza, J., Bossuat, J.P., Hubaux, J.P.: Multiparty homomorphic encryption from ring-learning-with-errors. Proc. Priv. Enhancing Technol. (CONF) (2021)
36. Nasr, M., Shokri, R., Houmansadr, A.: Machine learning with membership privacy using adversarial regularization. In: Proceedings of the 2018 ACM SIGSAC Conference on Computer and Communications Security, pp. 634–646 (2018)
37. Nasr, M., Shokri, R., Houmansadr, A.: Comprehensive privacy analysis of deep learning: Passive and active white-box inference attacks against centralized and federated learning. In: Symposium on Security and Privacy (S&P). IEEE (2019). https://doi.org/10.1109/SP.2019.00065
38. Papernot, N., Abadi, M., Erlingsson, U., Goodfellow, I., Talwar, K.: Semi-supervised knowledge transfer for deep learning from private training data. In: Proceedings of the International Conference on Learning Representations (ICLR), Toulon, France (2017)
39. Ren, L., Liu, Z., Li, F., Liang, K., Li, Z., Luo, B.: Privdnn: a secure multi-party computation framework for deep learning using partial DNN encryption. Proc. Priv. Enhancing Technol. **3**, 1–18 (2024)
40. Riazi, M.S., Weinert, C., Tkachenko, O., Songhori, E.M., Schneider, T., Koushanfar, F.: Chameleon: a hybrid secure computation framework for machine learning applications. In: Proceedings of the 2018 on Asia Conference on Computer and Communications Security, pp. 707–721 (2018)
41. Ruan, W., Xu, M., Fang, W., Wang, L., Wang, L., Han, W.: Private, efficient, and accurate: protecting models trained by multi-party learning with differential privacy. In: 2023 IEEE Symposium on Security and Privacy (SP), pp. 1926–1943. IEEE (2023)
42. Sav, S., et al.: Poseidon: privacy-preserving federated neural network learning. In: Network and Distributed System Security Symposium (NDSS). The Internet Society (2021)
43. Shejwalkar, V., Houmansadr, A.: Membership privacy for machine learning models through knowledge transfer. In: Proceedings of the AAAI Conference on Artificial Intelligence, vol. 35, pp. 9549–9557 (2021)
44. Shi, E., Chan, H., Rieffel, E., Chow, R., Song, D.: Privacy-preserving aggregation of time-series data. In: Annual Network & Distributed System Security Symposium (NDSS). Internet Society (2011)
45. Shokri, R., Shmatikov, V.: Privacy-preserving deep learning. In: Proceedings of the SIGSAC Conference on Computer and Communications Security (2015)
46. Shokri, R., Stronati, M., Song, C., Shmatikov, V.: Membership inference attacks against machine learning models. In: Symposium on Security and Privacy (SP). IEEE (2017)
47. Song, S., Chaudhuri, K., Sarwate, A.D.: Stochastic gradient descent with differentially private updates. In: 2013 IEEE Global Conference on Signal and Information Processing, pp. 245–248. IEEE (2013)

48. Tieleman, T., Hinton, G., et al.: Lecture 6.5-rmsprop: divide the gradient by a running average of its recent magnitude. COURSERA: Neural Netw. Mach. Learn. **4**(2), 26–31 (2012)
49. Tramer, F., Boneh, D.: Slalom: fast, verifiable and private execution of neural networks in trusted hardware. arXiv preprint arXiv:1806.03287 (2018)
50. Wagh, S., Gupta, D., Chandran, N.: Securenn: 3-party secure computation for neural network training. Proc. Priv. Enhancing Technol. (2019)
51. Wagh, S., Tople, S., Benhamouda, F., Kushilevitz, E., Mittal, P., Rabin, T.: Falcon: honest-majority maliciously secure framework for private deep learning. arXiv preprint arXiv:2004.02229 (2020)

Hallucination Detection in Large Language Models Using Diversion Decoding

Basel Abdeen[1(✉)] [iD], S. M. Tahmid Siddiqui[1] [iD], Meah Tahmeed Ahmed[1] [iD],
Anoop Singhal[2] [iD], Latifur Khan[1(✉)] [iD], Punya Parag Modi[1] [iD],
and Ehab Al-Shaer[3] [iD]

[1] The University of Texas at Dallas, Richardson, TX 75080, USA
{basel.abdeen,tahmid.siddiqui,meah.ahmed,lkhan}@utdallas.edu
[2] National Institute of Standards and Technology, Gaithersburg, USA
anoop.singhal@nist.gov
[3] Carnegie Mellon University, Pittsburgh, PA, USA
ehab@cmu.edu

Abstract. Large language models (LLMs) have emerged as a powerful tool for retrieving knowledge through seamless, human-like interactions. Despite their advanced text generation capabilities, LLMs exhibit hallucination tendencies, where they generate factually incorrect statements and fabricate knowledge, undermining their reliability and trustworthiness. Multiple studies have explored methods to evaluate LLM uncertainty and detect hallucinations. However, existing approaches are often probabilistic and computationally expensive, limiting their practical applicability.

In this paper, we introduce diversion decoding, a novel method for developing an LLM uncertainty heuristic by actively challenging model-generated responses during the decoding phase. Through diversion decoding, we extract features that capture the LLM's resistance to produce alternative answers and utilize these features to train a machine-learning model to develop a heuristic measure of the LLM's uncertainty. Our experimental results demonstrate that diversion decoding outperforms existing methods with significantly lower computational complexity, making it an efficient and robust solution for evaluating hallucination detection.

Keywords: large language models · hallucination detection · diversion decoding

1 Introduction

Recently, large language models (LLMs) have gained the world's attention as they started to exhibit a deep understanding of natural language and a solid grasp of the world's knowledge, prompting people to use them for knowledge retrieval instead of traditional search engines [2,11,21]. Although LLMs have

© IFIP International Federation for Information Processing 2025
Published by Springer Nature Switzerland AG 2025
S. Katsikas and B. Shafiq (Eds.): DBSec 2025, LNCS 15722, pp. 116–133, 2025.
https://doi.org/10.1007/978-3-031-96590-6_7

demonstrated high performance in various tasks, their reliability as a source of information is limited due to their tendency to hallucinate [12,14]. Hallucination is LLM behavior that arises when a model is uncertain of its knowledge, leading it to invent facts and generate fake information.

Multiple studies have attempted to tackle the LLM hallucination challenge by introducing various scores to develop heuristic measures for LLM uncertainty [6,9,14,18]. These studies proposed approaches that require an external knowledge base, use probabilistic approaches, or exhibit high computational complexity. Unlike these studies, this paper presents a deterministic and computationally efficient approach for quantifying LLMs' confidence without requiring any external components beyond an existing question-answering dataset. Our approach is inspired by state-of-the-art methodologies that leverage the relationship between consistency and confidence exhibited by LLMs [6,18,23]. When an LLM is confident, it tends to generate the correct answer in various syntactic forms while maintaining semantic similarity. Conversely, when the LLM lacks confidence, it produces semantically different answers for the same question through different decoding paths.

Unlike previous studies where multiple answers need to be sampled from an LLM [6,18,23], our approach, diversion decoding, requires generating two distinct answers as follows. We first prompt the LLM with a question and retrieve the greedy answer. Then, we prompt the LLM with the same question; however, whenever the LLM generates an answer that is semantically similar to the first one, we steer its generation toward a different answer. For a simple example, we ask the LLM, "What is the capital of France?" Assume that the first greedy answer is "Paris." We then prompt the LLM with the same question, but this time, whenever the LLM generates the word "Paris," we reject this generation and select the next possible token with the highest likelihood. We hypothesize that when the LLM is confident, it will keep trying to generate the same answer; otherwise, it is easy to steer it away toward a different answer. We captured various features of LLM behavior during diversion decoding and trained a machine learning model to develop a proxy measure of LLM uncertainty based on a labeled dataset. In our experiments, diversion decoding demonstrated robust performance in detecting hallucinations while requiring substantially less computational power compared to existing state-of-the-art approaches.

The remainder of this paper is structured as follows: Sect. 2 presents the motivation behind our approach. Section 3 defines the problem statement. Section 4 introduces the proposed diversion decoding method. Section 5 discusses the evaluation results. Section 6 reviews related work, and finally, Sect. 7 provides the conclusion, including limitations and directions for future research.

2 Motivation

Large language models (LLMs) have gained significant traction among individuals and organizations for various applications, including translation, summarization, chatbots, and knowledge retrieval. These applications range in complexity

Table 1. Example of LLM Hallucination from a Bard promotion tweet posted by Google in 2023 [4]

Prompt	What new discoveries from the James Webb Space Telescope (JWST) can I tell my 9-year-old about?
LLM Response	"...JWST took the very first pictures of a planet outside of our own solar system: the first-ever exoplanet image..."
Correct Info	The first pictures of exoplanets were taken by the European Southern Observatory's Very Large Telescope (VLT) in 2004, as confirmed by NASA

from simple question-answering systems to sophisticated customer assistance agents. Despite the widespread applicability of LLMs, there remain significant concerns about their reliability and trustworthiness [17]. One of the primary challenges to their reliability stems from their hallucination tendencies, where LLMs generate fabricated or nonfactual information. Table 1 illustrates an example of LLM hallucination in an open question-answering context.

In many use cases, incorrect decision-making by LLM-powered agents can result in significant financial loss or business disruption [17]. For example, LLMs are increasingly being integrated into automated cybersecurity systems for tasks such as malware detection, security automation, and cyber forensics [7]. Hallucinations in such systems can lead to inaccurate threat assessments, false alarms, or security misconfigurations that expose vulnerabilities. An LLM mistakenly flagging benign activity as malicious may cause disruptions, while failing to detect a genuine attack could leave critical systems exposed. Moreover, in regulated environments, where data accuracy and confidentiality are mandated by laws such as the General Data Protection Regulation (GDPR) and the Health Insurance Portability and Accountability Act (HIPAA), LLM hallucinations can result in compliance violations, legal repercussions, and reputational damage [5].

Despite ongoing efforts by AI experts to raise awareness about the risks of LLM hallucinations, users often accept LLM-generated outputs at face value, making them susceptible to fake information [1,12]. As a result, detecting and mitigating hallucinations remains a critical challenge in integrating LLMs into high-stakes applications. Effective methods for measuring and identifying hallucinations are essential for ensuring the reliability of LLMs in domains such as cybersecurity, healthcare, and finance. The stronger these detection mechanisms become, the more confidently LLMs can be deployed in critical decision-making systems.

3 Problem Statement

In this paper, we address the challenge of detecting LLM hallucinations by quantifying their confidence in their responses to factual questions. We introduce diversion decoding, a novel approach that leads to a proxy measure of an LLM's confidence in its greedy answer by deliberately attempting to steer it toward an alternative semantically different response. We use the degree of resistance exhibited by the model in deviating from its initial answer as a proxy measure of uncertainty. To quantify this resistance, we train a supervised machine learning model on a public dataset of factual question-answer pairs to predict whether a generated answer is true or hallucinated using features derived from diversion decoding. By quantifying LLM resistance, our approach provides a reliable estimation for LLM hallucination. Similar to recent studies [6,18], this work aims to use a proxy measure for the semantic uncertainty of an entire LLM-generated answer, beyond the uncertainty of individual tokens.

Our approach focuses on open question-answering tasks for factual questions. Unlike free-response questions, factual questions require a single, concise answer. The approach is particularly suited for developing proxy measures of uncertainty in open-source LLMs, where output token probabilities are accessible. Finally, we employ supervised learning to train a machine learning model on an existing question-answering dataset. This dataset plays a crucial role in distinguishing instances when LLM generate correct answers from those when they hallucinate by analyzing patterns in LLM behavior.

4   Approach

Diversion decoding helps develop a proxy for the LLM's uncertainty in answering a question by first generating the greedy answer and then forcing the model to produce a different response by diverting it away from the greedy answer during decoding. This process tests how "adamant" the LLM is about its initial response and, consequently, how certain it is of that answer.

Diversion decoding comprises three key components: a diversion decoder, a semantic similarity module, and an uncertainty assessment module. The diversion decoder prompts the LLM with a question, retrieves the greedy answer, and then compels the model to generate a second, distinct response. The semantic similarity module detects when the LLM attempts to reproduce the greedy answer and alerts the decoder to steer the generation away from that response. Finally, the uncertainty assessment module assesses the LLM's uncertainty based on the path it takes to generate the second answer. Figure 3 illustrates a high-level overview of the diversion decoding pipeline.

Figure 1 illustrates diversion decoding in action for the question, "What is the capital of France?" Each time the decoder generates "Paris," the similarity module rejects the response, forcing the decoder to explore alternative generation paths. Since this is a straightforward question that an LLM should be highly confident in answering, the model persistently attempts to generate "Paris" through different paths. In contrast, Fig. 2 demonstrates a case where the LLM was easily diverted from its greedy answer (Mississippi) to an alternative response (Utah). Unlike in the first example, where the LLM repeatedly attempted to generate the same answer through different routes, here, it readily produced a completely different response.

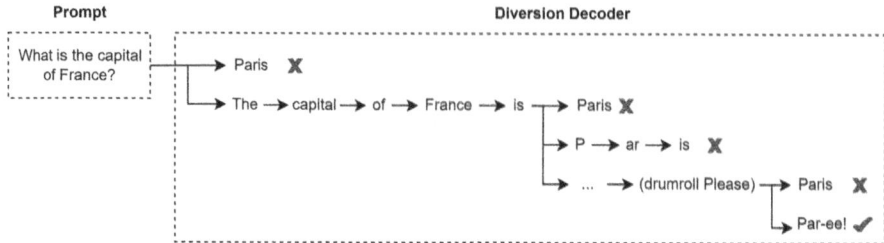

Fig. 1. Diversion decoding example when prompting the LLM with the question "What is the capital of France?" and getting Paris as the greedy answer. The LLM keeps trying to generate the answer "Paris" through different generation paths, demonstrating its confidence in the answer.

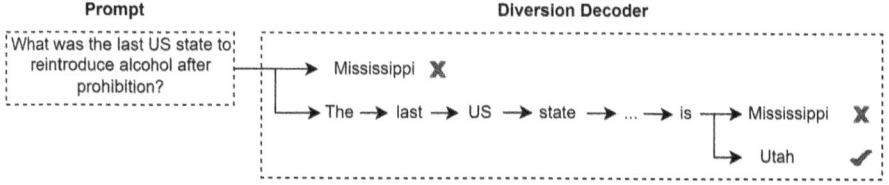

Fig. 2. Diversion decoding example when prompting the LLM with the question "What is the last US state to reintroduce alcohol after prohibition?" and getting Mississippi as the greedy answer. The LLM modified its answer from Mississippi to Utah after two rejections from the similarity module, demonstrating low confidence in its answer.

4.1 Diversion Decoding

LLM Decoding Background. LLMs generate a response to a prompt one token at a time. Given an input text, it generates an output token, appends it to the input, and then generates the next token. This process continues until the model produces a special token indicating the end of the response. At each step, the LLM generates a probability distribution over its predefined vocabulary. Based on a selected decoding strategy, the model chooses a token from this distribution. In greedy decoding, the LLM selects the token with the highest probability at each step. In top-k decoding, the model randomly selects a token from the k most probable tokens. In top-p (nucleus) decoding, the LLM samples a token from the smallest set of tokens whose cumulative probability mass reaches p. Moreover, sampling temperature modifies the Softmax distribution over possible next tokens. A higher temperature flattens the distribution, increasing randomness by making lower-probability tokens more likely. A lower temperature sharpens the distribution, concentrating probability on the most likely tokens, leading to more predictable and conservative outputs. In diversion decoding, we always select the greedy answer, which correlates to choosing top-k equals one or temperature equals zero.

Diversion Decoding. The diversion decoder first prompts the LLM with a question and generates a greedy answer. It then re-prompts the LLM with the same question but enforces the generation of a different response using the

---

Algorithm 1. Diversion Decoder Algorithm

1: **Input:** Large Language Model LLM, Question Q, Top-k parameter k, Similarity Threshold δ
2: **Output:** Greedy Answer G and a Distinct Answer R
3: Prompt LLM with Q and generate a greedy answer G
4: Re-prompt LLM with Q
5: Initialize $R \leftarrow \emptyset$
6: **while** End-of-response token not reached **do**
7:     Instruct LLM to generate probability distribution for next token
8:     Select top-k tokens with highest probabilities
9:     **for** each token t in top-k **do**
10:         Append the greedy word of t to R
11:         Get R similarity to G
12:         **if** Similarity $< \delta$ **then**
13:             Append the greedy word of t to R
14:             **break**
15:         **end if**
16:     **end for**
17:     **if** No token in top-k passes similarity check **then**
18:         Terminate response generation
19:     **end if**
20: **end while**
21: **Return** G and R

---

following approach. The decoder instructs the LLM to generate the probability distribution for the next token and selects the top-k tokens with the highest probabilities. It then attempts to generate a response by selecting the most probable token. If the similarity component approves the selected token, the decoder appends it to the prompt and proceeds to generate the next token. This process continues until the end-of-response token is reached. Conversely, if the similarity component rejects the generated token, the decoder selects the next highest probability token from the top-k candidates. This iterative process continues until either the similarity component approves a token, or all top-k tokens are exhausted, with none passing the similarity check. More formally, the token $\tilde{r}_i$ at decoding step i is selected according to the following rule:

$$\tilde{r}_i = \arg \max_{\substack{t \in \text{TopK}_i \\ \text{sim}(t,G) < \delta}} P_i\left(t \mid Q, \tilde{r}_1, \ldots, \tilde{r}_{i-1}\right) \tag{1}$$

where:

- Q: The input prompt.
- G: The greedy answer.
- $P_i(t \mid \cdot)$: The model's predicted probability of token t at step i.
- TopK$_i$: The top-k highest-probability tokens at step i
- $\text{sim}(t, G)$: The similarity between generated answer R with token t and the greedy answer G.
- δ: The similarity threshold.

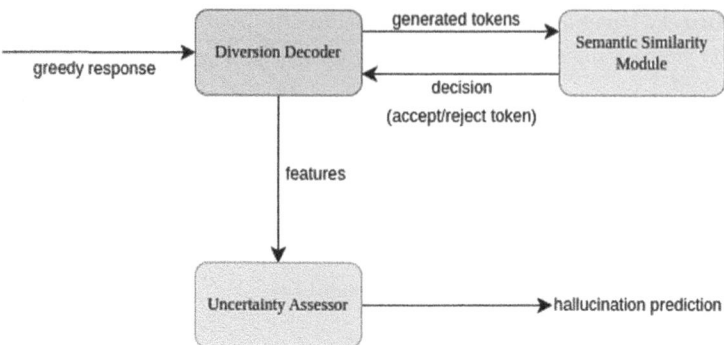

Fig. 3. Diversion decoding pipeline

Algorithm [1] showcases how our diversion decoding algorithm works. In lines 3–4, we prompt an LLM with a question, Q, to generate a greedy answer, G, and then we re-prompt the model with Q. We then begin an iterative process in line 6, which continues until the end-of-response token is reached. For each iteration, we generate the LLM's probability distribution for the next token (line 7), and we select the top k tokens with the highest probabilities (line 8). Here, k is a predefined value that is provided to the algorithm. We then enter an inner iterative loop that goes over each token in the queue of top k tokens. For each token, we form a greedy word by appending to it the highest likelihood tokens till the first space (line 10). This word-forming approach ensures that the semantic similarity module has the complete word context for accurate semantic comparison. We then extract the similarity score between the greedy answer G and the distinct answer R (line 11) and compare it to a predefined threshold, δ (line 12). If the similarity score is below the defined threshold, we append the token with its greedy word to our distinct answer, R (line 13), and break from the inner loop. Finally, if no token from the top-k queue passes the similarity check, we terminate the entire diversion decoding algorithm. The algorithm outputs the greedy answer, G, and the distinct answer, R.

Similarity Measure. The similarity component is designed to detect whether the decoder generates an answer that is semantically similar to the greedy answer. We implement a comprehensive similarity function that incorporates three distinct similarity metrics: sentence semantic similarity, word semantic similarity, and character-based similarity. These metrics were chosen based on their complementary strengths in capturing different aspects of textual similarity. Let A represent the generated answer concatenated with the next token candidate, and G represent the first greedy answer. The number of tokens in the greedy answer is denoted by L. We define auxiliary functions $last(t, n)$ and $first(t, n)$ to extract the last n words and first n words from text t, respectively. The function $encode(t)$ represents the semantic encoding of text t using all-mpnet-base-v2 model. The function $cos(x, y)$ computes the cosine similarity between vectors x and y. The complete similarity function $sim(A, G)$ is composed of several components. The first component, shown in Eq. (2), computes the sentence-level semantic similarity:

$$semantic\_sim1(A, G) = cos(encode(last(A, L + 1)), encode(G)) \qquad (2)$$

This semantic similarity metric captures the overall semantic relationship between the generated and greedy answers. The second component, defined in Eq. (3), focuses on word-level comparisons:

$$semantic\_sim2(A, G) = cos(encode(last(A, 1)), encode(first(G, 1))) \qquad (3)$$

The character-based similarity component, shown in Eq. (4), employs the longest common subsequence (LCS) algorithm:

$$character\_sim(A, G) = \frac{LCS(A, G)}{Length(G)} \qquad (4)$$

These three components are combined in the final similarity score computation, as shown in Eq. (5):

$$
\begin{aligned}
sim(A, G) = max(&semantic\_sim1(A, G), \\
&semantic\_sim2(A, G), \qquad\qquad (5)\\
&character\_sim(A, G))
\end{aligned}
$$

Equation (2) addresses the common phenomenon where LLMs generate introductory or framing text before providing the actual answer. To handle this behavior, we consider only the last L+1 words of the generated response. This is particularly evident in diversion decoding, where token rejection often leads the LLM to generate additional, semantically irrelevant introductory text. As demonstrated in Fig. 1, LLMs may produce verbose outputs such as "The capital of France is...(drumroll please)... Par-ee." By restricting our semantic comparison as shown in Eq. (2), we achieve significantly higher accuracy compared to analyzing the entire response.

Equation (3) serves a complementary purpose by focusing specifically on the first non-stop word of the greedy answer and the last generated token of the current generation. This approach proves particularly effective when dealing with lengthy greedy answers, as it enables early intervention in the decoding process before a substantial portion of the answer is generated.

The character-based similarity metric defined in Eq. (4) addresses an observed behavior in LLMs where, when forced to alter their response, they may generate concatenated words without proper spacing. This phenomenon can confound purely semantic similarity models, leading to false negatives in similarity detection. For instance, when the expected answer is "North Carolina," the LLM might generate "NorthCarolina" - a response that maintains character-level similarity despite lacking proper formatting. The LCS metric in Eq. (4) successfully captures these cases.

The maximum-based aggregation in Eq. (5) ensures that the highest similarity detected by any of the metrics is preserved in the final score, making the system more robust to various types of semantic equivalence. This multi-metric approach to similarity measurement demonstrates superior performance compared to single-metric approaches.

4.2 Uncertainty Assessment

After the decoder generates the second answer, the uncertainty assessment component aims to assign a persistence score to the greedy answer based on how resilient the LLM was against generating a different answer. Multiple attributes of the diversion decoding process can capture the LLM's uncertainty about its answer. For example, more rejections indicate that the model is more certain of its answer. However, in many cases, other features are essential to consider. For example, not all rejected tokens should be treated equally, as a rejected token with a higher likelihood demonstrates LLM certainty better than a rejected token with a low likelihood. Moreover, the LLM can have fewer rejections because it generates the end-of-response token before generating a full answer due to its certainty of the greedy answer.

Instead of using one metric to assess hallucination, we train a machine learning model using a dataset of open question-answer pairs - the TriviaQA dataset - as follows. First, we prompted the LLM with a question and obtained its greedy answer. The greedy answer is labeled correct if its ROUGE-L [19] similarity with the ground truth exceeded 0.3. Otherwise, it is considered a hallucination.

Second, we use diversion decoding to generate an answer that is semantically different from the greedy answer. Third, we collect the following six features from the diversion decoder: (1) the number of rejected tokens, (2) the sum of the negative log-likelihood of the rejected tokens, (3) the minimum negative log-likelihood of a rejected token, (4) the maximum negative log-likelihood of approved tokens, (5) the mean negative log-likelihood of all generated tokens, and (6) the length of the largest common substring between the greedy answer and the second-best answer. Finally, we applied this process to all questions in the dataset, and we trained a gradient-boosting model to predict if the greedy answer is hallucinated based on the extracted features and labels.

5 Evaluation

5.1 Dataset, Model and Metrics

We evaluate diversion decoding using TriviaQA, a large-scale open question-answering dataset [15]. TriviaQA was authored by trivia enthusiasts and contains a wide range of trivia questions in various domains, styles, and subjects (e.g., history, science, and culture), ensuring a comprehensive evaluation of diversion decoding.

The TriviaQA dataset is organized into two primary folders: one for reading comprehension and another for question answering. The unfiltered-web-dev.json file from the question-answering folder (version 1.0) contains 11,313 question-answer pairs, which were curated by trivia enthusiasts and supported by independently gathered evidence documents. We utilized 4,900 questions from this

Table 2. Example question-answer pair from our modified dataset file

Question	Where in England was actor Nigel Hawthorne born?
Aliases	"Cofantre", "Coventry (city)", "Coventry, Warwickshire", "Coventry", "Coventry, UK", "Coventry, England", "City of Coventry", "COVENTRY", "County Borough of Coventry", "Coventry (borough)", "Coventry City Council", "Coventry, United Kingdom", "Metropolitan Borough of Coventry"
Matched Wiki Entity Name	Coventry
Normalized Aliases	aliases converted to lowercase and stripped of special characters and punctuation
Normalized Value	coventry
Type	WikipediaEntity
Value	Coventry

particular file. Table 2 shows a sample from the dataset. Each question-answer pair consists of the question, the answer (value), variations of the correct answer (aliases), normalized versions of the answers, and metadata about the source of the answer (matched wiki entity name and the type of source).

We selected the Llama family of models [26] for our experiments because of its open-source accessibility, diversity in model sizes, and comparable performance to state-of-the-art closed-source models. Moreover, we used a 4-bit quantization of Llama to reduce memory usage and computational cost. Our experiments were all done using a single NVIDIA H100 GPU. We leveraged the Area Under the Receiver Operating Characteristic Curve (AUROC) for performance evaluation. Rather than defining a specific hallucination threshold, AUROC assesses the model's ability to differentiate between true positive and false positive classifications across a range of decision thresholds.

5.2 Experiments

Baselines. We evaluated diversion decoding against four baselines: predictive entropy [16], length-normalized predictive entropy [22], lexical similarity [8], and semantic entropy [6,18]. The predictive entropy is the conditional entropy of the generated tokens given the context.

$$H(W \mid X) = - \sum_{w \in V} P(w \mid X) \log P(w \mid X) \tag{6}$$

where X represents the given context, W is the next token to be generated, and V is the model's vocabulary. In sequential generation, the entropy at each

Table 3. Diversion decoding and baselines results

Model	Predictive entropy	Normalized predictive entropy	Lexical similarity	Semantic entropy	Diversion decoding
Llama 7B	67.0%	67.8%	64.4%	71.9%	**74.66%**
Llama 13B	70.1%	63.8%	61.7%	72.1%	**78.49%**

Table 4. Diversion decoding and baselines expansion ratio assuming n=10 for lexical similarity and semantic entropy

	Predictive entropy	Normalized predictive entropy	Lexical similarity	Semantic entropy	Diversion decoding
Expansion ratio	1	1	10	10	3.6

decoding step can be summed across the sequence to get the joint entropy:

$$H(Y \mid X) = \sum_{t=1}^{T} H(W_t \mid X, W_{<t}) \tag{7}$$

Length-Normalized Predictive Entropy adjusts the predictive entropy of longer sequences by dividing the joint log probability of each generated sequence by its length. Normalizing asserts that the expected uncertainty of generations is independent of sentence length. Lexical similarity measures the average similarity between the answers in a generated answer set by computing the average Rouge-L score for all pairs of sentences. Semantic entropy focuses on the meaning of text rather than the specific tokens used. It addresses "semantic equivalence," where different sentences can have identical meanings. The process involves sampling sequences from a language model, clustering sequences with the same meaning using a bi-directional entailment algorithm, and finally, calculating entropy over the distribution of meanings, summing probabilities of semantically equivalent sequences.

Training. We randomly selected 1,300 questions from the TriviaQA dataset to train our uncertainty estimation component. We trained a gradient-boosting classifier as we discussed in the diversion decoding section. We used log loss, a learning rate of 0.1, 100 estimators and the mean squared error with improvement score by Friedman to measure the quality of a split.

Results. We selected 3,600 random questions from TriviaQA to evaluate diversion decoding against the other baselines. We used Llama 2 models of 7 and 13 billion parameters. Table 3 presents the experimental results across different evaluation metrics, comparing the performance of Llama 7B and Llama 13B models. For the Llama 7B model, diversion decoding outperforms all other approaches, achieving an AUROC score of 74.66%. The second-best approach is semantic entropy, which attains a 71.9% score, followed closely by predictive entropy at 67.0%. Normalized predictive entropy and lexical similarity yield slightly lower performance at 67.8% and 64.4%, respectively. Similarly, for the Llama 13B model, diversion decoding again demonstrates superior performance, reaching an AUROC of 78.49%, showing a notable improvement over the 7B variant. Semantic entropy remains competitive with a score of 72.1%, maintaining consistency across model sizes. Predictive entropy and lexical similarity yield scores of 70.1% and 61.7%, respectively, while normalized predictive entropy shows a slightly lower performance at 63.8%.

Complexity Analysis. To assess the complexity of our approach compared to other methods, we compute the ratio of all generated tokens to the number of tokens in the initial response. We refer to this metric as the expansion ratio (ER), as it quantifies how much the generated response expands relative to the initial response. More formally, let $T_{init} \in \mathbb{N}$ denote the number of tokens in the initial response, and let $T_{gen} \in \mathbb{N}$ denote the total number of tokens after generation. The *Expansion Ratio* (ER) is defined as:

$$\mathrm{ER} := \frac{T_{gen}}{T_{init}} \tag{8}$$

While both our approach and existing methods use auxiliary models for semantic similarity or natural language inference, these models contain significantly fewer parameters than the large language model and can be safely ignored in our calculations.

In diversion decoding, the number of generated tokens varies across different questions based on the confidence of the large language model, as discussed in the diversion decoding section. To account for this variation, we empirically compute the ratio of generated tokens to the number of tokens in the greedy answer and report the median across our dataset of 4,900 examples. The results are presented in Table 4. Predictive entropy and normalized predictive entropy do not require any extra generation beyond the first response, thus, their expansion ratio is 1. On average, diversion decoding achieves an expansion ratio of 3.6, which is significantly lower than approaches that sample n responses, where the expansion ratio is n. For example, when 10 samples are sampled for lexical similarity or semantic entropy, the expansion ratio is 10.

5.3   Ablation Studies

In our experiments, we utilized a training dataset of 1,300 samples and a testing dataset of 3,600 samples, resulting in a training data ratio of approximately 26%. Despite the limited amount of training data, diversion decoding demonstrated robust performance, achieving AUROC scores of approximately 74% and 78% for the Llama 7B and 13B models, respectively. We conducted additional experiments with varying training data ratios to investigate further the extent of improvement that diversion decoding can achieve. Figure 4 illustrates the relationship between the AUROC score of diversion decoding and the training data

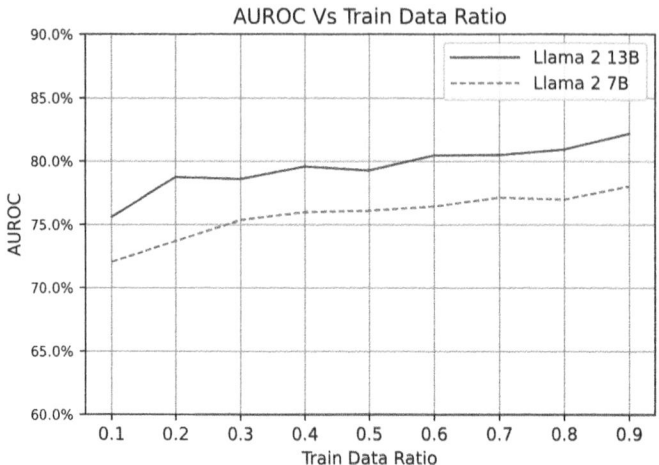

Fig. 4. Diversion decoding AUROC vs training data ratio

ratio in our dataset. As expected, increasing the amount of training data led to a significant performance boost. Notably, with a 90% training data ratio, the AUROC score reached approximately 82% for Llama 7B and around 78% for Llama 13B.

In our complexity analysis, we report the median expansion ratio of diversion decoding. In practice, LLMs may repeatedly generate the same response upon rejection, leading to a substantial increase in the number of generated tokens. To mitigate this, diversion decoding imposes a constraint on the number of generated tokens beyond the initial response. We represent this number as a ratio to the number of tokens in the initial response and denote it as a maximum generated token ratio (MGTR). More formally:

$$\text{MGTR} = \frac{T_g}{T_i}$$

where:

- T_g is the number of tokens generated beyond the initial response.
- T_i is the number of tokens in the initial response.

For users concerned with computational complexity, a trade-off exists between performance and token generation: reducing the maximum number of generated tokens can lower complexity while maintaining competitive results. To examine this relationship, we analyzed the impact of MGTR on AUROC scores using a training set ratio of 50%. The results, presented in Fig. 5, indicate a significant increase in AUROC when MGTR is below 9. Beyond this threshold, the AUROC score plateaus. Notably, even with a relatively low MGTR of 5, diversion decoding achieves competitive AUROC scores of approximately 74% and 78% for Llama 2 models with 7B and 13B parameters, respectively.

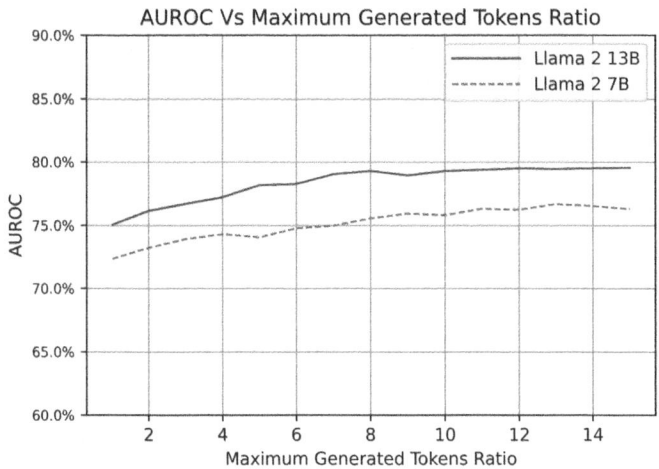

Fig. 5. Diversion decoding AUROC vs maximum generated tokens ratio

6   Related Work

The problem of hallucination detection and quantification has inspired several approaches. Maynez et al. [24] conducted a large-scale human evaluation on abstractive summarization models, revealing that even fluent summaries often contain hallucinations, and argued for entailment-based metrics over ROUGE to better capture faithfulness. Some studies tackle the problem by fact-checking the output against a verified knowledge base [10]. However, the size and extensiveness required of the knowledge base can be prohibitive, as relevant evidence must be present in the knowledge base before it can be used to challenge the large language model's output. Instead of querying an external database, researchers have also explored the possibility of getting the LLM to self-evaluate its confidence regarding the output [16,20]. Other proposed approaches take advantage of the model's token probabilities or hidden representations to identify sequences in the output that the model is less confident about [1,9]. Chen et al. [3] proposed INSIDE, which leverages the internal states of LLMs to compute an *EigenScore* measuring semantic dispersion across generations and uses feature clipping to reduce overconfident hallucinations. Researchers have also introduced RAGTruth, a specialized corpus for detecting hallucinations in fine-tuned LLM applications that utilize the retrieval-augmented generation (RAG) technique [25].

SelfCheckGPT [23] proposed comparing the LLM output against stochastically generated responses to check for divergence. It leverages the same LLM behavior that we take advantage of, wherein stochastically generated responses containing hallucinated facts are more likely to differ from each other. Uncertainty estimation methods have also demonstrated promising potential in identifying LLM hallucinations across multiple NLP tasks from different

Table 5. Comparison of different hallucination detection approaches. *"Num. Responses"*: number of responses each approach generates per query; *"Deterministic?"*: whether the approach consistently produces the same output given the same input; *"Retrieval Free?"*: whether the approach functions without reliance on external knowledge bases or RAG techniques; *"Finetuning Free?"*: whether it does not require model finetuning.

Approach	Num. Responses	Deterministic?	Retrieval Free?	Finetuning Free?
Semantic Uncertainty [6,18]	~10	✗	✓	✓
SelfCheckGPT [23]	~10	✗	✓	✓
RAGTruth [25]	1	✓	✗	✗
Diversion Decoding	~2	✓	✓	✓

domains [13]. Moreover, researchers introduced semantic uncertainty as a method for quantifying uncertainty in natural language, with the goal of extending beyond token-level probability to consider semantic equivalence among generated responses [6,18]. Assessing semantic uncertainty requires the following steps: (1) sampling M sequences given context from the predictive distribution of an LLM, (2) utilizing a bidirectional entailment algorithm to categorize semantically equivalent sequences together, and (3) calculating the semantic entropy after summing the probabilities of the sequences that were found to be semantically equivalent from the previous step.

Existing approaches exhibit two primary limitations. First, they are computationally expensive. For example, methods such as SelfCheckGPT and semantic entropy require generating multiple response samples (typically around ten) to achieve a reliable output. Given the high computational cost of running large language models (LLMs), these methods demand approximately ten times the resources needed for generating a single response, substantially increasing the cost of assessing uncertainty in LLM outputs. In contrast, our approach is significantly more efficient, requiring only two responses: one generated greedily and another obtained through a slightly more computationally intensive diversion strategy. Second, existing methods rely on probabilistic techniques, leading to variability in their results across different executions due to stochastic sampling from the response space. This inherent randomness reduces their reliability and practical applicability. In contrast, our approach is deterministic, ensuring consistent outputs without randomness. This determinism enhances interpretability, facilitates debugging, and improves usability, making our method more robust and practical for real-world applications. Table 5 presents a comparison between diversion decoding and various hallucination detection approaches. While diversion decoding requires only two responses, generating the second response is computationally more expensive, as analyzed in the evaluation section.

7   Conclusion, Limitations and Future Work

Despite the increasing adoption of LLMs in various applications, there remains a significant security risk of hallucinated LLM outputs going undetected. In this paper, we introduced diversion decoding as a method of developing a proxy measure for the LLMs' uncertainty and subsequently detecting hallucination in the output of LLMs. The approach consists of three main components: a diversion decoder, which forces the LLM to generate a semantically different answer to the greedy response; a semantic similarity module, which prevents the second answer from being similar to the greedy response; and an uncertainty assessment module, which is a trained machine learning model that develops a proxy for the uncertainty of the model. Our experimental results demonstrate that the proposed approach can achieve increased accuracy in the detection of hallucinations compared to other baselines.

Our approach focuses on assessing LLM hallucinations in the context of factual questions with concise answers. While this is a crucial aspect of evaluating language model reliability, LLMs have a wide range of use cases that extend beyond this specific task, including reading comprehension and problem-solving. In future work, we plan to improve diversion decoding techniques to handle a broader range of question formats beyond factual queries. Moreover, our current approach primarily focuses on open-source models due to their transparency and accessibility. However, with additional components, diversion decoding can also be adapted to closed-source LLMs by leveraging similar features. Finally, our approach employs traditional machine learning models, specifically gradient boosting, to detect hallucinations. We plan to experiment with more deep learning approaches, such as neural networks, to improve detection accuracy in future work.

Disclaimer. This paper identifies certain equipment, instruments, software, or materials to adequately describe the experimental procedure. Such identification is not intended to imply recommendation or endorsement of any product or service by NIST, nor is it intended to imply that the materials or equipment identified are necessarily the best available for the purpose. The use of Llama in our evaluation experiments is primarily because it is an open source model. We do not imply its recommendation or endorsement.

Acknowledgment. The research reported herein was supported in part by NIST grant number 60NANB24D143. Any opinions, findings, conclusions, and recommendations expressed in this material are those of the author(s) and do not necessarily reflect the views of NIST.

References

1. Azaria, A., Mitchell, T.: The internal state of an LLM knows when it's lying. In: Bouamor, H., Pino, J., Bali, K. (eds.) Findings of the Association for Computational Linguistics: EMNLP 2023, Singapore, pp. 967–976. Association for Computational Linguistics (2023). https://doi.org/10.18653/v1/2023.findings-emnlp.68. https://aclanthology.org/2023.findings-emnlp.68/

2. Brown, T., et al.: Language models are few-shot learners. Adv. Neural. Inf. Process. Syst. **33**, 1877–1901 (2020)

3. Chen, C., et al.: INSIDE: LLMs' internal states retain the power of hallucination detection. In: Proceedings of the 12th International Conference on Learning Representations (ICLR) (2024). https://arxiv.org/abs/2402.03744

4. Coulter, M., Bensinger, G.: Alphabet shares dive after Google AI chatbot Bard flubs answer in ad. Reuters (2023). https://www.reuters.com/technology/google-ai-chatbot-bard-offers-inaccurate-information-company-ad-2023-02-08/. Accessed 26 Feb 2025

5. Das, B.C., Amini, M.H., Wu, Y.: Security and privacy challenges of large language models: a survey. ACM Comput. Surv. **57**(6), 1–39 (2025)

6. Farquhar, S., Kossen, J., Kuhn, L., Gal, Y.: Detecting hallucinations in large language models using semantic entropy. Nature **630**(8017), 625–630 (2024)

7. Ferrag, M.A., et al.: Generative AI in cybersecurity: a comprehensive review of LLM applications and vulnerabilities. Internet Things Cyber-Phys. Syst. (2025)

8. Fomicheva, M., et al.: Unsupervised quality estimation for neural machine translation. Trans. Assoc. Comput. Linguist. **8**, 539–555 (2020)

9. Fu, J., Ng, S.K., Jiang, Z., Liu, P.: GPTScore: evaluate as you desire. In: Duh, K., Gomez, H., Bethard, S. (eds.) Proceedings of the 2024 Conference of the North American Chapter of the Association for Computational Linguistics: Human Language Technologies (Volume 1: Long Papers), Mexico City, Mexico, pp. 6556–6576. Association for Computational Linguistics (2024). https://doi.org/10.18653/v1/2024.naacl-long.365. https://aclanthology.org/2024.naacl-long.365/

10. Guo, Z., Schlichtkrull, M., Vlachos, A.: A survey on automated fact-checking. Trans. Assoc. Comput. Linguist. **10**, 178–206 (2022). https://doi.org/10.1162/tacl_a_00454. https://aclanthology.org/2022.tacl-1.11/

11. Hoffmann, J., et al.: Training compute-optimal large language models. In: Proceedings of the 36th International Conference on Neural Information Processing Systems. NIPS 2022. Curran Associates Inc., Red Hook (2022)

12. Huang, L., et al.: A survey on hallucination in large language models: principles, taxonomy, challenges, and open questions. ACM Trans. Inf. Syst. **43**(2), 1–55 (2025)

13. Huang, Y., et al.: Look before you leap: an exploratory study of uncertainty measurement for large language models. arXiv preprint arXiv:2307.10236 (2023)

14. Ji, Z., et al.: Survey of hallucination in natural language generation. ACM Comput. Surv. **55**(12), 1–38 (2023)

15. Joshi, M., Choi, E., Weld, D., Zettlemoyer, L.: TriviaQA: a large scale distantly supervised challenge dataset for reading comprehension. In: Barzilay, R., Kan, M.Y. (eds.) Proceedings of the 55th Annual Meeting of the Association for Computational Linguistics (Volume 1: Long Papers), Vancouver, Canada, pp. 1601–1611. Association for Computational Linguistics (2017). https://doi.org/10.18653/v1/P17-1147. https://aclanthology.org/P17-1147/

16. Kadavath, S., et al.: Language models (mostly) know what they know. arXiv preprint arXiv:2207.05221 (2022)
17. Kang, H., Liu, X.Y.: Deficiency of large language models in finance: an empirical examination of hallucination. arXiv preprint arXiv:2311.15548 (2023)
18. Kuhn, L., Gal, Y., Farquhar, S.: Semantic uncertainty: linguistic invariances for uncertainty estimation in natural language generation. arXiv preprint arXiv:2302.09664 (2023)
19. Lin, C.Y.: Rouge: a package for automatic evaluation of summaries. In: Text Summarization Branches Out, pp. 74–81 (2004)
20. Lin, S., Hilton, J., Evans, O.: Teaching models to express their uncertainty in words. arXiv preprint arXiv:2205.14334 (2022)
21. Long, X., et al.: Generative multi-modal knowledge retrieval with large language models. In: Proceedings of the Thirty-Eighth AAAI Conference on Artificial Intelligence and Thirty-Sixth Conference on Innovative Applications of Artificial Intelligence and Fourteenth Symposium on Educational Advances in Artificial Intelligence, pp. 18733–18741 (2024)
22. Malinin, A., Gales, M.: Uncertainty estimation in autoregressive structured prediction. arXiv preprint arXiv:2002.07650 (2020)
23. Manakul, P., Liusie, A., Gales, M.: SelfCheckGPT: zero-resource black-box hallucination detection for generative large language models. In: Bouamor, H., Pino, J., Bali, K. (eds.) Proceedings of the 2023 Conference on Empirical Methods in Natural Language Processing, Singapore, pp. 9004–9017. Association for Computational Linguistics (2023). https://doi.org/10.18653/v1/2023.emnlp-main.557. https://aclanthology.org/2023.emnlp-main.557/
24. Maynez, J., Narayan, S., Bohnet, B., McDonald, R.: On faithfulness and factuality in abstractive summarization. In: Proceedings of the 58th Annual Meeting of the Association for Computational Linguistics (ACL), pp. 1906–1919. Association for Computational Linguistics (2020). https://arxiv.org/abs/2005.00661
25. Niu, C., et al.: Ragtruth: a hallucination corpus for developing trustworthy retrieval-augmented language models. In: Proceedings of the 62nd Annual Meeting of the Association for Computational Linguistics (Volume 1: Long Papers), pp. 10862–10878 (2024)
26. Touvron, H., et al.: Llama 2: open foundation and fine-tuned chat models. arXiv preprint arXiv:2307.09288 (2023)

User and Data Privacy

Blockchain-Enhanced User Consent for GDPR-Compliant Real-Time Bidding

Cristòfol Daudén-Esmel[1]([✉]) [ID], Jordi Castellà-Roca[1] [ID], Alexandre Viejo[1] [ID], and Vicenç Torra[2] [ID]

[1] Departament d'Enginyeria Informàtica i Matemàtiques,
Universitat Rovira i Virgili, Tarragona, Catalonia, Spain
{cristofol.dauden,jordi.castella,alexandre.viejo}@urv.cat
[2] Department of Computing Science, Umeå University, Umeå, Sweden
vtorra@cs.umu.se

Abstract. Ensuring Real-Time Bidding compliance with GDPR and the ePrivacy Directive remains challenging. Existing solutions, like the IAB's Transparency and Consent Framework and OpenRTB, lack transparency and fail to secure legally valid user consent. We propose a blockchain-based framework that decentralizes consent management, giving users direct control. The system automates consent handling, provides immutable compliance proof, and includes a smartphone app for users to manage consent per website. Additionally, we introduce a specificity value for IAB Audience Taxonomy elements, helping users assess the privacy impact of sharing data. By enhancing autonomy, transparency, and accountability, our approach strengthens trust in programmatic advertising while maintaining GDPR compliance without disrupting the industry.

Keywords: General Data Protection Regulation (GDPR) · Real Time Bidding (RTB) · Blockchain · User Consent Management

1 Introduction

Every day, millions of users rely on free online services for information, entertainment, and communication. To sustain operations and generate revenue, most of these services rely on display advertising [9,12,23]. This model enables service providers (SPs) to monetize their platforms by allowing brands to target audiences through ads.

Programmatic advertising improves traditional display advertising by delivering personalized ads based on user data, including demographics, interests, and online behavior [24]. This approach strategically places ads to maximize engagement and relies heavily on tracking user activities, effectively making consumer data the "product" that fuels the online advertising ecosystem.

While programmatic advertising has gained traction due to its efficiency and targeting accuracy, it has also raised significant privacy concerns. The extensive

S. Katsikas and B. Shafiq (Eds.): DBSec 2025, LNCS 15722, pp. 137–155, 2025.
https://doi.org/10.1007/978-3-031-96590-6_8

collection of user data has sparked debates about the balance between advertising innovation and personal data protection, highlighting tensions between effective marketing and individual privacy rights.

To strengthen data protection rights and regulate personal data processing across various sectors, the European Union introduced the General Data Protection Regulation (GDPR) in 2018 [2]. Although its scope extends beyond online advertising, GDPR has significantly impacted programmatic advertising by granting users greater control over their personal information and enforcing stricter data processing requirements.

To address the compliance challenges posed by GDPR, the *Interactive Advertising Bureau Europe (IAB Europe)*, the leading federation representing the digital advertising industry in Europe [8], developed the *Transparency & Consent Framework (TCF)* [7] to establish a legal foundation for data processing within the programmatic advertising ecosystem. A key objective of the TCF was ensuring GDPR compliance for *real-time bidding (RTB)*, the protocol that enables advertisers to bid for digital ad space in real time. One of the most widely adopted RTB implementations in Europe is OpenRTB [11], a standardized framework that facilitates communication between publishers and advertisers. The TCF was designed to align OpenRTB's personal data processing with GDPR and the ePrivacy Directive [1], positioning it as a compliance solution for the industry.

Despite its goal of facilitating GDPR compliance, the TCF is not an open-access technical standard like those published by public standardization institutions. Instead, organizations must pay an annual membership fee of 1,200 EUR to IAB Europe and comply with a set of strict policies [25]. These policies define the requirements for participation in the framework, mandating that any company involved in personal data processing, such as adtech vendors, advertisers, publishers, and other intermediaries, be listed in a centralized Global Vendor List (GVL) maintained by IAB Europe. Additionally, they regulate how user consent must be obtained, stored, and transmitted, enforcing standardized procedures through Consent Management Platforms (CMPs) that rely on cookies and other tracking mechanisms. Although this structure aims to ensure regulatory compliance, it also restricts flexibility for businesses operating outside the framework, effectively making participation in the TCF a prerequisite for engaging in compliant programmatic advertising.

While the TCF was introduced as a compliance mechanism for GDPR, its restrictive nature and centralized control have drawn criticism. In particular, concerns have been raised about whether it genuinely ensures lawful and fair data processing within the RTB ecosystem. These concerns culminated in February 2022, when the Belgian Data Protection Authority (Belgian DPA) ruled against IAB Europe, questioning the legality of the TCF in the context of real-time bidding [3]. The decision concluded that OpenRTB, as structured under the TCF, violated the GDPR principles due to insufficient legal grounds for data processing and a lack of fairness. This ruling carries significant implications for the future of programmatic advertising in Europe, as it challenges the industry's reliance on consent-based frameworks and raises broader questions about the legitimacy of current data-driven advertising practices.

1.1   State of the Art

Research on digital advertising has primarily focused on three key areas: i) improving ad targeting and revenue generation from the advertiser's perspective; ii) analyzing the impact of digital ads on users, including consumer behavior, perception, and privacy concerns; and iii) exploring alternative strategies that reduce reliance on personal data while maintaining advertising effectiveness.

The first area, which has been the focus of much of the existing research, explores multiple strategies to enhance ad delivery and personalization. Some studies analyze user behavior through click-through logs to improve ad click-through rates [27,28], while others examine the broader ad exchange ecosystem, investigating time-dependent patterns in impressions, bids, and conversion rates to refine RTB mechanisms [29]. Additional approaches include recommendation systems that balance ad revenue and user experience [15], dynamic budget allocation strategies that optimize campaign spending [14], and analyses of how website quality influences ad performance and user engagement [21]. Although these studies have advanced targeted advertising and monetization, they rely heavily on extensive user data collection and often require user consent for data processing. However, obtaining meaningful and GDPR-compliant user consent remains a challenge, highlighting the need for alternative privacy-preserving approaches that reduce reliance on personal data.

Regarding the impact of digital advertising on users, research has highlighted significant privacy concerns, particularly related to user tracking, data leakage, and compliance with legal frameworks. Studies have shown that major advertising trackers can identify users with over 99.5% certainty after just 30 search result clicks [10] and that RTB can expose up to 27% of a user's browsing history to bidders [17]. These privacy risks have led to increased scrutiny over the adequacy of user consent in programmatic advertising. While regulatory efforts such as the GDPR and the California Consumer Privacy Act (CCPA) aim to strengthen user rights, research suggests that current consent mechanisms often fail to meet legal standards due to their complexity and lack of transparency [26]. The Belgian Data Protection Authority's ruling against IAB Europe further underscored these issues, concluding that the TCF does not ensure valid GDPR-compliant consent, given the challenges in informing users and managing data controller responsibilities [25]. These challenges call for new privacy-preserving approaches that can ensure compliance while minimizing reliance on personal data.

The third and final area of research examines the risks that digital advertising poses to user privacy and explores alternative approaches that reduce reliance on personal data. Traditional ad-matching schemes, such as the one proposed in [5], initially rely only on webpage content and ad features, avoiding direct user tracking. This limitation in data collection provides a basic form of privacy protection, as no personal user information is gathered. However, the approach also lacks adaptability since it does not incorporate user feedback. To improve performance, the authors later extend their model by incorporating ad impression and click data, which introduces tracking mechanisms. While this enhances targeting efficiency, it also increases data collection and reduces privacy protection. This transition reflects a common pattern in digital advertising research where efficiency improvements often come at the cost of greater data collection. These challenges highlight the need for GDPR-compliant privacy-preserving solutions that ensure effective advertising while respecting user consent.

In contrast, Provost et al. [18] propose a privacy-friendly approach to audience selection for online brand advertising by leveraging browsing behavior to infer quasi-social networks. Unlike traditional methods that rely on explicit user tracking, this approach constructs an anonymous network based on shared visits to user-generated content pages, such as social networking sites. The framework identifies potential brand audiences by selecting social-network neighbors of users who have previously exhibited brand affinity. A ranking mechanism based on brand proximity ensures that selected audiences show higher brand engagement while preserving user anonymity. The authors demonstrate that this method can effectively target relevant audiences without collecting personal identifiers or content data. However, it does not address broader issues of user consent and transparency, which are central to the objectives of this paper.

Finally, to address GDPR compliance issues in RTB and the TCF following their declaration as non-compliant by European authorities in February 2022, IAB Europe proposed two new initiatives: the *Vendor Compliance Program* and the *Global Accountability Platform*. The Vendor Compliance Program consists of both automated and manual monitoring on end-user devices to identify what information is collected by companies participating in the TCF. On the other hand, the Global Accountability Platform is an audited self-reporting system designed to provide accountability for the movement of RTB data between servers. However, as noted in [19], both initiatives face significant challenges, and the study questions whether the use of the TCF for RTB can be effectively monitored, audited, or secured.

As a result, there is still a need for a non-intrusive solution that ensures legal compliance in digital advertising while preserving the existing paradigm. Rather than replacing the system, targeted modifications should enhance user consent management, data privacy, and GDPR compliance without disrupting the industry.

1.2   Contributions and Organization of the Paper

This work addresses the challenges of ensuring GDPR and ePrivacy Directive compliance in real-time bidding (RTB) by proposing solutions that align these systems with current legislation. Specifically, we introduce a new framework that ensures compliance within the existing RTB model, focusing on the IAB's Transparency & Consent Framework (TCF) and OpenRTB implementations. At the core of this approach is user consent, which remains a fundamental requirement for legal compliance and trust in the adtech ecosystem.

Our approach builds on the blockchain-based access control system presented in [6] to decentralize user data collection and consent management. By shifting these processes from the current TCF system to a blockchain framework, our solution enhances transparency, security, and user control over personal data.

By design, this framework empowers users with greater control over their personal data within the adtech ecosystem. Additionally, it provides accessible and immutable evidence, enabling entities involved in the RTB process to verify user consent and demonstrate compliance with legal requirements.

The rest of this paper is organized as follows: Sect. 2 offers a brief overview of the technologies and concepts used in our contribution. Section 3 elaborates on the new scheme, detailing the design requirements, system architecture, and a high-level description of the protocols employed. Section 4 is dedicated to analyzing the functional, security and privacy aspects of the proposal. Finally, Sect. 5 presents the concluding remarks.

2 Background

This section provides an overview of the key technologies and concepts used in our contribution.

2.1 Programmatic Advertising and Real Time Bidding

Programmatic advertising [4] automates the purchase and sale of ad space through *Ad Exchanges*. It involves two main entities: *Supply-Side Platforms (SSPs)*, used by publishers to manage and sell ad inventory, and *Demand-Side Platforms (DSPs)*, used by advertisers to automate ad buying and campaign management.

Advertisers define their campaign objectives, target audience, and bid amounts via a DSP, while publishers use an SSP to manage available ad space and pricing. The Ad Exchange serves as a marketplace where SSPs and DSPs interact, with notable examples including Google Ad Exchange, Facebook Ad Exchange, and Microsoft Advertising Ad Exchange. Additionally, *Data Management Platforms (DMPs)* aggregate and analyze user data, enabling advertisers to refine their targeting strategies.

At the core of programmatic advertising is Real-Time Bidding (RTB), where ad inventory is bought and sold in real-time during a web page's loading process. When a user visits a website, an auction occurs within milliseconds, determining which ad will be displayed based on advertisers' pre-targeting criteria.

The RTB process, illustrated in Fig. 1, follows these steps:

1. Advertisers specify campaign details, including ads, target profiles, and bid amounts via DSPs.
2. A user visits a publisher's website, which has reserved ad space for programmatic sales.
3. The publisher sends a bid request to the SSP, including page details and user data.

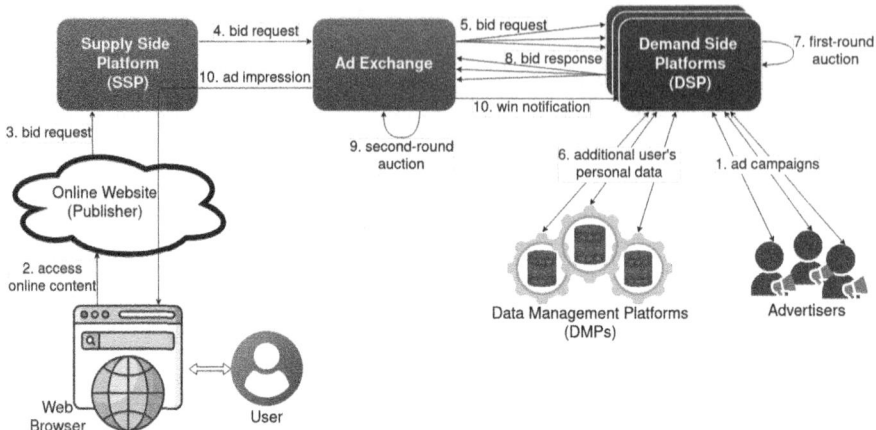

Fig. 1. Programmatic Advertising Scheme

4. The SSP forwards the request to the Ad Exchange.
5. The Ad Exchange relays the bid request to the connected DSPs.
6. DMPs may attach additional user-related metadata to the bid request sent to the RTB system. Then, the DSPs retrieve this additional user information and analyze the bid request.
7. Each DSP conducts an internal auction among relevant ad campaigns.
8. DSPs submit bids, specifying the amount and ad content.
9. The Ad Exchange selects the highest bid and runs a second-price auction, where the highest bidder pays slightly above the second-highest bid.
10. The winning ad is sent to the SSP and displayed on the publisher's webpage.

2.2   Pricing Model

The primary pricing model in real-time display advertising is CPM (Cost Per Thousand Impressions), where advertisers pay per 1,000 ad displays. Alternative models include CPC (Cost Per Click), charging per ad click, and CPA (Cost Per Acquisition), where payment occurs only after a user completes a specific action [22].

2.3   User Consent in IAB's Europe OpenRTB

In Programmatic Advertising, the IAB's TCF embeds user consent into OpenRTB bid requests [11], enabling DSPs and adtech vendors to verify consent before processing personal data for targeted ads. The bid request also includes user data for targeting and measurement.

Consent is stored as a Base64 string generated by the *Consent Management Platform (CMP)*, indicating: i) approved processing purposes, ii) authorized vendors, iii) legal basis (e.g., consent or legitimate interest), and iv) permitted data uses (e.g., personalized ads, analytics).

Upon receiving a bid request, DSPs and vendors check the consent string to determine processing permissions. If restrictions apply, they must exclude certain data or refrain from bidding. Advertisers must ensure compliance with a valid legal basis.

Despite these measures, OpenRTB fails to meet legal requirements (Sect. 1.1) due to insufficient transparency and user control. Additionally, bid requests expose user data—such as location, device details, and browsing history—raising privacy concerns over how this information is handled and shared.

2.4   Audience Taxonomy

Traditionally, data vendors, DMPs, and analytics providers have used custom taxonomies to segment audiences, leading to inconsistencies in data descriptions. Variability arises from diverse segmentation approaches, including demographic, interest-based, purchase intent, and psychographic classifications, making data comparability challenging.

To address this, the IAB Tech Lab introduced Audience Taxonomy 1.0[1], a standardized framework for labeling audience segments across different providers. This taxonomy ensures consistent classification of both first-party and third-party audience data. In this work, we analyze and adopt this taxonomy to define user profiles.

3   Proposal

In this section, we present the proposed solution for ensuring GDPR compliance in RTB while maintaining transparency and user control. First, we define the requirements that the system must meet to align RTB practices with privacy regulations. Next, we describe the system architecture, explaining how blockchain technology and a browser plug-in enable decentralized consent management. Finally, we detail the three-phase workflow of the framework: Configuration, where users define their privacy preferences; Web Browsing & Consent Enforcement, where consent is automatically applied during online activity; and Consent Management & Data Accountability, which allows users and regulatory authorities to monitor and verify data usage.

3.1   Requirements

In order to reconcile the TCF and RTB systems with GDPR, the following requirements must be fulfilled:

R1 User consent must be explicit, informed, and freely given, ensuring clarity in purpose, data usage, and user choice without implicit assumptions or misleading design.

---

[1] Audience Taxonomy: https://iabtechlab.com/standards/audience-taxonomy/.

R2 The integrity and authenticity of consents must be preserved.

R3 Users must be able to access, erase, and withdraw consent as easily as they give it.

R4 Users should have accessible records of visited publishers and involved trackers.

R5 Compliance with user preferences must be enforced across the adtech ecosystem.

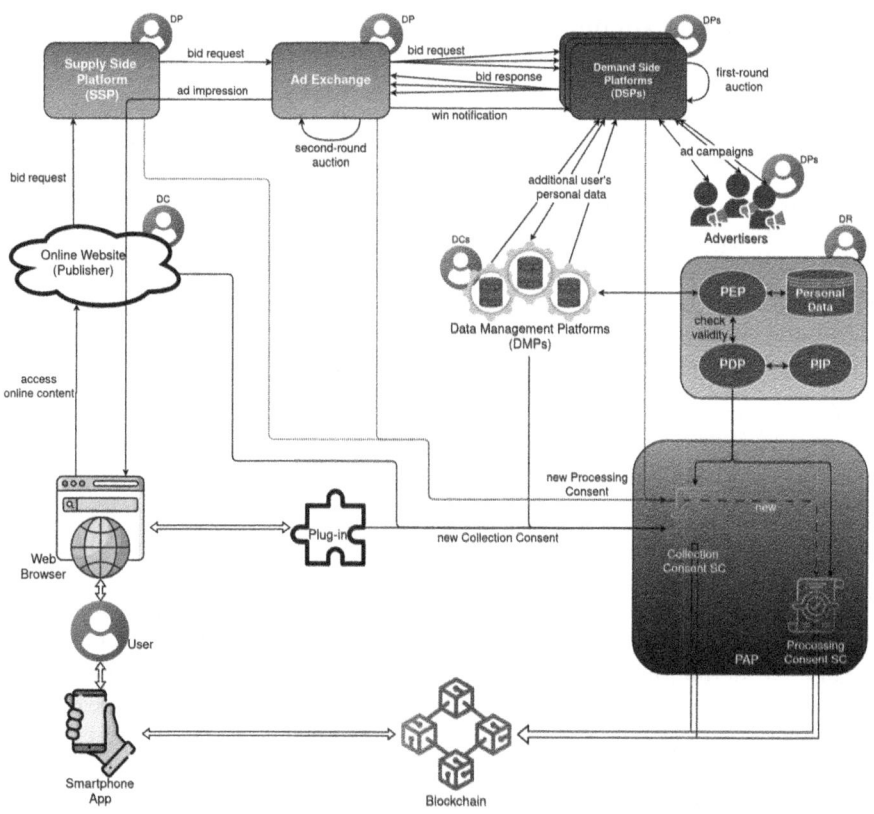

Fig. 2. Proposal Overview

3.2   System Architecture

To meet the legal requirements of OpenRTB, our solution decentralizes GDPR compliance verification and data management by leveraging a blockchain network, following the scheme in [6]. By storing user consents on-chain, we provide both users and adtech entities with immutable proof of granted permissions for data processing.

Figure 2 presents an overview of the system, where the browser extension (plug-in) plays a key role in consent management, serving as the user's access point. The plug-in, integrated into the OpenRTB model, ensures compliance without modifying the existing ecosystem. Once configured, it automates consent management based on the user's preferences, transparently handling data collection and processing. Additionally, it records visited sites and displayed ads for user review.

Under GDPR, adtech entities process personal data in two primary roles: Data Controllers (DCs), which determine the purpose and means of data processing, and Data Processors (DPs), which process data on behalf of a DC. In this context, Publishers and Data Management Platforms (DMPs) act as DCs because they collect and provide users' personal data for profiling in ad campaigns. Conversely, SSPs, DSPs, Ad Exchanges, and Advertisers function as DPs since they process this data during the advertising process. Additionally, the role of Data Recipient (DR) refers to the entity responsible for storing users' collected data. A DMP can also act as a DR if it directly stores the data. However, if storage is outsourced to a third party, then that third party assumes the role of DR.

Following [6], our system distinguishes between:

- *Data-Collection Consent:* Agreement between a user and a DC, specifying conditions for data collection in exchange for web content access.
- *Data-Processing Consent:* Agreement between a DP, DC, and user, outlining conditions under which the DP processes user data collected by the DC.

Additionally, a smartphone application provides users with a centralized interface to monitor, modify, and revoke consents in real-time. It also enables users to request data deletion, ensuring full control over their personal information in compliance with GDPR.

The system follows a three-phase workflow:

1. *Configuration:* Users define their privacy preferences, specifying which data can be collected and how it can be processed.
2. *Web Browsing & Consent Enforcement:* As users navigate the web, consent is automatically applied, and the RTB process operates within the predefined privacy settings.
3. *Consent Management & Data Accountability:* Users can monitor their consent history, track displayed ads, modify permissions, and request data deletion as needed.

3.3   Phase-1: Configuration

During the initial configuration, the user installs the plug-in, which enables control over personal data sharing with adtech entities. As part of this setup, the user specifies: i) the types of data she is willing to share; ii) the processing purposes she consents to by default; and iii) whitelisted or blacklisted vendors from the IAB Global Vendor List.

If a new entity, not previously approved, seeks access to user data for a specific purpose, it must first request explicit manual consent.

To help users assess their privacy exposure, the plug-in evaluates the worst-case scenario profile that could be constructed from the selected data. It then generates a privacy risk score ranging from 0 to 1, offering a clear, quantifiable measure of potential data exposure.

Since adtech entities use user profiling to categorize audiences for targeted advertising, understanding how shared data influences profiling is essential. The proposed system leverages this information to compute exposure levels, helping users make informed privacy decisions. The next subsections detail how user interests are structured, how the specificity of shared data is measured, and how this data is processed within the system to assess potential privacy risks.

User Profiling in Programmatic Advertising. User profiles in programmatic advertising are structured as topic distributions that reflect interests derived from browsing behavior. These profiles are built using elements such as keywords, website titles, and metadata, mapped to IAB's Audience Taxonomy (Sect. 2.4).

Our approach, based on Information Theory, measures the specificity of each taxonomy element using Inverse Document Frequency (IDF) [13]. The web, as the largest publicly available corpus of human knowledge, serves as a reference point to estimate the relative rarity of terms. The frequency with which a term appears across indexed web pages determines its specificity—less frequent terms provide more precise insights into user interests, while widely used terms offer broader categorizations [20].

For example, general terms such as "health" appear frequently across web content, making them less specific and revealing only broad user interests. In contrast, rare terms such as "lung cancer" occur far less often, making them more specific and offering deeper insights into user preferences.

To compute specificity, we analyze the hits (H) from web search engines. The IDF value for a term k is calculated as:

$$IDF(k) = -log(\frac{HC(k)}{total\_webs})$$ (1)

where $HC(k)$ is the number of search results for term k ($HC(k) = |H(k)|$), and $total\_webs$ is the estimated number of indexed websites (e.g., 400 billion in Google[2]).

To normalize specificity across different taxonomy levels, we define the Specificity (SP) metric as:

---

[2] Google's Index Size Revealed, 400 Billion Docs: https://zyppy.com/seo/google-index-size/.

$$SP(k) = \frac{IDF(k)}{-log(\frac{1}{total\_webs})} = \frac{-log(\frac{HC(k)}{total\_webs})}{-log(\frac{1}{total\_webs})} \quad (2)$$

This normalization ensures that specificity values remain within a consistent range, making it possible to compare different taxonomy elements effectively.

Hierarchy-Based Adjustments. The taxonomy used in this work follows a hierarchical structure, where higher-level categories are more general and lower-level categories are more specific. Consequently, the specificity of a non-leaf category depends on its own frequency as well as the aggregated contributions of its subcategories.

Since we are using hit counts to measure specificity, the HC value of a non-leaf category must be adjusted to reflect its overall presence in search results. Ideally, this would involve computing the union of unique search hits from all its subcategories along with its own hits:

$$HC(k) = \left| \left[\bigcup_{k' \in sonsOf(k)} H(k') \right] \cup H(k) \right| \quad (3)$$

However, accurately computing this union is computationally infeasible, as search results often overlap across subcategories or redirect to identical web content. To approximate this value efficiently, we define the adjusted hit count of a non-leaf category as:

$$HC(k) = |H(k)| + \max_{k' \in sonsOf(k)} |H(k')| \quad (4)$$

which follows the assumption:

$$HC(k) = \left| \left[\bigcup_{k' \in sonsOf(k)} H(k') \right] \cup H(k) \right| \geq \max_{k' \in sonsOf(k)} |H(k')| \quad (5)$$

This approximation ensures that higher-level categories retain a meaningful specificity score while remaining computationally efficient. The adjusted HC values are then used to compute IDF, ensuring that hierarchical dependencies are accounted for in the final specificity calculation.

Privacy Awareness and Exposure Calculation. The plug-in uses this specificity metric to help users assess their profile exposure when selecting allowed data categories. Once a user defines a personalized subset (P), their overall profile specificity (SP') is recursively computed:

$$SP'(k) = \begin{cases} \sum\limits_{k' \in sonsOf(k) \cap P} SP'(k'), & \text{if } NOT \text{ areLeafs}(sonsOf(k)) \\ \sum\limits_{k' \in sonsOf(k) \cap P} SP(k'), & \text{if areLeafs}(sonsOf(k)) \wedge \\ & |sonsOf(k) \cap P| < |sonsOf(k)| \quad (6) \\ SP(k), & \text{if areLeafs}(sonsOf(k)) \wedge \\ & |sonsOf(k) \cap P| = |sonsOf(k)| \vee \\ & |sonsOf(k) \cap P| = 0 \end{cases}$$

The final value is normalized between 0 and 1, enabling users to understand their privacy exposure level before consenting to data sharing.

3.4 Phase-2: Web Browsing and Consent Enforcement

When a user accesses a website with ad slots served through programmatic advertising, the publisher must obtain user consent before collecting and transmitting personal data to adtech entities.

In the proposed solution, instead of requiring the user to manually accept the publisher's terms via a TCF pop-up, the plug-in automatically provides the publisher with the user's preset privacy preferences. If the publisher agrees to these conditions, the plug-in generates a *Data-Collection Consent*, granting the user access to the content while allowing the publisher to collect personal data.

To share collected data with other RTB entities (DSPs, Ad Exchanges, and SSPs), the publisher must establish a *Data-Processing Consent* for each. If an entity is whitelisted in the plug-in's IAB Global Vendor List, the publisher generates the corresponding consent automatically. Otherwise, the publisher must request explicit user consent through the plug-in's API.

Both *Data-Collection* and *Data-Processing Consents* are encoded as Smart Contracts (SCs) on the Blockchain [6]. The plug-in manages all consents on behalf of the user, ensuring compliance. These SC references replace the TCF's TC string, which has been deemed non-compliant with current legislation.

Additionally, SSPs may enrich user data using Data Management Platforms (DMPs). In such cases, DMPs must have pre-obtained user consent to lawfully collect data, and SSPs must establish a *Data-Processing Consent* before using it, as detailed in [6].

Once all necessary consents are in place, the RTB protocol proceeds without modification, except when an SSP requests additional user data beyond what is included in the bid request. In this scenario, the SSP must verify a valid *Data-Processing Consent* between the user and the DMP supplying the data. The DMP, in turn, uses the proposed XACML extension to confirm consent validity before requesting the Data Recipient (DR) to provide the user's stored personal data.

Throughout this process, the plug-in records bid impressions for all displayed ads. The logged data includes: i) the winning advertiser's ID; ii) the user data shared by the publisher; iii) the amount paid for the impression; and iv) the reference to the Data-Collection Consent between the user and the publisher.

3.5 Phase-3: Consent Management and Data Accountability

During this phase, users can access and manage all generated consents, monitoring which entities collect and process their personal data and for what purposes. They can also modify or revoke these consents through a smartphone application, which interacts with Smart Contracts deployed on the Blockchain to ensure transparency and enforcement.

For data accountability, the plug-in records all displayed ads as the user browses the web. This enables users to verify whether advertisers had proper consent to use their data for targeted advertising.

Additionally, Supervisory Authorities can audit these records at any time to ensure adtech entities comply with legal requirements and operate within GDPR regulations.

4 Discussion

Section 3.1 defined key GDPR compliance requirements. This section evaluates their fulfillment through four propositions, each backed by supporting claims.

4.1 Proposition-1: User Consent for Data Collection and Processing is Explicit, Informed, and Specific to User Preferences

Upon installing the plug-in, users set their privacy preferences and assess their data exposure. These preferences generate a *Data-Collection Consent* when accessing services that request personal data for ads. A *Data-Processing Consent* ensures additional entities (e.g., SSPs, DSPs, Ad Exchanges) obtain explicit user authorization before accessing the data.

This proposition directly supports requirement R1, which mandates that consent be explicit, informed, and freely given. It is validated through the following claims:

Claim 1. *User consent preferences are explicitly defined during the plug-in setup.*

Proof. Upon installation, the plug-in requires users to configure their privacy settings via a user-friendly interface. Users specify: i) which personal data categories may be collected; ii) the duration for which data may be retained; and iii) which vendors from the IAB's Global Vendor List are pre-approved for data processing. Additionally, the plug-in provides transparency by evaluating and displaying the specificity of selected data categories, helping users understand their potential exposure based on the methodology in Sect. 3.3.

Claim 2. *A new Data-Collection Consent is generated whenever a user accesses an online service that collects personal data for advertising purposes.*

Proof. When a user visits a website that requires personal data for ad targeting, the plug-in ensures that the publisher adheres to the user's predefined privacy preferences. If the publisher agrees to these conditions, the plug-in generates a *Data-Collection Consent* contract between the user and the publisher. This contract specifies: i) the types of personal data the publisher may collect; ii) the retention period; and iii) the identity of the DR responsible for storing the collected data. This contract serves as explicit proof that the user has consented to data collection under the specified conditions.

Claim 3. *A new Data-Processing Consent is created whenever an additional entity requests to process user data collected by the publisher.*

Proof. If an SSP, DSP, Ad Exchange, or advertiser requests access to user data collected by the publisher, a *Data-Processing Consent* contract must be established. This contract specifies: i) the subset of personal data requested; ii) the processing purpose; and iii) the duration for which the data will be processed. The consent is linked to the original *Data-Collection Consent* to ensure that data usage remains traceable and compliant with user preferences.

Claim 4. *Data-processing consent requires explicit or implicit user approval.*

Proof. When a publisher creates a *Data-Processing Consent* request for an entity, the plug-in checks whether the entity is whitelisted and whether the requested data aligns with the user's predefined preferences. If both conditions are met, the consent is automatically validated. Otherwise, the user must manually approve or reject the request through a notification generated by the plug-in. This ensures that no personal data is shared beyond the user's explicit authorization.

4.2   Proposition-2: Generated Consents Maintain Integrity and Authenticity Throughout Their Lifecycle

The *Data-Collection* and *Data-Processing Consents* referenced in Claims 2 and 3 are stored as Smart Contracts on a public blockchain. Public blockchains are inherently tamper-resistant, ensuring transparency, integrity, and authenticity. Additionally, users interact with these contracts through asymmetric cryptographic key pairs, reinforcing security and non-repudiation.

This proposition directly supports requirement R2, which mandates that the integrity and authenticity of consents must be preserved. It is validated by the following claim:

Claim 5. *All Data-Collection and Data-Processing Consents established between the involved parties are securely stored on a public blockchain using immutable smart contracts.*

Proof. In the proposed system, *Collection Consent Smart Contracts* and *Processing Consent Smart Contracts* encode the respective agreements. Once deployed on the blockchain, these contracts inherit its immutability, authenticity, integrity, and irreversibility properties, ensuring that consents cannot be altered or forged [16].

4.3 Proposition-3: Users Retain Full Control over Their Consents and GDPR Rights

The proposed system allows users to manage consents via smart contracts, enabling them to: i) access their data; ii) request deletion; iii) control data collection and processing; iv) revoke consent anytime. As stated in Claim 5, consents are stored in Smart Contracts, providing users with methods to exercise their rights. The DR enforces access control through an XACML extension, verifying permissions recorded on the blockchain. *Collection-Consent Smart Contracts* encode agreements between users (data owners) and publishers (data collectors), ensuring secure and transparent access.

This proposition supports requirement R3, ensuring users can easily access, delete, and withdraw consent. The following claims support this:

Claim 6. *Smart contracts enable user rights management.*

Proof. The *Collection and Processing Consent Smart Contracts* implement methods that allow users to: i) revoke a *Data-Collection* or *Data-Processing Consent* (i.e., revokeConsent()); ii) modify which personal data can be collected or processed (i.e., modifyData()); and iii) request the DC to erase stored data (i.e., eraseData()).

Claim 7. *The DR enforces access control to user data through the XACML extension.*

Proof. The DR regulates access to user data using an XACML extension, ensuring compliance with granted permissions. The blockchain functions as the Policy Administration Point (PAP), maintaining access rights immutably. When a request is made: i) the Policy Enforcement Point (PEP) forwards it to the Policy Decision Point (PDP) for validation; ii) the PDP retrieves the corresponding *Collection-Consent SC* from the blockchain, verifies the user's public key (PK_{user}), and determines whether the requesting entity has the necessary permissions. This process guarantees that data access is only granted in accordance with the user's established consent.

4.4 Proposition-4: Users Have Direct Access to Their Consents and Ad Tracking Records

The proposed system allows users to review and manage all granted consents and collected data via the smartphone app (Claims 2, 3 and 7), ensuring compliance with their rights (Claim 6). Additionally, the plug-in logs ad impressions, summarizing displayed ads, involved entities, and personal data used for targeting. This transparency enables users to monitor data usage and detect potential misuse. If unauthorized processing is suspected, they can request an audit with a Supervisory Authority under GDPR.

This proposition supports requirements R6 and R7 by ensuring users have access to records of visited publishers, trackers, and adherence to their preferences across the adtech ecosystem. It is supported by the previous claims as well as the following:

Claim 8. *The Plug-in Captures All Bid Impressions and Related RTB Data.*

Proof. When a user visits a website displaying ads via RTB, the plug-in records bid impressions and associated data, including the advertiser, participating entities, ad category, and user data used in the selection process. This information is summarized and made accessible through the plug-in's interface, allowing users to review ad delivery details in a clear and structured manner.

5 Conclusions

This paper tackles GDPR and ePrivacy compliance in Real-Time Bidding (RTB) by decentralizing user consent management with blockchain. The proposed framework aligns IAB's TCF and OpenRTB with legal requirements, giving users direct control over their data while providing immutable proof for compliance.

A browser plug-in automates consent management based on user preferences, ensuring seamless browsing and transparency in data processing. A smartphone app allows users to monitor, modify, and revoke consents, while a specificity value in the IAB Audience Taxonomy helps assess privacy risks of shared data.

Future work includes implementing the solution, enforcing compliance without external audits, and evaluating usability, security, and economic feasibility across blockchain architectures.

Acknowledgments. This work was partially supported by the Wallenberg AI, Autonomous Systems and Software Program (WASP) funded by the Knut and Alice Wallenberg Foundation; and by the project Privacy-aware secure explainable data-driven models in federated learning (VR 2023-05531). Furthermore, this research is also supported by the project "HERMES" funded by the European Union NextGenerationEU/PRTR via INCIBE; by project PID2021-125962OB-C32 "SECURING/DATA" funded by MCIN/AEI/10.13039/501100011033/ FEDER, UE, and by the grant 2021SGR 00115 from the Government of Catalonia. The first author is also supported by the Spanish Government under an FPU grant (ref. FPU20/03254).

Appendix

The Taxonomy used in the work for user profile definition (IAB Tech Lab's Audience Taxonomy) has a total amount of 496 values under the *Interests* segment. These are organized in an architectural structure as can be seen in Fig. 3. In this figure, each node represents an element of the taxonomy and the color and size of the nodes indicate their height and their specificity. In order to calculate this specificity, first, we have performed a search of the different values on the Google search engine and then, we have applied the equation defined in Sect. 3.3 (Eq. 6). See Fig. 4, for a zoom of the branches *Academic Interests* and *Healthy Living* for a more detailed example of the labels.

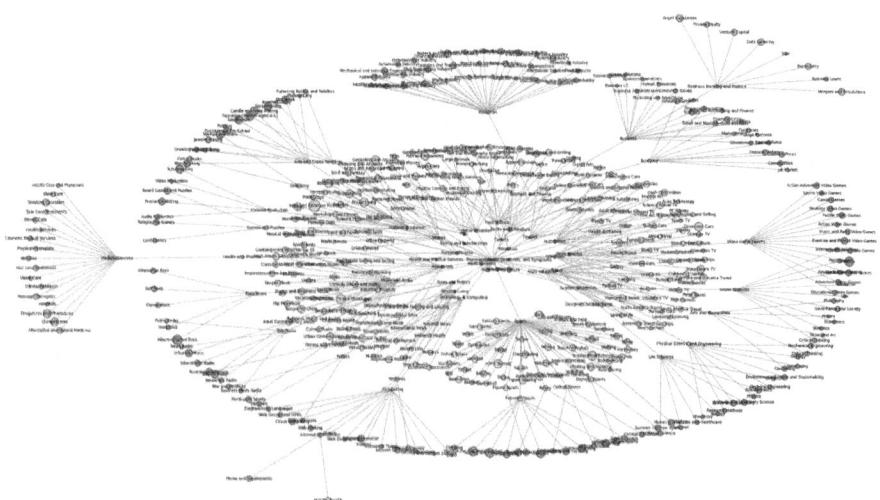

Fig. 3. Interests segment of the IAB Tech Lab's Audience Taxonomy

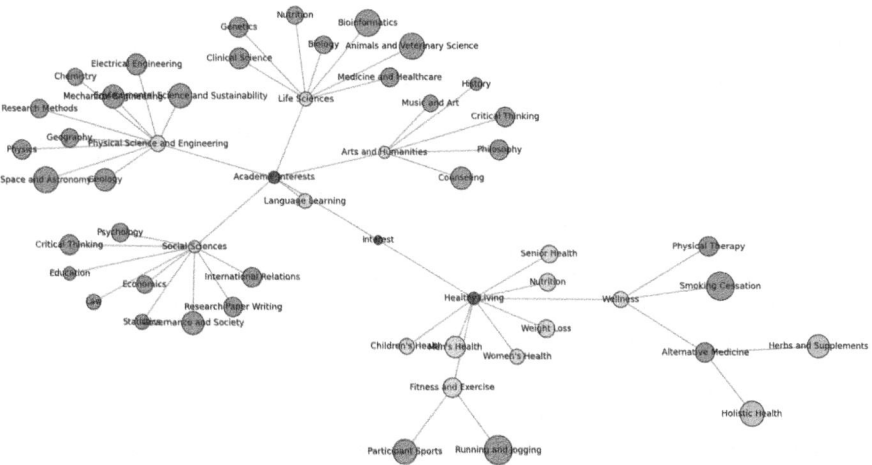

Fig. 4. Subset of Interests segment of the IAB Tech Lab's Audience Taxonomy

References

1. Directive 2002/58/EC of the European parliament and of the council of 12 July 2002 concerning the processing of personal data and the protection of privacy in the electronic communications sector (directive on privacy and electronic communications). Official J. Eur. Union L **201**, 37–47 (2002)
2. Regulation (EU) 2016/679 of the European parliament and of the council of 27 April 2016 on the protection of natural persons with regard to the processing of personal data and on the free movement of such data, and repealing directive 95/46/EC (general data protection regulation) (text with EEA relevance). Off. J. Eur. Union L 119 **59**, 1–88 (2016)
3. Belgian Data Protection Authority: IAB Europe held responsible for a mechanism that infringes the GDPR (2022). https://www.dataprotectionauthority.be/iab-europe-held-responsible-for-a-mechanism-that-infringes-the-gdpr. Accessed 26 Nov 2024
4. Busch, O.: The programmatic advertising principle. In: Programmatic Advertising: The Successful Transformation to Automated, Data-Driven Marketing in Real-Time, pp. 3–15. Springer (2015)
5. Chakrabarti, D., Agarwal, D., Josifovski, V.: Contextual advertising by combining relevance with click feedback. In: Proceedings of the 17th International Conference on World Wide Web, WWW 2008, pp. 417–426. Association for Computing Machinery, New York (2008)
6. Daudén-Esmel, C., Castellà-Roca, J., Viejo, A.: Blockchain-based access control system for efficient and GDPR-compliant personal data management. Comput. Commun. **214**, 67–87 (2024)
7. IAB Europe: IAB transparency and consent framework (2020). https://iabeurope.eu/transparency-consent-framework/. Accessed 26 Nov 2024
8. IAB Europe: IAB Europe Adex benchmark 2022 report (2023). https://iabeurope.eu/wp-content/uploads/2023/07/IAB-Europe_AdEx-Benchmark-2022_REPORT-1.pdf. Accessed 26 Nov 2024
9. Keywords Everywhere: 64 game-changing display advertising stats you need to know (2024). https://keywordseverywhere.com/blog/display-advertising-stats/. Accessed 29 Nov 2024
10. Gomer, R., Rodrigues, E.M., Milic-Frayling, N., Schraefel, M.: Network analysis of third party tracking: User exposure to tracking cookies through search. In: 2013 IEEE/WIC/ACM International Joint Conferences on Web Intelligence (WI) and Intelligent Agent Technologies (IAT), vol. 1, pp. 549–556 (2013)
11. Openrtb version 2.6 (2022). https://iabtechlab.com/standards/openrtb/
12. IAB: 2023 U.S. digital advertising industry hits new record (2023). https://www.iab.com/news/2023-u-s-digital-advertising-industry-hits-new-record-according-to-iabs-annual-internet-advertising-revenue-report/. Accessed 29 Nov 2024
13. Jain, A.: TF-IDF in NLP: Term frequency-inverse document frequency. Medium (2024). Accessed 05 Oct 2024
14. Liu, M., Yue, W., Qiu, L., Li, J.: An effective budget management framework for real-time bidding in online advertising. IEEE Access **8**, 131107–131118 (2020)
15. Malthouse, E.C., Hessary, Y.K., Vakeel, K.A., Burke, R., Fudurić, M.: An algorithm for allocating sponsored recommendations and content: unifying programmatic advertising and recommender systems. J. Advert. **48**(4), 366–379 (2019)
16. Mohanta, B., Panda, S., Jena, D.: An overview of smart contract and use cases in blockchain technology. In: 2018 9th International Conference on Computing, Communication and Networking Technologies (ICCCNT) (2018)

17. Olejnik, L., Minh-Dung, T., Castelluccia, C.: Selling off privacy at auction. In: Network and Distributed System Security Symposium (NDSS) (2014)
18. Provost, F., Dalessandro, B., Hook, R., Zhang, X., Murray, A.: Audience selection for on-line brand advertising: privacy-friendly social network targeting. In: Proceedings of the 15th ACM SIGKDD International Conference on Knowledge Discovery and Data Mining, KDD 2009, pp. 707–716. Association for Computing Machinery, New York (2009)
19. Ryan, J., Santos, C.: An unending data breach immune to audit? Can the TCF and RTB be reconciled with the GDPR? SSRN (2022)
20. Sanchez, D., Batet, M., Viejo, A.: Automatic general-purpose sanitization of textual documents. IEEE Trans. Inf. Forensics Secur. **8**(6), 853–862 (2013)
21. Shehu, E., Abou Nabout, N., Clement, M.: The risk of programmatic advertising: effects of website quality on advertising effectiveness. Int. J. Res. Mark. **38**(3), 663–677 (2021)
22. Start.io: Advertising pricing models (2025). https://www.start.io/glossary/advertising-pricing-models. Accessed 29 Jan 2025
23. Statista: Digital display advertising spending worldwide from 2022 to 2026 (2023). https://www.statista.com/statistics/235710/display-ad-spend-worldwide/. Accessed 29 Nov 2024
24. Statista: Programmatic advertising worldwide - statistics & facts (2023). https://www.statista.com/topics/2498/programmatic-advertising/. Accessed 29 Nov 2024
25. Veale, M., Nouwens, M., Santos, C.: Impossible asks: can the transparency and consent framework ever authorise real-time bidding after the Belgian DPA decision? Technol. Regul. 12–22 (2022)
26. Veale, M., Zuiderveen Borgesius, F.: Adtech and real-time bidding under European data protection law. German Law J. **23**(2), 226–256 (2022)
27. Wu, X., Yan, J., Liu, N., Yan, S., Chen, Y., Chen, Z.: Probabilistic latent semantic user segmentation for behavioral targeted advertising. In: Proceedings of the Third International Workshop on Data Mining and Audience Intelligence for Advertising, ADKDD 2009, pp. 10–17. Association for Computing Machinery, New York (2009)
28. Yan, J., Liu, N., Wang, G., Zhang, W., Jiang, Y., Chen, Z.: How much can behavioral targeting help online advertising? In: Proceedings of the 18th International Conference on World Wide Web, WWW 2009, pp. 261–270. Association for Computing Machinery, New York (2009)
29. Yuan, S., Wang, J., Zhao, X.: Real-time bidding for online advertising: measurement and analysis. In: Proceedings of the Seventh International Workshop on Data Mining for Online Advertising. ADKDD 2013. Association for Computing Machinery, New York (2013)

Enabling Right to be Forgotten in a Collaborative Environment Using Permissioned Blockchains

Anand Manojkumar Parikh[1], Shamik Sural[1(✉)], Vijayalakshmi Atluri[2], and Jaideep Vaidya[2]

[1] Indian Institute of Technology Kharagpur, Kharagpur, India
anandparikh4@gmail.com, shamik@cse.iitkgp.ac.in
[2] Rutgers university, Newark, USA
atluri@rutgers.edu, jsvaidya@business.rutgers.edu

Abstract. Any organization providing services to users typically requires the users to share some degree of personal information in order to access these services. However, users seldom have complete visibility or control over their own data, justifiably raising serious privacy concerns. Additionally, organizations are often inhibited from collaboration due to the increased risk of privacy breaches, and corresponding reporting requirements. Increasing privacy focused legislation worldwide such as the General Data Protection Regulation (GDPR) and the California Consumer Privacy Act (CCPA) create complex protection and reporting requirements that need to be systematically enforced. The Right To Be Forgotten (RTBF) recommendations included in GDPR essentially demand that every individual has the right to request for erasure of data pertaining to it, and thus in effect be forgotten from the system on demand. We propose a novel approach called CRISP (Consensus-enabled, Redactable, Immutable, Securely shareable, Provable) that uses permissioned enterprise blockchains for trustless interoperation among a network of identifiable organizations providing the ability to support RTBF. It combines off-chain data storage and distributed resource sharing with blockchain consensus mechanisms and decentralized access control. We describe the various components of CRISP and delineate the detailed steps of its operation. Results of an extensive set of experiments clearly establish the viability of our approach.

Keywords: GDPR, RTBF, Enterprise Blockchain, Interplanetary File System, HyperLedger Fabric, Access Control

1 Introduction

In today's information age, huge volumes of personal information and related transactional data of users are collected, analyzed, and shared by organizations running a variety of applications. It is increasingly being recognized that this data must be managed transparently without violating the user's right to privacy. Moreover, the data should not persist in the system for an indefinite period

S. Katsikas and B. Shafiq (Eds.): DBSec 2025, LNCS 15722, pp. 156–175, 2025.
https://doi.org/10.1007/978-3-031-96590-6_9

of time, but effectively be forgotten at the discretion of the individual to whom it pertains. The European Union's General Data Protection Regulation (GDPR) [1] contains the Right To Be Forgotten (RTBF) clause, which specifically embodies the requirement that every individual whose information is collected in a repository, must have the authority to request for removal of that data from further access by all/any other individuals/organizations when its legitimate usage is over. Likewise, the California Consumer Privacy Act (CCPA) and the Delete Act, enforced by the California Privacy Protection Agency, obligate data fiduciaries to maintain data accuracy and security while granting individuals the right to seek correction and erasure of data pertaining to them [2].

System level enforcement of the Right To Be Forgotten criteria comes with several technical challenges, which are further compounded when organizations are required to collaborate over tasks requiring multi-domain expertise. Collaborating users may need to operate in a trustless environment and uphold accountability. For example, banks often utilize the services of multiple fintech firms for investment consultancy that necessitates sharing of customer financial data with third parties. Likewise, hospitals may be required to share medical data of their patients with diagnostic facilities in an emergency. There are several other scenarios that require similar need based collaboration and hence, the associated necessity for enforcing RTBF. To address these challenges, in this paper, we present CRISP – a permissioned blockchain based approach that provides the ability to enforce RTBF in a distributed setting. While any permissioned blockchain could be used, a working implementation of CRISP uses HyperLedger Fabric (HLF) [3], an open source permissioned blockchain framework which is also arguably the most popular. Hence, in the rest of the paper, we will refer to HLF wherever we mention a permissioned blockchain.

A well-known limitation of blockchains is that they are not designed to store large files/datasets in the ledger blocks. CRISP overcomes this challenge by storing sensitive data off-chain using the inbuilt LevelDB database of HLF and the distributed file-system framework called IPFS (Interplanetary File System) [8]. To provide selective data access to different users, CRISP employs custom access control policies enforced via smart contracts. The term CRISP denotes the key properties of the proposed approach, namely, *Consensus-enabled*, *Redactable*, *Immutable*, *Securely shareable* and *Provable*. The primary contributions of this paper are summarized below. Specifically, CRISP enables:

i. Distributed access to data owned by a user (or a group of users) based on their preferences, while allowing modifications to it only on their consent.

ii. Redaction of the data immediately whenever and from wherever its owner(s) chooses, leaving behind minimal trace and ensuring no leakage of sensitive information to external parties.

iii. Independent verification of redaction by the owner(s) without requiring trust in a single centralized authority/organization through the extraction of a consensus based proof.

iv. Besides the above research contributions, we also make our entire code base publicly available on Github for furthering research in this field.

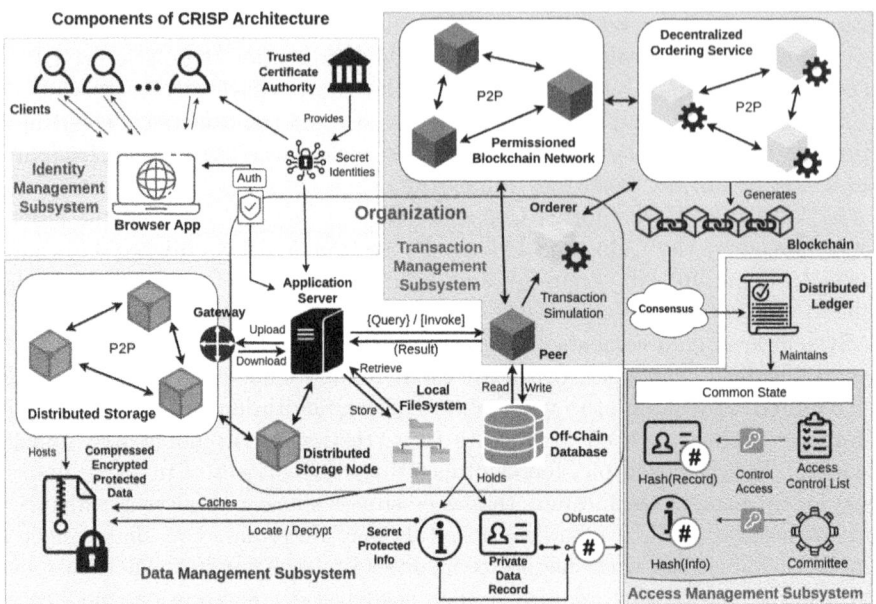

Fig. 1. Architecture Diagram of CRISP

To the best of our knowledge, CRISP is the first ever approach that simultaneously allows secure data sharing as well as accountable resource management in a distributed and trustless environment, while leveraging the fundamental concept of consensus to generate publicly verifiable proofs that guarantee each user's privacy and enforce their right to be forgotten.

2   CRISP Architecture and Operations

In this section, we first introduce the various components of CRISP and how different stakeholders interact with those components as depicted in Fig. 1. Next, we formalize the RTBF problem into a set of concrete statements. The protocols run by the components of CRISP and in what way the architecture is specialized for handling private data and protected data differently are then explained. Finally, we discuss how RTBF for its clients is guaranteed in CRISP.

2.1   Components of CRISP Subsystems

Consider a network consisting of organizations such as universities, medical facilities, legal institutions, etc. Each of these primarily hosts its clients' data under two scenarios. One is the private sensitive data pertaining to individuals (hereinafter called "private data"), e.g., patient medical records. The other is some shared data owned by a group of users, possibly spread across different organizations on which they wish to work by consensus of the group (hereinafter called "protected data"). An example use case of the latter is a multi-university army funded project. CRISP aims to meet the goals mentioned in Sect. 1 using its four subsystems (Fig. 1), namely, Data Management, Transaction Management, Access Management and Identity Management.

Data Management: To store private data records of its clients, each organization manages an off-chain database, which is directly accessible to peer nodes running smart contracts concerning the state of this data. On the other hand, to manage protected data jointly owned by a group of users, the organizations host a distributed storage system. Application servers of enrolled organizations are connected to it through a secure gateway for uploading and downloading protected data of collaborative groups based on the participants' requests.

Transaction Management: All the organizations in the network are connected through an append-only public permissioned blockchain [3], whose purpose is to immutably record transactions on clients' data. A transaction is executed by peer nodes belonging to different organizations and is considered valid only if it receives sufficient endorsements as defined by its endorsement policy. For deciding the total ordering of these transactions, which directly determines the state of the blockchain's ledger, organizations participate in a decentralized ordering service relying on a classical distributed consensus algorithm [11,21,26].

Access Management: Access to all kinds of data is managed by control structures present on the ledger, a copy of which is maintained by each peer node. Since this is publicly accessible by every organization and their clients, any sensitive information undergoes due obfuscation through a cryptographic hash [19] before getting registered on the ledger.

Identity Management: We assume the existence of a PKI (public-key infrastructure) who issues digital certificates to every individual and each organization, which is necessary for identification in the blockchain network. The application server of each organization allows its clients' access to CRISP after an authentication stage.

2.2   Formalization of the Problem

In this sub-section, we construct formal requirements translated from the informal goals set in Sect. 1. To identify every network participant – either an organization or an individual client, let each own a pair of private (secret) and public keys: $\langle sk, pk \rangle$, generated by a standard PKI procedure. Let $O = \{pk_{org1}, pk_{org2}, ...\}$ be the set of all organization identities. Each client belongs to exactly one organization, and is identified uniquely as $P = \langle pk_{org}, pk_{client} \rangle$, where *client* belongs to organization *org*. Let C be the set of all client identities in the network (refer to Table 2 in the Appendix).

Next, we represent client data in its most fundamental form – a sequence of bits of non-zero length, denoted by D. In case D does not exist in plain-text, but rather it is symmetrically encrypted using a key K, we replace D by K. Hence, our definition of D is either the raw data itself, or any information that is necessary and sufficient to retrieve the original data. At any instance, let data D be readable and writable by a set of client identities R and W, respectively. Additionally, let M be a set of members that jointly own this data and can decide to include/exclude identities in the sets R, W or even M. The exact procedure that members in M follow to decide this does not affect our modeling. Generically, it is represented by a sequence of bits V. The 4-tuple of sets $\langle R, W, M, V \rangle$, is summarized by notation A, the state of access control for D. Any data D can potentially be stored within multiple organizations' jurisdictions (i.e., their off-chain databases). To ensure D is never exposed to needless facilities, we track the set of organization identities owning a replica of D in a set F.

Formally, the state of the system concerning data D at any instance is characterized as $S = \langle D, F, A \rangle$. During its lifetime, i.e., before a user executes RTBF for D, a transaction T can change the state to $S' = \langle D', F', A' \rangle$. There are more factors affecting T than only the initial state S and the final state S'. Each transaction is always triggered by some client in the network, identified by its $P \in C$. It is intuitively obvious that transactions require a sequence of bits I as input. Moreover, each transaction must be endorsed by some set of peer nodes. Let the set $E \subseteq O$ be the set of organization identities that the endorsing peers belong to. Hence, a transaction is defined by $T = \langle S, S', P, I, E \rangle$.

In the context of this formalization (with all notations defined in Table 2 in the Appendix), the requirements of CRISP can be delineated as follows.

R1: Privacy of all client data (along with the respective client identities) must be preserved throughout and after its lifetime.

R2: Each transaction must be accountable (traceable) to the client that triggered it, given their identity.

R3: The proof of execution of every transaction must be freely available without dependency on a central authority.

To avoid repetition, all further discussion is in the context of data D. What immediately follows from R1 is that no state S or transaction T can ever be revealed in full to the entire network. Hence, the ledger contains only $X = \langle H[D], F, H[A] \rangle$ for a state S. Note that the input I to a transaction T is not relevant once it is successfully committed. I also potentially contains sensitive information, say bits of data D'. So, we do not retain I in the blockchain. Hence, we store a transaction $T = \langle S, S', P, I, E \rangle$ in the blockchain as $Y = \langle X, X', H[P], E \rangle$. Such a construction of Y automatically satisfies R2. Given a client identity P and a blockchain transaction Y, it can be checked easily if $H[P] = Y.H_P$, thereby adding accountability while preserving privacy. For ensuring R3, we propose that a transaction be endorsed by as many organizations as possible, i.e., maximize $|E|$. The motivation behind this is to make the state S strongly believable, as the result of all transactions T was voted by a large set of peers. Additionally, making E public (in the definition of Y) ensures any client can independently

---

Protocol 1 : Propose   (run on - server$_{org}$)

1: **function** PROPOSE (P, I)
2:     #‖Authenticate(P)‖   /*authenticate that P is a valid client*/
3:     I ← PreProcess (I)   /*pre-process input*/
4:     E ← EndorsementPolicy (I)   /*choose endorser set*/
5:     retval ← transmit(E,⟨H[P],I⟩,sig$_{org}$)   /*send for simulation (2)*/
6:     PostProcess (retval, I)   /*wait for commit and post-process*/
7: **end function**

Algorithm Set 1 : Utility Algorithms

1: **function** ENDORSEMENTPOLICY(I)
2:     **if** I.Modify **or** I.Replicate   /*If input contains any bits of D
3:         | **return** Q(F)   set policy as quorum of replica owners*/
4:     **end if**
5:     **return** Q(O)   /*default policy is quorum of all orgs*/
6: **end function**
1: **function** REPLICASET(F, H$_A$)
2:     F′ ← F   /*initialize new replica-set*/
3:     **for** f ∈ F′   /*for all replica organizations
4:     | participant ← false
5:     | **for** ⟨H$_{pkclient}$, H$_{pkorg}$⟩ ∈ H$_A$.H$_R$ ∪ H$_A$.H$_W$ ∪ H$_A$.H$_M$
6:     | | **if** H[f] = H$_{pkorg}$ if there is at least one
7:     | | | participant ← true   reader, writer or member
8:     | | **end if**   keep the organization
9:     | **end for**   in the new replica-set*/
10:    | **if** participant = false   /*otherwise, remove it*/
11:    | | F′ ← F′ - {f}
12:    | **end if**
13:        **return** F′
14: **end function**

---

verify if a transaction has indeed been voted by the necessary endorsers. This completely eliminates all dependencies on any single organization.

2.3   Operation of CRISP Protocols

Every organization runs certain protocols that guarantee privacy and security of client data and eventually aid in providing them RTBF by adhering to the requirements in Sub-Section 2.2. This sub-section presents the operational details of these protocols. For brevity, we do not present protocols that only query the state S, as they are fairly straightforward.

Protocol 1 - Propose. A client identity $P = \langle pk_{org}, pk_{client} \rangle \in C$ can propose that the current state $S = \langle D,F,A \rangle$ be changed to a new state $S' = \langle D',F',A' \rangle$. Every organization's application server gets these proposals from its clients which are of the following types based on the bits of the client's input I:

- $I.Modify$ $[D \neq D']$ - Overwrite current data D to $I.new\_data$.
- $I.Permit$ $[A \neq A']$ - Change access state A by some Δ. This incremental change is represented by the bits $I.\Delta_A$.
- $I.Replicate$ $[F' - F \neq \emptyset]$ - Create a new replica(s) of data D.
- $I.RTBF$ - Exercise the Right to be Forgotten.

The protocols in CRISP multiplex logic based on the input bits. First, the server locally authenticates the client to ensure only valid proposals are entertained. Next, the input is pre-processed before peers can simulate transactions on it (Sub-Section 2.4). Then, as per R3, for a strong provability argument, we must choose the maximal set of organizations to get an endorsement from. By default, the endorsement policy of any transaction is set as $E = Q(O)$, i.e., a quorum of all organizations in the network. A quorum of a set S is any majority subset of S, e.g., strictly more than one-half or two-thirds of S. However, we simultaneously need to preserve the privacy of data. If transactions that either modify ($I.Modify$) or share ($I.Replicate$) data, are endorsed by organizations other than those that already own a replica, that data is leaked. This adds a constraint $E \subseteq F$. Therefore, we set $E = Q(F)$ (Algorithm Set 1) in this case.

Next, the organization's server digitally signs the proposal $\langle H_P, I \rangle$ by the organization's identity, transmits it to the endorser set E for simulation (Protocol 2) on their peers, and waits for it to get committed (Protocol 3). Hashing the client's identity P in the proposal ensures its privacy. Also, the digital signature sig_{org} ensures that attackers cannot bypass the organization's security and propose malicious changes to the state. Finally, only transactions that receive identical results from a set of peers satisfying the endorsement policy get committed. Once the transaction is committed successfully in the blockchain, the server post-processes the return value and the input (Detailed in Sub-Section 3.1).

Protocol 2 - Simulate. A transaction is simulated by peers before its results are passed to the ordering service to be arranged in a block. This simulation is done through smart contracts in blockchain terminology. During this procedure, the peer has access to its copy of the ledger from where it reads its current hashed state $X = \langle H_D, F, H_A \rangle$. It verifies if hashed client identity H_P has access control to perform the changes proposed in the input before proceeding further. Lines 4–15 contain the core logic which updates the state S to S'. Note that, CRISP does not store the plain-text state S directly as $S = \langle D, F, A \rangle$ anywhere in the system. In context of an organization org, the off-chain database db_{org} stores plain-text data D and the ledger-copy $ledger_{org}$ stores the plain-text replica set F. The plain-text access state A is not stored anywhere at all. All changes to it (through $I.permit$) are done in the hashed form itself, represented by the operator $\oplus$ in Line 8 - it involves modifying some bits in $A.V$ leading to addition(s) or removal(s) of identities $P \in C$ from sets $A.R$, $A.W$ and $A.M$.

After any transition, Lines 16–20 constrain the replica-set to evict organizations having no participants in A (Algorithm Set 1). We simply add all organizations to the set $evicted\_orgs$ if its an RTBF operation. Lines 21–26 simulate a database delete and a database write for organizations removed from the replica-set and the ones retained in it, respectively. Note that every organization's peer

---

Protocol 2 : Simulate   (run on - peer$_{org}$)

1: **function** SIMULATE (H$_P$, I)
2:     X ← read (ledger$_{org}$)   /*get current hashed state*/
3:     #‖VerifyABAC (H$_P$, I, X.H$_A$)‖   /*verify H$_P$ is allowed access*/
4:     ⟨H$_{D'}$, F', H$_{A'}$,⟩ ← ⟨X.H$_D$, X.F, X.H$_A$⟩   /*set default values*/
5:     **if** I.modify   /*if data is modified
6:     | D' ← I.new_data   then copy new data
7:     | H$_{D'}$ ← H[D']   and construct hash*/
8:     **else if** I.permit   /*if permissions change then
9:     | H$_{A'}$ ← H$_{A'}$ ⊕ I.Δ$_A$ construct new hashed access state*/
10:    **else if** I.replicate   /*if data is replicated then
11:    | D' ← I.shared_data   copy shared data and verify
12:    | #‖H$_{D'}$ = H[D']‖   consistency with on-ledger hash
13:    | F ← F ∪ I.new_orgs   and add new orgs to replica list*/
14:    **else**   /*otherwise, its an RTBF operation
15:    | H$_{A'}$ ← ∅   so destroy the access state*/
16:    **end if**
17:    F' ← ReplicaSet(X.F, H$_{A'}$)   /*find out new replica set*/
18:    evicted_orgs ← X.F - F'   /*set of orgs to delete replicas from*/
19:    **if** I.RTBF   /*if its an RTBF operation, then forcefully delete
20:    | evicted_orgs ← O   data from everywhere*/
21:    **end if**
22:    **for** f ∈ evicted_orgs   /*for evicted organizations
23:    | delete(db$_f$, D')   simulate database delete*/
24:    **end for**
25:    **for** f ∈ F'   /*for participant organizations
26:    | write(db$_f$, D')   simulate database write*/
27:    **end for**
28:    X' ← ⟨H$_{D'}$, F', H$_{A'}$⟩   /*construct new hashed state*/
29:    write(ledger$_{org}$, X')   /*simulate ledger write*/
30:    Y ← ⟨X, X', H$_P$⟩   /*construct hashed transaction*/
31:    results[Y] ← ⟨D', retval⟩   /*store results temporarily*/
32:    gossip (X.F ∪ F', results[Y], sig$_{org}$)   /*gossip results*/
33:    broadcast (O, Y, sig$_{org}$)   /*broadcast transaction to all orgs' orderers*/
34: **end function**

---

which runs this smart contract, simulates the database delete and write operations on all the organizations. This is possible because these are not calls that require any actual interaction with the underlying database. The following is an example where this decentralization is useful:

- A client $P \in C$ of organization $org \in O$ executes an RTBF operation on one of their private data records D.
- At the time of simulation, *peer*$_{org}$ somehow failed to endorse this operation. Since the endorsement policy is $Q(O)$, another quorum of organizations $E \subseteq O$ ($org \notin E$) endorsed this transaction successfully.

Protocol 3 : Commit   (run on - peer$_{org}$)

1: **function** COMMIT (Y)
2:      **if** org $\in$ Y.X'.F'   /*if still a participant, then
3:      | write(db$_{org}$, results[Y].D')   perform actual database write*/
4:      **else**   /*but if evicted, then
5:      | delete(db$_{org}$, results[Y].D')   perform actual database delete*/
6:      **end if**
7:      write (ledger$_{org}$, Y.X')   /*perform actual ledger write*/
8:      append (blockchain$_{org}$, Y)   /*append transaction to blockchain*/
9:      transmit ({org}, results[Y].retval, sig$_{org}$)   /*return to server$_{org}$ (1)*/
10: **end function**

- Once the ordering service has packaged this transaction into a block, this data actually gets deleted whenever *peer$_{org}$* synchronizes *ledger$_{org}$* (Protocol 3).

After the simulations are complete, the peer constructs the new hashed state $X' = \langle H_D', F', H_A' \rangle$ and simulates a ledger write. The hashed transaction $Y' = \langle X, X', H^P \rangle$ is broadcast to the ordering service. It also generates a return value *retval* and stores appropriate results temporarily until the ordering service has packaged the transaction into a block. These peers participate in *gossip*, by which means they share the results, but only with past and present participating organizations. The invariant $E \subseteq F \cup F'$ is easily verifiable for any transaction. Hence, *gossip* ensures that peers that need the results, but which do not get picked as part of the endorsing quorum, still receive results to be committed.

Protocol 3 - Commit. In addition to simulating transactions, each peer asynchronously listens for blocks to be committed. We present the commit protocol at the transaction-level, but actually it runs at the block level. Since the ordering service totally-orders the transactions into blocks, both are equivalent. On receiving a hashed transaction Y to be committed, an organization *org* checks if it is either still a participant or has been evicted from the new replica-set. It then performs the necessary action of deleting or updating the data D' in db_{org}. Y does not contain D', but *org* knows D' either through direct participation as an endorser (i.e. *org* $\in E$), or through *gossip* (Protocol 2). Next, it writes the new hashed state $Y.X'$ to *ledger$_{org}$* and appends Y to *blockchain$_{org}$*. Finally, *peer$_{org}$* tranmits the results back to *server$_{org}$*, which intercepts and post-processes the *retval* (Details in Sub-Section 3.1).

2.4   Private and Protected Data

This sub-section discusses how the CRISP architecture adapts to fit the needs of security and privacy for both private and protected data.

Private Data. Private data contains personal sensitive attributes related to its owner, such as their name, address, contact information, medical records, etc.

For a client identity $P = \langle pk_{org}, \text{pk}_{client} \rangle$, CRISP stores this in db_{org} directly as plain-text D (Fig. 1). CRISP maintains the following invariants on private data.

- $F = \{org\}$: There can be no more than one replica of private data, which exists in db_{org}. Proposals of type *I.replicate* are disabled. It can be verified that the protocols (Sect. 2.3) never share private data with any organization other than *org*.
- $A.M = P$: P is the sole owner of D, hence member access is not granted to any other identity.
- $A.V = \emptyset$: The owner P can grant and revoke access to other clients. $P' \in C$ from the sets of readers $A.R$ and writers $A.W$. Hence, no additional information is required to maintain the access state A.

Protected Data. Protected data serves a different purpose compared to private data. It is a shared resource on which a group of users wish to operate on by consensus. This form of data can be arbitrarily large and unstructured. Blockchains are not designed to work well with reading/writing such large data from within smart contract execution environment. Hence, any protected data D is not directly stored inside db_{org} for any $org \in O$. Rather, CRISP considers the use of a distributed file system [8] running among organizations in the network. Enforcing selectivity in which nodes to store data on, is generally not easy in popular distributed filesystems, such as the Interplanetary File System (IPFS). Hence, to ensure the plain-text contents are not revealed to the nodes storing D, it is pre-processed as follows. It first undergoes lossless compression, and subsequent encryption by a random secret key K, to produce D' = *encrypt(comp(D),K)*. D' is uploaded to the IPFS service, which generates a *CID* (Content Identifier).

Since D is operated on by multiple users simultaneously, there may be concurrent write operations happening. Maintaining only a single version of this information will not suffice, so we keep the entire version history of D. Let us call the series of tuples *(CID, Key)* for each version v of data D its *protected information*. This information is necessary and sufficient to access D - for each version v, we require the *CID* to locate D' on the IPFS network and the secret key K to decrypt D' after decompression. Hence, we now use the notation D to denote the protected information, which has replaced its underlying protected data. This D is small - a list of byte arrays, each array being a concatenation of the *CID* and *Key* whose length is typically several bytes depending on the IPFS service implementation and choice of the encryption algorithm. It can now be conveniently stored in db_{org} so that peer nodes can directly operate on it through smart contracts.

For D, the access state A is governed by $A.V$, which represents a majority voting procedure. Members $A.M$ can grant and revoke votes for other clients $P' \in C$ to be members ($A.M$), readers ($A.R$) and writers ($A.W$). Any client P' that receives a quorum of votes, say strictly more than one-half of the total number of clients, can participate in this "committee" A with that role. Note

---

Protocol 4 : Verify

1: **function** VERIFY (P, k)	
2: cnt = 0	/*initialize count*/
3: **for** X ∈ blockchain$_{org}$	/*for all transactions in blockchain$_{org}$*/
4: | **if** X.H$_P$ = H[P]	/*if executed by client identity P*/
5: | | cnt ← cnt+1	/*increment count*/
6: | **end if**	
7: **end for**	
8: #‖cnt = k‖	/*check if cnt is equal to k*/
9: **end function**	

---

that, quorums in this voting procedure are unrelated to the quorums of peers required to satisfy a transaction's endorsement policies.

2.5   Provable RTBF

CRISP guarantees to provide each client the Right to be Forgotten. Every $org \in O$ is mandated to publish their blockchain copy $blockchain_{org}$ (and hence $ledger_{org}$) to the world. Making this information public allows clients to read the blockchain copies of all and any organization to verify if they are identical. There may be discrepancies because of the blockchain's replication lag or malicious peer nodes. In such case, copies not matching a majority can be easily discarded as being faulty. To verify that their RTBF has been rightfully executed, a client P maintains the count of transactions proposed by them so far. Given a correct blockchain copy, they can count the number of hashed transactions Y, where $Y.H_P = H[P]$. If both counts match, then all their transactions were committed successfully (Protocol 4). In the private data scenario, no one other than the owner P can execute the RTBF, so this technique suffices. For protected data, we slightly enhance the hashed transaction definition as $Y = \langle X, X', H_P, rtbf \rangle$, where boolean $rtbf$ denotes whether a transaction of type $I.RTBF$ was successfully executed or not. This allows any client $P \in C$ to verify if the RTBF has indeed been executed, by reading the blockchain.

3   Implementation and Evaluation

This section presents the details of our implementation of CRISP followed by results from an extensive set of experiments carried out over it to study its performance. We use HyperLedger Fabric (HLF)[1] as the permissioned blockchain at its core. For a proof of concept, we consider a network of five organizations, each having its cryptographic identities generated using HLF's Fabric-CA. Every organization owns two docker containers: a peer facility and an orderer node - all interconnected via a docker-network on localhost. For the distributed file

---

[1] https://hyperledger-fabric.readthedocs.io/en/latest/.

storage, we use IPFS Helia[2] to store the file chunks (blocks in IPFS terminology) in a local blockstore. For compressing protected data files, the gzip compression algorithm is used [17]. Symmetric encryption and subsequent decryption is done through 256-bit AES. The smart contracts (chaincodes in HLF terminology) were implemented in GoLang and the server code in NodeJS. The source code has been released through GitHub[3]. All the experiments were conducted on a client node machine with an AMD Ryzen7 4700U processor, 8 GB RAM and Ubuntu 22.04 distribution.

3.1   User Functionality

In this sub-section, we describe the functionality that our instantiation of CRISP provides to the clients. The organization servers expose an API to their users, consisting of a set of callable functions as listed in Table 3 in the Appendix, along with the type of operations performed. Types *Modify*, *Replicate*, *Permit* and *RTBF* are derived directly from Sect. 2.3. Operations of type *Query* only read the state. The type *Lifetime* represents operations which manage the lifetime of access control structures.

Functions [1 to 6] deal with private data *Record*s. Any client can always read and write to *Record*s owned by them. They can construct and destruct *ACL*s for these *Record*s as well as grant and revoke read and write accesses to/from other users, possibly from a different organization. Finally, they can exercise their Right To Be Forgotten for specified records and these are to be erased completely from the network. Subsequently, no one including the owner can access those records anymore, because they simply do not exist. However, on-chain hashes of all historical values of this data along with control-related transactions persist in the blockchain forever. But the data and the owner cannot be reconstructed from this information. Thus, user privacy is not violated and RTBF is guaranteed.

Functions [7 to 16] deal with protected data *File*s. A client can assemble a committee of members (possibly spread across organizations) to work on a shared protected data *File*. Members can grant and revoke votes to other users for being members, readers and writers. A user may join a committee as a member, reader or writer, given that they have gathered a quorum ($>1/2$) of votes for that access type from the existing members or leave a committee at any time it wishes. Readers can read the shared file and writers can write to the shared file, where each write appends a new version of the file into IPFS. A committee member can share a file with a newly joined participant organization for their users to use. Any committee participant (reader, writer or member) can check the validity of a file shared with them to ensure it has not been tampered with. As an optimization, when a client from organization *org* successfully checks the validity a protected data file D, $server_{org}$ caches a copy of its encrypted version D' from IPFS in its local filesystem (Fig. 1) for future access. Finally, each committee member may vote to exercise their RTBF for the shared file.

---

[2] https://helia.io/.

[3] https://github.com/anandparikh4/CRISP.

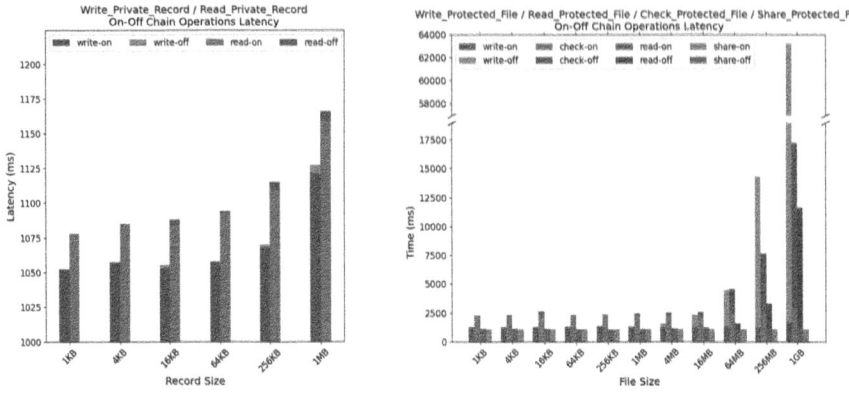

Fig. 2. Latency of (a) Private and (b) Protected Data Procedures

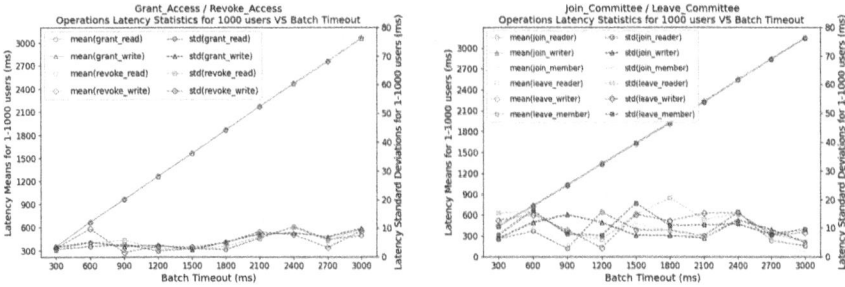

Fig. 3. Latency Statistics of (a) Private Access Control and (b) Protected Membership Modifications

When a quorum of members have voted for RTBF, the *retval* from Protocol 3 triggers the post-process operations on all servers - all traces of the file from the local filesystems holding it are deleted and the file on IPFS is marked for garbage collection. After a committee is marked for RTBF, all further operations on it or the underlying data are disabled and any committee member can disassemble the committee, ending the life cycle of the shared resource.

3.2   Experimental Results

In this sub-section, we study the latency of different functions listed in Table 3 in the Appendix. Figure 2(a) plots the latency of Write_Private_Record (Function 1) and Read_Private_Record (Function 2) for private data record size varying from 1 KB to 1 MB. The total latency of executing a function consists of the time for invoking transactions and evaluating queries (on-chain duration) as well as the server's backend latency (off-chain duration). Note that the X-axis starts from 1000 ms. It is observed that the off-chain durations are insignificant compared to the on-chain durations for all record sizes. Even after increasing the

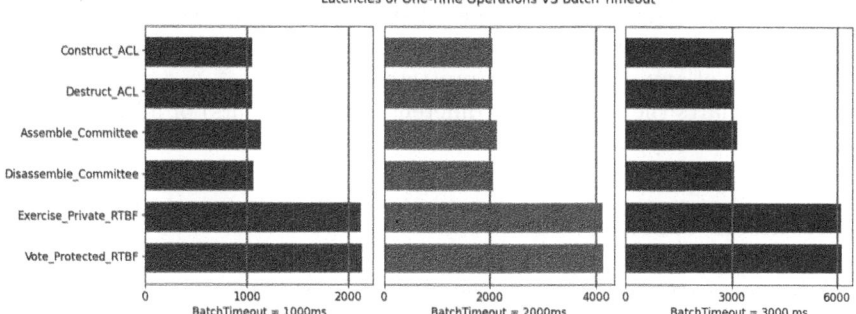

Fig. 4. Latency of One-Time Operations

record size from 1 KB to 1 MB, there is not more than a 10% variation in total latency. Next, in Fig. 2(b), we plot the latency of Write_Protected_File (Function 13), Check_Protected_File (Function 14), Read_Protected_File (Function 15) and Share_Protected_File (Function 16) for protected data file size varying from 1 KB to 1 GB. Each version of the file contains randomly generated ASCII characters for obtaining realistic benefits by compression (nearly 24% for most cases). It is observed that on-chain latency for all operations - write, check, read and share, is nearly identical for all file sizes. This is because, regardless of the file size, on-chain operations only deal with the small protected information objects. Additionally, the total latency stays nearly constant even for this large variation in file size, having minimal off-chain latency. For sizes less than 64 MB, the off-chain operations dominate drastically as cryptographic operations like encryption and decryption now take longer time.

Figure 3(a) has twin axes plotting the mean (left axis) and standard deviation (right axis) of latency of Grant_Access (Function 5) as well as Revoke_Access (Function 6) for N = 1000 users against a parameter "Batch Timeout" (BT). BT is part of the configuration of the ordering service, and is defined as the maximum amount of time the service waits for more transactions after receiving the first one before creating a new block. In the figure, it is seen that the mean time varies linearly with BT for both grant/revoke operations for either read/write type access control. Note the four overlapping mean lines in the figure. To emphasize that this mean is indeed a valid representative of the operation latency, we simultaneously plot the standard deviation (std) of the latency for the kth user on the twin axis (note the different scale). The stability of the four std lines and their small values as compared to the mean indicate that the mean is statistically significant. It is thus established that Batch Timeout is the only major contributing factor to operation latency, and the actual duration of simulation by the peer facilities is much smaller. The results for Grant_Vote (Function 9) and Revoke_Vote (Function 10) for access types "member", "reader" and "writer" are similar and hence omitted for brevity. Figure 3(b) plots the same statistics for Join_Committee (Function 11) and Leave_Committee (Function 12). Drawing the same inference again, note the six overlapping mean lines, and six stable std lines. We have covered the operations that take place most number of times in the lifetime of any data (private/protected).

Figure 4 charts the latency (for different batch timeouts) of all those operations that occur only once in its lifetime (Functions 3, 4, 7, 8, 17, 18).

4   Related Work

In this section, we review existing literature covering different aspects relevant to our work. First, we identify which data pertaining to an individual can be interpreted as private. Any data that constitutes personal attributes of an individual, or helps in identifying an individual directly or indirectly through additional information, is considered to be private data [14]. Such data could be stored as plaintext or in hashed or encrypted form to suit various security requirements [7]. Entering the realm of generative AI and LLMs, summary data or models which are learned from such private data using statistical or machine learning techniques may also be treated as private [12,23].

Next, we explore locations to store user data. Sensitive data pertaining to an individual, for instance their medical, banking or residential information can be maintained in private databases owned by the organization(s) managing the data. However, for a shared resource owned by multiple parties distributed across a network, such a local database server does not scale well. The Interplanetary File System, on the other hand, provides a decentralized data storage and sharing mechanism over peer-to-peer networks [8]. IPFS inherently has no access control layer in the sense that anyone with the Content Identifier (CID - which is the hash of a file's content) can locate and download the file from the IPFS service. To mitigate this, several approaches propose using a conjunction of IPFS based data storage with blockchain enabled authentication and access control mechanisms [28–30]. CRISP stores encrypted data files in a distributed manner whose addresses can be looked up via their unique CIDs stored in the IPFS distributed hash table. The blockchain is used to record transactions on the data in a tamper-proof manner over the peer-to-peer network.

Other off-chain approaches provide privacy by maintaining sensitive data in private databases, while storing only its hash on the blockchain [7,27]. The on-chain hash makes the actual data tamper-evident. The data stored outside can be erased upon receipt of an RTBF request from the user, thereby facilitating confidentiality while enforcing RTBF on demand. A blockchain model for healthcare with off-chain data storage and hash-based metadata is proposed in [6]. However, it depends on manipulation of local (off-chain) data structures to achieve RTBF, which is not provable to the end-user. Note that their RTBF guarantees are restricted to certain types of structured data.

The singular greatest limitation to achieving RTBF in blockchains is their immutability property [7,18]. So, the ability to modify blockchains under certain conditions in a controlled environment could create opportunities for allowing previously permanent information to now be forgotten. Chameleon hashing [20]

Table 1. Qualitative Comparison of CRISP and other Frameworks

Architecture	Core Security Paradigm	Distributed Big Data Sharing	Private Data Transactions	Data Modifications	RTBF
Bayle et al. [6]	Off-chain Hash	Unstructured	Strong	×	Centralized
Balistri et al. [5]	Off-chain Hash	×	Weak	×	Centralized
Makhdoom et al. [22]	Off-chain Hash	Structured Only	Strong	Accountable	Restricted
Tomaz et al. [32]	NIZKP + ABE	Unstructured	Strong	×	×
Ateniese et al. [4]	CH + MPC	×	×	Unaccountable	Exposed
Derler et al. [15]	CH + CP-ABE	×	×	Unaccountable	Exposed
Tian et al. [31]	PCH + BBT	×	×	Accountable	Exposed
Deuber et al. [16]	On-chain Voting	×	×	Accountable	Exposed
Botta et al. [9]	NIZKP	×	×	Accountable	Exposed
Nizamuddin et al. [25]	On-chain Voting	Unstructured	×	Accountable	×
Das et al. [13]	MPT	Unstructured	×	Accountable	×
CRISP	Off-chain Hash, On-Chain Voting	Unstructured	Strong	Accountable	Secret, Unrestricted, Decentralized

is one such possibility. In contrast to the SHA hashing schemes, which are collision resistant, chameleon hashes are collision tractable if a certain secret trapdoor key is known. The first proposal of using chameleon hashes with blockchains is [4]. It runs a multi-party computation in a decentralized setting to forge the hash that links the blockchain to actualize block-level redaction.

Chameleon hash functions are not the only means of achieving blockchain redaction. Deuber et al. [16] provide the first practical means of achieving redaction in public permissionless blockchains, such as Bitcoin [24] and Ethereum [10]. Changes suggested to the blockchain undergo on-chain consensus-based voting, considered successful only if pre-defined redaction policies are satisfied. Botta et al. [9] use non-interactive zero- knowledge proofs (NIZKPs) allowing each node to delete data without requiring to achieve consensus on the content to be deleted, while also preserving the public verifiability of transactions.

In Table 1, we make a qualitative examination of different architectures. The table clearly delineates the unique features of CRISP and firmly establishes it as a significant improvement over the current state-of-the-art in RTBF literature.

5   Conclusion and Future Directions

The CRISP approach, as proposed in this paper, enables secure sharing of both an individual's private data and a group's jointly-owned data, while allowing users to grant and revoke access control and also request modification or erasure of the same. We have also described in detail the data structures used, transaction endorsement policies, and the underlying algorithms for each operation in CRISP. The deletion of data is provable to the user making such a request. Our solution is thus user-centric and RTBF-compliant. Experimental results demonstrate the feasibility and efficiency of our implementation.

Regardless, there are still future possibilities to consider. Augmentation of CRISP, and possibly HLF's core itself, with chameleon hash functions can allow for trusted expungement of selected transactions within blocks and also entire blocks if desired, subject to certain conditions. This may help in clearing out even the anonymized historical remnants of user information from the blockchain. Adding infrastructure to CRISP for interoperating with permissionless blockchains such as Ethereum, might open up avenues for supporting larger networks.

A   Appendix

In this Appendix, we first list all the notations and definitions in one place for ease of reference (Table 2). We then enumerate (Table 3) the functions that have been referred in Sect. 3.

Table 2. Notations and Definitions

Notation	Definition
$\langle sk,pk \rangle$	Private and public keys of a participant
O	Set $\{pk_{org} \mid \forall\ org\}$ of all organization identities
C	Set $\{\langle pk_{org},\ pk_{client} \rangle \mid \forall\ client\}$ of all client identities
D	Sequence of bits representing client data
F	Set $F \subseteq O$, owning a replica of D
$A = \langle R,W,M,V \rangle$	Sets of readers, writers, members ($R,W,M \subseteq C$) and state of procedure defining ownership (V) for D
$S = \langle D,F,A \rangle$	State of the system concerning data D
$X = \langle H[D],F,H[A] \rangle$	Representation of hashed state S on the ledger
$T = \langle S,S',P,I,E \rangle$	A transaction carried out on state S of D
P	$\langle pk_{org},\ pk_{client} \rangle \in C$ who triggers T
I	Sequence of bits as input to T
E	Set $E \subseteq O$ who endorse T
$Y = \langle X,X',H[P],E \rangle$	Representation of hashed transaction T on the blockchain
$H^B = H[B]$	Cryptographic hash of B (a sequence of bits)
$g = G(e_1,e_2,...,e_n)\ H[g]$ $= G(H[e] \mid e \in g)$	Hash of a container g of type G = list/tuple/set (defined recursively)
$E = encrypt(B,K)\ B =$ $decrypt(E,K)$	Symmetric encryption and subsequent symmetric decryption of B by a key K
$B' = comp(B)\ B =$ $decomp(B')$	Lossless compression and subsequent deompression of B
sig_{org}	Digital signature of the identity $org \subseteq O$
$\#\|cond\|$	Evaluation of a boolean condition $cond.$ which terminates with failure if false
$Q(S)$	A quorum set of any set S

Table 3. User Functions

#	Function	Type
1	Write_Private_Record	Modify, Replicate
2	Read_Private_Record	Query
3	Construct_ACL	Lifetime
4	Destruct_ACL	Lifetime
5	Grant_Access	Permit
6	Revoke_Access	Permit
7	Assemble_Committee	Lifetime
8	Disassemble_Committee	Lifetime
9	Grant_Vote	Vote, Permit
10	Revoke_Vote	Vote, Permit
11	Join_Committee	Lifetime
12	Leave_Committee	Lifetime
13	Write_Protected_File	Modify, Replicate
14	Check_Protected_File	Validate
15	Read_Protected_File	Query
16	Share_Protected_File	Replicate
17	Exercise_Private_RTBF	Vote, RTBF
18	Vote_Protected_RTBF	Vote, RTBF

References

1. The European Union's General Data Protection Regulation (GDPR) (2016). https://gdpr-info.eu/
2. California Consumer Privacy Act (CCPA) (2018). https://cppa.ca.gov/regulations/
3. Androulaki, E., Barger, A., et al.: Hyperledger fabric: a distributed operating system for permissioned blockchains. In: Proceedings of the 13th EuroSys Conference, pp. 1–15 (2018)
4. Ateniese, G., Magri, B., Venturi, D., Andrade, E.: Redactable blockchain–or–rewriting history in bitcoin and friends. In: Proceedings of the European Symposium on Security and Privacy, pp. 111–126 (2017)
5. Balistri, E., Casellato, F., Giannelli, C., Stefanelli, C.: BlockHealth: blockchain-based secure and peer-to-peer health information sharing with data protection and right to be forgotten. ICT Express **7**(3), 308–315 (2021)
6. Bayle, A., Koscina, M., Manset, D., Perez-Kempner, O.: When blockchain meets the right to be forgotten: technology versus law in the healthcare industry. In: Proceedings of the 2018 IEEE/WIC/ACM International Conference on Web Intelligence, pp. 788–792 (2018)
7. Belen-Saglam, R., Altuncu, E., Lu, Y., Li, S.: A systematic literature review of the tension between the gdpr and public blockchain systems. In: Blockchain: Research and Applications, pp. 1–23 (2023)

8. Benet, J.: IPFS - Content Addressed, Versioned, P2P File System (IPFS Whitepaper) (2014)
9. Botta, V., Iovino, V., Visconti, I.: Towards data redaction in bitcoin. IEEE Trans. Netw. Serv. Manag. **19**(4), 3872–3883 (2022)
10. Buterin, V., et al.: A Next-Generation Smart Contract and Decentralized Application Platform (Ethereum Whitepaper) (2013)
11. Castro, M., Liskov, B., et al.: Practical byzantine fault tolerance. In: OsDI, vol. 99, pp. 173–186 (1999)
12. Cohen, A., Smith, A., Swanberg, M., Vasudevan, P.N.: Control, confidentiality, and the right to be forgotten. In: Proceedings of the ACM SIGSAC Conference on Computer and Communications Security, pp. 3358–3372 (2023)
13. Das, M., Tao, X., Liu, Y., Cheng, J.C.: A blockchain-based integrated document management framework for construction applications. Autom. Constr. **133**, 104001 (2022)
14. De Capitani Di Vimercati, S., Foresti, S., Livraga, G., Samarati, P.: Data privacy: definitions and techniques. Int. J. Uncertainty Fuzz. Knowl.-Based Syst. **20**(06), 793–817 (2012)
15. Derler, D., Samelin, K., Slamanig, D., Striecks, C.: Fine-Grained and Controlled Rewriting in Blockchains: Chameleon-Hashing Gone Attribute-Based. Cryptology ePrint Archive (2019)
16. Deuber, D., Magri, B., Thyagarajan, S.A.K.: Redactable blockchain in the permissionless setting. In: Proceedings of the 2019 IEEE Symposium on Security and Privacy (SP), pp. 124–138 (2019)
17. Deutsch, P.: GZIP File Format Specification Version 4.3. Technical report (1996)
18. Dutta, R., Das, A., Dey, A., Bhattacharya, S.: Blockchain vs GDPR in collaborative data governance. In: Proceedings of the 17th International Conference on Cooperative Design, Visualization, and Engineering, CDVE 2020, Bangkok, Thailand, pp. 81–92 (2020)
19. Gilbert, H., Handschuh, H.: Security analysis of sha-256 and sisters. In: International Workshop on Selected Areas in Cryptography, pp. 175–193 (2003)
20. Krawczyk, H., Rabin, T.: Chameleon Hashing and Signatures. Cryptology ePrint Archive (1998)
21. Lamport, L.: Paxos Made Simple. ACM SIGACT News (Distributed Computing Column) 32, 4 (Whole Number 121, December 2001), pp. 51–58 (2001)
22. Makhdoom, I., Zhou, I., Abolhasan, M., Lipman, J., Ni, W.: PrivySharing: a blockchain-based framework for privacy-preserving and secure data sharing in smart cities. Comput. Secur. **88**, 101653 (2020)
23. Moreno, J., Fernandez, E.B., Fernandez-Medina, E., Serrano, M.A.: Neuralyzer: a security pattern for the right to be forgotten in big data. In: Proceedings of the Conference on Pattern Languages of Programs, pp. 1–9 (2018)
24. Nakamoto, S.: Bitcoin: A Peer-to-Peer Electronic Cash System (Bitcoin Whitepaper) (2008)
25. Nizamuddin, N., Salah, K., Azad, M.A., Arshad, J., Rehman, M.: Decentralized document version control using ethereum blockchain and IPFS. Comput. Electr. Eng. **76**, 183–197 (2019)
26. Ongaro, D., Ousterhout, J.: In search of an understandable consensus algorithm. In: Proceedings of the 2014 USENIX Annual Technical Conference, pp. 305–319 (2014)
27. Politou, E., Casino, F., Alepis, E., Patsakis, C.: Blockchain mutability: challenges and proposed solutions. IEEE Trans. Emerg. Top. Comput. **9**(4), 1972–1986 (2019)

28. Singh, A., Sural, S., Sengupta, T., Sural, S.: Trusted sharing of autonomous vehicle crash data using enterprise blockchain and IPFS. In: Proceedings of the 5th ACM International Symposium on Blockchain and Secure Critical Infrastructure, pp. 11–24 (2023)

29. Steichen, M., Fiz, B., Norvill, R., Shbair, W., State, R.: Blockchain-based, decentralized access control for IPFS. In: Proceedings of the 2018 IEEE International Conference on Blockchain, pp. 1499–1506 (2018)

30. Tenorio-Fornés, A., Hassan, S., Pavón, J.: Open peer-to-peer systems over blockchain and IPFS: an agent oriented framework, pp. 19–24 (2018). https://doi.org/10.1145/3211933.3211937

31. Tian, Y., Li, N., Li, Y., Szalachowski, P., Zhou, J.: Policy-based chameleon hash for blockchain rewriting with black-box accountability. In: Proceedings of the 36th Annual Computer Security Applications Conference, pp. 813–828 (2020)

32. Tomaz, A.E.B., Do Nascimento, J.C., Hafid, A.S., De Souza, J.N.: Preserving privacy in mobile health systems using non-interactive zero-knowledge proof and blockchain. IEEE Access **8**, 204441–204458 (2020)

P-EDR: Privacy-Preserving Event-Driven Data Release Using Smart Contracts

Jingzhe Wang[✉] and Balaji Palanisamy

University of Pittsburgh, Pittsburgh, PA, USA
{jiw148,bpalan}@pitt.edu

Abstract. Timed Data Release (TDR) is a practical security mechanism designed to safeguard data until a specified time has elapsed. Recently, a more general paradigm, referred to as Event-driven Data Release (EDR) has gained attention. EDR enables data to be released based on the occurrence of a specified event. Existing blockchain-based constructions for EDR either neglect privacy considerations or restrict themselves to specialized message spaces (e.g., signatures) while achieving provable privacy guarantees. Despite its practical relevance, constructing a privacy-preserving EDR framework that supports general message spaces on blockchain with formal security guarantees remains an open challenge.

In this paper, we address this gap by introducing P-EDR, a privacy-preserving event-driven data release framework for general message spaces, built on smart contracts. P-EDR enables a data sender to encrypt its data, which can be securely released upon the occurrence of specified events. P-EDR incorporates a novel, tailored signature-based witness encryption, SGWE, designed to encrypt data messages within a general message space, contingent upon the presence of a valid signature of a referencing message. Using SGWE, decryption of ciphertext is only possible with a valid signature. We formally define the desired security model and present an efficient construction of SGWE. Additionally, we propose a practical design for P-EDR and we rigorously prove the security guarantees of our construction. Our experimental results for evaluating the performance of the proposed construction demonstrate the effectiveness of our approach.

Keywords: Event-driven Data Release · Blockchain · Smart Contract · Data Privacy

1 Introduction

Timed Data Release (TDR) is an essential mechanism for protecting sensitive data by ensuring its accessibility only after a specified time period. Numerous real-world applications benefit from TDR; for instance, in secure voting systems, ballots must remain confidential until the polling process is completed. In recent years, significant efforts have been dedicated to developing practical and decentralized TDR constructions, addressing various key aspects, including: (1)

© IFIP International Federation for Information Processing 2025
Published by Springer Nature Switzerland AG 2025
S. Katsikas and B. Shafiq (Eds.): DBSec 2025, LNCS 15722, pp. 176–195, 2025.
https://doi.org/10.1007/978-3-031-96590-6_10

safeguarding TDR against rational adversaries [11,12]; (2) leveraging reputation-based techniques to enhance resilience against attacks [19,21]; (3) augmenting TDR with controllable functionalities; and (4) ensuring reliability in TDR designs [22].

As a generalization of TDR, Event-driven Data Release (EDR) has emerged as a compelling paradigm. EDR allows the release of data based upon the occurrence of prescribed events. EDR is essential in various application scenarios. For example, in healthcare, patient records might be disclosed only upon verified requests from physicians, and in financial systems, funds could be released only after specific transaction conditions are satisfied.

Current approaches to constructing EDR often leverage blockchain technology to achieve decentralization. These approaches can be broadly categorized into three main directions: (1) The first direction, represented by works such as [7,13,24], aims at developing practical framework to enable event-driven execution on blockchain platforms. While such solutions effectively support event-driven paradigm, they fail to protect privacy. The second direction, exemplified by [8], focuses on protecting data privacy within EDR framework. However, while these approaches succeed in preserving privacy, they lack rigorous formal security analysis. The third direction emphasizes building provably secure EDR. For example, Madathil et al. [14] proposed *Oracle-based Conditional Payment (OCP)* , a system that facilitates privacy-preserving event-driven release of signature with formal security analysis. Despite its strong security guarantee, this approach is limited to a specific message space, such as signatures, thereby restricting its applicability to more general data message type. In light of these observations, we raise the following research question:

Is it possible to construct an efficient, privacy-preserving EDR for general message spaces on blockchains with formal security guarantees?

To this end, we propose P-EDR, a novel privacy-preserving event-driven data release framework offering formal privacy guarantees and implemented using smart contracts. Central to P-EDR is our proposed signature-based witness encryption scheme for general message space $m \in \{0,1\}^l$, coined as SGWE. This scheme enables encryption of messages with respect to target messages, such that decryption requires at least t valid signatures on the target message. We formally define the security of SGWE, provide an efficient construction, and prove its security under the Bilinear Diffie-Hellman assumption [3]. Building upon SGWE, we design P-EDR to support privacy-preserving event-driven data release by integrating SGWE with smart contracts. In this framework, a data sender selects a group of event publishers as candidates for event confirmation and encrypts a list of data messages $(m_j)_{j \in [k]}$ with respect to event messages $(\overline{m}_j)_{j \in [k]}$ using SGWE.Enc. A decentralized group of event publishers collaboratively confirm the occurrence of events. Upon noticing the occurrence of an event $\overline{m}$, the data receiver retrieves the event confirmation from the smart contract and decrypts the corresponding message using SGWE.Dec. The security of P-EDR naturally follows from that of SGWE.

We rigorously prove the security of SGWE. We implement both SGWE and P-EDR and conduct extensive evaluations. The results demonstrate that SGWE achieves high efficiency, while P-EDR incurs only a reasonable gas cost.

In summary, this paper makes the following key contributions:

- We propose SGWE, a signature-based witness encryption scheme for general message spaces, enabling data encryption corresponding to target messages.
- We introduce P-EDR, a privacy-preserving event-driven data release framework for general message spaces, constructed using smart contracts.
- We rigorously prove the security of SGWE and establish security result for P-EDR.
- We implement both SGWE and P-EDR and we demonstrate their efficiency through evaluations.

Roadmap. The paper is organized as follows. Section 2 provides an overview of PR-TDR. Section 3 introduces the preliminaries adopted in this paper. In Sect. 4, we formally define and construct SGWE. Section 5 presents the construction of P-EDR. In Sect. 6, we establish the security properties for both SGWE and P-EDR. Section 7 details the implementation and evaluation of PR-TDR. Section 8 reviews related work, and Sect. 9 concludes the paper.

2   P-EDR: An Overview

In this section, we provide an overview of our proposed P-EDR. We first sketch our proposed building block SGWE in Sect. 2.1. Then, we present the overview of P-EDR in Sect. 2.2.

2.1   SGWE: Signature-Based Witness Encryption for General Message Space

Let us consider a scenario where one wishes to encrypt a message $m \in \{0,1\}^l$ based on the occurrence of a referencing message $\overline{m}$. Decryption requires confirmation of the occurrence of $\overline{m}$. To address this requirement, SGWE provides a robust solution. At its core, SGWE leverages a group of n signers (*honest-majority*) who verify the occurrence of the referencing message $\overline{m}$ by submitting signatures on $\overline{m}$. Using SGWE, one can encrypt a list of data messages $(m_i)_{i \in [k]}$ corresponding to a list of referencing messages $(\overline{m}_j)_{j \in [k]}$ as follows: $c \leftarrow \mathsf{SGWE.Enc}((\overline{vk}_i)_{i \in [n]}, (m_j)_{j \in [k]}, (\overline{m}_j)_{j \in [k]})$ where $(\overline{vk}_i)_{i \in [n]}$ denotes the set of public signing keys held by the group of n signers.

To decrypt the j-th message m_j, the decryption process requires the ciphertext c, an aggregated signature σ_j on the reference message $\overline{m}_j$, a threshold set of signing public keys Q (at least t correct signing public keys), and the full set of public signing keys V. The decryption algorithm $\mathsf{SGWE.Dec}(j, c, \sigma_j, Q, V)$ will output m_j if the decryption conditions are satisfied. SGWE is a critical cryptographic building block of the P-EDR framework. A formal description of SGWE will be presented in Sect. 4.

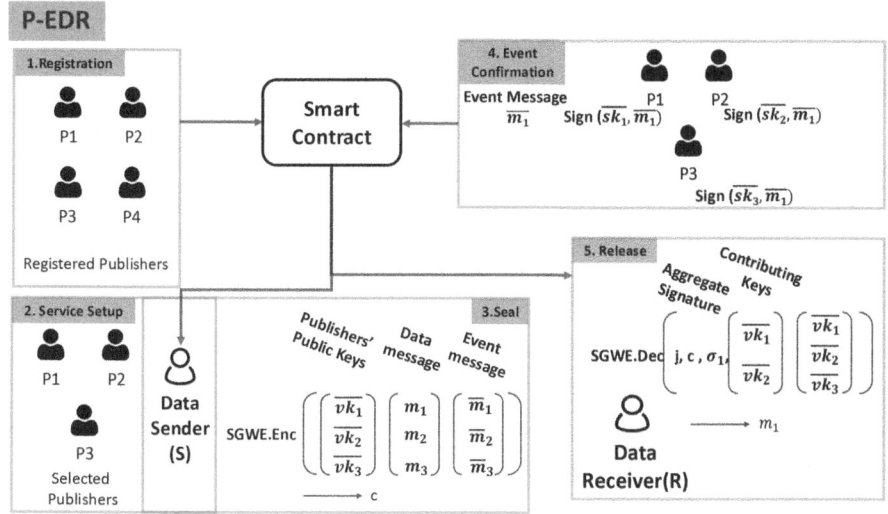

Fig. 1. P-EDR: Workflow

2.2 P-EDR: Workflow

P-EDR comprises the following key entities:

- *Data Sender*: The data sender S is responsible for preparing data, specifying the prescribed event messages, and identifying the data receiver. S encrypts the data with respect to the event messages and transmits it to the receiver.
- *Data Receiver*: The data receiver R stores the encrypted data sent by S and aims to decrypt the data after confirming that the corresponding event messages have occurred.
- *Event Publishers*: A decentralized set $\mathcal{P}$ of event publishers collaboratively confirms the occurrence of events.
- *Ethereum Blockchain*: Our framework utilizes the Ethereum blockchain to provide a smart contract service (denoted as $\mathcal{SC}$), which governs the event-driven data release process, particularly the event confirmation procedure.

P-EDR consists of five protocols: *Publisher Registration Protocol* ($\prod_{\text{reg}}$), *Service Setup Protocol* ($\prod_{\text{setup}}$), *Seal Protocol* ($\prod_{\text{seal}}$), *Event Confirmation Protocol* ($\prod_{\text{econf}}$), and *Release Protocol* ($\prod_{\text{release}}$). We use the example provided in Fig. 1 to illustrate the workflow.

At any point in time, any event publisher P_i can register with $\mathcal{SC}$ by invoking $\prod_{\text{reg}}$. Upon successful execution of $\prod_{\text{reg}}$, P_i's public signing key $\overline{vk_i}$ is published on $\mathcal{SC}$. Then, any data sender S wishing to initiate an event-driven data release service using P-EDR invokes $\prod_{\text{setup}}$ to select a group of event publishers, such as P_1, P_2, P_3, and specify the data receiver R. Following the setup, S prepares three distinct messages (m_1, m_2, m_3) and their corresponding event messages

$(\overline{m}_1, \overline{m}_2, \overline{m}_3)$. The confirmed occurrence of $\overline{m}_1$ enables decryption of m_1. To achieve this, S performs $\prod_{\text{seal}}$ to generate the ciphertext c by invoking:

$$c \leftarrow \text{SGWE.Enc}((\overline{vk}_1, \overline{vk}_2, \overline{vk}_3), (m_1, m_2, m_3), (\overline{m}_1, \overline{m}_2, \overline{m}_3)),$$

and transmits c to R. Suppose the event $\overline{m}_1$ occurs. The group of event publishers P_1, P_2, P_3 individually signs the event message $\overline{m}_1$ and submits their signatures to $\mathcal{SC}$. After verifying the signatures, $\mathcal{SC}$ aggregates them into a signature σ_1 for $\overline{m}_1$ and publishes it. These operations are governed by $\prod_{\text{econf}}$. Upon noticing the occurrence of $\overline{m}_1$, R consults $\mathcal{SC}$ to retrieve σ_1 and the set of verified publisher public keys $(\overline{vk}_1, \overline{vk}_2)$. Using these keys, R decrypts m_1 by invoking:

$$m_1 \leftarrow \text{SGWE.Dec}(1, c, \sigma_1, (\overline{vk}_1, \overline{vk}_2), (\overline{vk}_1, \overline{vk}_2, \overline{vk}_3)).$$

Here, we emphasize that event confirmation is achieved via signature verification. We assume that the event publishers operate under an honest-majority model [15]. The formal construction of P-EDR will be presented in Sect. 5.

3   Preliminaries

In this section, we present the key preliminaries adopted in our work.

3.1   Notations

We denote $r \leftarrow_\$ R$ to represent a value r chosen uniformly at random from a set R. The index set $[n]$ is defined as $\{1, \ldots, n\}$. The symbol $\subset$ denotes inclusion.

3.2   Bilinear Pairing

Definition 1 (Bilinear Pairing [3]). Let $\mathbb{G}_0$, $\mathbb{G}_1$, and $\mathbb{G}_T$ be three cyclic groups of prime order q, where $g_0 \in \mathbb{G}_0$ and $g_1 \in \mathbb{G}_1$ are generators. A **pairing** is an efficiently computable function $e : \mathbb{G}_0 \times \mathbb{G}_1 \rightarrow \mathbb{G}_T$ satisfying the following properties:

- **Bilinear:** For all $u, u' \in \mathbb{G}_0$ and $v, v' \in \mathbb{G}_1$, we have:

$$e(u \cdot u', v) = e(u, v) \cdot e(u', v), \quad \text{and} \quad e(u, v \cdot v') = e(u, v) \cdot e(u, v').$$

- **Non-degenerate:** $g_T := e(g_0, g_1)$ is a generator of $\mathbb{G}_T$.

3.3   Bilinear Diffie-Hellman Assumption

Definition 2 (Decisional Bilinear Diffie-Hellman [3]). Given the group settings $(\mathbb{G}_0, \mathbb{G}_1, \mathbb{G}_T)$ of prime order p, the Bilinear Diffie-Hellman (BDH) assumption states that no polynomial-time adversary can distinguish between the following two distributions:

$$(g_0, g_0^x, g_0^r, g_1, g_1^x, g_1^\alpha, g_T^{xr\alpha}) \quad \text{and} \quad (g_0, g_0^x, g_0^r, g_1, g_1^x, g_1^\alpha, g_T^y),$$

where $x, r, \alpha, y \leftarrow_\$ \mathbb{Z}_p$.

3.4   Shamir's Secret Sharing and Lagrange Interpolation

Shamir's Secret Sharing. The (t,n) secret sharing scheme proposed by Shamir [15] enables a secret s to be distributed among n participants such that any t or fewer shares reveal no information about s. To reconstruct the secret, at least t valid shares are required. This scheme generates shares $(s_1, s_2, \ldots, s_n)$ using a polynomial $f(x) \in \mathbb{F}[X]$ of degree at most $t - 1$, where $f(0) = s$ and $f(i) = s_i$ for $i \in [n]$.

Lagrange Interpolation. The reconstruction of the secret in Shamir's scheme relies on Lagrange interpolation. Given a set of supporting points $(\chi_1, y_1), \ldots, (\chi_k, y_k)$ over a finite field $\mathbb{Z}_p$ (where p is prime), the Lagrange basis polynomials are defined as:

$$L_i(x) = \prod_{j \in [k], j \neq i} \frac{x - \chi_j}{\chi_i - \chi_j}.$$

These polynomials satisfy $L_i(\chi_j) = 1$ if $i = j$ and $L_i(\chi_j) = 0$ otherwise. Using these, the interpolating polynomial is:

$$f(x) = \sum_{i \in [k]} L_i(x) y_i.$$

This polynomial has a degree at most $k - 1$ and passes through all given points.

3.5   Aggregatable Multi-signatures

An Aggregatable Multi-Signature scheme enables multiple signers to independently sign distinct messages, after which their signatures can be efficiently aggregated into a single compact signature. This aggregated signature can then be verified collectively against the corresponding set of messages and public keys. We will adopt the definition in [5] as follow:

Definition 3 (Aggregatable Multi-signatures). An aggregatable multi-signature scheme $\mathsf{Sig} = (\mathsf{KeyGen}, \mathsf{Sign}, \mathsf{Vrfy}, \mathsf{Agg}, \mathsf{AggVrfy}, \mathsf{Prove}, \mathsf{Valid})$ consists of seven algorithms defined as follows:

- $(\overline{vk}, \overline{sk}) \leftarrow \mathsf{KeyGen}(1^\lambda)$. This algorithm takes as input a security parameter λ and generates a key pair $(\overline{vk}, \overline{sk})$, where $\overline{vk}$ is the verification key and $\overline{sk}$ is the signing key.
- $\sigma \leftarrow \mathsf{Sign}(\overline{sk}, \overline{m})$. Given a signing key $\overline{sk}$ and a message $\overline{m}$, this algorithm produces a digital signature σ.
- $b \leftarrow \mathsf{Vrfy}(\overline{vk}, \overline{m}, \sigma)$. This algorithm verifies whether a given signature σ is valid for the message $\overline{m}$ under the verification key $\overline{vk}$, outputting a Boolean value b.
- $\sigma \leftarrow \mathsf{Agg}((\sigma_1, \ldots, \sigma_k), (\overline{vk}_1, \ldots, \overline{vk}_k))$. The aggregation algorithm takes a set of signatures $(\sigma_1, \ldots, \sigma_k)$ and the corresponding verification keys $(\overline{vk}_1, \ldots, \overline{vk}_k)$, producing a single aggregated signature σ.

– $b \leftarrow \mathsf{AggVrfy}(\sigma, (\overline{vk}_1, \ldots, \overline{vk}_k), (\overline{m}_1, \ldots, \overline{m}_k))$. This algorithm verifies an aggregated signature σ given a set of verification keys $(\overline{vk}_1, \ldots, \overline{vk}_k)$ and messages $(\overline{m}_1, \ldots, \overline{m}_k)$, returning a Boolean value b. If applied to a single signature, it behaves identically to Vrfy.

– $\pi \leftarrow \mathsf{Prove}(\overline{vk}, \overline{sk})$. Given a key pair $(\overline{vk}, \overline{sk})$, this algorithm generates a proof π using a hash function oracle H.

– $b \leftarrow \mathsf{Valid}(\overline{vk}, \pi)$. The validity-checking algorithm takes a verification key $\overline{vk}$ and a proof π, verifying its correctness using a hash function oracle H, and returns a Boolean value b.

For correctness, the scheme must satisfy both correctness and unforgeability properties. Furthermore, the algorithms Prove and Valid must form a zero-knowledge proof of knowledge for the relation $\mathcal{K} = \{(\overline{vk}, \overline{sk}) \mid \exists r \text{ such that } (\overline{vk}, \overline{sk}) \leftarrow \mathsf{KeyGen}(1^\lambda >; r)\}$.

In this paper, we instantiate the aggregatable multi-signature scheme by [5], satisfying the required properties mentioned above.

3.6   Blockchains

In our framework, we use *Ethereum* [23] as the underlying blockchain platform. Ethereum incorporates the concept of smart contracts [17], which are self-executing programs deployed and maintained on the Ethereum blockchain. Interacting with these smart contracts involves invoking functions, which incur a computational cost referred to as *gas* [4]. This gas cost is measured in Ether, Ethereum's native cryptocurrency [4].

4   SGWE: Signature-Based Witness Encryption for General Message Space

In this section, we formally introduce our proposed SGWE scheme. SGWE allows encryption of a list of k data messages $(m_j)_{j \in [k]}$ with respect to corresponding reference messages $(\overline{m}_j)_{j \in [k]}$, ensuring that each message m_j can only be decrypted if at least t valid signatures on the associated reference message $\overline{m}_j$ are provided. We begin by providing the formal definitions, followed by the security model that captures the desired security guarantees. Finally, we present the construction of SGWE.

4.1   Formal Definition

We now formally define our signature-based witness encryption scheme for a general message space $m \in \{0, 1\}^l$.

Definition 4. The proposed SGWE scheme consists of the following two algorithms:

- $c \leftarrow$ SGWE.Enc$((\overline{vk}_i)_{i \in [n]}, (\overline{m}_j)_{j \in [k]}, (m_j)_{j \in [k]})$. This algorithm takes as input a set of verification keys $(\overline{vk}_i)_{i \in [n]}$, a set of reference messages $(\overline{m}_j)_{j \in [k]}$, and the corresponding plaintext messages $(m_j)_{j \in [k]}$. It outputs a ciphertext c.
- $m \leftarrow$ SGWE.Dec(j, c, σ_j, Q, V). This algorithm takes as input a message index $j \in [k]$, a ciphertext c, an aggregate signature σ_j on $\overline{m}_j$, and two sets of verification keys, Q and V, corresponding to the aggregate signature scheme Sig. Here, Q represents the qualified subset of verification keys among V. The algorithm outputs the plaintext message m_j.

4.2 Security Model

We formally define the notion of correctness of SGWE below.

Definition 5. (Correctness) A t-out-of-n SGWE $=$ (Enc, Dec) is **correct** if, for all $\lambda \in \mathbb{N}$ and $k = \text{poly}(\lambda)$ no problablistic polynomial-time (PPT) adversary $\mathcal{A}$ can win the following experiment with more than negligible probability:

Correctness Expreiment - ExpCor

1. The Adversary $\mathcal{A}$ outputs the following items:
   - A message index id where id $\in [k]$.
   - A set V of verification keys regarding Sig, where $V = (\overline{vk}_1, ..., \overline{vk}_n)$.
   - A subset $Q \subset V$ of verification keys where $|Q| \geq t$.
   - Two lists of messages $(\overline{m}_i)_{i \in [k]}$ and $(m_i)_{i \in [k]}$.
   - An aggregate signature σ_{id} on reference message $\overline{m}_{id}$.
2. We say that $\mathcal{A}$ wins in this experiment if and only if both of the following conditions hold:

$$\text{Sig.AggVrfy}(\sigma_{id}, Q, (\overline{m}_{id})_{i \in |Q|}) = 1$$

$$\text{SGWE.Dec}(\text{id}, \text{SGWE.Enc}(V, (\overline{m}_i)_{i \in [k]}, (m_i)_{i \in [k]}), \ \sigma_{id}, Q, V) \neq m_{id}$$

We next formally define the security of SGWE. The security definition ensures that an adversary can obtain at most $n - t + 1$ keys but cannot query signatures on a reference message $\overline{m}_j$ corresponding to the selected index j that is being decrypted. Intuitively,

Definition 6. (Security) A (t, n)–SGWE based on the aggregate signature scheme Sig:=(KeyGen, Sign, Vrfy, Agg, AggVrfy, Prove, Valid) is **secure** if, for any $\lambda \in \mathbb{N}$ such that $t = poly(\lambda)$, and for any $k = poly(\lambda)$, subsets of messages $CM \subset [k]$, no probabilistic polynomial time (PPT) adversary $\mathcal{A}$ can achieve a non-negligible advantage in the following security experiment:

Security Expreiment - ExpSec

Setup

-   We assume that the hash function H is available to both the experiment and the adversary $\mathcal{A}$.
-   The experiment generates $(n-t+1)$ verification key pairs $(\overline{vk}_i, \overline{sk}_i) \leftarrow$ Sig.KeyGen(1^λ) and computes proof $\pi_i \leftarrow$ Sig.Prove$^H(\overline{vk}_i, \overline{sk}_i)$ for all $i \in \{t, ..., n\}$. The experiment then gives all (vk_i, π_i) to $\mathcal{A}$.
-   $\mathcal{A}$ provides the experiment with a set $VA = (\overline{vk}_1, ..., \overline{vk}_{t-1})$ of verification keys and a set $\Pi = (\pi_1, ..., \pi_{t-1})$ of corresponding proofs. If Sig.Valid$(\overline{vk}_i, \pi_i) = 0$ for any $i \in \{1, ..., t-1\}$, the experiment aborts. Otherwise, the experiment defines $V = (\overline{vk}_1, ..., \overline{vk}_n)$.

Phase-1 Query:

-   $\mathcal{A}$ makes signing query on reference message $\overline{m}$ corresponding to i-th verification key, denoted as $(i, \overline{m})$. If $i < t$, the experiment aborts. Otherwise, the experiment gets $\sigma_i \leftarrow$ Sig.Sign$(\overline{m}, sk_i)$ and returns it to $\mathcal{A}$.

Challenge:

-   $\mathcal{A}$ prepares challenge messages m_i^0, m_i^1 for $i \in CM$, messages $(m_i)_{i \in [k] \setminus CM}$, a list of reference messages $(\overline{m}_i)_{i \in [k]}$. If the signaure on any $\overline{m}_i$ for $i \in CM$ was queried before, the experiment aborts.
-   The experiment flips a coin $b \leftarrow_\$ \{0, 1\}$ and sets $m_i = m_i^b$ for all $i \in CM$. Then, $\mathcal{C}$ performs encryption $c \leftarrow$ SGWE.Enc$(V, (\overline{m}_i)_{i \in [k]}, (m_i)_{i \in [k]})$ and sends c to $\mathcal{A}$.

Phase-2 Query:

-   $\mathcal{A}$ can continue making signing queries on $(i, \overline{m})$ as long as $i \geq t$ and $\overline{m} \neq \overline{m}_i$ for all $i \in CM$.

Guess:

-   $\mathcal{A}$ outputs his guess b' on b

If $b' = b$, the experiment outputs 1, else outputs 0.

We then define $\mathcal{A}$'s advantage in the above experiment as:

$$\mathsf{Adv}^{\mathcal{A}}_{\mathsf{ExpSec}} = \left| \Pr[\mathsf{ExpSec}(\mathcal{A}, \lambda) = 1] - \frac{1}{2} \right|$$

4.3   SGWE: Construction

We now describe the construction of SGWE. In our scheme, each message $m_j \in \{0, 1\}^l$ for all $j \in [k]$, and the reference messages $\overline{m}_j \neq \overline{m}_{j'}$ for all $j, j' \in$

$[k], j = j'$. Our construction utilizes three hash functions: $H_0 : \{0,1\}^* \to \mathbb{G}_0$, $H_1 : \mathbb{G}_T \to \{0,1\}^\lambda$ and $H_2 : \{0,1\}^* \to \mathbb{Z}_p$.

SGWE.Enc$((\overline{vk}_i)_{i\in[n]}, (\overline{m}_j)_{j\in[k]}, (m_j)_{j\in[k]})$:

Sample $r \leftarrow_{\$} \mathbb{Z}_q$.

The following steps apply for each $j \in [k]$:

- Sample $b_{ji} \leftarrow_{\$} \mathbb{Z}_q$ for all $i \in \{0\} \cup [t-1]$
- Construct the polynomial $f_j(x) = \sum_{i=0}^{t-1} b_{ji}x^i$, ensuring that $f_j(0) = b_{j0}$
- Derive n different shares as follows: for $i \in [n]$, compute $\xi_i = H_2(\overline{vk}_i)$, and set $s_{ji} = f_j(\xi_i)$.
- Compute $c_{j1} = g_1^r$
- Compute $\alpha_j = g_T^{b_{j0}}$ and $h_j = H_1(\alpha_j)$
- Compute $c_{j2} = (e(H_0(\overline{m}_j), \overline{vk}_i)^r \cdot g_T^{s_{ji}})_{i\in[n]}$
- Compute $c_{j3} = h_j \oplus m_j$
- Compute the ciphertext $c_j = (c_{j1}, c_{j2}, c_{j3})$

Return $c = (c_j)_{j\in[k]}$.

SGWE.Dec(j, c, σ_j, Q, V): The decryption algorithm works as follows:

- Parse $c_j := (c_{j1}, c_{j2}, c_{j3})$
- Parse $V = (vk_1, ..., vk_n)$
- Parse Q as any subset of V of size at least t. Here, we denote I as the index sets for Q, where each $j' \in I$, $vk_{j'} \in Q$, and $|I| = t$.
- Compute $\xi_{j'} = H_2(vk_{j'})$ where $j' \in I$
- Derive Lagrange Coefficiencies as follows:

$$L_{j'} = \prod_{i\in I, i\neq j'} \frac{-\xi_i}{\xi_{j'} - \xi_i} \quad \text{for all } i \in I$$

- Compute

$$d = \frac{\prod_{j'\in I}(c_{j2_{j'}})^{L_{j'}}}{e(\sigma_j, c_{j1})} = g_T^{\sum L_{j'}s_{j'}} = g_T^{b_{j0}}$$

- Compute $h'_j = H_1(d)$.
- Recover the message: $m_j = h'_j \oplus c_{j3}$, and return m_j.

5 P-EDR: Privacy-Preserving Event-Driven Data Release Using Smart Contract

In this section, grounded on our proposed SGWE, we introduce our construction of P-EDR. P-EDR carefully integrates SGWE with smart contracts. Specifically, it allows a data sender to recruit a decentralized group of event publishers (*honest-majority*) responsible for validating event messages. The core component of P-EDR is our proposed event confirmation protocol, in which the event publishers collaboratively verify the occurrence of an event message assisted by the smart contract. In the following, we formally describe the detailed protocol.

5.1   P-EDR: Construction

P-EDR consists of five protocols: *Publisher Registration Protocol* ($\prod_{\text{reg}}$), *Service Setup Protocol* ($\prod_{\text{setup}}$), *Seal Protocol* ($\prod_{\text{seal}}$), *Event Confirmation Protocol* ($\prod_{\text{econf}}$), and *Release Protocol* ($\prod_{\text{release}}$). Details are as follows:

Event Publisher Registration Protocol $\prod_{\text{reg}}$: Each interested event publisher P_i registers with the smart contract $\mathcal{SC}$:

- Each event publisher P_i submits their public key $\overline{vk}_i$, proof π_i of key validity, and a deposit d to the smart contract $\mathcal{SC}$.
- $\mathcal{SC}$ verifies the validity of the key $\overline{vk}_i$ using $\mathsf{Sig.Valid}(\overline{vk}_i, \pi_i)$.
- If the verification passes, $\overline{vk}_i$ is added to the set V of registered public keys.
- If the verification fails, we skip the registration.

Service Setup Protocol $\prod_{\text{setup}}$: The sender S initiates the setup phase.

- The sender S registers the task id id and the associated reward r for the event publishers. Also, S specifies total number n of publishers needed and the receiver R.
- S attaches a signature σ_S to the message (id, r, n, R) using its private signing key, and S publishes the message to $\mathcal{SC}$.
- Upon receiving the message from S, $\mathcal{SC}$ does the following: (1) randomly select n publishers $\mathcal{P}_{\text{selected}} \subseteq \mathcal{P}$; (2) send $(\text{setup\_proposal}, id, n, r, \mathcal{P}_{\text{selected}})$ to the receiver R for approval. Upon receiving $(\text{accept\_setup}, id)$ from R: $\mathcal{SC}$ publishes $(\text{setup\_complete}, id, \mathcal{P}_{\text{selected}}, r)$. If no agreement is received within a timeout, $\mathcal{SC}$ outputs $(\text{setup\_rejected}, id)$

Seal Protocol $\prod_{\text{seal}}$: The seal protocol allows the data sender S to encrypt k different messages $(m_j)_{j \in [k]}$ with respect to k different event messages $(\overline{m}_j)_{j \in [k]}$. Details are as follows:

- The sender S queries the smart contract $\mathcal{SC}$ to retrieve the set of registered public keys V from the selected event publishers
- The sender encrypts the data $(\overline{m}_j)_{j \in [k]}$ with respect to $(\overline{m}_j)_{j \in [k]}$ by using our proposed SGWE scheme: $c \leftarrow \mathsf{SGWE.Enc}(1^\lambda, V, (\overline{m}_j)_{j \in [k]}, (m_j)_{j \in [k]})$.
- S then sends c to R.

Event Confirmation Protocol $\prod_{\text{econf}}$: The event confirmation phase confirms the occurrence of event $\overline{m}$ by verifying signatures. Details are as follows:

- Each event publisher signer P_i computes a signature σ_i on the event message $\overline{m}$ using their private signing key $\overline{sk}_i$:

$$\sigma_i \leftarrow \mathsf{Sig.Sign}(\overline{sk}_i, \overline{m}).$$

- The event signature signature σ_i is submitted to the smart contract $\mathcal{SC}$.

- $\mathcal{SC}$ verifies the signatures using:

$$\mathsf{Sig.Verify}(\overline{vk}_i, \overline{m}, \sigma_i).$$

- If the verification fails, $\mathcal{SC}$ will penalize P_i's deposit d.
- Once at least t valid signatures are collected, $\mathcal{SC}$ aggregates them into:

$$\mathsf{AggSig} \leftarrow \mathsf{Sig.Agg}((\sigma_i)_{i \in S}, (\overline{vk}_i)_{i \in S}),$$

where S is the set of event publishers who provided valid signatures.
- $\mathcal{SC}$ records the event $\overline{m}$ along with the aggregated signature AggSig and the corresponding public signing keys.
- $\mathcal{SC}$ publishes $(\overline{m}, \mathsf{AggSig}, S)$.

Release Protocol $\prod_{\mathbf{release}}$: If the data receiver R notices event $\overline{m_j}$ has occurred, R will consult $\mathcal{SC}$ for conformation of $\overline{m}_j$ and then perform decryption. Details are as follows:

- On noticing the occurrence of the event, the receiver R queries the smart contract $\mathcal{SC}$ to verify the occurrence of event $\overline{m}_j$. If $\mathcal{SC}$ returns $\bot$, R will continue waiting. Otherwise, if $\mathcal{SC}$ returns (AggSig, S), R will do the following procedures to release the data:
- Use the aggregated signature AggSig and public keys S to run the decryption algorithm:

$$m_j \leftarrow \mathsf{SGWE.Dec}(j, c, \mathsf{AggSig}, S, V).$$

- Output m_j.

6   Security Analysis

6.1   SGWE: Security Proof

Theorem 1. (Correctness) SGWE satisfies correctness provided that the hash function H_2 is collision-resistant.

Proof. See Appendix 1.

Theorem 2. (Security) Assuming that H_0, H_1, and H_2 are modeled as random oracles, SGWE is secure under the Decisional Bilinear Diffie-Hellman (DBDH) assumption in $(\mathbb{G}_0, \mathbb{G}_1)$.

Proof. See Appendix 2.

6.2   P-EDR: Security Analysis

Building upon the security guarantees of SGWE and the assumption that event publishers follow an *honest-majority* model, we establish the following security properties for P-EDR.

Theorem 3. P-EDR satisfies correctness, provided that SGWE is correct.

Theorem 4. P-EDR preserves privacy, assuming the security of SGWE.

7   Evaluations

In this section, we present the implementation and performance evaluation of PR-TDR.

7.1   Implementation

We implemented SGWE in Rust [6] and utilized arc_bls12_381 [1] for operations over the BLS12-381 curve. Additionally, we implemented the modified aggregate signature scheme proposed by [5]. For P-EDR, we developed the five protocols in *Solidity* [18] and deployed the smart contract in a local Ethereum testing environment provided by Ganache [16]. All experiments were conducted on a MacBook Pro.

7.2   SGWE Performance Evaluations

We evaluated the running time of SGWE.Enc and SGWE.Dec across four (t, n) configurations, maintaining a ratio of $\frac{t}{n}, = \frac{2}{3}$, namely an honest-supermajority setting: $(6, 9)$, $(12, 18)$, $(16, 24)$, and $(24, 36)$. The encryption time results for SGWE.Enc are presented in Fig. 2a. From Fig. 2a, it can be observed that the running time of SGWE.Enc increases as n grows. This behavior aligns with our design principle, where shares are prepared for each $\overline{vk}_i$, $i \in [n]$. The decryption time results for SGWE.Dec are shown in Fig. 2b. We observe that the decryption time also increases as t grows. This is attributed to the construction of SGWE, which requires at least t valid signatures to successfully perform decryption.

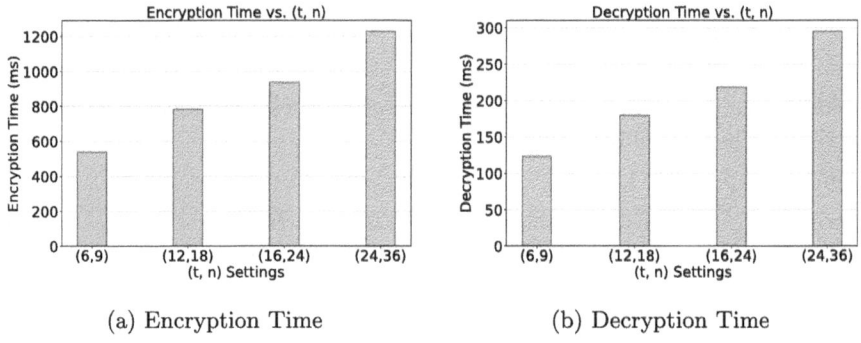

(a) Encryption Time   (b) Decryption Time

Fig. 2. Encryption Time and Decryption Time of SGWE

7.3   P-EDR Performance Evaluations

In this section, we evaluate the performance of the event confirmation protocol Π_{econf} in terms of gas cost. The gas cost analysis is conducted under four different threshold settings, with the results presented in Fig. 3. From the figure, it is evident that the gas cost increases as t grows. This is attributed to the design of our protocol, where the smart contract must verify at least t signatures to confirm an event message.

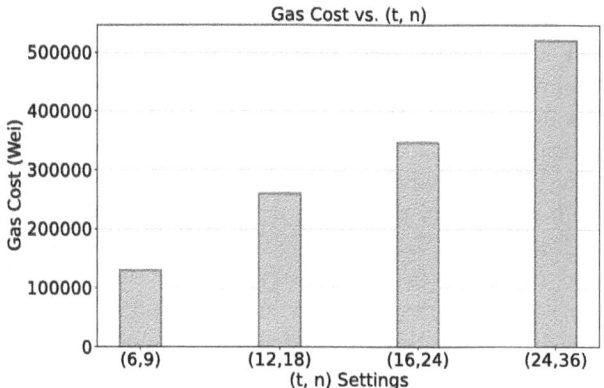

Fig. 3. Event Confirmation Gas Cost

8   Related Work

8.1   Timed Data Release

A significant body of research has been dedicated to developing distributed and decentralized solutions for Timed Data Release (TDR) that ensure data privacy until a designated release time [2,9–12,19–21]. Foundational work by Li et al. [9,10] introduced attack-resilience analysis and assessed the security properties of TDR mechanisms. Subsequent research by Li et al. [11,12] and Bacis et al. [2] integrated game theory with smart contracts to mitigate threats posed by rational adversaries in decentralized TDR environments.

To address vulnerabilities from both rational and malicious adversaries, Wang et al. [19,21] designed a reputation-aware TDR framework implemented on the Ethereum blockchain. Building on this, Wang et al. [20] later introduced controllable primitives to enhance the flexibility of TDR systems. More recently, PR-TDR [22] has provided an efficient, privacy-preserving, and formally secure TDR solution, ensuring reliable data release.

Despite these advancements, current TDR frameworks are limited in their ability to systematically support privacy-preserving, event-driven data release. In this paper, we propose P-EDR, a rigorous design that extends TDR capabilities to enable secure and privacy-preserving event-driven data release.

8.2   Event-Driven Execution Models on Blockchain

Event-driven execution on blockchains has attracted growing interest in recent years. EventWarden [13] introduces an event-driven proxy service over Ethereum-like blockchains, allowing users to outsource transaction execution. Kaleem et al. [7] propose an event-driven smart contract platform that addresses scalability and performance issues in blockchain ecosystems. Zhao et al. [24] introduce SigVM, a blockchain virtual machine designed to support event-driven programming, enhancing automation and flexibility.

While these solutions advance event-driven execution, they do not adequately address data privacy concerns. To fill this gap, Karanjai et al. [8] developed a privacy-preserving event-based transaction system using Zero-Knowledge Proofs (ZKPs). Although effective in protecting data confidentiality, this system lacks formal security guarantees. Madathil et al. [14] introduced Oracle-based Conditional Payment (OCP), a privacy-preserving event-driven payment protocol with formal security guarantees. However, OCP is limited to processing data in the form of signatures, restricting its applicability to more general data formats.

In contrast, the proposed P-EDR framework supports general data formats, ensuring privacy while providing formal security guarantees. This expands the applicability of privacy-preserving, event-driven blockchain systems, overcoming the limitations of prior work.

9   Conclusion

In this paper, we present P-EDR, a systematic framework for privacy-preserving event-driven data release for general message spaces using smart contracts. P-EDR enables secure event-driven data release while ensuring provable privacy guarantees. To achieve this, we first introduce SGWE, a signature-based witness encryption scheme designed for general message space $m \in \{0,1\}^l$. Leveraging SGWE, we carefully design P-EDR, which consists of five core protocols implemented via smart contracts. We formally define the desired security properties of SGWE and provide rigorous proofs of its security. Additionally, we implement SGWE and demonstrate its efficiency. P-EDR is implemented on Ethereum, and our performance evaluations confirm that P-EDR achieves gas efficiency.

Acknowledgement. This material is based upon work supported by the National Science Foundation under Grant #2020071. Any opinions, findings, and conclusions or recommendations expressed in this material are those of the authors and do not necessarily reflect the views of the National Science Foundation.

Appendix 1: Proof of Theorem 1

Proof. To prove this, we provide a sequence of hybrids:

<u>Hybrid$_0$</u>: This is the correctness experiment defined in ExpCor.

Hybrid_1: This hybrid is the same as Hybrid_0, except that in the lagrange coefficients derivation step if $H_2(\overline{vk}_i) = H_2(\overline{vk}_j)$ for $i \neq j$, the hybrid aborts. By the collision-resistant property of H_2, the probability that $\mathcal{A}$ can distinguish Hybrid_1 from Hybrid_0 is negligible. Thus, the output of executing Hybrid_1 with $\mathcal{A}$ is computationally indistinguishable from Hybrid_0, and the adversary's advantage in Hybrid_0 is the same as in Hybrid_1, except with negligible probability.

Next, it remains to show that $\mathcal{A}$'s successful probability in Hybrid_1 as defined is 0. Now, we assume that the adversary $\mathcal{A}$ outputs the following items: (1)A message index id where $\mathsf{id} \in [k]$; (2) A set V of verification keys regarding Sig, where $V = (\overline{vk}_1, ..., \overline{vk}_n)$; (3) A qualified subset $Q \subset V$ of verification keys where $|Q| \geq t$; (4) A list of reference messages $(\overline{m}_i)_{i \in [k]}$ and messages $(m_i)_{i \in [k]}$;(5) An aggregated signature σ_{id} on reference message $\overline{m}_{\mathsf{id}}$. As defined in our construction, here we let I denote the index set for which we have $j' \in I$ for $\overline{vk}_{j'} \in Q$. To win in Hybrid_1, we must have

$$\mathsf{Sig.AggVrfy}(\sigma_{\mathsf{id}}, Q, (\overline{m}_{\mathsf{id}})_{i \in |Q|}) = 1$$

which gives us

$$e(\sigma, g_1) = \prod_{j'=1}^{I} e(H_0(\overline{m}_{\mathsf{id}}), vk_{j'})^{L_{j'}} \quad \text{where } vk_{j'} = g_1^{x_{j'}} \text{ for } x_{j'} \in \mathbb{Z}_q$$

Given the above, we should show that

$$\mathsf{SGWE.Dec}(\mathsf{id}, \mathsf{SGWE.Enc}(V, (\overline{m}_i)_{i \in [k]}, (m_i)_{i \in [k]}), \sigma_{\mathsf{id}}, Q, V) = m_{\mathsf{id}}$$

Based on our construction, $\mathsf{SGWE.Enc}(V, (\overline{m}_i)_{i \in [k]}, (m_i)_{i \in [k]})$ yields a set of cipertext $c = (c_j)_{j \in [k]}$. Specifically, we have $c_j = (c_{j1}, c_{j2}, c_{j3})$ where

$$c_{j1} = g_1^r, \quad c_{j2} = (e(H_0(\overline{m}_j), \overline{vk}_i)^r \cdot g_T^{s_{ji}})_{i \in [n]}, \quad c_{j3} = h_j \oplus m_j$$

Here, $s_{ji} = f_j(\xi_i)$ where f_j is the polynomial that corresponds to j-th message $\overline{m}_j$ such that $f_j(0) = b_{j0}$. It is worth noting that $\xi_i = H_2(\overline{vk}_i)$ and $\overline{vk}_i \neq \overline{vk}_{i'}$ for any $vk_i, vk_{i'} \in V$, and due to the collision resistance of H_2, we have $\xi_i \neq \xi_{i'}$ for $i \neq i'$. Then, focusing on the message index id, we have the decryption as follows

$$d_{\mathsf{id}} = \frac{\prod_{j' \in I} (c_{\mathsf{id}2_{j'}})^{L_{j'}}}{e(\sigma_{\mathsf{id}}, c_{\mathsf{id}1})} = \frac{\prod_{j' \in I} (e(H_0(\overline{m}_{\mathsf{id}}), \overline{vk}_{j'})^{r \cdot L_{j'}} \cdot g_T^{s_{\mathsf{id}j'} \cdot L_{j'}})}{e(\sigma_{\mathsf{id}}, g_1)^r} = g_T^{\sum_{j' \in I} L_{j'} s_{\mathsf{id}j'}}$$

$$= g_T^{b_{\mathsf{id}0}}$$

The last step in the above equation holds since $|I| \geq t$ and $s_{\mathsf{id}i} \neq s_{\mathsf{id}i'}$, the lagrange interpolation $\sum L_{j'} s_{\mathsf{id}j'}$ will correctly reconstruct $f_{\mathsf{id}}(0) = b_{\mathsf{id}0} = \sum_{j' \in I} L_{j'} s_{\mathsf{id}j'}$. Thus, $d_{\mathsf{id}} = g_T^{b_{\mathsf{id}0}}$ is correctly computed. Next, we have $h'_{\mathsf{id}} = H_1(d_{\mathsf{id}})$. Finally, performing $h'_{\mathsf{id}} \oplus c_{\mathsf{id}3} = m_{\mathsf{id}}$. This completes the proof for correctness.

Appendix 2: Proof of Theorem 2

Proof. We prove it by using contradiction. Assume that $\mathcal{A}$ is a PPT adversary that can break SGWE with ϵ advantage. Our task is to construct a PPT distinguisher $\mathcal{D}$ to solve BDH problem with ϵ advantage.

Information Available to $\mathcal{D}$: In our security reduction, $\mathcal{D}$ will receive problem instances of BDH. We denote tuple $(g_0, g_0^x, g_0^\alpha, g_1, g_1^x, g_1^r, g_T^{x\alpha r})$ as a BDH tuple and $(g_0, g_0^x, g_0^\alpha, g_1, g_1^x, g_1^r, g_T^y)$ as a random tuple.

Given that VA is the set of verification keys provided by $\mathcal{A}$, we denote $I = [t-1]$ as the index set of verification keys $\overline{vk}_i$ selected by $\mathcal{A}$. Here, $\overline{vk}_i = g_1^{x_i}$ and $\overline{sk}_i = x_i$ for all $i \in I$. Due to the extractable proof of knowledge property of Sig, D has access to the secret signing key $x_i, \forall i \in I$. Similarly, we denote $\overline{I} = \{t, ..., n\}$ as the index set of honest parties' verification key $\overline{vk}_i$ where $i \in \overline{I}$.

Auxiliary Information: We provide several key terms calculation here:

- Randomly sample $\xi_i \leftarrow_\$ \mathbb{Z}_q$ for all $i \in [n]$.
- For $i \in \overline{I}$, we draw $x_i' \leftarrow_\$ \mathbb{Z}_q$
- Define a polynomial $L'(x) = \prod_{j \in I} \frac{x - \xi_j}{-\xi_j}$
- The reduction sets $(H_0, \tau_0) \leftarrow S(0, 1^\lambda)$. Sets a counter $\mathsf{ctr} = 1$.

Next, we detail how to simulate the verification keys $\overline{vk}_i$ for $i \in \overline{I}$, random-oracle queries H_0, H_1 and H_2, signature queries for $\overline{m}$ such that $\overline{m} \neq \overline{m}_i$, $i \in CM$, and the ciphertext c.

Verification Keys: We simulate $\overline{vk}_i$ for $i \in \overline{I}$ as :

$$\overline{vk}_i = (g_1^x)^{L'(\xi_i)} \cdot g_1^{x_i'} = g_1^{L'(\xi_i)x + x_i'} = g_1^{\tilde{x}_i}$$

Here, $x_i' \leftarrow_R \mathbb{Z}_p$. Due to x_i' being randomly distributed in $\mathbb{Z}_p$, $L'(\xi_i)x + x_i'$ is also.

Hash Query: Before moving to the detail, we first show the simulation for random oracles $\mathcal{D}$ initializes three empty list $\mathcal{L}_0$, $\mathcal{L}_1$, and $\mathcal{L}_2$.

- $H_0 : \{0,1\}^* \to \mathbb{G}_0$, every query to H_0 for target reference message $\overline{m}$ such that $\overline{m} \neq \overline{m}_i$ where $i \in CM$ will be answered as follows: If $\overline{m}$ has ever been queries, then retrieves $(\overline{m}, \alpha_{\overline{m}})$ from $\mathcal{L}_0$. If not, $\mathcal{D}$ chooses $\alpha_{\overline{m}} \leftarrow_\$ \mathbb{Z}_q$, and add $(\overline{m}, \alpha_{\overline{m}})$ to $\mathcal{L}_0$. $\mathcal{D}$ outputs $g_0^{\alpha_{\overline{m}}}$.
- $H_1 : \mathbb{G}_T \to \{0,1\}^\lambda$: Let the incoming query be α, if $\mathcal{L}_1$ has an entry (α, h_α) for α, then return h_α. Otherwise, randomly sample $h_\alpha \leftarrow_\$ \{0,1\}^\lambda$ and add h_α to $\mathcal{L}_1$ and return h_α.
- $H_2 : \{0,1\}^* \to \mathbb{Z}_q$: Assume we initially add $(\overline{vk}_i, \xi_i)$ where $i \in [n]$ to $\mathcal{L}_2$. If the incomming query $\overline{vk}_{i'}$ has already been an entry in $\mathcal{L}_2$, retrieve $(\overline{vk}_{i'}, \xi_{i'})$ and return $\xi_{i'}$. Otherwise, choose $\xi_{i'} \leftarrow_\$ \mathbb{Z}_q$, and return $\xi_{i'}$ and add $(\overline{vk}_i', \xi_{i'})$ to $\mathcal{L}_2$.

Signature Query: Signature on $\overline{m}$ where $\overline{m} \neq \overline{m}_i$ for $i \in CM$.

$$\sigma = ((g_0^x)^{L'(\xi_i)} \cdot g_0^{x_i'})^{\alpha \overline{m}} = g_0^{\tilde{x}_i \alpha \overline{m}} = g_0^{\alpha \overline{m} \cdot \tilde{x}_i} = H_0(\overline{m})^{\tilde{x}_i}$$

Challenge Ciphertext: Before detailing the calculation of the challenge ciphertext, we first have the following auxiliary terms: For all $i \in I$, sample b_{j0}, s_{ji} uniformly at random. By setting the points $(0, b_{j0}), (\xi_i, s_{ji})$ for $i \in I$, we confirm a uniquely defined polynomial f_j where $f_j(0) = b_{j0}$ with degree $t - 1$. Next, we calculate the challenge ciphertext as follows:
For c_{j1} and c_{j2} for all $j \in [k]$, we have

- $c_{j1} = g_1^r$
- c_{j2} is calculated as follows: For simulating c_{j2} we consider two cases for $i \in I$ and $i \in \overline{I}$. For $i \in I$, based on the extractaness of the signature, we can get the secret key $x_i \in \mathbb{Z}_p$. Thus, we have

$$c_{j2} = e(g_0^{\alpha \overline{m}_j}, g_1^r)^{x_i} \cdot g_T^{s_{ji}} = e(H_0(\overline{m}_j), g_1^r)^{x_i} \cdot g_T^{s_{ji}}$$
$$= e(H_0(\overline{m}_j), g_1^{x_i})^r \cdot g_T^{s_{ji}} = e(H_0(\overline{m}_j), \overline{vk}_i)^r \cdot g_T^{s_{ji}}$$

Then, for $i \in \overline{I}$, we derive $s_{ji} = f_j(\xi_i)$ for all $i \in \overline{I}$. Then, we calculate c_{j2} as follows:

$$c_{j3} = e(g_0^x, g_1^r)^{L_0'(\xi_i)\alpha \overline{m}_j} \cdot e(g_0, g_1^r)^{\alpha \overline{m}_j \cdot x_i'} \cdot g_T^{s_{ji}}$$
$$= e(g_0^{\alpha \overline{m}_j}, g_1^{L_0'(\xi_i)xr}) \cdot e(g_0^{\alpha \overline{m}_j}, g_1^{rx_i'}) \cdot g_T^{s_{ji}}$$
$$= e(g_0^{\alpha \overline{m}_j}, g_1^{L_0'(\xi_i)xr + rx_i'}) \cdot g_T^{s_{ji}}$$
$$= e(H_0(\overline{m}_j), g_1^{(L_0'(\xi_i)x + x_i')r}) \cdot g_T^{s_{ji}}$$
$$= e(H_0(\overline{m}_j), \overline{vk}_i)^r \cdot g_T^{s_{ji}}$$

Regarding c_{j3}, we have:

- For all $j \in [k] \setminus CM$, we set $c_{j3} = H_1(g_T^{b_{j0}}) \oplus m_j$ where $H_1(g_T^{b_{j0}})$ comes from H_1 query.
- For all $j \in CM$, the challenge set, we sample $z_j \leftarrow_\$ \mathbb{Z}_q$ and set $c_{j3} = H_1(A \cdot g_T^{z_j}) \oplus m_j$ where $A = g_T^{x\alpha r}$ or g_T^y, which we will analyze in detail next.

Then, we shall show two parts:

- If given the BDH tuple $(g_0, g_0^x, g_0^\alpha, g_1, g_1^x, g_1^r, g_T^{x\alpha r})$, $\mathcal{D}$ perfectly simulates the experiment ExpSec from $\mathcal{A}$'s view, based on definition, $\mathcal{A}$'s advantage in this simulation is at least ϵ.
- If given the random tuple$(g_0, g_0^x, g_0^\alpha, g_1, g_1^x, g_1^r, g_T^y)$, then in $\mathcal{D}$'s simulation, $\mathcal{A}$'s advantage is 0.

We next detail how to simulate each above. Now, let us assume that $\mathcal{D}$ is given the BDH tuple, that is $(g_0, g_0^x, g_0^\alpha, g_1, g_1^x, g_1^r, g_T^{x\alpha r})$.

- c_{j3} is calculated as follows: for $j \in CM$, given the BDH tuple $g_T^{x\alpha r}$, we first choose $z_j \leftarrow_\$ \mathbb{Z}_q$ and derive

$$c_{j3} = H_1(g_T^{x\alpha r} \cdot g_T^{z_j}) \oplus m_j = H_1(g_T^{x\alpha r+z_j}) \oplus m_j$$

Since in this case, the simulator perfectly simulates the view defined in ExpSec, thus the adversary $\mathcal{A}$ has at least ϵ advantage. Next, we will consider the case $\mathcal{D}$ is given a random tuple $(g_0, g_0^x, g_0^\alpha, g_1, g_1^x, g_1^r, g_T^y)$. The only difference here is c_{j3}. In this case, we have

- for $j \in CM$, given g_T^y, we have

$$c_{j3} = H_1(g_T^y) \oplus m_j$$

In this case, $\mathcal{A}$'s advantage is 0. In summary, $\mathcal{D}$ will have at least ϵ to distinguish the tuples. This completes the proof.

References

1. The arc-bls12 381 Project. arc_bls12_381: A rust implementation of the bls12-381 curve. https://github.com/arkworks-rs/curve-bls12-381. Accessed 28 Jan 2025
2. Bacis, E., Facchinetti, D., Guarnieri, M., Rosa, M., Rossi, M., Paraboschi, S.: I told you tomorrow: practical time-locked secrets using smart contracts. In: Proceedings of the 16th International Conference on Availability, Reliability and Security, pp. 1–10 (2021)
3. Boneh, D., Shoup, V.: A graduate course in applied cryptography. Draft 0.5 (2020)
4. Buterin, V.: Ethereum: a next generation smart contract & decentralized application platform (2014). https://ethereum.org/en/whitepaper/. Accessed 10 May 2024
5. Döttling, N., Hanzlik, L., Magri, B., Wohnig, S.: Mcfly: verifiable encryption to the future made practical. In: International Conference on Financial Cryptography and Data Security, pp. 252–269. Springer (2023)
6. Mozilla Foundation. The rust programming language. https://www.rust-lang.org
7. Kaleem, M., et al.: An event driven framework for smart contract execution. In: Proceedings of the 15th ACM International Conference on Distributed and Event-Based Systems, pp. 78–89 (2021)
8. Karanjai, R., Xu, L., Gao, Z., Chen, L., Kaleem, M., Shi, W.: Privacy preserving event based transaction system in a decentralized environment. In: Proceedings of the 22nd International Middleware Conference, pp. 286–297 (2021)
9. Li, C., Palanisamy, B.: Emerge: self-emerging data release using cloud data storage. In: 2017 IEEE 10th International Conference on Cloud Computing (CLOUD), pp. 26–33. IEEE (2017)
10. Li, C., Palanisamy, B.: Timed-release of self-emerging data using distributed hash tables. In: 2017 IEEE 37th International Conference on Distributed Computing Systems (ICDCS), pp. 2344–2351. IEEE (2017)
11. Li, C., Palanisamy, B.: Decentralized privacy-preserving timed execution in blockchain-based smart contract platforms. In: 2018 IEEE 25th International Conference on High Performance Computing (HiPC), pp. 265–274. IEEE (2018)

12. Li, C., Palanisamy, B.: Decentralized release of self-emerging data using smart contracts. In: 2018 IEEE 37th Symposium on Reliable Distributed Systems (SRDS), pp. 213–220. IEEE (2018)
13. Li, C., Palanisamy, B.: Eventwarden: a decentralized event-driven proxy service for outsourcing arbitrary transactions in ethereum-like blockchains. In: 2020 IEEE International Conference on Web Services (ICWS), pp. 9–16. IEEE (2020)
14. Madathil, V., Thyagarajan, S.A., Vasilopoulos, D., Fournier, L., Malavolta, G., Moreno-Sanchez, P.: Cryptographic oracle-based conditional payments. Cryptology ePrint Archive (2022)
15. Shamir, A.: How to share a secret. Commun. ACM **22**(11), 612–613 (1979)
16. Truffle Suite. Ganache (2023). https://trufflesuite.com/ganache/. Accessed 01 May 2024
17. Szabo, N.: Formalizing and securing relationships on public networks. First Monday (1997)
18. Solidity Team. Solidity programming language (2023). https://soliditylang.org. Accessed 01 May 2024
19. Wang, J., Palanisamy, B.: Attack-resilient blockchain-based decentralized timed data release. In: IFIP Annual Conference on Data and Applications Security and Privacy, pp. 123–140. Springer (2022)
20. Wang, J., Palanisamy, B.: CTDRB: controllable timed data release using blockchains. In: International Conference on Security and Privacy in Communication Systems, pp. 231–249. Springer (2022)
21. Wang, J., Palanisamy, B.: Securing blockchain-based timed data release against adversarial attacks. J. Comput. Secur. 1–29 (2023)
22. Wang, J., Palanisamy, B.: PR-TDR: privacy-preserving and reliable timed data release. In: 2024 43rd International Symposium on Reliable Distributed Systems (SRDS), pp. 115–125 (2024)
23. Wood, G., et al.: Ethereum: a secure decentralised generalised transaction ledger. Ethereum Project Yellow Paper **151**(2014), 1–32 (2014)
24. Zhao, Z., Beillahi, S. M., Song, R., Cai, Y., Veneris, A., Long, F.: Sigvm: enabling event-driven execution for truly decentralized smart contracts. Proc. ACM Program. Lang. **6**(OOPSLA2), 673–698 (2022)

Performance-Efficient Anti-fingerprinting for Privacy

Lars Tomer Yavor[1] and Anne V. D. M. Kayem[2(✉)] [ID]

[1] Hasso-Plattner-Institute for Digital Engineering, University of Potsdam,
Potsdam, Germany
`lars.yavor@student.hpi.uni-potsdam.de`
[2] Department of Computer Science, University of Exeter, Exeter, UK
`a.v.kayem@exeter.ac.uk`

Abstract. In modern browsers, interactive 3D graphics are enabled by the WebGL component, which also serves as a vector for browser fingerprinting. Browser fingerprinting offers the benefit of allowing web application service providers to capture data about a web user's browsing activity and as such establish user authenticity. One drawback of fingerprinting, however, is that the data collected can reveal unique (private) details about a user's browsing behaviours which is in contravention of digital privacy laws such as the GDPR. To address this issue, anti-browser fingerprinting solutions such as randomising or blocking WebGL parameters have been proposed. However, these solutions face challenges with detectability and web compatibility, often resulting in performance degradation and poor user experience. In this paper, we propose a performance-efficient anti-browser fingerprinting mechanism for WebGL that is robust to detectability and offers improved user experience. We achieve this by extending the *JShelter* browser extension by: (1) generating realistic and valid WebGL parameters, reducing the likelihood of detection while preserving the functionality of visited websites; and (2) enhancing the spoofing (randomisation) mechanism in *JShelter*, to ensure that the spoofed values are indistinguishable from those of real hardware configurations. The results of our empirical study indicate reduced WebGL related errors in *JShelter* from over 150 to zero. Additionally, the modified *JShelter* version transfers data more efficiently and achieves faster speeds compared to the unmodified version, thus improving privacy, usability, and compatibility.

Keywords: Anti-fingerprinting · Browser Privacy · Performance

1 Introduction

The prevalence of web applications and the requirement to comply with privacy legislation impose a need for stateless tracking mechanisms such as browser fingerprinting [14]. While privacy legislation such as the GDPR requires transparency with respect to all user tracking forms several web application providers fail to do so when fingerprinting is concerned [12,18].

Published by Springer Nature Switzerland AG 2025
S. Katsikas and B. Shafiq (Eds.): DBSec 2025, LNCS 15722, pp. 196–210, 2025.
https://doi.org/10.1007/978-3-031-96590-6_11

Typically, fingerprinting is used to establish user authenticity when other forms of verification are not available. For instance, when an IP address of a user is not constant, such as if the user browses sometimes from their home network and at other times from their university network. IP addresses are highly likely to differ for each network despite the fact that the user uses the same device [3]. In contrast to cookies, web application service providers are not explicitly required by law to inform their users about the fingerprinting tracking activities they conduct. This opens up pathways for privacy breaches, due to the lack of transparency in the user details collected and the storage agreements [7,14]. For instance, in May 2023 Facebook was fined 1.2 billion euros by the European Data Protection Board (EDPB) for Meta's transfers of personal (sensitive) data, starting in July 2020, to the U.S., on the basis of standard contractual clauses [5,8,13].

To increase user awareness of browser fingerprinting and to guard against fingerprinting multiple web applications offer options to allow users to check their own fingerprint and its uniqueness [2,4,6,9]. However, from the performance and usability standpoint, anti-fingerprinting mechanisms suffer from two issues namely: *detectability* and *reduced effectiveness* both of which negatively impact performance and discourage adoption. *Detectability* refers to the fact that web applications wanting to conduct fingerprinting can, by analysing various parameters (e.g. IP address, operating system, ...), determine if an accessing browser is employing anti-fingerprinting. When this is the case, some applications will police traffic from such browsers by delaying data transfers (e.g. by employing pro-fingerprinting priority algorithms). *Lack of effectiveness* refers to the negative impact these delays have on the performance of the web application from the client-end, thereby reducing the attractiveness of adopting anti-fingerprinting mechanisms (negatively impacting usability) and negatively impacting privacy (through reduced anti-fingerprinting adoption).

In this paper, we focus on adversaries who want low-effort and fast identification of users to support targeted advertising [15]. We minimise *detectability* and improve *effectiveness* of anti-fingerprinting mechanisms with a parameter spoofing and an anti-traffic policing mechanism. The parameter spoofing (randomisation) mechanism works by identifying and anonymising anti-fingerprinting parameters, and the anti-traffic policing mechanism improves anti-fingerprinting performance. As a proof-of-concept, we extended the JShelter browser extension (which is privacy-preserving and offers anti-fingerprinting) to integrate WebGL[1] parameter spoofing to enable anti-fingerprinting. WebGL is a key component in browsers that enables 3D graphics and offers realistic opportunities for fingerprinting. Currently, the JShelter extension randomises WebGL parameters without verifying the validity of the generated values. This often results in unrealistic or inconsistent outputs, making the spoofing mechanism more easily detectable. Results from our empirical study indicate reduced WebGL related errors in *JShelter* from over 150 to zero. Additionally, the modified *JShelter* ver-

---

[1] https://github.com/polcak/jsrestrictor/issues/166.

sion transfers data more efficiently and achieves higher speeds compared to the unmodified version, thus improving privacy, usability, and compatibility.

The paper is structured as follows. In Sect. 2 we discuss related work on browser fingerprinting and anti-fingerprinting. In Sect. 3, we present our proposed anti-fingerprinting approach and follow this in Sect. 4, with a discussion of empirical results. We offer concluding statements in Sect. 5.

2   Related Work

There are three key anti-fingerprinting approaches [15] namely: (1) **Homogeneity** such as in the case of the Tor Browser to support anonymity. All Tor Browser users have by-default the same sized displays and information obtainable from HTTP headers or JavaScript APIs is modified to ensure homogeneity across users[2]; (2) **randomisation** which works by randomising fingerprinting information for every website to minimise detectability. This approach is implemented in the Brave browser[3]; and (3) **Detect and/ or block** fingerprinting attempts, e.g., NoScript blocks JavaScript[4] and therefore information that can be obtained over JavaScript.

With **Homogeneity** the idea is to create a fingerprint that is the same for each user. This leads to non-unique fingerprints for these users to ensure anonymity. Tor tries to make it harder for websites to differentiate between their users. This approach can be effective, but always depends on the size of a browser's user base. Furthermore, it presents two disadvantages. Web applications that know that the fingerprint distinguishes users (especially if the user base is small) can potentially detect that a privacy-preserving tool is in place. The other disadvantage is that the user will have to provide the same information, which is difficult to guarantee [15]. **randomisation** requires that the values selected be realistic values; otherwise, this approach leads to web rendering inconsistencies. This increases the complexity of randomisation and makes having some sort of data structure necessary from which realistic, random values are loaded. Reading such data structures can increase website loading times and therefore downgrade users browsing experience. Furthermore, randomisation can lead to inconsistent browser behavior making it hard for users to trust the reliability of the anti-fingerprinting application. While **Detect and/ or block** approaches are time sensitive in that the fingerprinting must be detected and blocked from the HTTP header and in a time-efficient way [15]. In the case of WebGL, Brave's strict mode[5] blocks most of the information that can be requested from the browser. This behavior leads to disruptions in the browsing experience which then influences the user experience.

Other anti-fingerprinting approaches include ones centered around blocking *JavaScript* which is an effective in that the browser fingerprinting relies mostly

---

[2] https://tb-manual.torproject.org/anti-fingerprinting/.

[3] https://brave.com/privacy-updates/3-fingerprint-randomisation/.

[4] https://noscript.net/.

[5] https://github.com/brave/brave-browser/issues/9189.

on requesting information from a user's browser via *JavaScript* [4, 10]. However, since *JavaScript* powers many features of websites and disabling it leads to inconsistent web application rendering. This makes blocking *JavaScript* an effective solution but not a privacy preserving method that ensures user usability.

3   System Architecture

To create and implement our anti-fingerprinting approach, we embed a 3D graphics rendering tool into a browser extension with the goal of assessing the impact of our proposed randomisation (spoofing) and anti-traffic policing mechanisms.

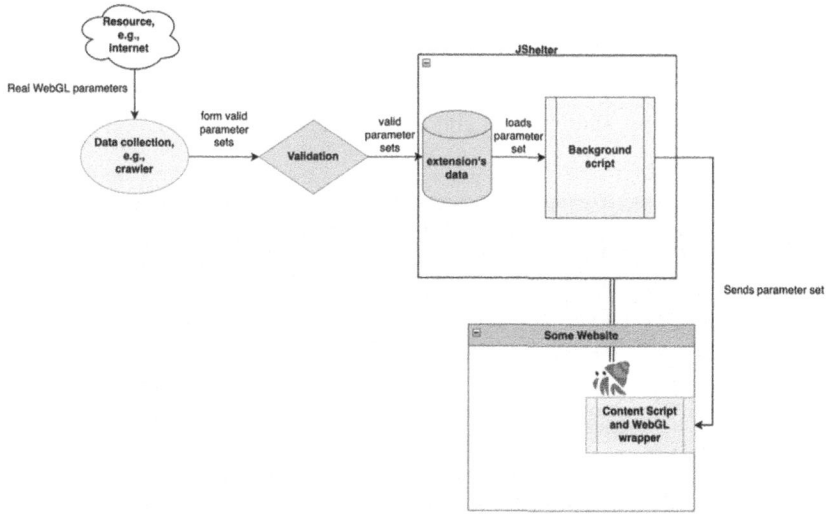

Fig. 1. Overview of System Architecture.

As shown in Fig. 1, fingerprinting data is collected via a crawler which then transfers valid parameter sets to a validation tool. The validation tool assesses the parameter sets provided to determine which ones form valid parameter sets that browser fingerprinting tools will be looking at. This data is then passed to the JShelter component, which loads the parameter set into the database. These parameters are then randomised to minimise detectability and block traffic policing parameters. WebGL is then used as a case study to show the impact of minimising detectability and block traffic policing parameters on the rendering of a web page with 3D content.

The relations and data flow between the components is shown in Fig. 1. First, realistic parameters need to be gathered and validated to ensure their correctness and realism. Second, the parameter sets are made accessible for the browser extension, e.g., by storing them in the extension. When the extension is active it loads parameters via the background script and sends them to the content script which can then intercept WebGL requests authentic and provide values to the requesting website. This architecture ensures that the wrapper can return realistic, valid and spoofed WebGL parameters. It bases on a reliable coordination between background script, content script and wrapper.

WebGL 2.0 supports rendering low-level 3D figures in HTML5 canvas elements. It is a plugin-free and an open-web standard, supported by most browser vendors like Apple (Safari), Google (Chrome), Microsoft (Edge), and Mozilla (Firefox). Figure 2 shows the process of graphic data flow from an application through the GPU to the frame buffer. The application sends vertices which contain information about the graphic model that the GPU should render. In *vertex processing* stage the provided data is modified by the vertex shader to determine the coordinates of each vertex in the frame buffer. The new ordered 2D vertices are handed over to the next stage - the *rasterizer* where the GPU calculates which pixel in the framebuffer is affected by the graphic model. After this stage is completed, the colour of the pixels is modified during the *fragment processing* stage by the fragment shader, and the graphic model displayed.

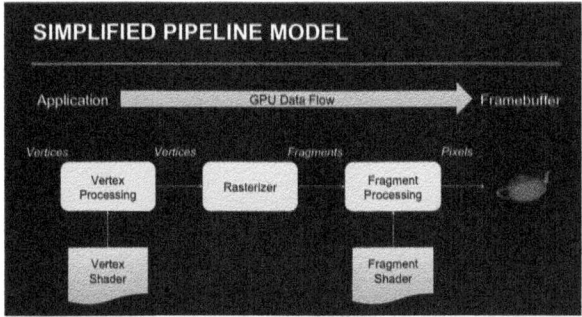

Fig. 2. Figure shows rendering pipeline of a graphic model. Source: [1].

JShelter is a browser extension designed to enhance privacy. It intercepts and modifies web requests, including WebGL API calls, ensuring users' privacy is maintained. This extension is available for both Chromium-based browsers and Firefox, offering flexibility across different browser platforms. It provides privacy for users with different in depth knowledge about privacy. They achieve this by giving users the choice of different levels of privacy strictness [15]. JShelter employs two levels of anti-fingerprinting - on the strictest level it blocks any request. This level is for user who willingly accept the option of poor web page rendering in favour of privacy. The less strict level uses randomised values but has the caveat that an observer (adversary) could detect that a privacy preserving tool is in place and block the user.

To achieve real-time randomisation (spoofing) of WebGL parameters, it is necessary to intercept, load, and send WebGL parameters. For these reasons we use existing and new components of JShelter. JShelter provides a WebGL wrapper which intercepts WebGL API requests by websites and responds them with spoofed values. The wrapper runs as part of the content script, which is a script only activated per site during load time. In this content script a random number is generated based on the domain. This number is constant for the domain during the whole browsing session which means even if the page gets reloaded this number stays the same. When a WebGL API request is intercepted, the wrapper determines the requested value. As shown in Fig. 3, JShelter retrieves the value from a parameter set corresponding to the random constant calculated earlier. These parameter sets ensure: (1) The values are realistic and correctly grouped (i.e., valid combinations are returned together) and (2) Consistency across the same domain within a session. To get such parameter sets and to be able to send them, the following components need to be in place and interact with the WebGL wrapper: (1) **Data collection and storage**: It needs a data set of valid parameter set, in case of this work a web crawler was used. The parameter set have to be in respect to the underlying user's operating system. Since randomly combined parameters might fail in being valid, it needs a validation step to ensure the correctness of a formed parameter set; and (2) **Parameter loading**: To access the parameter in real-time it is necessary to load the data into the content script. Since browser extension can only access certain data location and only by its background scripts, it is favorable to store the parameter sets in some data section of the extension. That ensures that it is accessible by the background script of the extension, which is a script that always runs when an extension is enabled in a browser. The background script needs to load the parameter sets and send it asynchronously to the content script which can then process it. Since the wrapper runs within the content script the wrapper has at this step access to the parameter sets.

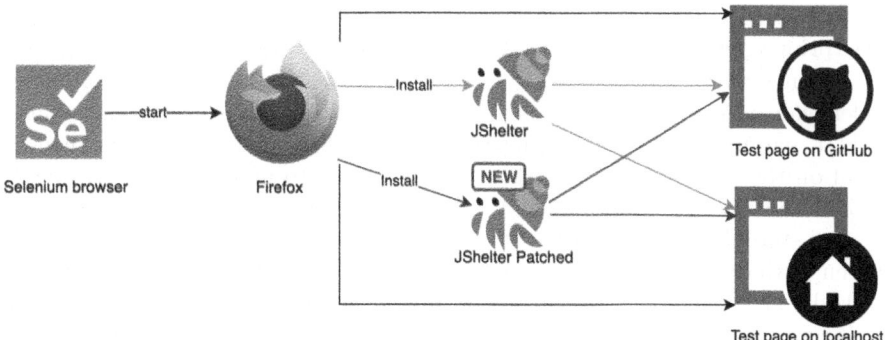

Fig. 3. Testing Architecture.

To minimise detectability and to increase web compatibility of JShelter, it is important to ensure to have real and valid parameter sets of WebGL values. A web crawler is used to collect real values (such as those in *Web3DSurvey*[6]) and minimise detectability. When values are realistic it makes them more indistinguishable from actual hardware parameters. To ensure that these values are correctly combined, tests of *the Khronos Group* are used to verify that parameters are compatible when combined. This also decreases the likelihood of detectability and poor web page rendering due to wrong combinations of WebGL parameters. Finally, to ensure that the parameter sets can be processed by the content script we employ asynchronous data transfer to ensure the content script runs efficiently. This minimises the risk of blocking by counter-anti-fingerprinting tools, thereby improving web page rendering and usability.

This paper aligns with Brave's approach in using random, session-consistent values but extends it to WebGL spoofing. Unlike Brave's browser-specific solutions, we embed the anti-fingerprinting measures into a browser extension (JShelter), thus offering cross-platform accessibility [15]. Furthermore, Brave doesn't handle WebGL which is an added novelty of our approach in which we tackle the WebGL fingerprinting issue by employing random, operating system dependent, realistic values, which we believe might be a valuable addition to JShelter and/or privacy focused web browsers.

4   Empirical Analysis

We focus on anti-fingerprinting measurements in the Firefox browser. The main focus is on fingerprinting via WebGL, which is an already studied and widely used tracking method [11,16,17]. In particular on Ubuntu LTS 23.10 and macOS Ventura 13.2.1, which means other operating systems like Windows, iOS or Android are not covered by this paper. All experiments were executed on a MacBook Pro with a 2,9 GHz 6-Core Intel Core i9 CPU, an Intel UHD Graphics 630 GPU and 32 GB 2400 MHz DDR4 RAM, the macOS Ventura 13.2.1 operating system.

To ensure the validity and repeatability of the tests for WebGL's anti-fingerprinting measures, a controlled and consistent test environment was set up. The main goal was to assess the behavior of the patched JShelter extension under realistic settings and to ensure that it provides valid, randomly generated WebGL parameters without losing web compatibility. The test environment is based on the Selenium framework, which was used to automate browser interactions and run the tests. Selenium allows developers to precisely control the browser state, ensuring consistent testing across multiple iterations. Firefox was chosen as the browser due to its focus on privacy as written in their manifesto[7]. Geckodriver version 0.35.0 was used to interact with Firefox.

We modified the browser configuration to accept self-signed certificates, to ensure that the sites with self-signed HTTPS certificates proceeded without interference from security warnings. Self-signed HTTPS certificates for locally hosted test pages were necessary because WebGL parameters can only be

---

[6] https://web3dsurvey.com/.
[7] https://www.mozilla.org/en-US/about/manifesto/

retrieved in a secure context[8]. To prevent cached data or previous session data from influencing the test results, all storage methods—such as cookies, cache, and local storage—were disabled. An isolated, default browser profile was used to eliminate the possibility of installed extensions or custom configurations affecting the test results. The test pages were locally hosted, to ensure availability and allow direct control over the environment to simulate realistic WebGL scenarios.

Each test began with the initialization of a new, clean browser session, ensuring that no state from previous sessions influenced the tests. Depending on the test variant no extension, the patched JShelter extension or the unmodified JShelter extension was then loaded, and the initial responses of the WebGL APIs were examined to verify the correct functionality of the extension. During the tests, the automated browser interacted with local test pages that emulated typical WebGL application scenarios, such as rendering 2D objects or requesting WebGL parameters. The behavior of the patched extension was observed under these controlled conditions to ensure consistency and reliability.

To validate the correctness of parameter combinations we use tests from the *Khronos Group* which maintains the WebGL standard. These tests cover multiple scenarios to ensure correct functionality and web compatibility of the generated WebGL parameters.

1. **Context-creation** aims to create a large number of WebGL contexts, that are needed to start with rendering/ displaying WebGL graphics. This ensures that the parameters fit to create a valid WebGL context.
2. **Many-draw-calls** triggers many draw and update calls per WebGL context. This helps to evaluate the speed of responsiveness of the WebGL API.
3. **Shader-with-too-many-uniforms** tests that vertex shaders and fragment shaders function as expected. Since vertex and fragment shaders are a fundamental part of WebGL this checks that they are working properly.
4. **gl-get-calls** ensures that getting WebGL parameter values through WebGL API works and is in the expected type. Furthermore, it checks that the parameters are combined in a valid fashion, e.g., `MAX_VERTEX_UNI FORM_BLOCKS` should be greater than or equal 12[9].
5. **gl-get-tex-parameter** tests texture parameters for validity. Since the extension of this work manipulated also texture parameters, this test is supportive to ensure the behavior is correct.
6. **get-extension** checks that get extension works as expected and is constant also for multiple requests.
7. **promoted-extensions** ensures that extensions that are crucial are reachable by the API. These extension tests are essential in ensuring that the patched extension is not changing anything regarding the extensions behavior.

In addition, a manual test was conducted to check compatibility with real web applications by testing the website https://dddance.party/, which uses the WebGL library *Three.js*[10], to assess the impact of anti-fingerprinting measures

---

[8] https://developer.mozilla.org/en-US/docs/Web/Security/Secure_Contexts.

[9] https://registry.khronos.org/OpenGL-Refpages/gl4/html/glGet.xhtml.

[10] https://threejs.org/

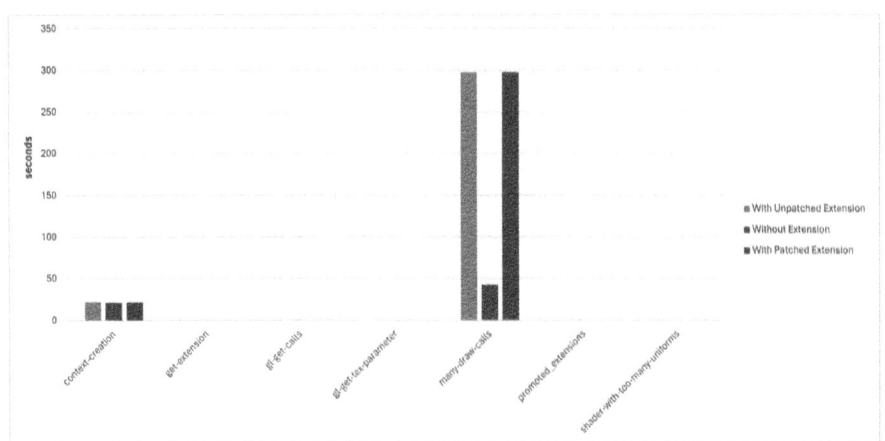

Fig. 4. Total run time in seconds for 20 test runs per test variant.

on the display and functionality of complex 3D graphics. These tests were to ensure that the modified JShelter extension not only provides data protection, but also ensures compatibility and functionality of WebGL-based applications.

The results showed that the modified JShelter extension fully met the validation requirements. The Khronos Group tests, including context-creation, gl-get-calls and shader-with-too-many-uniforms, were passed without error. This confirmed that the returned WebGL parameters were correct and compatible with the specifications. Compared to the unmodified JShelter version, which generated errors in some tests, the modified version performed significantly better.

As shown in Fig. 4 in most cases the extension (patched or unmodified) does not affect the run time of WebGL 2.0 process. Significant differences are observed when comparing between browser without *JShelter* and with *JShelter* when the website triggers multiple draw calls. In this scenario, both the extension patched and unpatched versions of the *JShelter* extension are approximately 7 times slower. From the users' perspective, this means slow graphic rendering, for example, a website with a lot of graphics would render slower. Furthermore, the runtime difference between the patched and unmodified (unpatched) version is insignificant because the information is sent in the same fashion to the requesting website. Reading a data set and calculating a random parameter set can increase the runtime (see Fig. 4), but this point could perhaps be addressed by caching certain sent responses and instead of rereading values, the cached response could be sent to the requested website. This way, the runtime can be reduced. Despite the fact that the run times of the official *Khronos Group* test are relatively similar between the patched and unpatched versions of JShelter, there are still performance differences as visualized in Fig. 5. The Fig. 5 shows that the unpatched extension after 20 automatic tests runs flags multiple test fails while the patched version did not. The test failures occur when the param-

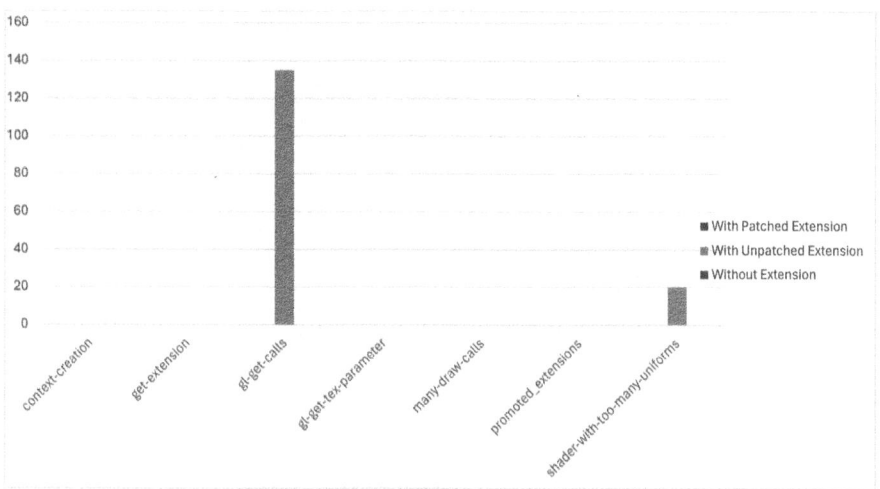

Fig. 5. Total Number of Errors over 20 runs.

Fig. 6. Outcome when visiting https://dddance.party/ with unmodified JShelter.

eter set is checked for validity. Also creating proper shaders lead to errors when Firefox is running with the not patched version. In the manual tests WebGL objects might be rendered incorrectly when random, invalid values are returned. An example of such behavior can be seen in Fig. 6, where one figure's colours are not rendered. Furthermore, instead of moving and dancing as expected the figures are all in the same stiff posture. Since this website's purpose is to play with dancing creatures this incorrect rendering affects the usability of the website.

Fig. 7. Outcome when visiting https://dddance.party/ with plain Firefox.

Fig. 8. Outcome when visiting https://dddance.party/ with patched JShelter.

By contrast, the test run without any browser extension (see Fig. 7) and of the one with the patched browser extension (see Fig. 8) are quite similar. The only differences are the timestamp of the screenshot, which is why the creatures are not completely synchronised. This validates improved usability by using our WebGL anti-fingerprinting approach.

Lastly, we look at performance by visiting a page of a green future plan for living at www.kubota.com/futurecube/. Rendering the 3D graphics of this website leads to different CPU temperature and potentially performance differences in graphics rendering.

Figure 9 shows the temperature increase during execution without JShelter is higher than for the runs with JShelter. Furthermore, the unpatched version creates higher CPU temperatures faster than the patched version which indicates that the unpatched extension leads to more CPU cycles and is less efficient from the processing viewpoint.

The frame rendering times differ significantly when https://www.kubota.com/futurecube/ is visited. When visited without any extension ($\tilde{1}$ ms) compared to with the patched extension the average rendering time for a frame is

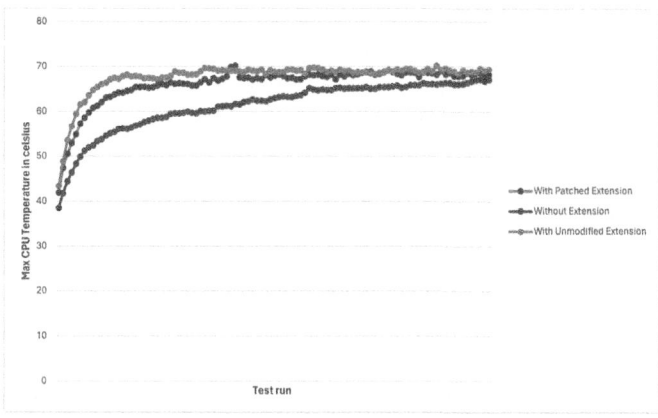

Fig. 9. Temperature Variations when Visiting https://www.kubota.com/futurecube/

strongly distinct ($\tilde{1}90$ ms). Running with the patched extension slows the frame rendering times for users and therefore affects the usability and performance of a visited WebGL website negatively. The patched version outperforms slightly the unmodified version of JShelter in terms of the total transferred data in bytes (see Fig. 10).

Even though the total amount of transferred data differs only in a few mega bytes it again indicates a lesser performance of the unmodified (unpatched) extension compared to the patched one. When both this information are combined, the peak of the patched extension data transfer occurs in relatively shorter frame time (mean: 40 s) than the one of the unmodified one. Furthermore, the

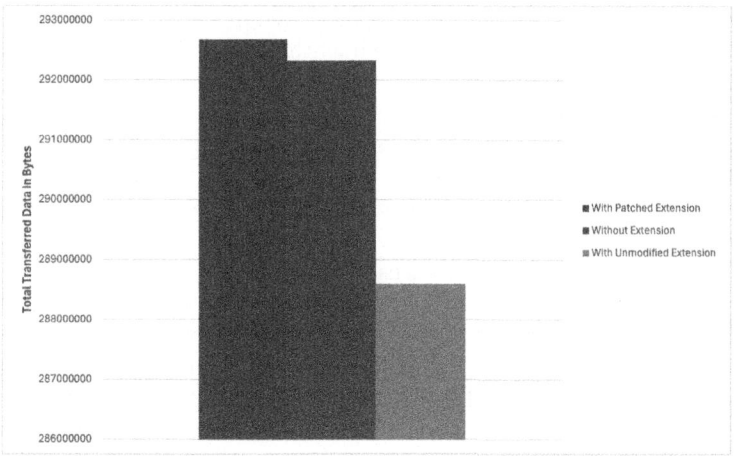

Fig. 10. Total transferred data by visiting https://www.kubota.com/futurecube/

highest value of average frame time still makes up to nearly 2% of the data the unmodified extension transferred which is twice as much as for the patched one. Of all transferred data the patched extension sent more than 50% were sent in 40 or less seconds. While the unmodified (unpatche) version sent only 23% of their total data in 40 or less seconds.

Overall, this shows that the patching JShelter's WebGL anti-fingerprinting measurements did improve their performance regarding WebGL rendering.

5   Conclusion

In this paper, we presented a performance-efficient anti-browser fingerprinting mechanism for WebGL that is robust to detectability and offers improved user experience. We achieved this by extending the *JShelter* browser extension by: (1) generating realistic and valid WebGL parameters, reducing the likelihood of detection while preserving the functionality of visited websites; and (2) enhancing the spoofing (randomisation) mechanism in *JShelter*, to ensure that the spoofed values are indistinguishable from those of real hardware configurations.

We showed that by improving JShelter's anti-fingerprinting measures for WebGL parameters, it is possible to implement privacy measures that provide realistic and consistent values for WebGL parameters without compromising compatibility with web applications or usability. The added benefit of this work is that it can also be adopted by other privacy-focused browser extensions such as *PrivacyBadger* or *Ghostery*.

The results of our empirical study indicate reduced WebGL related errors in *JShelter* from over 150 to zero. Additionally, the modified *JShelter* version transfers data more efficiently and achieves faster speeds compared to the unmodified version, thus improving privacy, usability, and compatibility. Our proposed solution safely manipulates WebGL parameters while preserving performance and compatibility. The user experience is also improved by increasing web compatibility compared to existing approaches such as the unmodified JShelter extension. In essence, it provides a good balance between data protection and functionality.

As future work, one important direction is the integration of the developed solution directly into browsers such as Firefox to overcome the limitations of browser extensions, especially in terms of performance. A direct implementation in the browser could minimise runtime problems and realise additional optimisations, such as more efficient caching. This could also potentially be expanded to include mobile browsers and devices.

Our current solution is based on a limited amount of data, mainly from the Web3D Survey and the Khronos Group. Future work could expand this database by collecting values for a wider range of operating systems and GPUs to increase the robustness of the solution. This could potentially be integrated into an adaptive system that dynamically adjusts WebGL parameters based on contextual information, such as the target website or browser, to achieve high protection without compromising performance.

References

1. Angel, E., Haines, E.: An interactive introduction to WEBGL and three.JS. In: ACM SIGGRAPH 2017 Courses. SIGGRAPH '17. Association for Computing Machinery, Los Angeles (2017). isbn: 9781450350143. https://doi.org/10.1145/3084873.3084875

2. Budington, B.: Panopticlick: fingerprinting your web presence. USENIX Association, San Francisco (2016)

3. Datta, A., Lu, J., Tschantz, M.C.: Evaluating anti- fingerprinting privacy enhancing technologies. In: The World Wide Web Conference. WWW '19, pp. 351–362. Association for Computing Machinery, San Francisco (2019). isbn: 9781450366748. https://doi.org/10.1145/3308558.3313703

4. Eckersley, P.: How unique is your web browser? In: Atallah, M.J., Hopper, N.J. (eds.) PETS 2010. LNCS, vol. 6205, pp. 1–18. Springer, Heidelberg (2010). https://doi.org/10.1007/978-3-642-14527-8_1

5. EDPB. 1.2 billion euro fine for Facebook as a result of EDPB binding decision (2023). https://www.edpb.europa.eu/news/news/2023/12-billion-euro-fine-facebook-result-edpb-binding-decision_en

6. Fietkau, J., et al.: The elephant in the background: a quantitative approach to empower users against web browser fingerprinting. In: Proceedings of the 20th Workshop on Workshop on Privacy in the Electronic Society. WPES '21, pp. 167–180. Association for Computing Machinery, Virtual Event (2021). isbn: 9781450385275. https://doi.org/10.1145/3463676.3485599

7. Iqbal, U., Englehardt, S., Shafiq, Z.: Fingerprinting the fingerprinters: learning to detect browser fingerprinting behaviors. In: 2021 IEEE Symposium on Security and Privacy (SP), pp. 1143–1161 (2021). https://doi.org/10.1109/SP40001.2021.00017

8. Jaeger, D., et al.: Analysis of publicly leaked credentials and the long story of password re-use. In: ResearchGate (2018). Accessed 11 July 2024. https://www.researchgate.net/profile/David-Jaeger-3/publication/327623664_Analysis_of_Publicly_Leaked_Credentials_and_the_Long_Story_of_Password_Re-use/links/6313bcdc1ddd44702131c7e8/Analysis-of-Publicly-Leaked-Credentials-and-the-Long-Story-of-Password-Re-use.pdf

9. Laperdrix, P., Rudametkin, W., Baudry, B.: Beauty and the beast: diverting modern web browsers to build unique browser fingerprints. In: IEEE Symposium on Security and Privacy (SP), pp. 878–894. IEEE (2016). https://doi.org/10.1109/SP.2016.57. https://inria.hal.science/hal-01285470

10. Lin, X., et al.: Fashion faux pas: implicit stylistic fingerprints for bypassing browsers' anti-fingerprinting defenses. In: 2023 IEEE Symposium on Security and Privacy (SP), pp. 987–1004 (2023). https://doi.org/10.1109/SP46215.2023.10179437

11. Lin, X., et al.: Phish in sheep's clothing: exploring the authentication pitfalls of browser fingerprinting defenses . In: 31st USENIX Security Symposium (USENIX Security 22), pp. 1651–1668. USENIX Association, Boston (2022). isbn: 978-1-939133-31-1. https://www.usenix.org/conference/usenixsecurity22/presentation/lin-xu

12. Matte, C., Bielova, N., Santos, C.: Do cookie banners respect my choice? Measuring legal compliance of banners from IAB Europe's transparency and consent framework (2020). arXiv: 1911.09964

13. Mayer, J.R., Mitchell, J.C.: Third-party web tracking: policy and technology. In: 2012 IEEE Symposium on Security and Privacy, pp. 413–427 (2012). https://doi.org/10.1109/SP.2012.47
14. Mudassar, M., et al.: An analysis of browser and machine fingerprinting techniques. In: 2023 International Conference on Business Analytics for Technology and Security (ICBATS), pp. 1–8 (2023). https://doi.org/10.1109/ICBATS57792.2023.10111174
15. Polcak, L., et al.: JShelter: give me my browser back (2023). arXiv: 2204.01392
16. Salomatin, A., Iskhakov, A., Meshcheryakov, R.: Proactive detection of attacks on APCS accounts based on analysis of user identification graphical attributes. In: 2022 International Russian Automation Conference (RusAutoCon), pp. 831–835 (2022). https://doi.org/10.1109/RusAutoCon54946.2022.9896378
17. Wu, S., et al.: Rendered private: making GLSL execution uniform to prevent WebGL-based browser fingerprinting. In: 28th USENIX Security Symposium (USENIX Security 19), pp. 1645–1660. USENIX Association, Santa Clara (2019). isbn: 978-1-939133-06-9. https://www.usenix.org/conference/usenixsecurity19/presentation/wu
18. Xiang, A., Pei, W., Yue, C.: PolicyChecker: analyzing the GDPR completeness of mobile apps' privacy policies. In: Proceedings of the 2023 ACM SIGSAC Conference on Computer and Communications Security. CCS '23, pp. 3373–3387. Association for Computing Machinery, Copenhagen (2023). isbn: 9798400700507. https://doi.org/10.1145/3576915.3623067

Trusted Platform and Privacy Management in Cyber Physical Systems: The DUCA Framework

Antonio Muñoz[1]([✉])(ID), Javier Lopez[1](ID), Cristina Alcaraz[1](ID), and Fabio Martinelli[2]

[1] Network, Information and Computer Security Lab (NICS), Languages and Computer Science Department, University of Malaga, Malaga, Spain
{anto,javierlopez,alcaraz}@uma.es

[2] Security Group Istituto di Informatica e Telematica - IIT, National Research Council - C.N.R., Pisa, Italy
Fabio.Martinelli@iit.cnr.it

Abstract. This paper explores the application of the DUCA (Data Usage Control and Compliance Architecture) framework for privacy management in Cyber-Physical Systems (CPS). DUCA integrates Privacy-by-Design (PbD) principles, Privacy-Enhancing Technologies (PETs), and context-aware policy enforcement to support regulatory compliance and protect data throughout its lifecycle. A key focus of this work is the integration of Secure Elements (SEs)—including Trusted Execution Environments (TEE), Trusted Platform Modules (TPM), and Intel SGX—to enable privacy protection during data processing, complementing traditional safeguards for data at rest and in transit. The framework also supports emerging standards such as DICE and MARS to facilitate scalable trust management in heterogeneous CPS environments. We present DUCA's modular architecture and evaluate its applicability across representative use cases, including smart grids, eHealth, and AI-enabled infrastructures, demonstrating its effectiveness in enforcing privacy without compromising functionality.

Keywords: Privacy Management · Secure Elements · Privacy-by-Design · Data Usage Control · Cyber-Physical Systems · GDPR Compliance

1 Introduction

Cyber-Physical Systems (CPS) are increasingly central to sectors such as energy, healthcare, transportation, and manufacturing, where the interplay between digital intelligence and physical processes enables real-time, data-driven decision-making. However, the dynamic, distributed, and heterogeneous nature of CPS introduces significant challenges for privacy and security, particularly regarding the protection of sensitive data throughout its lifecycle. Ensuring robust privacy in these environments requires not only regulatory compliance—such as

© IFIP International Federation for Information Processing 2025
Published by Springer Nature Switzerland AG 2025
S. Katsikas and B. Shafiq (Eds.): DBSec 2025, LNCS 15722, pp. 211–230, 2025.
https://doi.org/10.1007/978-3-031-96590-6_12

adherence to the General Data Protection Regulation (GDPR)—but also the integration of security mechanisms that operate effectively at both software and hardware levels.

Traditional privacy strategies, rooted in Privacy-by-Design (PbD) principles, employ Privacy-Enhancing Technologies (PETs) such as anonymization, pseudonymization, encryption, and differential privacy. While effective for securing data at rest and in transit, these techniques often fall short when it comes to safeguarding data during computation—a critical stage in CPS where information is actively processed and acted upon in real time. This limitation has prompted interest in Secure Elements (SEs), such as Trusted Execution Environments (TEEs), Trusted Platform Modules (TPMs), and Intel Software Guard Extensions (SGX), which enable privacy policy enforcement within tamper-resistant hardware contexts.

This work is conducted within the scope of the DUCA (Data Usage Control and Compliance Architecture) project, which investigates scalable, policy-driven approaches to privacy in CPS. DUCA combines PETs, dynamic and context-aware policy enforcement, and Secure Elements into a modular architecture that supports compliance and privacy-aware data usage. In this paper, we focus specifically on the integration and evaluation of Secure Elements within this framework, analyzing their suitability for runtime enforcement of privacy policies in heterogeneous CPS scenarios.

The main contribution of this work lies in the detailed examination of how hardware-based Secure Elements can be employed to extend privacy protection to data-in-use, addressing a gap in conventional PET-centric frameworks. We provide a comparative analysis of SE technologies—including TEE, TPM, SGX, SEV, DICE, and MARS—highlighting their trade-offs in terms of isolation guarantees, attestation capabilities, performance, and applicability across CPS domains. Furthermore, we demonstrate the relevance of these technologies through three representative use cases: smart grids, eHealth, and big data analytics, each with distinct operational and regulatory constraints.

The remainder of the paper is structured as follows. Section 2 presents background and related work on privacy management in CPS. Section 3 describes the DUCA architecture and its privacy-relevant components. Section 4 examines the integration of Secure Elements and analyzes their capabilities. Section 5 presents representative application scenarios and evaluation insights. Finally, Sect. 6 concludes the paper and outlines directions for future work.

2 Background and Related Work

Ensuring privacy in Cyber-Physical Systems (CPS) has become a pressing challenge as these systems manage vast volumes of sensitive data across interconnected and dynamic infrastructures. Unlike conventional IT environments, CPS operate in real-time contexts where continuous data flows introduce complex privacy risks. These challenges have led to the adoption of Privacy-by-Design (PbD) principles and Privacy-Enhancing Technologies (PETs), integrating privacy directly into system architectures.

Historically, privacy evolved from the notion of "the right to be alone" [1] to the modern concept of information privacy, centered on individuals' control over personal data [2]. The General Data Protection Regulation (GDPR) [3], enforced since 2018, formalizes these principles, mandating not only protection measures but also demonstrable compliance. PbD, codified in GDPR Article 25 [4] and conceptualized by Cavoukian [5], promotes the proactive embedding of privacy throughout the system lifecycle. DUCA adopts PbD not just as a regulatory response but as a core design principle, embedding protections from the outset—particularly vital in CPS environments characterized by high-frequency processing of sensitive data.

CPS tightly integrate computational and physical components [6,7], and are deployed in critical sectors such as energy, healthcare, manufacturing, and transportation [8–10]. Their heterogeneity, inclusion of legacy technologies, and diverse operational contexts pose privacy and security challenges. For instance, in healthcare, CPS handle sensitive patient data under strict confidentiality requirements [11]. DUCA addresses these risks through a distributed, adaptable framework that ensures consistent enforcement of privacy policies across components and stakeholders with distinct obligations. This approach mitigates risks such as service disruption or public safety threats by embedding privacy within both data management and decision-making processes.

DUCA operationalizes PbD through the use of PETs including data minimization, anonymization, and user-centric privacy controls [12]. These technologies secure data across its lifecycle—from collection and processing to storage and sharing—without compromising utility. Complementing this, DUCA incorporates privacy risk assessment tools that support early vulnerability detection and continuous monitoring, essential for real-time CPS. Transparent interfaces further empower users to manage privacy preferences, reinforcing GDPR principles and supporting DUCA's sustainable deployment.

PETs such as anonymization and pseudonymization reduce re-identification risks, while encryption safeguards data at rest and in transit [13]. Differential privacy enhances analytics by introducing statistical noise, maintaining aggregate utility while protecting individual identities. DUCA integrates these PETs with dynamic, policy-driven enforcement mechanisms, allowing adaptation to regulatory and operational demands across domains.

Beyond technical controls, CPS privacy governance requires policy management, auditing, and accountability [14]. DUCA supports context-aware privacy enforcement that adapts controls to data types and operational contexts. Mechanisms such as audit trails and secure logging establish transparency, enabling compliance verification and fostering trust.

The DUCA framework builds upon prior research emphasizing the need for adaptable and modular privacy management. Approaches using digital twins for dynamic policy adjustment [15] and privacy architectures such as Sovereign [16] and Eden [17] demonstrate the viability of embedded privacy in complex environments. DUCA extends these concepts by combining PbD and PETs throughout the system lifecycle and across heterogeneous CPS deployments.

3   DUCA Architecture and Privacy-Oriented Integration

The DUCA (Data Usage Control and Compliance Architecture) framework is designed to support privacy-preserving, regulation-compliant data usage in complex CPS environments, including smart grids, healthcare systems, and large-scale analytics infrastructures. It adopts a modular architecture that integrates Privacy-Enhancing Technologies (PETs), dynamic usage control, and hardware-based Secure Elements (SEs) to protect data throughout its lifecycle.

Figure 1 provides an overview of DUCA's main components. The DSA Lifecycle Infrastructure (DLI) manages the specification and storage of Data Sharing Agreements (DSAs) through a user interface, a policy authoring tool that converts high-level rules into controlled natural language (CNL), and a DSA Mapper that translates these policies into enforceable formats (e.g., U-XACML). The DSA Store enables persistence and retrieval of DSAs.

The DLI connects to the DSA Enforcement Infrastructure (DEI), which interprets and enforces usage policies in real time. Supporting this process are two additional layers: the Common Security Infrastructure (CSI), which provides identity management, encryption services, and auditing; and the Advanced Security Infrastructure (ASI), which handles PET integration and anonymization functions. Together, these components ensure that privacy policies are enforceable, traceable, and adaptable across distributed CPS components.

To validate the flexibility of the architecture, DUCA has been applied to several representative use cases. In smart grid systems, anonymization modules within ASI and enforcement via DEI ensure that real-time consumption data is protected using Intel SGX enclaves. In big data analytics, DUCA combines PETs (e.g., differential privacy) with CSI's auditing and enforcement capabilities to regulate large-scale query operations. In transportation systems, DUCA supports the definition of context-aware DSAs through the DLI, while CSI handles identity abstraction and consent tracking, and ASI ensures anonymization prior to data release.

A key feature of DUCA is its integration of Secure Elements to support privacy policy enforcement during computation—an area typically underserved by software-only approaches. TEEs such as ARM TrustZone and Intel SGX isolate execution environments, enabling secure analytics. TPMs provide attestation and secure key storage, while confidential computing platforms such as AMD SEV facilitate encrypted processing at the virtualization layer. Unlike previous frameworks relying solely on software controls [14,18], DUCA embeds hardware-backed trust anchors that enhance resilience against privileged-level attacks.

This integration of Secure Elements complements existing PETs and reinforces DUCA's capacity to enforce privacy policies across all stages of the data lifecycle. It specifically addresses the challenge of protecting data during use—a critical vulnerability in CPS—by executing sensitive operations within hardware-isolated environments. This prevents privacy policies from being bypassed even by privileged software components, thereby enhancing compliance assurance and improving system resilience in real-time settings.

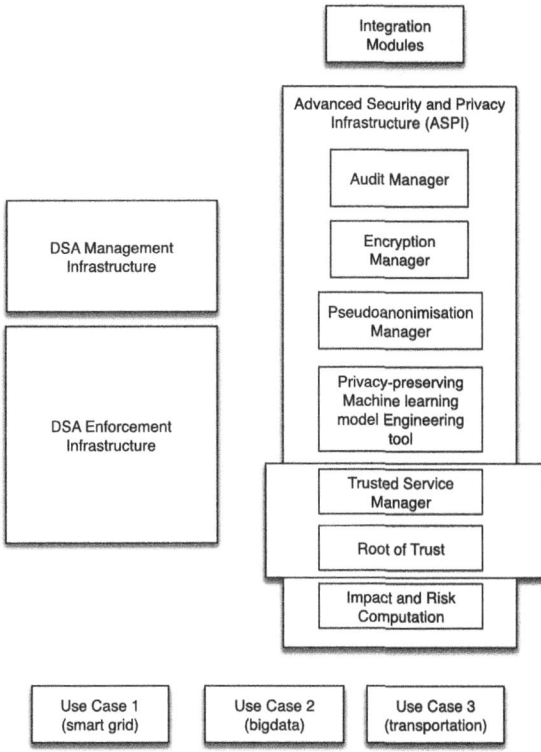

Fig. 1. DUCA Architecture

4   Secure Elements in DUCA: Comparative Analysis and Selection Criteria

The DUCA framework incorporates SE such as TEE, TPM, and Intel Software Guard Extensions (SGX) to ensure robust and tamper-resistant enforcement of privacy policies, especially during data processing, a well-known gap in traditional privacy frameworks.

Table 1 presents a technical comparison of common secure elements used in CPS. It contrasts their isolation levels, latency overhead, memory constraints, platform compatibility, and typical use cases.

Figure 2 presents a comparative overview of all Secure Elements integrated or considered within DUCA, namely TPM 2.0, Intel SGX, AMD SEV, TEE (e.g., TrustZone), DICE, and MARS. Each element is assessed across five critical dimensions: isolation level, latency overhead (normalized inversely), memory capacity, platform flexibility, and resistance to side-channel attacks. Values are normalized on a scale from 1 to 5 to facilitate visual comparison and support evidence-based selection in Cyber-Physical System (CPS) contexts.

Table 1. Technical Comparison of Secure Elements for CPS Integration

SE	Isolation	Latency	Memory	Platform	Example
TEE	Medium (isolated OS world)	Low (10–30%) [19]	Moderate (OS shared)	ARM, Mobile, IoT	Smart meters, connected vehicles, medical devices [20]
TPM 2.0	High (discrete chip)	Very Low (sub-ms) [21]	N/A	Windows, Linux, IoT	Device attestation, secure boot, key management [22]
Intel SGX	Very High (enclave-based)	Medium–High (20–60%) [23]	Strict (128 MB pre-SGX2)	Intel CPUs	eHealth analytics, encrypted ML, smart grid optimization [24]
AMD SEV	High (VM-level isolation)	Low (VM encryption) [25]	High (full VM encryption)	AMD EPYC servers	Secure cloud data processing, federated learning [25]
DICE	Low–Medium (device-level identity chaining)	Negligible	Minimal (low footprint)	Constrained IoT, ARM Cortex-M	Secure identity for IoT, low-power CPS nodes [26]
MARS	High (modular, attestation-focused)	Low–Medium (platform-dependent)	Flexible (scalable)	General-purpose, Edge/Cloud	Dynamic trust in heterogeneous CPS, fog computing [27, 28]

TPM 2.0 excels in device attestation with negligible latency and broad platform compatibility, making it a foundational element for secure bootstrapping and key management. Intel SGX provides the highest isolation for secure computation, though it is constrained by limited memory and reduced platform flexibility. TEEs offer balanced performance for latency-sensitive CPS tasks, particularly at the edge, while AMD SEV supports scalable virtual machine-level privacy enforcement in cloud infrastructures.

DICE exhibits minimal overhead and maximal flexibility, making it ideal for constrained IoT nodes and low-power CPS environments requiring lightweight identity derivation. MARS contributes enhanced modularity and scalability for attestation and measurement, addressing the trust management needs of heterogeneous, cloud-edge CPS deployments. Collectively, this comparison informs the strategic selection of Secure Elements tailored to specific privacy, performance, and trust requirements in diverse CPS scenarios.

The integration of secure elements into CPS must be guided by application-specific requirements such as real-time responsiveness, data sensitivity, and trust assurance. The selection of the appropriate hardware-based security primitive depends on the operational context, performance constraints, and the level of isolation needed to mitigate threats. This subsection outlines key deployment recommendations tailored to different CPS environments.

Latency-Sensitive CPS (e.g., Smart Grids, Autonomous Vehicles): Implement TEE (e.g. TrustZone) to enforce privacy policies on the edge with minimal overhead. TEEs enable real-time decision making without significant delay, as demonstrated in privacy-preserving smart metering systems [29].

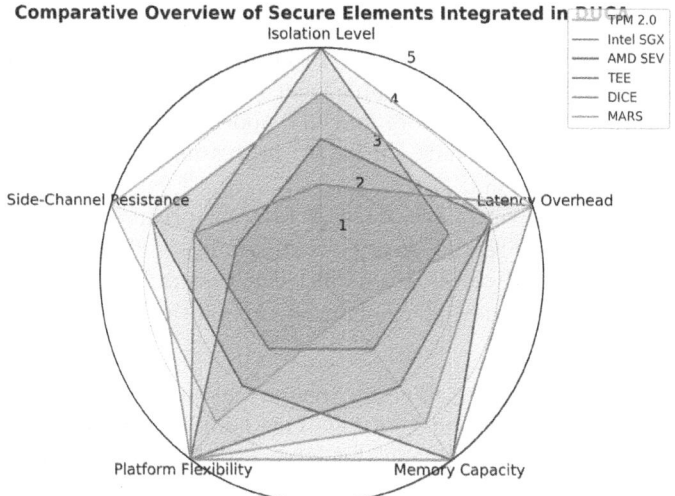

Fig. 2. Comparative overview of Secure Elements integrated or considered in DUCA. The radar chart evaluates TPM 2.0, Intel SGX, AMD SEV, TEE (e.g., TrustZone), DICE, and MARS across five critical dimensions: isolation level, latency overhead (inverted), memory capacity, platform flexibility, and side-channel resistance. Scores are normalized (1–5) for comparative visualization.

Data-Intensive Environments (e.g., Healthcare, Big Data Analytics): Use Intel SGX or AMD SEV to process sensitive data securely. SGX enclaves are ideal for the isolated computation of encrypted health data [30]. AMD SEV, by encrypting entire virtual machines, enables secure analytics in federated learning setups [31].

Device Trust Establishment: TPMs offer hardware-backed attestation and secure key storage, critical in environments requiring proof of device integrity (e.g., in smart manufacturing and IoT deployments) [32].

Although secure elements bring significant benefits for CPS integration, each technology introduces inherent limitations and trade-offs that must be considered during system design. Factors such as memory constraints, performance overhead, and vulnerability to specific attack vectors can affect their suitability for certain applications. This subsection highlights key technical drawbacks associated with leading secure element architectures.

- *SGX Limitations:* Prior to SGX2, enclave memory is limited to 128MB. Paging induces significant performance penalties. SGX is vulnerable to side-channel attacks (e.g. Foreshadow [33]), requiring careful mitigation.
- *TEE Constraints:* TEEs share system resources with the OS, which can pose risks if the OS is compromised. TrustZone's limited cryptographic acceleration restricts complex computation.
- *TPM Boundaries:* TPMs do not support data processing. Their role is limited to key storage, attestation, and secure boot, necessitating complementarity with TEEs/SGX.

DUCA adopts a hybrid Secure Element (SE) integration model in which TPMs are deployed on all CPS nodes to ensure device integrity and secure bootstrapping. TEEs are used to enforce local, context-aware privacy policies on edge devices, such as smart sensors and IoT nodes. In addition, SGX enclaves are used to protect sensitive data during AI processing or analytics in cloud or fog computing environments.

This modular approach allows DUCA to scale privacy enforcement while optimizing for performance and security contextually.

While DUCA currently leverages mainstream Secure Elements (TEE, TPM, SGX), emerging technologies offer enhanced capabilities for privacy protection in CPS.

Intel SGX2: SGX2 introduces dynamic memory management, allowing enclave memory to expand or shrink at runtime. This addresses SGX's earlier 128MB limitation and improves performance for large-scale analytics [34].

ARM Realm Management Extension (RME): An evolution of TrustZone, ARM RME supports finer-grained isolation and improved security management. RME introduces Realms, isolated from both the OS and the hypervisor, which improves the privacy enforcement of edge devices [35].

RISC-V Keystone Enclave: Keystone is an open source, flexible TEE designed for RISC-V platforms. It enables customized enclave security, which is potentially suitable for low-cost CPS nodes and IoT systems [36].

Confidential AI Accelerators: Hardware such as NVIDIA Confidential GPUs and Intel TDX (Trusted Domain Extensions) aims to extend enclave-like protections to GPU and virtualized AI workloads, a promising direction for DUCA's secure AI analytics.

DUCA Roadmap: DUCA's architecture is modular, enabling seamless integration of these next-generation SEs. Future versions will support SGX2 and RME, enhancing scalability and security in complex CPS deployments.

In addition to mainstream Secure Elements such as TPM 2.0 and Intel SGX, the DUCA framework can be extended to incorporate alternative trusted computing standards, enhancing flexibility and platform compatibility. *Trusted Platform Module (TPM) 2.0* provides secure storage for cryptographic keys and hardware-backed attestation capabilities, essential for device integrity validation in Cyber-Physical Systems (CPS) [21]. TPM 2.0 is widely supported across operating systems and hardware, and has been standardized by the Trusted Computing Group (TCG) to ensure robust security baselines [22]. We can see how DICE and MARS offer lightweight identity derivation and modular attestation capabilities respectively, complementing traditional SEs for diverse CPS scenarios.

Complementing TPM 2.0, the DICE offers a lightweight and scalable alternative. DICE, also standardized by TCG, is designed for constrained devices, enabling secure device identity derivation and trust establishment without requiring a discrete TPM. Its minimal resource requirements make DICE particularly suitable for IoT nodes and low-power edge devices in CPS deployments [37].

Moreover, *Measurement and Attestation Roots (MARS)* represents an emerging framework that emphasizes flexible attestation mechanisms and trust anchors tailored for diverse platforms. MARS enables fine-grained measurement of system states and supports scalable trust establishment across heterogeneous CPS environments [37]. Its modular design accommodates dynamic CPS infrastructures, aligning with DUCA's goals of real-time, context-aware privacy enforcement.

By supporting TPM 2.0, DICE, and MARS, DUCA can adapt trust enforcement mechanisms to diverse operational environments—ranging from high-resource cloud platforms to resource-constrained edge nodes. This flexibility enhances DUCA's ability to manage privacy risks dynamically, ensuring that data usage policies are enforced securely even in heterogeneous and evolving CPS landscapes.

4.1 SE-Based Policy Enforcement

Secure Elements (SEs) serve as hardware-based anchors for the enforcement of privacy and security policies in CPS. Unlike frameworks that implement privacy enforcement exclusively in software [14,18], DUCA relies on SEs to provide trusted execution environments that isolate sensitive computations from the rest of the system stack. This design enhances the enforcement of privacy policies by mitigating risks of tampering or bypass, especially during the data-in-use phase.

Trusted Platform Modules (TPMs) offer a hardware root of trust and enable cryptographic attestation, secure boot, and key sealing. While effective for system integrity verification, TPMs do not provide runtime execution isolation. Trusted Execution Environments (TEEs), such as ARM TrustZone, allow execution of code in a secure world that is isolated from the normal world, offering moderate protection against compromised OS layers but often requiring hardware-specific integration.

Intel Software Guard Extensions (SGX) provide stronger guarantees by allowing designated code to run within enclaves—isolated memory regions that are protected even from privileged software, including the OS and hypervisor. This capability makes SGX particularly suitable for enforcing privacy policies tied to specific data processing tasks. DUCA leverages this feature to ensure that analytics or access decisions on sensitive data are carried out within hardware-protected contexts.

Emerging standards such as DICE (Device Identifier Composition Engine) and MARS (Measurement and Attestation Roots) extend these principles by enabling scalable identity management and layered attestation across resource-constrained CPS components. Their integration into DUCA supports device-level privacy assertions and supply-chain trust anchoring.

By embedding enforcement mechanisms within SEs, DUCA enhances the resilience of CPS against advanced adversaries and complements PETs by securing data not only at rest or in transit but also during computation. The framework supports dynamic and context-aware privacy policies that are evaluated and enforced in real time, tailored to operational context, user roles, and risk posture.

Table 2. Comparison of Secure Elements for CPS Privacy Enforcement

Technology	Isolation	Attestation	Performance	Enforcement Scope
TPM	None (boot-time only)	Supported	Low impact	System integrity verification
ARM TrustZone	Medium (dual-world)	Limited	Low to medium	Secure execution on mobile/IoT
Intel SGX	High (enclaves)	Supported	High for I/O-bound tasks	In-enclave policy enforcement
DICE	None (identity derivation)	Supported	Minimal overhead	Hardware-based device identity
MARS	Not isolation-based	Supported	Minimal overhead	Root-of-trust attestation across platforms

Table 2 summarizes key properties of Secure Elements relevant for privacy enforcement in CPS, comparing their isolation level, attestation support, performance overhead, and scope of enforcement.

5   Application Scenarios and Privacy-Preserving Strategies in Cyber-Physical Systems

This section provides an in-depth overview of three specific use cases addressed by the DUCA project. The following scenarios illustrate how TPM 2.0, SGX, SEV, TEE, and emerging standards such as DICE and MARS are used contextually to enhance privacy enforcement and trust assurance in diverse CPS applications.

5.1   Use Case 1: Smart Grids and Surveillance Systems

The increasing deployment of smart grids enhances efficiency and reliability in energy distribution, but also raises significant privacy concerns, particularly with the integration of surveillance systems that collect data from public environments. Addressing these concerns requires robust security mechanisms to ensure data confidentiality, integrity, and compliance with privacy regulations. End-to-end encryption [38] and real-time pseudonymization techniques such as keyed hash functions [4] have been proposed to secure data transmission and mitigate identity linkage risks in IoT-enabled infrastructures. DUCA builds upon these methodologies by embedding them into a comprehensive data usage control architecture that enforces policies dynamically across interconnected smart grid devices.

A study by [39] explores the privacy challenges in Industry 4.0, emphasizing the importance of differential privacy, federated learning, and homomorphic encryption to secure large-scale, AI-driven data operations. DUCA aligns with these strategies, ensuring privacy-preserving analytics and compliance with GDPR and CCPA by PbD principles and PETs into its core.

The Sovereign framework [40] offers a decentralized smart home model utilizing Named Data Networking (NDN) and data-centric security to enable local control of IoT devices, eliminating reliance on external cloud services. DUCA draws on this approach for privacy-aware data handling in smart grids, emphasizing decentralized control and end-to-end encryption.

Further, a comprehensive review [41] categorizes IoT security frameworks into encryption-based solutions, identity management techniques, and self-protecting data models. DUCA incorporates homomorphic encryption, k-anonymity, and policy enforcement mechanisms to ensure regulatory compliance and data protection even across domain boundaries.

Blockchain's immutability and secure data-sharing capabilities [42] support GDPR compliance through pseudonymization and encryption. DUCA adopts blockchain-based measures to safeguard data throughout its lifecycle. Burnable pseudo-identities [43] enable anonymous, unlinkable interactions in blockchain systems, aligning with DUCA's approach to privacy-centric identity management in CPS.

GDPR-compliant SIEM frameworks [44] highlight early-stage pseudonymization and sanitizable digital signatures for secure and auditable data processing. DUCA integrates these techniques to maintain data usability for security incident detection while protecting personal information.

Overall, DUCA systematically addresses privacy and security challenges in smart grids and surveillance systems through the integration of PETs, decentralized control, and dynamic policy enforcement. Future research includes AI-driven privacy risk assessment and enhanced real-time adaptation of privacy policies.

Enhancing Smart Grid Privacy with Secure Elements: DUCA strengthens privacy protections using Secure Elements:

- *TPM*: Attests the authenticity of smart meters, ensuring trusted data sources.
- *Intel SGX*: Enables real-time grid optimization within secure enclaves, protecting sensitive energy data during processing.
- *TEE*: Enforcement of privacy policies within isolated execution environments, safeguarding energy consumption patterns.
- *DICE*: Provides a lightweight, hardware-backed identity derivation for constrained IoT nodes, enabling trust establishment with minimal overhead.
- *MARS*: Facilitates scalable, platform-independent attestation for heterogeneous smart grid infrastructures, enhancing dynamic policy enforcement.

5.2 Use Case 2: Usage Control for eHealth: Trust-Aware Cooperative Services in Mobility

The domain of eHealth, particularly in scenarios enabled by cooperative and cooperative automated mobility (CCAM), presents complex challenges related to data integrity, trust, and privacy. The continuous exchange of sensitive medical and mobility data increases exposure to potential breaches, particularly when data traverse heterogeneous infrastructures. Distributed ledger technologies (DLTs) have been used to ensure data authenticity and traceability [45], yet these solutions often lack integrated pseudonymization and encryption, leaving personal information vulnerable during transmission.

DUCA addresses this gap by incorporating real-time encryption and pseudonymization of IoT device identities, alongside dynamic context aware data sharing policies. These policies adapt based on factors such as asset location and role, and are enforced with remote attestation techniques to verify the trustworthiness of third-party nodes, thereby ensuring end-to-end data integrity and compliance.

A review by [46] identifies the major privacy challenges in blockchain systems, such as linkage transaction and smart contract vulnerabilities, and proposes cryptographic solutions including Secure Multi-Party Computation (SMPC), Zero Knowledge Proofs (ZKP), homomorphic encryption, and differential privacy. These align with DUCA's objective of enabling secure, privacy-preserving analytics and support for Self-Sovereign Identity (SSI) models, which enhance user control over personal data.

Complementary research by [47] presents a Pseudonym Revocation System (PRS) for IoT healthcare, utilizing elliptic curve cryptography (ECC) to manage pseudonym lifecycles without centralized control. DUCA integrates these principles to balance patient privacy with regulatory compliance.

In addition, a mobile library [48] to anonymize FHIR-compliant health data prior to transmission enables local processing and consent-based data sharing, an approach consistent with DUCA's emphasis on minimizing raw data exposure. Similar objectives are reflected in the methods of minimization of offline data and pseudonymization in real time by [49], further supporting DUCA's strategy.

The EDEN framework [50], employing federated learning for privacy-preserving location data management, illustrates the potential to balance data utility with privacy, informing the approach of DUCA in securing mobility-related eHealth data.

Enhancing eHealth Privacy with Secure Elements: DUCA strengthens privacy in mobile healthcare environments through:

- *Intel SGX*: Enables secure analytics on encrypted patient data within enclaves, preventing unauthorized access.
- *TPM*: Verifies the integrity of mobile healthcare and telemedicine devices, ensuring that only authenticated nodes handle sensitive data.
- *ARM TrustZone*: Executes privacy policies securely on mobile and IoT healthcare devices, protecting data at the edge.

- *DICE*: Supports secure identity chaining for lightweight mobile health devices, ensuring trusted data collection and transmission.
- *MARS*: Enables real-time attestation of third-party healthcare nodes, supporting dynamic and context-aware data sharing policies.

Through these Secure Elements, DUCA ensures robust, context-aware, and regulation-compliant privacy protection across dynamic and distributed eHealth ecosystems.

5.3   Use Case 3: Usage Control for Big Data and AI

Big Data and AI applications pose substantial challenges in managing personal data, especially under stringent privacy regulations such as GDPR. Traditional data protection techniques—anonymization, differential privacy, and homomorphic encryption [51]—provide foundational safeguards but often fall short when data traverse heterogeneous environments, including local and cloud-based infrastructures. DUCA addresses these limitations by enabling flexible, granular data protection through seamless enforcement of data usage policies across diverse platforms. Its architecture integrates PETs to ensure compliance and data security even in evolving threat landscapes.

A comprehensive review by [52] explores privacy risks in Beyond 5G (B5G) and 6G networks, such as unauthorized surveillance and AI-driven re-identification. The study advocates for decentralized AI, homomorphic encryption, and differential privacy—approaches DUCA adopts for privacy-preserving analytics throughout the data lifecycle.

In addition, [53] examines privacy in location-based services via centralized and federated frameworks like MOOD and SAFER. These systems assess privacy risks and enforce protections prior to data publication, supporting DUCA's implementation of PbD in AI environments and federated privacy assessments.

Research by [18] on Data-Centric Security (DCS) using Apache Ranger highlights dynamic data masking and role-based access control, aligning with the aim of DUCA to embed privacy policies in AI infrastructure. Automation via REST APIs enhances DUCA's scalability and interoperability.

Furthermore, [54] presents digital twins in System-of-Systems (SoS) architectures to dynamically manage pseudonymization and encryption critical to DUCA's context-aware privacy enforcement in AI-driven applications. The de-identification techniques explored by [55], including k-anonymity and l-diversity, inform the balance of DUCA between data protection and analytic utility.

Lastly, [56] discusses attribute-centric anonymization and synthetic data generation using Generative Adversarial Networks (GANs). DUCA leverages these methods to enable privacy-preserving AI model training while minimizing personal data exposure.

Enhancing Big Data Privacy and AI Security with Secure Elements: DUCA integrates Secure Elements to ensure privacy-compliant and secure analytics:

- *Intel SGX/AMD SEV*: Supports privacy-preserving machine learning on encrypted data within secure enclaves, maintaining model and data integrity.
- *TPM*: Verifies the authenticity and integrity of the data sources, mitigating the risks of adversarial data poisoning.
- *TEE*: Executes privacy-preserving analytics in isolated environments, enabling dynamic enforcement of privacy policies across cloud and edge infrastructures.
- *MARS*: Provides scalable trust attestation across federated AI infrastructures, ensuring trustworthiness of diverse computing environments during model training and data exchange.

Through these technologies, DUCA enhances AI-driven decision-making while ensuring GDPR compliance and scalable big data privacy protection. While DICE is optimized for constrained environments and is therefore less applicable in this context, MARS contributes effectively to federated trust management by enabling scalable and reliable attestation across diverse AI infrastructures.

5.4   Transversal to Three-Use Cases

Beyond the specific use cases presented, several complementary research efforts contribute transversally to DUCA's privacy-preserving objectives, particularly to advance compliance, data security, and the effective integration of PETs. A comprehensive review [57] of PETs in the automotive sector identifies technological parallels relevant to smart grids, eHealth, and AI analytics, supporting DUCA's adoption of differential privacy, homomorphic encryption, federated learning, and secure multi-party computation. This review also highlights the complexity of cross-organizational data sharing—an inherent challenge addressed within DUCA's modular and policy-driven architecture.

To illustrate how DUCA operationalizes PbD, PETs, and dynamic policy enforcement, Fig. 3 outlines its privacy management framework. This model demonstrates DUCA's embedded privacy protections throughout CPS infrastructures, ensuring regulatory compliance while maintaining data utility and operational efficiency.

In line with this, Privacy Level Agreements (PLAs) [58] formalize user-defined privacy preferences within Industrial Data Spaces, complementing DUCA's model-based enforcement of data minimization and purpose limitation. Additionally, scalable anonymization techniques, such as clustering-based k-anonymity with α-deassociation [59], are applicable across DUCA's healthcare and smart grid domains.

A dual layer protection strategy combining blowfish encryption with pseudonymization [60] aligns with DUCA's security model for data confidentiality, particularly during inter-domain sharing. In the IoT context, the categorization of pseudonyms into short-term, session-based, and location-based types [61] informs DUCA's identity management mechanisms, enhancing secure communication in CPS environments.

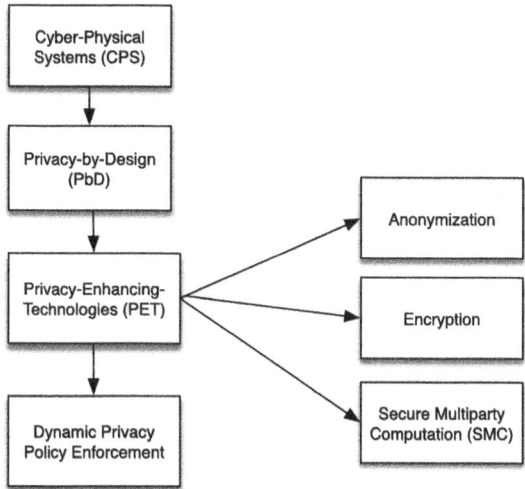

Fig. 3. DUCA Privacy Management Framework: Integration of PbD, PETs, and Dynamic Policy Enforcement

Moreover, the application of homomorphic encryption to text mining services [5] exemplifies the potential for privacy-preserving analytics, an approach that DUCA extends to surveillance systems and AI-driven decision-making.

Taken together, these contributions reinforce DUCA's commitment to robust, scalable, and regulation-compliant privacy management across diverse CPS applications. Future research will aim to further enhance DUCA's capabilities in privacy-preserving AI, adaptive policy refinement, and real-time privacy risk assessment, thereby supporting its continued evolution as a comprehensive and forward-looking privacy framework.

6   Discussion and Conclusions

Designing privacy-aware Cyber-Physical Systems (CPS) remains a complex challenge due to their dynamic, distributed, and heterogeneous nature. The DUCA framework addresses these demands through a holistic Privacy-by-Design (PbD) approach, embedding protection mechanisms across the entire data lifecycle—from generation to storage and sharing—while supporting real-time CPS functionalities.

At its core, DUCA integrates Privacy-Enhancing Technologies (PETs) to enable fine-grained control over data processing without compromising analytical utility. Techniques such as anonymization, pseudonymization, encryption, and differential privacy are combined with adaptive, context-aware policy enforcement to ensure continuous alignment with evolving regulations like the GDPR. This architectural flexibility allows DUCA to accommodate the distinct regulatory and operational needs of various domains, including energy, healthcare, and mobility.

The practical applicability of DUCA has been demonstrated across diverse use cases—ranging from smart grids and industrial systems to AI-enabled healthcare—confirming its ability to reconcile robust privacy protection with the performance constraints inherent to CPS. A key differentiator of DUCA is its integration of Secure Elements (SEs), such as Trusted Execution Environments (TEE), Trusted Platform Modules (TPM), and Intel SGX. These components enable secure, tamper-resistant execution of privacy policies, enhancing trustworthiness across data in use, in transit, and at rest—surpassing the capabilities of software-only approaches.

Further extending its capabilities, DUCA incorporates emerging trusted computing technologies like DICE and MARS. DICE offers lightweight identity derivation and attestation suited for resource-constrained devices, supporting edge trust establishment with minimal overhead. MARS provides scalable, modular attestation mechanisms for heterogeneous infrastructures. DUCA's modular architecture supports seamless integration of such components, ensuring adaptability as new standards and SE technologies evolve.

Despite its strengths, DUCA must address ongoing challenges related to scalability, interoperability, and dynamic policy orchestration. Large-scale CPS introduce complexities in achieving low-latency policy enforcement across diverse infrastructures. Interoperability is further hindered by varied data formats, protocols, and legacy components. Moreover, SE integration entails trade-offs involving system complexity, energy consumption, and performance overhead.

Future work will focus on developing autonomous, adaptive policy orchestration mechanisms, potentially leveraging machine learning for real-time privacy risk assessment and automated policy tuning. The integration of advanced privacy-preserving AI techniques—such as federated learning, secure multi-party computation, and homomorphic encryption—can further enable compliant analytics without compromising confidentiality. Additionally, DUCA's modular design should continue evolving to accommodate emerging cryptographic primitives and SE standards with minimal system disruption.

In summary, DUCA delivers a comprehensive and adaptable solution for privacy management in CPS. Through its fusion of dynamic policy enforcement, extensive PET integration, and hardware-backed security, it provides scalable, regulation-compliant privacy safeguards. Its demonstrated versatility and extensibility position DUCA as a reference architecture for the next generation of privacy-aware cyber-physical infrastructures.

Acknowledgments. This work has been supported by the EU project DUCA under GA No 101086308 (HORIZON-MSCA-2021-SE-01).

Disclosure of Interests. Authors have no competing interests.

References

1. Warren, S.D., Brandeis, L.D.: The right to privacy. Harv. Law Rev. **4**(5), 193–220 (1890)
2. Westin, A.F.: Privacy and Freedom. Atheneum, New York (1967)
3. Tsohou, A., Kokolakis, G.: GDPR in practice: privacy statements and fair processing. Comput. Law Secur. Rev. **36**, 105406 (2020)
4. European Parliament and Council: Regulation (EU) 2016/679 of the European parliament and of the council of 27 April 2016 on the protection of natural persons with regard to the processing of personal data and on the free movement of such data, and repealing directive 95/46/EC (general data protection regulation), article 25: Data protection by design and by default. Off. J. Eur. Union 1–88 (2020)
5. Cavoukian, A.: Privacy by design: the 7 foundational principles. Information and Privacy Commissioner of Ontario (2011)
6. Cárdenas, A.A., Amin, S., Sastry, S.: Research challenges for the security of control systems. In: Proceedings of the 3rd Conference on Hot Topics in Security, pp. 1–6. USENIX Association (2008)
7. Lee, E.A.: Cyber-physical systems: design challenges. In: Proceedings of the 11th IEEE International Symposium on Object and Component-Oriented Real-Time Distributed Computing (ISORC), pp. 363–369. IEEE (2008)
8. Broy, M.: Cyber-physical systems - innovation durch software-intensive eingebettete systeme. Informatik-Spektrum **35**, 61–66 (2012)
9. Khaitan, S.V., McCalley, J.D.: Design techniques and applications of cyberphysical systems: a survey. IEEE Syst. J. **9**(2), 350–365 (2015)
10. Zhong, R., Feng, X., Li, Q.: Cyber-physical systems in intelligent manufacturing. Adv. Robot. **31**(19–20), 1175–1190 (2017)
11. Baloyi, E., Le Guennec, D.: Privacy in cyber-physical systems: issues and solutions. Int. J. Cyber-Phys. Syst. (IJCS) **4**(2), 40–58 (2019)
12. Hoepman, J.-H.: Privacy design strategies. In: IFIP International Information Security Conference, pp. 446–459. Springer (2014)
13. Cha, S., Lee, H., Kang, H.K.: Privacy-enhancing technologies: a review. J. Inf. Process. Syst. **15**(1), 1–16 (2019)
14. Mont, M., Harrison, K., Clark, J.R.: Privacy management for portable healthcare records. In: Proceedings of the 18th IEEE Symposium on Computer-Based Medical Systems (CBMS), pp. 459–464. IEEE (2005)
15. Zemskov, A.D., et al.: Security and privacy of digital twins for advanced manufacturing: a survey, arXiv preprint arXiv:2412.13939 (2024)
16. Volkmann, M., Tripathi, S.S., Kaven, S., Frank, C., Skwarek, V.: Privacy in local energy markets: a framework for a self-sovereign identity based P2P-trading authentication system. In: 2023 IEEE 21st International Conference on Industrial Informatics (INDIN), pp. 1–7. IEEE (2023)
17. Vargaftik, S., Basat, R.B., Portnoy, A., Mendelson, G., Itzhak, Y.B., Mitzenmacher, M.: Eden: communication-efficient and robust distributed mean estimation for federated learning. In: International Conference on Machine Learning, pp. 21984–22014. PMLR (2022)
18. Ponchione, L.: Implementation of policies in data-centric security solutions: a case study. Ph.D. dissertation, Politecnico di Torino (2023)
19. Suzaki, K., Nakajima, K., Oi, T., Tsukamoto, A.: TS-perf: general performance measurement of trusted execution environment and rich execution environment on intel SGX, arm trustzone, and RISC-V keystone. IEEE Access **9**, 133520–133530 (2021)

20. Akgün, M., Soykan, E.U., Soykan, G.: A privacy-preserving scheme for smart grid using trusted execution environment. IEEE Access **11**, 9182–9196 (2023)
21. Camenisch, J., Chen, L., Drijvers, M., Lehmann, A., Novick, D., Urian, R.: One TPM to bind them all: fixing TPM 2.0 for provably secure anonymous attestation. In: IEEE Symposium on Security and Privacy (SP), pp. 901–920. IEEE (2017)
22. Fernandez, E.B., Muñoz, A.: A cluster of patterns for trusted computing. Int. J. Inf. Secur. **24**(1), 72 (2025)
23. Weichbrodt, N., Aublin, P.-L., Kapitza, R.: SGX-perf: a performance analysis tool for intel SGX enclaves. In: Proceedings of the 19th International Middleware Conference, pp. 201–213 (2018)
24. Rajeh, Z.M., Alhomdy, S.A., Thabit, F.: Secure authentication in smart home environment using SGX and biometrics: survey. In: 2024 1st International Conference on Emerging Technologies for Dependable Internet of Things (ICETI), pp. 1–10. IEEE (2024)
25. Atiiq, S.A., Risdianto, A.C.: Demystifying AMD SEV performance penalty for NFV deployment. In: Proceedings of the 2024 13th International Conference on Networks, Communication and Computing, pp. 1–8 (2024)
26. Jäger, L., Petri, R.: Dice harder: a hardware implementation of the device identifier composition engine. In: Proceedings of the 15th International Conference on Availability, Reliability and Security, pp. 1–8 (2020)
27. Trusted Computing Group: TCG Cyber Resilient Module and Building Block Requirements Version 1.00, Rev. 0.08. Trusted Computing Group, TCG Specifications (2020). https://trustedcomputinggroup.org/resource/
28. Trusted Computing Group: TCG Reference Integrity Manifests (RIM) Information Model Version 1.00, Rev. 0.16. Trusted Computing Group, TCG Specifications (2020). https://trustedcomputinggroup.org/resource/tcg-reference-integrity-manifest-rim-information-model/
29. Sultan, S.: Privacy-preserving metering in smart grid for billing, operational metering, and incentive-based schemes: a survey. Comput. Secur. **84**, 148–165 (2019)
30. Birrell, E., Gjerdrum, A., van Renesse, R., Johansen, H., Johansen, D., Schneider, F.B.: SGX enforcement of use-based privacy. In: Proceedings of the 2018 Workshop on Privacy in the Electronic Society, pp. 155–167 (2018)
31. Zobaed, S., Amini Salehi, M.: Confidential computing across edge-to-cloud for machine learning: a survey study. Softw. Pract. Exp. (2025)
32. Safford, D.R., Wiseman, M.: Hardware rooted trust for additive manufacturing. IEEE Access **7**, 79211–79215 (2019)
33. Van Bulck, J., et al.: Foreshadow: extracting the keys to the intel {SGX} kingdom with transient {Out-of-Order} execution. In: 27th USENIX Security Symposium (USENIX Security 2018), pp. 991–1008 (2018)
34. Lutsch, A., El-Hindi, M., Heinrich, M., Ritter, D., IstvÁĄn, Z., Binnig, C.: Benchmarking analytical query processing in intel SGXv2, arXiv preprint arXiv:2403.11874 (2024)
35. Kaplan, M., Raj, H., Scarlata, V., Vinayagamoorhty, K.: Enabling realms with the arm confidential compute architecture. USENIX (2021). https://www.usenix.org/publications/loginonline/enabling-realms-arm-confidential-compute-architecture
36. Lee, D., Kohlbrenner, D., Shinde, S., Asanović, K., Song, D.: Keystone: an open framework for architecting trusted execution environments. In: Proceedings of the Fifteenth European Conference on Computer Systems, pp. 1–16 (2020)
37. Said, S., Hajlaoui, J.E., Omri, M.N.: A survey on the optimization of security components placement in internet of things. J. Netw. Syst. Manage. **32**(4), 77 (2024)

38. Dhinakaran, D., Sankar, S., Selvaraj, D., Raja, S.E.: Privacy-preserving data in IoT-based cloud systems: a comprehensive survey with AI integration, arXiv preprint arXiv:2401.00794 (2024)
39. Tanisha, J., Rajesh, P., Singh, R., Adhip, K., Stuti, K., Ajitha, D.: Privacy and data protection challenges in industry 4.0: an AI-driven perspective (2024)
40. Zhang, Z., Yu, T., Ma, X., Guan, Y., Moll, P., Zhang, L.: Sovereign: self-contained smart home with data-centric network and security. IEEE Internet Things J. 9(15), 13808–13822 (2022)
41. Al-Hasnawi, A., Niu, Y., Tawfeq, J.F., Pradhan, M.R., Salahat, M., Ghazal, T.M.: IoT security frameworks: a comparative review with a focus on privacy. In: 2024 2nd International Conference on Cyber Resilience (ICCR), pp. 1–10. IEEE (2024)
42. Campanile, L., Iacono, M., Marulli, F., Mastroianni, M., et al.: Privacy regulations challenges on data-centric and IoT systems: a case study for smart vehicles. In: IoTBDS, pp. 507–518 (2020)
43. Gutiérrez-Agüero, I., Anguita, S., Larrucea, X., Gomez-Goiri, A., Urquizu, B.: Burnable pseudo-identity: a non-binding anonymous identity method for ethereum. IEEE Access 9, 108912–108923 (2021)
44. Menges, F., et al.: Towards GDPR-compliant data processing in modern SIEM systems. Comput. Secur. 103, 102165 (2021)
45. Asante, M., Epiphaniou, G., Maple, C., Al-Khateeb, H., Bottarelli, M., Ghafoor, K.Z.: Distributed ledger technologies in supply chain security management: a comprehensive survey. IEEE Trans. Eng. Manage. 70(2), 713–739 (2021)
46. Bernabe, J.B., Canovas, J.L., Hernandez-Ramos, J.L., Moreno, R.T., Skarmeta, A.: Privacy-preserving solutions for blockchain: review and challenges. IEEE Access 7, 164908–164940 (2019)
47. Bermad, N.: Pseudonym revocation system for IoT-based medical applications. Available at SSRN 4865840
48. Dimopoulou, S., Symvoulidis, C., Koutsoukos, K., Kiourtis, A., Mavrogiorgou, A., Kyriazis, D.: Mobile anonymization and pseudonymization of structured health data for research. In: Seventh International Conference on Mobile and Secure Services (MobiSecServ), pp. 1–6. IEEE (2022)
49. Kangwa, M.: Prevention of personally identifiable information leakage in ecommerce using offline data minimization and online pseudonymisation. Ph.D. dissertation, The University of Zambia (2023)
50. Khalfoun, B., Ben Mokhtar, S., Bouchenak, S., Nitu, V.: Eden: enforcing location privacy through re-identification risk assessment: a federated learning approach. Proc. ACM Interact. Mob. Wearable Ubiquitous Technol. 5(2), 1–25 (2021)
51. Salas, J., Domingo-Ferrer, J.: Some basics on privacy techniques, anonymization and their big data challenges. Math. Comput. Sci. 12, 263–274 (2018)
52. Sandeepa, C., Siniarski, B., Kourtellis, N., Wang, S., Liyanage, M.: A survey on privacy for B5G/6G: new privacy challenges, and research directions. J. Ind. Inf. Integr. 30, 100405 (2022)
53. Khalfoun, B.: Privacy preserving location based services: from centralized to federated approaches. Ph.D. dissertation, INSA de Lyon (2022)
54. Jost, T.E.: Privacy management for cyber-physical systems - a system of systems architecture based on digital twins (2021)
55. Baumer, K.: Identification and evaluation of concepts for privacy-enhancing big data analytics using de-identification methods on wrist-worn wearable data. Ph.D. dissertation, Technische Universität München (2020)
56. Majeed, A.: Attribute-centric and synthetic data based privacy preserving methods: a systematic review. J. Cybersecur. Priv. 3(3), 638–661 (2023)

57. Garrido, G.M., Schmidt, K., Harth-Kitzerow, C., Klepsch, J., Luckow, A., Matthes, F.: Exploring privacy-enhancing technologies in the automotive value chain, arXiv e-prints, pp. arXiv–2209 (2022)

58. Ahmadian, A.S., Jürjens, J., Strüber, D.: Extending model-based privacy analysis for the industrial data space by exploiting privacy level agreements. In: Proceedings of the 33rd Annual ACM Symposium on Applied Computing, pp. 1142–1149 (2018)

59. Onesimu, J.A., Karthikeyan, J., Sei, Y.: An efficient clustering-based anonymization scheme for privacy-preserving data collection in IoT based healthcare services. Peer-to-Peer Netw. Appl. **14**(3), 1629–1649 (2021)

60. Fazal, R., Shah, M.A., Khattak, H.A., Rauf, H.T., Al-Turjman, F.: Achieving data privacy for decision support systems in times of massive data sharing. Clust. Comput. 1–13 (2022). https://doi.org/10.1007/s10586-021-03514-x

61. Akil, M., Islami, L., Fischer-Hübner, S., Martucci, L.A., Zuccato, A.: Privacy-preserving identifiers for IoT: a systematic literature review. IEEE Access **8**, 168470–168485 (2020)

Database and Storage Security

Bloom Filter Look-Up Tables for Private and Secure Distributed Databases in Web3

Shlomi Dolev$^{(\boxtimes)}$ ⓘ, Ehud Gudes ⓘ, and Daniel Shlomo

Ben-Gurion University of the Negev, Beer-Sheva, Israel
{dolev,ehud}@cs.bgu.ac.il, danshl@post.bgu.ac.il

Abstract. The rapid growth of decentralized systems in the Web3 ecosystem has introduced numerous challenges, particularly in ensuring data security, privacy, and scalability [3,8]. These systems rely heavily on distributed architectures, requiring robust mechanisms to manage data and interactions among participants securely.

One critical aspect of decentralized systems is key management, which is essential for encrypting files, securing database segments, and enabling private transactions. However, securely managing cryptographic keys in a distributed environment poses significant risks, especially when nodes in the network can be compromised [9].

This research proposes a decentralized database scheme specifically designed for secure and private key management. Our approach ensures that cryptographic keys are not stored explicitly at any location, preventing their discovery even if an attacker gains control of multiple nodes. Instead of traditional storage, keys are encoded and distributed using the BFLUT (Bloom Filter for Private Look-Up Tables) algorithm [7], which enables secure retrieval without direct exposure.

The system leverages OrbitDB [4], IPFS [1], and IPNS [10] for decentralized data management, providing robust support for consistency, scalability, and simultaneous updates. By combining these technologies, our scheme enhances both security and privacy while maintaining high performance and reliability.

Our findings demonstrate the system's capability to securely manage keys, prevent unauthorized access, and ensure privacy, making it a foundational solution for Web3 applications requiring decentralized security.

Keywords: Bloom Filter · Private Secure Data Base · Web3

1 Introduction

The rise of decentralized systems in the Web3 environment introduces unique challenges in securely and efficiently managing critical data [3]. While Web3 provides transparency, self-sovereignty, and decentralized data sharing without

Partially supported by the Israeli Science Foundation (Grant No. 465/22), the Rita Altura Trust Chair in Computer Science, and the Frankel Center for Computer Science.

© IFIP International Federation for Information Processing 2025
Published by Springer Nature Switzerland AG 2025
S. Katsikas and B. Shafiq (Eds.): DBSec 2025, LNCS 15722, pp. 233–250, 2025.
https://doi.org/10.1007/978-3-031-96590-6_13

reliance on central intermediaries, its peer-to-peer (P2P) architecture requires robust mechanisms to ensure privacy, security, and conflict-free updates [11]. These challenges are amplified by the need to maintain availability and consistency in a distributed network where multiple nodes participate in data storage and dissemination.

One of the key considerations in decentralized systems is how to balance privacy and accessibility. While data must remain accessible to authorized users, it is essential to prevent unauthorized access and ensure that even if some nodes are compromised, sensitive information remains secure. Traditional approaches often rely on explicit data storage, which can expose sensitive information to potential attacks or breaches.

In this research, we propose a novel decentralized database scheme designed to securely store and retrieve keys without directly storing them. Unlike conventional systems, where sensitive data or keys are explicitly stored, our scheme encodes information in a distributed manner across the network by using a combination of advanced technologies. This ensures that even if certain nodes are compromised, the encoded information cannot be reconstructed or exploited by attackers.

Our system leverages the following components:

OrbitDB and CRDTs: OrbitDB [4] is a distributed database built on IPFS [1], enabling decentralized storage without centralized intermediaries. It supports various database types, such as logs, key-value stores, and document-based systems, making it adaptable for decentralized environments.

A key feature is its use of CRDTs (Conflict-Free Replicated Data Types) [5], which ensure data consistency across nodes by allowing concurrent updates without conflicts.

IPNS (InterPlanetary Name System): IPNS [10] is a protocol for persistent addressing in decentralized networks, built on top of IPFS [1].

In IPFS, files are addressed by their content identifier (CID), which changes whenever the content is modified. This dynamic nature complicates access to frequently updated files, as older references become obsolete.

IPNS solves this by associating a fixed, cryptographically signed name with the file's changing CID, allowing seamless access to the latest version. In our system, this ensures reliable data retrieval, even as files are updated, simplifying management in distributed environments with frequent modifications.

BFLUT (Bloom Filter for Private Look-Up Tables): At the core of our solution is the BFLUT algorithm [7], which encodes keys into secure, distributed representations. This approach avoids explicitly storing cryptographic keys, ensuring that they cannot be directly exposed or reconstructed, even if an attacker gains access to certain nodes in the network.

BFLUT is built upon the Bloom Filter technique, a probabilistic data structure that efficiently verifies whether an element is present in a set without storing the element itself. This enables BFLUT to securely encode keys by activating specific bits in the Bloom Filter, determined by hash functions applied to the key's components.

This mechanism is vital for our decentralized database, as it allows us to manage keys securely and privately, enabling efficient key retrieval while maintaining robust protections against unauthorized access (ref. Sect. 4.2).

This work contributes to the design and analysis of a secure decentralized database, specifically focusing on efficient key encoding and retrieval. By addressing privacy and scalability concerns, our approach lays the foundation for secure, reliable, and efficient Web3-based applications.

The rest of this paper is structured as follows: Sect. 2 discusses related work, Sect. 3 highlights the key advantages of our approach, Sect. 4 outlines the methodology, and Sect. 5 presents the analysis of our scheme. Finally, discussions and conclusions appear in Sect. 6. Many details are omitted from this extended abstract.

2 Related Work

Key management and secure data distribution are critical aspects of decentralized systems. Two significant studies provide insights into current approaches and their limitations, particularly regarding **secret sharing schemes** and **threshold cryptography**.

Secure and Effective Key Management Using Secret Sharing Schemes in Cloud Computing (2020). This study [6] explores the use of secret sharing schemes (SSS) to enhance key management in cloud environments. The approach involves dividing a secret into multiple shares, distributed across different nodes. A predefined threshold of shares is required to reconstruct the key, thereby reducing the risk of single points of failure and improving overall security in cloud setups.

However, there are notable limitations:

1. **Centralized Dependency:** The reliance on cloud providers for the distribution and reconstruction of shares means that data still resides within centralized systems, which is contrary to the decentralized philosophy of Web3.
2. **Reconstruction Delays:** Share reconstruction in dynamic or unreliable environments can introduce significant delays.

Secure Key Management in Distributed Systems: Challenges and Solutions (2023). This study [2] builds on the principles of secret sharing by incorporating threshold cryptography for robust key management in distributed networks. Unlike traditional approaches, this method enables operations directly on the shares without requiring full reconstruction. This improves fault tolerance, as the system can function even if certain nodes are unavailable, and enhances resilience to failures.

While the approach provides theoretical improvements:

1. **Computational Overhead:** Performing operations on shares without full reconstruction increases computational complexity, especially in large-scale systems with numerous nodes.
2. **Threshold-Based Complexity:** Systems requiring frequent key updates or decentralized storage face challenges in maintaining efficient operations, as the threshold model adds complexity to key updates.

Relevance to Our Work. The literature review explores decentralized systems like IPFS [1] and OrbitDB [4], which provide reliable, self-sovereign data storage in Web3 environments. It also examines conflict management methods, particularly CRDTs [5], which ensure consistency in distributed updates, and Bloom Filter-based techniques, such as BFLUT [7], for private data retrieval.

While each of these tools operates independently, this research combines these methodologies. Existing solutions mainly focus on secure key management in controlled or semi-controlled environments like hybrid cloud systems. In contrast, our approach is designed for fully decentralized Web3 environments, offering:

1. **Decentralized File Representation:** Utilizing BFLUT for bitwise modifications, reducing false positives in key retrieval on IPFS.
2. **True Decentralization:** Eliminating reliance on a single entity, enhancing security and privacy in distributed storage.

3   Key Advantages of the Proposed System

High Privacy. The system leverages the BFLUT (Bloom Filter for Private Look-Up Tables) algorithm to encrypt and securely store data. This algorithm encodes data so that it can only be accessed through a controlled retrieval mechanism. This design prevents direct exposure of sensitive information, even in cases of system breaches.

Consistency and Concurrent Updates. Using CRDTs (Conflict-Free Replicated Data Types), the system supports concurrent updates while maintaining absolute consistency across all nodes. This decentralized update mechanism eliminates the need for central synchronization, ensuring that data remains accurate and up-to-date across the entire network.

Efficient and Secure Data Distribution. The system distributes data intelligently across different nodes in the network, where each fragment of the database is stored on a separate node. This approach ensures balanced workload distribution, high availability, and fast access to required data without relying on a single point of failure. The optimized distribution mechanism also facilitates efficient file management and retrieval within the network.

Security and Resilience in a Decentralized Environment. The system is designed so that each node stores only data fragments. In contrast to traditional databases, where all the information is stored in a single geographic location and could be lost entirely due to accidental deletion or failure, our approach distributes the data across multiple nodes. This ensures that such a catastrophic loss does not occur.

In the event of a node failure, the data remains accessible through other nodes, maintaining availability and integrity. Moreover, even if all the files associated with a specific bit of a key were to be deleted, the system can still proceed with key extraction by treating all possible values for that bit as valid. Advanced encryption methods prevent unauthorized access, while the distributed nature ensures that even attacks targeting multiple nodes cannot compromise the data's availability or integrity.

The combination of these technologies enables the creation of a distributed, secure, and efficient database tailored to the complex requirements of the Web3 environment. Our solution addresses the intersection of privacy, availability, and update management, representing a significant advancement in distributed data management.

4 Methodology

Before delving into the implementation details, we first examine the general structure and the BFLUT data structure, which forms the backbone of the proposed system. BFLUT is the core mechanism for secure and efficient data encoding and storage in a decentralized environment, ensuring privacy and seamless access.

4.1 Introduction: System Purpose and General Structure

The proposed system provides a secure, decentralized database within the Web3 environment. Data entries are stored as files on distributed nodes, with their references managed using a key-value structure in **OrbitDB**, a distributed database optimized for decentralized storage. Each key-value pair is structured as follows:

Key: A unique identifier generated using a hash function.

Value: A reference to a file stored on a specific node in the network.

Since files in the system are addressed by theirContent Identifier (CID)—a hash of their content—any modification results in a new CID, invalidating previous references. To maintain persistent access, the system employs InterPlanetary Name System (IPNS), which associates a fixed, cryptographically signed name with the latest CID. This ensures that even when a file is updated, its reference remains valid and accessible.

Each file is stored on a limited number of nodes to enhance privacy, scalability, and fault tolerance, reducing reliance on any single entity. The system ensures reliable and secure decentralized data storage and retrieval by integrating OrbitDB for efficient key-value management and IPNS for dynamic file referencing.

4.2   BFLUT: A Secure Encoding Mechanism

The BFLUT (Bloom Filter for Private Look-Up Tables) algorithm is a secure and compact encoding mechanism designed to encode and store data while ensuring privacy. It leverages the principles of Bloom Filters, which allow the system to verify the existence of data without revealing or storing the data itself. This technique ensures that sensitive information remains protected even in decentralized environments.

Encoding involves activating specific bits in a Bloom Filter table based on hash functions. These bits are strategically chosen to represent the data in a secure and distributed manner, avoiding the direct storage of raw data.

Example: Storing and Searching Data. Consider a user named "John Smith" associated with the value '0110'. The encoding and storage process involves computing a hash of "John Smith" with the prefix '0' and activating the corresponding bit in the Bloom Filter table, represented as $H(JohnSmith0)$. Subsequently, additional bits are activated for the following prefixes:
$H(JohnSmith01)$, $H(JohnSmith011)$, and $H(JohnSmith0110)$.

This process ensures that all prefixes of the value are securely encoded in the system. By activating these bits in the Bloom Filter table, the system creates a distributed representation of the data that can be securely retrieved. When the system stores these activated bits, they are effectively linked to the user's name and associated prefixes. This linkage allows the system to verify the existence of data while maintaining its encoded form, ensuring privacy and security.

To retrieve the value associated with the key "John Smith," the system follows this process:

1. Check the bits at $H(JohnSmith0)$ and $H(JohnSmith1)$. If none of them are active, it can be concluded that the key does not exist in the system.
2. If a bit is active for one of the prefixes (e.g., $H(JohnSmith0)$), continue checking the subsequent prefixes: $H(JohnSmith00)$ or $H(JohnSmith01)$.
3. Repeat this process, appending additional prefixes, until the desired value length is reached (assuming the length is known).

BFLUT inherently allows for the possibility of false positives, where certain bits may appear active even if the corresponding value does not exist. However, if no solution is found, it can be conclusively determined that the key does not exist in the system. This will be elaborated upon later (Ref. Fig. 1).

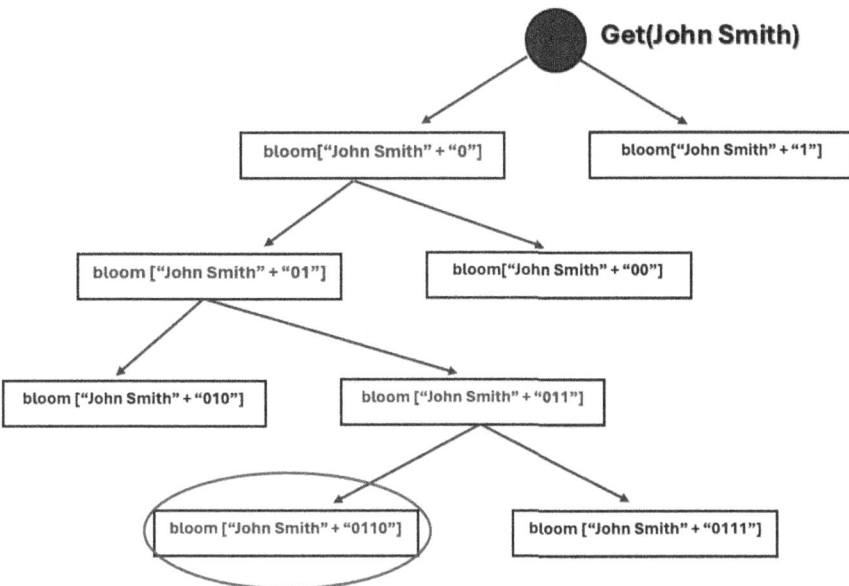

Fig. 1. Get value from BFLUT example

4.3 System Implementation

Having understood the system's structure and the role of BFLUT, we now delve into the details of the system's implementation, including its initialization, data insertion, and retrieval processes.

Introduction: A System for Key Management Based on Username and Password. Let us consider a system designed to securely store and retrieve keys based on a username and password, for example, "John Smith" with the password "password". In this system, the username and password are not stored in their raw form; rather, they are used as inputs to derive a unique key (KEY). This key is chosen from a predefined range of values (in this example, binary values 0 or 1) and is managed in a distributed and secure manner across the network.

When the correct username and password are provided, the system computes a mapping that yields the corresponding key (KEY). This derived key is then encrypted and stored across multiple nodes, ensuring that even if part of the network is compromised, the sensitive credentials are not exposed. The raw data (i.e., the username and password) is never stored directly, so the security of the system is maintained by safeguarding only the encrypted key.

Step 1: System Initialization and File Allocation. During initialization, the system creates a distributed database with N files, each containing M bits, initially set to 0. It also generates N unique hash addresses as keys, each pointing to a node storing a file in the distributed network. This design ensures balanced load distribution, resilience to failures, and consistent data accessibility (Ref. Fig 2).

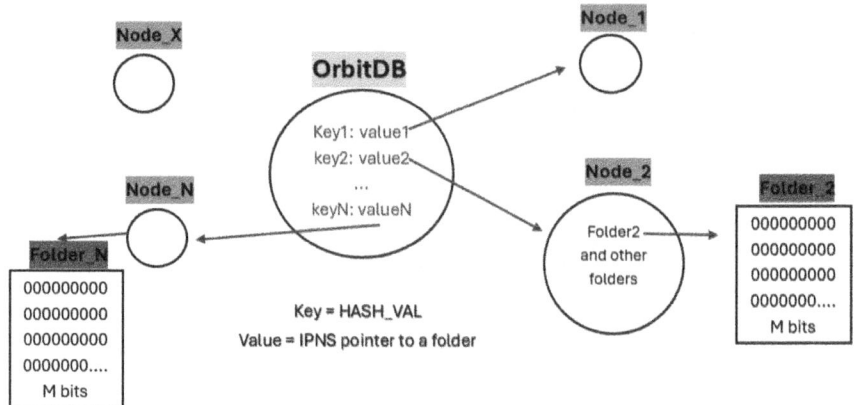

Fig. 2. Step 1 - System Initialization

Step 2: Inserting a New Key. When a new key needs to be added to the system for a given username and password, the process follows these steps:

1. **Generate a Random Key:** The system generates a random key of length L bits (e.g., 16 bits). For instance, suppose the generated key is Key $=$ 1000111000010010.
2. **Calculate Hash Values Using BFLUT:** The system calculates Hash values for each prefix of the key, combining the username, password, and the prefix.
   For example, for this key $= 1000111000010010$: $F(JohnSmith, password, 1)$ $F(JohnSmith, password, 10)$ $F(JohnSmith, password, 100)$ and $etc.$
3. **Locate the Nearest File:** For each Hash value, the system uses OrbitDB to locate the nearest key by comparing the numerical distance between the target hash and the stored keys in the database. The "nearest key" is determined as the one with the smallest absolute difference from the target hash. This key serves as a pointer to the IPNS address of the file where data related to that prefix is stored. This ensures efficient lookup and retrieval of data distributed across the network.
4. **Turn on the bits in the File:** The system accesses the file via the IPNS address associated with the nearest key. The Hash value is divided into equal parts, with each part representing locations in the file where bits are turned on.

5. **Update the File:** After turning on the bits, the file is saved back into the IPFS system, generating a new CID. The IPNS address is updated to always point to the latest version of the file. These steps repeat for all prefixes of the key until the insertion process is complete (Ref. Fig. 3).

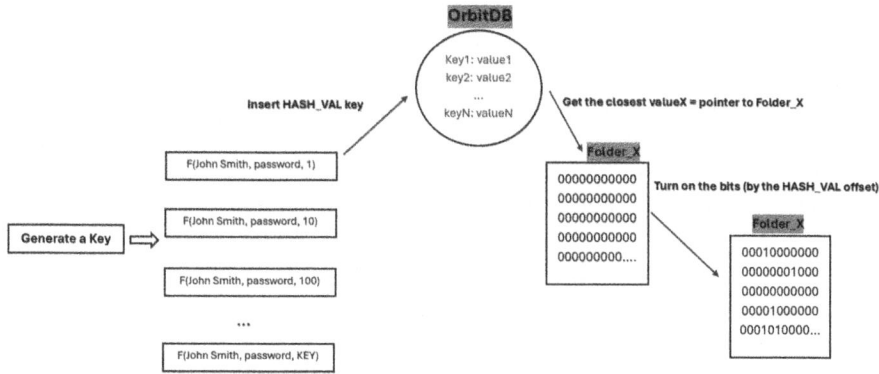

Fig. 3. Step 2 - Insert a new key.

Step 3: Retrieving a Key Using BFLUT. When a key needs to be retrieved from the system based on a username and password, the process follows these steps:

1. **Calculate Hash Values for Retrieval:** For the given username and password, the system calculates Hash values for all possible prefixes of the key. For example: F(John Smith, password, 0) F(John Smith, password, 1)
2. **Locate the Nearest File:** For each Hash value, the system uses OrbitDB to locate the nearest key, which points to the relevant file where the bits are stored.
3. **Verify the Presence of Information:** The system accesses the file via the IPNS address and checks if the required bits are turned on at the appropriate locations. If the bits are present, the information is considered valid, and the system proceeds to check the remaining prefixes.
4. **Reconstruct the Key:** The process continues for all prefixes until the full key of length L bits is reconstructed. For example, if the bits for PREFIX = $1, 10, 100, 1000$ are turned on and the required key length is 16 bits (and all prefixes are valid up to the 16th bit), the system successfully concludes that the entire key is present and retrieves the key 1000111000010010.

4.4   Complete Example

The following is a complete example of how the system works to insert a key and securely store its data across the network.

1. **Generating a New Key:** The system begins by generating a random Hash key and receiving the username and password as input. For example: Username: `user123`, Password: `password123`, and Random Key: `ab12cd34ef56`. This unique key will be used to organize and locate information in the system.
2. **Hashing Prefixes:** The system iterates through each prefix of the generated key, combining the prefix with the username and password to calculate a Hash value. For the key `ab12cd34ef56`, the prefixes are `a`, `ab`, `ab1`, `ab12`, and so on up to the full key. For each prefix, the system computes a Hash using the formula:

$$\text{Hash} = \text{hash}(\text{username} + \text{password} + \text{prefix})$$

   For example, for the prefix `ab12`, the computed Hash would be `5678abcd`.
3. **Locating the Nearest File:** For each calculated Hash, the system identifies the closest key in the database using Hash proximity. For example, if the Hash for the prefix `ab12` is `5678abcd`, and the database contains keys such as `1234abcd`, `5678efgh`, and `9101ijkl`, the closest key is determined to be `5678efgh`. The value associated with this key is the IPNS address of a file, which the system retrieves from the database.
4. **Updating the File:** The system accesses the file corresponding to the retrieved IPNS address and updates specific bits in the file based on the positions derived from the Hash values. For example, if the bit positions are `4, 8, 16`, these bits in the file are turned on. The updated file is uploaded back to IPFS, generating a new CID. The IPNS address for the key is updated to point to this new CID. This process continues for every prefix of the key, ensuring that all associated files are updated with consistent bit modifications based on the Hash values.

   This iterative approach ensures that data is stored securely and that the system can later verify the information by recalculating and checking the specific bit patterns. By using the closest key mechanism, the system effectively distributes and organizes information across the network.

4.5   Decentralized Write Operations Without OrbitDB

OrbitDB serves as a platform for key storage in our decentralized system. It can be replaced with a more distributed approach, where each node maintains a table mapping addresses to specific nodes, ensuring efficient data distribution.

Inspired by Ripple's trust model, we propose publishing a list of trusted nodes in a public and verifiable manner, akin to a blockchain. This approach ensures transparency and trust within the decentralized system.

When a user needs to write data, they first compute the relevant target nodes responsible for storing the bits. The user then directly interacts with these nodes to store the data, which improves performance.

This method prevents a single point of control over stored information, ensuring that data remains truly decentralized. Furthermore, a protocol can be defined to regulate write permissions, controlling the frequency and conditions under which data can be written. By implementing such mechanisms, we establish a fair, scalable, and secure decentralized storage system.

5 Analysis

In this study, we analyze a system based on the BFLUT data structure, designed to securely and efficiently store keys in a decentralized manner. The system operates by activating bits in files using unique keys and a specific Hash process. However, due to the characteristics of the data structure, there is a probability of encountering a False Positive where a key may point to data that does not actually belong to the intended user.

This section aims to analyze the probability of False Positives under different scenarios, identify the system's limitations, and optimize various parameters. Additionally, the analysis aims to evaluate the number of file accesses required to extract a single key based on the given system parameters.

For the purpose of this analysis, we make the following assumptions:

1. All files in the system are treated as a single unified file, with a length equal to the sum of all individual file lengths.
2. The processes of bit activation and retrieval are applied uniformly across the unified file.

5.1 Analysis Overview

Before delving into the specific analyses, we define the key parameters used throughout this research:

- N: The total number of keys stored currently in the system.
- F: The total number of bits in the system, calculated as the product of the number of files and the length of each file.
- L: The length of each key, typically represented in binary.
- U: The number of segments into which the Hash address is divided, used to determine the bit activation for each prefix.

These analyses provide insights into balancing security, scalability, and resource efficiency in decentralized environments.

5.2   General Calculations

1. For a single key, in one iteration of $PREFIX$, the number of bits activated is:
$$\frac{L}{U}$$

2. Over all iterations across the entire key (L), the total number of bits activated is:
$$L \cdot \frac{L}{U}$$

3. The probability that a specific bit remains unactivated by a single key is:
$$1 - \frac{L \cdot \frac{L}{U}}{F}$$

4. The probability that a specific bit remains unactivated after N keys is:
$$\left(1 - \frac{L \cdot \frac{L}{U}}{F}\right)^{N}$$

5. The probability that any bit is activated at least once:
$$1 - \left(1 - \frac{L \cdot \frac{L}{U}}{F}\right)^{N}$$

6. The probability that all the bits activated by the next key $(N+1)$ are already activated:
$$\left(1 - \left(1 - \frac{L \cdot \frac{L}{U}}{F}\right)^{N}\right)^{L \cdot \frac{L}{U}}$$

This represents the probability of a False Positive.

Specifically, for a search of length L, if in every iteration of the search all the bits corresponding to the key's prefixes are lit in their designated positions (as calculated in step 6), the system will incorrectly determine that the key exists. This happens due to overlaps caused by other inserted keys activating those specific bits, leading to a False Positive result.

The probability of this happening depends on the number of keys already inserted (N), the total memory size (F), and the ratio of activated bits (L/U), as described in the formula for step 6.

5.3   Analysis Details

In the following analysis, the keys will be treated as having a length of 64 hexadecimal characters (equivalent to 256 bits). Each analysis will focus on specific parameters by fixing some variables and substituting relevant values:

Analysis 1: Balancing Key Length (L) and Segment Division (U). When analyzing the ratio of activated bits (α) in distributed systems utilizing the BFLUT mechanism, the selection of parameters U and L significantly impacts system behavior. Notably, the base of the key representation (binary, hexadecimal, etc.) does not directly affect system performance, as the activated bits are treated as indices. Thus, the focus is placed on the number of activated bits and their ratio relative to the system parameters.

The activated bit ratio (α) represents the proportion of bits in the system that are turned on, serving as a critical parameter for balancing system efficiency and the probability of False Positives (P_{FP}). A commonly desired ratio is $\alpha = 0.5$, where half the bits in the system are activated. This ratio helps reduce the probability of False Positives while maintaining sufficient inactive bits to support efficient searches.

To achieve the desired α, the number of activated bits is calculated as:

$$\alpha = \frac{\text{Activated Bits}}{F} = \frac{N \cdot L^2 \cdot \frac{1}{U}}{F},$$

where N is the number of keys, L is the key length, U is the number of segments, and F is the total number of bits in the system. Solving for U:

$$U = \frac{N \cdot L^2}{\alpha \cdot F}.$$

A higher U value reduces activated bits per iteration, lowering False Positives but also decreasing validations, which may cause early failures. Conversely, a lower U value increases activations, improving validation but raising False Positives.

Similarly, increasing L raises the False Positive rate, emphasizing the need to optimize U based on system-specific factors like the number of keys (N), memory size (F), and efficiency requirements.

Analysis 2: Effect of Number of Keys N. We will analyze the impact of N on the probability of False Positives while keeping $L = 64$, $U = 4$, and $F = 2^{21} \cdot 150$ (representing the size of each file in bits multiplied by the number of files).

Using these values, the formula for the probability of False Positives becomes:

$$\left(1 - \left(1 - \frac{64 \cdot \frac{64}{4}}{2^{21} \cdot 150}\right)^N\right)^{64 \cdot \frac{64}{4}}$$

As N increases, the probability of a False Positive also increases, as more keys activate additional bits in the system, raising the chance of collisions. Below are the probabilities for different values of N:

- For example $N = 500,000$: The probability of a False Positive is approximately 5.77×10^{-93} (negligible).

The table provides a detailed breakdown of the calculations for all the tested values of N.

For a detailed visualization, refer to Appendix A.

This demonstrates that as the number of keys grows, the system's ability to distinguish between keys diminishes, leading to a higher likelihood of False Positives (Table 1).

Table 1. False Positive Probability as a Function of N.

N	Computed Result
100000	0.00e+00
200000	0.00e+00
300000	6.91e-211
400000	6.99e-142
500000	5.77e-98
600000	9.53e-69
700000	8.83e-49
800000	6.71e-35
900000	3.87e-25
1000000	3.21e-18

Analysis 3: Minimum Storage Size (F) for Given P_{FP}. In this analysis, we calculate the minimum F required to support N keys with a specified False Positive probability (P_{FP}). By fixing the parameters N, L, U, we evaluate the required storage size F for varying P_{FP} values.

The formula to calculate F is derived as follows:

$$F \geq \frac{L^2}{U \cdot \left(1 - \left(1 - P_{FP}^{\frac{U}{L^2}}\right)^{\frac{1}{N}}\right)}$$

We fixed $N = 500,000$, $L = 64$, and $U = 4$ for this calculation. The required F values for different False Positive probabilities (P_{FP}) are shown below:

- For $P_{FP} = 10^{-6}$: The required F is approximately $56.61 \cdot 2^{21}$ bytes.
- For $P_{FP} = 10^{-9}$: The required F is approximately $62.43 \cdot 2^{21}$ bytes.
- For $P_{FP} = 10^{-12}$: The required F is approximately $67.33 \cdot 2^{12}$ bytes.

These results demonstrate the relationship between the desired false-positive probability and the required storage size (F). Each file in the system is assumed to have a size of 2^{21} bytes. Thus, the system will require between 55 and 70 files for the given probabilities. As P_{FP} decreases (i.e., stricter False Positive requirements), the required storage size increases significantly. For a detailed visualization, refer to Appendix A.

Analysis 4: Analysis of Expected Number of File Accesses. In a distributed system, the expected number of file accesses is a critical metric for understanding the efficiency and resource usage of the system. This metric helps evaluate the system's performance and scalability.

Formally, for a discrete random variable X, the expected value is defined as:

$$E[X] = \sum_{x \in \text{Range}(X)} x \cdot P(X = x)$$

where $P(X = x)$ is the probability that X takes the value x.

Problem Statement. Suppose the system contains K files in total and a key length L. These accesses may include repeated visits to the same file. The goal is to calculate the expected number of unique files accessed when retrieving data for a key.

Derivation of the Expected Number of Unique Accesses. In this calculation, we consider the key length to be 256 bits. At each step, we check both possible values (0 and 1), meaning each step involves two operations. Since the total number of steps is equal to the key length, the total number of operations is 2L = 256 * 2

Thus, the expected number of unique files when we have a system with 16 files is given by:

$$E[X] = K \cdot \left(1 - \left(1 - \frac{1}{K}\right)^{2L}\right)$$

If we also consider false positives, there may be a few additional file accesses. However, if P_{FP} is very small, this additional number of accesses remains negligible.

5.4   Simulation

In this simulation, we examined the process of key extraction in a distributed system using IPFS, IPNS, and OrbitDB. The goal was to reconstruct a key while minimizing file accesses.

Key Findings. Initially, in our simulation, we set m, the number of files, to 100. Unlike binary search (logarithmic complexity, checking two options per step), our approach expanded the search space by testing all 16 possible hexadecimal characters (0 to f) at each step. This significantly increased the initial search size.

Each extraction attempt validated all 16 extensions, causing an exponential growth in checks. Unlike binary search, where each step halves the search space, our method evaluated all potential values, leading to a higher number of unique file accesses (Table 2).

Realizing that the number of file accesses was likely to be very high, especially given the large number of files, we adjusted our approach. We reduced the number of files to 50 while increasing their size. This will limit the number of accessed files to 50.

Since multiple files may reside on the same cluster (node), the actual number of physical accesses is much lower. Finding the right balance between the number of files and their size is key to optimizing performance and secure distribution.

Table 2. False Positive Probability as a Function of N.

Username	Password	NumberOfUniqueFiles
"alice12"	securePass1!	95
bob-smith	bobRocks42@	98
charlie.dev	charlieCode99$	96
david-w	DavidPass123*	97
emma.l	emmaLovesCats!	95
frank-t	FrankStrongP@ss	97
grace.hopper	graceCode42#	95
henry-m	HenrySafePass1!	96
isabella-99	BellaSecret$22	98
jack-admin	AdminJack#2024	94

6   Discussion and Conclusions

Secure Key Management Without Centralized Storage. The proposed system effectively manages cryptographic keys in a decentralized environment without explicitly storing them. Leveraging BFLUT and IPFS ensures that key recovery remains secure even if multiple or even all nodes are compromised, as long as the prefix used in the hash, for example, is the username, and the password is unknown. The bits maintained by each node result from a cryptographic hash function (SHA) and thus do not leak information. Furthermore, when nodes may act adversarially, information retrieval is still possible by adding intermediate error-correcting codes (during the writes), correcting partial retrievals, and continuing to retrieve the entire information. Denial of service regarding too many writes by (non-allowed) users should be monitored and restricted by each node to ensure a limited number of writes. As for reads, the distribution of nodes that maintain the database and the possibility to tolerate errors yields a possibility to cope with erasures, too. More details are deferred to the full version.

Optimizing File Count and Size for Performance. Initial simulations with 100 files resulted in excessive file accesses. By reducing the number of files to 50 while increasing their size, the system achieved **47–50** accesses per run, striking a better balance between efficiency and resource utilization.

A   Appendix

See Figs. 4 and 5.

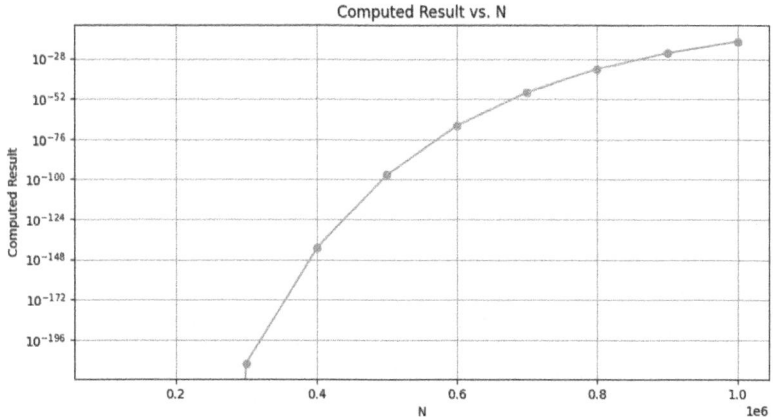

Fig. 4. False Positive Probability as a Function of N.

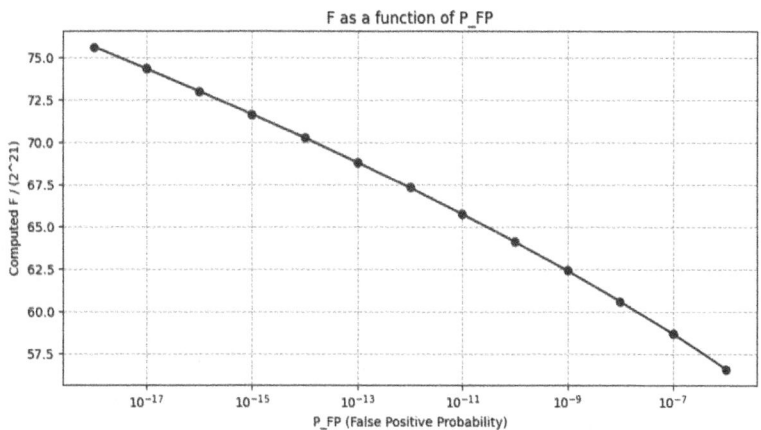

Fig. 5. Required F as a function of P_{FP} for fixed $N = 500,000$, $L = 64$, and $U = 4$.

References

1. Benet, J.: IPFS - content addressed, versioned, P2P file system. arXiv preprint arXiv:1407.3561 (2014)
2. Brown, A., Green, B.: Secure key management in distributed systems: challenges and solutions. IEEE Trans. Cloud Comput. 1–12 (2023)
3. Cachin, C.: Blockchain and consensus protocols: a tutorial. Inria Research Report (2017)
4. OrbitDB Contributors. Orbitdb: A decentralized database for peer-to-peer applications (2023). Accessed 22 Nov 2024
5. CRDT.Tech. Crdts: Conflict-free replicated data types (2023). Accessed 22 Nov 2024
6. Doe, J., Smith, J.: Secure and effective key management using secret sharing schemes in cloud computing. Int. J. Cloud Appl. Comput. (IJCAC) **10**(3), 45–63 (2020)
7. Dolev, S., Gudes, E., Segev, E., Ullman, J., Weintraub, G.: BFLUT bloom filter for private look-up tables. In: Proceedings of the CSCML 2022. LNCS, vol. 13301, pp. 499–505. Springer (2022)
8. Gutierrez, C., et al.: Blockchain security and privacy in practice: challenges and future directions. In: Proceedings of the ACM Conference on Advances in Cryptography (2022)
9. Heilman, E., Kendler, A., Zohar, A., Goldberg, S.: Eclipse attacks on bitcoin's peer-to-peer network. In: 24th USENIX Security Symposium (USENIX Security 2015), pp. 129–144. USENIX Association (2015)
10. Protocol Labs. IPNS (interplanetary name system) documentation (2023). Accessed 22 Nov 2024
11. Zongming, X., Cheng, J.: A survey of peer-to-peer content distribution technologies. J. Supercomput. **37**(3), 243–259 (2005)

Purpose Filter: A Space-efficient Purpose Metadata Storage

Paulo R. P. Amora$^{(\boxtimes)}$ ⓘ, Francisco D. B. S. Praciano ⓘ, and Javam C. Machado ⓘ

LSBD, Universidade Federal do Ceará, Fortaleza, Brazil
{paulo.amora,daniel.praciano,javam.machado}@lsbd.ufc.br

Abstract. In this paper, we attack the problem of storing purpose and consent metadata. This special kind of data brings a constraint where a false positive signifies the violation of a regulation. Our approach allows necessary metadata for purpose and consent maintenance and enforcement to be efficiently organized as a custom filter data structure to enhance metadata storage and fast retrieval. Contrary to other filters in the literature, we show that our approach guarantees that no false positives occur to the users' consent. We analyze the configuration knobs of this data structure, discuss improvements, and our experimental results show that our method outperforms a more traditional approach of storing a foreign key to refer to a purpose storage table.

Keywords: Digital Rights Management · Data Structures · Databases

1 Introduction

Personal data have become a first-class citizen in the domain of user applications. As a result, government agencies have acted to balance the power dynamic between users and companies, empowering users by providing rights over any ceded data through regulations such as GDPR [8], CCPA [4], and LGPD [14].

These regulations require the user who provides the data must provide consent, in a well-informed manner, for what purpose applications may process their data. Database Management Systems (DBMS) usually store data collected by online applications. The Database Administrator (DBA) is responsible for modeling how data will be stored and also what should be stored, falling under their responsibility for the correct modeling of stated purposes and consent provided by users. Consent metadata must be stored to enable enforcement. Storing each user's consent data presents a problem where the amount of metadata can overcome the actual data. The consent enforcement is a task that is performed very frequently in this scenario and must be fast to not create overhead in the database query processing.

Purpose-based access control is not a new problem, with works like [1,3,22] providing solutions to this problem, however, they store this metadata directly on

© IFIP International Federation for Information Processing 2025
Published by Springer Nature Switzerland AG 2025
S. Katsikas and B. Shafiq (Eds.): DBSec 2025, LNCS 15722, pp. 251–270, 2025.
https://doi.org/10.1007/978-3-031-96590-6_14

the database, using tables. More recently, with the legal support provided by new regulations, new works such as [6,13,18,24] discuss other forms of storing this metadata, either as surrogate keys or alongside data, internal to the database.

In this work, we introduce Purpose Filter, a data structure designed to store purpose metadata while allowing fast verification of data associated to a purpose.

This work provides the following contributions:

– A zero FPR filter data structure to store and verify purpose and consent;
– A formalization of this data structure with its parameters;
– Insights on how to apply this data structure to store purpose and consent;
– An empirical evaluation of the data structure behavior on different proportions of accepted/denied consents, backing our formalization;
– Experimental evaluation performed against our main competitors on consent storage approach.

This paper is organized as follows: Sect. 2 defines and models purpose and consent definition and modeling. Section 3 presents the data structure and justify how it guarantees compliance, it also details construction and probing algorithms. Section 4 provides an experimental evaluation of our data structure against a more traditional storage approach. Section 5 discusses related work. Section 6 concludes the paper while providing directions for future work.

2   Purpose Metadata

To model our filter, we first state our understanding on purpose and what data is necessary to enforce purpose. In this fashion, we use the following entities, definitions, and claims.

From GDPR [8], we define three entities:

Data Owner: The party who provides the data. They have all rights pertaining to data processing and usage and may object to this use. Therefore, they can consent to which purposes the Controller assigns to their data.

Data Processor: The party who intends to process data from the Data Owners. They must clearly state what ends they will use the retrieved data and how they will consume it.

Data Controller: The party that stores the data collected from Data Owners and provide them to Data Processors. According to the Owners' requests, they manage the access permissions of personal data, actively allowing or denying access to data.

Figure 1a shows the relationship between Data Owner and Data Controller. Data Controller configures the existing purposes, adding the purpose metadata. Whenever the Data Owner provides data to the Data Controller (e.g., sign up for

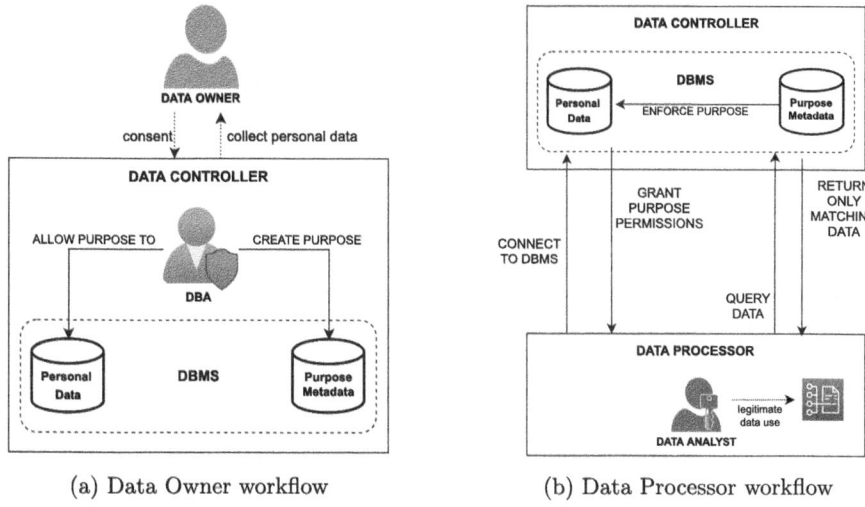

(a) Data Owner workflow   (b) Data Processor workflow

Fig. 1. Data workflows

a service, allow the Data Controller to read stored cookies), the Data Controller will present the existing purposes, and the Data Owner will either accept or reject their data usage by Data Processors. The purpose creation process requires active intervention by a DBA. However, the Data Controller can perform the assignment automatically, be it the DBA or a configured DBMS. This is where our filter will be positioned, in storing these purpose and consent data.

Figure 1b shows the relationship between Data Controller and Data Processor. When the Data Processor queries the Data Controller's DBMS, the DBMS links a preconfigured purpose to the Data Processor. The DBMS processes queries sent by the Processor and uses the purpose metadata to enforce purpose-based access control over any personal data queried by the Data Processor. Therefore, only data from Data Owners that consented to the processing purpose will be returned to the Data Processor. To the data analyst querying the database, this enforcement happens transparently. There are no changes in connecting to the database or querying data.

To ensure that the Owner's consents are being respected, the Data Controller defines and uses a purpose verification function to verify that only allowed tuples return. The Data Controller must return only data in which the processing purposes match the assigned purposes.

Example: For the remainder of this work, we will consider the following environment: Ten people, indexed from 1 to 10, one purpose, and owner consent will be either Positive (P) or Negative (N), and these will be grouped in two sets, namely the allow set and deny set. For the sake of simplicity, we will also assume that each element will hash to only one position in the filter.

$$Allow\_set = \{P_1, P_2, P_3, P_4\}$$

$$Deny\_set = \{N_5, N_6, N_7, N_8, N_9, N_{10}\}$$

3   Purpose Filter

To store and query purpose metadata in an efficient way, we propose a filter-based data structure, named Purpose Filter. Purpose Filter is composed of multiple filters layered upon one another, each layer responsible for a different type of verification. A design inspired by Cascaded Bloom Filters [25] and Stacked Filters [5], with the distinct objective of succinctly representing a data set and querying purpose data without violating purpose properties and definitions.

Each purpose is created as a Purpose Filter and all positive or negative consents pertaining are used in filter construction. We build the *allow* and *deny* sets using the tuple id or any unique identifier of this register in the database, such as an OID. Being a succinct structure, we store a representation of this tuple id within the filter through hashing. Whenever a query attempts to read personal data from a table, before retrieving this data from the disk, the tuple ids which are retrieved from the DBMS Catalog, before data is actually scanned. The IDs are confronted against the correspondent filter, and only the accepted tuples are returned. This verification can be cheap when the filter is in memory, since it only costs an access to the filter to ensure tuple acceptance. Details about this cost are provided in Sect. 3.6. Due to the constraint of only returning allowed tuples, we cannot allow a false positive tuple.

Purpose Filter layers can be of any compatible type of filter. We define compatible by having the same primitive behavior as a Bloom Filter [2]. Therefore, Cuckoo Filters [7], Counting Quotient Filters [17], and XOR Filters [9] are examples of compatible filters. In this work we focus on the construction of Purpose Filter using Bloom Filter layers.

3.1   Filter Construction

Purpose Filter is built by layering filters one on top of the other, alternating the layers between positive and negative. The final data structure may have more than one pair of filters, however it will always have an even number of layers. Algorithm 1 provides a high-level view while Algorithm 3 in the Appendix provides more detail.

The construction takes two sets, one positive of known elements in the set and one negative of known elements not in the set. The positive set is the allow set. The negative set is the complement of the allow set, i.e. the deny set. We also set a target false negative rate (FNR), which we use as criterion to stop the construction process. Lines 3 to 6 show what happens during construction, two layers are created per iteration, the positive set is inserted in the first layer and

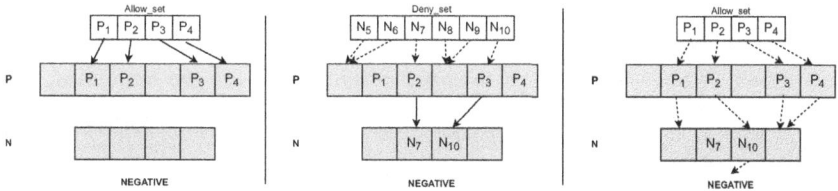

Fig. 2. Purpose Filter construction.

the negative set is tested against this layer (lines 3 and 4). Then, any accepted elements from the negative set are inserted in the second layer and the positive set is tested (lines 5 and 6). This process repeats until a target FNR is reached or it cannot be reduced further. Since the size of the sets dimnishes over the iterations, subsequent layers are smaller, and the final data structure may have the form of a funnel.

Algorithm 1: Constructor function

Data: Positive set P, Negative set N, False Positive Rate FPR, # of hashs k
Result: Constructed Purpose Filter

1 initialize filter ;
2 **while** *FNR threshold not achieved or FNR not changed* **do**
3 | insert positive elements from P in a new layer;
4 | test negative elements from N on this layer and discard the true negatives;
5 | insert negative elements from N in a new layer;
6 | test positives elements from P on this layer and discard the true positives;
7 **end**

The size of each layer is calculated in Sect. 3.5, being dependent on the type of filter used in every layer. We perform the calculation for Bloom Filters, and we show that on average, the biggest layer is the first layer, dominating the cost.

Our main goal is to achieve a zero false positive rate (0 FPR). From our consent modeling, we have a constraint that no data should be provided when the user does not give consent. We can derive that while no false positives may occur, a false negative is acceptable, because it does not violate the constraint. Regular filters may reduce the false positive rate (FPR) but do not guarantee a 0 FPR. A false positive defeats the system compliance; therefore, we ensure that we have a 0 FPR.

We achieve the 0 FPR through Theorem 1. To start, we provide two claims, which must be true to Purpose Filter.

Claim. A tuple z is deemed positive if rejected by a negative layer of the filter

Claim. A tuple z is deemed negative if rejected by a positive layer of the filter or reaches the end of the filter.

Theorem 1. *Be PF a Purpose Filter; D the complete dataset; P, N, U distinct subsets of D such as $D = P + N + U$. P are the positive elements used in construction, N the negative used in construction and U are the undefined, which are elements of D not used in construction. If $U = \emptyset$ and the end of the filter returns negative, we achieve a 0 FPR.*

Through Theorem 1 we prove that there is a design for a filter structure that represents purpose and stores consent metadata, complying to these data constraints of avoiding a false positive. The proof for Theorem 1 is in the Appendix.

To show the construction process we go to our example. Figure 2 presents three phases of the building structure: the leftmost figure represents the beginning of construction, where the first layer is populated by the *Allow_set*. We already show the negative layer for clarity, but as Algorithm 3 shows, the layers are built incrementally. In the center figure we have the second step, which is to get the *Deny_set* and test it against the positive layer. As the dashed arrows show, $\{N_5, N_6, N_8, N_9\}$ do not survive the first filter; therefore, they can be safely discarded as true negatives. The survivors $\{N_7, N_{10}\}$ are added to the negative layer, represented by the solid arrows. Then, in the rightmost figure, we return to the *Allow_set*, to verify how they behave when checked by the negative layer. As we can see from the dashed arrows, $\{P_1, P_3, P_4\}$ are rejected by the negative layer, meaning that they are true positives. $\{P_2\}$ goes through the negative layer; however, the end of the filter dictates that any element that passes through every layer will be deemed negative.

The proper steps to guarantee Theorem 1 are taken during Purpose Filter construction and data probing. The positive set is built with all the relevant elements. All other relation tuples are added as the negative set to guarantee that all elements are used. That ensures the first condition, of $U = \emptyset$. All elements are known during filter construction because they are all tuples in the relation.

3.2   Filter Probing

After construction, the filter uses a probing function to respect both definitions used in Theorem 1, which Algorithm 2 shows. That ensures the second condition, i.e., the filter returns negative at the end.

Algorithm 2: Probing function

Data: Tuple x, Purpose Filter pf
Result: true, if tuple is definitely in set; false, otherwise
1 **for** $i = 0$ to pf.layers.length-1 **do**
2 | **if** pf.layers[i].lookup(x) $==$ false **then**
3 | | return ((i mod 2) $==$ 1);
4 | **end**
5 **end**
6 return false;

To verify consent for a given tuple, the filter tests whether the tuple is accepted or rejected for each layer. If it is accepted, the algorithm moves to the next layer. If rejected, the filter evaluates on which layer it was rejected. If it is a positive layer (odd-numbered layers), the filter returns negative. If it is a negative layer (even-numbered layers), the filter returns positive. If the algorithm reaches the end of the filter, it returns negative.

The cost to probe is in the worst case, the cost to check each layer. During construction process we verify that not so many layers are constructed after the first pair. For 10 million ids used on our experiments, the filter had 4 layers. Therefore, it is still a fast check. We provide further analysis in Subsect. 3.6.

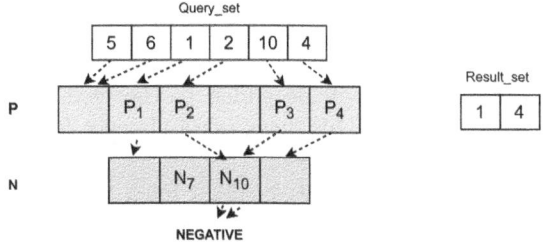

Fig. 3. Probe example

Figure 3 shows an example of query posed to the DBMS, where we shall assume that the predicates would return tuple ids $\{1, 2, 4, 5, 6, 10\}$. From our running example, we know that from the intended result set, only $\{1, 2, 4\}$ consented to their data to be returned. The filter ensures that only consented tuple ids return, filtering out tuple ids $\{5, 6\}$ on the first layer. Tuple id $\{10\}$ is accepted by the first layer, however, since it was added in the second layer, it reaches the end of the filter and is filtered out. Positive tuple ids $\{1, 4\}$ are rejected by the second layer, being added to the result set. Positive tuple id $\{2\}$ though, collides with negative tuple id $\{10\}$, and is accepted by the negative layer, being discarded. Finally, the result_set is built with the surviving tuple ids $\{1, 4\}$, and $\{2\}$ was discarded as a false negative.

With these changes, we achieve a purpose representation that is smaller in size than a usual solution, e.g., store the purposes as a new attribute [24]. Purpose Filter also complies with the requirement of not allowing any registers outside the purpose to be wrongly returned. Another benefit is that by embedding Purpose Filter into the operator execution, no query rewriting or additional statements are required. All the logic is executed within query processing, avoiding processing overhead when executing queries, and providing an extra security layer for SQL malicious manipulation.

The collateral effect is to have a false negative rate. That is inherent to the data representation performed by the filter. However, purpose-aware query processing is respected. We evaluate how this false negative rate evolves over data proportions of positive and negative, and conclude that the number is small enough, most often near zero. More details, including the modeling of this false negative rate are available in Subsect. 3.4.

3.3   Filter Maintenance

In the case that new personal data is added, the Purpose Filter must be updated before any probing of new data, since we are restricted by Theorem 1 that the unknown set must be empty. As consent can be allowed or denied, this new element will be part of the positive or negative set.

If the element is part of the positive set, it must be inserted into the top layer of the filter, which is positive. This operation is enough to ensure consistency of the filter. However, to dampen the growth of the FNR, this element can follow through the layers of the filter, being tested against the next layer (negative). If it yields a false negative, it will be added to the next positive layer, until it reaches the end of the filter. This gives extra chances for the element to be correctly classified as a true positive.

If the element is part of the negative set, it must be inserted in the second topmost layer of the filter, which is the first negative layer of the filter. Unlike the previous decision, the negative element must be inserted in every negative layer until it reaches the end of the filter. The reason behind this is that if there is a negative layer that does not "see" this element, it may reject it, yielding a false positive, which is unacceptable.

Bloom filters by definition do not support deletes, but other structures such as Cuckoo Filters [7] and Counting Quotient Filters [17] do support deletion, and are compatible as layers of Purpose Filter, as long as all are the same. Modification of a consent can be seen as a delete-and-insert operation. Inserts were already covered, let us focus on deletes.

To delete a positive entry, it is only necessary to remove it from the topmost layer of the filter. This may increase the FNR because other entries may be affected because of the removal of a given entry (e.g. hash collisions).

An issue rises when deleting negative entries, because they may incur in false positives in the negative layers. Currently, this is a limitation, although it is more probable that a user removes consent after granting it instead of the contrary.

3.4   Information Loss

The foundation of Purpose Filter, and purpose-based access control in general, is to restrict unwarranted access to all data, allowing only authorized tuples to be returned as a query result. Therefore, within the same dataset, a given query Q posed to a compliant DBMS may return fewer tuples than the same query in a noncompliant DBMS. Consequently, it is important to model this information loss accordingly. We will use FNR for the false negative rate of the filter and FPR_i for the false positive rate of the i-th layer. Just to clarify, FNR applies to the entire filter, while FPR_i refers to each layer.

The possible outputs are: True positive, True negative, False Negative. Since we are interested in false negatives, the probability of a positive element reaching the end of the filter is the same as that it being accepted by every layer. So we must associate the probabilities of it being accepted in the positive layers (half of the filter) and negative layers (other half).

Since the element is positive, the probability that it is accepted by a positive layer is 1, therefore we can ignore the even layers in the FNR calculation:

$$TotalFNR = \prod_{i=0}^{\frac{\#L}{2}} FPR\_L_{2i+1} \tag{1}$$

3.5   Space Allocation

As expected, the allocation of space for filter layers depends on the set size that will be inserted. For the first layer, $nPos$ is the positive set size and $nNeg$ the negative set, however, for each subsequent layer, $nPos$ and $nNeg$ corresponds only to the survivors. We have positive survivors, which yielded a pass when they should have been rejected from a negative layer and negative survivors, which have the same behavior from a positive layer. The expected size of the positive survivor set at a layer i is:

$$nPos_i = nPos * FPR_i * \prod_{j=0}^{i} FPR_{2j}$$

Similarly, the expected size of the negative survivor set at a layer i is:

$$nNeg_i = nNeg * FPR_{i+1} * \prod_{j=1}^{i} FPR_{2j-1}$$

Summing all the Bloom Filter layers we obtain:

$$TotalSize = \sum_{i=0}^{\frac{\#L}{2}} \frac{(nPos_{2i} * \log p_{2i})}{(\log 2)^2} + \frac{(nNeg_{2i+1} * \log p_{2i+1})}{(\log 2)^2} \tag{2}$$

By examining the productories, we can observe that the survivor set size diminishes very fast, since we have a product of very small values (the FPRs).

3.6   Costs

To quantify the costs of the purpose filter, we establish two constants c_{ins} and c_{prb}, which means the cost of inserting an element into a layer and the cost of detecting the layer for the element. For Bloom Filters, $c_{ins} = c_{prb} = k$, since the operations are bound for the k hash functions used.

Building Cost. To build each layer, we insert every element of the corresponding set and then probe it using the opposite set. For a positive layer we have:

$$c_{ins} * (nPos_i) + c_{prb} * (nNeg_i)$$

And for a negative layer:

$$c_{ins} * (nNeg_i) + c_{prb} * (nPos_i)$$

The resulting build cost is the sum of these costs for each layer

$$BuildCost = \sum_{i=0}^{\frac{\#_L}{2}} c_{ins} * (nPos_{2i}) + c_{prb} * (nNeg_{2i})$$
$$+ c_{ins} * (nNeg_{2i+1}) + c_{prb} * (nPos_{2i+1}) \quad (3)$$

Observe that in the last pair of layers, the term $c_{prb} * (nPos_{2i+1})$ does not exist.

The time complexity for construction is bound by $O(k*(nPos+p*nNeg)*l)$, where k is the amount of hash functions, nPos and nNeg are the sizes of the positive and negative set, p is the FPR of the layer and l is the quantity of layers.

Query Cost. The query cost is either the sum of the rejection probability of each layer, or the probability that it is accepted by all layers. For positive and negative elements, the cost is bound by:

$$QueryCost \leq \max\{\sum_{i=0}^{\frac{\#_L}{2}} c_{prb} * (1 - FRR_i), \prod_{i=0}^{\frac{\#_L}{2}} c_{prb} * FRR_i\} \quad (4)$$

Therefore, the time complexity is bound by $O(kl)$ for each element.

3.7   Optimizing Filter Construction

We can fine-tune the construction process by making use of three constraints: space, target FPR_0, and target FNR. If there are space limitations, the FNR may vary, because we need to adjust the number of bits per element. Do note that the build threshold may impact on the amount of subsequent layers, but in general, as already shown, the bulk of storage space is used by the first layer. By affixing FPR_0, we do not hinder the total FNR of the structure, as the experiments will show.

3.8   Purpose and Consent Modeling Using Purpose Filter

Consent may be given as a blanket term (i.e., the owner consents to the usage of all their data or denies all). For each purpose, a filter is created, and each user consent (allow/deny) is added to the filter. In this scenario, only one filter per purpose is needed, as we only have one consent per tuple. Consent can also be given as a fine-grained collection of consents for each attribute of the tuple. This is called cell-level consent [12]. For cell-level consent, we build a filter for each attribute and each purpose. The consents for a given purpose are presented as a list of allow/deny for each attribute, which is why all consents for a given attribute are applied to a purpose filter.

To avoid redundant checks on the filter, a query or transaction may hold the intermediate result from the scan operator in memory, and reuse it, reducing the overhead on more complex queries such as nested queries or long transactions.

4 Experimental Evaluation

A first version of Purpose Filter was implemented alongside Purpose Scan [19]. The current version was implemented using Java 21, where the following experiments were performed.

4.1 Evaluation Setup

Experiments were run in a Lenovo Thinkpad machine with an Intel Core I7 10510U 1.8 GHz, with 16 GB of RAM using JVM version 21.

To represent the personal data tuple ids in the database, we generated 10 million random unique integers. This set was then partitioned into our positive and negative sets according to the experiment proportion.

We used Bloom Filters [2] as the filter layers of the Purpose Filter. We used Google Guava's fixed MurmurHash3 implementation with 32-bits as our hash function. To calculate the Nth hash positions, we used the double hashing technique from Mitzenmacher [16]. Every experiment was run 5 times, and the presented results are the average of these runs.

We compare how much space is used by the data structure in comparison with an approach of storing each purpose alongside the tuple as a 1-byte attribute, simulating a foreign key binding that tuple to a purpose table. We partition our dataset into x% positives and (100-x)% negatives. We vary the proportion in increments of 5%, beginning at 5% and going until 95%. We perform 2 experiments, one with a set amount of bits and one with a target FPR for the first layer, calculating the optimal number of bits and storage size. We also compare the storage overhead with Sieve [18] and Hippocratic Databases, using the implementation from [12]. Additional experiments regarding the number of layers and their sizes are presented in the Appendix.

4.2 Fixed Size

In this subsection, the experiments discuss the configuration, where we set the number of bits used to represent each element in four configurations: 3-bit, 5-bit, 7-bit, and 9-bit.

Storage Space. In this experiment, we observe how the data structure grows according to the proportion of positive and negative elements. Figure 4a presents how the space consumption varies in this window. The x-axis represents the proportion of the positive set, seen as a sliding window (5% positives, 95% negatives; 10% positives, 90% negatives, and so on). The y-axis represents the amount of space consumed in bits compared to the baseline approach. The legend indicates the configuration, from left to right equal to the stated configurations above. The bar above indicates the storage used by our baseline, which is constant (8-bits times 10 m tuples).

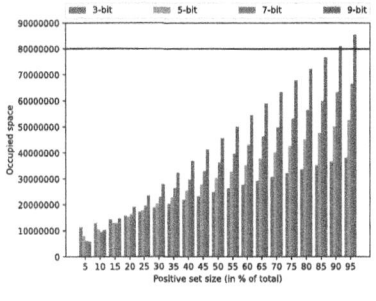

(a) Variation of space used.

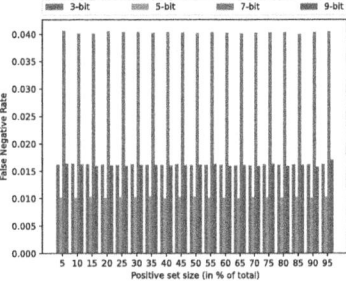

(b) Variation of FNR.

Fig. 4. Experiments for fixed size

We observe that the amount of storage space used increases with the positive set proportion, i.e., when there are more positive elements, the filter size increases. This happens because the first layer has all positives inserted into it, and while the filter sees all negative elements during construction, only the negative elements accepted by the first layer during construction are added to the negative layer.

Because of the small proportion of positive items in the beginning, the first layer in lower-bit configurations yields more false positives. Therefore, the negative survivor set becomes very large. With more bits, this phenomenon ceases to exist, which is why, as the proportion becomes more balanced, the expected behavior (more bits = bigger filter size) becomes the norm.

Another interesting observation is that even with 9 bits per element, which would be more than the baseline, the total filter size only overcomes the baseline when there are more than 90% positives. This result comes from our filter construction, which leans heavier on the positive set size, instead of the baseline, which would be a constant value.

Knowing that the amount of bits used to represent elements impacts the False Negative Rate, we follow to the next experiment.

False Negative Rate. In this experiment, we observe how the False Negative Rate (FNR) varies when the proportion of positive and negative elements change.

Figure 4b presents how this FNR varies over. The x-axis represents the size of the positive set. The y-axis represents the percentage of false negatives returned by the filter. The legend indicates the configuration, from left to right equal to the stated configurations above. The build threshold was set as a 5% false negative rate for the filter.

The FNR remains very close for different positive set sizes and the same configuration, showing resilience from the filter with varying positive set sizes. The variation shown, especially on the 7-bit configuration, comes from the number of layers. While the 3 and 5-bit had 6 layers, therefore, they needed three iterations of the algorithm to finish, and the 7-bit finished with 2 layers, being the turning point of the decision process. Upon observing this result, we executed with a threshold of 3%, and the FNR falls to around 0.1%, but it builds 4 layers instead of 2.

4.3 Fixed FPR_0

In this experiment, we fix the FPR of the first layer, from 1% to 10%, and observe how the full structure behaves on storage space and FNR. Given the amount of data to be presented, we select four positive set proportions, 5%, 30%, 55%, 90%, to present our data.

Storage Space. In this experiment, we observe how the data structure grows according to the proportion of positive and negative elements. Figure 5a presents how the space consumption varies over the selected values. The x-axis represents the size of the positive set. The y-axis represents the amount of space consumed in bits when compared to the baseline approach. The legend indicates the configuration, from left to right equal to the stated configurations above. The bar above indicates the storage used by our baseline, which is constant (8-bits times 10 m tuples).

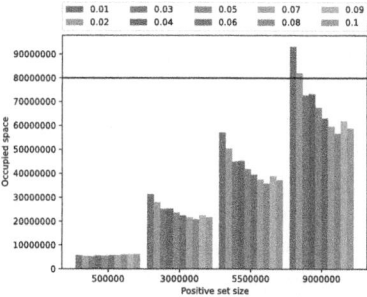

(a) Variation of space used.

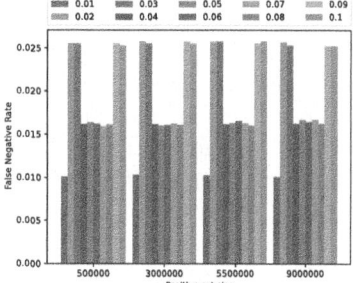

(b) Variation of FNR.

Fig. 5. Experiments for fixed FPR_0

We observe that the amount of storage space used decreases with increasing FPR_0. This happens because to achieve a low FPR on the first layer, we need to allocate more bits. This behavior is more apparent when the positive set size is large enough.

We also observe a slight bump up from 8% to 9%. That is also due to the threshold, where 8% has 6 layers in the filter and 9% goes to 8 layers, adding a little more size.

The storage size comparison to the baseline was already discussed; therefore, we skip it to avoid repetition.

False Negative Rate. In this experiment, we observe how the False Negative Rate (FNR) varies when the proportion of positive and negative elements change. Figure 5b presents how this FNR varies over. The x-axis represents the size of the positive set. The y-axis represents the percentage of false negatives returned by the filter. The legend indicates which FPR was fixed for the first layer. Once again, the build threshold was set to 5%.

By fixing an FPR to the first layer, we add a step of figuring out the optimal size of the Bloom Filter layer. We also observed that although the subsequent layers are not bound and yield a rather large FPR, the full filter FNR remains bounded. This is also reflected in space-saving for filter storage.

Going back to Fig. 5b, we observe that we do have a raise in the FNR for the 0.02 and 0.03 FPR configurations. Upon closer observation, we see that this is also when the construction threshold is near; with the 0.04 FPR onwards, the construction process adds 2 more layers, further reducing the FPR. What we also observe is that although the space required to store the filter decreases when we advance on the FPR, the FNR remains mostly constant. This behavior happens because of the calculation of the optimal size. Since we use a *log* base 2, the number of bits remains mostly unchanged from 0.04 to 0.08, highlighting that upper bounds may give the best cost-benefit relationship with regard to FNR and storage size.

4.4   Comparison with Other Works

To compare with other consent storage approaches, we ran a benchmark configuration of TPC-H with 1 million tuples on the CUSTOMER table and compared the space used on each approach. Purpose Scan [19] with Purpose Filter as the purpose storage, in the fixed size configuration of 5-bit per tuple id. Sieve [18] configured to query CUSTOMER and Hippocratic Databases with the extra attribute using the implementation from [12]. Figure 6 shows the comparison.

The y-axis shows the storage space used in bytes for each approach, lower is better. The x-axis shows the proportion of all the elements that are in the positive set. We observe that the other works have a fixed size, independent of the positive set size. Hippocratic DB (in orange and circles) stores less data than Sieve (purple, single slash), adding this overhead to query processing as added predicates that are evaluated upon query processing. Sieve constructs indexes auxiliary to data storage, increasing the amount of metadata stored.

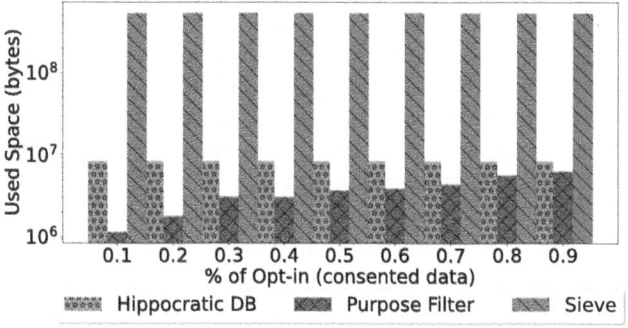

Fig. 6. Comparison with other works

We can see that depending on the positive set size, we (red, cross slash) achieve around half an order of magnitude below Hippocratic Databases and almost 3 orders of magnitude below Sieve, storing less than 10 MB versus almost 1 GB, highlighting the gain in storage size.

Although our approach scales size with the positive set size, we see from the experiment that even with 90% of the consents being positive, we are still below Hippocratic DB, matching what was observed from our previous experiments, in Fig. 4a.

Discussion. From these experiments, we observe a trade-off between storage space and the completeness of the results. Although it is a characteristic of the filter, it can be established dynamically based on the number of tuples and the size of the positive set. Considering scenarios where most of the Data Owners consent to their data being used to fully use a service, it is reasonable to expect that the positive set be the majority. Even with the highest level of FNR, 95.9% of the positive results are returned, which, in numbers, are 6,713,000 tuples of 7,000,000, which should not bring drawbacks to OLAP processing, being composed of aggregates and machine learning, as there is a small amount of data being excluded.

We also point out that these experiments were executed using a 5% threshold to stop adding layers to the filter. If the low FNR is more important, this threshold can be lowered, although a little more storage space will be used because of the extra layers.

We also identify that the threshold is as important to the resulting filter size and performance. By only changing the threshold in our experiment, we achieved a far better FNR by increasing our filter size by 4%. Depending on the application, this trade-off can be highly exploited.

5 Related Work

Purpose metadata storage is discussed in several works that address purpose-based access control, with many not showing concern with metadata growth.

SchengenDB [13] proposes to store purpose metadata alongside the tuple as a bitmap, and even proposing some kind of encoding/compressing of this data, based on Huffman encoding [10]. Compliance by Construction [23] proposes a method of storing personal data in user shards, accessible only through materialized views that may replicate data, using more space. GDPRBench [24] explores the impact of storing regulation metadata as new attributes, showing that for personal data, space can increase in almost 6 times by storing metadata, justifying why more specialized approaches are necessary. Sypse [6] uses data partitioning, surrogate keys and storing purpose data in tables. Machado and Amora [15] survey the impacts on DBMS storage for each challenge brought by new regulations, suggesting ways to address metadata explosion in a GDPR-compliant database. Other works [1,3,18,20,22,26] store purpose data as restricted tables in the DBMS, requiring metadata to be constructed over this metadata.

Data growth can be fought against by using filters to succinctly represent data, in a trade-off between space and false positives. Bloom Filters [2], Cuckoo Filters [7], Counting Quotient Filters [17] Stacked Filters [5], and XOR Filters [9] are examples of filter structures that achieve low storage sizes in comparison to data and a very low false positive rate. Due to the nature of purpose data, a false positive represents a wrongful retrieval of personal data, defeating the goal of purpose access guarantee.

More recently, EGH Filters [11] and Revirego et al. [21] propose filters with a false positive free set. [11] define the false positive free zone as a function of defective elements, which is a small subset of the universe. [21] define the false positive free set as a subset of the universe, leaving unknown elements with a nonzero probability of false positives. Note that for our problem domain, both are insufficient because the volume of data may be big (Purpose Filters scale with size) and do not allow false positives once the universe is known.

6   Conclusion and Future Work

This work presents Purpose Filter, a space-saving data structure for purpose metadata. The construction process ensures a 0 FPR data structure and probing for purpose metadata is fast. This metadata is stored efficiently, achieving in the worst case 80% of the occupied space when storing the purpose metadata explicitly. This space saving becomes relevant as the number of purposes increase.

As future works, we envision some avenues of research, given that this is a first step towards a compliant data management solution. Optimizations include the grouping of filters to represent some sort of hierarchy between purposes, as well as fine tuning of the parameters to provide an optimal setup for a set of other constraints, and a method to reuse already built filters to reduce the creation overhead. The internal filters may also be changed, as this work used Bloom Filters as the storage layer, other filters can be applied. Lastly is to address more requirements brought by these regulations, such as efficient auditing, delete guarantees and effective personal data representation i.e. represent adequately all data pertaining to a user.

Acknowledgments. This research was partially supported by CAPES (grant #88887.609129/2021), by CNPQ (grant #316729/2021-3), LSBD/UFC and IFCE.

Appendix

Construction Algorithm

Algorithm 3: Constructor function

Data: Positive set P, Negative set N, False Positive Rate FPR, # of hashs k
Result: Constructed Purpose Filter

1 filter = ;
2 finished = false;
3 filter.layers = {};
4 **while** *finished == false* **do**
5   R_set = {} // Elements that survive probing
6   **if** *filter.layer_counter % 2 == 0* **then**
7   build layer with appropriate size ;
8   **for** *i=0 to P.length* **do**
9   layer.insert(P[i]);
10   **end**
11   **for** *j=0 to N.length* **do**
12   **if** *layer.probe(N[j]) == true* **then**
13   R_set.add(N[j])
14   **end**
15   **end**
16   N = R_set // Update negative elements to only survivors
17   filter.layers.add(layer);
18   **end**
19   **else**
20   build layer with appropriate size;
21   **for** *i=0 to N.length* **do**
22   layer.insert(N[i]);
23   **end**
24   **for** *j=0 to P.length* **do**
25   **if** *layer.probe(P[j]) == true* **then**
26   R_set.add(P[j])
27   **end**
28   **end**
29   P = R_set // Update positive elements to only survivors
30   filter.layers.add(layer);
31   finished = FNR_is_ok();
32   **end**
33 **end**
34 **return** *filter*;

In Algorithm 3, lines 7 and 20 refer to an "appropriate size". When building the Purpose Filter, we have two correlated variables, the number of hashes k and the layer FPR. If the number of hashes is passed, the layer is constructed with a predefined size being a proportion of the positive set, yielding an FPR variation. If FPR is passed, the size of the first layer and the number of hashes are estimated using the positive set size, then these calculated variables are used as parameters for the construction. On line 31, we have a function that rechecks the full filter False Negative Rate, if it is below a given threshold (e.g. the target FPR of the first layer) or did not change, the filter is considered complete.

Proof for Theorem 1
Proof. Take elements $x, y \in D$. If $U = \emptyset$, be $x \in P$ and $y \in N$. During filter construction, x is inserted in the top layer and either is rejected by the next negative layer, directly below, or is inserted two layers below, in the next positive layer; y is either rejected by the topmost layer or inserted in the next negative layer. After construction, when we probe the filter for x, x either is rejected by a negative layer (true positive) or reach the end of the filter (false negative); when we probe for y, y is rejected by a positive layer (true negative) or reach the end of the filter (true negative). Since any element in D is only part of P or N, it is not possible to have a false positive. ∎

Experiments for Number of Layers and Layers' Sizes

Table 1. Number of layers and pair sizes for different fixed sizes.

Config	# layers	Pair 1 size	Pair 2 size	Pair 3 size	Pair 4 size	Total Size
3-bit, 5500000	6	19,910,272	5,037,184	1,277,312	–	26,224,768
5-bit, 5500000	4	29,770,496	3,008,512	–	–	32,779,008
7-bit, 5500000	2	39,773,888	–	–	–	39,773,888
7-bit, 5500000*	4	39,772,416	1,614,720	–	–	41,387,136

Table 2. Number of layers and pair sizes for different fixed FRRs.

Config	# layers	Pair 1 size	Pair 2 size	Pair 3 size	Pair 4 size	Total Size
0.02 FRR, 5500000	4	46,998,400	3,566,272	–	–	50,564,672
0.04 FRR, 5500000	6	39,962,432	4,308,096	1,092,352	–	45,362,880
0.08 FRR, 5500000	6	30,349,888	4,435,840	1,121,216	–	35,906,944
0.1 FRR, 5500000	8	29,838,016	4,769,216	1,911,040	768,512	37,286,784

We selected four configurations from the fixed size and four from the fixed FRR. To maintain a standard of comparison, all data were collected using the positive set size 55%. From the first table, we already see that more layers do not necessarily mean that the filter will be larger. As we have a smaller representation of data, we may incur more false positives, needing more layers. As mentioned before, the 7-bit configuration falls near our defined threshold for creating more layers, because of that, we see the high FNR for this configuration. To better explore this phenomenon, we present in the fourth row an additional experiment for the 7-bit configuration using a threshold of 0.03 FNR for our cutoff on filter construction (Tables 1 and 2).

As the results show, we add 2 more layers but the overall space does not increase as much. What is more interesting is that in this configuration the FNR for the filter falls to 0.1%, a better result than all other configurations.

For the second table, where we see the increased FNR on the first and last of the selected results, we observe that for a higher FRR, size decreases as expected, however, if it is too relaxed, the number of false results will increase significantly and result in an larger filter size, because of the error.

References

1. Agrawal, R., Bird, P., Grandison, T., Kiernan, J., Logan, S., Rjaibi, W.: Extending relational database systems to automatically enforce privacy policies. In: ICDE, pp. 1013–1022. IEEE Computer Society, Tokyo (2005)
2. Bloom, B.H.: Space/time trade-offs in hash coding with allowable errors. Commun. ACM **13**(7), 422–426 (1970)
3. Byun, J., Li, N.: Purpose based access control for privacy protection in relational database systems. VLDB J. **17**(4), 603–619 (2008)
4. CCPA: California Consumer Privacy Act (2018). https://oag.ca.gov/privacy/ccpa. Accessed 07 Oct 2021
5. Deeds, K., Hentschel, B., Idreos, S.: Stacked filters: learning to filter by structure. Proc. VLDB Endow. **14**(4), 600–612 (2021)
6. Deshpande, A.: Sypse: privacy-first data management through pseudonymization and partitioning. In: CIDR, pp. 1–8 (2021). https://www.cidrdb.org/
7. Fan, B., Andersen, D.G., Kaminsky, M., Mitzenmacher, M.: Cuckoo filter: practically better than bloom. In: CoNEXT, pp. 75–88. ACM (2014)
8. Regulation, G.: Regulation (EU) 2016/679 of the European Parliament and of the Council of 27 April 2016 on the protection of natural persons with regard to the processing of personal data and on the free movement of such data, and repealing Directive 95/46. Off. J. Eur. Union **59**, 1–88 (2016)
9. Graf, T.M., Lemire, D.: Xor filters: faster and smaller than bloom and cuckoo filters. CoRR arxiv:1912.08258 (2019)
10. Huffman, D.A.: A method for the construction of minimum- redundancy codes. In: Proceedings of the IRE 40, vol. 9, pp. 1098–1101 (1952)
11. Kiss, S.Z., Hosszu, É., Tapolcai, J., Rónyai, L., Rottenstreich, O.: Bloom filter with a false positive free zone. IEEE Trans. Netw. Serv. Manag. **18**(2), 2334–2349 (2021)
12. Konstantinidis, G., Holt, J., Chapman, A.: Enabling personal consent in databases. Proc. VLDB Endow. **15**(2), 375–387 (2021)

13. Kraska, T., Stonebraker, M., Brodie, M., Servan-Schreiber, S., Weitzner, D.: Schen-genDB: a data protection database proposal. In: Gadepally, V., et al. (eds.) DMAH/Poly -2019. LNCS, vol. 11721, pp. 24–38. Springer, Cham (2019). https://doi.org/10.1007/978-3-030-33752-0_2

14. LGPD: Lei Geral de Proteção de Dados (2018). http://www.planalto.gov.br/ccivil_03/_ato2015-2018/2018/lei/L13709compilado.htm. Accessed 07 Oct 2021

15. Machado, J.C., Amora, P.R.P.: The impact of privacy regulations on DB systems. J. Inf. Data Manag. **12**(5) (2021)

16. Mitzenmacher, M.: Balanced allocations and double hashing. In: SPAA, pp. 331–342. ACM (2014)

17. Pandey, P., Bender, M.A., Johnson, R., Patro, R.: A general-purpose counting fil-ter: making every bit count. In: SIGMOD Conference, pp. 775–787. ACM, Chicago (2017)

18. Pappachan, P., Yus, R., Mehrotra, S., Freytag, J.: Sieve: a middleware approach to scalable access control for database management systems. Proc. VLDB Endow. **13**(11), 2424–2437 (2020)

19. Praciano, F.D.B.S., Amora, P.R.P., Abreu, I.C., Machado, J.C.: Purpose scan: a purpose-aware access method. In: Heterogeneous Data Management, Polystores, and Analytics for Healthcare - VLDB 2022 Workshops, Poly and DMAH (2022)

20. Pun, S.: Prisql: a privacy preserving sql language (2010). https://doi.org/10.11575/PRISM/10182. https://prism.ucalgary.ca/handle/1880/104364

21. Reviriego, P., Sánchez-Macián, A., Walzer, S., Dillinger, P.C.: Approximate mem-bership query filters with a false positive free set. CoRR arxiv:2111.06856 (2021)

22. Rizvi, S., Mendelzon, A.O., Sudarshan, S., Roy, P.: Extending query rewriting techniques for fine-grained access control. In: SIGMOD Conference, pp. 551–562. ACM, France (2004)

23. Schwarzkopf, M., Kohler, E., Frans Kaashoek, M., Morris, R.: Position: GDPR compliance by construction. In: Gadepally, V., et al. (eds.) DMAH/Poly -2019. LNCS, vol. 11721, pp. 39–53. Springer, Cham (2019). https://doi.org/10.1007/978-3-030-33752-0_3

24. Shastri, S., Banakar, V., Wasserman, M., Kumar, A., Chidambaram, V.: Under-standing and benchmarking the impact of GDPR on database systems. Proc. VLDB Endow. **13**(7), 1064–1077 (2020)

25. Tripunitara, M.V., Carbunar, B.: Efficient access enforcement in distributed role-based access control (RBAC) deployments. In: SACMAT, pp. 155–164. ACM (2009)

26. Wang, L., Neet al.: Data capsule: a new paradigm for automatic compliance with data privacy regulations, pp. 3–23. CoRR arxiv:1909.00077 (2019)

Secure and Reliable Digital Wallets: A Threat Model for Secure Storage in eIDAS 2.0

Zahra Ebadi Ansaroudi[1]([⊠])(iD), Amir Sharif[1]([⊠])(iD), Giada Sciarretta[1](iD), Francesco Antonio Marino[3](iD), and Silvio Ranise[1,2](iD)

[1] Center for Cybersecurity, FBK, Trento, Italy
{zebadiansaroudi,asharif,g.sciarretta,ranise}@fbk.eu
[2] Department of Mathematics, University of Trento, Trento, Italy
[3] Italian Government Printing Office and Mint, Rome, Italy
fa.marino@ipzs.it

Abstract. The revised eIDAS regulation (eIDAS 2.0) advocates a shift back to user control over digital credentials, introducing the European Digital Identity Wallet. This shift aims to enhance privacy by allowing citizens to disclose personal data in a controlled manner selectively. As the keys to which the credentials are bound must be stored securely, a secure storage mechanism is essential—one that is not only secure but also accessible through the available technology stack and compliant with eIDAS 2.0.

In support of the European Digital Identity Wallet, the EU Commission published an Architecture and Reference Framework together with a set of Implementing Acts to ensure interoperable solutions. However, the current versions only identify a high-level set of requirements and do not provide insights on satisfying them through actionable implementations. Secure storage is a crucial aspect that remains inadequately addressed, highlighting the need for comprehensive security and privacy guidelines to ensure a robust solution. To address this gap, we provide a threat model explicitly designed for the secure storage component of the wallet. This allows for identifying potential threats and a set of effective controls to secure the implementations and serves as a practical tool to assist architects in making informed decisions when selecting an implementation that best meets their system's security and privacy requirements. In addition, it reinforces essential assurance activities, such as certification, testing, and attestation required by the eIDAS 2.0 to maintain a trusted state for secure storage.

Keywords: Digital Identity Wallet · Secure Storage · Threat Model

1 Introduction

In the modern digital landscape, digital identity wallets have become critical for securely managing and storing user credentials, playing a central role in elec-

© IFIP International Federation for Information Processing 2025
Published by Springer Nature Switzerland AG 2025
S. Katsikas and B. Shafiq (Eds.): DBSec 2025, LNCS 15722, pp. 271–289, 2025.
https://doi.org/10.1007/978-3-031-96590-6_15

tronic identification and trust services. Within the European Union (EU), the European Digital Identity Wallet (EUDIW) initiative, introduced under the new electronic Identification, Authentication, and Trust Services (eIDAS 2.0) regulation, represents a significant advancement toward secure and user-centric digital identities [17]. To ensure interoperability and security, the European Commission has proposed the EUDIW Architecture and Reference Framework (ARF), which outlines technical guidelines and best practices for EU member states to implement secure and privacy-preserving wallet solutions [18].

A crucial component of the EUDIW security architecture is the Wallet Secure Cryptographic Device (WSCD), responsible for secure key management, authentication processes, and cryptographic operations. Given its role in handling these operations, the security of WSCD is essential to guarantee the confidentiality and integrity of user data both within the EUDIW, and during its interaction with the EUDIW on the user's device. Here, the concepts of trust, trustworthiness, assurance, and attestation, in turn, are crucial to maintaining the security and reliability of users' personal and sensitive data, such as cryptographic key material protected by WSCD [29,45].

In this context, "trust" refers to users' confidence in the EUDIW implementation and, more specifically, their certainty that the WSCD operates securely and as intended; it is subjective and influenced by past experiences, manufacturer reputation, and transparency in security practices. Trustworthiness is the objective quality of the WSCD, reflecting its ability to consistently perform secure operations, resist threats, and comply with standards such as FIPS 140-3 [35] or Common Criteria [14], which is also mandated by eIDAS 2.0 regulation [3,17]. Assurance encompasses the processes that demonstrate and validate this trustworthiness, such as testing and certification. Attestation adds a real-time verification layer, offering cryptographic evidence that the WSCD remains in a trusted state. These concepts are interlinked: trust arises from perceived trustworthiness, which is reinforced through assurance mechanisms and maintained over time through attestation [7,43]. As assurance mechanisms play an enhanced role in sustaining trust, they must go beyond static evaluations. While certification and rigorous testing provide assurance for WSCD during the production phase, real-time verification during its operation is necessary to maintain trust. This can be achieved through attestation, typically via signed statements or cryptographic certificates, proving the WSCD remains untampered and compliant with security policies.

To make such efforts effective, it is essential to develop a comprehensive threat model. Threat modeling plays a critical role in ensuring trustworthiness, as it enables the proactive identification and mitigation of attack vectors before they can be exploited. This is particularly vital for EUDIW solutions, which manage personal data such as identification data. A structured threat model informs the design of protective measures and security controls that reduce exposure to these risks.

For example, the WSCD must be hardened against threats that could compromise users' private keys, thereby undermining the trust placed in the

EUDIW. Threat modeling allows for such risks to be systematically identified and addressed through targeted controls. It is also interlinked with assurance activities: for certification, a robust threat model ensures that regulatory requirements are met while accounting for real-world attack scenarios. In testing, it directs efforts—such as penetration testing and vulnerability scanning—toward the most critical attack surfaces. In attestation, it defines the parameters that must be continuously verified to confirm the WSCD remains in a trusted state.

Despite its centrality, threat modeling is not yet adequately addressed in existing regulatory frameworks and technical guidelines, leaving a critical gap. While the Implementing Act (IA) [16] defines high-level security requirements and the ARF provides technical guidance, neither includes a detailed and systematic threat modeling methodology tailored to WSCD implementations. This gap creates uncertainty about specific threats, vulnerabilities, and asset risks, potentially exposing WSCD architectures to sophisticated threats such as side-channel exploits, unauthorized key extraction, or software tampering [6,37,48].

To address these limitations, this paper proposes a structured threat modeling approach tailored specifically to WSCD deployments within the EUDIW framework. Building on our prior research [46], which examined general EUDIW threats, we extend our analysis by explicitly focusing on secure storage threats, vulnerabilities, and necessary controls relevant to various WSCD architectures. Our contributions are:

- Systematically identifying, categorizing, and contextualizing threats applicable to WSCD using established frameworks such as STRIDE [32] and LINDDUN [30].
- Mapping identified threats and vulnerabilities to effective security controls in alignment with ARF and eIDAS 2.0 regulatory requirements.
- Providing a reference threat model to assist Wallet Providers and EU regulators in developing secure and privacy-preserving WSCD solutions.

By establishing threat modeling as a key component of assurance—integrating testing, certification, and attestation—we aim to significantly enhance the security and reliability of EUDIW implementations, ultimately contributing to a robust digital identity infrastructure across the EU.

Paper Structure. Section 2 presents the method we follow to perform the WSCD threat modeling in the context of EUDIW that provides a brief explanation of the WSCD components, and our threat characterization. In Sect. 3, we report our findings and share lessons learned. Section 4 contrasts our approach with related works. We summarize the main results and provide insights for future work in Sect. 5.

2   WSCD Threat Modeling

This section describes the method used for WSCD threat modeling, building upon our previous work in [46], which involves the following steps:

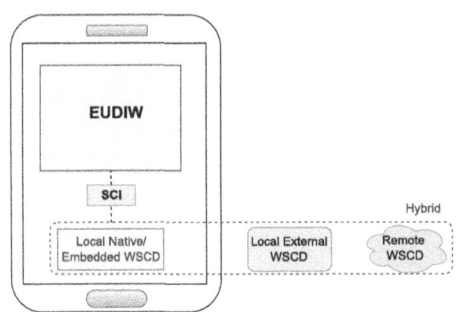 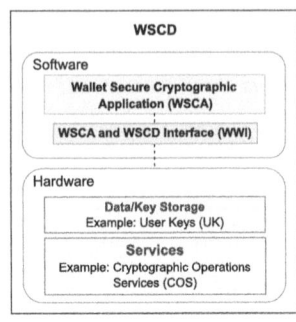

(a) WSCD within the EUDIW ecosystem.   (b) Internal components of WSCD.

Fig. 1. Overview of WSCD in the EUDIW ecosystem and its internal components. The Interfaces, Assets, and Services are detailed in Table 2.

Context Establishment is an initial step to provide a complete understanding of the WSCD component. It helps to pinpoint the critical assets and understand how the WSCD component interacts with EUDIW.

Threat Characterization focuses on identifying potential threats and attack scenarios relevant to the WSCD. It categorizes threats by their sources, categories, and the assets they target. Additionally, it outlines vulnerabilities, along with the security controls needed to mitigate the identified threats.

2.1   Context Establishment

The EUDIW is an application developed by an entity called "Wallet Provider" in the ARF [18]. The EUDIW, when installed on a User device, is a user-controlled application that allows them to store and manage their digital credentials such as their personal identification data, or mobile driving licenses.

According to the ARF [18], the EUDIW can be implemented as a single mobile application. This application integrates multiple components to support its core functions, primarily the secure issuance and presentation of credentials. A key component in the EUDIW ecosystem, as shown in Fig. 1 is the Wallet Secure Cryptographic Device (WSCD), which is hardware-backed storage and manages keys and implements cryptographic suites and mechanisms essential for credential issuance and presentation. The WSCD itself includes many components at the hardware level, including data or key storage, and many services which you can find in Fig. 1. We further list all of them in Table 2 and describe them in Sect. 2.2. Additionally, the EUDIW includes a Wallet Secure Cryptographic Application (WSCA), which leverages the WSCD's capabilities via two interfaces: the Secure Cryptographic Interface (SCI) between the EUDIW and WSCA, and the WSCA and WSCD Interface (WWI) between the WSCA and WSCD. While the former is specifically designed to manage cryptographic assets and execute cryptographic operations using the WSCD, the latter is specifically designed to enable communication between the WSCA and the WSCD. The security of the WSCD component is of great importance to avoid the release of credentials to an EUDIW that cannot securely store private keys as highlighted in Annex 2 of ARF (WUA_08 requirement) [18]. The security and capabilities of the WSCD can be attested by the Wallet Provider by acquiring a key attestation from the WSCD component of the EUDIW. This attestation is known as Wallet Unit Attestation (WUA) as defined by the ARF [18], which is issued by the Wallet Provider and ensures that the keys used for key binding of credentials reside in a trusted WSCD.

As illustrated in Fig. 1 and Table 1, WSCDs can be configured in diverse architectures. Local hardware-based solutions include on-device modules—such as processor-native environments (e.g., Trusted Execution Environments (TEEs) or integrated security co-processors) and embedded Secure Elements (SEs), such as Embedded Subscriber Identity Modules (eSIMs)—as well as external, user-

Table 1. Comparison of WSCD Types

Feature	Secure Element (SE)	Trusted Execution Environment (TEE)	Hardware Security Module (HSM)
Deployment Type	Local (Embedded and External)	Local Native	Remote
Form Factor	Embedded SE: Integrated chip on device motherboard (e.g., eSIM, Android StrongBox) External SE: Portable, often card-based (e.g., smart cards, secure USB tokens)	Logic integrated within main CPU architecture (e.g., Android Keystore) Dedicated security coprocessor (e.g., Apple Secure Enclave)	Standalone appliances or server modules (e.g., rack-mounted, in data centers)
Advantages	High security, widely used in IoT and mobile devices External SEs: Portable, easy to replace or upgrade	Flexible, integrates with existing hardware, supports secure software updates, offers strong performance	High security and performance, suitable for enterprise and critical infrastructure
Limitations	Embedded SEs: Less flexible, difficult to upgrade External SEs: Limited processing power, may not integrate seamlessly with other hardware	Requires specific hardware support, implementation complexity	High cost, large form factor, requires specialized hardware

held SEs (e.g., Java-based smart cards). Remote solutions, such as Hardware Security Modules, provide centralized key management and high security from data centers. Hybrid setups combine on-device and remote approaches for balanced security, scalability, and flexibility. Building on this architectural diversity, Table 1 provides a detailed overview of these WSCD types by comparing them across key aspects: form factor, advantages, and limitations. Specifically, for local, processor-native TEEs, the table highlights their embedded form factor, flexible updates, and security profile compared to the Rich Operating System (Rich OS)- the main, general-purpose OS like Android or iOS - but with a different security profile compared to dedicated SEs and HSMs. In contrast, embedded SEs typically integrate seamlessly at the hardware level, although upgrading them can be challenging, while external SEs are portable but often have limited processing power. Alternatively, remote solutions such as HSMs in secure data centers provide high-level security, centralized cryptographic key and operational security management (monitoring, audits). However, they may introduce additional costs and complexity and generally require constant connectivity.

2.2   Threat Characterization

In the following, we present our main results concerning the list of identified assets and threats.

Assets. We categorize the assets into data, services, and interfaces that require protection as highlighted in Table 2, with illustrative examples shown in Fig. 1. For example, secure storage within the hardware boundary of WSCD contains data assets, while key management and cryptographic services enable secure cryptographic operations using them. Overall, grouped by function and importance, these assets support secure operations within the EUDIW. Data assets involve sensitive information such as cryptographic keys and authentication data. Service assets include essential cryptographic functions, such as key management and secure communication. Finally, interface assets enable secure interactions between the WSCD, WSCA, and the EUDIW.

Threats. We consider threats as any potential violations of the WSCD security or privacy, including unauthorized access, data modification. We identified a list of **23** threats, here we report a subset of **10** threats, which are summarized in Table 3 and are later discussed in a discussion section. Due to page limits, for each threat, we selectively report relevant attack techniques, vulnerabilities, and controls rather than providing a comprehensive list. Readers interested in a complete list with detailed information can refer to our companion website [4]. Table 3 includes:

- **Threat Category (TC)**: The entry in the threat category categorizes each threat using two established frameworks: STRIDE [32] and LINDDUN [30]. STRIDE, developed by Microsoft, serves as a mnemonic for security threats, covering Spoofing (SP), Tampering (TA), Repudiation (RE), Information Disclosure (ID), Denial of Service (DS), and Elevation of Privileges (EP).

Table 2. Asset Categorization in WSCD Threat Modeling

Category	Asset	Description
Data	User/Holder Keys (UK)	Symmetric and asymmetric keys (e.g., private keys) managed by the WSCA, essential for cryptographic operations and securing sensitive user interactions within the EUDIW
	WSCD Authentication Data (WAD)	Credentials and authentication tokens, such as the PIN/passwords, required for secure access to the WSCD resources and services
	Client Application Data (CAD)	Holder-specific data, such as credentials, provided by the EUDIW for cryptographic functions; requires confidentiality and integrity protection
	WSCD Data (WD)	Core application code, such as the WSCA code, libraries, and sensitive WSCD security data, including secure keys, logs, support keys, key management information, and update code packages
Service	Key Management Services (KMS)	Services for key generation, secure access, rotation, and secure destruction within the WSCD to maintain controlled and protected key lifecycles
	Cryptographic Operations Services (COS)	Essential cryptographic functions such as encryption/decryption, digital signing, verification, and hashing, ensuring data confidentiality, authenticity, and integrity within the EUDIW context
	Authentication Services (AS)	Authentication mechanisms for verifying the identity of the Holder and the authorized device accessing the WSCD
	Access Control Services (ACS)	Authorization and monitoring services, including audit logging, to control and oversee access to the WSCD resources
	Secure Communication Services (SCS)	Encrypted transmission using protocols like TLS/SSL to secure data in transit, with end-to-end encryption and message integrity checks
	Data Protection Services (DPS)	Encryption and integrity protection measures for securely stored data, safeguarding against unauthorized access and tampering
	Backup and Recovery Services (BRS)	Services for securely backing up and recovering keys and critical data to prevent data loss and ensure resilience
	WSCD-specific Security Services (WSS)	Dedicated security mechanisms, including tamper detection, secure boot, and application isolation, to protect against physical and logical threats
Interface	Secure Cryptographic Interface (SCI)	Interface facilitating secure data exchange between the EUDIW and the WSCA, ensuring controlled cryptographic interactions
	WSCD and WSCA Interface (WWI)	Interface governing secure data flow between the WSCD and the WSCA, ensuring data integrity and enforcing access control

LINDDUN focuses on privacy threats, including Linkability (LN), Identi-fiability (IF), Non-Repudiation (NR), Detectability (DT), Data Disclosure (DD), Unawareness/Unintervenability (UU), and Non-Compliance (NC).

Table 3. An excerpt of threats to the WSCD in the EUDIW ecosystem.

T1. Data Disclosure involves compromise of Holder data, which is potentially accessed physically or remotely [21, 38].

TC: ID, DD

AT: (AT1) Side-channel attack (e.g., the attacker extracts side-channel information by monitoring physical leakages like power consumption, electromagnetic emissions to infer secrets like cryptographic keys, or other sensitive data without direct access to the IC internals)

V: Weak cryptographic protection (V1), Weak access control mechanisms (V2), Insecure communication channels (V4), Poor credential management (V7)

AA: UK, WAD, CAD, WSD, SCS, DPS, SCI, WWI

C: Isolation (Physical and Logical) (C1), Side-Channel mitigation (C4), Data encryption (C7), Integrity protection (C8), Secure communication channels (C19)

AW: All

T2. Data Manipulation involves the threat actor trying to manipulate the Holder data in storage or during transfer [20, 21, 44].

TC: SP, TA, DD

AT: (AT19) Man-in-the-Middle (e.g., an attacker intercepts and alters communication between the User and the WSCD, allowing them to capture credentials and impersonate the User to gain unauthorized access and manipulate the data)

V: Weak access control mechanisms (V2), Lack of data integrity mechanisms (V5), Weak authentication mechanisms (V6), Insufficient or Inadequate code signing/verification (V10)

AA: UK, WAD, CAD, WAPD, WSD, SCS, DPS, COS, KMS, SCI, WWI

C: Integrity protection (C8), Key management (C10), Access control (C17), Secure communication channels (C19)

AW: All

T4. Physical Tamping involves the threat actor trying to modify or exploit the physical security measures to access WSCD [20, 23, 26, 36].

TC: EP, DS, TA, NC, DT

AT: (AT5) Perturbation (e.g., an attacker could attempt to introduce intentional disturbances or variations to a system's environment to induce errors or reveal sensitive information and extract confidential data)

V: Inadequate physical security (V8), Weak key management practices (V13)

AA: All WSCD assets

C: Tamper-Resistant hardware (C2), Anti-tampering (C13), Self-testing (C25), Security audits (C26)

AW: All

T6. Key Disclosure/Compromise involves unauthorized access to the plain text form of a secret key, allowing direct reading, copying, or compromising of the key by an attacker [38, 49].

TC: ID, EP, NC

AT: (AT25) Attacks to cryptographic algorithm implementations (e.g., Attacker targets the implementation of cryptographic algorithms within the WSCD, such as exploiting weaknesses in random number generators to predict cryptographic keys or breaking encryption due to implementation flaws)

V: Weak cryptographic protection (V1), Weak access control mechanisms (V2), Weak authentication mechanisms (V6), Poor credential management (V7)

AA: UK, KMS

C: Secure cryptographic implementation (C6), Data encryption (C7), Key management (C10), Zeroization of keys (C27)

AW: All

T12. WSCD Malfunction involves a WSCD fault, which is causing security properties to weaken or fail [49].

TC: TA, NC

AT: (AT2) Fault injection (e.g., an attacker intentionally introduces faults or errors into a system or device to cause malfunction and reveal sensitive information. This can be done by inducing physical perturbations during cryptographic computation or by algorithm parameter manipulation)

V: Inadequate error handling (V14)

AA: All WSCD assets

C: Monitoring and logging (C21), Self testing (C25), Security audits (C26), Error handling (C32)

AW: All

(*continued*)

Table 3. (*continued*)

T15. Unauthorized Code Execution involves the threat actor trying to import malicious code into WSCD to disclose or modify sensitive data. Includes executing malicious applications with illegal byte-code sequences or invalid parameters [19, 23].

TC: TA, NC, ID, DD

AT: (AT24) Software/firmware modification (e.g., the attacker modifies the software/ firmware of the WSCD, introducing vulnerabilities or backdoors that can be exploited to compromise its security)

V: Improper validation of integrity check value (V11), Improper input validation (V12), Insecure card and applet management (V18), Vulnerable applet execution controls (V19)

AA: All WSCD assets

C: Secure debug (C14), Control flow integrity (C15), Secure firmware and software update (C24), Secure APIs (C28)

AW: TEE, SE

T18. Unauthorized Card Management involves the threat actor trying to perform unauthorized card management operations (e.g., by impersonating the card issuer or applet provider) to take benefit of the privileges or services granted to this actor on the card and perform fraudulent operations like loading, installing, deleting, extracting, or personalizing an applet, or updating privileges [21].

TC: TA, SP, EP, NC

AT: (AT16) Key replacement (e.g., the attacker replaces a valid card issuer key with a malicious one to gain unauthorized access or control)

V: Insecure card and applet management (V18)

AA: WAPD, WSS, WSD, KMS, ACS

C: Secure card and applet management (C22)

AW: SE

T20. Applet/ Application Impersonation involves a threat actor forging the identity of a trusted entity (e.g., an applet in an SE or a Trusted Application (TA) in a TEE) to gain unauthorized access to WSCD resources, services, or data. Examples include impersonating a TA in a TEE environment or a legitimate applet in a SE [23, 36].

TC: SP, ID, EP, DD

AT: (AT16) Key replacement (e.g., the attacker replaces a TEE trusted key, or an issuer's public key, with a malicious one to gain unauthorized access or control)

V: Insecure card and applet management (V18), Vulnerable applet execution controls (V19)

AA: WAD, AS, ACS

C: Access control (C17)

AW: TEE, SE

T21. WSCD Cloning involves the threat actor trying to copy WSCD-related data from one device to another, making the second device accept it as genuine [23].

TC: SP, ID, EP, DD

AT: (AT7) External DRAM probing (e.g., an attacker tries to retrieve the TEE code or data by probing data on an external RAM bus to analyze the TEE behavior, to find vulnerabilities in the TEE and use this vulnerability to attack the TEE)

V: Inadequate data cloning protection (V20)

AA: All WSCD assets

C: Data cloning protection (C30)

AW: TEE

T22. RAM Exploitation involves the attacker gaining access to device RAM, potentially accessing sensitive runtime data like cryptographic keys, authentication data, or other confidential information [23].

TC: ID, EP, DD, NC

AT: (AT10) Breach of memory isolation (e.g., An attacker can try to directly access and modify TEE memory contents by exploiting a flaw in hardware memory isolation)

V: Improper input validation (V12), Lack of memory protection (V22)

AA: UK, WAD, WSS

C: Secure boot (C5), Secure I/O (C11), Memory protection (C12), Security audits (C26), Secure APIs (C28)

AW: TEE

- **Attack Techniques (AT)**: Describes strategies that attackers use to exploit threats, which are taken from academic literature [33, 43, 48], and technical reports [19–21, 44].
- **Vulnerabilities (V)**: Highlights weaknesses like weak cryptographic protection, which could be exploited by specific threats, which are taken from widely recognized standards [37, 38].
- **Affected Assets (AA)**: Identifies impacted elements like Secure Communication Services (SCS) under specific threats.
- **Controls (C)**: Lists measures such as Strong Authentication to counteract threats like **T1.** Data Disclosure. The identified controls are mostly taken from the technical reports [19–21, 44].
- **Affected WSCD (AW)**: Reports the affected WSCD type for each threat.

3   Discussion

In our threat modeling, we identified **23** distinct threats, **23** vulnerabilities, **32** controls, and **28** attack techniques extracted from various sources, including widely recognized standards (e.g., OWASP [38, 39]), technical reports [19–21, 44], and academic studies [8, 33, 47]. The identified threats apply to various WSCD solutions, including TEE, SE (embedded and external), and HSM. These WSCD types as mentioned in Sect. 2.1, and shown in Table 1 represent different categories outlined in the ARF: local native, local embedded, local external, and remote, reflecting the diversity of secure storage technologies used within the EUDIW framework.

The insights gained from our threat modeling analysis form the basis for the following lessons learned:

- Of the **23** identified threats, **16** (69.6%) apply to all WSCD types, **2** (8.7%) apply only to TEE, another **2** (8.7%) apply only to SE, and **3** (13%) apply to both TEE and SE. This classification per architecture type, highlights better the trade-offs between WSCD types as it provides per-architecture threat profiling. To elaborate, let us consider "T22. Ram Exploitation", TEE-based solutions are vulnerable specifically to this threat, where an attacker may access sensitive runtime data due to the reliance on software-based isolation mechanisms to protect sensitive data during runtime. This reliance, coupled with the shared use of hardware resources between secure and non-secure environments, can make TEEs vulnerable to attacks that exploit weaknesses in the software stack or runtime memory management [23]. While this is not the case for other WSCD types. Similarly, SE-based solutions (e.g., smart cards or eSIMs) face additional risks, such as "T18. Unauthorized Card Management", which necessitates extra security measures tailored to their architecture [21].
- Among our list of threats, "T4. Physical Tampering", "T5. Faulty Update Code Package", "T12. WSCD Malfunction", "T13. Functionality Abuse", "T15. Unauthorized (Ill-formed) Code Execution", and "T21. WSCD Cloning" deserves the most attention to mitigate as if these threats are carry out, the

results are the comprise of all WSCD assets. Given that, these require the highest priority for mitigation efforts.

– Information Disclosure (**13** out of **23**) and Elevation of Privilege (**12** out of **23**) are the most common security threat category identified in our analysis. Both threats involve sensitive data, whether contained in WSCD storage, transferred between WSCD and authenticated external entities using a client application (e.g., EUDIW), or transmitted between physically separate components of the WSCD. The impact of Elevation of Privilege is particularly severe, as it enables attackers to gain unauthorized access to WSCD functions and data, potentially leading to misuse or unauthorized cryptographic operations. In contrast, the impact of Information Disclosure is less immediate but can provide attackers with data that could be leveraged for more specialized attacks in subsequent stages.

– Non Compliance (**16** out of **23**) and Data Disclosure (**8** out of **23**) are our analysis's most prevalent privacy threats. While Non-Compliance is a critical threat to avoid, as failure to adhere to regulations could expose User's data to unauthorized access and result in hefty fines from regulatory authorities, the impact in the case of Data Disclosure can be a significant risk as the attacker can access the User's sensitive data such as their private keys which enables attackers to decrypt User's stored credentials.

– Integrity Protection (C8), Key Management (C10), Authentication (C16), Access Control (C17), Secure Card and Applet Management (C22), Security Audits (C26), and Secure APIs (C28) deserve additional attention in contrast to the other controls as they are mitigating multiple threats (**4** up to **10** threats) if implemented. Rather than C22 and C26, which are SE and HSM-specific controls, the rest are applicable to all WSCD types.

– Access Control (C17), Authentication (C16), Security Audits (C26), and Key Management (C10) are among the top security and privacy controls within our analysis; however, each also involves a trade-off between robust security and ease of implementation. Access Control (C17) requires not only complex policy management (e.g., role-based or attribute-based) but also demands continuous alignment within the WSCD that can lead to various challenges within the implementation. To elaborate, let's consider the case of local native and embedded SEs WSCD types. In the context of local native WSCD solutions, access control enforcement relies heavily on the host operating system's authentication, authorization, and process isolation mechanisms. Vulnerabilities or misconfigurations in the OS can compromise policy enforcement. Furthermore, in the case of embedded SEs, as they often have limited memory, processing power, and bandwidth, these constraints lead to imposing limitations on how access control logic is enforced (e.g., limited policy complexity, and limited secure storage). However, in case this control is implemented properly, it effectively mitigates threats such as unauthorized access (T17), impersonation (T3), and data disclosure (T1). In the context of Authentication (C16), it is important to have a balance between security and usability. While this control can be integrated at a fundamental level by integrating well-established protocols and APIs to safeguard access to the WSCD, it may generate user inconvenience if the solution necessitates frequent or multi-step credential verification processes. Despite its relative ease, it remains effective in preventing unauthorized credential use and reducing impersonation attempts (T3). Security Audits (C26) demand specialized logging and analysis tools, raising both the expertise needed to maintain and analyze them. This continuous scrutiny ensures that Wallet Providers remain well-informed about potential vulnerabilities, ultimately contributing to a more robust security posture. Finally, Key Management (C10)—encompassing advanced cryptographic techniques and ensuring reliable key generation, distribution, and storage—poses a more demanding control to implement. However, it is highly effective in mitigating threats such as key disclosure (T6), thereby ensuring that private keys remain protected against a broad range of security threats targeting the WSCD.

Practical Considerations. Integrating WSCDs into the EUDIW framework requires a careful balance between stringent security requirements—particularly compliance with the eIDAS High assurance level as mandated by the ARF—and practical challenges like user convenience and offline functionality. Building on our earlier work [3] that highlighted these complexities, we further examine the intricate trade-offs in WSCD selection. To support Wallet Providers in making informed development decisions, we define the following set of criteria:

- **User Reachability**: Accessibility and user adoption potential of the WSCD technology.
- **Security:** WSCD compliance with the eIDAS High assurance requirement, as specified under Common Criteria (CC) vulnerability assessment AVA_VAN.5, whether nationally or at the EU level [3,14].
- **User Convenience:** Smooth, intuitive user experience and user-centric design.
- **Offline Use:** determines whether the WSCD technology meets the requirement to operate without network connectivity.
- **Backup and Restore:** WSCD support for secure backup and restore of hardware-bound keys.

Each of the WSCD solutions is analyzed in the following based on the listed criteria, with a summary provided in Table 4.

Local Native. Local native WSCD solutions, such as TEEs are more widely implemented across a broader range of devices, thus satisfying the high range of user reachability. Concerning security, these solutions provide a baseline level of security (CC AVA_VAN.3), which does not meet the eIDAS High assurance requirement. Users need to set a password or biometric within the EUDIW solution to enable access to the WSCD functionalities, thereby ensuring a seamless user experience. Lastly, as the cryptographic materials and WSCA are hosted locally on the user's device, this WSCD type can easily support offline use-cases. Moreover, the keys are bound to the device WSCD and together with the other cryptographic materials are not exportable.

Embedded SEs. These WSCD solutions, such as eSE (e.g., Strongbox in Android), or eSIM are starting to become more accessible in the markets. According to a report published by Counterpoint [13], half a billion eSIM-capable devices were shipped worldwide in 2023 and it is estimated that by 2028 most of the European population will have an eSIM-capable device [1]. From a security standpoint, many embedded SEs—such as those found on high-end phones—already hold high-assurance CC certifications (CC AVA_VAN.5), whereas eSIM implementations generally still require that evaluation to demonstrate the security guarantees needed for EUDIW use cases. Because the SE resides entirely on the user's device, these solutions deliver seamless convenience and naturally support offline operation. However, like local TEEs, their keys are permanently bound within the SE and cannot be exported, so no backup or key-migration functionality is available.

External SEs. These WSCD solutions, typically take the form of NFC-enabled smart cards—most commonly government-issued identity (ID) cards—that act as portable WSCDs. Their adoption is hindered by the still-limited penetration of NFC-capable smartphones and the fact that mandatory issuance of ID cards only began in August 2021 [15]. The provided ID cards by member states are generally certified to CC AVA_VAN.5. Concerning user's convenience, smart cards do not provide a user-friendly experience as it requires the user to carry and tap their card for each interaction. On the plus side, because only NFC connectivity is needed, they fully support offline use cases. As with other local WSCD types, the cryptographic keys are permanently bound to the SE and cannot be exported, so no backup or restore functionality is available.

HSMs. Hardware Security Modules are widely adopted in the industry in different use cases for encryption, decryption, digital signature, authentication, and payments, as they must be deployed in the cloud—separate from the user's device—reachability is not a problem, since accessing HSMs from the EUDIW is merely a matter of implementing an API call. Regarding security, HSMs can meet the eIDAS High assurance requirement when certified under CC AVA_VAN.5. User convenience is low, as interactions between the EUDIW and a remote HSM require strong user authentication that can add an additional burden on the user experience. However, HSMs do not support offline use cases as the EUDIW needs to be connected to the internet to access the remote modules. As HSMs operate in cloud environments, they routinely allow encrypted key backups and disaster recovery mechanisms as part of standard operational procedures. The backups remain protected (e.g., encrypted) and can be restored to a compatible HSM without exposing the actual private keys in the clear.

To sum up and synthesize our findings, we highlight the following key insights:

– Among local mobile solutions, embedded SEs, such as Android's StrongBox (on CC AVA_VAN.5-certified high-end devices) or eSIMs, offer superior security through tamper-resistant hardware for cryptographic operations. However, their adoption is limited: StrongBox is primarily available on select Samsung models and a few Google Pixel devices, covering only a small percentage of the European mobile market [27, 31]. This coverage could expand if Apple's Secure Enclave achieves compliance with eIDAS High, enhancing security. For eSIMs, adoption is similarly constrained but projected to reach high penetration by 2028 [1]. Nevertheless, a significant portion of users remain reliant on less secure alternatives (e.g., TEEs)—certified only at CC AVA_VAN.3 or external/remote options—certified at AVA_VAN.5 but hindered by usability and connectivity challenges—limiting their immediate suitability.

- HSMs provide a promising level of the eIDAS High assurance requirement (CC AVA_VAN.5), satisfying ARF mandates, but their integration into the EUDIW presents substantial challenges for Wallet Providers. First, developing a robust interface to connect the EUDIW with secure back-end modules is complex. Second, additional security measures are required to safeguard front-end interactions with these HSMs. Moreover, practical concerns—such as limited offline support and the need for scalable, high-performance back-end systems—make HSM deployments costly and intricate, potentially deterring widespread adoption.

- As a transitive solution, local native TEEs (e.g., Qualcomm's TEE [22]) offer broad reachability across mid-range and budget devices, despite providing only baseline security (CC AVA_VAN.3), which falls short of the eIDAS High assurance requirement (CC AVA_VAN.5) [16]. A phased approach leveraging TEEs initially ensures immediate accessibility and user adoption while embedded SEs and HSMs mature in terms of market penetration, certification, and cost-effectiveness. This strategy balances usability and security, addressing current needs while preparing for robust, standardized implementations.

Table 4. Trade-off Analysis of WSCD Technologies

WSCD Type	User Reachability	Security (CC AVA_VAN.x)	User Convenience	Offline	Backup
Local Native (TEEs)	High (widespread)	Basic (CC AVA_VAN.3, not eIDAS High)	High	Yes	No
Local embedded SEs	Growing (eSIM 2028)	Cert. req., potential eIDAS High	High	Yes	No
Local external SEs	Low (NFC limits)	Certified (CC AVA_VAN.5, eIDAS High)	Low	Yes	No
Remote HSMs	High (cloud API)	Certified (CC AVA_VAN.5, eIDAS High)	Low	No	Yes (encrypted)

4   Related Works

Several studies underscore the crucial role of threat modeling methodologies when combined with secure storage technologies to enhance system security. For example, research has effectively applied STRIDE and DREAD frameworks alongside TEEs and SEs. These efforts address threats like spoofing, data disclosure, denial of service, and unauthorized access across various systems [12, 25, 34, 42], consistently demonstrating the benefits of secure storage in protecting sensitive operations and data identified through threat modeling. Complementing these high-level treatments, component-level threat analyses have shown that assumed "trusted" hardware boundaries often conceal critical vulnerabilities. For instance, Cerdeira et al. cataloged numerous implementation flaws and insecure interfaces in ARM TrustZone TEEs, enabling attackers to escape the secure world and compromise the non-secure world [11]. Brasser et al. demonstrated how code-reuse and state-rollback techniques can bypass Intel SGX enclave isolation guarantees [9]. Likewise, Park et al. showed that a single side-channel trace is sufficient to recover private keys from hardware cryptocurrency wallets [40], and Kepkowski et al. revealed how timing side-channels can defeat phishing-resistant protections in FIDO2 authenticators [28]. In the smartcard domain, Ahmed et al. found that embedding secrets in a tamper-resistant SE with HSM-backed recovery significantly mitigates threats from device theft and malware [2]. Industry protection profiles such as EN 419221-5, the ANSSI CC Protection Profile, and the GlobalPlatform Protection Profiles further enumerate attacker capabilities and prescribe hardware countermeasures [5,10,21]. Finally, broader STRIDE- and attack-tree-based surveys by Grüner et al. and Pöhn et al. confirm that while secure enclaves raise the cost of attack, a comprehensive component-level threat model is essential to cover all TEE, SE, and HSM variant-specific risks [24,41].

Taken together, these system-level and component-level studies establish that formal threat modeling paired with hardware roots of trust is both necessary and effective.

Within the EUDIW framework, where the WSCD functions as secure storage, the IA [16] itself provides a foundational, high-level threat identification that acknowledges potential threats to WSCDs within the ecosystem. However, this initial assessment remains at a high level, and importantly, it does not delve into detailed threat modeling of the internal components and diverse architectural implementations of this critical secure storage.

Similarly, our previous threat modeling work [46] performed a general threat modeling of the EUDIW ecosystem. While it focused on the main entities and primary operational phases like credential issuance and presentation, it intentionally considered the WSCD as a secure storage black box, explicitly leaving its internal threat landscape out of scope.

As non of the aforementioned studies, nor the EUDIW IA offer a component-level threat model for the WSCD, this paper presents a targeted and structured threat model focused precisely on the WSCD. Our study offer a granular analysis of threats and vulnerabilities across different WSCD architectures relevant to the EUDIW ecosystem.

5   Conclusion

The introduction of EUDIW under the eIDAS 2.0 regulation represents a significant step towards giving back the users control over their data. The ARF offers a general reference architecture, and the IA provides foundational guidelines for implementing EUDIW solutions. However, their broad, high-level approach fails to adequately address critical security and privacy aspects, such as secure storage mechanisms. While certification and testing may ensure WSCD security during the production phase, real-time verification during operation is crucial. In this context, threat modeling is key to strengthening security. A clear threat model ensures that WSCD solutions meet regulatory requirements and address real-world attacks, enhancing security beyond compliance. Without it, critical threats like side-channel attacks, key extraction, or software tampering may be missed, leaving systems vulnerable. Despite its crucial role, threat modeling has not been adequately addressed in the existing ARF and IA documents, leaving a critical gap.

This research paper fills the identified gap by presenting a structured and targeted threat model specifically tailored to secure storage—also referred to as WSCD—within the EUDIW framework. Leveraging STRIDE and LINDDUN frameworks, our research identifies, contextualizes, and categorizes potential threats, mapping them to vulnerabilities, attack scenarios, and impacted assets. Furthermore, we listed a set of actionable security controls to mitigate these threats and to address the ARF requirements. The developed reference model not only serves as a practical tool for Wallet Providers, enabling the design of secure and privacy-preserving EUDIW implementations, but also guides assurance activities to reinforce certification, testing, and attestation. By addressing the evolving threat landscape and aligning with the eIDAS 2.0 standards, this work contributes to a more robust digital identity ecosystem, ultimately improving user trust and security. As a preliminary step to conducting an accurate and effective risk assessment, knowing what potential threats exist is essential.

In future work, we plan to enhance our threat model by incorporating a control-based risk assessment methodology that systematically quantifies risks and maps them to specific security controls, ensuring alignment with best practices. In addition, by indicating the priority or mandatory implementations per each control, we aim to assist the Wallet Providers to take an informed decision by implementing the most effective measures for risk reduction. This will highlight how EUDIW risk levels evolve with different deployments of WSCD and based on the implementation of selected controls.

Acknowledgements. This work has been partially supported by a joint laboratory between FBK and the Italian Government Printing Office and Mint and by the project SERICS (PE00000014) under the MUR National Recovery and Resilience Plan funded by the European Union - NextGenerationEU.

The work of Silvio Ranise has also been supported by the Italian Ministry of University's Progetti di Ricerca di Rilevante Interesse Nazionale (PRIN) 2022 program under the "Postquantum Identification and Encryption Primitives: Design and Realization (POINTER)" (2022M2JLF2) project funded by the European Union - NextGenerationEU.

References

1. Abiresearch: eSIM in the Consumer and M2M Markets (2023). https://www.abiresearch.com/news-resources/chart-data/esim-market
2. Ahmed, K.A., Saraya, S.F., Wanis, J.F., Ali-Eldin, A.M.: A blockchain self-sovereign identity for open banking secured by the customer's banking cards. Future Internet **15**(6), 208 (2023)
3. Ansaroudi, Z.E., Sciarretta, G., De Maria, A., Ranise, S.: Navigating secure storage requirements for eudi wallets: a review paper. EURASIP J. Inf. Secur. **2025**(1), 2 (2025)
4. Ansaroudi, Z.E.: Secure and reliable digital wallets: a threat model for secure storage (2025). https://st.fbk.eu/complementary/DBSEC2025
5. ANSSI WG17: Common Criteria Protection Profile – Cryptographic Module for Trust Service Providers. Technical report, Common Criteria Portal (2016). https://www.commoncriteriaportal.org/files/ppfiles/ANSSI-CC-PP-2016_05%20PP.pdf. version 0.15
6. Barker, E.: Nist special publication 800-57 part 1 revision 5- recommendation for key management (2020)
7. Bastian, P., Kraus, M., Fischer, J.: Concepts for secure wallets in decentralized identity ecosystems. HMD Praxis der Wirtschaftsinformatik (2023)
8. Bouffard, G., Thampi, B.N., Lanet, J.-L.: Detecting laser fault injection for smart cards using security automata. In: Thampi, S.M., Atrey, P.K., Fan, C.-I., Perez, G.M. (eds.) SSCC 2013. CCIS, vol. 377, pp. 18–29. Springer, Heidelberg (2013). https://doi.org/10.1007/978-3-642-40576-1_3
9. Brasser, F., Müller, U., Dmitrienko, A., Kostiainen, K., Capkun, S., Sadeghi, A.R.: Software grand exposure:{SGX} cache attacks are practical. In: 11th USENIX Workshop on Offensive Technologies (WOOT 17) (2017)
10. CEN: EN 419221-5:2018 Protection Profiles for TSP Cryptographic Modules – Part 5: Cryptographic Module for Trust Services. Technical report, iTeh Standards (2018). https://standards.iteh.ai/catalog/standards/cen/3e27cc07-2782-4c65-81b7-474d858a471c/en-419221-5-2018
11. Cerdeira, D., Santos, N., Fonseca, P., Pinto, S.: Sok: understanding the prevailing security vulnerabilities in trustzone-assisted tee systems. In: 2020 IEEE Symposium on Security and Privacy (SP), pp. 1416–1432. IEEE (2020)
12. Chen, K.: Confidential high-performance computing in the public cloud. IEEE Internet Comput. **27**(1), 24–32 (2023)
13. Counterpoint: G+D, Thales, Idemia Pacesetters in 2023 eSIM Enablement Rankings (2024). https://www.counterpointresearch.com/insights/gd-thales-idemia-pacesetters-in-2023-esim-enablement-rankings/
14. ENISA: Cybersecurity certification–eucc, a candidate cybersecurity certification scheme to serve as a successor to the existing sog-is (2021). https://www.enisa.europa.eu/publications/cybersecurity-certification-eucc-candidate-scheme-v1-1.1
15. European Commission: Regulation (EU) 2019/1157 of the European Parliament and of the Council of 20 June 2019 on strengthening the security of identity cards of Union citizens and of residence documents issued to Union citizens and their family members exercising their right of free movement (2019). https://eur-lex.europa.eu/legal-content/EN/TXT/?uri=CELEX:32019R1157
16. European Commission: reference standards, specifications and procedures for a certification framework for eID Wallets (2024). https://eur-lex.europa.eu/legal-content/EN/TXT/?uri=OJ:L_202402981

17. European Union: Regulation of the European Parliament and of The Council Amending Regulation (Eu) No 910/2014 as Regards Establishing a Framework for a European Digital Identity (2021). https://eur-lex.europa.eu/legal-content/EN/TXT/?uri=CELEX:52021PC0281
18. European Union: The European Digital Identity Wallet (2025). https://eu-digital-identity-wallet.github.io/eudi-doc-architecture-and-reference-framework/1.10.0/
19. European Union Agency for Cybersecurity (ENISA): Cybersecurity Certification: EUCC, a candidate cybersecurity certification scheme to serve as a successor to the existing SOG-IS. Technical report, ENISA (2021). https://www.enisa.europa.eu/publications/cybersecurity-certification-eucc-candidate-scheme-v1-1.1
20. Federal Office for Information Security (BSI): Common Criteria Protection Profile Cryptographic Service Provider: BSI-CC-PP-0104-2019. Protection profile (pp), Common Criteria Portal (2019). https://commoncriteriaportal.org/files/ppfiles/pp0104b_pdf.pdf
21. GlobalPlatform: GlobalPlatform Technology Secure Element Protection Profile V1. Technical report, GlobalPlatform (2021). https://commoncriteriaportal.org/files/ppfiles/CCN-CC-PP-5-2021.pdf
22. GlobalPlatform: Globalplatform technology: The cornerstone of trust and interoperability for the european union digital identity wallet (2023). https://globalplatform.org/wp-content/uploads/2023/03/GP_EUDI_Wallet_White_Paper_v1.0_PublicRelease_signed.pdf
23. GlobalPlatform Technology: Tee protection profile version 1.3 (2020). https://globalplatform.org/specs-library/tee-protection-profile-v1-3/
24. Grüner, A., Mühle, A., Lockenvitz, N., Meinel, C.: Analyzing and comparing the security of self-sovereign identity management systems through threat modeling. Int. J. Inf. Secur. **22**(5), 1231–1248 (2023)
25. Huq, N., Gibson, C., Vosseler, R.: Driving security into connected cars: threat model and recommendations. Trend Micro (2020)
26. Joy, A., Soh, B., Zhang, Z., Parameswaran, S., Jayasinghe, D.: Physical and software based fault injection attacks against tees in mobile devices: a systemisation of knowledge. arXiv preprint arXiv:2411.14878 (2024)
27. Kantar: Google pixel celebrates a record global quarter (2023). https://www.kantar.com/north-america/inspiration/technology/google-pixel-celebrates-a-record-global-quarter
28. Kepkowski, M., Hanzlik, L., Wood, I., Kaafar, M.A.: How not to handle keys: timing attacks on fido authenticator privacy. arXiv preprint arXiv:2205.08071 (2022)
29. Kramer, M.: Trust and trustworthiness in computer systems. Commun. ACM **54**(8), 40–48 (2011)
30. LINDDUN: LINDDUN Privacy Threat Modeling Framework. https://linddun.org/
31. Lopez, J.: Canalys: In q1 2023, global high-end smartphones will grow by 4.7% (2023). https://www.techgoing.com/canalys-in-q1-2023-global-high-end-smartphones-will-grow-by-4-7/
32. Microsoft: STRIDE Threat Modeling Framework. https://learn.microsoft.com/en-us/azure/security/develop/threat-modeling-tool
33. Muñoz, A., Ríos, R., Román, R., López, J.: A survey on the (in)security of trusted execution environments. Comput. Secur. **129**, 103180 (2023). https://doi.org/10.1016/j.cose.2023.103180
34. Nagy, R., Bak, M., Papp, D., Buttyán, L.: T-raid: tee-based remote attestation for iot devices. In: International ISCIS Security Workshop (2021)

35. National Institute of Standards and Technology (NIST): FIPS 140-3: Security Requirements for Cryptographic Modules. Technical report, National Institute of Standards and Technology (2019). https://csrc.nist.gov/pubs/fips/140-3/final

36. Oracle: Java card system – open configuration protection profile (2020). https://www.commoncriteriaportal.org/files/ppfiles/pp0099V2b_pdf.pdf

37. (OWASP), T.O.W.A.S.P.: Cryptographic storage cheat sheet. https://cheatsheetseries.owasp.org/cheatsheets/Cryptographic_Storage_Cheat_Sheet.html. Accessed May 2024

38. OWASP Foundation: OWASP Cryptographic Storage Cheat Sheet (2024). https://cheatsheetseries.owasp.org/cheatsheets/Cryptographic_Storage_Cheat_Sheet.html

39. OWASP Foundation: Using a Broken or Risky Cryptographic Algorithm (2024). https://owasp.org/www-community/vulnerabilities/Using_a_broken_or_risky_cryptographic_algorithm

40. Park, D., Choi, M., Kim, G., Bae, D., Kim, H., Hong, S.: Stealing keys from hardware wallets: a single trace side-channel attack on elliptic curve scalar multiplication without profiling. IEEE Access **11**, 44578–44589 (2023)

41. Pöhn, D., Grabatin, M., Hommel, W.: Analyzing the threats to blockchain-based self-sovereign identities by conducting a literature survey. Appl. Sci. **14**(1), 139 (2023)

42. Pöhn, D., Grabatin, M., Hommel, W.: Modeling the threats to self-sovereign identities. Gesellschaft für Informatik (2023)

43. Rana, S., Parast, F.K., Kelly, B., Wang, Y., Kent, K.B.: A comprehensive survey of cryptography key management systems. J. Inf. Secur. Appl. **78**, 103607 (2023)

44. Realia Technologies S.L.: Perfil de Protección HSM Realia Technologies S.L. Technical report, Realia Technologies S.L. (2011). https://www.commoncriteriaportal.org/files/ppfiles/PP%20HSM%20REALIA%202.0.pdf

45. Schoen, S., Pohlmann, N.: Remote attestation and trusted execution environments: enabling secure communication. J. Comput. Secur. **17**(5), 503–530 (2009)

46. Sharif, A., Ansaroudi, Z.E., Sciarretta, G., Pöhn, D., Mollaeefar, M., Hommel, W., Ranise, S.: Protecting digital identity wallet: a threat model in the age of eidas 2.0. In: Risks and Security of Internet and Systems. Springer, Cham (2025). https://doi.org/10.1007/978-3-031-89350-6_6

47. Stajnrod, R., Ben Yehuda, R., Zaidenberg, N.J.: Attacking trustzone on devices lacking memory protection. J. Comput. Virol. Hack. Techn., 1–11 (2022)

48. Szefer, J.: Survey of microarchitectural side and covert channels, attacks, and defenses. J. Hardware Syst. Secur. **3**(3), 219–234 (2019)

49. Thales: Thales luna k7 cryptographic module security target (2022). https://www.commoncriteriaportal.org/files/epfiles/[DD]%20002-010985-001_Luna-PCIe-HSM7_CC_SecurityTarget_RevM.pdf

Differential Privacy

Facility Location Problem Under Local Differential Privacy Without Super-Set Assumption

Kevin Pfisterer[1]([⊠])[iD], Quentin Hillebrand[2][iD],
and Vorapong Suppakitpaisarn[2][iD]

[1] Technical University of Munich, Munich, Germany
kevin.pfisterer@tum.de
[2] The University of Tokyo, Bunkyo City, Japan
quentin-hillebrand@g.ecc.u-tokyo.ac.jp, vorapong@is.s.u-tokyo.ac.jp

Abstract. In this paper, we introduce an adaptation of the facility location problem and analyze it within the framework of local differential privacy (LDP). Under this model, we ensure the privacy of client presence at specific locations. When n is the number of points, Gupta et al. [5] established a lower bound of $\Omega(\sqrt{n})$ on the approximation ratio for any differentially private algorithm applied to the original facility location problem. As a result, subsequent works have adopted the super-set assumption, which may, however, compromise user privacy. We show that this lower bound does not apply to our adaptation by presenting an LDP algorithm that achieves a constant approximation ratio with a relatively small additive factor. Additionally, we provide experimental results demonstrating that our algorithm outperforms the straightforward approach on both synthetically generated and real-world datasets.

Keywords: Privacy in location-based services · Local differential privacy · Facility location · Approximation algorithms

1 Introduction

The facility location problem is a well studied problem in combinatorial optimization and operations research. Given a set of locations, costs for opening facilities, and a metric for the distance between locations, the goal is to open a set of facilities and connect clients to the facilities with minimal costs. The problem is NP-hard and therefore research focused on developing heuristic approaches and approximation algorithms since the 1960's [9,13]. The problem finds application in several fields such as data mining, bioinformatics and machine learning [3]. It can be formalized as follows.

Definition 1 (Facility location problem [1]). *Given the tuple $(V, d, \boldsymbol{f}, \boldsymbol{b})$ where V is the set of locations with $|V| = n$, (V, d) is a metric, $\boldsymbol{f} \in \mathbb{R}^n_{\geq 0}$ indicates*

© IFIP International Federation for Information Processing 2025
Published by Springer Nature Switzerland AG 2025
S. Katsikas and B. Shafiq (Eds.): DBSec 2025, LNCS 15722, pp. 293–310, 2025.
https://doi.org/10.1007/978-3-031-96590-6_16

the facility costs for every location $v \in V$, and $\boldsymbol{b} \in \{0,1\}^n$ indicates if a client is present at location $v \in V$. The objective of the facility location problem is to find a set of locations $S \subseteq V$ which minimizes:

$$cost_d(S; \boldsymbol{b}) = \sum_{s \in S} f_s + \sum_{v \in V} b_v d(v, S) \tag{1}$$

with $d(v, S) = \min_{s \in S} d(v, s)$. The first part of Eq. 1 is called facility costs while the latter one is called connection costs.

With the development of the differential privacy (DP) by Dwork et al. [2], recent research applied DP to the facility location problem to ensure privacy for clients. The idea of differential privacy is to ensure that the inclusion or exclusion of a single data point does not significantly affect the solution, thereby protecting individual privacy. The concept measures a system's privacy leakage using a parameter called the privacy budget, denoted as ε. An algorithm is referred to as an ε-DP mechanism if it has a privacy budget of ε.

Differential private algorithms deploy basic privacy mechanisms such as the exponential mechanism [11] or the Laplace mechanism [2] depending on the domain of the solution. Both mechanisms introduce a degree of uncertainty about the correctness of the solution. The Laplace mechanism does this by adding a noise drawn from the Laplace distribution to the solution while the exponential mechanism assigns output probabilities to categorical solution proportional to their utility.

DP requires a trusted curator that runs the algorithm and has access to the private information. This introduces a single point of failure and makes the curator prone to malicious attacks or human errors. Local differential privacy (LDP) [8] solves this issue by restricting the access of private data to the clients themselves. LDP algorithms are split into two parts. The first one runs locally and applies a privacy mechanisms to the private data to generate a noisy version. The noisy data is then sent to an aggregation server that computes a solution to the problem based on the noisy input.

There are works applying DP to the facility location model. Gupta et al. [5] were the first to apply DP to the uniform facility location problem. In this setting all locations have the same facility costs. They showed that any differentially private algorithm for the uniform facility location problem has an approximation ratio of $\Omega(\sqrt{n})$ when n is the number of points.

This lead to the introduction of the super-set output setting [1,5]. Here, the output of the algorithm for the facility location problem is a set $R \subseteq V$ of potential facilities. Every client is then connected according to a predefined connection rule to one of the facilities in R. The actual set of opened facilities S is then the set of locations in R that have at least one connected client. Under this super-set output setting, they provide an ε-DP algorithm with expected costs of at most

$$OPT \cdot O(\log n \log \Delta) \cdot \frac{\log \Delta}{\varepsilon} \log \frac{n \log^2 \Delta}{\varepsilon} \tag{2}$$

where OPT is the optimal value and $\Delta = \max\limits_{u,v \in V} d(u,v)$. It uses results from Fakcharoenphol et al. [4] to approximate any arbitrary metric by a distribution over hierarchically well-separated trees (HST) with distortion $O(\log n)$. The algorithm then takes an HST as input and outputs a super-set of facilities.

In [3], Esencayi et al. improve upon the results of Gupta et al. for the facility location problem under the ε-DP model with super-set output setting. They showed that there exists an algorithm with an approximation ratio of $O(\frac{1}{\varepsilon})$ under the HST metric and therefore an algorithm with approximation ratio of $O(\frac{\log n}{\varepsilon})$ for any arbitrary metric. Furthermore, they proved that the approximation ratio of any ε-DP algorithm is lower bounded by $\Omega(\frac{1}{\sqrt{\varepsilon}})$ even under a HST metric and the super-set output setting.

Cohen-Added et al. [1] were the first to study the facility location problem under local differential privacy (LDP) in 2022. They provide an ε-LDP algorithm that achieves an $O(n^{1/4}/\varepsilon^2)$ approximation ratio under the HST metric for the non-uniform facility location problem. The algorithm applies the randomized response mechanism, a special variant of the exponential mechanism, on the location side to private data. It uses an HST together with the noisy data from every location to output a super-set of facilities. The clients are then connected based on a lowest common ancestor rule to facilities. Furthermore, they proved a lower bound of $O(n^{1/4}/\sqrt{\varepsilon})$ for the approximation ratio of any non-interactive ε-LDP algorithm.

1.1 Our Contribution

Although most works on differentially private facility location algorithms assume the super-set assumption, this compromises user privacy. Revealing only facilities that connect to at least one user discloses information about users. This concern motivates us to explore a practical setting for the facility location problem, where we can design an LDP algorithm with a constant approximation ratio and a relatively small additive factor. We show experimentally that the proposed algorithm outperforms the straightforward solution on synthetically generated data and a dataset based on real world data from the city Chiang Mai, Thailand.

We introduce the Facility Location Problem with Linear Facility Costs. In this setting, the objective is to assign a capacity to each opened facility, enabling it to serve up to its designated limit of clients. Additionally, facility costs scale linearly with capacity, meaning that the higher a facility's capacity, the greater the cost to establish it. We demonstrate that this problem is no longer NP-hard and can be optimally solved in polynomial time. Also, the negative result by Gupta et al. no longer applies in our setting, allowing us to design efficient ε-LDP algorithms without relying on the super-set output setting.

To obtain an ε-LDP algorithm for this setting, one can deploy the Laplace mechanism locally and then compute the capacities based on the noisy input. When the algorithm operates with a failure probability α, we show that this simple approach achieves an expected upper bound on the cost of $\left(1 + \frac{2}{\varepsilon} \ln \frac{2n}{\alpha}\right) OPT$. The resulting approximation ratio is $O(\ln n)$.

We propose an algorithm to further improve that trivial algorithm. For this algorithm, we assume that, for an input where every location $v \in V$ has at least $\gamma^2 \ln^2 n$ locations with a distance of at most δ away, we propose an ε-LDP algorithm that bounds the total costs by $(1 + \frac{2}{\varepsilon} \ln \frac{2n}{\alpha} \frac{1}{\gamma \ln n}) OPT + 4\delta n b_{avg}$, when b_{avg} is the average number of client per location. We observe that the approximation ratio $\left(1 + \frac{2}{\varepsilon} \ln \frac{2n}{\alpha} \frac{1}{\gamma \ln n}\right) = O(1)$, and the additive term $4\delta n b_{avg}$ remains small compared to overall cost when δ is sufficiently small.

Finally, we demonstrate that our ε-LDP algorithm outperforms the straightforward approach on both synthetically generated datasets and a real-world instance based on data from Chiang Mai, Thailand. We use the Matérn cluster point process to generate clustered instances that simulate cities with densely populated neighborhoods. Furthermore, we use the Poisson point process to generate instances with uniformly at random distributed locations. We show that, for both generations processes with varying generation parameters and for the real-world instance, our theorems provide input parameters for our ε-LDP algorithm resulting in lower cost solutions compared to the straightforward approach.

2   Local Differential Privacy

The following definition formally introduces L_1 local differential privacy (LDP).

Definition 2 (L_1-LDP [8]). *Let $\varepsilon > 0$. A randomized query $\mathcal{R}$ satisfies L_1 ε-local differential privacy (ε-LDP) if, for any possible local inputs $b, b' \in \mathbb{Z}$ such that $|b - b'| = 1$, and any possible outcome set S,*

$$\Pr[\mathcal{R}(b) \in S] \leq e^{\varepsilon} \Pr[\mathcal{R}(b') \in S].$$

An algorithm $\mathcal{A}$ is said to be L_1 ε-LDP if, for any local node, and any sequence of queries $\mathcal{R}_1, \ldots, \mathcal{R}_\kappa$ posed the node, where each query $\mathcal{R}_j$ satisfies ε_j-local differential privacy (for $1 \leq j \leq \kappa$), the total privacy loss is bounded by $\varepsilon_1 + \cdots + \varepsilon_\kappa \leq \varepsilon$. The algorithm is referred to as non-interactive if the number of queries to each user is one, and those queries are independent to each other.

In the following section, we explain our rationale for employing the notion of L_1-LDP in this paper.

Definition 3 (L_1-Sensitivity [2]). *The L_1-sensitivity of a function $f : \mathbb{Z} \to \mathbb{R}$ is the smallest value $S(f)$ such that, for all $b, b' \in \mathbb{Z}$ such that $|b - b'| = 1$, the following holds:*

$$\|f(b) - f(b')\|_1 \leq S(f)$$

Definition 4 (L_1 Local Laplacian Query [6]). *For any function $f : \mathbb{Z} \to \mathbb{R}$ and input $b \in \mathbb{Z}$, the following mechanism, known as the Laplace mechanism, is defined as:*

$$LM_f(b) = f(b) + Y$$

where Y is drawn from $Lap(S(f)/\varepsilon)$. The L_1 local Laplace mechanism satisfies L_1 ε-LDP.

Since this paper exclusively employs the L_1 version of ε-LDP, we omit the L_1 prefix. In other words, when we mention ε-LDP, sensitivity, and the local Laplacian query, we are referring to the L_1 ε-LDP, L_1-sensitivity, and the L_1 local Laplacian query, respectively.

3 Our Setting: Facility Location with Linear Facility Costs (FL-Linear)

In this section, we formally present our adaptation of the traditional facility location problem, referred to as Facility Location with Linear Facility Costs (FL-Linear). We later demonstrate that this problem can be optimally solved in polynomial time.

3.1 Problem Statement

Definition 5 (FL-Linear). *The Facility Location with Linear Facility Costs is defined by the input tuple* $(V, d, \boldsymbol{f}, \boldsymbol{b})$ *where* V *defines the set of locations with* $|V| = n$, (V, d) *is a metric,* $\boldsymbol{f}$ *indicates the facility costs for every location* $v \in V$, *and* $\boldsymbol{b} = [b_v]_{v \in V} \in \mathbb{N}_{>0}^n$ *indicates the amount of clients present at location* $v \in V$. *The goal is to find a set of locations* $S \subseteq V$ *with capacities* $(k_s)_{s \in S}$ *and a connection function* $h : V \to S$ *that minimize the costs*

$$cost_d(S, h, d) = \sum_{s \in S} k_s f_s + \sum_{v \in V} b_v d(v, h(v)) \tag{3}$$

Furthermore, every facility must be able to serve all of its connected clients. Let $L_v = \{u \in V : h(u) = v\}$ *denote the set of connected locations to a facility* $v \in S$. *Then the following equation must hold for all* $v \in S$:

$$\sum_{u \in L_v} b_u \le k_v \tag{4}$$

In contrast to the original problem, every facility $v \in S$ now has a capacity k_v assigned to it. Furthermore, the facility to which a location is connected to is now given as an output by the connection function h. Previous research on the original problem defined a connection rule (e.g. connect location to closest open facility) and only outputted a super-set of opened facilities.

Since a location appears in the dataset only if at least one person resides there, we assume that every location has at least one client present, i.e., $b_v > 0$. In Sect. A, we relax this assumption and derive a bound based on the ratio between clients and locations.

The FL-Linear problem finds application in real-world scenarios such as in the setting of placing evacuation shelters. The costs for providing space, food, water and, equipment like first aid kits depends on the amount of people it is designed to shelter. Therefore, it is reasonable to determine the facility cost based on the number of individuals relocating to the facility.

Privacy Assumption. We adopt the assumption from previous works that the set of locations, the distances between them, and the facility costs at each location are publicly available information. The only data kept private is the number of individuals at each location, denoted as **b**. This assumption is motivated by the problem of placing facilities for evacuation [14]. In such scenarios, the distances between buildings and the costs of constructing evacuation facilities at each site are known. However, the presence of an individual at a specific location is sensitive information. Revealing the number of individuals at each location could risk disclosing this sensitive data.

We consider the value $b_u \in \mathbb{Z}$ as local data. To safeguard an individual's location, we seek a mechanism that ensures others cannot distinguish between b_u and b'_u when $|b_u - b'_u| = 1$, which corresponds to the presence or absence of the person at node u. For this reason, we adopt the privacy notion of L_1 ε-LDP in this work.

3.2   Non-private Optimal Algorithm

By introducing linear facility costs based on the capacity, the problem becomes easier and we can find a polynomial time algorithm to solve it. For a fixed location v the costs it induces is independent on the connection of other locations. We say that $v \in V$ is connected to $u \in V$ if $h(v) = u$. Finding the optimal facility u, a location v should be connected to, is now a local decision:

$$h(v) = \arg\min_{u \in V}(f_u + d(u, v)) \tag{5}$$

For each location, we determine the optimal location to which it is connected. We define the set of locations that have at least one connection as

$$M = \{v \in V : \exists u \in V \text{ such that } h(u) = v\} = \{v \in V : h(v) = v\}.$$

For any marked location $v \in M$, let $L_v = \{u \in V : h(u) = v\}$ denote the set of locations assigned to v. The facility at v is then opened with a capacity corresponding to the total demand of the clients connected to it:

$$k_v = \sum_{u \in L_v} b_u.$$

In the base algorithm, no privacy mechanism is applied. Consequently, the algorithm has full knowledge of the exact client demands b_u and can set facility capacities accordingly. As a result, every location is optimally connected, leading to a globally optimal solution. The computation can be performed in polynomial time.

4   Straightforward Algorithm: Laplace Mechanism with Margin

To keep the amount of clients b_v of a location v private, we introduce a local differential private algorithm that uses the Laplace mechanism to ensure privacy and opens facilities based on a noisy number of clients. Every location $v \in V$ adds a Laplacian noise parameterized by the privacy budget ε to their private number of clients b_v to generate a noisy variant b'_v. Afterwards, it sends b'_v to the aggregation server. On the server side the optimal assignments and capacities are computed based on $\mathbf{b'} = [b'_v]_{v \in V}$.

Algorithm 1: ε-LDP algorithm with laplacian mechanism and margin

---

Data: V, $\boldsymbol{f}$, $\boldsymbol{b}$, privacy budget ε, failure probability α
Result: connection function h', capacities k'
begin

    Location Side:
    for $v \in V$ **do**
        $b'_v \longleftarrow b_v + Lap(1/\varepsilon)$
        Send b'_v to server

    Server Side:
    for $v \in V$ **do**
        $h'(v) \longleftarrow \arg\min_{u \in V} f_u + d(u, v)$
    $M' \longleftarrow \{v \in V : h'(v) = v\}$
    for $v \in M'$ **do**
        $L'_v \longleftarrow \{u \in V : h'(u) = v\}$
        $N'_v \longleftarrow \sum_{u \in L'_v} b'_u$
        $k'_v \longleftarrow N'_v + \frac{2}{\varepsilon}\sqrt{|L'_v|} \ln \frac{2n}{\alpha}$
    return h', k'

On the server side, Algorithm 1 mirrors the steps of the non-private algorithm by first computing the optimal connections between locations. We leverage the key observation that for any location v,

$$h(v) = \arg\min_{u \in V} \left(b_v f_u + b_v d(u, v)\right) = \arg\min_{u \in V} \left(f_u + d(u, v)\right) = h'(v),$$

which means we do not need direct access to the private value b_v to calculate $h'(v)$. The main distinction between the two approaches arises during the capacity computation. In the optimal assignment, the capacity can be set exactly to the number of clients. However, in the private setting, the noisy estimate b'_v may underestimate the true client count b_v. Without an additional margin, this underestimation would lead to an immediate failure at location v. Consequently, we add a margin of $\frac{2}{\varepsilon}\sqrt{|L'_v|} \ln \frac{2n}{\alpha}$ to the noisy count of connected clients N'_v to ensure that the total failure probability does not exceed α.

4.1   Analysis

We first show that Algorithm 1 ensures privacy for the presence of individuals.

Theorem 1. *Algorithm 1 satisfies ε-LDP.*

Proof. The presence or abscence of an individual at location v changes b_v by at most 1. Hence, the L_1-sensitivity is 1. Algorithm 1 locally adds Laplacian noise drawn from $Lap(1/\varepsilon)$ to b_v and therefore satisfies ε-LDP.   □

In the following we show that the output by Algorithm 1 satisfies the capacity constraint with a probability of $1 - \alpha$ and if they are satisfied the expected costs are bounded by $(1 + \frac{2}{\varepsilon} \ln \frac{2n}{\alpha})OPT$. Let E_v denote the event that a failure occurs at location $v \in M'$. This means more clients are connected to v than it has capacity: $\sum_{u \in L'_v} b_u > k'_v$. For a failure to occur, the Laplacian noise added to the clients in L'_v must be larger than the margin added to v, i.e.

$$\left| \sum_{u \in L'_v} Lap(1/\varepsilon) \right| > \frac{2}{\varepsilon} \sqrt{|L'_v|} \ln \frac{2n}{\alpha} \tag{6}$$

We first bound $\Pr[E_v]$, and then apply union bound to derive a bound for the total failure probability. For the first part, we use the following results.

Theorem 2 (Xian et al. [15]). *Let $X_1, ..., X_k \sim Lap(b)$ be independent, then for $t \geq 2b\sqrt{k} \ln \frac{2k}{\beta}$,*

$$\Pr\left[\left| \sum_{i=1}^{k} X_i \right| \leq t \right] \geq 1 - \beta \tag{7}$$

From Theorem 2, a bound on $\Pr[E_v]$ follows by setting t according to the margin.

Theorem 3. *The total failure probability of Algorithm 1 is bounded by α.*

Proof. Let $v \in M$, then it will be opened with a capacity of

$$k'_v = N'_v + \frac{2}{\varepsilon} \sqrt{|L'_v|} \ln \frac{2n}{\alpha} \tag{8}$$

A failure occurs if the capacity is smaller than the actual number of connected clients.

$$\Pr\left[N_v > N'_v + \frac{2}{\varepsilon} \sqrt{|L'_v|} \ln \frac{2n}{\alpha} \right] \leq \Pr\left[\left| \sum_{u \in L'_v} Lap(1/\varepsilon) \right| > \frac{2}{\varepsilon} \sqrt{|L'_v|} \ln \frac{2n}{\alpha} \right] \tag{9}$$

Given the total failure probability α, by Theorem 2 with $k = |L'_v|$ and $\beta_v = \frac{|L'_v|}{n}\alpha$ it follows that for $t \geq \frac{2}{\varepsilon} \sqrt{|L'_v|} \ln \frac{2n}{\alpha}$,

$$\Pr[E_v] \leq \frac{|L'_v|}{n}\alpha. \tag{10}$$

By applying union bound we get a bound on the total failure probability,

$$\sum_{v \in M} \Pr[E_v] \leq \frac{\alpha}{n} \sum_{v \in M} |L'_v| = \alpha. \tag{11}$$

□

Theorem 4. *Assuming no failures occur, the expected cost of the solution produced by Algorithm 1 is at most*

$$\left(1 + \frac{2}{\varepsilon} \ln \frac{2n}{\alpha}\right) OPT.$$

Proof. Recall that the optimal cost OPT can be divided into the connection cost, denoted by OPT_{conn} and the facility cost OPT_{fac}, i.e. $OPT = OPT_{conn} + OPT_{fac}$. Computing the connection function $h' : V \to V$ does not involve private information. Since no failure occurs, h' is a valid solution and will be the same as the connection function h from the optimal non-private algorithm. Therefore, the connection costs are the same as in the optimal solution:

$$\sum_{v \in V} b_v d(v, h'(v)) = OPT_{conn} \tag{12}$$

Since, the connection function is the same, also the set of marked locations M' is the same as M. Algorithm 1 opens $v \in M'$ with a capacity of $k'_v = N'_v + \frac{2}{\varepsilon}\sqrt{|L'_v|}\ln\frac{2n}{\alpha}$. This gives expected facility costs of

$$E\left[\sum_{v \in M'}\left(N'_v + \frac{2}{\varepsilon}\sqrt{|L'_v|}\ln\frac{2n}{\alpha}\right)f_v\right] = OPT_{fac} + \frac{2}{\varepsilon}\ln\frac{2n}{\alpha}\sum_{v \in M'}\sqrt{|L'_v|}f_v \tag{13}$$

Finally, we obtain that our cost is

$$OPT_{conn} + OPT_{fac} + \frac{2}{\varepsilon}\ln\frac{2n}{\alpha}\sum_{v \in M'}\sqrt{|L'_v|}f_v \leq \left(1 + \frac{2}{\varepsilon}\ln\frac{2n}{\alpha}\right)OPT. \tag{14}$$

$\sum_{v \in M'}\sqrt{|L'_v|}f_v$ can be bounded with OPT since every location has at least one client and therefore a facility is opened with a capacity of at least $|L'_v|$ in the optimal case. □

In this paper, we do not incorporate penalty costs for facility failures. Our analysis can be extended to account for such failures by introducing an appropriate penalty function and using Theorem 3 to bound the expected total costs.

5   Our Algorithm: ε-LDP Algorithm with Reconnection

The margin added to every marked node $v \in M'$ in Algorithm 1 depends on the number of connected locations $|L'_v|$. This leaves the question whether the total margin added can be decreased while keeping the upper bound on the failure probability. In the last step of the analysis of Algorithm 1, we bounded $\sum_{v \in M'}\sqrt{|L'_v|}f_v$ with OPT. In this section, we describe how by merging close facilities, we can create less facilities with higher capacities and therefore find a better bound for $\sum_{v \in M'}\sqrt{|L'_v|}f_v$. This decreases the multiplicative error from $\mathcal{O}(\log n)$ to constant under an additional assumption about the distribution of the locations while introducing an additive error.

Additional Assumption. In the following we assume that no location is isolated from all other locations. Formally, for a given $\delta > 0$, let $B(v, \delta)$ denote the ball of radius δ centered on the location $v \in V$. A location $u \in V$ is contained in the ball $B(v, \delta)$ if $d(u, v) \leq \delta$. We assume that for $\delta > 0, \gamma \geq 1$ and every location $v \in V$:

$$|B(v, \delta)| \geq \gamma^2 \ln^2 n \tag{15}$$

With $\gamma = 1$, $n = 10,000,000$, and $\delta = 1$ km, our assumption implies that each household has at least 259.79 other households within a 1 km radius. Given that the average Japanese household size in 2022 was 2.25, this corresponds to approximately 585 inhabitants within the same area, resulting in a population density of 186 inhabitants per square kilometer. This confirms that our assumption remains valid even in small village settings. For cases focusing on densely populated areas, such as Tokyo, which has a population density of 6,300 people per square kilometer [12], our assumption is even more strongly supported.

5.1 Description of ε-LDP Algorithm with Reconnection

The ε-LDP algorithm with reconnection follows the same steps as Algorithm 1. On the location side the Laplace mechanism is used to ensure ε-LDP. Then it computes the optimal assignment $\hat{h}$ and the set of marked locations $\hat{M}$ without using private data.

Instead of immediately opening every marked location with a margin as done in Algorithm 1, we select a maximal set of marked locations that are pairwise at least a distance of 2δ apart. This ensures that no two facilities opened are within 2δ of each other. To compute this set, we first construct the graph $G = \left(\hat{M}, \ \left\{\{u, v\} : u, v \in \hat{M}, \ d(u, v) \leq 2\delta\right\}\right)$. Then, we run a greedy algorithm to determine a maximal independent set I in G. In this process, the algorithm repeatedly selects the node with the lowest facility value for which none of its neighbors has already been chosen, ensuring that every pair of nodes in I is separated by at least 2δ.

Before computing the capacities for the facilities in I, we update the connection function $\hat{h}$. For every $v \in I$, we connect all nodes in $B(v, \delta)$ to v. Moreover, all locations not covered by any ball are connected to the optimal location restricted to the set I. Finally, similar to Algorithm 1, we add a margin of $\frac{2}{\varepsilon} \sqrt{|\hat{L}_v|} \ln \frac{2n}{\alpha}$ to the capacity, on top of the number of connected clients $\hat{N}_v$.

5.2 Analysis

The reconnection algorithm uses the same Laplace privacy mechanism as Algorithm 1. Therefore, the proof of ε-LDP is straightforward.

Theorem 5. *Algorithm 2 satisfies ε-LDP.*

Proof. Similar to Theorem 1, the absence or presence can change b_v by at most 1, resulting in a sensitivity of 1. Algorithm 2 applies the local Laplace mechanism by adding Laplacian noise with parameter $1/\varepsilon$. □

Algorithm 2: ε-LDP algorithm with reconnection

Data: V, $\boldsymbol{f}$, $\boldsymbol{b}$, privacy budget ε, failure probability α, δ
Result: connection function $\hat{h}$, capacities $\hat{k}$
begin

> **Location Side:**
> **for** $v \in V$ **do**
>> $b'_v \longleftarrow b_v + Lap(1/\varepsilon)$
>> Send b'_v to server
>
> **Server Side:**
> **for** $v \in V$ **do**
>> $\hat{h}(v) \longleftarrow \arg\min_{u \in V} f_u + d(u, v)$
>
> $\hat{M} \longleftarrow \{v \in V : \hat{h}(v) = v\}$
> $G \longleftarrow (\hat{M}, \{\{u, v\} : u, v \in \hat{M}, d(u, v) \le 2\delta\})$
> $I \longleftarrow$ maximal independent set of G
> **for** $v \in I$ **do**
>> $\hat{h}(u) \longleftarrow v$ for all $u \in B(v, \delta)$
>
> **for** $u \in V$ s.t. $\nexists v \in I$ with $u \in B(v, \delta)$ **do**
>> $\hat{h}(u) \longleftarrow \arg\min_{v \in I} f_v + d(u, v)$
>
> **for** $v \in I$ **do**
>> $\hat{L}_v \longleftarrow \{u \in V : \hat{h}(u) = v\}$
>> $\hat{N}_v \longleftarrow \sum_{u \in \hat{L}_v} b'_u$
>> $\hat{k}_v \longleftarrow \hat{N}_v + \frac{2}{\varepsilon}\sqrt{|\hat{L}_v| \ln \frac{2n}{\alpha}}$
>
> **return** $\hat{h}, \hat{k}$

In the following, we analyze the costs of the output of ε-LDP algorithm with reconnection (Algorithm 2).

Lemma 1. $|\hat{L}_v| \ge \gamma^2 \ln^2 n$ for every $v \in I$.

Proof. Because the set I has the property that the balls $B(u, \delta)$ for all $u \in I$ do not overlap, reconnecting all nodes in $B(v, \delta)$ to v together with the assumption that $|B(v, \delta)| \ge \gamma^2 \ln^2 n$ establishes the lemma. □

We bound the additional costs that occur due to the reconnection and then bound the costs of the additional capacity used to open facilities compared to the optimal assignment.

Lemma 2. *The extra reconnection cost, given by*

$$\sum_{u \in V} b_u(f_{\hat{h}(u)} + d(u, \hat{h}(u))) - OPT,$$

is bounded above by $4\delta n b_{avg}$ *when* $b_{avg} = \frac{1}{n} \sum_{v \in V} b_v$.

Proof. Consider a location $v \in I$ from the maximal independent set. Since v is in I, it is opened as a facility in both the optimal solution and in the solution produced by Algorithm 2. We begin by bounding the cost of reconnecting every node in $B(v, \delta)$ to v.

Take any $u \in B(v, \delta)$ so that $d(u, v) \leq \delta$. Let $w \in M$ be such that $h(u) = w$; that is, in the optimal solution u is connected to w, but in the modified solution $\hat{h}(u) = v$ (i.e. u is reconnected to v).

In the optimal solution, the cost associated with u is $b_u(f_w + d(u, w))$, while in the reconnected solution the cost is $b_u(f_v + d(u, v))$. Because both v and w are marked in the optimal assignment, each prefer being connected to itself rather than to the other, which gives us:

$$f_v < f_w + d(v, w) \quad \text{and} \quad f_w < f_v + d(v, w).$$

Using these inequalities along with the triangle inequality, we can bound the reconnection cost:

$$b_u(f_v + d(u, v)) < b_u(f_w + d(v, w) + d(u, v)) \leq OPT_u + 2b_u\delta,$$

when OPT_u is the cost for u in the optimal solution, i.e. $OPT_u = b_u(f_{h(u)} + d(u, h(u)))$. This shows that reconnecting the node u from w to v increases the costs by at most $2b_u\delta$.

We now bound the cost of reconnecting nodes that are not within a δ-distance of any location in I. In Algorithm 2, the optimal assignment for such nodes is made to a node in I. Let $u \in V$, $v \in I$, and $w \in M$ be such that $h(u) = w$ and $\hat{h}(u) = v$. Moreover, assume that there is no $x \in I$ satisfying $d(x, u) \leq \delta$; otherwise, we would have applied the previous case.

As before, we want to bound the cost incurred by u under the solution $(\hat{h}, \hat{k})$, which is $b_u(f_v + d(v, u))$. Because u was reconnected to v, it follows that w was not selected in the maximal independent set. By the properties of such a set, there must exist a neighbor of w in G that belongs to I; denote this neighbor by v. Hence, we have $d(v, w) \leq 2\delta$.

Using this, we obtain

$$b_u(f_v + d(v, u)) \leq b_u(f_w + d(w, u) + 2d(v, w)) \leq OPT_u + 4b_u\delta.$$

This shows that the extra cost for reconnecting node u is at most $4\delta b_u$. Summing over all nodes in V gives an overall additional reconnection cost bounded by $\sum_{u \in V} 4\delta b_u \leq 4\delta\, n\, b_{avg}$. □

We are now ready to demonstrate the main statement of this paper.

Theorem 6. *Algorithm 2 has a failure probability of at most α. Moreover, when it succeeds, its expected cost is bounded by*

$$\left(1 + \frac{2}{\varepsilon}\ln\frac{2n}{\alpha}\frac{1}{\gamma\ln n}\right)OPT + 4\delta nb_{avg}.$$

Proof. The failure probability is established using an argument analogous to that in Theorem 3. Moreover, by Lemma 1 we have

$$\sum_{v \in I} \sqrt{|\hat{L}_v|} f_v \leq \frac{1}{\gamma \ln n} \sum_{v \in I} |\hat{L}_v| f_v \leq \frac{1}{\gamma \ln n} OPT.$$

Following a similar reasoning as in Theorem 4, the lemma statement then follows.

$\square$

When ε, α, and γ are constants, the multiplicative factor $\left(1 + \frac{2}{\varepsilon} \ln \frac{2n}{\alpha} \frac{1}{\gamma \ln n}\right)$ remains $O(1)$. Additionally, if the locations are sufficiently dense (i.e., δ is small), the additive term $4\delta n b_{avg}$ becomes negligible compared to OPT. While we assume $b_v \geq 1$ for all $v \in V$ in this section, we present an analysis for the case where $b_v \geq 0$ in Appendix A.

6   Experimental Results

In this section, we evaluate the private algorithms with various parameter settings on both synthetically generated and real-world datasets, comparing their performance against the non-private algorithm. We generate synthetic instances using two distinct methods. The first employs the Matérn cluster point process [7,10], which creates clustered instances where each cluster simulates a densely populated neighborhood. By adjusting the generation parameters, we can control both the number of neighborhoods (centers) and the number of households (locations) within each neighborhood. The second method uses a Poisson point process, where the number of locations is drawn from a Poisson distribution, and these locations are then uniformly distributed across a simulation window. Our results show that for all instances, there exists a value of δ such that the private reconnection algorithm outperforms the straightforward approach. We provide further experimental results in Appendix B.

6.1   Synthetic Instances

We generate the locations' positions using the Matérn cluster point process [7]. The process takes the tuple $(n, \gamma, \delta_{\text{gen}})$ as input, where n is the expected total number of locations, γ is a scaling parameter, and δ_{gen} defines the clustering radius. Let n_{centers} be the number of centers generated and n^i_{daughter} the number of locations around center i. We require two conditions:

1. Each center should have at least $\gamma^2 \ln^2 n$ locations within δ_{gen} in expectation, i.e. $\mathbb{E}[n^i_{\text{daughter}}] \geq \gamma^2 \ln^2 n$.
2. The total expected number of locations should be n, i.e. $\mathbb{E}\left[\sum_{i=1}^{n_{\text{centers}}} n^i_{\text{daughter}}\right] = n$.

We model n^i_{daughter} as a Poisson random variable with parameter $\lambda_{\text{daughter}}$ and n_{centers} as a Poisson random variable with parameter λ_{centers}. Since the expected value of a Poisson distribution equals its λ-parameter, we set $\lambda_{\text{daughter}} = \gamma^2 \ln^2 n$, so that $\mathbb{E}[n^i_{\text{daughter}}] = \gamma^2 \ln^2 n$. To ensure that the total expected number of locations is n, we choose $\lambda_{\text{centers}} = \frac{n}{\lambda_{\text{daughter}}}$, since then $\mathbb{E}[n_{\text{centers}}] \cdot \mathbb{E}[n^i_{\text{daughter}}] = \lambda_{\text{centers}} \cdot \lambda_{\text{daughter}} = n$.

The process first samples $n_{\text{centers}} \sim \text{Poisson}\left(\frac{n}{\gamma^2 \ln^2 n}\right)$ and distributes these centers uniformly at random on a 1×1 simulation window. For each center, it samples $n_{\text{daughter}} \sim \text{Poisson}(\gamma^2 \ln^2 n)$. Then, for each location, a radial coordinate is drawn uniformly from $[0, \delta]$ and an angular coordinate from $[0, 2\pi]$, which are subsequently converted to Cartesian coordinates. Because each location lies at most δ away from its center, the overall simulation window expands to $(1 + 2\delta) \times (1 + 2\delta)$.

We generate the number of clients per location from a Gaussian distribution with a mean of 2.5 and a standard deviation of 1.5. The resulting b_v values are then rounded to the nearest integer and restricted to the interval $[0, 8]$. For the facility costs at each location, we draw values from a uniform distribution over a specified interval.

Our Results. Figure 1 shows the normalized costs of the private reconnection algorithm in comparison with the optimal non-private and straightforward private algorithm. In this benchmark δ is increased from 0 to 1 with a step size of 0.01 for the private reconnection algorithm. For every δ, 1000 instances are generated with $n = 1000, \gamma = 2, \delta_{gen} = 0.2$. The private algorithms are executed with $\varepsilon = 0.1$ and $\alpha = 0.1$. It can be seen that for clustered instances the reconnection algorithm outperforms the straightforward approach for any δ. Furthermore, the reconnection algorithm performs better in comparison to the straightforward approach if no locations with facility costs close to 0 exist. For locations with facility costs of almost 0 it is more likely that they connect all of the other close locations anyways. Therefore, the reconnection part reconnects fewer locations leading to more similar solutions.

Figure 2a depicts the performance of the private reconnection algorithm on instances generated by a Poisson point process [10]. The generation process first samples the number of locations $n_{locations}$ according to a Poisson distribution with parameter $\lambda = n$ and then generates $n_{locations}$ locations uniformly at random distributed on a 1×1 simulation window.

In Fig. 2b the algorithms are compared for an varying privacy budget ε from 0.01 to 1 with a step width of 0.001. For every ε, 100 instances are generated with $n = 1000, \gamma = 2, \delta_{gen} = 0.2, f_v \in [0.1, 0.3]$. The private algorithms are executed with $\alpha = 0.1$ and the reconnection algorithm uses $\delta = 0.2$. The outcome aligns with the theoretical results. A smaller ε leads to a bigger coefficient $\frac{2}{\varepsilon}$ in the multiplicative approximation ratio. The reconnection algorithm keeps the influence of this coefficient small by introducing the additional additive error which is independent of ε.

Figure 3a shows the costs depending on the size of the instances. For $n \in [100, 5000]$ with a step size of 100, 500 instances with $\delta_{gen} = 0.2, \gamma = 2$ and $f_v \in [0.1, 0.3]$ are generated. The private algorithms are executed with $\varepsilon = 0.1$

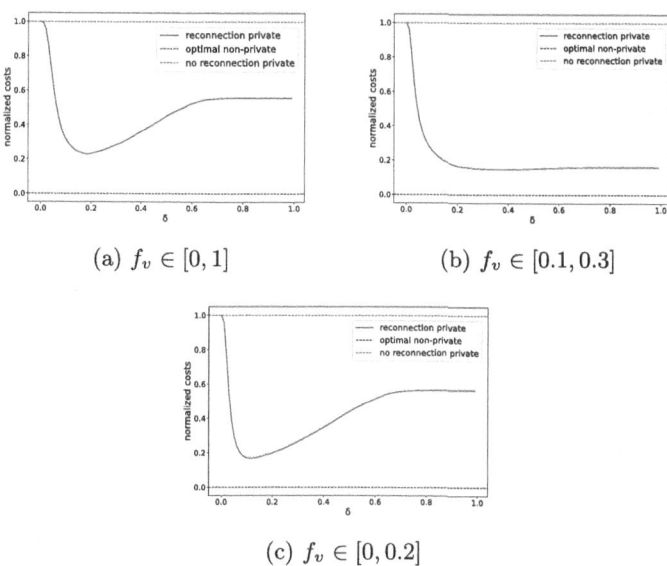

(a) $f_v \in [0,1]$ (b) $f_v \in [0.1, 0.3]$

(c) $f_v \in [0, 0.2]$

Fig. 1. Normalized costs for varying δ and facility cost ranges on clustered instances

and $\alpha = 0.1$. Furthermore, the reconnection algorithm is also executed with $\delta = 0.2$. In alignment with the previous results, the reconnection algorithm outperforms the straightforward algorithm.

6.2   Real-World Instances

For an application of the algorithm to the real world we generate a set of data according to the technique described in "Submodularity Property for Facility Locations of Dynamic Flow Networks" [14]. It uses data from the project "Urban Observatory and Citizen Engagement by Data-driven and Deliberative Design: A Case Study of Chiang Mai City" to generate a set of locations with clients. We expand this data by first normalizing the position of the locations to a 1×1 window and then uniformly at random assign facility costs from the interval $[0.1, 0.3]$. The dataset consists of 431 different locations. Over 100 instances, the private algorithms were executed with $\varepsilon = 0.1$ and $\alpha = 0.1$.

Our Results. Figure 3b shows that for $\delta = 0.1$ the reconnection algorithm outperforms the straightforward approach. With this we can conclude that by executing the reconnection algorithm with a correctly chosen δ our private reconnection algorithm outperforms the straightforward approach.

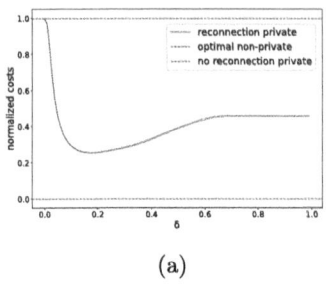
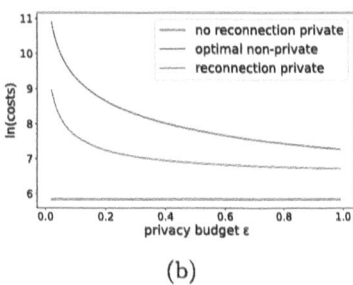

|(a)|(b)|

Fig. 2. (a) Normalized costs against varying δ for Poisson point process instances (b) Impact of different privacy budgets ε on clustered instances

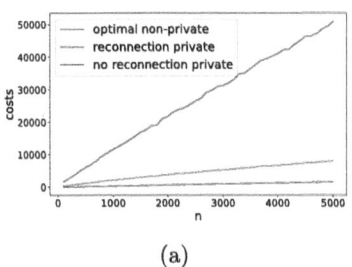
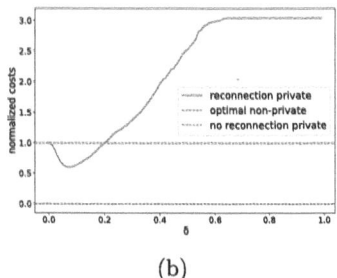

|(a)|(b)|

Fig. 3. (a) Costs for varying n on clustered instances (b) Normalized costs for varying δ on real-world instances

7   Conclusion and Future Works

Without the super-set assumption, releasing results for the facility location problem under LDP leads to large errors because the noise added to each location is significant relative to its original value. In this work, we introduce an algorithm called "re-connection" that aggregates several values. This approach ensures that the aggregated original value is sufficiently large, so that the relative impact of the noise is reduced. As a result, our algorithm achieves a constant approximation ratio with only a small additive error. In the next version we plan to include further experiments on real-world datasets. We believe that this technique can be extended to other algorithms operating under LDP, and we are currently exploring its application to additional combinatorial optimization problems.

Acknowledgments. Quentin Hillebrand is partially supported by KAKENHI Grant 20H05965, and by JST SPRING Grant Number JPMJSP2108. Vorapong Suppakitpaisarn is partially supported by KAKENHI Grant 21H05845 and 23H04377. The authors express their gratitude to Phapaengmuang Sukkasem and Suphanat Chaidee for providing the real-world dataset used in this study. This research was conducted while Kevin Pfisterer was at The University of Tokyo, and the authors also thank Hiroshi Imai and Kunihiko Sadakane for hosting him.

A Additional Theoretical Results When $b_v \geq 0$

In this section we provide an analysis of our ε-LDP Algorithm 2 that does not require the presence of at least one client at every location. Thus far, we assumed that every location hosts at least one client ($b_v \geq 1$ for all $v \in V$). This assumption was essential for establishing $\sum_{v \in M'} \sqrt{|L_v'|} f_v \leq OPT$ in Sect. 4 and $\sum_{v \in I} \sqrt{|\hat{L}_v|} f_v \leq OPT/(\gamma \ln n)$ in Sect. 5. Without this assumption, scenarios with many facilities but only one client per location would lead to a poor approximation—since the optimum (OPT) depends on the number of clients, while the private algorithm's costs depend on the number of locations.

In this section, we relax the assumption that every location has at least one client and instead require conditions on the facility costs and the overall client-to-location ratio. In particular, we now allow $b_v \in \mathbb{N}_{\geq 0}$. Moreover, we assume that the ratio $\eta = \frac{f_{max}}{f_{min}}$ is constant and define $\nu = \frac{N}{n}$ as the ratio between the total number of clients and the number of locations.

As previously discussed, we need a revised bound on $\sum_{v \in I} \sqrt{|\hat{L}_v|} f_v$. We observe that

$$\sum_{v \in I} \sqrt{|\hat{L}_v|} f_v \leq \frac{f_{max}}{\gamma \ln n} \sum_{v \in I} |\hat{L}_v| = \frac{f_{max}}{\gamma \ln n} \frac{N}{\nu} \leq \frac{1}{\gamma \ln n} \frac{\eta}{\nu} OPT.$$

Using this inequality, we follow the arguments in the proof of Theorem 4 to derive an upper bound on the total expected cost: $\left(1 + \frac{2}{\varepsilon} \ln \frac{2n}{\alpha} \frac{1}{\gamma \ln n} \frac{\eta}{\nu}\right) OPT + 4\delta n b_{avg}$. When ε, α, γ, η, and ν are constants, we obtain that the multiplicative factor $\left(1 + \frac{2}{\varepsilon} \ln \frac{2n}{\alpha} \frac{1}{\gamma \ln n} \frac{\eta}{\nu}\right)$ remains $O(1)$.

B Additional Experimental Results

In this section we provide further experimental results on synthetically generated instances that illustrate the performance of our ε-LDP reconnection Algorithm 2 compared with the private straightforward and optimal solution.

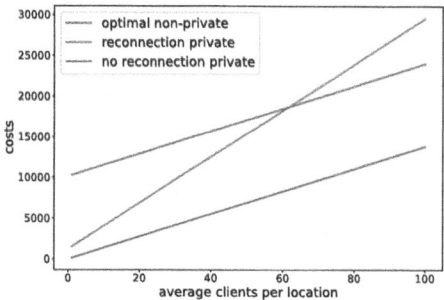

Fig. 4. Costs for varying b_{avg} on clustered instances

Our Results. Figure 4 presents the algorithm costs as the average number of clients per location, b_{avg}, increases. For this analysis, 100 instances are generated with parameters $n = 1000$, $\delta_{gen} = 0.2$, and $\gamma = 2$. In each instance, every location is assigned the same number of clients, b_{avg}. The algorithms are executed for values of b_{avg} ranging from 1 to 100, and the costs are averaged across all instances. The private algorithms are run with parameters $\alpha = 0.1$, $\varepsilon = 0.1$, and $\delta = 0.2$.

The results illustrate the impact of b_{avg} on the additive costs of the private reconnection Algorithm 2. Additionally, they indicate that for scenarios where the average number of clients is below 75 (e.g., individuals within a household), our algorithm outperforms the straightforward approach.

References

1. Cohen-Addad, V., Esencayi, Y., Fan, C., Gaboradi, M., Li, S., Wang, D.: On facility location problem in the local differential privacy model. In: AISTATS 2022, pp. 3914–3929 (2022)
2. Dwork, C., McSherry, F., Nissim, K., Smith, A.: Calibrating noise to sensitivity in private data analysis. In: Halevi, S., Rabin, T. (eds.) TCC 2006. LNCS, vol. 3876, pp. 265–284. Springer, Heidelberg (2006). https://doi.org/10.1007/11681878_14
3. Esencayi, Y., Gaboardi, M., Li, S., Wang, D.: Facility location problem in differential privacy model revisited. Adv. Neural Inf. Process. Syst. 32 (2019)
4. Fakcharoenphol, J., Rao, S., Talwar, K.: A tight bound on approximating arbitrary metrics by tree metrics. In: Proceedings of the Thirty-Fifth Annual ACM Symposium on Theory of Computing, pp. 448–455 (2003)
5. Gupta, A., Ligett, K., McSherry, F., Roth, A., Talwar, K.: Differentially private combinatorial optimization. In: SODA 2010, pp. 1106–1125 (2010)
6. Hillebrand, Q., Suppakitpaisarn, V., Shibuya, T.: Unbiased locally private estimator for polynomials of Laplacian variables. In: KDD 2023, pp. 741–751 (2023)
7. Illian, J., Penttinen, A., Stoyan, H., Stoyan, D.: Statistical Analysis and Modelling of Spatial Point Patterns. John Wiley & Sons, Hoboken (2008)
8. Kasiviswanathan, S.P., Lee, H.K., Nissim, K., Raskhodnikova, S., Smith, A.: What can we learn privately? SIAM J. Comput. 40(3), 793–826 (2011)
9. Kuehn, A.A., Hamburger, M.J.: A heuristic program for locating warehouses. Manag. Sci. 9(4), 643–666 (1963)
10. Last, G., Penrose, M.: Lectures on the Poisson Process, vol. 7. Cambridge University Press, Cambridge (2017)
11. McSherry, F., Talwar, K.: Mechanism design via differential privacy. In: FOCS 2007, pp. 94–103 (2007)
12. Ministry of Health, Labour and Welfare, Japan: Summary report of comprehensive survey of living conditions 2022 (2023). https://www.mhlw.go.jp/english/database/db-hss/dl/report_gaikyo_2022.pdf. Accessed 26 Feb 2025
13. Stollsteimer, J.F.: A working model for plant numbers and locations. J. Farm Econ. 45(3), 631–645 (1963)
14. Suriya, P., Suppakitpaisarn, V., Chaidee, S., Sukkasem, P.: Submodularity property for facility locations of dynamic flow networks. In: ATMOS 2023, pp. 10:1–10:13 (2023)
15. Xian, R., Li, Q., Kamath, G., Zhao, H.: Differentially private post-processing for fair regression. In: ICML 2024 (2024)

Can Differentially Private Fine-Tuning LLMs Protect Against Privacy Attacks?

Hao Du[1]([✉]), Shang Liu[2]([✉]), and Yang Cao[3]([✉])

[1] Hokkaido University, Sapporo, Japan
`hao.du.y4@elms.hokudai.ac.jp`
[2] China University of Mining and Technology, Xuzhou, China
`shang@cumt.edu.cn`
[3] Institute of Science Tokyo, Tokyo, Japan
`cao@c.titech.ac.jp`

Abstract. Fine-tuning large language models (LLMs) has become an essential strategy for adapting them to specialized tasks; however, this process introduces significant privacy challenges, as sensitive training data may be inadvertently memorized and exposed. Although differential privacy (DP) offers strong theoretical guarantees against such leakage, its empirical privacy effectiveness on LLMs remains unclear, especially under different fine-tuning methods. In this paper, we systematically investigate the impact of DP across fine-tuning methods and privacy budgets, using both data extraction and membership inference attacks to assess empirical privacy risks. Our main findings are as follows: (1) Differential privacy reduces model utility, but its impact varies significantly across different fine-tuning methods. (2) Without DP, the privacy risks of models fine-tuned with different approaches differ considerably. (3) When DP is applied, even a relatively high privacy budget can substantially lower privacy risk. (4) The privacy-utility trade-off under DP training differs greatly among fine-tuning methods, with some methods being unsuitable for DP due to severe utility degradation. Our results provide practical guidance for privacy-conscious deployment of LLMs and pave the way for future research on optimizing the privacy-utility trade-off in fine-tuning methodologies.

Keywords: Fine-tuning LLMs · Differential Privacy · Attacks

1 Introduction

In recent years, large language models (LLMs), including GPT-4, LLaMA, and PaLM, have significantly advanced natural language processing (NLP), enabling diverse applications such as content generation, machine translation, question answering, and code completion. These models achieve remarkable proficiency in understanding and generating human-like text by training on extensive datasets, typically drawn from publicly available internet resources. However, when faced

© IFIP International Federation for Information Processing 2025
Published by Springer Nature Switzerland AG 2025
S. Katsikas and B. Shafiq (Eds.): DBSec 2025, LNCS 15722, pp. 311–329, 2025.
https://doi.org/10.1007/978-3-031-96590-6_17

with more specific downstream tasks, pre-trained LLMs need to be fine-tuned in order to achieve optimal performance and results [33].

Fine-tuning has become a crucial approach for adapting LLMs to specialized downstream tasks, enabling these models to achieve state-of-the-art performance across various fields. However, as modern LLMs continue to grow in scale, fully fine-tuning their large number of parameters can lead to excessive computational resource consumption. To address this issue, parameter-efficient fine-tuning (PEFT) methods [15, 21] have been introduced, significantly reducing the number of adjustable parameters and consequently lowering resource requirements. Nevertheless, fine-tuning often involves sensitive data, raising considerable privacy concerns, such as vulnerability to data extraction and membership inference attacks, which can compromise the confidentiality of information used during the fine-tuning process.

In this context, differentially private optimization algorithms have emerged as a widely adopted approach to mitigate privacy risks during the fine-tuning of LLMs. These algorithms integrate differential privacy (DP) principles by introducing carefully calibrated noise into gradient updates during training, effectively restricting the influence of individual data points on the resulting model parameters. A prominent example is differentially private stochastic gradient descent (DP-SGD) [1], which modifies traditional stochastic optimization by clipping per-sample gradients and adding calibrated noise. Consequently, this method ensures that the contribution of any individual data point remains indistinguishable within the overall model behavior. DP-SGD thus offers strong privacy guarantees, enabling models to leverage sensitive datasets without compromising individual data privacy.

Although DP offers strong theoretical privacy guarantees, its empirical privacy effectiveness on LLMs remains unclear, especially under different fine-tuning methods. Existing studies [13, 23, 25, 27, 29] have not thoroughly examined how DP influences empirical privacy risks or its effectiveness in mitigating a range of privacy attacks. Lukas et al. [23] investigated the leakage of personally identifiable information (PII) in LLMs and assessed DP's impact on privacy risks. However, their study focused solely on full fine-tuning and considered only a single privacy budget scenario, without exploring PEFT approaches. Similarly, Fu et al. [13] evaluated the defense provided by DP training against membership inference attacks but limited their experiments exclusively to the LoRA method. Panda et al. [29] examined privacy auditing methods in LLMs; however, their evaluation was constrained to a single privacy budget and lacked diversity in fine-tuning methods. Although some analyses have addressed model privacy risks across different fine-tuning strategies, these studies exhibit various shortcomings. Mireshghallah et al. [27] conducted a comprehensive analysis of memorization in autoregressive models; however, the membership inference attack techniques and fine-tuning methods they employed are now outdated. Additionally, one paper [25] focused specifically on the privacy risks of different PEFT methods. However, their experiments primarily relied on the exposure metric from data extraction attacks to evaluate model memorization, which does not provide a complete picture. Furthermore, the experimental results for LoRA and prefix-tuning reported in their paper differ from our findings, as detailed in *Remark 2*.

To address the gap between theoretical guarantees and real-world privacy attacks, this paper systematically investigates the impact of DP on fine-tuning LLMs, with considering on both full and parameter-efficient fine-tuning (PEFT) methods. We evaluate how different privacy budgets affect model utility and empirical privacy risk using two representative attack techniques: data extraction and membership inference. Our study spans multiple fine-tuning strategies and model sizes to ensure broad applicability. Key contributions of this work include:

(1) A comprehensive comparison of the privacy-utility trade-off across fine-tuning methods under DP constraints.
(2) Empirical evidence showing that full fine-tuning and LoRA offer favorable trade-offs, while prefix-tuning suffers from severe utility degradation.
(3) Practical insights for selecting fine-tuning strategies in privacy-sensitive applications. These findings serve as a foundation for optimizing private fine-tuning in future LLM deployments.

2   Related Work

2.1   Parameter-Efficient Fine-Tuning (PEFT)

Fine-tuning is a fundamental process for adapting pre-trained models to downstream tasks, enabling them to leverage the vast knowledge captured during pretraining. While traditional full fine-tuning updates all parameters of a model, achieving high task-specific performance, it is computationally expensive and prone to overfitting, especially with limited data. To overcome these challenges, many Parameter-Efficient Fine-Tuning (PEFT) methods [3,16,18,19,22,35] have been proposed, offering more efficient alternatives. These methods vary in their approach, striking different balances between parameter efficiency, adaptability, performance, expanding the range of available fine-tuning methods.

Full Fine-tuning [10] (FFT) updates all parameters of a model, providing maximum flexibility and allows the model to fully adapt to the task. However, it is computationally intensive and requires substantial data to avoid overfitting [15], making it less practical for resource-constrained scenarios. Prefix-tuning [19] adds trainable prefix vectors at every Transformer layer, interacting with input through attention mechanisms. Compared to Prompt-tuning, it allows dynamic adjustment of intermediate representations, improving adaptability for complex tasks, but slightly increases computational cost due to its per-layer modifications. LoRA [16] uses low-rank decomposition of weight matrices and fine-tunes only the low-rank components. It maintains a effective balance between parameter efficiency and task performance, making it highly applicable in large-scale models and complex tasks. P-tuning [22] addresses the limitation of traditional prompt-based learning which is unstable by introducing continuous prompt embeddings that are learned during training. These embeddings are concatenated with discrete prompts and input tokens, allowing the model to adapt more effectively to specific tasks.

2.2 Differential Privacy (DP)

Differential privacy (DP) [11] was originally developed to provide strong privacy guarantees in statistical databases by ensuring that query results do not reveal sensitive information about any individual record. DP-SGD (Differentially Private Stochastic Gradient Descent) [1] incorporates this concept into training by clipping gradients and injecting noise, limiting the influence of any single data point. After DP-SGD, many DP training methods aim to reduce the computational and memory overhead of per-example gradient clipping, enhance efficiency, and improve the trade-off between privacy and utility. Ghost Clipping [12] approximates the per-sample clipping without explicitly calculating each gradient, thereby reducing the computational and memory overhead.

Book Keeping [6] works by recording and reusing the output gradients computed during the initial backward pass. This avoids the need for a second back-propagation (required by earlier methods like GhostClip) to compute per-sample gradient norms. By "book-keeping" the output gradients, the method significantly reduces both time and memory overhead, bringing the efficiency of differentially private training closer to that of standard (non-DP) training. In our work, we employed the Book Keeping approach for DP training to ensure differential privacy. Specifically, we utilized the open-source fastDP [2] library to implement this method.

2.3 Membership Inference Attack

Membership inference attacks (MIAs) are designed to determine whether specific data points were included in a model's training set, thereby posing considerable risks to sensitive information such as clinical records and user preference datasets. Recent research has investigated the underlying mechanisms, vulnerabilities, and effects of MIAs on LLMs, illuminating various attack strategies and factors that affect model susceptibility. Mireshghallah et al. [28] proposed an MIA based on Likelihood Ratios, using the original model as a reference. Their work also conducted a preliminary investigation into how different fine-tuning methods affect the effectiveness of the attacks. Jagannatha et al. [17] conducted a black-box MIA on clinical language models, employing a Threshold-Based Attack to identify which samples were included in fine-tuning across models of varying sizes.

SPV-MIA [13] further increased the AUC for membership inference attacks on LLMs to over 90%. Their method eliminates the need for attackers to access an external reference dataset. Instead, the adversary prompts the target LLM to generate texts, which form a reference dataset used to fine-tune a reference model. By comparing the target model's sampling probability with that of the reference model, the method calibrates the inherent biases. Specifically, in the probabilistic variation assessment, it generates slight, symmetrical paraphrases of a text to approximate the local variation (similar to a second derivative) of the probability function. This variation signal, after calibration, serves as a robust indicator to determine if the text was part of the training set. In our work, we chose SPV-MIA as the membership inference attack method to evaluate the model's privacy risk.

2.4   Data Extraction Attack

Data extraction and reconstruction attacks reveal a critical vulnerability in LLMs, enabling adversaries to retrieve sensitive data, including personally identifiable information (PII), from both the models' outputs and internal representations. These vulnerabilities underscore the importance of assessing security risks when deploying LLMs in sectors that handle sensitive or proprietary information, such as healthcare, finance, and customer service. Recent researches have explored a variety of data extraction techniques, highlighting the increasing success of these attacks [9]. Early research on data extraction primarily focused on retrieving pre-training data. Carlini et al. [8] attempted to extract sensitive information that was inadvertently memorized during language model training. They also introduced the *exposure* metric to quantify the extent to which a model memorizes specific data, significantly influencing subsequent research. Lukas et al. [23] focused on extracting personal identifiable information (PII) from models under varying conditions, proposing more advanced extraction and reconstruction attacks. In our work, we employed a basic prompt attack and used the exposure metric to quantify risk, which will be detailed in the next section.

3   Methodology

In this paper, we evaluate the privacy risks of language models by implementing two types of privacy attacks: a data extraction attack and a membership inference attack (MIA). For the data extraction attack, we employ a prompt attack to attempt to extract a canary, a sample that is artificially inserted into the original dataset to simulate sensitive data, embedded in the fine-tuning dataset. Regarding the MIA, we adopt SPV-MIA [14], the current state-of-the-art method specifically designed for language models. To protect the fine-tuning dataset, we utilize differential private fine-tuning.

3.1   Data Extraction Attack

Adversary's Capability. Our method simulates a typical black-box adversary, which means an adversary is limited to black-box queries and cannot access the underlying model or its internal weights. In this setting, the adversary can submit crafted prompts to the model and observe its outputs. Additionally, we assume that the adversary has partial knowledge of the fine-tuning dataset. This may include access to some of the training samples or general information about the data distribution. This combination of query access and auxiliary data constitutes the adversarial capability in our experiments.

Threat Model. We designed a simple prompt-based method to simulate a data extraction scenario for evaluating model privacy risk. First, we selected an open-source dataset and inserted repeated canary samples, which is equivalent to 0.25% of the total training samples, into its training set. The 0.25% proportion was chosen because it does not overly distort the dataset distribution while being sufficient for the model to memorize the canary, as evidenced by the fact that, in the absence of DP, full fine-tuning can fully output the canary sample. The canary sample consists of a sentence containing a *secret code*. We then fine-tuned the model using this modified training set and evaluated its perplexity on the validation set. After fine-tuning, we provided a prompt (specifically, a partial prefix of the complete canary sentence) to generate 1,000 unique candidate outputs. We will detail the generation method in the following subsection. Next, we computed the cross-entropy loss for each candidate relative to the true canary sample, ranked these losses to obtain a rank, and finally used this rank to calculate the exposure detailed in **Definition 1.** A higher exposure indicates that the model has a stronger memorization of the canary, implying a higher privacy risk. We employed two kind of attacks. In the weak attack, the model is provided only with the prefix that precedes the *secret code* and is expected to generate the complete *secret code*. In the strong attack, the model is challenged to output only the final character of the *secret code*. We carry out these two attacks in order to simulate scenarios where the adversary has different levels of prior knowledge.

Definition 1. Exposure.

$$\textbf{exposure}_f(s) = \log_2|C| - \log_2\left(\textbf{rank}_f(s)\right) \tag{1}$$

We follow the definition [8] in our study. The candidate space C represents the number of candidates generated during the generation rather than every possible character combination of the same length as the secret string s.

Candidates Generation. Given that the target canary and candidate outputs share a common prefix, we use stochastic decoding techniques to generate a diverse set of candidate texts. Specifically, we employ sampling strategies such as temperature scaling, top-k, and nucleus (top-p) sampling to produce multiple outputs from the fine-tuned model. We apply truncation to ensure that all candidate outputs maintain the same length. This generation process is iterated until a predefined number of unique candidate texts is obtained, ensuring a comprehensive representation of the model's output distribution under similar input conditions.

Design Motivation. In data extraction research, exposure is frequently used as a risk metric. In Carlini et al. [8] 's original study, the candidate space was defined as all possible character combinations. However, when the target string is long, this approach results in an enormous candidate space that is impractical to compute. An alternative [25] involves manually selecting similar targets from the dataset, such as similar English names, to form the candidate space. Yet, this method requires extensive data processing and remains impractical for large datasets. To address these challenges, we designed a method in which the model itself generates candidate outputs. It is important to emphasize that, strictly speaking, our approach is not a true attack but rather an evaluation technique to assess the model's risk of memorizing sensitive information. By simulating an adversary using a prompt to extract data, we can measure the model's exposure and thus its privacy risk. Our experiments have demonstrated that this method is effective.

3.2   Membership Inference Attack

For the Membership Inference Attack, we adopted SPV-MIA [13]. We implemented the attack using the open-source SPV-MIA code [31]. To ensure compatibility with DP training and PEFT, we integrated fastDP and Hugging Face's PEFT library into the original code, enabling it to support PEFT-based DP training as well as perform inference and data generation.

Adversary's Capability. The adversary in SPV-MIA operates in a black-box environment, meaning they can only submit crafted prompts and observe the model's outputs. Additionally, it is assumed that the adversary may have partial information about the training data distribution.

Threat Model. Instead of relying on pre-existing data, the adversary uses the target language model to generate candidate reference texts that approximate the training data's distribution. These self-generated texts are then used to fine-tune a reference model. The core of SPV-MIA is a probabilistic variation metric that quantifies how much the target model memorizes a specific record. This metric is defined as the expectation of the second-order directional derivative of the model's probability function:

$$\tilde{p}_\theta(x) := \mathbb{E}_z \left[z^\top H_p(x) z \right],\tag{2}$$

where $H_p(x)$ is the Hessian of the probability function $p_\theta(x)$.

$$A_{\text{our}}(x, \theta, \hat{\theta}) = 1 \left[\tilde{p}_\theta(x) - \tilde{p}_{\hat{\theta}}(x) \geq \tau \right],\tag{3}$$

where $\hat{\theta}$ is the self-prompt reference model, and τ is the threshold for membership inference.

The difference serves as a robust membership signal that does not solely depend on overfitting.

4   Experiments

4.1   Key Findings Takeaway

The following key findings summarize the main trends observed in our experiments and provide guidance on the trade-offs between model utility and privacy protection:

(1) DP reduces model utility, with lower privacy budgets causing greater degradation. Full fine-tuning and LoRA exhibit strong robustness, whereas prefix-tuning suffers significantly, particularly in larger models.

(2) Without DP, full fine-tuning and LoRA are prone to extreme memorization, resulting in very high exposure and MIA risk, while prefix-tuning and P-tuning naturally offer better privacy protection.

(3) With DP training, both exposure and MIA risk are significantly reduced across all methods, with full fine-tuning and LoRA benefiting most; however, further lowering the privacy budget has only marginal effects on MIA AUC.

(4) In terms of privacy-utility trade-off, full fine-tuning achieves the best overall balance. Among the PEFT approaches, LoRA excels in preserving utility and P-tuning offers superior privacy protection, whereas prefix-tuning is not recommended due to its severe utility loss under DP.

4.2   Experimental Setup

Environment. The experiments were conducted on a Linux server running Ubuntu 22.04.5 LTS. Our environment used Python 3.10 with PyTorch 1.13.0 and CUDA 11.6, alongside key libraries such as Transformers and fastDP. The server featured dual NVIDIA A6000 GPUs (totaling 96 GB of VRAM), an AMD EPYC 7313P CPU, and 503 GB of system memory, providing a robust platform for training and evaluating our models under DP and various fine-tuning methods.

Datasets. In our study, we employed two datasets for fine-tuning the language model: **Wikitext-2-v1** [26] and **AG News** [36]. **Wikitext-2-v1** is a high-quality corpus derived from English Wikipedia articles. It contains 36718 samples for training and 3760 samples for validation. **AG News** is a widely recognized dataset used primarily for text classification tasks. It contains 120000 samples for training and is known for its concise yet diverse content.

For the data extraction attack, we utilize the entire Wikitext-2-v1. The canary sample is *The secret code is hzdh0831.* The method for constructing the training set is detailed in methodology. In the Membership Inference Attack, we extract 10,000 samples from the AG News' train-set to form the training set, which represents the member set in the context of the attack. Additionally, we extract 1,000 samples from AG News' test-set to serve as the evaluation set, which simultaneously functions as the non-member set.

Models. We employ two autoregressive language models: GPT-2 and GPT-2 XL [30]. GPT-2 is an autoregressive model based on the transformer architecture, pre-trained on a diverse corpus of web text. It is well-known for its ability to generate coherent and contextually relevant text, making it a popular choice for language modeling tasks. GPT-2 XL, the largest variant in the GPT-2 family, contains a significantly higher number of parameters, which allows it to capture more intricate language patterns and deliver enhanced performance on complex tasks. GPT-2 has 124M parameters while GPT-2 XL has 1.5B parameters.

For the fine-tuning methods, we adopt full fine-tuning as our baseline. Additionally, we explore three popular parameter-efficient fine-tuning (PEFT) approaches: prefix-tuning, LoRA, and P-tuning, which are detailed in Sect. 3. For PEFT of GPT-2, we use 8 as the rank of LoRA, 30 as the length of virtual tokens in Prefix-tuning and P-tuning, 128 as the size of hidden encoder in P-tuning. These methods are implemented using the peft [24] module available in the Transformers [34] library, enabling us to compare their performance in terms of utility and privacy risks. In two attack experiments, we fine-tuned for 10 epochs for the target model and used early-stopping to prevent overfitting.

Differential Privacy Mechanism. We employ DP-Adam to provide sample-level differential privacy protection for the fine-tuning dataset. Specifically, we utilize fastDP [4,5,7], a library that enables differentially private optimization of PyTorch models. FastDP implements gradient clipping based on Book-Keeping approach to achieve DP. It can integrate seamlessly with our chosen PEFT methods and language models.

Metrics. For model utility analysis, we use perplexity as the evaluation metric in both experiments. In the prompt attack experiment, we measure the risk of privacy leakage using the exposure metric, which is detailed in Sect. 3. For the membership inference attack (MIA) experiment, we employ SPV-MIA as the attack method and assess its effectiveness using the AUC (Area Under the Curve) and ASR (Attack Success Rate) metrics.

4.3 Impact of Differential Privacy on Model Utility

We plotted the perplexity of fine-tuned models against different privacy budgets across two settings in Fig. 1. Without the application of DP, all three PEFT methods exhibit perplexity levels comparable to full fine-tuning, with LoRA even matching the full fine-tuning performance. This indicates that, in the absence of DP, the selected PEFT approaches can maintain high utility, with LoRA showing the best performance.

However, once noise is introduced via DP, the utility of the models degrades across all fine-tuning methods. As the privacy budget decreases (i.e., as more noise is injected), the perplexity of the models increases. We fine-tuned both GPT-2 and GPT-2 XL on Wikitext-v2. The results reveal that, with the exception of prefix-tuning, all fine-tuning methods yield lower perplexity on DP-trained GPT-2 XL compared to GPT-2, indicating enhanced utility for larger models. However, prefix-tuning exhibits the opposite behavior. GPT-2 XL fine-tuned with prefix-tuning shows higher perplexity, suggesting that DP severely impacts its utility. The anomalous behavior of prefix-tuning on larger models warrants further investigation and validation. Notably, the extent of the perplexity's increase varies among the methods; prefix-tuning shows the most pronounced deterioration in utility, while FFT and LoRA continue to maintain relatively good performance. A possible explanation for these observations is that methods like FFT and LoRA distribute the DP-induced noise across a larger set of parameters or incorporate it into low-rank updates, which mitigates its adverse effects. In contrast, prefix-tuning relies heavily on a small set of learned prompt representations to condition the model's output. Consequently, the noise has a disproportionate impact on these few parameters, leading to a significant decline in their effectiveness and, therefore, a marked drop in utility.

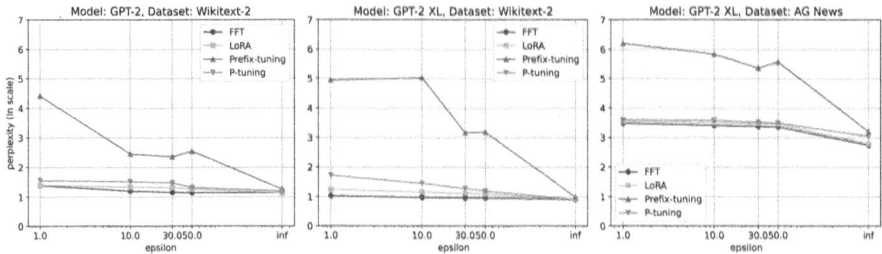

Fig. 1. Perplexity as a function of the privacy budget ϵ for various fine-tuning methods. The x-axis represents the privacy budget, while the y-axis shows the model perplexity in *ln* scale (with lower values indicating higher utility). Trends in the figure illustrate the impact of different DP budgets on model utility across various fine-tuning methods.

Remark 1. DP reduces model utility, with lower privacy budgets causing greater degradation. LoRA and full fine-tuning are relatively robust, while prefix-tuning suffers severe utility loss. Notably, although larger models typically yield higher utility at the same privacy budget, prefix-tuning exhibits a counterintuitive drop.

4.4   Impact of Differential Privacy on Empirical Privacy Risk

To evaluate the impact of DP on models' empirical privacy risk, we performed two attacks on GPT-2 obtained by different fine-tuning methods which is detailed in Sect. 3.

Data Extraction. We plotted the exposure metric against the privacy budget ϵ for various fine-tuning methods in Fig. 2.

Without applying any DP mechanism, both FFT (full fine-tuning) and LoRA exhibit extremely high exposure, reaching the maximum possible level. This

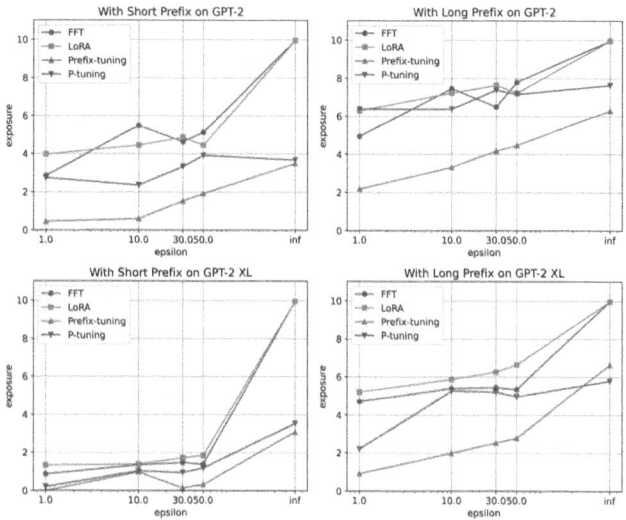

Fig. 2. Exposure as a function of the privacy budget ϵ for different fine-tuning methods. The four subplots display results for two model sizes and two attack scenarios. The top two subplots correspond to GPT-2, while the bottom two correspond to GPT-2 XL. The left subplots represent the weak attack (Short Prefix), and the right subplots represent the strong attack (Long Prefix). These trends illustrate how DP training affects model exposure across varying privacy budgets and attack strengths.

indicates that these models can directly output the secret code embedded in the canary, thus posing a significant privacy risk. An adversary can easily extract sensitive information by simply providing an appropriate prompt. In contrast, prefix-tuning and P-tuning inherently offer a degree of privacy protection, as their exposure is much lower than FFT and LoRA with no DP mechanism. We hypothesize that it is related to the location of the fine-tuned parameters within the model. Methods like FFT and LoRA modify parameters that are distributed across key layers (such as the self-attention and feed-forward networks) which are directly involved in generating outputs and encoding detailed information from the training data. This broader and deeper integration allows these methods to capture and retain more specific patterns and even sensitive details. In contrast, techniques like prefix-tuning and P-tuning adjust only a small set of additional parameters—typically in the form of prompt embeddings or similar auxiliary tokens—that are less tightly coupled with the core model representations. This more limited and peripheral update results in a lower capacity for memorization.

After introducing DP noise, the results show distinct behaviors across the fine-tuning methods. For FFT and LoRA that tend to develop strong memorization of the training data, the application of DP leads to a significant reduction in exposure even at a high privacy budget (e.g., $\epsilon = 50$). This indicates that DP is highly effective in mitigating the memorization—and thus the privacy risk— of sensitive data in these models. Conversely, for prefix-tuning and P-tuning, although the introduction of DP noise does lower exposure, the reduction is less pronounced. We speculate that this may be because these two methods, particularly in smaller models like GPT-2, do not form strong memorization in the first place, leaving less room for DP to further reduce exposure. Furthermore, as the privacy budget decreases, there is a general trend of declining exposure, which suggests that a stricter privacy budget does indeed enhance privacy protection. However, compared to the initial drop in exposure observed when DP was first applied, the subsequent decreases are not as significant.

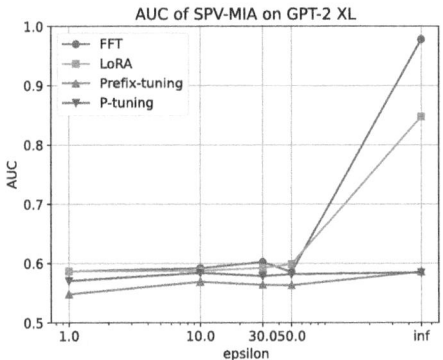

Fig. 3. MIA attack performance as a function of privacy budget ϵ on GPT-2 XL. This plot illustrates how the effectiveness of membership inference attacks (as measured by AUC) varies with different privacy budgets. Each point represents the MIA performance under a specific ϵ value.

Another interesting finding is that, when mitigating prompt attacks, DP proved more effective on GPT-2 XL than on GPT-2, as shown by a more pronounced decrease in exposure. One possible explanation is that larger models have more parameters, allowing them to better absorb and distribute the noise introduced by DP. This dilution of noise effects on individual parameters reduces the model's tendency to memorize specific training data, thereby enhancing privacy protection under the same privacy budget.

Remark 2. Without DP, full fine-tuning and LoRA result in very high exposure, which contradicts previous studies that reported LoRA as having the lowest exposure. In contrast, prefix-tuning and P-tuning naturally provide better privacy protection. When DP is applied, exposure decreases significantly, and lower privacy budgets lead to even lower exposure. Moreover, more complete prompts tend to increase privacy risk. Larger models exhibit lower exposure than smaller ones under the same privacy budget.

Membership Inference Attack. In our MIA experiments, we observed some intriguing phenomena and we plot the results in Fig. 3. Without DP, both FFT and LoRA were extremely vulnerable to MIA, achieving AUC values exceeding 80% and FFT reaching as high as 97.8%, which clearly indicates a very high privacy risk. We attribute this vulnerability to the strong memorization capabilities inherent in FFT and LoRA, leading these methods to effectively capture and reproduce sensitive information from the training data. In contrast, prefix-tuning and P-tuning exhibited substantially lower AUC values (around 60%) in the absence of DP, consistent with our findings from the prompt attack experiments. To eliminate the influence of model architecture, we fine-tuned GPT-J [32] on the same dataset without DP. The results show that GPT-J fine-tuned with P-tuning and prefix-tuning still maintains a low AUC of around 0.6 against SPV-MIA. These results suggest that prefix-tuning and P-tuning naturally offer a degree of privacy protection by limiting the memorization of individual training samples, which is consistent with our findings in the data extraction.

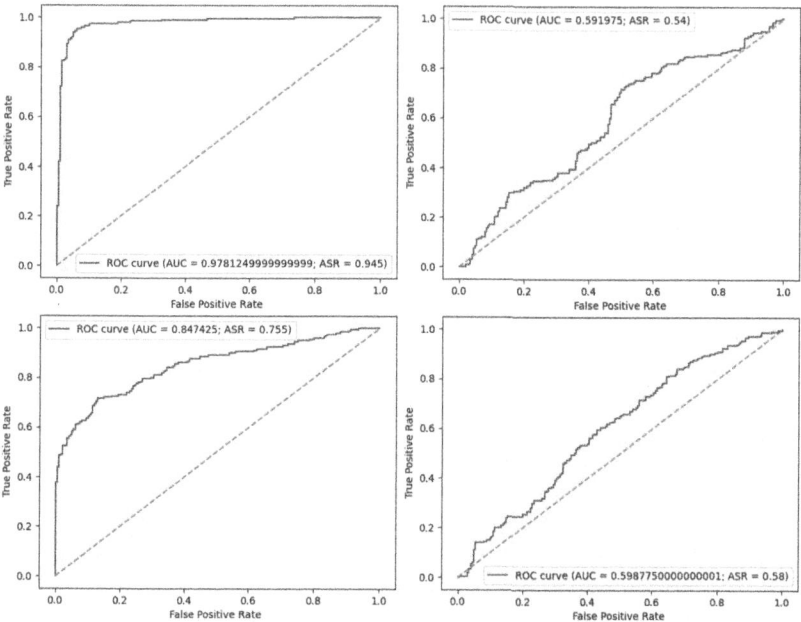

Fig. 4. ROC Curves for Membership Inference Attacks (MIA) on Models with and without DP Training. The top two subplots show the ROC curves for full fine-tuning (FFT) before DP training and after DP training (with $\epsilon = 10$), while the bottom two subplots depict the corresponding results for LoRA. The ASR (Attack Success Rate) is indicated in the plots. This figure demonstrates that DP training significantly mitigates the effectiveness of MIA attacks, as reflected in the substantial degradation of the ROC curves when DP is applied.

Upon introducing a DP mechanism, all four fine-tuning methods experience a substantial reduction in AUC. In particular, FFT and LoRA see dramatic decreases, with all methods converging to approximately 58% AUC. We plotted the ROC curves of GPT-2 XL under SPV-MIA before and after DP training in Fig. 4. It can be seen that DP training significantly reduces the attack threat on LoRA and full fine-tuning.

However, further lowering the privacy budget beyond this point does not yield a more pronounced decline in AUC. One potential explanation for this plateau is that the initial application of DP introduces enough noise to disrupt the memorization signals exploited by the attacks, effectively reducing vulnerability across the board. Once these signals are sufficiently obfuscated, additional noise, which is achieved by further lowering the privacy budget, offers diminishing returns in terms of additional privacy gains. In fact, even with a privacy budget of $\epsilon = 1$, DP guarantees that the success rate of MIA remains below 73%, which is still higher than the AUC values observed in current MIAs. This may imply that current MIA methods are still insufficient in their ability to effectively attack models trained with DP.

Remark 3. Without DP, full fine-tuning and LoRA exhibit extremely high MIA risk, whereas prefix-tuning and P-tuning inherently offer some privacy protection, consistent with our previous findings. Once DP training is introduced, the MIA risk decreases for all fine-tuning methods, with reductions being particularly significant for full fine-tuning and LoRA. Notably, even at very high privacy budgets, DP still provides substantial protection against MIA, though further changes in the privacy budget have little impact on the AUC.

4.5   Trade-Off Between Utility and Privacy

Achieving an optimal trade-off between utility and privacy remains a critical objective. To evaluate how different fine-tuning methods balance utility and privacy protection under DP, we plotted the relationship between exposure and perplexity as well as AUC and perplexity for each fine-tuning method, as shown in Fig. 5. In these plots, every point on a curve corresponds to the model's performance under a specific privacy budget. We interpret a better privacy-utility trade-off as a situation where a model maintains low perplexity while also keeping exposure and AUC low; therefore, curves that are generally closer to the lower-left corner indicate superior trade-offs. It is important to note that the rightmost point on each curve represents $\epsilon = \infty$ (i.e., no DP), and when considering trade-offs under DP, this point can be disregarded.

Based on the plots, under DP the curves for full fine-tuning are consistently closer to the lower-left corner in both graphs. This indicates that full fine-tuning achieves the best privacy-utility trade-off under DP. We attribute this to the large number of trainable parameters in full fine-tuning, which enables the model to better absorb and mitigate the impact of DP-induced noise while still protecting privacy.

Among the PEFT methods, both LoRA and P-tuning demonstrate a favorable trade-off. Specifically, the curve for P-tuning is positioned further left, suggesting a stronger advantage in privacy protection, whereas the curve for LoRA is shifted slightly to the right, reflecting better utility preservation. In contrast, prefix-tuning under DP leads to excessively high perplexity, severely compromising model utility. Although it offers relatively strong privacy protection, the excessive loss in utility—likely due to the model's diminished capacity to memorize—renders prefix-tuning unsuitable for DP training in its current form. This suggests a need for developing DP training methods tailored specifically for prefix-tuning.

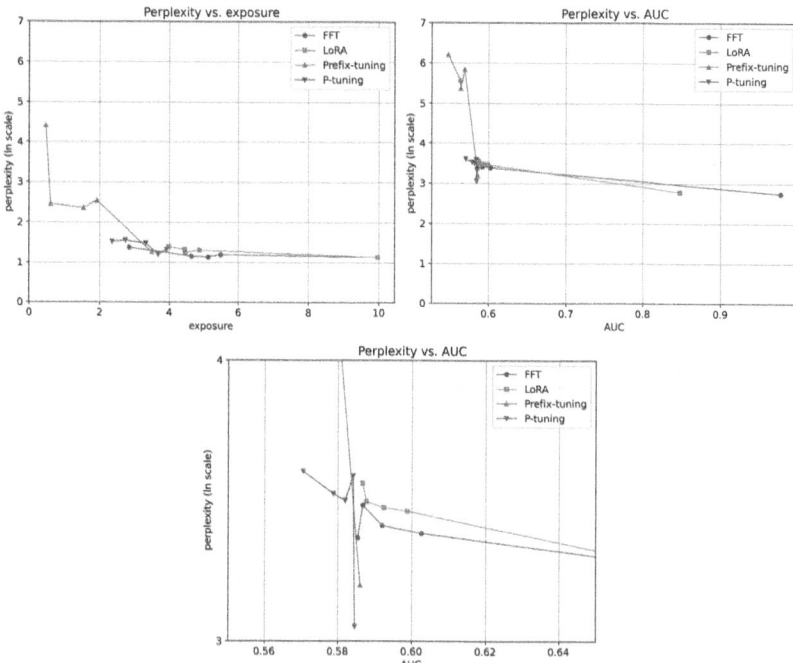

Fig. 5. Trade-off between model privacy risk and utility. The left panel plots exposure versus perplexity, while the right panel shows AUC versus perplexity, with perplexity on the vertical axis in both plots. In each curve, the rightmost point corresponds to the model trained without DP. We have enlarged part of the right panel to better observe the relationship between the curves.

In summary, full fine-tuning appears to be the best option under DP due to its high privacy-utility trade-off. However, given the substantial computational resources and time required for full fine-tuning, it is often impractical with large models. Among the PEFT approaches, LoRA is recommended when model utility is the primary concern, whereas P-tuning is preferable when stronger privacy protection is desired. We do not recommend using prefix-tuning under DP training because of its severe impact on utility. It is important to note that prefix-tuning and P-tuning naturally offer a certain degree of privacy protection even without DP. Therefore, if reducing privacy risk is the primary concern and DP training is not feasible, these methods are attractive alternatives.

Remark 4. Under DP, full fine-tuning achieves the best privacy-utility trade-off, as it maintains low perplexity and low exposure/AUC. Among the PEFT methods, LoRA and P-tuning offer promising results. P-tuning excels in privacy protection, while LoRA better preserves utility. In contrast, prefix-tuning suffers from excessively high perplexity under DP, severely impairing utility, and is therefore not recommended. These findings suggest that while full fine-tuning is optimal, practical constraints make PEFT methods attractive; among them, LoRA is preferable when utility is paramount, and P-tuning when privacy is the main concern.

5   Future Work

While our study offers valuable insights into the impact of privacy budgets on model utility and protection across fine-tuning methods, it is limited in several ways. Our experiments focused solely on the GPT-2 family, which may not capture the full range of behaviors exhibited by other architectures or larger language models. Additionally, we limited our analysis to standard differentially private optimization algorithms, even though recent advances have introduced specialized DP methods for PEFT, such as RAFT [20], which might offer improved trade-offs between utility and privacy. Our exploration of PEFT parameter configurations was also restricted to a few settings, leaving open questions about how different configurations might affect model performance and privacy risk. Furthermore, our evaluation was based on a narrow set of datasets, which may not fully represent the diversity of real-world data distributions and their associated privacy challenges. Future work should address these limitations by incorporating a broader range of models, exploring diverse DP methods (especially those tailored for PEFT), systematically varying parameter settings, and utilizing more varied datasets to enhance the generalizability and robustness of the findings.

6   Conclusion

In this work, we investigated the impact of DP on the utility and empirical privacy risk of LLMs fine-tuned with various methods, including both full fine-tuning and parameter-efficient fine-tuning methods. Our experiments demonstrate that while DP effectively reduces model exposure and membership inference risks, it also degrades utility, with the extent of degradation varying significantly across different fine-tuning methods. Moreover, our analysis of the privacy-utility trade-off reveals that, under DP, full fine-tuning achieves the best overall balance; however, practical considerations such as resource constraints make PEFT methods, particularly LoRA and P-tuning, attractive alternatives depending on whether the emphasis is on preserving utility or ensuring privacy. Overall, our findings provide valuable guidance for selecting fine-tuning strategies under DP constraints and set the stage for future research aimed at optimizing the trade-off between model performance and privacy protection in large-scale language models.

Acknowledgement. This work is partially support by JSPS KAKENHI JP23K24851, JST PRESTO JPMJPR23P5, JST CREST JPMJCR21M2.

References

1. Abadi, M., et al.: Deep learning with differential privacy. In: Proceedings of the 2016 ACM SIGSAC Conference on Computer and Communications Security, pp. 308–318 (2016)
2. awslabs: fast-differential-privacy: Fast, memory-efficient, scalable optimization of deep learning with differential privacy. https://github.com/awslabs/fast-differential-privacy (2024). v2.1 release (2024). Accessed 05 May 2025
3. Ben Zaken, E., Goldberg, Y., Ravfogel, S.: BitFit: simple parameter-efficient fine-tuning for transformer-based masked language-models. In: Proceedings of the 60th Annual Meeting of the Association for Computational Linguistics, pp. 1–9 (2022)
4. Bu, Z., Chiu, J., Liu, R., Zha, S., Karypis, G.: Zero redundancy distributed learning with differential privacy. arXiv preprint arXiv:2311.11822 (2023)
5. Bu, Z., Wang, Y.X., Zha, S., Karypis, G.: Differentially private bias-term fine-tuning of foundation models. In: Workshop on Trustworthy and Socially Responsible Machine Learning, NeurIPS 2022 (2022)
6. Bu, Z., Wang, Y.X., Zha, S., Karypis, G.: Differentially private optimization on large model at small cost. In: Proceedings of the 40th International Conference on Machine Learning (2023)
7. Bu, Z., Wang, Y.X., Zha, S., Karypis, G.: Differentially private optimization on large model at small cost. In: International Conference on Machine Learning, pp. 3192–3218. PMLR (2023)
8. Carlini, N., Liu, C., Kos, J., Úlfar Erlingsson, Song, D.: The secret sharer: evaluating and testing unintended memorization in neural networks (2019)
9. Das, B.C., Amini, M.H., Wu, Y.: Security and privacy challenges of large language models: a survey. ACM Comput. Surv. **57**(6), 1–39 (2025)
10. Devlin, J.: Bert: pre-training of deep bidirectional transformers for language understanding. arXiv preprint arXiv:1810.04805 (2018)
11. Dwork, C.: Differential privacy. In: International Colloquium on Automata, Languages, and Programming, pp. 1–12 (2006)
12. Feyisetan, O., Diethe, T., Drake, T.: Leveraging hierarchical representations for preserving privacy and utility in text . In: 2019 IEEE International Conference on Data Mining, pp. 210–219 (2019)
13. Fu, W., Wang, H., Gao, C., Liu, G., Li, Y., Jiang, T.: Practical membership inference attacks against fine-tuned large language models via self-prompt calibration. arXiv preprint arXiv:2311.06062 (2023)
14. Fu, W., Wang, H., Gao, C., Liu, G., Li, Y., Jiang, T.: Membership inference attacks against fine-tuned large language models via self-prompt calibration. In: The Thirty-Eighth Annual Conference on Neural Information Processing Systems (2024)

15. Han, Z., Gao, C., Liu, J., Zhang, J., Zhang, S.Q.: Parameter-efficient fine-tuning for large models: a comprehensive survey. Trans. Mach. Learn. Res. (2024)
16. Hu, E.J., et al.: LoRA: low-rank adaptation of large language models. In: International Conference on Learning Representations (2022)
17. Jagannatha, A., Rawat, B.P.S., Yu, H.: Membership inference attack susceptibility of clinical language models. arXiv preprint arXiv:2104.08305 (2021)
18. Lester, B., Al-Rfou, R., Constant, N.: The power of scale for parameter-efficient prompt tuning. In: Proceedings of the 2021 Conference on Empirical Methods in Natural Language Processing, pp. 3045–3059 (2021)
19. Li, X.L., Liang, P.: Prefix-tuning: optimizing continuous prompts for generation. In: Proceedings of the 59th Annual Meeting of the Association for Computational Linguistics and the 11th International Joint Conference on Natural Language Processing, pp. 4582–4597 (2021)
20. Li, Y., Tan, Z., Liu, Y.: Privacy-preserving prompt tuning for large language model services. arXiv preprint arXiv:2305.06212 (2023)
21. Liu, H., et al.: Few-shot parameter-efficient fine-tuning is better and cheaper than in-context learning. In: Oh, A.H., Agarwal, A., Belgrave, D., Cho, K. (eds.) Advances in Neural Information Processing Systems (2022)
22. Liu, X., et al.: GPT understands, too. AI Open **5**, 208–215 (2024)
23. Lukas, N., Salem, A., Sim, R., Tople, S., Wutschitz, L., Zanella-Béguelin, S.: Analyzing leakage of personally identifiable information in language models. In: 2023 IEEE Symposium on Security and Privacy, pp. 346–363 (2023)
24. Mangrulkar, S., Gugger, S., Debut, L., Belkada, Y., Paul, S., Bossan, B.: Peft: state-of-the-art parameter-efficient fine-tuning methods (2022). https://github.com/huggingface/peft
25. Marchyok, L., Carlini, N., Kurakin, A., Hong, S.: Evaluating privacy risks of parameter-efficient fine-tuning (2025)
26. Merity, S., Xiong, C., Bradbury, J., Socher, R.: Pointer sentinel mixture models (2016)
27. Mireshghallah, F., Uniyal, A., Wang, T., Evans, D., Berg-Kirkpatrick, T.: An empirical analysis of memorization in fine-tuned autoregressive language models. In: Goldberg, Y., Kozareva, Z., Zhang, Y. (eds.) Proceedings of the 2022 Conference on Empirical Methods in Natural Language Processing, pp. 1816–1826. Association for Computational Linguistics, Abu Dhabi, United Arab Emirates (2022)
28. Mireshghallah, F., Uniyal, A., Wang, T., Evans, D.K., Berg-Kirkpatrick, T.: An empirical analysis of memorization in fine-tuned autoregressive language models. In: EMNLP, pp. 1816–1826 (2022)
29. Panda, A., Tang, X., Choquette-Choo, C.A., Nasr, M., Mittal, P.: Privacy auditing of large language models. In: The Thirteenth International Conference on Learning Representations (2025)
30. Radford, A., Wu, J., Child, R., Luan, D., Amodei, D., Sutskever, I.: Language models are unsupervised multitask learners (2019)
31. tsinghua-fib-lab: ANeurIPS2024_SPV-MIA: Practical Membership Inference Attacks against Fine-tuned Large Language Models via Self-prompt Calibration (2024). https://github.com/tsinghua-fib-lab/ANeurIPS2024_SPV-MIA. commit df01b14. Accessed 05 May 2025
32. Wang, B., Komatsuzaki, A.: GPT-J-6B: a 6 billion parameter autoregressive language model (2021). https://github.com/kingoflolz/mesh-transformer-jax
33. Wei, J., et al.: Finetuned language models are zero-shot learners. In: International Conference on Learning Representations (2022). https://openreview.net/forum?id=gEZrGCozdqR

34. Wolf, T., et al.: Transformers: state-of-the-art natural language processing. In: Proceedings of the 2020 Conference on Empirical Methods in Natural Language Processing: System Demonstrations, pp. 38–45. Association for Computational Linguistics (2020)

35. Xu, L., Xie, H., Qin, S.Z.J., Tao, X., Wang, F.L.: Parameter-efficient fine-tuning methods for pretrained language models: A critical review and assessment. arXiv preprint arXiv:2312.12148 (2023)

36. Zhang, X., Zhao, J.J., LeCun, Y.: Character-level convolutional networks for text classification. In: NIPS (2015)

Attackers and Attack Detection

Metadata Assisted Supply-Chain Attack Detection for Ansible

Pandu Ranga Reddy Konala, Vimal Kumar$^{(\boxtimes)}$, David Bainbridge,
and Junaid Haseeb

School of Computing and Mathematical Sciences, University of Waikato,
Hamilton 3240, New Zealand
{pkonala,vkumar,davidb,jhaseeb}@waikato.ac.nz

Abstract. This study examines metadata-assisted detection of supply chain attacks in Infrastructure as Code (IaC), focusing on metadata's role in identifying security smells. Metadata, including dependency relationships and author records, provides insights into IaC scripts but remains underutilized by detection tools. The evaluation of static IaC smell detection tools highlights their limitations in incorporating metadata analysis. To address this, a methodology integrating metadata and dependency analysis was developed to identify security smells in dependency chains. An analysis of 482 Ansible Galaxy repositories identified vulnerabilities in 45 dependency chains, including reliance on deprecated dependencies (CWE-477), hard-coded credentials (CWE-798), and improper file permissions (CWE-280). Additionally, three repositories contained security vulnerabilities associated with output (CVE-2024-8775) and logging (CVE-2017-7550). The findings highlight the necessity of integrating metadata analysis with static code analysis for detecting security smells. This approach enhances IaC security and mitigates risks related to supply chain attacks.

Keywords: Infrastructure as Code (IaC) · Ansible · Dependency management · Vulnerability detection · Supply chain attacks · Metadata

1 Introduction

Software supply chain attacks/poisoning occur when malicious code is injected into the software development and distribution process. Notable incidents include the 2018 attack on the Node.js *eslint-scope* package, where attackers exploited a stolen *npm* token to release a malicious version designed to exfiltrate *npm* tokens from dependent machines [51]. Similarly, in 2022, a large-scale attack on a WordPress plugin and theme developer compromised 40 themes and 53 plugins, impacting over 360,000 active websites [20].

While such previous attacks primarily targeted traditional software, the scope of software development has expanded significantly. Developers now engage in

© IFIP International Federation for Information Processing 2025
Published by Springer Nature Switzerland AG 2025
S. Katsikas and B. Shafiq (Eds.): DBSec 2025, LNCS 15722, pp. 333–350, 2025.
https://doi.org/10.1007/978-3-031-96590-6_18

operations such as infrastructure management, which is managed through Infrastructure as Code (IaC). It shares similarities with traditional software development such as presence of rich metadata and versioning, particularly in its reliance on external components and repositories. Developers rarely create all components independently, instead utilizing prebuilt IaC dependencies, which may originate from the same or different authors. One analysis of GitHub repositories showed that open source projects, on average, rely on 180 external components [16]. These dependencies, in turn, rely on other dependencies, creating a more complex software supply chain and consequently a larger attack surface.

Despite the increased adoption of IaC in software development workflows, existing research on software supply chain security primarily focuses on traditional software, leaving gaps in understanding how supply chain vulnerabilities manifest in IaC environments. IaC repositories contain rich metadata—including version history, dependency relationships, licensing, platform compatibility, and authorship—yet current security mechanisms do not fully leverage this metadata for supply chain vulnerability assessment.

This work investigates supply chain attacks in the context of IaC by analyzing dependencies and metadata associated with IaC repositories. Metadata plays a critical role in identifying potential attack vectors, such as tracing transitive dependencies and detecting poisoned repositories. By systematically examining metadata-driven relationships, this work provides a methodology for detecting supply chain vulnerabilities in IaC, addressing a critical gap in current security approaches.

To achieve this, we begin by examining the extent to which existing IaC smell detection tools incorporate metadata parameters in their analyses. This allows us to assess whether these tools effectively capture metadata-driven security concerns or if there are omissions that leave IaC repositories vulnerable. Next, we explore how dependency information within metadata fields can be leveraged to identify repositories that exhibit security smells, shedding light on how metadata can serve as a valuable asset in security assessment. Finally, we evaluate the susceptibility of Ansible software to supply chain attacks, identifying possible vulnerabilities to supply chain attacks by analyzing the dependency chain through metadata.

By structuring our study around these investigative directions, we aim to provide a comprehensive understanding of how metadata can enhance security assessments in IaC.

2   Background

Supply chain attacks represent a cybersecurity risk, as demonstrated by incidents that reveal vulnerabilities across industries. The Colonial Pipeline ransomware attack, which leveraged a compromised password, disrupted fuel distribution in the United States, affecting gasoline and jet fuel along the East Coast [33]. Likewise, JBS, a meat producer, faced a supply chain ransomware attack attributed to the REvil group, interrupting operations in Australia, Canada, and the United States [34].

The PyPI supply chain attack in 2024 targeted the Python Package Index (PyPI), a repository for Python libraries [41]. Attackers uploaded malicious packages that appeared legitimate, exploiting the trust embedded in open-source ecosystems. These packages included malware intended to exfiltrate information from compromised systems, posing risks to organizations that inadvertently integrated them. This incident exposed weaknesses in open-source supply chains and emphasized the need to verify dependencies prior to their inclusion in software projects.

Hossain Faruk et al. [18] investigated software supply chain security by examining vulnerabilities that adversaries can exploit at multiple points of the software development lifecycle. Their study highlights that reliance on open-source or third-party code necessitates measures to protect the software supply chain from malicious activities. The authors identified issues in software supply chain security to enhance organizational awareness and best practices in this field. They reviewed existing methods and frameworks for securing the software supply chain, offering insights into prevention, detection, assessment, and remediation of security issues.

Duan et al. [15] examined package managers for interpreted languages, specifically PyPI (Python), *npm* (Node.js), and RubyGems (Ruby), to detect malicious packages. Their approach employed use of regular expressions to build heuristic rules derived from known supply chain attacks and malware studies, integrating both static and dynamic code analysis. Additionally, metadata-based heuristics, including package names, authorship, popular packages with different authors, and version information, were incorporated. A dependency analysis further identified vulnerabilities such as single points of failure and risks associated with unmaintained packages.

Ohm et al. [35] conducted a comprehensive review of 20 publications focused on identifying and detecting software supply chain attacks. The reviewed studies were categorized into six groups: rules and heuristics, typosquatting, differential analysis, machine learning methods, anomaly detection, and clustering. Notably, six of these studies integrated metadata analysis with both static and dynamic code analysis, highlighting the significance of metadata in detecting supply chain attacks. The authors concluded that no single approach is universally effective; instead, employing multiple strategies can help identify malicious behaviors across various environments. They emphasized the need for future research adopting a multimodal approach for detecting security-breaching packages. Despite this progress in software supply chain security, similar studies focusing on IaC scripts—particularly those that incorporate metadata for attack detection—are currently lacking, represents a promising area for further research.

2.1 Infrastructure as Code

Although existing studies are primarily focused on software code and security incidents, yet the use of IaC for building, orchestrating, and maintaining software systems prompts an inquiry into whether IaC may experience supply chain attacks in the same manner as code. This issue arises because IaC and code share many common features. This subsection considers two aspects: the general concept of IaC and the ways developers and system administrators interact with it. The IaC technology stack is divided into three categories [50]:

- *Infrastructure provisioning* automates the allocation and management of hardware resources for deploying infrastructure components.
- *Configuration management* encodes system setups to maintain software environments.
- *Image building* generates machine and container images in standardized formats.

These categories collectively support automation in provisioning, configuration, and image-building procedures, facilitating IT operations. IaC is generally set up using either a standalone script or a group of scripts organized within a repository, collectively designed to accomplish a specific task. These scripts can be executed on a single system or across multiple systems. A typical example [26] of an IaC script (`main.yml`) is shown in Listing I:

Listing I: Sample Ansible Script

```
- name: Install Nginx
  hosts: web_servers
  become: yes
  tasks:
    - name: Install Nginx
      apt:
        name: nginx
        state: present
```

These IaC scripts are typically shared by developers or system administrators through technology specific code bases such as Ansible Galaxy or platforms such as GitHub. When scripts are downloaded using the software's command line interface, metadata is retrieved before the script itself. An example of metadata obtained from Ansible Galaxy [2] is shown in Listing II:

Listing II: Metadata of Sample Ansible Script

```
{"id": 56789,"upstream_id": null,
  "created": "2024-02-05","modified": "2024-02-05",
  "username": "devops_admin",
  "github_repo": "ansible-role-nginx","github_branch": "main",
  "name": "nginx","description": "Install Nginx",
  "summary_fields": {"dependencies": [
      {"id": 10, "name": "security.hardening"},
      {"id": 11, "name": "common.utils"}],
    "namespace": {"id": 3050,"name": "devops_admin"},
    "provider_namespace": {
      "id": 205,"name": "devops_admin",
      "repository": {"name": "ansible-role-nginx"},
      "tags": ["webserver", "nginx", "http"],
      "versions": [{"name": "1.1"},{"name": "1.0"}]},
    "download_count": 342560}}
```

The metadata retrieved from Ansible Galaxy provides detailed information about the IaC script through various key fields. This data is necessary for ensuring management of infrastructure automation processes. It provides essential information about the script, such as its dependencies, supported platforms, version requirements, and licensing, which enables developers and system administrators to assess compatibility and compliance before deployment. Metadata also facilitates traceability by identifying the script's origin, authorship, and version history, helping teams address issues and implement updates effectively. Additionally, usage metrics like download counts and community engagement provide valuable information about a script's reliability and level of adoption. While these metrics promote script reuse and collaboration, poor management can expose systems to potential vulnerabilities.

3   State-of-the-Art IaC Smell Detection Tools

Software tools employ different mechanisms for processing input and generating output. Ohm et al. [35] conducted a survey of traditional software tools, where each tool in their respective studies described its approach to handling input and output data [35]. Similarly, we examine how static vulnerability analysis tools for IaC scripts process input and output data to identify security vulnerabilities. We define the term 'level of analysis' where the levels indicate the assessment scope and influence the types of vulnerabilities that can be detected. This study identifies two levels of analysis in static vulnerability assessment: single file analysis, and repository-level analysis.

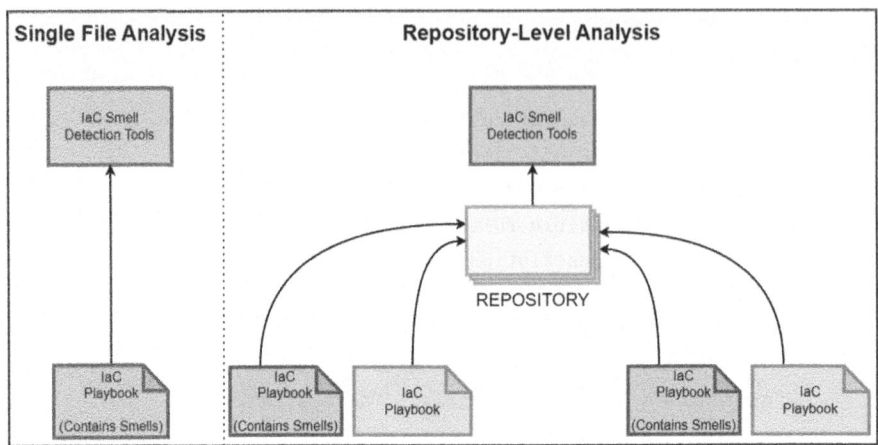

Fig. 1. Levels of Analysis

3.1   Level 1: Single File Analysis

Single file analysis, as shown in Fig. 1, evaluates individual IaC files in isolation, identifying localized misconfigurations, security smells, syntactical errors, etc. This level examines hardcoded secrets, insecure configurations, and non-compliant syntax. Tools such as `ansible-lint` [49] and `yamllint` [12] verify that Ansible scripts conform to fundamental standards, while policy-as-code frameworks, including Checkov [6] and KICS [9], ensure that each file meets predefined security and compliance benchmarks.

This approach does not consider interdependencies between files or the broader operational context. It establishes a baseline of file-level security, ensuring that vulnerabilities are addressed before integration into larger systems.

3.2   Level 2: Repository-Level Analysis

Repository-level analysis, as shown in Fig. 1, expands the scope to assess an entire repository as a cohesive unit. This level detects cross-file issues that may not be identifiable through single file analysis, such as variable reuse, conflicting configurations, and role or module misconfigurations.

Policy-as-code tools, including Open Policy Agent (OPA) [36] and Checkov [6], are used at this level to enforce compliance and maintain consistency with organizational standards. By analyzing interactions between IaC components, this level provides insights into security issues that emerge when multiple files operate together.

Table 1. Static Code Analysis Tools to Detect Smells for IaC Software

Tool Name	Year	IaC Software Category	Availability	Levels of Analysis	Metadata Analysis
ACID [38]	2020	Configuration Management	Opensource	Repository Level	No
BARREL [7]	2018	Infrastructure Provisioning	Opensource	Single File	No
⋆ Checkov [6]	2021	Infrastructure Provisioning	Hybrid	Single File, Repository Level	No
⋆ CloudSploit [3]	2020	Infrastructure Provisioning	Proprietary	Repository Level	Unknown
CookStyle [10]	2016	Configuration Management	Opensource	Single File, Repository Level	No
DeepIaC [5]	2020	Configuration Management	Opensource	Single File	No
Foodcritic [43]	2011	Configuration Management	Opensource	Repository Level	No
GLITCH [42]	2022	Configuration Management	Opensource	Single File, Repository Level	No
Häyhä [25]	2021	Infrastructure Provisioning	Opensource	Single File	No
⋆ KICS [9]	2020	All	Opensource	Single File	No
Puppeteer [46]	2016	Configuration Management	Opensource	Repository Level	No
RADON [14]	2021	Configuration Management	Opensource	Single File, Repository Level	No
Rehearsal [45]	2016	Configuration Management	Opensource	Repository Level	No
SecGuru [19]	2014	Infrastructure Provisioning	Proprietary	Unknown	No
SecureCode [13]	2020	Configuration Management	Proprietary	Repository Level	No
⋆ Semgrep [44]	2020	All	Opensource	Single File	No
SLAC [40]	2021	Configuration Management	Opensource	Repository Level	No
SLIC [39]	2019	Configuration Management	Opensource	Repository Level	No
⋆ SNYK IaC [47]	2023	Infrastructure Provisioning, Image Building	Proprietary	Single File, Repository Level	No
SODALITE [24]	2020	Infrastructure Provisioning	Opensource	Single File, Repository Level	No
Sommelier [8]	2017	Infrastructure Provisioning	Opensource	Single File	No
⋆ SonarQube [48]	2016	Infrastructure Provisioning, Image Building	Hybrid	Repository Level	No
TAMA [17]	2022	Configuration Management	Opensource	Repository Level	No
⋆ tfsec [4]	2019	Infrastructure Provisioning	Opensource	Single File, Repository Level	No

⋆ - Tools that are developed and maintained by private organizations, suggesting a high probability of them being proprietary.

3.3 Analysis of IaC Smell Detection Tools

An analysis of static IaC smell detection tools from both industry and academic sources, initially conducted by Konala et al. [22], was expanded to examine the mechanisms employed by these tools. Our study was guided by two questions:

1. What levels of analysis are implemented by these tools? (To understand how these tools process input and output data).
2. Do the examined tools analyze metadata parameters retrieved from the IaC codebase's APIs? (To examine how these tools process metadata).

Our analysis as shown in Table 1, for static code analysis tools for IaC, reveals that 3 out of 10 examine both single file and repository levels, while 4 out of 10 focus exclusively on repository-level analysis and 3 out of 10 only perform single file analysis. Regarding availability, 7 out of 10 of surveyed tools are open-source solutions, 2 out of 10 are proprietary, and 1 out of 10 offer hybrid licensing models. Of these tools, 3 out of 10 are commercially developed by private organizations, while 7 out of 10 are developed within research environments. This distinction matters because commercially developed tools often prioritize for production ready environments whereas research-based tools typically emphasize experimentation. Despite this diversity in approaches, a critical finding is that none of the examined tools incorporate metadata analysis, significantly limiting their ability to detect supply chain attacks.

The examination of supply chain attacks in the context of both traditional software and IaC, along with the analysis of metadata and the capabilities of smell detection tools, offers insights into the current state of research in this domain, as discussed in Sect. 2 and summarized in Table 1. However, several gaps remain. The key gaps identified are:

– **Lack of methods for IaC:** Current methods for detecting supply chain attacks mainly target traditional software code and related codebases, as outlined in Sect. 2. In contrast, research on IaC security is still in its infancy and needs further development [22].
– **Limited functionality of IaC tools:** Current static vulnerability assessment tools for IaC detect various smells but lack the capability to process and analyze metadata at all levels, leaving them vulnerable to supply chain attacks.

3.4 Summary

Cyber attackers are taking advantage of vulnerabilities is supply chain of software ecosystems, as evidenced by events at Colonial Pipeline [33], JBS [34], and PyPI [41]. Prior work has investigated open-source dependencies, package managers, and security methods to detect code that breaches security [15,18,40]. IaC, which automates infrastructure provisioning and configuration, may also be exposed to such attacks because it shares properties with software code. Current IaC smell detection tools analyze files and repositories but do not examine metadata, which diminishes their ability to guard against attacks that seek to exploit this. Further investigation is necessary to address this by integrating metadata analysis into IaC vulnerability assessment.

4   Methodology

To overcome the limitations identified in existing tools, it is essential to broaden the analytical scope beyond individual files and repositories to encompass their interdependencies as well. To achieve this, a methodology was devised that incorporates metadata analysis and dependency traversal to identify susceptible repositories.

The proposed methodology begins with selecting a repository for analysis. Upon selection, the repository's metadata information is retrieved and its dependency data is extracted. Using the extracted dependency information, associated dependency repositories are identified, and their metadata is also retrieved. This process is repeated iteratively, traversing the dependency chain until no additional dependencies remain.

Algorithm 1. Supply-Chain Attack Detection Methodology

1: **Input:** Primary repository R
2: **Output:** Identified vulnerabilities $\mathcal{V}_{\text{total}}$ mapped to CWE [1] and known CVE [32]
3: **Notation:**
4:     r – repository being analyzed (primary or dependency)
5:     $\mathcal{M}(r)$ – metadata associated with repository r
6:     $\mathcal{D}(r)$ – set of direct dependencies of repository r
7:     $\mathcal{A}(r)$ – analysis performed on repository r
8:     $\mathcal{V}(r)$ – vulnerabilities identified in repository r
9:     $\mathcal{T}(R)$ – transitive closure of all dependencies
10: **Dependency Discovery:**
11: Initialize: $\mathcal{T}(R) \leftarrow \emptyset$
12: **repeat**
13:     **for** each repository $r \in \{R\} \cup \mathcal{T}(R)$ **do**
14:         Retrieve metadata: $\mathcal{M}(r)$
15:         Extract direct dependencies: $\mathcal{D}(r)$
16:         Update transitive dependency set: $\mathcal{T}(R) \leftarrow \mathcal{T}(R) \cup \mathcal{D}(r)$
17:     **end for**
18: **until** $\mathcal{D}(r) = \emptyset, \forall r \in \mathcal{T}(R)$
19: **Static Vulnerability Analysis:**
20: **for** each repository $r \in \{R\} \cup \mathcal{T}(R)$ **do**
21:     Perform static analysis: $\mathcal{A}(r) \rightarrow \mathcal{V}(r)$
22: **end for**
23: **Vulnerability Aggregation:**
24: $\mathcal{V}_{\text{total}} \leftarrow \bigcup_{r \in \{R\} \cup \mathcal{T}(R)} \mathcal{V}(r)$
25: **return** $\mathcal{V}_{\text{total}}$

Once all the repositories in a dependency chain have been identified, static code analysis is performed on each repository. This analysis evaluates both the source code and metadata across the entire dependency chain. By including dependency repositories and their metadata in the analysis, this approach enables the identification of supply chain attacks, such as poisoned dependencies, that could compromise the security of the overall system. This methodology, as presented in Algorithm 1, provides a systematic approach for addressing the limitations of existing tools within the IaC ecosystems.

For each primary repository R, Algorithm 1 outputs a dependency tree $\mathcal{T}(R)$. For each repository r in $\{R\} \cup \mathcal{T}(R)$, the Algorithm outputs a set of vulnerabilities $\mathcal{V}(r)$. The set of vulnerabilities $\mathcal{V}(r)$ is obtained by performing static code analysis ($\mathcal{A}(r)$), as outlined by Konala et al. [23], focusing on code security attributes such as deprecated keywords, hard-coded credentials, improper file permissions, logging and monitoring failures, and insecure default configurations to evaluate individual repositories.

4.1 Dataset Overview

Data obtained from Ansible Galaxy [2] served as the primary dataset for this study. Although the presented methodology can be generalizable to other code management platforms that provide metadata access, Ansible Galaxy was specifically chosen due to its structured repository format, containing distinct Ansible roles and collections. This facilitates straightforward extraction and subsequent analysis without the necessity for further filtering. Conversely, platforms such as GitHub encompass repositories with diverse code types and functionalities, thus necessitating additional preprocessing steps to isolate relevant Ansible-specific content. Consequently, Ansible Galaxy was selected to simplify the implementation of the methodology, yet its applicability is not constrained exclusively to this platform. Furthermore, the selection was motivated by the diversity of repositories available in Ansible Galaxy, along with its built-in quality mechanisms.

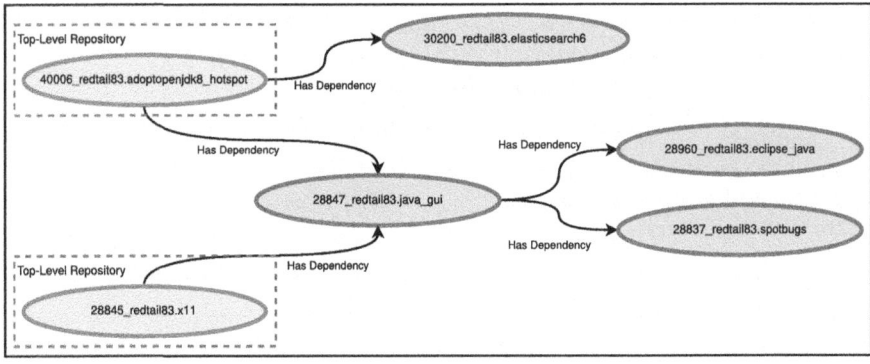

Fig. 2. Example of dependency chains from the dataset

Of the 31,076 repositories that were examined, 27,801 showed no dependencies, while 3,275 had identifiable dependencies. It must be noted that many repositories contain code directly copied from sources. In such cases dependencies and therefore their vulnerabilities cannot be identified in a straightforward manner. Consequently, only repositories from the latter category were considered for detailed analysis. From these, 268 repositories and their associated dependency chains [37] were selected based on metadata completeness. Completeness, in this context, refers to the thorough population of essential metadata fields, including repository descriptions, dependency information, versioning history, author details, and other relevant data, without omissions. Ensuring metadata completeness is crucial for performing a reliable dependency chain analysis, as required by our proposed methodology.

Figure 2, illustrates an example of dependency chains derived from our dataset. Collectively, the selected 268 dependency chains involved 482 repositories, providing the foundation for subsequent analysis. The primary objective of this analysis was to pinpoint top-level repositories and investigate if they were vulnerable due to security smells not in their code but in the code of their dependencies. Here, top-level repositories are defined as those operating exclusively as downstream consumers without themselves serving as dependencies.

5 Findings and Discussion

The analysis of the Ansible Galaxy dataset, following Algorithm 1, revealed security smells within IaC dependency chains. A total of 45 dependency chains, involving 40 repositories, were found to contain vulnerabilities that could enable supply chain attacks both currently and in the future. Subsequently, the study focused on a detailed examination of these vulnerable dependencies, specifically aiming to:

- Map identified security smells to the CWE framework.
- Map identified security smells with known CVEs.

The following subsections provide an discussion of these analyses.

5.1 Security Smells Mapping To CWE

Our analysis revealed that security smells were primarily linked to the use of deprecated keywords and modules. The distribution of these security smells indicated that out of the 40 repositories that were studied, 95% of the repositories contained deprecated components, which can be associated with the Use of Obsolete Function security weakness (CWE-477) [28]. This reliance on outdated repositories utilizing unmaintained versions of Ansible suggests that developers have not migrated their scripts to the latest versions.

Furthermore, additional security concerns were identified, with hard-coded database credentials present in 1 repository representing 2.5% of the repositories under consideration, corresponding to CWE-798 (Use of Hard-Coded Credentials) [29]. Similarly, improper file permissions were observed in 2.5% of the repositories, aligning with CWE-280 (Improper Handling of Insufficient Permissions or Privileges) [27]. These findings indicate potential security risks within IaC scripts, emphasizing the need for improved security practices in dependency management and script maintenance.

Temporal Analysis of Repository Releases. Figure 3 presents an analysis of the latest release dates for repositories within the dependency chain, providing further support for observations related to the Use of Obsolete Function CWE-477 [28]. The histogram analysis indicates a mean release date of November 2018 and a median release date of May 2018, highlighting a significant gap of approximately seven years at the time of our study (January 2025). This prolonged period without updates increases the risks associated with relying on outdated dependencies. Furthermore, to substantiate this claim, an examination of Ansible releases [11] reveals that the number of deprecated keywords increases with each new version, further emphasizing the challenges posed by outdated infrastructure.

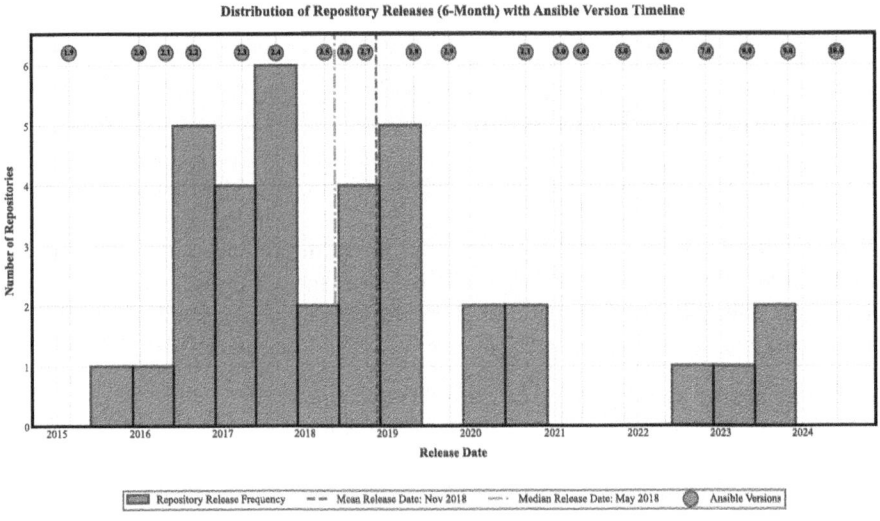

Fig. 3. Timeline Histogram of Repository Releases Over 6 Months with Ansible Versions

5.2 Author Activity Analysis

In addition to the code-based analysis, repositories and their authors were examined based on contribution records, specifically the last commit information derived from repository metadata. Repositories were classified into 5 categories based on whether contributions occurred within a six-month timeframe, corresponding to the typical update cycle for Ansible. Authors were categorized based on their involvement in single or multiple repositories and further distinguished as either individual contributors or organizational entities. Moreover, the analysis provides a count of repositories that are potentially susceptible to present or future supply chain attacks for each category if vulnerable dependency repositories are utilized, as outlined in Table 2.

Table 2. Repository & Author Contribution Analysis

Category	Repository Activity	Author Activity	Author Status	Vulnerable Repositories	Cumulative Downloads
C1	inactive	active	single	21	941,327
C2	inactive	active	org	9	34,370
C3	inactive	inactive	single	5	227
C4	active	active	single	3	7,100,309
C5	inactive	inactive	org	2	72

While many vulnerable repositories within the dependency chain are no longer actively maintained, their authors often continue contributing to other projects (e.g., Categories C1, C2). Given their continued activity, it is conceivable that they may recognize the associated risks and take proactive measures to mitigate them. However, security risks become significant when a repository remains unmaintained for an extended period, particularly when its author is inactive (Category C3). This risk is exacerbated when an unmaintained repository is linked to an inactive author from an organizational entity (Category C5), increasing the likelihood of RepoJacking supply chain attacks [21] involving IaC scripts. Notably, our analysis identified a repository containing hard-coded database credentials, classified as CWE-798 (Use of Hard-Coded Credentials). Such vulnerabilities could be exploited by malicious actors to carry out Repo-Jacking attacks, compromising the security of dependent systems.

To gain deeper insights into the extent of vulnerabilities in Ansible Galaxy, Table 3 aggregates the data from the detailed classification by summarizing the total number of affected repositories across the defined categories from Table 2. With 117 repositories identified as potentially vulnerable to compromise, this table provides an overall view of the impact, highlighting the distribution of vulnerabilities within the ecosystem. Categories C1 and C4 account for the majority of the affected repositories, suggesting that even projects with active contributions can be at risk due to vulnerable dependencies. Conversely, the counts in Categories C3 and C5 are particularly concerning given their association with inactive repositories and authors, which may impede the timely application of security patches. Together, these findings underscore the critical need for continuous monitoring and proactive mitigation strategies to address vulnerabilities in IaC environments and safeguard against supply chain attacks.

Table 3. Number of Affected Repositories

Category	Total Affected Repositories
C1	47
C2	19
C3	6
C4	43
C5	2

5.3   Security Smells Mapping To Known CVE

Building on the repository and author contribution analysis, the mapping of publicly known CVEs [32] associated with Ansible revealed three affected repositories. These repositories represent a range of activity statuses and author types, highlighting diverse security risks within the IaC ecosystem.

The first repository, maintained by an active individual author, is a widely used project with a high download count (4,389,601), reflecting extensive adoption within the community. Despite its active maintenance, it is associated with CVE-2024-8775 [31], which has a CVSS v3.1 base score of 5.5, indicating a moderate security risk. This suggests that even actively maintained repositories may harbor vulnerabilities that can affect downstream projects.

The second repository, although maintained by an active individual author, has been inactive for some time and has a relatively low download count (1,567). It is also affected by CVE-2024-8775, illustrating how vulnerabilities can persist across different repositories and dependency chains, regardless of their popularity or level of maintenance. The inactivity further increases the security risk, as the absence of updates reduces the likelihood of timely patching.

The third repository, managed by an organizational author, is inactive and has a minimal download count (41). However, it is associated with CVE-2017-7550 [30], a critical vulnerability with a CVSS v3.1 base score of 9.8. The presence of such a high-severity CVE in an unmaintained repository raises significant concerns about potential exploitation, especially in the context of supply chain attacks.

This analysis aligns with prior findings that inactive repositories managed by organizations represent a notable security risk. These repositories can serve as attack vectors, allowing vulnerabilities in dependencies to facilitate lateral movement within systems. The identification of CVEs in both actively and inactively maintained repositories emphasizes the need for continuous monitoring and proactive security measures to mitigate threats in IaC environments.

5.4   Limitations and Future Work

Current practices for detecting vulnerabilities in dependency chains rely predominantly on static analysis methods that examine code without executing it. Such methods may not capture vulnerabilities that manifest when code segments from separate repositories interact during execution. While static analysis may overlook these dynamic interactions, their combination during runtime could lead to behavior that compromises system security.

Additionally, we acknowledge a limitation in the temporal analysis discussed in Subsect. 5.1. This analysis, which involves calculating mean and median release dates, is affected by the dominance of older releases, resulting in a graph that disproportionately reflects repositories with earlier dates. Establishing whether recent repositories exhibit improved security standards would require additional supporting data. However, determining this falls outside the scope of the current study, which primarily focuses on metadata and supply-chain attack detection.

Future work should focus on developing and integrating dynamic analysis methods that assess code during execution, especially for infrastructure as code. Expanding the investigation to include alternative approaches beyond static analysis could help capture vulnerabilities that are otherwise hidden, thereby reducing the chance of supply chain attacks.

6   Conclusion

This study analyzed the vulnerability of IaC to supply chain attacks, highlighting limitations in existing static smell detection tools, which lack the capability to incorporate metadata analysis. By applying a methodology that integrates metadata and dependency repository analysis, security smells were identified within Ansible dependency chains, including reliance on deprecated dependencies (CWE-477 [28]), hard-coded credentials (CWE-798 [29]), and improper file permissions (CWE-280 [27]). Additionally, the analysis identified vulnerabilities associated with CVE-2024-8775 [31] and CVE-2017-7550 [30] in three repositories.

The findings indicate the necessity for developing tools that integrate metadata analysis with security assessments to address supply chain risks in IaC environments. Future research should extend the methodology by incorporating dynamic analysis and evaluating security smells across multiple IaC platforms to establish security guardrails within IaC ecosystems against supply chain attacks.

Acknowledgement. We appreciate the valuable feedback provided by the reviewers. The authors would also like to acknowledge funding support from the New Zealand Ministry of Business, Innovation, and Employment (MBIE) for project UOWX1911, "Artificial Intelligence for Human-Centric Security".

References

1. Common weakness enumeration. https://cwe.mitre.org/index.html
2. Ansible Community: Ansible Galaxy (2023). https://galaxy.ansible.com/
3. Aqua: Cloudsploit. https://cloudsploit.com/
4. aquasecurity: tfsec. https://github.com/aquasecurity/tfsec
5. Borovits, N., et al.: Deepiac: Deep learning-based linguistic anti-pattern detection in IaC. In: Proceedings of the 4th ACM SIGSOFT International Workshop on Machine-Learning Techniques for Software-Quality Evaluation, MaLTeSQuE 2020, pp. 7–12. Association for Computing Machinery, New York (2020). https://doi.org/10.1145/3416505.3423564
6. BridgeCrew: Checkov. https://www.checkov.io/
7. Brogi, A., Canciani, A., Soldani, J.: Modelling and analysing cloud application management. In: Dustdar, S., Leymann, F., Villari, M. (eds.) Service Oriented and Cloud Computing, pp. 19–33. Springer, Cham (2015)
8. Brogi, A., Di Tommaso, A., Soldani, J.: Sommelier: a tool for validating TOSCA application topologies. In: Pires, L.F., Hammoudi, S., Selic, B. (eds.) Model-Driven Engineering and Software Development, pp. 1–22. Springer, Cham (2018)
9. Checkmarx: Kics. https://www.kics.io/
10. Chef: Cookstyle (2023). https://github.com/chef/cookstyle
11. Community, A.: Releases and Maintenance. Red Hat, Inc. (2025). https://docs.ansible.com/ansible/latest/reference_appendices/release_and_maintenance.html
12. Cunin, A.: 'yamllint' documentation: a linter for YAML files (2023). https://yamllint.readthedocs.io
13. Dai, T., Karve, A., Koper, G., Zeng, S.: Automatically detecting risky scripts in infrastructure code. In: Proceedings of the 11th ACM Symposium on Cloud Computing, SoCC 2020, pp. 358–371. Association for Computing Machinery, New York (2020). https://doi.org/10.1145/3419111.3421303
14. Dalla Palma, S., Di Nucci, D., Palomba, F., Tamburri, D.A.: Within-project defect prediction of infrastructure-as-code using product and process metrics. IEEE Trans. Softw. Eng. **48**(6), 2086–2104 (2022). https://doi.org/10.1109/TSE.2021.3051492
15. Duan, R., Alrawi, O., Kasturi, R.P., Elder, R., Saltaformaggio, B., Lee, W.: Towards measuring supply chain attacks on package managers for interpreted languages. In: Proceedings of the Network and Distributed System Security Symposium (NDSS) (2021). https://doi.org/10.14722/ndss.2021.23055, https://www.ndss-symposium.org/wp-content/uploads/ndss2021_1B-1_23055_paper.pdf
16. GitHub Inc.: The state of the octoverse (2020). https://octoverse.github.com/2019/. Accessed 07 Jan 2025
17. Hassan, M.M., Rahman, A.: As code testing: characterizing test quality in open source ansible development. In: 2022 IEEE Conference on Software Testing, Verification and Validation (ICST), pp. 208–219 (2022). https://doi.org/10.1109/ICST53961.2022.00031
18. Hossain Faruk, M.J., Tasnim, M., Shahriar, H., Valero, M., Rahman, A., Wu, F.: Investigating novel approaches to defend software supply chain attacks. In: 2022 IEEE International Symposium on Software Reliability Engineering Workshops (ISSREW), pp. 283–288 (2022). https://doi.org/10.1109/ISSREW55968.2022.00081
19. Jayaraman, K., Bjørner, N., Outhred, G., Kaufman, C.: Automated analysis and debugging of network connectivity policies. Microsoft Res. 1–11 (2014)

20. Kasturi, R.P., et al.: Mistrust plugins you must: a large-scale study of malicious plugins in WordPress marketplaces. In: 31st USENIX Security Symposium (USENIX Security 22), pp. 161–178. USENIX Association, Boston (2022). https://www.usenix.org/conference/usenixsecurity22/presentation/kasturi

21. Kim, M., Jung, W., Lee, S., Kwon, T., Kim, E.T.: Code repository vulnerability focusing on repojacking. In: 2023 14th International Conference on Information and Communication Technology Convergence (ICTC), pp. 1880–1884 (2023). https://doi.org/10.1109/ICTC58733.2023.10392354

22. Konala, P.R.R., Kumar, V., Bainbridge, D.: SoK: static configuration analysis in infrastructure as code scripts. In: IEEE International Conference on Cyber Security and Resilience, CSR 2023, Venice, Italy, 31 July–2 August 2023, pp. 281–288. IEEE (2023). https://doi.org/10.1109/CSR57506.2023.10224925

23. Konala, P.R.R., Kumar, V., Bainbridge, D., Haseeb, J.: A framework for measuring the quality of infrastructure-as-code scripts (2025). https://arxiv.org/abs/2502.03127

24. Kumara, I., et al.: Towards semantic detection of smells in cloud infrastructure code, pp. 63–67 (2020). https://doi.org/10.1145/3405962.3405979

25. Lepiller, J., Piskac, R., Schäf, M., Santolucito, M.: Analyzing infrastructure as code to prevent intra-update sniping vulnerabilities. In: Groote, J.F., Larsen, K.G. (eds.) Tools and Algorithms for the Construction and Analysis of Systems, pp. 105–123. Springer, Cham (2021)

26. Meijer, B., Hochstein, L., Moser, R.: Ansible: Up and Running, 3rd edn. O'Reilly Media, Sebastopol (2022)

27. Mitre: About CWE-280: Improper Handling of Insufficient Permissions or Privileges (2018). https://cwe.mitre.org/data/definitions/280.html

28. MITRE: About CWE-477: use of obsolete function (2018). https://cwe.mitre.org/data/definitions/477.html

29. MITRE: About CWE-798: Use of hard-coded credentials (2018). https://cwe.mitre.org/data/definitions/798.html

30. MITRE Corporation: CVE-2017-7550: Ansible Jenkins Plugin Module Exposes Passwords in Remote Host Logs (2017). https://nvd.nist.gov/vuln/detail/CVE-2017-7550

31. MITRE Corporation: CVE-2024-8775: Exposure of Sensitive Information in Ansible Vault Files Due to Improper Logging (2024). https://nvd.nist.gov/vuln/detail/CVE-2024-8775

32. MITRE Corporation: Common Vulnerabilities and Exposures (CVE) (2025). https://cve.mitre.org/

33. Nahta, P.: Securing the digital supply chain: challenges, innovations, and best practices in cybersecurity (2025). https://doi.org/10.4018/979-8-3693-8357-5.ch008

34. Ofori-Yeboah, A., Addo-Quaye, R., Oseni, W., Amorin, P., Agangmikre, C.: Cyber supply chain security: a cost benefit analysis using net present value. In: 2021 International Conference on Cyber Security and Internet of Things (ICSIoT), pp. 49–54 (2021). https://doi.org/10.1109/ICSIoT55070.2021.00018

35. Ohm, M., Stuke, C.: SoK: practical detection of software supply chain attacks. In: Proceedings of the 18th International Conference on Availability, Reliability and Security, ARES 2023, Association for Computing Machinery, New York (2023). https://doi.org/10.1145/3600160.3600162

36. Open Policy Agent: Open Policy Agent (OPA) (2025). https://www.openpolicyagent.org/

37. Palo Alto Networks: What is dependency chain abuse? (2023). https://www.paloaltonetworks.com/cyberpedia/dependency-chain-abuse-cicd-sec3

38. Rahman, A., Farhana, E., Parnin, C., Williams, L.: Gang of eight: a defect taxonomy for infrastructure as code scripts. In: 2020 IEEE/ACM 42nd International Conference on Software Engineering (ICSE), pp. 752–764 (2020). https://doi.org/10.1145/3377811.3380409

39. Rahman, A., Parnin, C., Williams, L.: The seven sins: security smells in infrastructure as code scripts. In: 2019 IEEE/ACM 41st International Conference on Software Engineering (ICSE), pp. 164–175 (2019). https://doi.org/10.1109/ICSE.2019.00033

40. Rahman, A., Rahman, M.R., Parnin, C., Williams, L.: Security smells in ansible and chef scripts: a replication study. ACM Trans. Softw. Eng. Methodol. **30**(1) (2021). https://doi.org/10.1145/3408897

41. Research, J.S.: Revival hijack: Pypi hijack technique exploited, 22k+ packages at risk (2024). https://jfrog.com/blog/revival-hijack-pypi-hijack-technique-exploited-22k-packages-at-risk/

42. Saavedra, N., Ferreira, J.F.: Glitch: automated polyglot security smell detection in infrastructure as code (2022). https://doi.org/10.48550/ARXIV.2205.14371, https://arxiv.org/abs/2205.14371

43. Schwarz, J., Steffens, A., Lichter, H.: Code smells in infrastructure as code. In: 2018 11th International Conference on the Quality of Information and Communications Technology (QUATIC), pp. 220–228 (2018). https://doi.org/10.1109/QUATIC.2018.00040

44. Semgrep: Semgrep. https://semgrep.dev/

45. Shambaugh, R., Weiss, A., Guha, A.: Rehearsal: a configuration verification tool for puppet. In: Proceedings of the 37th ACM SIGPLAN Conference on Programming Language Design and Implementation, PLDI 2016, pp. 416–430. Association for Computing Machinery, New York (2016). https://doi.org/10.1145/2908080.2908083

46. Sharma, T., Fragkoulis, M., Spinellis, D.: Does your configuration code smell? In: 2016 IEEE/ACM 13th Working Conference on Mining Software Repositories (MSR), pp. 189–200 (2016)

47. SNYK: Snykiac. https://snyk.io/product/infrastructure-as-code-security/

48. Sonar: Sonarqube. https://www.sonarsource.com/products/sonarqube/

49. Thames, W., contributors: ansible-lint - checks playbooks for practices and behavior that could potentially be improved (2023). https://ansible-lint.readthedocs.io

50. Wang, R.: Infrastructure as Code, Patterns and Practices: With Examples in Python and Terraform. ITpro Collection, Manning (2022)

51. Zhu, H.: Postmortem for malicious packages published on July 12th, 2018 (2018). https://eslint.org/blog/2018/07/postmortem-for-malicious-package-publishes/

Diffusion-Based Adversarial Purification for Intrusion Detection

Mohamed Amine Merzouk[1,2,3(✉)], Erwan Beurier[2,3], Reda Yaich[3],
Nora Boulahia-Cuppens[2], Frédéric Cuppens[2], and Foutse Khomh[1,2]

[1] Mila - Québec AI Institute, Montréal, Canada
mohamed-amine.merzouk@polymtl.ca
[2] Polytechnique Montréal, Montréal, Canada
[3] IRT SystemX, Palaiseau, France

Abstract. The rise of sophisticated cyberattacks has fueled the adoption of machine learning (ML) techniques in intrusion detection systems; however, the emergence of adversarial examples poses a critical challenge, allowing malicious actors to bypass detection or generate false alerts. In response, this paper introduces a novel approach to adversarial purification in intrusion detection utilizing diffusion models, which have demonstrated promising capabilities in various domains. Our research is the first to explore the effectiveness of these models specifically within the context of network intrusion detection. We conduct a thorough analysis of diffusion model parameters, revealing optimal configurations that enhance adversarial robustness while maintaining the integrity of normal performance. Notably, we provide insights into the intricate relationship between diffusion noise and the number of diffusion steps and leverage them to optimize the diffusion process. Our comprehensive experiments across two prominent datasets and against five different adversarial attacks underscore the strong purification potential of diffusion models, marking a pivotal contribution to enhancing the resilience of intrusion detection systems against adversarial threats. For further research, we make our implementation code is publicly available on Github.

1 Introduction

Intrusion detection stands out as one of the most formidable challenges in cybersecurity, especially with the increasing sophistication of cyberattacks. Unfortunately, traditional signature-based approaches reach their limit against previously unknown threats, also called zero-days. As such, the integration of Machine Learning (ML) techniques has emerged as a promising avenue for enhancing the detection capabilities of intrusion detection systems.

However, the advent of adversarial examples [8,32] poses a severe obstacle to the reliability of ML, specifically in critical tasks such as intrusion detection. They are generated from regular data instances by adding a meticulously crafted perturbation that misleads an ML model. Applied to network data, they enable cyber attackers to either evade ML-based intrusion detection systems or flood the network with false alerts.

© IFIP International Federation for Information Processing 2025
Published by Springer Nature Switzerland AG 2025
S. Katsikas and B. Shafiq (Eds.): DBSec 2025, LNCS 15722, pp. 351–370, 2025.
https://doi.org/10.1007/978-3-031-96590-6_19

In response to the escalating threat of adversarial attacks, research efforts have been directed toward designing effective countermeasures. Among the various defensive approaches, adversarial purification has emerged as a compelling solution to remove the adversarial perturbation from data before processing it. This defense is particularly interesting for intrusion detection, as it can be integrated upstream of the model without retraining. Recent work [22] has demonstrated promising purification performance using diffusion models [11,27].

Diffusion models are generative models inspired by the dynamics of diffusion processes in physics [27]. They consist of a forward process that gradually adds noise to initial data and a backward process that reconstructs that data using a deep neural network. Because diffusion models are trained using examples drawn from the original data distribution, the reconstructed data is expected to adhere to the same distribution, even when the initial data is an adversarial example. Thus, they can be used for adversarial purification: removing the perturbation from adversarial examples to classify them correctly. Furthermore, since they are not explicitly trained on adversarial examples, their purification performance is not limited to a specific adversarial attack.

Despite the recent attention given to adversarial purification with diffusion models, there remains a notable gap in understanding their potential in the context of intrusion detection. This paper fills that gap by studying the purification effects of diffusion models and demonstrating their effectiveness on network intrusion detection. By conducting a comprehensive analysis of the diffusion parameters, we identify optimal configurations maximizing the adversarial robustness with limited impact on the regular performance. We show the effectiveness of our method on two network datasets (UNSW-NB15 [21] and NSL-KDD [34]) and against state-of-the-art adversarial attacks. Moreover, to our knowledge, this is the first investigation of the relationship between the number of diffusion steps and the optimal amount of diffusion noise for adversarial purification. Our findings demonstrate that the optimal amount of diffusion noise depends not on the number of diffusion steps but rather on the amount of adversarial perturbation.

2   Background and Related Work

This section introduces the major approaches to adversarial defense, provides some background on diffusion models, and reviews the literature on diffusion models in intrusion detection systems and adversarial purification.

Adversarial Defenses. The following presents three dominant approaches to defend against adversarial examples [41].

Adversarial training consists of training the model with adversarial examples in addition to the training data [8,18]. Despite its effectiveness, this technique has several drawbacks: (*i*) it requires the retraining of the model and significantly lengthens the training duration, and (*ii*) it protects only against adversarial examples generated with the methods it was trained on.

Adversarial detection consists of a separate classifier deployed upstream of the ML model that detects and discards adversarial examples before they are fed to the model [2]. It is plug-and-play and does not require retraining. Several supervised and unsupervised techniques exist; interested readers may refer to [2] for a detailed review. Unfortunately, adversarial detection also depends on the adversarial attacks on which it was trained. Moreover, since it is a classifier, it can be fooled to some extent [5].

Adversarial purification consists of a separate model deployed upstream of the ML model that removes the perturbation from adversarial examples before they are fed to the model [29,31]. This approach is also plug-and-play, and the purification models are typically trained independently of the ML model. Adversarial purification does not require retraining, and it is, in many cases, independent of the adversarial attacks. This paper focuses on the adversarial purification approach using diffusion models [22].

Adversarial Defenses in Intrusion Detection. ML models and neural networks, in particular, have demonstrated state-of-the-art performance at the intrusion detection task [4]. The threat of adversarial samples has thus been taken seriously and several works can be found on adversarial defenses in network-based intrusion detection. Most of these works focus on a variety of adversarial training techniques [1,35,36,43]. Notably, [1,35], and [36] use Generative Adversarial Networks (GANs) to augment the databases for training a classifier, demonstrating the efficiency of adversarial defenses in the context of intrusion detection.

Diffusion Models. Diffusion models are a class of generative models that leverage the diffusion processes used in physics to learn complex data distributions and samples from them [11,27]. Instead of modeling the distribution like VAEs [14] and GANs [7], they model the process of transforming a simple distribution (e.g., Gaussian noise) into the target distribution through a sequence of steps. They consist of two Markov processes: a *forward* and a *reverse* process.

In the *forward process*, each step involves adding Gaussian noise to the data over T steps until no structure remains; it corresponds to a smooth transition from the complex data distribution to a Gaussian distribution (latent space). The amount of noise added at each step depends on the variance schedule β. In the *reverse process*, each step reverts the corresponding forward step—removes the diffusion noise—to reconstruct the original data distribution. Since the reverse process is mathematically intractable, it is approximated with deep neural networks. In this work, we use discrete diffusion steps, but the continuous case can also be applied; it requires solving stochastic differential equations [30].

In the following, we provide the intuition into the theory behind diffusion models. We consider a dataset x_0 with unknown distribution $x_0 \sim q(x_0)$. For a given number T of steps, we consider the Markov chain $(x_t)_{t \leq T}$ with transitions

$$q(x_{t+1}|x_t) = \mathcal{N}\left(x_{t+1}; \sqrt{1 - \beta_{t+1}}x_t, \beta_{t+1}I_n\right), \tag{1}$$

that is, we gradually add Gaussian noise with a given variance $(\beta_t)_{t \leq T}$ to the data. If we define $\bar{\alpha}_t = \prod_{i=1}^{i=t} (1 - \beta_i)$, then the cumulative noise addition from the clean data to step t is written:

$$q(x_t|x_0) \simeq \mathcal{N}\left(x_t; \sqrt{\bar{\alpha}_t}x_0, (1 - \bar{\alpha}_t) I_n\right). \tag{2}$$

Equation 2 describes the *forward process* of diffusion models. Note that to ensure the diversity of generated data the variance schedule should guarantee that the data resembles a Gaussian distribution at the end of the forward process:

$$q(x_T|x_0) \simeq \mathcal{N}(x_T; 0, I_n). \tag{3}$$

The *reverse process* consists of generating examples from the original data distribution using the reverse Markov chain; it starts from a Gaussian distribution with transitions

$$p(x_t|x_{t+1}) = \mathcal{N}(x_{t+1}; \mu_\theta(x_t, t), \Sigma_\theta(x_t, t)), \tag{4}$$

where θ represents the parameters of the deep neural network used to estimate the diffusion noise to be removed.

Adversarial Purification with Diffusion Models. Adversarial purification is the process of removing the perturbation from adversarial examples to classify them correctly. This process can be seen as a generative task and approached with diffusion models. The gradual addition of Gaussian noise in the forward step submerses the adversarial perturbation, but the data becomes too noisy to be correctly classified. Thus, the reverse step reconstructs the data in the original distribution without adversarial perturbations.

Furthermore, the forward process does not need to complete T steps and reach a Gaussian distribution. There should be enough added noise to submerse the adversarial perturbation, but not too much, as it damages the data structure and decreases the accuracy. The forward process should stop at the optimal diffusion step t^*, where the diffusion noise suffices to remove the adversarial perturbation while preserving the structure for the classification [22].

After this concept was introduced in [22], later work leveraged guided diffusion models for adversarial purification [37,39]. Authors in [16] train a robust guidance with an adversarial loss and apply it to the reverse process. Diffusion models are also used to purify backdoors in poisoned models [26].

Diffusion Models in Intrusion Detection. Intrusion detection systems benefit greatly from the automation provided by ML, including deep learning [10,17,28]. However, network intrusion datasets are often imbalanced; benign traffic outweighs malicious traffic. Due to their generative capabilities, diffusion models are successfully applied in data augmentation for balancing network datasets [9,33,44]. The diffusion model can also detect intrusion by learning the

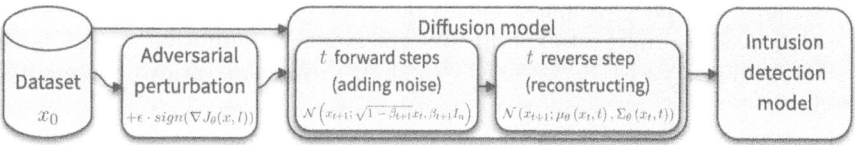

Fig. 1. Methodology scheme: dataset instances x_0 undergo adversarial perturbation, the diffusion model's purification, and then the intrusion detection classification.

distribution of benign traffic. The difference between the original and reconstructed data is then used to detect malicious traffic [38, 40].

However, to our knowledge, no prior research has investigated the adversarial purification potential of diffusion models in the context of intrusion detection. This paper represents the foremost initiative to address diffusion-based adversarial purification in intrusion detection.

3   Methodology

As shown in Fig. 1, our methodology consists of a diffusion model deployed upstream of the intrusion detection model. The diffusion model serves as a "filter" that removes adversarial perturbations. It adds noise to the data for several steps t and reconstructs it through the reverse diffusion process involving the diffusion neural network. The data, whether original or adversarial, are first purified by the diffusion model and then fed to the intrusion detection model to determine if they are benign or malicious.

The intrusion detection model is a Fully Connected Neural Network (FCNN) with fixed hyperparameters throughout the experiments. It comprises a fully connected neural network with 5 hidden layers of 256, 512, 1024, 512, and 256 Rectified Linear Units (ReLU). It is trained for $10,000$ epochs, and the parameters are optimized using Adam with a learning rate of 10^{-5}.

The literature presents more sophisticated architectures of intrusion detection [12]. However, FCNNs are advantageous due to their simplicity and interpretability, providing a clear baseline without the confounding factors and biases of sophisticated architectures. Simple models facilitate theoretical analysis, reproducibility, and benchmarking, enabling easier comparisons. Moreover, insights gained from FCNNs can be generalized to improve more complex models.

The diffusion models are trained according to [11, Algorithm 1]. We consider T discrete diffusion steps. Instead of having a separate neural network for each timestep [27], we encode the timesteps as sinusoidal embeddings and add them to each layer of the diffusion neural network [11].

The purification results are recorded across the diffusion steps. For each $t \in [1, T]$, we apply t forward diffusion steps to the data instance x_0 to get x_t; then we apply t reverse diffusion steps to x_t to get $\hat{x}_0$, the reconstruction of x_0.

The variance schedule β is linearly distributed (T evenly spaced values between β_1 and β_T). Across different experiments, the number of diffusion steps T is 100 or 1000, while β_1 varies between 10^{-5} and 10^{-4}, and β_T varies between 10^{-4} and 10^{-1}.

The diffusion neural networks are fully connected neural networks with 10 hidden layers; each hidden layer typically consists of 960 ReLU units, except for the experiments that compare neural network architectures. The diffusion neural networks are trained for $200,000$ epochs, where each epoch consists of predicting a random step of the reverse process for each dataset instance. The loss function is a Mean Squared Error (MSE), and the parameters are optimized using AdamW with a learning rate of 10^{-4}.

The metrics recorded during the experiments evaluate two aspects of diffusion models: (i) the reconstruction performance by recording the reconstruction loss (MSE between the original data and the reconstructed data) for a diffusion step t, and (ii) the adversarial purification performance by feeding the reconstructed data to the intrusion detection model and recording its accuracy.

The optimal diffusion step $t^* \in [1, T]$ is the step that maximizes the intrusion detection accuracy on adversarial examples [22]. It should be large enough to dilute the adversarial perturbation with diffusion noise. However, the larger it is, the more data structure it dilutes, which decreases the test accuracy.

Implementation. All experiments are carried out on two prominent, publicly available, network datasets: NSL-KDD [34], which has been widely used as a standard benchmark in network intrusion detection research and allows for direct comparison with a vast body of previous major work in intrusion detection; and UNSW-NB15 [21] a more recent dataset which is representative of modern network traffic [24]. The latter was created using real network traffic from the IXIA PerfectStorm tool, providing more realistic and diverse attack scenarios compared to older datasets. For further details on the implementation of our experiments, we make our code publicly available[1].

4   Results

In this section, we present the results of our experiments. We first analyze the reconstruction loss and the accuracy of the intrusion detection model on reconstructed data. We compare the robustness of the intrusion detection model with respect to the level of diffusion applied to the data. We aim to find the optimal diffusion step t^* that removes the adversarial perturbation and increases the robustness while minimizing the repercussions on non-adversarial data.

Furthermore, we analyze the impact of several diffusion parameters on the purification performance: the number of steps T, the initial variance β_1, and the

---

[1] Github repository: https://github.com/mamerzouk/adversarial-purification/.

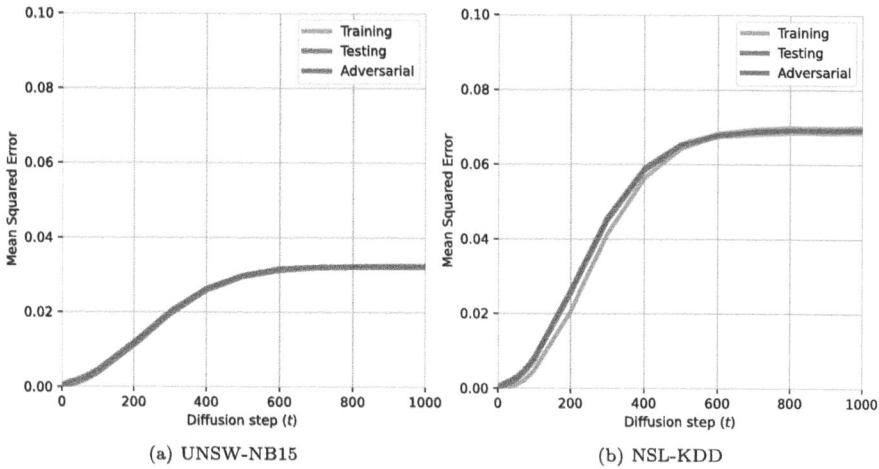

Fig. 2. Reconstruction loss over the diffusion steps t

final variance β_T. Finally, we study the impact of the adversarial perturbation amplitude ϵ on the optimal diffusion step t^* and compare our purification model against five state-of-the-art adversarial attacks. The figures present the results on both UNSW-NB15 and NSL-KDD; the values are the mean and standard deviation over 10 randomly initialized runs.

Unless otherwise noted, the diffusion models in these experiments use the standard diffusion parameters proposed in the previous work [11]: $\beta_1 = 10^{-4}$, $\beta_T = 0.02$, and $T = 1000$.

Reconstruction Loss and Accuracy over t. Figure 2 shows the reconstruction loss over the diffusion steps t, while Fig. 3 shows the accuracy of the intrusion detection model on the same reconstructed data over the diffusion steps t.

Figure 2 shows that the reconstruction loss increases similarly for all three sets, the lines even overlap on UNSW-NB15.Indeed, as noise is added gradually, the data structure is slowly destroyed.The more diffusion steps are applied, the more noise is added, and the harder it is to reconstruct precisely the data. After 600 steps, the reconstruction loss plateaued around 0.03 and 0.07 on UNSW-NB15 and NSL-KDD, respectively.Moreover, we notice that the reconstruction loss on adversarial examples is slightly superior to that on the original testing set.The difference in the reconstruction losses can also be used as an indicator for detecting adversarial examples.This avenue is not investigated in this paper, as adversarial detection approaches are out of our scope.

The accuracy curve in Fig. 3 corroborates the previous results: the training and testing accuracy decrease as the diffusion step increases due to the damaged data structure.It becomes more challenging for the intrusion detection model to distinguish benign and malicious traffic, which decreases its accuracy. After 600 steps, the reconstructed data is too noisy to be classified correctly.

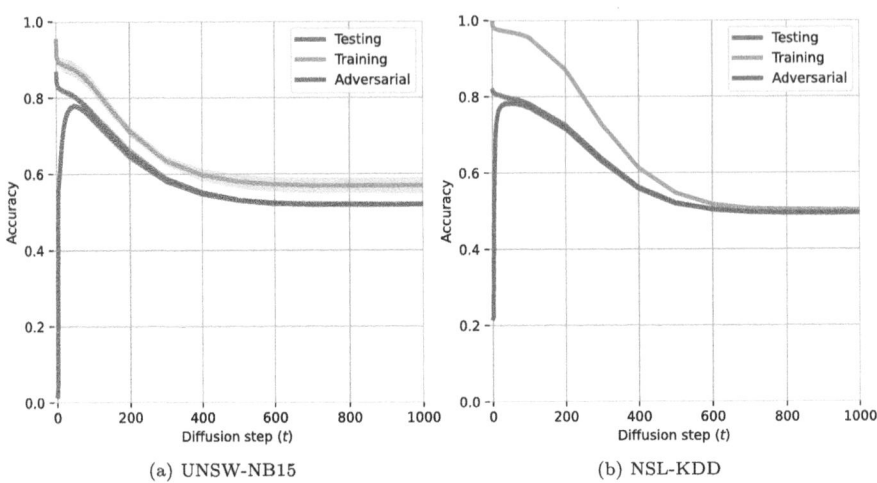

(a) UNSW-NB15   (b) NSL-KDD

Fig. 3. Intrusion detection accuracy over the diffusion steps t (Color figure online)

Purification Performance. In order to evaluate the robustness of the intrusion detection after the diffusion model's purification, we focus on the red line in Fig. 3, which represents the accuracy of the intrusion detection model on adversarial examples. Those adversarial examples were generated from the testing set using the targeted Fast Gradient Sign Method (FGSM) with a perturbation amplitude $\epsilon = 0.03$. At step 0, before purification, the accuracy on adversarial data is 0.02, while it is 0.86 on the original test data, indicating that the adversarial attack succeeded in misleading the intrusion detection model. After a few diffusion steps, the adversarial accuracy increases drastically. The added diffusion noise dilutes the adversarial perturbation that misleads the model while preserving enough data structure for a good classification. After 44 steps, the adversarial accuracy peaks at 78% while the test accuracy is 80%. This diffusion step t^* is optimal as it maximizes the accuracy on adversarial examples while minimizing the impact on the non-adversarial test data. This result empirically shows the purification capabilities of diffusion models in intrusion detection.

After the peak, the structure damage due to the addition of diffusion noise decreases the adversarial accuracy. Since the adversarial perturbation has been removed, the difference between the test and adversarial accuracy disappears; it is below 0.01 after $t = 90$. Both values decrease until they reach random classification when the reconstructed data is too noisy.

Variance Schedule. The variance of the Gaussian noise added at step t of the diffusion process is denoted β_t. It follows a linear distribution of T evenly spaced values between β_1 and β_T. The variance schedule is an essential parameter of the diffusion process; we hypothesize that it is also critical to the purification capabilities of diffusion models. In the following, we study the impact of the variance schedule β on the purification capabilities of the diffusion model through

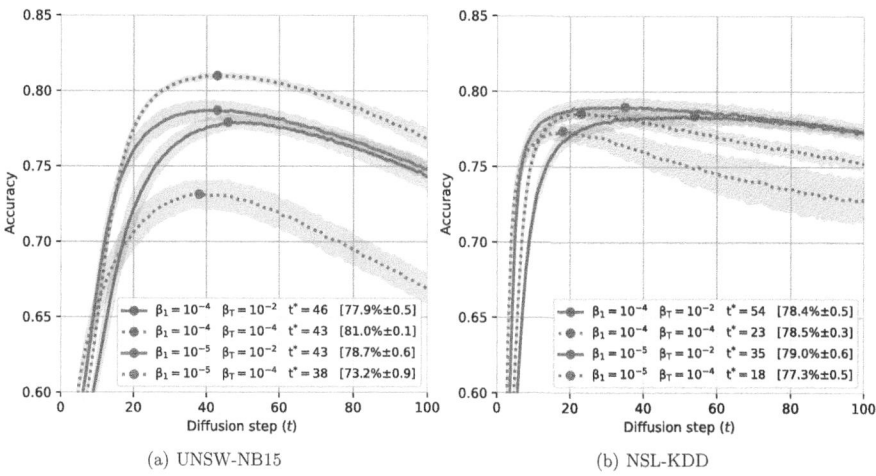

Fig. 4. Intrusion detection accuracy over diffusion step t for different β_1. Continuous lines for $\beta_T = 10^{-2}$ and dotted lines for $\beta_T = 10^{-4}$. The marker indicates the maximum accuracy reached at the optimal diffusion step t^*.

the accuracy of the intrusion detection model on purified examples. Using a fixed $T = 1000$, we vary both β_1 and β_T to find an optimal schedule.

Figure 4 shows the impact of β_1, the first value of the variance schedule. If we focus on the continuous lines, corresponding to $\beta_T = 10^{-2}$, we do not see a significant difference between the two values of β_1. However, with a smaller β_T, the difference between β_1 becomes significant. The dotted lines, corresponding to $\beta_T = 10^{-4}$, show a large difference between the two values of β_1. As the final β decreases, the difference between the accuracy of the two β_1 values increases. The impact of the initial variance β_1 is therefore linked to the length of the variance schedule $\beta_T - \beta_1$ and becomes less significant as the interval increases. This result suggests that β_T plays an influential role in the purification.

Figure 5 shows the impact of β_T, the final variance of the diffusion schedule. The figure shows an increasing accuracy with smaller β_T values. The intuition is that as β_T decreases, the interval between successive variance values decreases, which makes the noising more gradual and easier for the neural network to reconstruct. On UNSW-NB15, the maximum accuracy value is $81\% \pm 0.1$ at $t^* = 43$, it was reached with the smallest value $\beta_T = 10^{-4}$, which represents a constant variance schedule (since $\beta_1 = 10^{-4}$). On NSL-KDD, the maximum accuracy value is very close between when $\beta_1 \leq 10^{-2}$, but $\beta_1 \leq 10^{-4}$ is the earliest to achieve 78.5 ± 0.3 after only $t^* = 23$.

Number of Diffusion Steps T. In addition to the initial and final perturbation values β_1 and β_T, the diffusion process is characterized by the number of diffusion steps T. This parameter determines the granularity of the diffusion since a larger number of steps T makes the step size smaller.

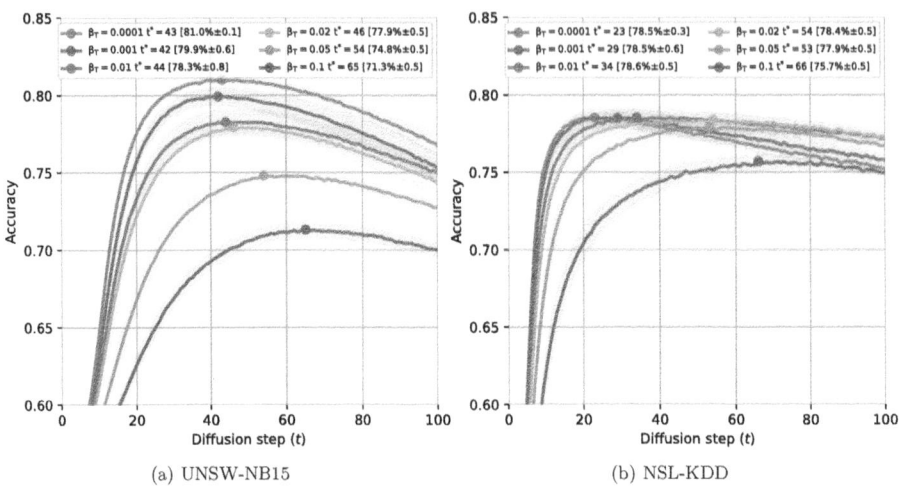

Fig. 5. Intrusion detection accuracy over diffusion step t for different β_T

In the following, we study how the number of diffusion steps T affects the optimal diffusion steps t^*. We compare diffusion models with $T = 100$ and $T = 1000$ with respect to the optimal diffusion step t^* and identify how it translates to an equivalent amount of noise.

Figure 6 shows the impact of the number of diffusion steps T over three references: the diffusion step t, the variance step β_t, and the composed variance σ_t^2. This experiment uses the standard diffusion parameters to focus the analysis on when the optimum is recorded rather than its value. With the optimal variance interval recorded in Fig. 5, $\beta_1 = \beta_T = 10^{-4}$, the 1000-step diffusion model largely over-performs the 100-step one on UNSW-NB15, as shown in Fig. 11 (Appendix A).

In the first part of Fig. 6, we see the accuracy across the diffusion step t. The $T = 100$ diffusion model reaches its optimum at $t^* = 19$ and $t^* = 11$, while the $T = 1000$ reaches its optimum at $t^* = 46$ and $t^* = 54$ on UNSW-NB15 and NSL-KDD, respectively. This indicates a slower evolution when $T = 1000$, which is coherent since the variance steps are smaller. Therefore, we plot the same values with respect to the variance steps β_t to find a similarity. In the second part of Fig. 6, the x-axis corresponds to β_t and covers the whole interval from 0 to $\beta_T = 0.02$. However, the optimum is still reached at distant values of β. For $T = 100$, it is reached with $\beta^* = 0.0037$ and $\beta^* = 0.0021$, while for $T = 1000$, it is reached with $\beta^* = 0.0010$ and $\beta^* = 0.0012$ in UNSW-NB15 and NSL-KDD, respectively.

β_t is the amount of variance applied at the diffusion step t, but it does not correspond to the total variance applied to the initial data x_0. Indeed, the diffusion forward process is a composition of Gaussian distributions with gradual variances β_t. The total (composed) variance σ_t^2 of such composition is the sum of the individual variances, $\sigma_t^2 = 1 - \bar{\alpha}_t$ (Eq. 2).

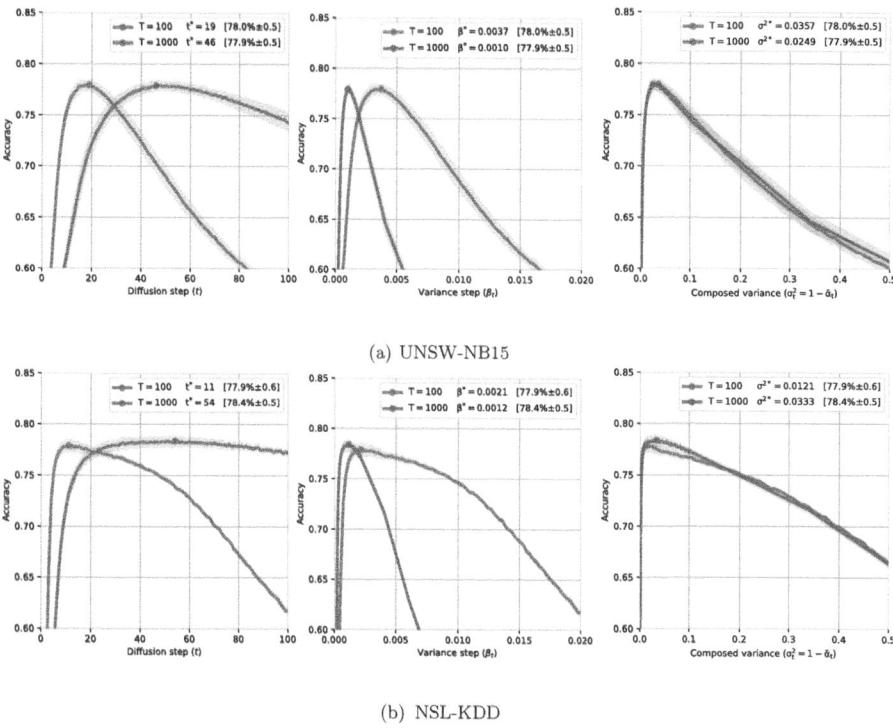

(a) UNSW-NB15

(b) NSL-KDD

Fig. 6. Intrusion detection accuracy over t, β_t, and σ_t^2 for different number of diffusion steps T

The third part of Fig. 6 shows the accuracy across the composed variance σ_t where the two lines overlap, indicating a similar accuracy regardless of the number of diffusion steps T. The optimum is reached at $\sigma_t^2 = 0.0249$ and $\sigma_t^2 = 0.0333$ for $T = 1000$, and $\sigma_t^2 = 0.0357$ and $\sigma_t^2 = 0.0121$ for $T = 100$ on UNSW-NB15 and NSL-KDD, respectively. Considering the scale of σ_T^2 in Fig. 6, the optimum values are relatively close. We note from this experiment that the optimal noise added σ^{2*} approaches 0.03, which corresponds to the adversarial perturbation amplitude ϵ used in these experiments. This result suggests a dependence between the optimal noise amount and the perturbation amplitude.

Adversarial Perturbation Amplitude ϵ. Beyond the diffusion parameters, the purification performance of diffusion models depends on the amount of adversarial perturbation ϵ added to the data. Figure 7 shows the accuracy of the intrusion detection model on increasing ϵ values. It demonstrates how the purification performance decreases as the perturbation amplitude increases. The accuracy at t^* goes from $79.8\% \pm 0.5$ and $79.5\% \pm 0.5$ when $\epsilon = 0.01$ to $76.3\% \pm 0.5$ and $77.5\% \pm 0.5$ when $\epsilon = 0.05$ on UNSW-NB15 and NSL-KDD, respectively. Another pattern is that it takes more diffusion steps to reach an optimum as ϵ

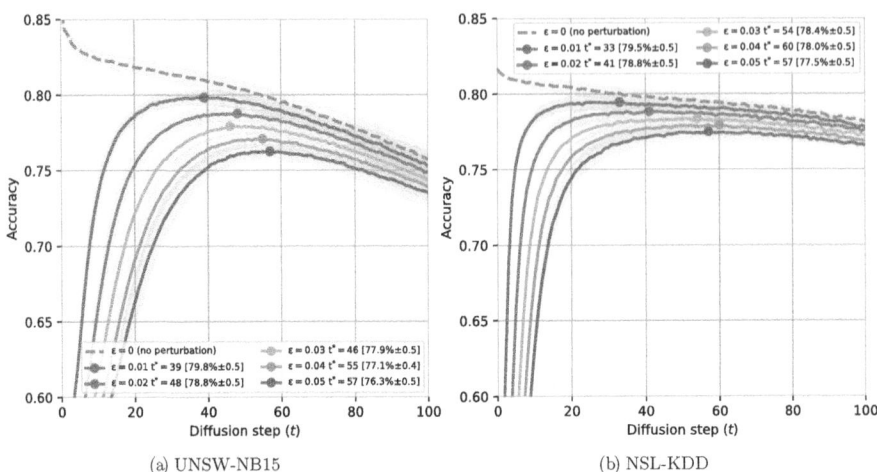

(a) UNSW-NB15   (b) NSL-KDD

Fig. 7. Intrusion detection accuracy over the diffusion step t for different adversarial perturbation amplitudes ϵ generated with FGSM (Color figure online)

increases. The two phenomena are linked: the diffusion model needs to add more perturbation to dilute a larger ϵ, thus taking more diffusion steps. However, the test accuracy (purple line) decreases as more noise is added. Since it represents an upper bound on the adversarial accuracy, it causes the optimal adversarial accuracy to decrease as ϵ increases.

Adversarial Attacks. The efficiency of adversarial examples also depends on the method used to generate them. Various methods exist, each optimizing different distance norms and criteria. While previous experiments show how diffusion models considerably improve the adversarial accuracy of intrusion detection models, they have only been tested on one adversarial attack (FGSM). Here, we study how the purification performance is generalized to other adversarial examples' generation methods. We compare five well-established methods, namely: DeepFool [20], Jacobian-based Saliency Map Attack (JSMA) [23], Fast Gradient Sign Method (FGSM) [8], Basic Iterative Method (BIM) [15], and Carlini&Wagner's L_2 attack [6].

Figure 8 shows the adversarial accuracy of the intrusion detection model for the adversarial attacks and the testing set baseline. We note that the diffusion models successfully purify adversarial examples from all 5 generation methods. However, the optimal adversarial accuracy and diffusion step vary from one method to the other. Carlini&Wagner's attack is the most resistant to adversarial purification, with a maximum adversarial accuracy of $73.9\% \pm 2$ and $75.8\% \pm 0.8$ on UNSW-NB15 and NSL-KDD, respectively. The optimum is reached after only 17 steps on UNSW-NB15, 2.7 times faster than FGSM. On NSL-KDD, the adversarial accuracy is stable between 30 and 100, making t^* less accurate.

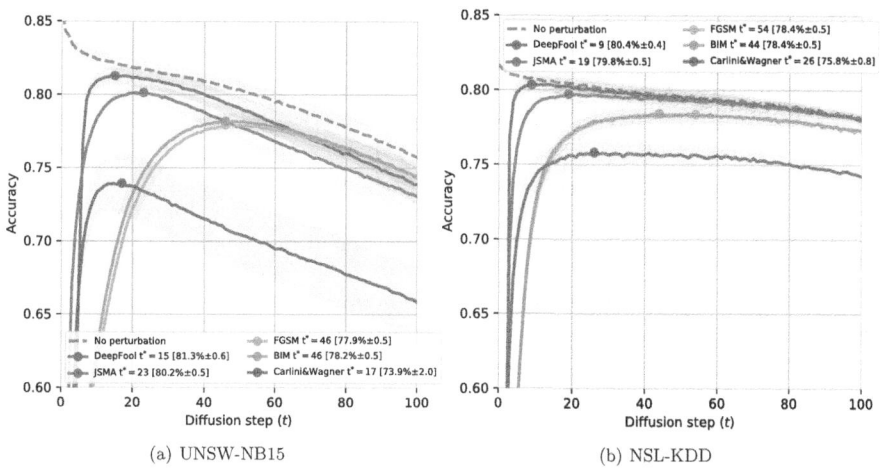

(a) UNSW-NB15   (b) NSL-KDD

Fig. 8. Accuracy over the diffusion step t for different adversarial attacks

FGSM and BIM achieve similar performance; FGSM reaches a maximum of $77.9\% \pm 0.5$ and $78.4\% \pm 0.5$, while BIM reaches a maximum of $78.2\% \pm 0.5$ and $78.4\% \pm 0.5$ on UNSW-NB15 and NSL-KDD, respectively. The optimal diffusion steps are also very close between the two. This similarity is explained by the fact that BIM is based on FGSM; it applies small FGSM steps iteratively (100 in our experiments) to optimize the adversarial examples. However, the iterative approach does not make BIM's adversarial examples more robust to our diffusion-based adversarial purification. The diffusion models achieve the highest purification performance on DeepFool's adversarial examples, with a maximum accuracy of $81.3\% \pm 0.6$ and $80.4\% \pm 0.4$ on UNSW-NB15 and NSL-KDD, respectively, closely followed by JSMA with a maximum accuracy of $80.2\% \pm 0.5$ and $79.8\% \pm 0.5$ on UNSW-NB15 and NSL-KDD, respectively. DeepFool and JSMA also had the fastest-growing adversarial accuracy values among other attacks, almost reaching the testing accuracy upper bound.

5   Discussion

Diffusion Neural Network. The size of the neural network has a considerable impact on the reconstruction loss of the diffusion model. Larger neural networks converge faster and reach lower reconstruction loss values due to their capacity to model more complex patterns and learn better representations. The main obstacle to using larger neural networks is that they take longer to process the data, making the training and reconstruction longer. The diffusion neural network should be hyperparameterized with particular attention to domain-specific time constraints, especially in network intrusion detection, where the reaction time is critical.

In addition to the size of the diffusion neural network, other hyperparameters impact the reconstruction loss and, potentially, the purification performance. The choice of the loss function, the optimization algorithm, and the learning rate affect the convergence time and help find better optimums. Finally, fully connected neural networks can be replaced with more sophisticated neural network architectures that model the diffusion process more precisely. In sum, optimizing diffusion neural networks is a promising avenue for improving the reconstruction loss, the purification performance, and even the processing time of diffusion models.

Variance Schedul β. The variance schedule determines the amount of noise added at each step of the forward diffusion process. In the experiments, the schedule is linear—it consists of T evenly space values between β_1 and β_T. This schedule is essential for adversarial purification, since adding too little noise does not remove the adversarial perturbation, and too much noise corrupts the data structure. The importance of β_1, the variance of the first diffusion step, depends on the total length of the diffusion schedule $\beta_T - \beta_1$. When the schedule is small, the choice of the starting value makes a considerable difference in the purification capabilities. As the difference between β_1 and β_T increases, β_1 is less significant since it has little impact on the rest of the variance values.

On the other hand, the last value β_T has a more significant impact on the variance schedule, which also extends to the purification performance. In the standard setting, where $T = 1000$, $\beta_1 = 10^{-4}$, and $\beta_T = 0.02$, a smaller value of β_T leads to a better adversarial accuracy. The best purification performance was recorded with the smallest value $\beta_T = \beta_1 = 10^{-4}$, which describes a constant variance schedule.

As opposed to generative models, diffusion models in adversarial purification do not require the forward process to reach a Gaussian distribution $\mathcal{N}(x_T; 0, I_n)$ after T steps. Therefore, there is more freedom in choosing the diffusion parameters to optimize the adversarial accuracy.

Number of Diffusion Steps T. The number of diffusion steps affects multiple aspects of the diffusion process. It determines the size of the variance schedule β and its values since there are T evenly spaced values. In the best-performing case $\beta_T = \beta_1 = 10^{-4}$, the number of diffusion steps makes a considerable difference in favor of a larger T. Having the same variance schedule divided into more variance steps allows the neural network to learn more details about the applied noise, which are then helpful to accurately reconstruct the data in the reverse process.

The number of diffusion steps also affects the optimal diffusion step t^*; it happens earlier in the process when T is smaller. This is explained by the fact that the diffusion steps t do not correspond to an equivalent variance step β_t. However, even when considering β_t instead of t, the reconstruction curve does not match. This is because the β_t values are gradually added to the data (Eq. 1) according to the variance step; they do not represent the total variance applied to the data. Instead, we consider the variance of the composition, $\sigma_t^2 = 1 - \bar{\alpha}$, which makes the values of $T = 100$ and $T = 1000$ match. The total variance that maximizes the adversarial accuracy, σ^{2*} is very close between the two different T values. Furthermore, the optimal variance σ^{2*} approaches the value of the perturbation amplitude ϵ, demonstrating the dependence of the diffusion noise on the adversarial perturbation.

In sum, diffusion models with more diffusion steps achieve better adversarial accuracy with an optimal variance schedule. However, it takes more steps to reach optimum, translating into a longer purification time. Thus, the choice of T should also consider the time constraints that characterize the application domain.

Adversarial Perturbation Amplitude. The diffusion-based adversarial purification effectively removes adversarial perturbations from network traffic data. However, the effectiveness of this method varies slightly depending on the nature of the adversarial examples. In the case of adversarial examples generated with FGSM, the parameter ϵ determines the amount of perturbation added to the data. As the ϵ increases, more noise is required to dilute the perturbation, making the optimum occur later in terms of diffusion steps. Another side effect is that the extra required noise also dilutes some of the data structure, thus decreasing the test accuracy, representing an upper bound to the adversarial accuracy. Therefore, the maximum adversarial accuracy decreases as ϵ increases.

Adversarial Attacks. In addition to the perturbation amplitude ϵ, the purification process is sensitive to the adversarial examples' generation method. The results show a considerable gap in the adversarial accuracy between different methods. In particular, DeepFool and JSMA are easier to purify and approach the upper bound of the test accuracy after a few diffusion steps, and FGSM and BIM achieve close performance due to their similarities. Carlini&Wagner's L_2 adversarial examples are the most resistant to purification; this is due to its iterative nature and the choice of the objective function [5, Section 2.6]. Nonetheless, our method still recovers up to 75% of the original test accuracy.

Adversary's Constraints. The adversarial example generation method and the adversarial perturbation amplitude are both parameters controlled by the adversary when they generate adversarial examples. However, they are constrained in the amount of perturbation they can add. A larger adversarial perturbation can increase the chances of being detected, cancel the purpose of the data, or even break its consistency, especially for highly structured data like network traffic [3,19].

While we acknowledge the importance of data consistency and structure in network traffic, the state-of-the-art adversarial attacks we use were mainly developed for computer vision tasks; thus they perturb all data features without awareness of their structure. In our experiments, we consider the worst-case scenario in which the attacker perturbs all data features, establishing a lower bound on the robustness of our method. If additional constraints are imposed on the attacker, we hypothesize that our defense method can only perform better compared to the worst-case scenario assumed in our experiments. However, in order to optimize the diffusion parameters, the design of real-world diffusion-based adversarial purification models should consider a realistic threat model.

Comparison with Other Defenses We acknowledge that our method is only evaluated against the baseline test accuracy. We argue that our results cannot be directly compared to other defense techniques for three reasons:

1. We could not find any research addressing adversarial purification, or any post-training defense, in intrusion detection. This gap in the literature indicates that our approach represents a novel contribution to the field.
2. The adversarial defenses presented in Sect. 2 applied to different intrusion detection datasets: [1] uses CICIDS2017 [25] and several other datasets; [36] and [42] use CICIDS2018 [25]; [35] uses KDD99.
3. The they also use different metrics: F1 score and FNR in [1]; attack success rate and other metrics in [42]; while [36] and [35] use accuracy.

6   Conclusion

Diffusion models are a promising approach to adversarial purification. Their seamless integration with existing systems and generalization across attack methods make them particularly interesting in the context of intrusion detection.

Throughout this paper, we have demonstrated the effectiveness of diffusion models in mitigating the threat of adversarial examples against intrusion detection. We have compared several diffusion neural network sizes, which show that larger neural networks yield lower loss values despite their increased demands in time and computational resources. Our analysis of the variance schedule indicates the importance of the final variance β_T in determining the purification performance, with smaller values achieving the highest accuracy. Furthermore, we have shown that the optimal amount of diffusion noise σ^{2^*} is nearly constant regardless of the number of diffusion steps T and that it approaches the value of the perturbation amplitude ϵ. However, in terms of purification performance, diffusion models with a larger T display better adversarial accuracy despite requiring more diffusion steps. Finally, we benchmarked our method against five state-of-the-art adversarial attacks and an increasing perturbation amplitude.

While scalability and computational complexity remain the main challenges for diffusion models in intrusion detection, especially for inline detection, we envision future research endeavors to refine and optimize diffusion models for practical deployment. As novel adversarial attacks emerge and challenge adversarial defenses [13], our future work will focus on adapting diffusion-based purification to these attacks. Ultimately, complementing diffusion models with other defensive techniques remains necessary to prevent a single point of failure.

Acknowledgments. This work was supported by Mitacs through the Mitacs Accelerate International program and the CRITiCAL chair. It was enabled in part by support provided by Calcul Québec, Compute Ontario, the BC DRI Group, and the Digital Research Alliance of Canada. This work has also received support from the French government through the "France 2030" program, as part of the IRT SystemX Program CYBELIA.

A   Additional Results

This appendix provides additional results on the training reconstruction loss of the diffusion models and the impact of the number of diffusion steps T on

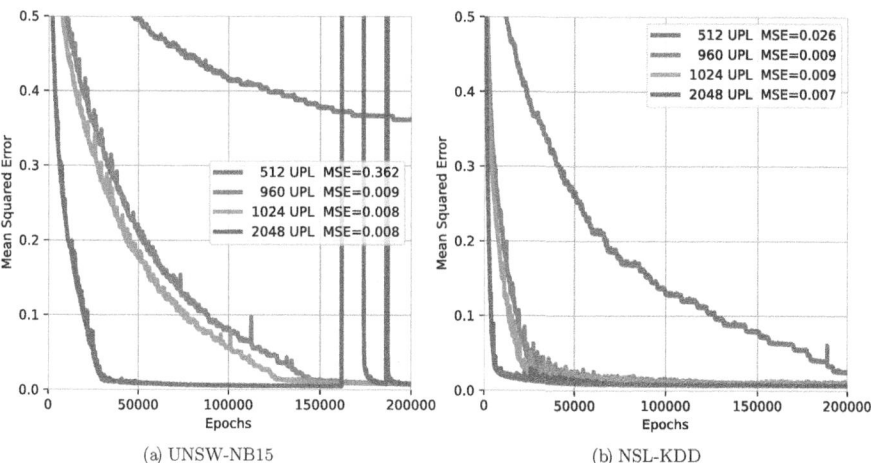

(a) UNSW-NB15   (b) NSL-KDD

Fig. 9. Reconstruction loss over training epochs for different neural network sizes

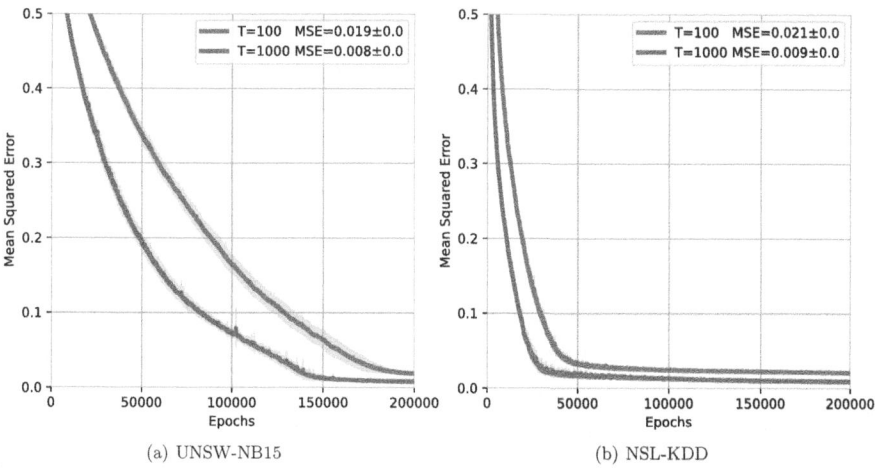

(a) UNSW-NB15   (b) NSL-KDD

Fig. 10. Reconstruction loss over training epochs for $T = 100$ and $T = 1000$

purification performance. These details contribute to a deeper understanding of the optimal configurations for maximizing adversarial robustness and minimizing computational costs (Figs. 9,10 and 11).

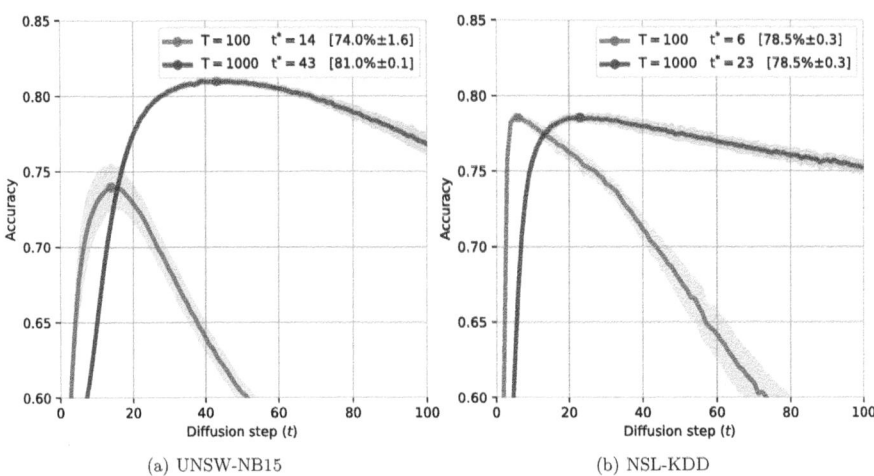

(a) UNSW-NB15   (b) NSL-KDD

Fig. 11. Accuracy over the diffusion step t for different number of diffusion steps t using the optimal variance interval recorded in Fig. 5: $\beta_1 = \beta_T = 10^{-4}$

References

1. Abdelaty, M., Scott-Hayward, S., Doriguzzi-Corin, R., Siracusa, D.: GADoT: GAN-based adversarial training for robust DDoS attack detection. In: IEEE Conference on Communications and Network Security (CNS) (2021)
2. Aldahdooh, A., Hamidouche, W., Fezza, S.A., Déforges, O.: Adversarial example detection for DNN models: A review and experimental comparison. Artif. Intell. Rev. (2022)
3. Apruzzese, G., Andreolini, M., Ferretti, L., Marchetti, M., Colajanni, M.: Modeling realistic adversarial attacks against network intrusion detection systems. Digital Threats (2022)
4. Buczak, A.L., Guven, E.: A survey of data mining and machine learning methods for cyber security intrusion detection. IEEE Commun. Surv. Tutorials (2016)
5. Carlini, N., Wagner, D.: Adversarial examples are not easily detected: bypassing ten detection methods. In: ACM Workshop on Artificial Intelligence and Security (2017)
6. Carlini, N., Wagner, D.: Towards evaluating the robustness of neural networks. In: IEEE Symposium on Security and Privacy (SP) (2017)
7. Goodfellow, I.J., et al.: Generative Adversarial Nets. In: Advances in Neural Information Processing Systems (2014)
8. Goodfellow, I.J., Shlens, J., Szegedy, C.: Explaining and harnessing adversarial examples. In: International Conference on Learning Representations (2015)

9. Han, F., Ye, P., She, C., Duan, S., Wang, L., Liu, D.: Mmid-bench: a comprehensive benchmark for multi-domain multi-category intrusion detection. IEEE Trans. Intell. Veh. (2024)

10. He, K., Kim, D.D., Asghar, M.R.: Adversarial machine learning for network intrusion detection systems: a comprehensive survey. IEEE Commun. Surv. Tutorials (2023)

11. Ho, J., Jain, A., Abbeel, P.: Denoising diffusion probabilistic models. In: Advances in Neural Information Processing Systems (2020)

12. Javaid, A., Niyaz, Q., Sun, W., Alam, M.: A deep learning approach for network intrusion detection system. EAI Endorsed Trans. Secur. Saf. (2016)

13. Kang, M., Song, D., Li, B.: Diffattack: evasion attacks against diffusion-based adversarial purification. In: Advances in Neural Information Processing Systems (2023)

14. Kingma, D.P., Welling, M.: Auto-encoding variational bayes (2022). arXiv:1312.6114

15. Kurakin, A., Goodfellow, I.J., Bengio, S.: Adversarial examples in the physical world. In: International Conference on Learning Representations (2017)

16. Lin, G., Tao, Z., Zhang, J., Tanaka, T., Zhao, Q.: Robust diffusion models for adversarial purification (2024). arXiv:2403.16067

17. Liu, H., Lang, B.: Machine learning and deep learning methods for intrusion detection systems: a survey. Appl. Sci. (2019)

18. Madry, A., Makelov, A., Schmidt, L., Tsipras, D., Vladu, A.: Towards deep learning models resistant to adversarial attacks. In: International Conference on Learning Representations (2018)

19. Merzouk, M.A., Cuppens, F., Boulahia-Cuppens, N., Yaich, R.: Investigating the practicality of adversarial evasion attacks on network intrusion detection. Ann. Telecommun. 1–13 (2022). https://doi.org/10.1007/s12243-022-00910-1

20. Moosavi-Dezfooli, S.M., Fawzi, A., Frossard, P.: Deepfool: a simple and accurate method to fool deep neural networks. In: IEEE Conference on Computer Vision and Pattern Recognition (2016)

21. Moustafa, N., Slay, J.: Unsw-nb15: a comprehensive data set for network intrusion detection systems (unsw-nb15 network data set). In: 2015 Military Communications and Information Systems Conference (MilCIS) (2015)

22. Nie, W., Guo, B., Huang, Y., Xiao, C., Vahdat, A., Anandkumar, A.: Diffusion models for adversarial purification. In: International Conference on Machine Learning (2022)

23. Papernot, N., McDaniel, P., Jha, S., Fredrikson, M., Celik, Z.B., Swami, A.: The limitations of deep learning in adversarial settings. In: IEEE European Symposium on Security and Privacy (EuroS P) (2016)

24. Ring, M., Wunderlich, S., Scheuring, D., Landes, D., Hotho, A.: A survey of network-based intrusion detection data sets. Comput. Secur. (2019)

25. Sharafaldin, I., Lashkari, A.H., Ghorbani, A.A.: Toward generating a new intrusion detection dataset and intrusion traffic characterization. In: 4th International Conference on Information Systems Security and Privacy (2018)

26. Shi, Y., Du, M., Wu, X., Guan, Z., Sun, J., Liu, N.: Black-box backdoor defense via zero-shot image purification. In: Advances in Neural Information Processing Systems (2023)

27. Sohl-Dickstein, J., Weiss, E., Maheswaranathan, N., Ganguli, S.: Deep unsupervised learning using nonequilibrium thermodynamics. In: International Conference on Machine Learning (2015)

28. Sohn, I.: Deep belief network based intrusion detection techniques: a survey. Expert Syst. Appl. (2021)
29. Song, Y., Kim, T., Nowozin, S., Ermon, S., Kushman, N.: Pixeldefend: leveraging generative models to understand and defend against adversarial examples (2017). arXiv:1710.10766
30. Song, Y., Sohl-Dickstein, J., Kingma, D.P., Kumar, A., Ermon, S., Poole, B.: Score-based generative modeling through stochastic differential equations. In: International Conference on Learning Representations (2021)
31. Srinivasan, V., Rohrer, C., Marban, A., Müller, K.R., Samek, W., Nakajima, S.: Robustifying models against adversarial attacks by langevin dynamics. Neural Netw. (2021)
32. Szegedy, C., et al.: Intriguing properties of neural networks. In: International Conference on Learning Representations (2014)
33. Tang, B., Lu, Y., Li, Q., Bai, Y., Yu, J., Yu, X.: A diffusion model based on network intrusion detection method for industrial cyber-physical systems. Sensors (2023)
34. Tavallaee, M., Bagheri, E., Lu, W., Ghorbani, A.A.: A detailed analysis of the KDD cup 99 data set. In: IEEE Symposium on Computational Intelligence for Security and Defense Applications (2009)
35. Usama, M., Asim, M., Latif, S., Qadir, J., Al-Fuqaha, A.: Generative adversarial networks for launching and thwarting adversarial attacks on network intrusion detection systems. In: 15th International Wireless Communications & Mobile Computing Conference (IWCMC) (2019)
36. Wang, J., Pan, J., AlQerm, I., Liu, Y.: Def-ids: An ensemble defense mechanism against adversarial attacks for deep learning-based network intrusion detection. In: 2021 International Conference on Computer Communications and Networks (ICCCN) (2021)
37. Wang, J., Lyu, Z., Lin, D., Dai, B., Fu, H.: Guided diffusion model for adversarial purification (2022). arXiv:2205.14969
38. Wang, Y., Ding, J., He, X., Wei, Q., Yuan, S., Zhang, J.: Intrusion detection method based on denoising diffusion probabilistic models for UAV networks. Mob. Netw. Appl. (2023)
39. Wu, Q., Ye, H., Gu, Y.: Guided diffusion model for adversarial purification from random noise (2022). arXiv:2206.10875
40. Yang, C., Wang, T., Yan, X.: Ddmt: denoising diffusion mask transformer models for multivariate time series anomaly detection (2023). arXiv:2310.08800
41. Yuan, X., He, P., Zhu, Q., Li, X.: Adversarial examples: attacks and defenses for deep learning. IEEE Trans. Neural Netw. Learn. Syst. (2019)
42. Zhang, C., Costa-Pérez, X., Patras, P.: Adversarial attacks against deep learning-based network intrusion detection systems and defense mechanisms. IEEE/ACM Trans. Netw. (2022)
43. Zhang, K., Zhou, H., Zhang, J., Huang, Q., Zhang, W., Yu, N.: Ada3diff: defending against 3d adversarial point clouds via adaptive diffusion. In: ACM International Conference on Multimedia (2023)
44. Zhang, W., Chen, Z., Chen, D., Li, J., Pan, Y.: Did-ids: a novel diffusion-based imbalanced data intrusion detection system. In: IEEE International Conference on Information, Communication and Networks (ICICN) (2023)

Feature Identification and Study of Attackers' Behaviours Using Honeypots

Junaid Haseeb[1(✉)], Masood Mansoori[2], and Ian Welch[3]

[1] School of Computing and Mathematical Sciences, University of Waikato,
Hamilton, New Zealand
junaid.haseeb@waikato.ac.nz
[2] Canberra School of Professional Studies, University of New South Wales (UNSW),
Canberra, ACT, Australia
m.mansoori@unsw.edu.au
[3] School of Engineering and Computer Science, Victoria University of Wellington,
Wellington, New Zealand
ian.welch@vuw.ac.nz

Abstract. Investigating the attack process followed by automated scripts, tools or botnets and their threat actors is a widely researched area in the cyber security. There has also been emphasis on differentiating attacks performed by humans considering their adaptability which poses a greater threat. Limited number of features such as slower typing speed and typing mistakes in commands issued by human attackers on the compromised systems have been used to detect their presence. This paper presents a study of human attackers by deploying 15 honeypots in five locations worldwide, collecting and analysing attack data for two months. We propose a comprehensive feature set based on characteristics and patterns of issued commands and the usage of alphanumeric, modifiers, cursor and other keys in the attack process. We used these features to distinguish human attackers interacting with honeypots. Moreover, five case studies are discussed to provide insights into actions performed in the attack process. The results show various actions performed by human attackers ranging from executing basic commands for getting device information to more advanced actions such as downloading files, running scripts and removing traces of their activities.

Keywords: Honeypots · IoT · Human attackers · Bots · Deception

1 Introduction

Modern cyber attacks are becoming increasingly sophisticated [14]. To provide better defence, it is necessary to understand the attack process in detail and characterise different types of attackers behind them. Both aspects are connected. The first is about identifying steps taken to perform the attack process, tools, and techniques used; and the second directly influences the first, as various types of attacker may follow different attack processes. The exploitation process

© IFIP International Federation for Information Processing 2025
Published by Springer Nature Switzerland AG 2025
S. Katsikas and B. Shafiq (Eds.): DBSec 2025, LNCS 15722, pp. 371–389, 2025.
https://doi.org/10.1007/978-3-031-96590-6_20

followed for various cyber attacks and specifically the behaviours of botnets targeting Internet of Things (IoT) devices to perform Distributed Denial of Service (DDoS) attacks have been extensively studied [2,5,21,25,36,42]. There also exist human attackers, and they possess unique characteristics that differentiate them from bots. Existing studies detect human attackers considering they are susceptible to making mistakes while typing attack commands on target systems, their typing speed is slower and commands are sent character by character or copied and pasted [6,11,28,31,41]. However, these studies use a limited set of features to detect human attackers and only cover general behaviour.

Why to Study the Behaviour of Human Attackers? Accurately identifying human attackers is an important concern in understanding attack behaviour and their adaptability in the attack process. For example:

- Human attackers can change their attack actions according to the situation, whereas bots operate based on a pre-programmed or pre-defined set of instructions.
- There is a high probability that human attackers will perform the attack process differently according to their skills, domain knowledge, and available resources. On the other hand, the probability of performing similar actions as part of an attack process is higher for bots operated by the same botnet or following the same script.
- Humans can respond to their failed attack actions differently, e.g., they can look for the errors in issued commands and then correct them, can repeat the same command to give it another try or execute another command. In comparison, bots may continue to perform attack actions even if the failure follows the sequence as they are programmed.
- The intentions of human attackers performing attack actions can vary based on what they discover during each phase of the attack process. On the other hand, bots may be limited to achieving a specific goal, such as using the resources of infected devices for DDoS attacks.
- Defending against human attackers is a complex process as humans can think out of the box and perform counter-operations against defensive actions. However, bots are more likely to be rigid in their responses of defensive actions if they can make any response at all.

This paper focusses on identifying human attackers and providing a deeper understanding of how they interact with a target system and studying their attack process. Honeypots are security systems used as decoys allowing attackers to interact with them. As a result, honeypots help in monitoring, analysing, understanding, and modelling attackers' behaviours [12,14]. Honeypots have been widely used to lure attackers into attacking them and then analyse captured attacks to obtain useful information [5,8,23,25,29,33,42]. In this paper, we conduct a large experiment by deploying 15 instances of a medium-interaction honeypot, i.e., Cowrie[1], in five locations including North America, Europe (Amsterdam), South East Asia (Singapore), Australia, and New Zealand for two months.

---

[1] Cowrie SSH/Telnet Honeypot (https://github.com/cowrie/cowrie).

Three instances of honeypots are deployed in each location to capture and analyse attacks. The contributions made by this research include:

- A comprehensive set of features to identify human attackers is proposed. Our feature set includes identifying: 1) instruction patterns, i.e., sending attack commands; 2) usage of modifier keys when pressed simultaneously with alphanumeric keys and function keys; 3) usage of cursor control keys pressed with modifier keys; 4) usage of other keys, e.g., Backspace, Tab, Enter, Spacebar, Delete and 5) usage of shortcut keys for copy, paste, exit and enter.
- We validated our features by analysing the collected data and observing the use of controls, modifiers, cursor and shortcut keys for human attackers as opposed to automated attacks. Furthermore, we found that human attackers made typographical and spelling errors and spent a considerable amount of time getting information about devices once they successfully logged into the target system.
- We also analysed five case studies to discern the characteristics of human attackers in terms of attack actions performed to exploit devices and potential intentions. The analysis shows that within an interactive Shell, they combine the typing of commands character by character with pasting commands from a buffer. The intentions of attacks vary from obtaining basic information to downloading, installing malware files, and removing any traces of attack activities.

2   Related Work

This section discusses existing studies differentiating human attackers from automated attacks, bots, and botnets. We then provide details on the behaviour of human attackers performing cyber attacks reported in the literature.

2.1   Categorising Human Attackers

Barron and Nikiforakis [6] labelled attack sessions performed by humans in their deployed honeypots using three methods. The first method examines whether an attacker pressed Backspace or Delete when interacting with the system by sending a series of commands. The reason for using these indicators is that humans are susceptible to making mistakes while typing. The second method calculates time deltas between keystrokes and maximum delta for each session is obtained. This was assumed that human attackers type slower and the maximum delta value will be higher. The third method they applied was to define the threshold value for the maximum delta. If the value exceeds the specified threshold, the attack session is labelled as human. Udhani et al. [37] identified behavioural traits for human attackers based on the analysis of connection requests received on the honeypot. Their included features are the number of requests, attacker's target, frequency of requests, and passwords used. They defined threshold values for all features to identify human attackers such as if the number of requests is ≤ 10 per minute, targeting different machines ≤ 2 per day, the frequency of requests are ≤ 3 per second and typing default/alphanumeric passwords with a speed of ≤ 3 characters per second.

Filippoupolitis et al. [11] profiled human attackers through observable (i.e. speed, mistakes, antiforensics and success) and nonobservable (i.e. skill, education, risk, gender, goal) features. Observable features were measured based on attackers' activities on a system, and for non-observable features, participants filled in the questionnaire. They applied machine learning techniques to create realistic human profiles. In real-time, a new attack was labelled being performed by human if it matches with a profile. Otherwise, the attacker was indicated as a bot. Nicomette et al. [28] identify intruders as humans based on typographical errors that are corrected using `Backspace` and data sent to the server as character-per-character or blocks (using keyboard shortcuts such as paste).

Wagener et al. [41] designed "Heliza", a high-interaction honeypot in which the concept of insult was introduced responding to attackers' commands. In cases where attackers become overwhelmed and respond to insults, it is considered an indicator of a human attacker performing manual attacks. Another characteristic reported that indicates a high probability of a human attacker is typographic errors in commands. Dang et al. [9] conducted an extensive study to understand attacks on IoT devices. As part of their software honeypot design, they keep track of the terminal's window size event, which they reported as an indicator for detecting the presence of human attackers.

Kemppainen and Kovanen [18] analysed the command data to differentiate if a bot programme or a human produced them. They defined criteria for bot programmes as if: 1) the timestamps of commands are consistent or almost consistent; 2) fixed delays between commands; 3) attack process keep executing commands despite the failure of actions; and 4) in separate sessions, only one command executed and repeated. Variations observed in the above criteria potentially refer to human attackers, as the study mentioned, if one or more criteria is fulfilled, commands are executed by a computer programme. Ramsbrock et al. [31] also labelled some of the attacks carried out manually based on typographical errors in commands.

Keystroke dynamics is another concept for distinguishing between users based on their typing patterns. One of its key application areas is user authentication [32]. The extracted features are related to the timing of the press, release, and hold key [32], the time difference between pressing and releasing a similar key or similar key and a key next to it [30]. The research on keystroke dynamics has been expanded to differentiate between humans and automated attacks/bots. For example, using text-based CAPTCHAs and extracting the information related to press, release, and hold times of keys [3]. Other studies detected malicious linked accounts spreading fake news [26], improved bot detection [10], found fake social media profiles by grouping them based on similar typing patterns [22].

2.2   Behaviour of Human Attackers

Barron and Nikiforakis [6] reported their observations for human attackers once they have logged into the honeypots as: 1) they execute more commands than required to explore compromised system or may make typo errors and then correct them, and 2) they are more focused on listing user files, documents, and exploring information in them. Nicomette et al. [28] categorised two main steps of an attack process and analysed that second step, that is, intrusion, performed mostly by humans. Activities involved as part of this step after gaining access to the honeypot include: 1) changing the password; 2) downloading malicious programmes mainly using wget; 3) if downloading failed, generally the attackers return to the honeypot after several days and execute the same commands; 4) when downloading is successful, attackers uncompressed the file, and 5) use writable directories to hide malicious activities and create their directories inside. Their study also mentioned three other activities that included SSH port scanning, using IRC clients to connect with botmasters, and gaining root privileges [28]. Other studies discussed attackers' intentions, skill level, and attack actions. However, these studies are mainly focused on discussing the behaviour of IoT botnets [2,4,5,21,25,36,42] or attackers in general [9,31,38].

2.3   Key Findings

The features identified in the studies discussed above are suitable to represent the general behaviour of human attackers. However, these features are very well known and it is possible that bots can be programmed to mimic general human behaviour to write commands at various typing speeds, randomly adding delays, and pressing Backspace or Delete keys. Understanding the behaviour of human attackers is an important concern, and there is a need to consider additional features that can be used to detect human attackers. This includes considering other possible usages of keystrokes such as Spacebar, Enter while typing commands, shortcuts, cursor, and other keys. In terms of explicitly discussing the behaviour of human attackers while performing cyber attacks, as far as we know, there exist very few studies. Attacks are evolving continuously, and there is a need to further study human behaviour performing these attacks.

This paper attempts to fill the gaps by introducing a set of features to detect human attackers and report observations collected by analysing multiple case studies of attacks performed by human attackers. The findings reported in this paper resulted from conducting a large experiment to deploy 15 honeypots with different configurations at five geographic locations around the world.

3   Experimental Setup and Data Collection

This section discusses experiment details, honeypots setup, and data collection performed.

3.1   Honeypot System

In the experimental design, we initially need to choose a base honeypot system as the target decoy system. We assume that attackers mostly target the platforms, systems, services, or devices which are wide spread and easy to exploit.

Recently, the IoT market has grown exponentially with its emergence [1,19]. IoT devices support a broad application area, including home automation, industrial control systems, healthcare, and smart cities [4]. However, IoT devices are resource restricted, designed with poor security measures, and their associated configuration and maintenance flaws make them an easy target to infect with malware and use them performing DDoS attacks [1,5,20,27,29]. Simulating the behaviour of IoT devices is not an easy task due to their highly heterogeneous nature [13,24]. Taking this into account, we define a more general criterion for the selection of honeypots based on the findings reported in existing studies [4,5,29] related to how botnets operate to exploit IoT devices:

1. Simulating Secure Shell (SSH) and Telnet protocols. These protocols are used by IoT devices [40,43]
2. Allowing attackers to login into the system to further explore their exploitation process.
3. Providing access to the simulated Shell environment where attackers can interact and execute commands.
4. Providing support for Linux commands.
5. Allowing attackers to access and manipulate the file system, such as downloading, uploading, and removing directories and files.

Cowrie is a medium interaction honeypot that meets the above criteria and has been assigned to the list of IoT honeypots by existing studies [12,34]. Therefore, we decided to use Cowrie as the base honeypot system for our experiment.

3.2   Honeypot Setup Configurations

We used two variants of the Cowrie honeypot for this experiment. One is a default honeypot and the other is custom honeypot.

Default Honeypot: In this variant, we used the Cowrie honeypot with default settings and configured it to receive connection requests on ports 22 and 23 for the SSH and Telnet protocols, respectively. Cowrie with these settings was able to provide essential services according to the criteria above such as simulating a command-based terminal for Shell interaction and execute Linux commands, file system, and a user profile to mimic an appropriate environment.

Custom Honeypot: One of the challenges with the deployment of a honeypot is its inherent suspectable nature considering that a honeypot is designed to simulate an environment. Attackers apply various techniques to detect if they are interacting with a real system [17]. Specifically talking about the Cowrie honeypot, existing studies [7,35,39] have also mentioned various techniques which can be used to detect this honeypot when default configurations are used.

Srinivasa et al. [35] discussed that generating dynamic response, maintaining libraries used for honeypot development, and increasing interaction are among the list of countermeasures to be used against detection fingerprinting attempts made by attackers. Cabral et al. [7] proposed that the advancement of various Cowrie configurations helps avoid detection. Haseeb et al. [16] also theoretically discussed that Cowrie honeypot configurations can be changed to mimic IoT specific profiles, and increasing deception can help avoid detection.

According to the criteria discussed above, the default Cowrie variant will provide the required services. However, the focus of this study is on investigating the behaviour of human attackers. Considering that human attackers are more sophisticated and upon detection of a honeypot, they may leave the system without providing useful information. Therefore, we decided to use another variant of Cowrie, which we call a custom honeypot. The honeypot configurations and components relevant to increasing deception, avoiding detection, and increasing exposure were customised. For modifications discussed below, some of the information for currently running processes and about device were taken from a real device, i.e., cloud-based storage device.

- *Device information:* The default configurations of the honeypot related to showing device information were changed, such as host name, hardware, and software information.
- *Processes information:* The process information was added to the list of processes currently running in the honeypot.
- *Username and password:* The password list was limited to accepting five possible combinations of username and password. This was to make sure that we only did not capture attack campaigns and automated attacks. We included two log-in credentials (one of them with minor modification) in the list which were reported as the part of the Mirai (IoT malware) source code[2].
- *Welcome message:* Welcome message and banner information were changed for simulated Shell environment. This is shown to the attackers once they gain access to the device.
- *Interactive timeout:* The interactive timeout was increased to ten minutes to capture longer activities of attackers. This refers to increasing the time for interactive sessions to terminate.
- *User profile:* The information for default user was changed to another user. For this purpose, all related files were updated to contain the same information about the user profile.
- *Commands support:* The top command dynamically listed the processes running rather than showing a static message.

3.3   Deployment Model

We deployed 15 default and custom honeypot instances in five different geographical locations. The underlying operating system for the machines with honeypots

---

[2] https://github.com/jgamblin/Mirai-Source-Code.

installed was Ubuntu, i.e., a Linux distribution. The honeypots were operational for two months in North America, Europe (Amsterdam), South East Asia (Singapore), Australia, and New Zealand. The purpose of choosing various locations was to collect large attack data. Deploying all honeypots on one location will limit the analysis, as attacks may be location specific.

We deployed one instance of default honeypot and two instances of custom honeypot (each containing a specific user information) in each location. The rationale behind making these deployment decisions cover various aspects and assumptions such as: 1) the custom honeypots are resilient to get into the device and there are high chances that attacks captured on them are not automated attacks which break into the devices as the result of brute force or dictionary attacks; 2) it will enable us to determine how increasing deception as a result of increased restriction on access credentials for the honeypot can affect the type of attack captured and 3) to convince attackers for the custom honeypots that they are accessing real devices in case they are successful in detecting default honeypot on any of the locations.

3.4   Data Collection

Data collection was carried out for two months. Our honeypots stored data in the form of events such as executing commands, downloading and uploading files, and log-in attempts. We did not ask for any personal information such as name, email, address etc. when interacting with deployed honeypots. Also, source IP addresses were masked before data analysis.

When an attacker connects to the honeypot, a unique identifier is assigned, that is, the session id. All information in various events was extracted through session id representing an attacker's activities in each attack session. For our analysis in this study, we limit our scope to interactive attack sessions only, where attackers interact with the system through a command-line system (Shell environment) to perform the attack process. Details on the number of interactive attack sessions received in default and custom honeypots are provided in Fig. 1 and Fig. 2, respectively. It can be seen that there is a significant difference in the number of interactive attack sessions on default and custom honeypots. The reason behind this could be that custom honeypots were resilient to default unrestricted login attempts as we set a specific list of username and password combinations. However, in default honeypots, attackers were allowed to log in with any username and password combination.

4   Feature Identification and Characterising Humans Attackers

In order to differentiate different types of attacker, we need to identify a set of potential features that represent the characteristics of humans.

4.1 Feature Identification

Our feature identification process is based on domain knowledge and the following features are identified:

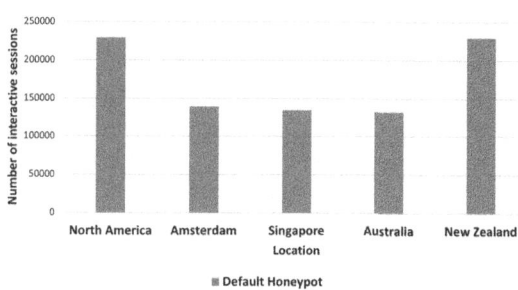

Fig. 1. Interactive sessions on default honeypots

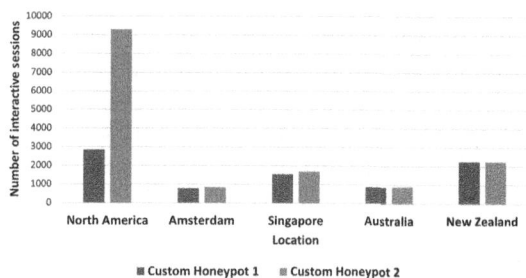

Fig. 2. Interactive sessions on custom honeypots

- *Instruction pattern:* We initially studied how a human attacker interacts and executes commands to carry out the attack process. The possible options could be: 1) commands are executed one by one so that each time an instruction (command or multiple commands using separators) is completed, the attacker hits the `Enter` key to execute and 2) multiple instructions (commands) are executed at once such that an attacker can paste multiple instructions together. However, in this case, `New Line` will be automatically recorded. Also, for the second case, `Enter` may be pressed at the end once the commands are pasted. *Resulting Features:* 1) `Enter` and 2) `New Line and Enter`.
- *Typing pattern:* We explored typing patterns such as if an attacker inserts (i.e., types) specific characters as part of an instruction (i.e., command). In such cases, if the "space" key is pressed during typing, this indicates that a human attacker types instructions (i.e. commands) character by character (e.g., `uname -a`). *Resulting Feature:* `Spacebar`.

- *Typographical errors:* There is a high probability that humans make mistakes while typing commands and correct them using `Backspace` or `Delete` keys. It is also possible that the space bar is pressed consecutively by mistake while typing. Such as writing a command with more than one space in between, e.g. `uname   -a`. *Resulting Features:* 1) `Backspace`; 2) `Delete` and 3) `Consecutive_Spacebar`.
- *Modifier keys:* We explored modifier keys such as `Shift and Ctrl` pressed by attackers. These keys separately do not perform any operation. However, it is important to detect these keys when pressed simultaneously with alphanumeric and function keys as they pass special instructions to the Shell and associated system and can indicate the presence of human attackers. Many operations can be performed when modifier keys are pressed with alphanumeric keys. Although we consider all the alphanumeric and function keys when pressed with modifier keys, in this paper we present common operations that can be performed by applying modifier keys as well as other keys as features. *Resulting Features:* 1) `Ctrl-c` (copy); 2) `Ctrl-v` (paste); 3) `Ctrl-d` (exit the terminal); 4) `Ctrl-j` (New Line); 5) `Ctrl-l` (clear screen) and 6) `Ctrl-m` (Enter).
- *Cursor keys:* We also looked for the use of cursor keys during a session, as they are solid indicators of a human attacker adding or removing characters at a specific location in the command. *Resulting Features:* 1) `Left`; 2) `Right`; 3) `Up` and 4) `Down`. `Up and Down` can also be used to check for previously executed commands. We also consider whether these cursor keys are pressed simultaneously with modifier keys such as `Ctrl` or `Shift`.
- *Other keys:* We also looked at other keys that can potentially be pressed to simplify terminal features (e.g., Tab to autocomplete, Page Up and Down to navigate a long stream of text). *Resulting Features:* 1) `Tab`; 2) `Clear`; 3) `Insert`; 4) `Home`; 5) `Page Up`; 6) `Page Down`; 7) `End`; 8) `Delete` and 9) `Esc` (escape).

The identified features discussed above cover a representative set of the potential characteristics of human attackers when they interact with the compromised system to exploit it. The features discussed above are not limited to only considering typographical errors in commands for sending data but allow us to think about many possible scenarios where human attackers can be detected.

4.2   Analysis

We analysed interactive attack sessions captured across all of the honeypots based on features mentioned above. First, we sort the commands in all sessions according to the time stamp. Many sessions were found to execute an identical or similar set of commands with variations in arguments and follow the same sequence, representing similar attack patterns. A major portion of the attack sessions on each machine could be represented using only three to five attack patterns. Overall, the attack sessions representing these patterns demonstrated the many of the following combined patterns:

– Were logged by multiple honeypots deployed in different locations
– Issued identical or similar set of instructions, including similar commands and identical sequences
– Were repeated for a number of days
– Were initiated by multiple sources in different geographical locations
– Had near-identical session duration on different deployed honeypots

This shows that most of the recorded attacks (around more than 90%) are automated, persistent, or are the result of campaigns by automated tools. Further supporting this observation; most of the attack sessions recorded did not include identified features associated with human attackers. We could only identify the presence of New Line which indicated that multiple commands were executed sequentially as the presence of Enter key to send instructions separately.

In our data set, attack sessions were recorded on default and custom honeypots deployed in various locations in which features discussed above associated with human attackers were present, as shown in Fig. 3. For example, Enter and New Line were pressed by attackers when executing commands in most attack sessions. However, features such as Ctrl-x, Ctrl-z, Left, Right were found in fewer attack sessions. These sessions with the presence of the above-mentioned features represented the behaviour of human attackers in terms of interacting with systems for exploitation.

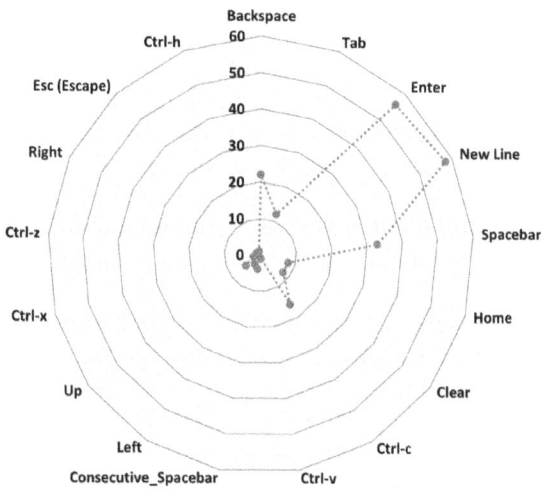

Fig. 3. Presence of identified features in attack sessions.

4.3   Observations

We report our observations as follows by analysing the attack sessions in which the above mentioned features were found:

– Human attackers interacting with the terminal press `Enter` to execute instruction(s). It is possible that attackers send an instruction as a single command, multiple commands with separators or multiple instructions (commands). `Enter` key is pressed at the end, for execution. It can be seen from Fig. 3 that in almost all of the attacks, `New Line` and `Enter` found together.
– During the interaction, human attackers use a combination of typing commands as a character by character or paste commands using mouse clicks. We can generalise our observation as: 1) short commands, e.g., (`ls -a`, `cat .bash_history`, `cd ..`, `uname -a`, `rm -rf`) are typed and `Spacebar` was used. This gives a good indication of the presence of human attackers and 2) long commands, multiple commands were combined using separators and/or multiple commands were pasted.
  It can be seen from Fig. 3 that in many attacks, `Spacebar` was present as a feature. Other attacks, where `Spacebar` was not recorded mostly comprised of commands such as `top`, `w` in which the above discussed scenario of pressing the `Enter` key helped to indicate the presence of human attackers. These commands were found to be typed in the terminal character by character.
– Typographical errors are recorded when humans type commands followed by `Backspace` key to correct them. Multiple consecutive `Backspace` keys were also used to remove commands by attackers when attackers decided to change the command before execution. Another interesting finding is that to make corrections; attackers also used cursor keys such as `Left`, `Right` along with `Backspace` key to remove specific character(s) in commands which were potentially mistyped.
– Human attackers also made other types of errors while typing commands. These included 1) pressing `multiple Consecutive_Spacebar`; 2) mistyping commands, e.g., (`ngproc`, `uanem a-`) which must be (`nproc`, `uname -a`) respectively and, 3) pressing wrong keys, e.g., `ls =a` instead of `ls -a`.
– Human attackers also used various shortcut keys, e.g., `Ctrl-c`, `Ctrl-v`, `Ctrl-x`, `Ctrl-z`, `Ctrl-h`. `Ctrl-c` was not only pressed for copying but also to stop the execution of the current command (i.e. process). `Ctrl-v` may be pressed for paste operations. However, in most of the captured attacks, mouse clicks was observed to be used for pasting commands. `Ctrl-x` and `Ctrl-z` were also found which are generally used for cut and undo operations. `Ctrl-h` was found which is the shortcut used for deleting the character before the cursor. `Up` cursor key was also used as a shortcut to traverse the history of typed commands and execute them respectively.
– Other keys such as `Tab`, `Home`, `Clear` and `Esc` were also found in attacks we investigated which were associated with human attackers, as shown in Fig. 3.
– We also observed attackers' behaviour when their issued commands were not successfully executed. One of the possible reasons for failing to execute the command could be due to the mistyped instructions e.g. `ls =a`. In these scenarios, mistyped commands were followed by commands containing the correct syntax e.g. `ls -a`.
  Another possible reason for failure is that the command was not supported by

the underlying operating system i.e. Cowrie honeypot, or the results were not those expected by the attacker. For example, we observed repeated similar commands with variations such as using different editors if one were not supported e.g. vim `config.json` followed by vi `config.json`.

– The most common observed behaviour for human attackers was to spend considerable time to perform following two activities. The first activity is discovering knowledge about the device. We found that in most of the attacks, a combination of commands such as `ifconfig`, `top`, `uname -a`, `w` and `nproc` were executed. These commands are supported by Linux-based operating systems and are fairly standard in the reconnaissance phase of an attack process, as indicated by IoT Kill Chain [15]. The second observed activity was exploring directories, files and permissions by attackers. Commands related to activities associated with changing of file and directories, including creation and removal of dummy files and folders, listing, changing ownership and permissions are commonly found in attacks performed by human attackers.

The above discussion concludes that the existence of identified features allows accurate categorisation of attack sessions performed by human attackers, assuming that most automated tools have not been designed to possess these features. Moreover, other observations related to activities performed by human attackers were also discussed.

5   Case Studies

Extending our discussion, we present five case studies of human attackers representing different behaviours in terms of interacting with honeypots and their potential intentions of attack actions.

Attacker 1: This attacker successfully logged into honeypots deployed in North America, Europe (Amsterdam), Australia, and New Zealand. Generally, this attacker initiated only a single attack session in which multiple commands were initially typed to obtain device information. Subsequently, a series of commands was pasted to clear traces of attacks by removing command history and log-in details. The attacker then attempted to download a file from a URL address and execute it in some cases. The title of the downloaded file indicated a script designed to perform log cleaning. The attack process consists, therefore, of successfully breaking in, getting device information, and hiding traces of the activity.

The attack pattern for the attacker was different in the cases where the attacker returned to the honeypots over multiple sessions. In such cases, the attacker kept checking the basic details about the device. This is similar to the attack pattern discussed above. However, the attacker was not interested in removing traces of their activities; instead, downloading files from various URL addresses, extracting, installing, and removing them were part of the actions performed.

The features identified in this study were also present in the attack sessions performed by this attacker. These include pressing **Backspace, Ctrl-c, Tab,**

Spacebar keys multiple times during the attack process. In addition, the attacker spent considerable time on the decoy system performing the attack process. Other observed behaviours were the relative considerable delay following the execution of `top` command. The reason behind the delay could potentially be the attacker observing the simulated output for device and process information such as running processes, CPU and available memory information, and number of connected users. Snippets of commands from various attacks performed by this attacker are provided in Fig. 4.

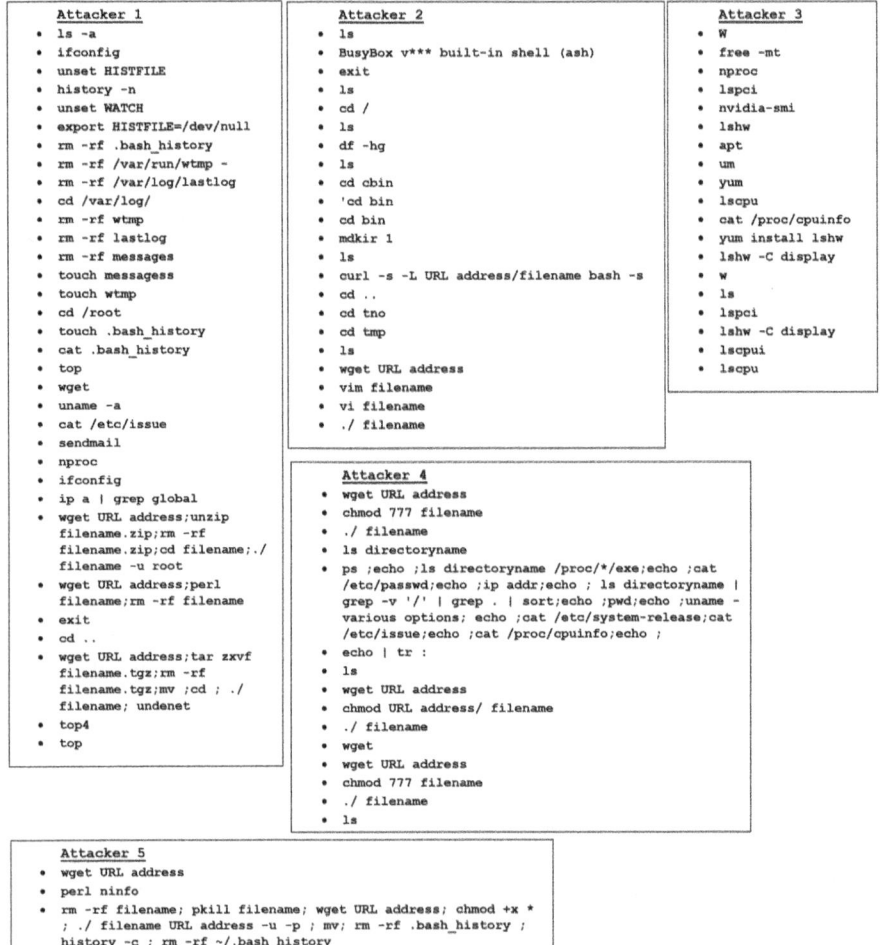

Fig. 4. Commands executed by attackers in various sessions

Attacker 2: This attacker successfully logs into the three instances of our honeypots deployed in Singapore. Commands typed in attack sessions were mostly intended to explore and list files and directories. The attacker also pasted a command to download a file from a URL address. In general, this attacker had limited interaction with the system. The attacker used the cursor keys and pressed `Backspace,` `Tab`, and `Enter` keys during command typing and execution. Snippets of commands from various attacks performed by the attacker are provided in Fig. 4.

Attacker 3: This attacker successfully logs into two honeypots deployed in Australia. Commands typed in attack sessions focused on obtaining basic information about the device, such as CPU information, logged-in users, and memory and hardware information. This attacker used cursor keys, pressed `Backspace,` `Tab,` `Enter` and shortcut keys such as `Ctrl-x,` `Ctrl-z` and `Ctrl-c` during typing and execution of commands. Snippets of commands from various attacks performed by the attacker are provided in Fig. 4.

Attacker 4: This attacker successfully log into a honeypot deployed in New Zealand and performed two attack sessions. In one of the sessions, the attacker executed multiple commands together as a single instruction collecting device information. The main commands used were intended to download files, assign appropriate execution permissions to the downloaded files, and install them accordingly. We identified the use of features `Ctrl-h,` `Backspace,` and `Enter` keys during the typing and execution of commands. Snippets of commands from various attacks performed by the attacker are provided in Fig. 4.

Attacker 5: This attacker successfully logs into a honeypot deployed in Amsterdam and performs two attack sessions. In one of the sessions, the attacker executed multiple commands combined as a single instruction to terminate several processes, download files, assign permissions, execute downloaded files, and remove traces of these activities by erasing Shell history. The attacker logged into the system in the next attack session and changed password. During the attack sessions, this attacker pressed `Enter,` `Spacebar` to type and execute commands. Snippets of commands from various attacks performed by the attacker are provided in Fig. 4.

The cases discussed above show that human attackers can perform various attack actions. Some of the attackers were limited to typing basic commands with typographical errors. Others were able to write more advanced commands such as downloading malware files, extracting them, assigning permissions, and removing traces of their activities. The features identified in this paper were also observed in these attacks, which helped to detect the presence of human attackers.

6 Limitations and Future Work

This study can be further extended by collecting and analysing data from human participants in a controlled environment. The process will involve the challenge of minimising the subjective bias introduced by the confounding variables in the experiment. The external validity of the study and generalising them to attackers on the Internet will also be questioned depending on the number of participants and their selection process. Another dimension of extending this work is to prepare bots with AI-based solutions which can mimic human behaviours while typing attack commands. The interaction of such bots can be further analysed with identified feature set to differentiate between bots and humans. The process can be challenging when bots can accurately mimic human typing behaviour. However, adding more contextual details in terms of command execution may reveal the human-specific behaviour.

7   Conclusion

We conducted a large experiment by deploying 15 server honeypots in various locations around the world and collected data. Analysing the captured attacks, we proposed a set of features covering behavioural characteristics of human attackers when they interact with a target system through a command-line interface. Existing studies were limited to typographical errors made by humans and slower typing speed. We discussed other scenarios including command patterns and the usage of modifier, cursor control, and other keys and how these features assist in detecting human attackers. Further, extending our analysis, we discussed various case studies of human attackers and reported our observations. They perform an attack process combining typing commands character by character and pasting the entire commands and executed commands with typographical mistakes. The intentions of executing attacks ranged from obtaining basic information to downloading and installing malicious files and removing traces.

Acknowledgments. This work was supported by the Cyber Security Research Programme - Artificial Intelligence for Automating Response to Threats from the Ministry of Business, Innovation and Employment (MBIE) of New Zealand as a part of the Catalyst Strategy Fund under grant MAUX1912. We also thank Hyunwoo Kim for help with a script writing task.

References

1. Al-Hadhrami, Y., Hussain, F.K.: DDoS attacks in IoT networks: a comprehensive systematic literature review. World Wide Web **24**(3), 971–1001 (2021). https://doi.org/10.1007/s11280-020-00855-2
2. Ali, I., et al.: Systematic literature review on IoT-based botnet attack. IEEE Access **8**, 212220–212232 (2020)
3. Alsuhibany, S.A., Alreshoodi, L.A.: Detecting human attacks on text-based captchas using the keystroke dynamic approach. IET Inf. Secur. **15**(2), 191–204 (2021)
4. Angrishi, K.: Turning internet of things (IoT) into internet of vulnerabilities (IoV): IoT botnets. arXiv preprint arXiv:1702.03681 (2017)

5. Antonakakis, M., et al.: Understanding the Mirai botnet. In: 26th USENIX Security Symposium (USENIX Security 2017), pp. 1093–1110 (2017)
6. Barron, T., Nikiforakis, N.: Picky attackers: quantifying the role of system properties on intruder behavior. In: Proceedings of the 33rd Annual Computer Security Applications Conference, pp. 387–398. Association for Computing Machinery (2017)
7. Cabral, W.Z., Valli, C., Sikos, L.F., Wakeling, S.G.: Advanced cowrie configuration to increase honeypot deceptiveness. In: IFIP International Conference on ICT Systems Security and Privacy Protection, pp. 317–331. Springer (2021)
8. Carrillo-Mondéjar, J., Roldán-Gómez, J., Gómez, J., Villafranca, S.R., Suarez-Tangil, G.: Stories from a customized honeypot for the IoT. J. Internet Technol. **25**(1), 117–127 (2024)
9. Dang, F., et al.: Understanding fileless attacks on Linux-based IoT devices with HoneyCloud. In: Proceedings of the 17th Annual International Conference on Mobile Systems, Applications, and Services, pp. 482–493. Association for Computing Machinery (2019)
10. DeAlcala, D., et al.: BeCAPTCHA-type: biometric keystroke data generation for improved bot detection. In: Proceedings of the IEEE/CVF Conference on Computer Vision and Pattern Recognition, pp. 1051–1060 (2023)
11. Filippoupolitis, A., Loukas, G., Kapetanakis, S.: Towards real-time profiling of human attackers and bot detection. In: Proceedings of the 7th International Conference on Cybercrime Forensics Education and Training (CFET). Canterbury Christ Church University, UK (2014)
12. Franco, J., Aris, A., Canberk, B., Uluagac, A.S.: A survey of honeypots and honeynets for Internet of Things, industrial Internet of Things, and cyber-physical systems. IEEE Commun. Surv. Tutor. **23**(4), 2351–2383 (2021)
13. Guarnizo, J.D., et al.: SIPHON: towards scalable high-interaction physical honeypots. In: Proceedings of the 3rd ACM Workshop on Cyber-Physical System Security, pp. 57–68. Association for Computing Machinery (2017)
14. Han, X., Kheir, N., Balzarotti, D.: Deception techniques in computer security: a research perspective. ACM Comput. Surv. (CSUR) **51**(4), 1–36 (2018)
15. Haseeb, J., Mansoori, M., Welch, I.: A measurement study of IoT-based attacks using IoT kill chain. In: 2020 IEEE 19th International Conference on Trust, Security and Privacy in Computing and Communications (TrustCom), pp. 557–567. IEEE (2020)
16. Haseeb, J., Mansoori, M., Welch, I.: Failure modes and effects analysis (FMEA) of honeypot-based cybersecurity experiment for IoT. In: 2021 IEEE 46th Conference on Local Computer Networks (LCN), pp. 645–648. IEEE (2021)
17. Ilg, N., Duplys, P., Sisejkovic, D., Menth, M.: A survey of contemporary open-source honeypots, frameworks, and tools. J. Netw. Comput. Appl. **220**, 103737 (2023)
18. Kemppainen, S., Kovanen, T.: Honeypot utilization for network intrusion detection. In: Cyber Security: Power and Technology, pp. 249–270. Springer (2018)
19. Koohang, A., Sargent, C.S., Nord, J.H., Paliszkiewicz, J.: Internet of Things (IoT): from awareness to continued use. Int. J. Inf. Manage. **62**, 102442 (2022)
20. Kuang, B., Fu, A., Susilo, W., Yu, S., Gao, Y.: A survey of remote attestation in Internet of Things: attacks, countermeasures, and prospects. Comput. Secur. **112**, 102498 (2022)
21. Kumari, P., Jain, A.K.: A comprehensive study of DDoS attacks over IoT network and their countermeasures. Comput. Secur. **127**, 103096 (2023)

22. Kuruvilla, A., Daley, R., Kumar, R.: Spotting fake profiles in social networks via keystroke dynamics. In: 2024 IEEE 21st Consumer Communications & Networking Conference (CCNC), pp. 525–533. IEEE (2024)

23. Lingenfelter, B., Vakilinia, I., Sengupta, S.: Analyzing variation among IoT botnets using medium interaction honeypots. In: 2020 10th Annual Computing and Communication Workshop and Conference (CCWC), pp. 0761–0767. IEEE (2020)

24. Luo, T., Xu, Z., Jin, X., Jia, Y., Ouyang, X.: IoTCandyJar: towards an intelligent-interaction honeypot for IoT devices. Black Hat (2017)

25. Marzano, A., et al.: The evolution of bashlite and mirai IoT botnets. In: 2018 IEEE Symposium on Computers and Communications (ISCC), pp. 00813–00818. IEEE (2018)

26. Morales, A., et al.: Keystroke biometrics in response to fake news propagation in a global pandemic. In: 2020 IEEE 44th Annual Computers, Software, and Applications Conference (COMPSAC), pp. 1604–1609. IEEE (2020)

27. Neshenko, N., Bou-Harb, E., Crichigno, J., Kaddoum, G., Ghani, N.: Demystifying IoT security: an exhaustive survey on IoT vulnerabilities and a first empirical look on Internet-scale IoT exploitations. IEEE Commun. Surv. Tutor. **21**(3), 2702–2733 (2019)

28. Nicomette, V., Kaâniche, M., Alata, E., Herrb, M.: Set-up and deployment of a high-interaction honeypot: experiment and lessons learned. J. Comput. Virol. **7**(2), 143–157 (2011)

29. Pa, Y.M.P., Suzuki, S., Yoshioka, K., Matsumoto, T., Kasama, T., Rossow, C.: {IoTPOT}: analysing the rise of {IoT} compromises. In: 9th USENIX Workshop on Offensive Technologies (WOOT 2015) (2015)

30. Pisani, P.H., Lorena, A.C.: A systematic review on keystroke dynamics. J. Braz. Comput. Soc. **19**(4), 573–587 (2013). https://doi.org/10.1007/s13173-013-0117-7

31. Ramsbrock, D., Berthier, R., Cukier, M.: Profiling attacker behavior following SSH compromises. In: 37th Annual IEEE/IFIP International Conference on Dependable Systems and Networks (DSN 2007), pp. 119–124. IEEE (2007)

32. Raul, N., Shankarmani, R., Joshi, P.: A comprehensive review of keystroke dynamics-based authentication mechanism. In: International Conference on Innovative Computing and Communications: Proceedings of ICICC 2019, vol. 2, pp. 149–162. Springer (2020)

33. Saputro, E.D., Purwanto, Y., Ruriawan, M.F.: Medium interaction honeypot infrastructure on the internet of things. In: 2020 IEEE International Conference on Internet of Things and Intelligence System (IoTaIS), pp. 98–102. IEEE (2021)

34. Srinivasa, S., Pedersen, J.M., Vasilomanolakis, E.: Open for hire: attack trends and misconfiguration pitfalls of IoT devices. In: Proceedings of the 21st ACM Internet Measurement Conference, pp. 195–215. Association for Computing Machinery (2021)

35. Srinivasa, S., Pedersen, J.M., Vasilomanolakis, E.: Gotta catch'em all: a multi-stage framework for honeypot fingerprinting. Digit. Threats: Res. Pract. **4**(3), 1–28 (2023)

36. Sutheekshan, B., Basheer, S., Thangavel, G., Sharma, O.P.: Evolution of malware targeting IoT devices and botnet formation. In: 2024 IEEE International Conference on Computing, Power and Communication Technologies (IC2PCT), vol. 5, pp. 1415–1422. IEEE (2024)

37. Udhani, S., Withers, A., Bashir, M.: Human vs bots: detecting human attacks in a honeypot environment. In: 2019 7th International Symposium on Digital Forensics and Security (ISDFS), pp. 1–6. IEEE (2019)

38. Valli, C., Rabadia, P., Woodward, A.: Patterns and patter-an investigation into SSH activity using kippo honeypots. In: 11th Australian Digital Forensics Conference. SRI Security Research Institute, Edith Cowan University, Perth, Western Australia (2013)
39. Vetterl, A., Clayton, R.: Bitter harvest: systematically fingerprinting low-and medium-interaction honeypots at internet scale. In: 12th USENIX Workshop on Offensive Technologies (WOOT 2018) (2018)
40. Vidal-González, S., et al.: Analyzing IoT-based botnet malware activity with distributed low interaction honeypots. In: World Conference on Information Systems and Technologies, pp. 329–338. Springer (2020)
41. Wagener, G., Dulaunoy, A., Engel, T., et al.: Heliza: talking dirty to the attackers. J. Comput. Virol. **7**(3), 221–232 (2011)
42. Wang, A., Liang, R., Liu, X., Zhang, Y., Chen, K., Li, J.: An inside look at IoT malware. In: International Conference on Industrial IoT Technologies and Applications, pp. 176–186. Springer (2017)
43. Wang, B., Dou, Y., Sang, Y., Zhang, Y., Huang, J.: IoTCMal: towards a hybrid IoT honeypot for capturing and analyzing malware. In: ICC 2020 - 2020 IEEE International Conference on Communications (ICC), pp. 1–7. IEEE (2020)

Access Control and Internal Controls and Audit Process

Supporting Delegation in Outsourced ICA Process

Sabrina De Capitani di Vimercati[1], Sara Foresti[1]([⊠]),
Stefano Paraboschi[2], Sara Petrilli[1], and Pierangela Samarati[1]

[1] Università degli Studi di Milano, Milan, Italy
{sabrina.decapitani,sara.foresti,pierangela.samarati}@unimi.it,
sara.petrilli@studenti.unimi.it
[2] Università degli Studi di Bergamo, Dalmine, Italy
stefano.paraboschi@unibg.it

Abstract. We consider the problem of enforcing corporate governance control relying on cloud-based services. Extending previous work, we focus in particular on the support of delegation of the director privileges, enabling their dynamic and temporary assignment to a vice-director. Like previous work, our control relies on encrypted tags, which are here extended addressing the challenges introduced by dynamic delegation which operates on a time dimension orthogonal to the corporate governance control process. Our solution enables delegation while ensuring a vice-director to enjoy the director privileges only when delegation is active and not to operate as director for operations the vice-director has processed as employee (separation of duties). Our tag construction ensures integrity of the dynamic delegation control and protection against tag tampering.

Keywords: Cloud-based services · outsourcing · internal controls and audit process · delegation · separation of duties

1 Introduction

Cloud-based applications and services represent today a convenient alternative to on-premises solutions for the management of applications and processes, due to their scalability, efficiency, and cost benefits. Adoption of cloud-based solutions for sensitive or critical applications requires, however, particular care, to ensure confidentiality and integrity of the data and process are properly considered. In this paper, we consider the enforcement of corporate governance control with cloud-based services and, specifically of the *Internal Controls and Audit* (ICA) functions, aimed at verifying the compliance of the operations generated and elaborated within an organization with internal rules, regulations, and laws. More concretely, we consider a three-phase ICA process, which is the most common in companies that have to comply with market regulations, like bank and financial institutions. In this context, companies are organized in units, which

S. Katsikas and B. Shafiq (Eds.): DBSec 2025, LNCS 15722, pp. 393–412, 2025.
https://doi.org/10.1007/978-3-031-96590-6_21

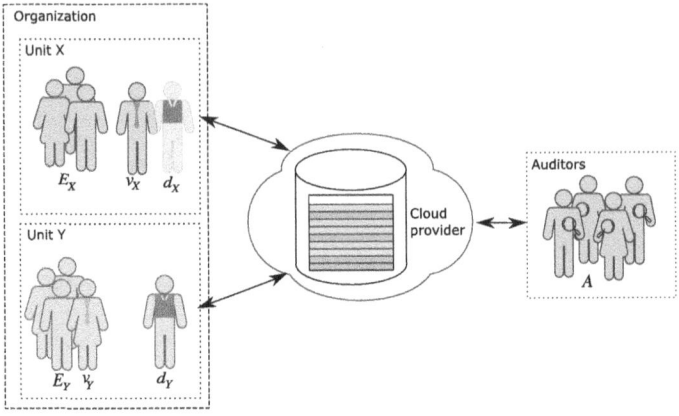

Fig. 1. Reference scenario

generate and process operations (e.g., a bank operating through branches and processing money withdrawal and deposit), and each operation goes through three phases. Each phase is under the control of a different subject, who is in charge of verifying different aspects of the operation and produces a report for the phase. The first (*employee*) phase is executed by an employee of the unit where the operation has been processed. The second (*director*) phase is executed by the director of the unit where the operation has been processed. The third (*auditor*) and final phase is executed by an independent auditor external to the company. Operations and reports should be visible only to auditors and to the employees and director of the unit where the operation has been processed, and each report can be generated only by a subject with the role (employee, director, auditor) for the report. Also, a report can be updated only by the subject who generated it, and only during the corresponding phase.

The approach in [4] for enforcing the ICA process, while relying on cloud-based services, assumes all subjects to be available for the execution of their phase. However, since each unit has one director only, absence of the director prevents execution of the second phase of the ICA process for all the operations processed at the unit, which remain therefore blocked as a phase cannot start before the completion of the previous one. While the block in the operativity of the unit caused by the absence of its director can be easily solved when managing the ICA process on-premises by simply delegating an employee of the unit (the vice-director), enforcing delegation in the cloud introduces complications since the cloud provider is assumed to simply provide services and execute requested actions while remaining unaware of the ICA process.

In this paper, we build on the approach in [4], extending and revising it to enable delegation of the director privileges. With reference to Fig. 1, the goal is to support dynamic delegation enabling a vice-director (e.g., v_X in the figure) to take on the director privileges for the operations in their unit. Our solution leverages tags associated with operations and units to support the execution of the ICA phases, which corresponds to write actions executed at the server and regulated by such tags (which enable the enforcement of access regulations). Our approach supports the intrinsically dynamic nature of delegation without the need to rewrite the tags of operations and permits the vice-director to operate on behalf of the director only when delegation is active, independently from the status of the operation at the time of activation/deactivation of delegation (e.g., on operations for which the first phase terminated before delegation). Also, our approach enforces separation of duties, preventing the vice-director from performing the first and second phase of control on a same operation, thus guaranteeing the involvement of three different subjects in the ICA process of each operation (independently from who performed the first phase of control). Our tag construction ensures integrity of the dynamic delegation control and protection against tag tampering. The main advantage of our solution is the direct support of the ICA process, including delegation, while leveraging basic services of the cloud provider.

The remainder of this paper is organized as follows. Section 2 illustrates the basic concepts on which our work is based. Section 3 characterizes the aspects to take into account for supporting dynamic delegation of the director's role. Section 4 describes our solution for supporting delegation of the director's privileges in the ICA process. Section 5 illustrates the pseudocode of the procedures implementing our solution. Section 6 discusses related work. Finally, Sect. 7 concludes the paper. The Appendix shows that our procedures correctly enforce the write controls on reports and tags.

2   ICA Process in the Cloud

In this section, we illustrate the basic concepts of the approach proposed in [4] for enforcing the ICA process in the cloud. Since our focus is on the management of delegation, we limit the concepts to those affected by delegation and simplify notation to refer to a single unit. The approach leverages symmetric encryption and a hierarchical organization of keys associated with the different subjects (and groups thereof) of the ICA process. Each individual subject s (i.e., employee e, director d, auditor a), the set E of employees of each unit (with $d \notin E$), and the set A of auditors is associated with a key known also to the provider. Hierarchical key organization enables each individual subject s (and the provider) to derive the key of the group to which s belongs. Denoting key assignment with $\phi(s)$ and key derivation with $\rightsquigarrow$, this is formally expressed as $\forall e \in E, a \in A :$ $\phi(e) \rightsquigarrow \phi(E), \phi(a) \rightsquigarrow \phi(A)$. In the following, we will also use k_s to denote the key assigned to a subject s and known to the provider, that is, $\phi(s) = k_s$.[1]

---

[1] While in the original model a prime superscript was used to denote encryption keys shared with the provider (in contrast to the keys known only to subjects and used for reading and writing reports) and their assignment function, focusing only on the controls on tags regulating write operations, which are based on keys shared with the provider, in this paper we simplify notation and omit such superscript.

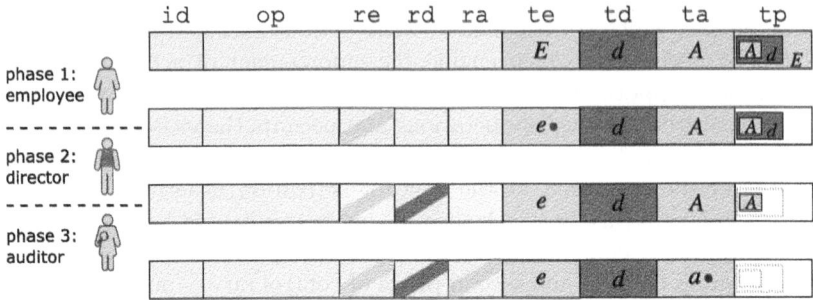

Fig. 2. Evolution of the reports and tags for an operation

Regulation of write privileges on reports relies on the use of tags, which are random values encrypted with keys shared with the service provider. For each unit, a (precomputed) strip of tags is defined. This strip is attached to every operation of the unit at generation time, and evolves as the ICA process for the operation progresses. The strip has four tags: a tag for each report (te for employee report re, td for director report rd, and ta for auditor report ra), and a phase tag (tp). The random values encrypted in the tags are all different (to prevent subjects from operating outside their role) and each report tag is encrypted with the key of the subjects allowed to write the corresponding report (k_E for te, k_d for td, and k_A for ta). The phase tag has three layers of encryption, each using the key of the subjects authorized to perform one of the three phases. More precisely, the random value within the phase tag is encrypted (as an onion) with k_A, then k_d, then k_E. The phase tag evolves as the ICA process progresses regulating the start and end of each phase. Intuitively, a subject will be authorized to operate on a report only if proving ability to decrypt both the report tag and the phase tag. Hence, when the process for an operation starts, only employees will be able to operate. When the employee phase is completed, the outer layer of the phase tag is peeled, enabling the second phase in which only the director would be able to operate. Similarly, when the second phase completes and the third is enabled, only auditors can operate.

Using dot notation to refer to the different fields of an operation (including the operation identifier id, the operation content op, reports, and tags), a subject s will be authorized for a write operation on a report $o.r*$, with $* \in \{e,d,a\}$, only if proving ability to decrypt the corresponding report tag $o.t*$ and the phase tag $o.tp$. Denoting with W the write actions to be authorized and with λ the function assigning keys to tags (i.e., identifying the keys used for encrypting tags), write control is formally captured by the following property.

Property 1 (Write control). For each subject s, operation o, and report $o.r*$, with $* \in \{e,d,a\}$: write$(s,o.r*) \in$ W iff $\phi(s) \leadsto \lambda(o.t*) \land \phi(s) \leadsto \lambda(o.tp)$.

Figure 2 summarizes the evolution of reports and tags for an operation. In the figure, for simplicity, we specify for each tag the subjects who can derive the corresponding encryption key. Note that when an employee e (auditor a, resp.) starts the employee phase (auditor phase, resp.), they overwrite the value for te (ta, resp.) with a new random value encrypted with their own key k_e (k_a, resp.). This prevents updates to the report by other employees (auditors, resp.). In the figure, a bullet denotes this change in the random value of a tag.

3   Delegation in the ICA Process

The execution of the ICA process regulated by tags as above relies on the presence of all the subjects authorized to perform its three phases. While the first (employee) phase and last (auditor) phase can be executed by any of the subjects operating in the required role (i.e., any employee or any auditor, resp.), the second phase can be executed only by the director. If the director is temporarily unavailable (e.g., for a sick leave) the ICA process would remain blocked for all operations for which the second phase has not been performed. Our goal is to extend the ICA process allowing the director to delegate their privileges to a *vice-director*, denoted v, also - and otherwise - operating as a regular employee. While in principle simple, the consideration of delegation introduces several complications.

First, delegation is *dynamic* and its activation/deactivation operates on a time dimension orthogonal to the phases of the ICA process. When activated, delegation should enable the vice-director to perform the second phase also for operations that have originated, and/or whose first phase was even started or completed, before the delegation became active. When deactivated, it should prevent the vice-director from performing the second phase on any operation, even on those that originated, or whose first phase was executed, when the delegation was active. This orthogonal and dynamic lifetime of the delegation requires rethinking the precomputed director tag and phase tag (for its middle layer), statically attached to the operations at their creation.

Second, with the vice-director operating as a regular employee, but also acquiring director's privileges when delegated, care must be taken to ensure the vice-director not to execute the director phase for operations for which the vice-director executed the first phase. With control delegated to the server simply expressed as control on tags (the service provider should remain agnostic with respect to the process itself), the enforcement of this *separation of duties* should be embedded in tags themselves, hence again it requires rethinking the precomputed tag strip (intuitively, treating differently the operations for which the vice-director performed the first phase).

Third, again with the vice-director dynamically acquiring privileges to perform the second phase, care must be taken with respect to potential vulnerabilities of the control, which could be exposed to tampering with the tag strip enabling passing write controls for operations that should not be granted.

In the next section, we redefine tags to address the three challenges above.

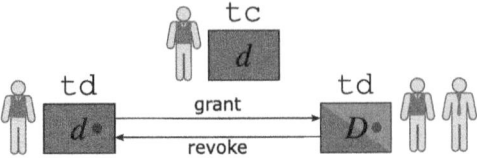

Fig. 3. Evolution of the director tag

4   Tag Management for Delegation Enforcement

In the following, we describe our solution for supporting director's role delegation addressing the aspects discussed in the previous section. In particular, we illustrate how to support dynamic delegation (Sect. 4.1), while enforcing separation of duties (Sect. 4.2), and ensuring integrity of the tag control process and of tag evolution (Sect. 4.3).

4.1   Dynamic Delegation

As noted, delegation is dynamic and its validity span is orthogonal with respect to the phases of the ICA process. While in the original approach the director tag was static throughout an operation life time and equal for all operations of the same unit, with delegation the director tag needs to change dynamically. This makes the precomputed director tag in the tag strip attached to operations not suitable in presence of delegation. As a matter of fact, maintaining such tag, would require rewriting it for the tag strip of all the existing operations that have not completed the second phase. A further complicating factor is the management of the middle layer of the phase tag associated with operations, which cannot be simply rewritten.

The above observations suggest two requirements: first, the need for a director tag that can be decrypted by both the director and the vice-director (this latter only if delegation is active); second, a detachment of the director tag with respect to operation records. We accommodate them by considering a key, denoted k_D, which can be derived by both the director and vice-director (i.e., $k_d \leadsto k_D$, and $k_v \leadsto k_D$). We use key k_D (in contrast to k_d) for the middle layer of the phase tag tp, hence enabling its decryption also by the vice-director. We also define, for each unit u, a single director tag u.td, which applies to all the operations of the unit. Being detached from operations, this tag can dynamically change to activate/deactivate delegation as needed. Like in the original model, the tag is a random value encrypted with the unit's director key (i.e., k_d). To activate delegation, the director overwrites the tag using a new random value and key k_D. To deactivate delegation the director overwrites it, again using a new random value, and key k_d. Delegation can be activated and de-activated as needed. To note that activation/deactivation requires not only changing the key with which the tag is encrypted, but also using a new random value to avoid

(a) regular employee   (b) vice-director

Fig. 4. Structure of the tags at initialization time for operations generated by regular employees (a) and by the vice-director (b)

replay attacks. Figure 3 illustrates the change of tag u.td when delegation is activated/deactivated, introducing our graphical (double-colored) notation for the tag accessible also to the vice-director (i.e., encrypted with key k_D). Again, the bullet in the tag denotes the change of the underlying random value. Note that the director tag can be written only by the director, who is the only subject who can activate/deactivate delegation. Analogously to write operations on reports, write actions on u.td are controlled through a tag, denoted u.tc, defined at the unit level, and encrypted with key k_d.

Write control (Property 1) needs then to be revised to consider the director tag now associated with the unit (in contrast to the operation). The property is revised as follows, changing the management of write operations on the director report with reference to director tag u.td (in contrast to o.td).

Property 2 (Write control with delegation). For each subject s, operation o, and report o.r* with * $\in$ {e,d,a}:

- write(s,o.r*) $\in$ W, with * $\in$ {e,a}, iff $\phi(s)\rightsquigarrow\lambda(o$.t*$) \wedge \phi(s)\rightsquigarrow\lambda(o$.tp$)$;
- write(s,o.rd) $\in$ W iff $\phi(s)\rightsquigarrow\lambda(u$.td$) \wedge \phi(s)\rightsquigarrow\lambda(o$.tp$)$.

4.2 Separation of Duties

With the vice-director also (and otherwise) operating as a regular employee care must be taken to avoid the vice-director to perform both the first (employee) and second (director) phase for an operation as this would violate separation of duties. To ensure this, we remove the vice-director from the set E of employees, treating v as a separate subject. We then consider two different tag strips, one for operations processed by regular employees (i.e., for which a regular employee performed the first phase) and the other for operations processed by the vice-director. The tag strip for operations processed by regular employees is defined as illustrated above, that is, the employee tag te (and the external layer of the phase tag tp) is encrypted with key k_E and the middle layer of the phase tag is encrypted with key k_D (derivable by both the director and the vice-director, see Fig. 4(a)). The tag strip for operations processed by the vice-director (when operating as an employee) have the employee tag te (and the external layer of the phase tag tp) encrypted with key k_v and the middle layer of the phase tag encrypted with key k_d (see Fig. 4(b)). The exclusion of the vice-director from the set E of employees (i.e., $k_v \not\rightarrow k_E$) ensures that the vice-director cannot use

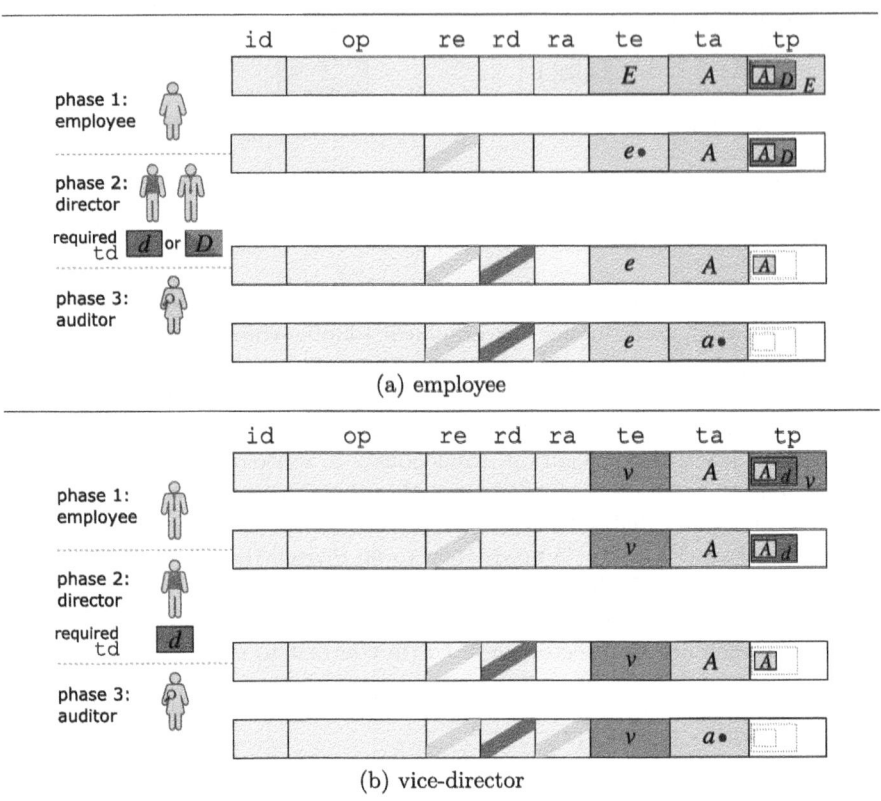

Fig. 5. Evolution of the reports and tags for an operation generated by a regular employee (a) and by the vice-director (b)

the regular employee tag strip. The use of k_d for the middle layer of the phase tag of the vice-director's strip ensures that the vice-director will not be able to execute the second phase for operations that the vice-director processed, and for which the vice-director executed the first phase. Formally, the generation of the two tag strips is captured by the following property.

Property 3 (Tag strip generation). The tag strip $\langle \texttt{te,ta,tp} \rangle$ associated with an operation o is computed as follows:

- $o.\texttt{te}= \text{Enc}(\sigma, k_1)$;
- $o.\texttt{ta}= \text{Enc}(\sigma', k_A)$;
- $o.\texttt{tp}= \text{Enc}(\text{Enc}(\text{Enc}(\sigma'', k_A), k_2), k_1)$

where $\sigma \neq \sigma' \neq \sigma''$ are random values, $k_1{=}k_v$ and $k_2{=}k_d$ if o is generated by v, or $k_1{=}k_E$ and $k_2{=}k_D$ if o is generated by a regular employee.

Figure 5 illustrates the evolution of the tags for operations processed by a regular employee and by the vice-director.

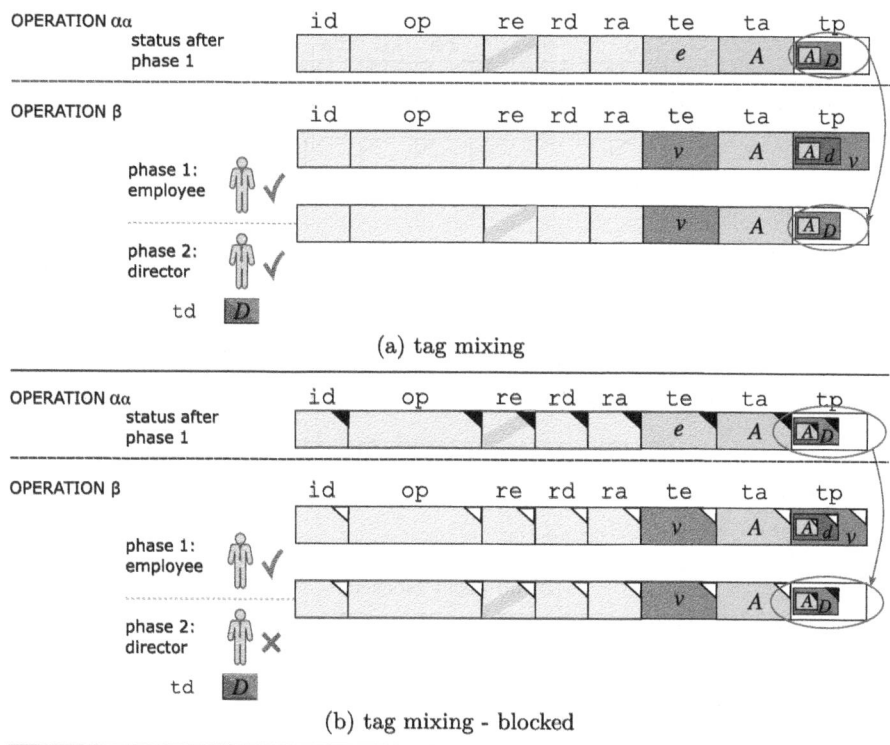

(a) tag mixing

(b) tag mixing - blocked

Fig. 6. An example of tag mixing (`tp` of operation α after phase 1 used for operation β)

4.3 Ensuring Tag Integrity

Although the use of two different tag strips guarantees the proper execution of the ICA process with delegation without violating the separation of duties principle, the generation of tags must be done with care to avoid possible vulnerabilities. In particular, the mixing of tags from different strips (Fig. 6) as well as the phase tag not properly peeled (Fig. 7) can cause an unexpected evolution of the ICA process that the cloud provider cannot detect.

– *Tag mixing.* Consider two operations, one generated by a regular employee (α) and another one generated by the vice-director (β), for which the first phase has been completed. Switching the phase tag of the two operations would permit the vice-director, in case delegation is active, to complete the second phase for operation β for which the vice-director also performed the first phase (Fig. 6(a)). Indeed, the vice-director would be able to decrypt both `td` and the (middle layer of the) phase tag, both encrypted with key k_D, thus proving to the provider the authorization to write report `rd`. To avoid mixing tags of different operations, tags should be tied to operations including the operation identifier (Fig. 6(b), where the operation identifier is represented

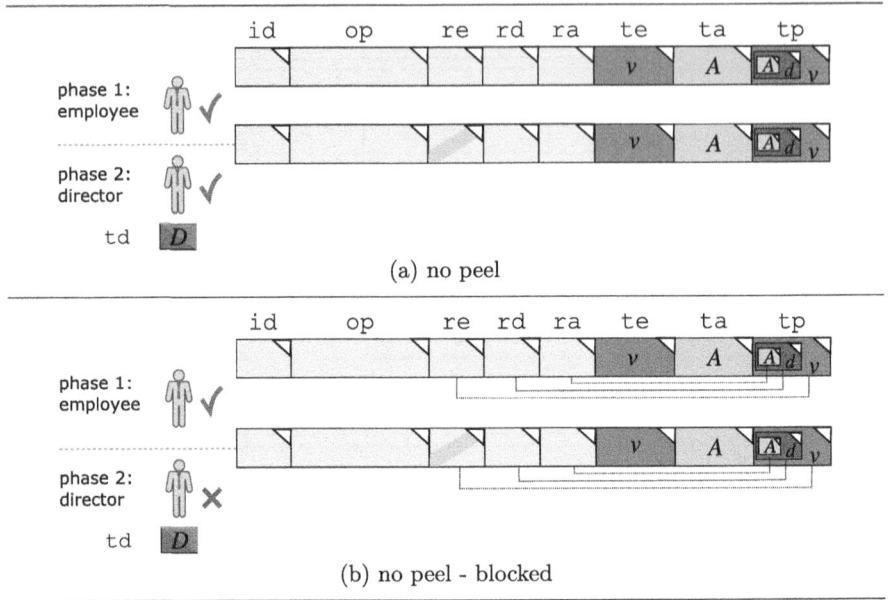

Fig. 7. An example of not peeled phase tag

with a triangle of different color in the top left corner of the fields in the operation record).

– *No peel.* Consider an operation generated by the vice-director and assume that, at the end of the first phase, the external layer of the phase tag is not peeled. In case delegation is active, the vice-director would be able to decrypt both td, encrypted with k_D, and tp, encrypted with k_v, thus gaining write access to rd (Fig. 7(a)). Note that the vice-director could gain access to rd for such an operation also before the completion of the first phase, or even before its start. To avoid situations where the external layer of the phase tag is used for regulating write access to rd, the layers of tp should include a reference to the phase they regulate (Fig. 7(b)).

To tie tags with operations, we add a unique operation identifier within tags. To permit the verification of the correspondence between the phase of the ICA process and the layer of the phase tag, we introduce in each layer a reference to the corresponding phase. Tag strip generation (Property 3) is revised as follows.

Property 4 (Tag strip generation (revised)). The tag strip $\langle \text{te},\text{ta},\text{tp} \rangle$ associated with an operation o is computed as follows:

– $o.\text{te}= \text{Enc}(\sigma\|o.\text{id}, k_1)$;
– $o.\text{ta}= \text{Enc}(\sigma'\|o.\text{id}, k_A)$;
– $o.\text{tp}=\text{Enc}(\text{Enc}(\text{Enc}(\sigma''\|o.\text{id}\|\text{a}, k_A)\|o.\text{id}\|\text{d}, k_2)\|o.\text{id}\|\text{e}, k_1)$

where $\sigma \neq \sigma' \neq \sigma''$ are random values, $k_1 = k_v$ and $k_2 = k_d$ if o is generated by v, or $k_1 = k_E$ and $k_2 = k_D$ if o is generated by a regular employee.

In the following, we use notation $[o.\mathtt{t}*].\mathtt{id}$ to refer to the operation identifier in tag $o.\mathtt{t}*$, and $[o.\mathtt{tp}].\mathtt{ph}$ to refer to the phase reported in the phase tag. Note that, even including the operation (and phase) identifier, tags are always generated starting from a random value since otherwise anyone could prove ability to decrypt tags, being the operation identifier publicly available. The random values used to generate tag strips are all different, that is, tags of the same or of different operations are generated from different random values.

Write control (Property 2) is revised as follows to consider operation identifiers within tags and phase reference in the layers of the phase tag.

Property 5 (Write control with delegation (revised)). For each subject s, operation o processed at unit u, and report $o.\mathtt{r}*$ with $* \in \{\mathtt{e,d,a}\}$:

- $\mathtt{write}(s, o.\mathtt{r}*) \in \mathrm{W}$, with $* \in \{\mathtt{e,a}\}$, iff $\phi(s) \rightsquigarrow \lambda(o.\mathtt{t}*) \wedge \phi(s) \rightsquigarrow \lambda(o.\mathtt{tp}) \wedge o.\mathtt{id} = [o.\mathtt{t}*].\mathtt{id} = [o.\mathtt{tp}].\mathtt{id} \wedge [o.\mathtt{tp}].\mathtt{ph} = *$;
- $\mathtt{write}(s, o.\mathtt{rd}) \in \mathrm{W}$ iff $\phi(s) \rightsquigarrow \lambda(u.\mathtt{td}) \wedge \phi(s) \rightsquigarrow \lambda(o.\mathtt{tp}) \wedge o.\mathtt{id} = [o.\mathtt{tp}].\mathtt{id} \wedge [o.\mathtt{tp}].\mathtt{ph} = \mathtt{d}$.

Analogously to the write control on reports, also the evolution of tags is regulated (the evolution of the ICA process requires report and tag updates). The rules governing tag updates are similar to those regulating report updates. A subject is authorized to write a report tag $\mathtt{t}*$ (with $* \in \{\mathtt{e,a}\}$) if the subject would also be authorized to write the corresponding report $\mathtt{r}*$ (i.e., the first condition in Property 5 holds also for tags $\mathtt{te}$ and $\mathtt{ta}$). Only the director is authorized to write $\mathtt{td}$. A subject is authorized to write the phase tag $\mathtt{tp}$ if the subject can decrypt the phase tag, as well as the report tag corresponding to the exposed layer of the phase tag, and the operation identifier matches with the one of the phase tag and of the provided report tag (e.g., the subject can decrypt $\mathtt{tp}$ and $\mathtt{te}$, $[o.\mathtt{tp}].\mathtt{ph} = \mathtt{e}$, and $o.\mathtt{id} = [o.\mathtt{te}].\mathtt{id} = [o.\mathtt{tp}].\mathtt{id}$). Note that, checking the ability of a subject to decrypt a report tag besides the phase tag, prevents subjects who can decrypt the phase tag to terminate a phase when not responsible for it. Write control on tags is formally captured by the following property.

Property 6 (Write control on tags). For each subject s, operation o processed at unit u, and tag $o.\mathtt{t}*$ with $* \in \{\mathtt{e,a,p}\}$ and tag $u.\mathtt{td}$:

- $\mathtt{write}(s, o.\mathtt{t}*) \in \mathrm{W}$, with $* \in \{\mathtt{e,a}\}$, iff $\phi(s) \rightsquigarrow \lambda(o.\mathtt{t}*) \wedge \phi(s) \rightsquigarrow \lambda(o.\mathtt{tp}) \wedge o.\mathtt{id} = [o.\mathtt{t}*].\mathtt{id} = [o.\mathtt{tp}].\mathtt{id} \wedge [o.\mathtt{tp}].\mathtt{ph} = *$;
- $\mathtt{write}(s, u.\mathtt{td}) \in \mathrm{W}$, iff $\phi(s) = \lambda(u.\mathtt{tc})$;
- $\mathtt{write}(s, o.\mathtt{tp}) \in \mathrm{W}$ iff $\phi(s) \rightsquigarrow \lambda(o.\mathtt{tp}) \wedge o.\mathtt{id} = [o.\mathtt{tp}].\mathtt{id} \wedge ((\phi(s) \rightsquigarrow \lambda(o.\mathtt{te}) \wedge [o.\mathtt{tp}].\mathtt{ph} = \mathtt{e} \wedge o.\mathtt{id} = [o.\mathtt{te}].\mathtt{id}) \vee (\phi(s) \rightsquigarrow \lambda(u.\mathtt{td}) \wedge [o.\mathtt{tp}].\mathtt{ph} = \mathtt{d}) \vee (\phi(s) \rightsquigarrow \lambda(o.\mathtt{ta}) \wedge [o.\mathtt{tp}].\mathtt{ph} = \mathtt{a} \wedge o.\mathtt{id} = [o.\mathtt{ta}].\mathtt{id}))$.

Delegation(u,$action$) /* client-side; perform $action$ on director's role at unit u * /
1: σ_d=Dec(u.tc, k_d) /* decryption of tag regulating write operations over u.td */
2: **if** $action$==activate **then** /* activate delegation */
3:   key=k_d, new_key=k_D
4: **else** /* deactivate delegation */
5:   key=k_D; new_key=k_d
6: σ=Dec(u.td, key)
7: randomly generate σ'
8: new_tag=Enc(σ', new_key)
9: **Write_TD**(u, σ, σ_d, new_tag, new_key)

Write_TD(u, σ, σ_d, new_tag, new_key) /* provider-side; check σ and σ_d to verify if u.td */
1: **if** σ==Dec(u.td, λ(u.td)) AND /* can be overwritten with new_tag encrypted with new_key */
   σ_d==Dec(u.tc, λ(u.tc)) **then**
2:   u.td=new_tag
3:   λ(u.td)=new_key

Fig. 8. Procedures for activating and deactivating delegation

We conclude this section observing that the tag strip $\langle$te,ta,tp$\rangle$ associated with an operation does not need to be created when the operation is generated, but it can be precomputed in advance as discussed in [4]. The only difference in our approach compared to [4] is that, since our tags include the operation identifier, we precompute a set of tag strips for each unit, together with operation identifiers. When a new operation is generated, it is associated with an identifier and the appropriate tag strip depending on who has generated the operation (a regular employee or the vice-director).

5   Management of Delegation and Write Operations

In this section, we describe the pseudocode of the activation and deactivation of delegation (Sect. 5.1) and of write operations on reports (Sect. 5.2).

5.1   Delegation

Figure 8 illustrates the pseudocode implementing the activation and deactivation of delegation. Procedure **Delegation** is invoked by the director d of a unit u and takes as input the unit u of the director and the $action$ (activation or deactivation) that the director wishes to perform. We assume that before executing the procedure, the director tag has been correctly generated, meaning that the tag was initially encrypted with key k_d. The procedure first decrypts the tag u.tc governing write operations over u.td (line 1). It then determines the key (variable key) protecting the director tag and the new key (variable new_key) that will be used for encrypting the director tag (lines 2–5). The value of these keys depends on the action to be enforced. In case of activation, the tag must be decrypted with key=k_d (i.e., the key associated with the subject executing the procedure) and re-encrypted with new_key=k_D (i.e., the key shared with the vice-director and that the subject calling the procedure should derive starting from their own key); $key=k_D$ and $new\_key=k_d$, otherwise. The procedure then decrypts the director tag u.td with key (line 6), generates a new random value σ' (line 7), and encrypts it with new_key (line 8). The procedure finally invokes **Write_TD** operating at the provider side (line 9).

Procedure **Write_TD** takes as input the unit u (i.e., the unit of director d), values σ and σ_d obtained from procedure **Delegation** through the decryption of tags u.td and u.tc, respectively, the new director tag new_tag computed by procedure **Delegation**, and the new key new_key used for encrypting new_tag. **Write_TD** verifies whether σ and σ_d match the decryption of u.tc and u.td, respectively (line 1). If this is the case, the cloud provider concludes that procedure **Delegation** has been called by the director of unit u. Procedure **Write_TD** can then overwrite the director tag u.td with new_tag (line 2). The procedure also updates the identifier of the encryption key now protecting u.td (line 3). We note that the checks on σ and σ_d (line 1) guarantee that only the director of a unit can activate delegation since the tag regulating write operations on the director tag (i.e., tag u.tc) is encrypted with a key known to the director only.

5.2   Write Reports and Tags

Figure 9 illustrates the pseudocode implementing the evolution of an ICA phase. When a subject s needs to perform an ICA phase over an operation, s invokes procedure **ICA_Phase**, which takes as input the operation identifier id, the unit u of the operation, and the phase $phase$ of the ICA process. Depending on the value of variable $phase$, the procedure identifies the report r to be generated/updated, and the corresponding report tag and decrypts it (lines 2–5). The procedure then decrypts the phase tag tp, obtaining triple (σ_p, id_p, p) (line 6). Note that a subject s can decrypt a tag if and only if the subject can derive the key used for encrypting the tag. Otherwise, the decryption operation does not produce a meaningful result.

For the employee and auditor phases, if the operation identifier reported in the decrypted report tag and phase tag matches the operation identifier o.id, the procedure generates a new random value σ', computes a new report tag new_tag concatenating σ' with o.id and encrypting it with the key of the employee/auditor who started the phase, and writes it in the operation record by invoking procedure **Write_Tag** executed at the provider (lines 7–11). Procedure **ICA_Phase** then checks if the operation identifiers in the phase tag id_p and in the report tag id_r correspond to the input id and if the input $phase$ corresponds to the phase in the phase tag. If this is the case, the considered tags are those associated with operation o and therefore procedure **ICA_Phase** proceeds with the generation/update of the report of interest and writes it in the operation record by invoking procedure **Write_Report** executed at the provider (lines 12–15). Finally, procedure **ICA_Phase** completes the ICA phase by invoking procedure **Peel_Phase_Tag**, which operates at the provider and removes the exposed encryption layer of the phase tag.

ICA_Phase(*id, u, phase*) /* client-side; write report of *phase* for operation *id* at unit *u* */
1: let o in O s.t. $o.\text{id}=id$
2: **case** *phase* **of**
3:   **e:** $r=o.\text{re}$, $(\sigma_r, id_r)=\text{Dec}(o.\text{te}, \lambda(o.\text{te}))$ /* $\phi(s)\leadsto\lambda(o.\text{te})$ */
4:   **d:** $r=o.\text{rd}$, $\sigma_r=\text{Dec}(u.\text{td}, \lambda(u.\text{td}))$, $id_r=id$ /* $\phi(s)\leadsto\lambda(u.\text{td})$ */
5:   **a:** $r=o.\text{ra}$, $(\sigma_r, id_r)=\text{Dec}(o.\text{ta}, \lambda(o.\text{ta}))$ /* $\phi(s)\leadsto\lambda(o.\text{ta})$ */
6: $(\sigma_p, id_p, p)=\text{Dec}(o.\text{tp}, \lambda(o.\text{tp}))$ /* $\phi(s)\leadsto\lambda(o.\text{tp})$ */
7: **if** ($p==phase==$e OR $p==phase==$a) AND $id_r==id_p==o.\text{id}$ **then** /* start ICA *phase* */
8:   randomly generate σ'
9:   $new\_tag=\text{Enc}(\sigma'\|o.\text{id}, k_s)$ /* with s the invoking subject */
10:   $new\_key=k_s$
11:   **Write_Tag**(*id*, σ_r, σ_p, *new_tag, new_key, phase*)
12: **if** $id_r==id_p==o.\text{id}$ AND $p==phase$ **then** /* generate/modify and write the report */
13:   $r=$Decrypt $o.r$
14:   $r=$Update and encrypt r
15:   **Write_Report**(*id, u*, σ_r, σ_p, r, *phase*)
16:   **Peel_Phase_Tag**(*id, u*, σ_r, σ_p, *phase*) /* finalize ICA *phase* */

Write_Tag(*id*, σ_r, σ_p, t, k, *phase*) /* provider-side; check σ_r and σ_p to verify if */
1: let o in O s.t. $o.\text{id}=id$ /* tag of *phase* for operation *id* can be set to t encrypted with k */
2: **case** *phase* **of**
3:   **e:** $t=o.\text{te}$
5:   **a:** $t=o.\text{ta}$
6: **if** $(\sigma_r, id)==\text{Dec}(t, \lambda(t))$ AND $(\sigma_p, id, phase)==\text{Dec}(o.\text{tp}, \lambda(o.\text{tp}))$ **then**
7:   $t=t$; $\lambda(t)=k$

Write_Report(*id, u*, σ_r, σ_p, r, *phase*) /* provider-side; check σ_r and σ_p to verify if */
1: let o in O s.t. $o.\text{id}=id$ /* report of *phase* for operation *id* at unit *u* can be set to r */
2: **case** *phase* **of**
3:   **e:** $r=o.\text{re}$, $t=o.\text{te}$
4:   **d:** $r=o.\text{rd}$, $t=u.\text{td}$
5:   **a:** $r=o.\text{ra}$, $t=o.\text{ta}$
6: **if** ((*phase*==d AND $\sigma_r==\text{Dec}(t, \lambda(t))$) OR $(\sigma_r, id)==\text{Dec}(t, \lambda(t))$) AND
   $(\sigma_p, id, phase)==\text{Dec}(o.\text{tp}, \lambda(o.\text{tp}))$ **then** $r=r$

Peel_Phase_Tag(*id, u*, σ_r, σ_p, *phase*) /* provider-side; check σ_r and σ_p to verify if */
1: let o in O s.t. $o.\text{id}=id$ /* phase tag at *phase* of operation *id* at unit *u* can be peeled */
2: **case** *phase* **of**
3:   **e:** $t=o.\text{te}$
4:     **if** $\lambda(o.\text{te})==k_{v_u}$ **then** $key=k_{d_u}$ /* keys of vice-director (v_u) and director (k_{d_u}) of unit *u* */
5:     **else** $key=k_{D_u}$ /* key shared between director and vice-director of unit *u* */
6:   **d:** $t=u.\text{td}$, $key=k_A$
7:   **a:** $t=o.\text{ta}$, $key=$NULL
8: **if** ((*phase*==d AND $\sigma_r==\text{Dec}(t, \lambda(t))$) OR $(\sigma_r, id)==\text{Dec}(t, \lambda(t))$) AND
   $(\sigma_p, id, phase)==\text{Dec}(o.\text{tp}, \lambda(o.\text{tp}))$ **then** $o.\text{tp}=\sigma_p$; $\lambda(o.\text{tp})=key$

Fig. 9. Execution of a ICA phase

Procedure **Write_Tag** enforces Property 6 and is executed by the provider.
It verifies whether subject s is authorized to write a report tag (i.e., $o.\text{te}$ or $o.\text{ta}$)

by checking whether: 1) the input value σ_p corresponds to the decryption of the phase tag (i.e., subject s can derive $\lambda(o.\text{tp})$), 2) the input value σ_r corresponds to the decryption of the report tag (i.e., subject s can derive $\lambda(o.\text{t*})$), 3) the input operation identifier id matches the identifier reported in the report and phase tags, and 4) the input phase corresponds to the phase reported in the phase tag. If these checks succeed, the provider can conclude that s is authorized to write the report tag, and updates it with the value received as input.

Analogously, procedure **Write_Report** enforces Property 5 and is executed by the provider. It verifies whether subject s is authorized to write a report (i.e., $o.\text{re}$ or $o.\text{rd}$ or $o.\text{ra}$) by checking whether: 1) the input value σ_p corresponds to the decryption of the phase tag (i.e., subject s can derive $\lambda(o.\text{tp})$), 2) the input value σ_r corresponds to the decryption of the report or director tag (i.e., subject s can derive $\lambda(o.\text{te})$ or $\lambda(u.\text{td})$ or $\lambda(o.\text{ta})$); 3) the (employee or auditor) report tag and the phase tag are those associated with the operation of interest (i.e., the input operation identifier id matches with the identifier in the tags), and 4) the input phase corresponds to the phase reported in the phase tag. If these checks succeed, the provider can conclude that s is authorized to write the report, and modifies it according to the input value.

Procedure **Peel_Phase_Tag** takes the same input as procedure **Write_Report** and performs the same checks. If the checks succeed, **Peel_Phase_Tag** removes the exposed layer of the phase tag.

6   Related Work

The adoption of cloud services for data storage and management provides numerous advantages but also introduces several issues related to, for example, the reliability of cloud providers and the lack of control of data owners over their data and processing (e.g., [3,6,9,10,15,17]). The problem of protecting data and computations (confidentiality and integrity) when moving to the cloud has been widely studied. Solutions protecting the confidentiality of outsourced data are often based on owner-side encryption (e.g., [7]), thus preventing exposure of sensitive information if the cloud provider is compromised. Owner-side encryption, however, rules out any processing of data. Many efforts have been then dedicated to the design of approaches for supporting computations over encrypted data (e.g., [5,7,11,13]). With respect to integrity, solutions have been proposed for verifying not only that data are correctly stored at the cloud provider but also the integrity of data processing results (e.g., [18]).

A line of research related to our work focuses on the problem of enforcing access control on outsourced data. Approaches addressing this problem either rely on attribute-based encryption (ABE) (e.g., [16,19]), or combine selective encryption and key derivation strategies (e.g., [3,12]) to translate read access privileges into the knowledge of the keys necessary to decrypt data. ABE is a public key encryption schema that can be combined with ABS (Attribute-Based Signature) for regulating write actions over resources (e.g., [8,14]). While effective, solutions relying on ABE are less efficient than our proposal due to their adoption of asymmetric encryption. Our proposal is inspired by approaches lever-aging selective encryption for access control enforcement. Selective encryption uses symmetric encryption and enforces access control policies by properly regu-lating the keys to be used for resource encryption and to be distributed to users. Key derivation strategies (e.g., [1]) enable users to derive, from the distributed keys, the ones used for encryption. Selective encryption approaches have also been enhanced to enforce selective write privileges (e.g., [2]). While similar to our proposal, these techniques cannot be directly used for enforcing the ICA process, because of the peculiarities of the considered scenario and of the intrin-sically dynamic nature of authorizations while the process evolves.

The problem of moving the ICA process to the cloud has been first addressed in [4]. However, this proposal does not consider the potential block in the oper-ativity of a unit caused by the absence of the director responsible for the second phase of the ICA process of all operations of the unit. We have then enhanced this solution to enable the delegation of the director privileges, while preventing the delegated subject to perform more than one phase of the ICA process.

7   Conclusions

We addressed the problem of enforcing corporate governance internal control and audit functions while relying on cloud-based services for their execution. Extending previous work, we considered in particular the support of delega-tion, enabling directors to dynamically and temporarily delegate their privileges to vice-directors. Support of dynamic delegation required rethinking the (pre-defined and static) encrypted tags attached to operations. Our solution pro-vides support of delegation while ensuring separation of duties and correctness of the control against possible misbehavior and tag tampering. Our work leaves room for extensions, including the support of alternative delegation (e.g., non-predefined vice-director, enforcement of two-person-rules for acquiring director's privileges), and consideration of additional functionalities of governance con-trol (e.g., preventing subjects to perform employee, director, or audit control on operations for which they may be in conflict of interest).

Acknowledgements. This work was supported in part by the EC under projects GLACIATION (101070141) and EdgeAI (101097300), by the Italian MUR under PRIN project POLAR (2022LA8XBH), and by project SERICS (PE00000014) under the MUR NRRP funded by the EU - NGEU. Project EdgeAI is supported by the Chips Joint Undertaking and its members including top-up funding by Austria, Belgium, France, Greece, Italy, Latvia, Netherlands, and Norway under grant agreement No. 101097300. Views and opinions expressed are however those of the authors only and do not necessarily reflect those of the European Union, the Chips Joint Undertaking, or the Italian MUR. Neither the European Union, nor the granting authority, nor Italian MUR can be held responsible for them.

Correctness

We first show that **Delegation** procedure updates the director tag in accordance with the status of delegation.

Lemma 1. *Procedure* **Delegation** *in Fig. 8 guarantees that for each unit u, $\phi(s) \rightsquigarrow \lambda(u.\mathtt{td})$ iff $s=d$, or $s=v$ and delegation is active.*

Proof. We assume that the director tag is correctly generated and encrypted when procedure **Delegation** is called and that the caller of the procedure is the director d of unit u. We now distinguish two cases, depending on the action (activate or deactivate) input to the procedure.

- **Delegation**(u,activate). The procedure first decrypts the control tag $u.\mathtt{tc}$, obtaining value σ_d. The director tag is encrypted with k_d that only d can derive. The procedure can then decrypt the director tag (obtaining value σ), generate a new random value, and re-encrypt the new random value with k_D (*new_tag*) that both d and v can derive. The verification of whether the caller of **Delegation** is authorized to overwrite the director tag with *new_tag* (i.e., to activate delegation) is verified by the provider through procedure **Write_TD**, which checks whether both σ_d and σ match with the decryption of $\lambda(u.\mathtt{tc})$ and $\lambda(u.\mathtt{td})$, respectively. If this is the case, **Write_TD** activates delegation by overwriting $u.\mathtt{td}$ with *new_tag* and assigning $\overline{k}_D$ to $\lambda(u.\mathtt{td})$. After the activation of delegation, $\phi(s) \rightsquigarrow \lambda(u.\mathtt{td})$, with $s \in \{d,v\}$.
- **Delegation**(u,deactivate). The procedure first decrypts the control tag $u.\mathtt{tc}$, obtaining value σ_d. The director tag is encrypted with k_D that d and v can derive. The procedure can then decrypt the director tag with k_D, generate a new value, and re-encrypt the new value with k_d that only subject d can derive. Again, the verification of whether the caller of **Delegation** is authorized to overwrite the director tag with *new_tag* (i.e., to deactivate delegation) is verified by the provider through procedure **Write_TD**. If such a check succeeds, **Write_TD** overwrites $u.\mathtt{td}$ with *new_tag*, and assigns k_d to $\lambda(u.\mathtt{td})$. As a consequence, delegation is deactivated and $\phi(s) \rightsquigarrow \lambda(u.\mathtt{td})$, with $s=d$. □

We now show that **Peel_Phase_Tag** procedure correctly decrypts the phase tag of an operation.

Lemma 2. *Procedure* **Peel_Phase_Tag** *in Fig. 9 guarantees that for each object o, phase tag o.tp is correctly decrypted.*

Proof. The procedure takes as input the id of an operation, the unit u where operation id has been processed, two secret values σ_r and σ_p, and the current ICA *phase*. Depending on the current *phase*, the procedure determines the key needed for decrypting the next layer of the phase tag. The procedure then checks whether the decryption of $o.\mathtt{tp}$ produces a triple that corresponds to $(\sigma_p, id, phase)$, and the input value σ_r corresponds to the decryption of the director tag ($phase=d$) or the input id and σ_r correspond to the decryption of the report tag ($phase=e$ or $phase=a$). If the control succeeds, the procedure assigns σ_p to $o.\mathtt{tp}$, meaning that the current layer of the phase tag is correctly removed. □

We are now ready to prove that the procedures in Fig. 9 satisfy Property 5.

Theorem 1 (Correct enforcement of write control). *Procedure* **ICA_Phase** *guarantees that for each subject s and operation o, Property 5 is satisfied.*

Proof. We assume that before starting the ICA process, the tags associated with the operations have been correctly generated and processed. We distinguish two cases: *1)* the subject invoking the procedure is an employee or an auditor and the phase is e or a, and *2)* the subject invoking the procedure is the director or the vice-director and the phase is d.

- *Case 1.* The procedure decrypts both the report tag corresponding to the input value *phase* (i.e., te if *phase*=e or ta if *phase*=a) obtaining pair (σ_r, id), and the phase tag obtaining triple (σ_p, id, p). If there is a match among the identifier provided as input and the ones obtained from the decryption of the report and phase tags and the phase tag exposes the encryption layer corresponding to the input *phase*, the procedure calls **Write_Report**. Procedure **Write_Report** checks whether the report and phase tags have been correctly decrypted (input σ_r and σ_p), the operation identifier (input *id*) matches the identifier reported in the tags, and the input phase *phase* corresponds to the phase reported in the phase tag. The check performed by **Write_Report** succeeds only if: 1) $\phi(s) \rightsquigarrow \lambda(o.\text{t}*)$ (with t*=te or t*=ta) because only in this case σ_r can correspond to the value that the cloud provider obtains with the decryption of the report tag; 2) $\phi(s) \rightsquigarrow \lambda(o.\text{tp})$ because only in this way σ_p can correspond to the value that the cloud provider obtains with the decryption of the phase tag; 3) the input *id* corresponds to the identifiers that the cloud provider obtains from the decryption of the report and phase tags; 4) the input *phase* corresponds to the phase that the cloud provider obtains from the decryption of the phase tags. The report is then written only if Property 5 is satisfied.

- *Case 2.* For the operation o the employee phase has been already executed as the requesting input *phase* is d. Procedure **Peel_Phase_Tag** has then removed the external layer (Lemma 2) of the phase tag that now exposes the layer corresponding to the director phase. The **ICA_Phase** procedure decrypts both the director tag obtaining value σ_r, and the phase tag obtaining triple (σ_p, id, p). If the operation identifier (input *id*) matches the identifier reported in the phase tag, and the input phase *phase* corresponds to the phase reported in the phase tag, the procedure calls **Write_Report** that, as before, checks whether the director and phase tags have been correctly decrypted (input σ_r and σ_p), the operation identifier (input *id*) matches the identifier reported in the phase tag, and the input phase *phase* corresponds to the phase reported in the phase tag. This check succeeds only if: 1) $\phi(s) \rightsquigarrow \lambda(o.\text{td})$ meaning that s is the director or, if the delegation is active (Lemma 1), the vice-director; 2) $\phi(s) \rightsquigarrow \lambda(o.\text{tp})$ because only in this way σ_p can correspond to the value that the cloud provider obtains with the decryption of the phase tag; 3) *id* corresponds to the identifiers that the cloud provider obtains from the decryption of the director and phase tags; 4) *phase* corresponds to the phase that the cloud provider obtains from the decryption of the phase tags. The report is then written only if Property 5 is satisfied.

References

1. Atallah, M., Blanton, M., Fazio, N., Frikken, K.: Dynamic and efficient key management for access hierarchies. ACM TISSEC **12**(3), 18:1–18:43 (2009)
2. De Capitani di Vimercati, S., Foresti, S., Jajodia, S., Livraga, G., Paraboschi, S., Samarati, P.: Enforcing dynamic write privileges in data outsourcing. COSE **39**, 47–63 (2013)
3. De Capitani di Vimercati, S., Foresti, S., Jajodia, S., Paraboschi, S., Samarati, P.: Encryption policies for regulating access to outsourced data. ACM TODS **35**(2), 12:1–12:46 (2010)
4. De Capitani di Vimercati, S., Foresti, S., Paraboschi, S., Samarati, P.: Enforcing corporate governance controls with cloud-based services. IEEE TSC **17**(6), 3583–3596 (2024)
5. Ding, X., Wang, Z., Zhou, P., Choo, K., Jin, H.: Efficient and privacy-preserving multi-party skyline queries over encrypted data. IEEE TIFS **16**, 4589–4604 (2021)
6. Gritzalis, S., Yannacopoulos, A., Lambrinoudakis, C., Hatzopoulos, P., Katsikas, S.: A probabilistic model for optimal insurance contracts against security risks and privacy violation in IT outsourcing environments. IJIS **6**, 197–211 (2007)
7. Hacigümüş, H., Iyer, B., Mehrotra, S., Li, C.: Executing SQL over encrypted data in the database-service-provider model. In: Proceedings of SIGMOD, Madison, WI, USA (2002)
8. Huang, Q., Yang, Y., Shen, M.: Secure and efficient data collaboration with hierarchical attribute-based encryption in cloud computing. Futur. Gener. Comput. Syst. **72**, 239–249 (2017)
9. Jhawar, R., Piuri, V., Samarati, P.: Supporting security requirements for resource management in cloud computing. In: Proceedings of CSE, Paphos, Cyprus (2012)
10. Jhawar, R., Piuri, V., Santambrogio, M.: A comprehensive conceptual system-level approach to fault tolerance in cloud computing. In: Proceedings of SysCon, Vancouver, BC, Canada (2012)
11. Li, F., Ma, J., Miao, Y., Liu, X., Ning, J., Deng, R.H.: A survey on searchable symmetric encryption. ACM CSUR **56**(5), 119:1–119:42 (2024)
12. Miklau, G., Suciu, D.: Controlling access to published data using cryptography. In: Proceedings of VLDB, Berlin, Germany (2003)
13. Poh, G., Chin, J., Yau, W., Choo, K.K.R., Mohamad, M.: Searchable symmetric encryption: designs and challenges. ACM CSUR **50**(3), 40:1–40:37 (2017)
14. Ruj, S., Stojmenovic, M., Nayak, A.: Privacy preserving access control with authentication for securing data in clouds. In: Proceedings of CCGrid, Ottawa, Canada (2012)
15. Xie, S., Mohammady, M., Wang, H., Wang, L., Vaidya, J., Hong, Y.: A generalized framework for preserving both privacy and utility in data outsourcing. IEEE TKDE **35**(1), 1–15 (2023)
16. Xu, S., Ning, J., Huang, X., Li, Y., Xu, G.: Untouchable once revoking: a practical and secure dynamic EHR sharing system via cloud. IEEE TDSC **19**(6), 3759–3772 (2022)

17. Zahid, M., Shafiq, B., Vaidya, J., Afzal, A., Shamail, S.: Collaborative business process fault resolution in the services cloud. IEEE TSC **16**(1), 162–176 (2023)
18. Zhang, B., Dong, B., Wang, W.: Integrity authentication for SQL query evaluation on outsourced databases: a survey. IEEE TKDE **33**(4), 1601–1618 (2021)
19. Zhang, Y., Deng, R., Xu, S., Sun, J., Li, Q., Zheng, D.: Attribute-based encryption for cloud computing access control: a survey. ACM CSUR **53**(4), 83:1–83:41 (2021)

Transaction Logs in Access Control: Leveraging an Under-Utilized Data Source

Sascha Kern[1], Thomas Baumer[1(✉)], Raphael Neudert[1],
and Günther Pernul[2]

[1] Nexis GmbH, Rudolf-Vogt-Straße 6, 93053 Regensburg, Germany
{sascha.kern,thomas.baumer,raphael.neudert}@nexis-secure.com
[2] University of Regensburg, Universitätsstraße 31, 93053 Regensburg, Germany
guenther.pernul@ur.de

Abstract. Maintaining access control policies is an ongoing process to ensure required but not excessive authorizations. Organizations thus leverage various data sources to ease this maintenance. Among these data sources are access control matrices, attributes, access logs, and transaction logs. While research reasonably covers the former data sources, the potential of transaction logs remains untapped. We pave the way for transaction logs as a data source in access control by (i) expressing them with a formalization, (ii) pinpointing them in typical Identity and Access Management (IAM) infrastructures, and (iii) grounding them in IAM processes. We conclude that access control transaction logs are valuable data sources for improving analytical capabilities for IAM.

Keywords: Access Control · Transaction Logs · Data Quality

1 Introduction

Existing research has devoted considerable attention to the initial creation of high-quality access control policies [12,23]. Once created, policies lose quality due to changing environmental conditions, incorrect or suboptimal policy adjustments, or over-granting [29]. Access control policies must thus be maintained in an ongoing manner to remain accurate. This is intuitive for static access control models like Role-Based Access Control (RBAC). Dynamic models, like e.g. Attribute-Based Access Control (ABAC), which grant access based on attribute values, cannot eliminate this problem either, since their policies also reflect the organizational context at the time of creation and can become outdated due to changes in the environment (e.g., new regulatory requirements, organizational structures or application systems). In practice, it is prevalent to analyze access control policies manually to identify inaccurate authorizations, e.g., by Access Reviews [18]. The effectiveness of manual maintenance is limited, as authorization data is often vast and challenging to analyze [20].

Approaches that aim to automate parts of policy maintenance exist. Still, they are limited by the availability and quality of required data [21]: The most

© IFIP International Federation for Information Processing 2025
Published by Springer Nature Switzerland AG 2025
S. Katsikas and B. Shafiq (Eds.): DBSec 2025, LNCS 15722, pp. 413–424, 2025.
https://doi.org/10.1007/978-3-031-96590-6_22

important and readily available data types are the access control matrix and attributes. The access control matrix and its variants describe the effective authorizations defined by the access control policies. At the same time, attributes offer valuable context information that helps understand policies' semantics and identify patterns and outliers. However, these data only describe the current state of access control, which is likely outdated and thus equally erroneous, as in the policies. Therefore, policy maintenance with no further data reproduces existing errors and is limited to environments with high data quality. Another data source used for policy maintenance is access logs [34]. They allow for identifying inaccurate authorizations by analyzing which authorizations have been invoked in a certain period. However, the availability of access logs can be limited, and their use requires a certain level of interpretation.

We introduce transaction logs as a data source for maintaining access control policies. Transaction logs are structured change histories for relevant IAM data. We provide a formal definition and show that transaction logs are available in IAM infrastructures. We ground the validity of access control transaction logs in IAM processes. Finally, we conduct a case study with a real-world enterprise to verify our findings. In summary, the contributions of this work are as follows:

C1 *We formalize transaction logs in access control.*
C2 *We locate transaction logs in typical, centralized IAM infrastructures.*
C3 *We ground the analytical value of transaction logs in IAM processes.*

This work is structured as follows. We position our work with related work in Sect. 2. Section 3 analyzes the utilization of transaction logs in three steps: (i) We formalize transaction logs in IAM. (ii) We analyze how to locate transaction logs in IAM infrastructures. (iii) We ground the validity of transaction logs on typical IAM processes. Section 4 concludes this work.

2   Related Work

Research proposes methods to improve the quality of access control policies. They differ in terms of the addressed quality dimensions and required data. We present relevant approaches along with their respective data reliance and known limitations. Table 1 summarizes the known data usages and limitations.

The *access control matrix* displays the authorizations granted by a policy set as they are. Theoretically, it can identify patterns in existing authorizations and adjust them to remove outliers. For example, one identity sharing all authorizations except one with ten other identities could be assigned the missing authorization. However, without further data to provide context information, the analytical power of the access control matrix is limited. Some authors propose visualizations based on the access control matrix to improve the data understanding of policy engineers [22,25]. Other works that process the access control matrix to improve policy quality typically use it to recreate existing authorizations, while modifying policies to improve other quality dimensions such as complexity [6,33], redundancy, or the number of conflicts [26].

Table 1. Data types and their known uses and limitations for access control policy maintenance.

Data Category	Known Use	Known Limitations
Access Control Matrix	Recreating authorizations	Analytical power
Attributes	Identifying authorization patterns and outliers	Detectable inaccuracies Attribute and ACP quality
Access Logs	Estimating inaccurate authorizations with access invocations	Availability Sensitive data Detectable inaccuracies
Transaction Logs	Draw authorization insights from IAM processes	No formalization or localization Missing grounding

Attributes provide valuable information about real-world meanings of access control policies. They are commonly used by policy mining approaches to create semantically meaningful policies. We argue ABAC mining approaches might serve as blueprints for attribute-based policy maintenance. Note that using ABAC policies alone does not fully eliminate the problem of policy maintenance, since the attribute rules can outdate just like other access control models. Suppose no data other than the present state attributes and the access control matrix are available. In that case, policy maintenance is limited to outlier detection, and only a relatively small fraction of authorizations can be identified as inaccurate. Moreover, outlier detection approaches are limited by their strong reliance on attribute quality and authorization accuracy. Thus, a policy set cannot be maintained if its quality is too low.

Several approaches use *access logs* to identify excessive authorizations [14,30], missing authorizations [4], or both [5,19]. Access logs are records of historic permission invocations in the form $\langle S, O, A, R \rangle$, with S being the subject that requests access, O and A being the requested object and action, and R being the response returned by the access control mechanism, i.e., a *permit* or *deny* decision. The shared concept for identifying excessive authorizations with access logs is to search for authorizations not used in a certain period (e.g., last year). Authorizations that are not needed are excessive and can thus be removed according to the principle of least privilege. However, if a user holds an excessive authorization and uses it, it cannot be detected using access logs. Missing authorizations are identified by analyzing authorization requests that were denied. However, this method requires further interpretation since the mere request of an authorization does not necessarily mean that an identity *should* have it. Regarding availability, core applications like operating and database management systems often generate detailed access logs. In contrast, higher-level applications tend to create fewer, as it is not a prioritized use case. Another limitation can stem from legal requirements, as access logs enable user monitoring, which is restricted by some privacy protection laws. Access logs can be a valuable data source for identifying inaccurate authorizations. However, their utilization can be limited by their availability, the sensitivity of their content, and the amount of inaccuracies they can reveal. Some approaches like [15,30] also use access logs to identify behavior anomalies, e.g., many access requests that occurred within a short period, and revoke the related authorizations. However, these authorizations are not revoked for being excessive, but as an immediate threat response.

Transaction logs are structured records of data changes. Changes to access control policies and digital identities are particularly relevant in access control. Transaction logs allow for the tracking of changes that have occurred and the restoration of previous data states. Despite inconsistent terminology, they are a well-established data type used in other application fields of IT, e.g., database systems [9], software version control systems [7], or digital ledger technologies [3]. Some authors have emphasized the analytical value of (structured) data change logs in IAM: Molloy et al. [24] propose to identify job change events, recognizable by the pattern of an identity losing and receiving several authorizations within a short time frame, to determine semantically meaningful permission groupings for roles. They also argue that historical update information can be used to identify legacy permissions that should no longer be authorized altogether. Mitra et al. [23] propose to use transaction logs to identify outdated roles that require maintenance. Both Strembeck [31] and Fuchs et al. [10] name trace management as requirements for role model maintenance that provide role engineers with valuable context information. Hein et al. [16] use transaction logs to enable administrators to rollback suboptimal changes to a role set. Hunt et al. [17] also suggest standardizing transaction logs for the provisioning standard System for Cross-domain Identity Management (SCIM) and name replication of IAM systems as a possible use case. However, none of these works introduces a formalization or analyzes the infrastructure localization of transaction logs or their utilization for policy maintenance.

This work offers a foundation for analyzing authorization structures with transaction logs. Established IAM processes provide a structure for the analysis. To the best of our knowledge, this is the first work to formally define transaction logs in the context of access control.

3   Transaction Logs in Identity and Access Management

This section examines how transaction logs can be used to provide analysis support for the maintenance of access control policies. Section 3.1 formally defines transaction logs. Section 3.2 examines where transaction logs can be collected from a schematic IAM infrastructure. Section 3.3 grounds access control transaction logs in typical IAM processes.

3.1   Formalization of Transaction Logs

For a precise and common notation throughout our work, we formalize transaction logs, including their preliminaries, the transactions themselves, and their

interactions. We show that transaction logs for access control do not differ substantially from related concepts for database systems or version control. Figure 1
depicts the basic idea of transactions and their interactions, which we detail in
the following paragraphs.

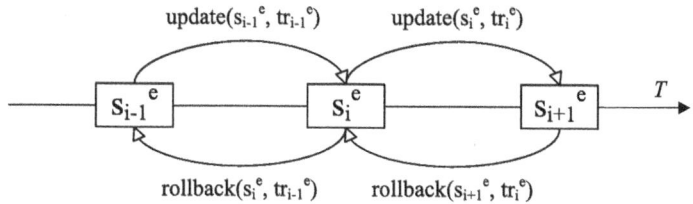

Fig. 1. Transactions and their interactions.

Preliminaries

Let E be the set of all entities, A the set of all attributes assignable to entities,
and V the set of all attribute values.

- $e \in E$ is an entity.
- $a \in A$ is an attribute.
- $v \in V$ is an attribute value.

Entities have an arbitrary set of attributes assigned, and an attribute can have an
arbitrary amount of values. For access control, entities refer to digital identities
or access control policies.

States

- An entity e has an arbitrary amount of states $s^e \in S^e$. $S^e = \{\varnothing, s_1^e, ... s_n^e\}$
  describes a sequence of $n + 1$ states of an entity $e \in E$, with $\varnothing$ being the
  empty state. The states are ordered by their occurrence in time. We follow
  that s refers to an entity $e \in E$ at a specific time.

Transactions

- $TR^e = \{tr_{create}^e, tr_1^e, ..., tr_{n-1}^e, tr_{delete}^e\}$ is the sequence of transactions for an
  entity e. It contains the descriptions of state changes, ordered by their occurrence over time.
- We define a transaction $tr^e \in TR^e$ with the tuple $\langle a, v, t \rangle$. A transaction tr_i^e
  describes a single state change $s_i^e \rightarrow s_{i+1}^e$. Along with a and v, it contains a
  timestamp t that allows ordering the transactions in TR^e.
- We define a *create* transaction $tr_{create}^e = \langle \varnothing, \varnothing, t \rangle$. It describes the initial
  creation of e as it is added to E.
- We define a *delete* transaction $tr_{delete}^e = \langle \varnothing, \varnothing, t \rangle$. It describes the removal of
  e from E.

While transactions describe state changes of entities, interactions use transactions to transition between states.

Interactions

- We define an update function $update(s_i^e, tr_i^e) = s_{i+1}^e$. Thus, by applying the next transaction tr_i^e to a given data state s_i^e, the data state is transitioned forward $(s_i^e \rightarrow s_{i+1}^e)$.
- $update(\varnothing, tr_{create}^e)$ creates the first non-empty state s_1^e.
- $update(s_n^e, tr_{delete}^e)$ creates the empty state $\varnothing$.
- We define a rollback function $rollback(s_i^e, tr_{i-1}^e) = s_{i-1}^e$. Thus, by applying the previous transaction tr_{i-1}^e in a rollback function, a state is transitioned backward $(s_i^e \rightarrow s_{i-1}^e)$.
- $rollback(\varnothing, tr_{delete}^e)$ creates the last non-empty state s_n^e.
- $rollback(s_1^e, tr_{create}^e)$ creates the empty state $\varnothing$.

Transaction thus enable two interactions with entity states: update and rollback. While the update function proceeds the entity state forward in time, the rollback function reverses the entity to a previous state. Both functions thus compute previous or new transactions to reach the desired entity states.

Transaction Log

- We define a transaction log $L \supset TR^e, \forall e \in E$, i.e. the sequence of transactions observed in a given time span for all observed entities. A transaction log entry is thus a single transaction for a specific entity.

Finally, transaction logs are the main focus of our study. Along with the current data states for these entities, transaction logs allow to analyze data changes, and to restore previous data states. Since this depiction of transaction logs is not specific to access control, we consider access control transaction logs a subset of transaction logs in general computer science.

3.2   Localization in IAM Infrastructures

We analyze the availability of transaction logs in centralized IAM infrastructures. We introduce a schematic architecture of centralized IAM and analyze transaction logs' sources and collection constraints.

Schematic IAM Infrastructure. An IAM infrastructure controls user authentication and authorization. Due to the limited scope of this work, we do not consider the authentication details and focus on centralized IAM infrastructures typical for mid to large-sized organizations [8]. To execute user authorization, an IAM infrastructure must store user identities, policies, and supplemental data (e.g., department structures). While this data is not limited to a specific type of storage system, it is often found in relational databases, HR systems, directory systems, or meta-directories [1,11]. Any application system that relies on authorization functionality is a target for access control and is thus called a *target system*. An IAM infrastructure can include numerous target systems such as workstations or business application systems (e.g., a banking

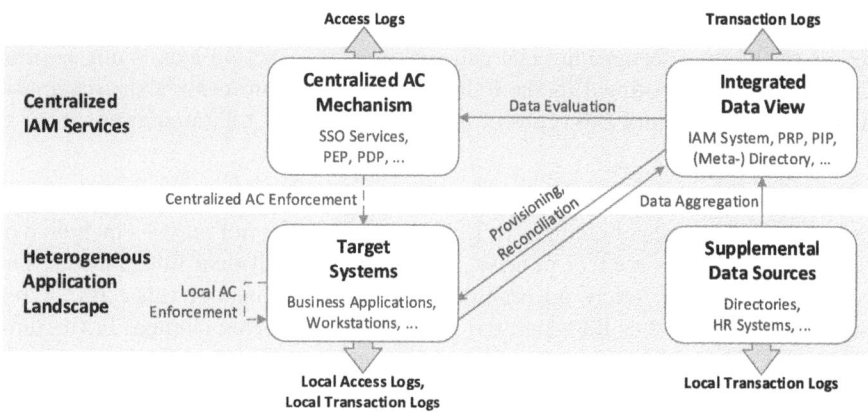

Fig. 2. Schematic centralized [8] IAM infrastructure and possible log data generation.

system). The mechanism that evaluates polices to enforce the defined authorizations is called an *access control mechanism* [27]. It can either reside locally within the target system (which is the isolated model [8]) or exist as a central service in the IAM infrastructure, as defined e.g. by the eXtensible Access Control Markup Language (XACML) standard, Single Sign On (SSO) standards like Open Authorization (OAuth) or the Security Assertion Markup Language (SAML), or provision standards like SCIM or Service Provisioning Markup Language (SPML).

To enable modeling and managing access control policies throughout an organization, an IAM infrastructure must aggregate data from the numerous target systems and supplemental data sources in an integrated data view [1,11]. This data view includes the authorizations, user identities (and possibly additional information), and the policies defining the resulting authorizations. Common examples of systems providing centralized IAM data views are industrial IAM systems, the Policy Retrieval Point (PRP) and Policy Information Point (PIP) of the XACML standard, (meta-) directories, or relational database views. For decentralized access control mechanisms to work, newly created or changed user identities and access control policies must be provisioned into the target systems in a *provisioning process*, and data inconsistencies must be identified and rectified in a *reconciliation process*. These data aggregation and synchronization tasks are commonly executed by IAM systems (like SailPoint IIQ, One Identity Manager, Oracle IAM, or Microsoft Entra), which also offer extensive logging and data overview functionality. A centralized access control mechanism can reduce or eliminate the need for data provisioning and reconciliation but requires high system interoperability and data standardization.

In summary, the schematic IAM services operate on two infrastructure layers: The heterogeneous application landscape includes numerous target systems and supplemental data sources. On top of it resides a centralized IAM service layer, including an integrated IAM data view and possibly a centralized access control mechanism. Any application may generate various types of log data, e.g. error records or debug information. The generation of transaction logs is not as arbitrary and will be examined in the following. Figure 2 summarizes the schematic IAM infrastructure and the types of log data generated by its components.

Localization of Transaction Logs. As defined in Sect. 3.1, transaction logs are structured records of changes to IAM data. The relevant entities include digital identities, access control policies, and possibly additional information. The integrated data view offers an organization-wide summary of this data. A full transaction log can thus be generated by simply monitoring changes in the integrated data view and logging them in a structured way. This is trivial since it only requires logging all observed create, update, and delete operations on the relevant data, a standard functionality in common database management systems. Industrial IAM systems also need to generate detailed change logs by default to comply with legal regulations[1] which require organizations to track when and how employees were granted rights and how access control rules were modified. Since an integrated IAM data view is a prerequisite for the organization-wide modeling and management of access control policies, we argue that transaction logs are easy to obtain. On principle, these transactions can also be logged locally throughout the heterogeneous application landscape. However, utilizing local transaction logs requires log collection and normalization effort.

3.3   Grounding Transaction Logs on IAM Processes

Transaction log entries provide analytical value because they document events that can be mapped to meaningful real-world activities. IAM Processes provide a structure for such activities to be located and analyzed. A process instance (i.e., a single process execution) spans over a certain execution time and covers a set of logged events that document its execution. Mapping logged events to a process is not always trivial: It requires identifying the process from the log events and then determining which events were part of which process instance. The process mining research domain provides valuable tools for this mapping [32]. For the maintenance of access control policies, IAM processes that change existing authorizations or the composition of policies are especially interesting. Several of these processes are standardized to a certain degree and documented in frameworks such as identity life cycle models, policy life cycle models, or capability maturity models [28]. This section analyzes three exemplary processes and their possible mapping to transaction logs: Joiner, Mover, and Access Review. We selected them because of their wide adoption and clear grounding for access control transaction logs.

---

[1] Global, national, and federal regulation efforts on IAM are numerous and heterogeneous in detail. Notable examples include audited compliance or certifications, like the Sarbanes-Oxley Act (SOX), the Basel Accords, the European General Data Privacy Regulation (GDPR), or the ISO 27000 standards.

The Joiner Process is executed when a person enters an organization. It includes the creation of a digital identity with its respective attributes, as well as the initial assignment of the permissions that the person requires. Typical events documenting the creation of a digital identity are new employee records in an HR system or user accounts in numerous target systems. In these examples, new authorizations can be assigned by roles, directory groups, or target system-specific permissions. Identified instances of the Joiner process can reveal a lot of information as they show a complete digital identity that receives all required authorizations shortly after its creation.

Over-granting causes digital identities to accumulate authorizations. As a result, users typically have significantly more authorizations than they should have according to the principle of least privilege. According to an estimate by practitioners, the proportion of excessive authorization commonly amounts to more than 20% of total authorizations [2]. Maintenance approaches that rely on an organization's current attributes and access control matrix are prone to reproducing these errors [21]. The authorizations granted in the Joiner process are unlikely to contain many excessive authorizations since no accumulation has yet taken place. The initially set attributes are also guaranteed to be timely and likely of high data quality. Therefore, the Joiner Process can provide a better data foundation for policy maintenance than an organization's current attributes and access control matrix. At the same time, the Joiner process provides a complete picture of the digital identities and authorizations at the time of their creation, meaning that it allows the identification of complex authorization patterns.

The Mover Process is executed when a person changes their affiliation within the organization, e.g., the department, cost center, or job title. Due to changes in the person's responsibilities, a Mover process execution is often accompanied by changes in their authorizations. A Mover process execution shows in the transaction logs through attribute changes, e.g., a new value for the attribute department, or through a digital identity losing and receiving multiple authorizations in a short time span. The Mover process allows the identification of strong correlations between attributes and authorizations without requiring knowledge of the full authorization structure: If changes of authorizations or attributes frequently occur together, this indicates that they depend on one another. However, identifying complex attribute patterns can be challenging since a Mover process does not necessarily need to change all attributes required for an authorization. For example, employees might require the permission *Network Access for External IT Employees* after moving from marketing to the IT department. If employees were already externals, the Mover process would only show the attribute change *department = IT*, but not *employee type = external*. Consequently, it is easier to detect excessive authorizations with Mover processes than missing ones, since a digital identity missing either one of these attributes would imply that it should not inherit this permission. In contrast, detecting missing permissions requires knowing the complete pattern.

The Access Review Process aims to identify excessive authorizations (and possibly other errors affecting access control policies, e.g. inaccurate attributes).

It is periodically carried out by employees who check the authorizations of subjects in their responsibility (e.g. department heads). If an excessive authorization is found, it is revoked [18]. Access Review executions are thus shown in transaction logs through their authorization revocation events. They are a valuable source for analysis because they show confirmed errors in the access control matrix. Like access logs, these identified inaccuracies provide a ground truth that can be used to search for further errors. Groll et al. provide formalizations for the analysis of Access Review results. They propose an approach that identifies further excessive authorizations based on past Access Review decisions [13].

Further Implications. Due to over-granting, access control transaction logs are likely to contain more entries that document users receiving authorization than authorization revocations. Furthermore, frequent over-granting causes authorization grant entries to be inaccurate, more likely than revocation entries. This means that revocation entries are potentially more valuable for analysis than grants but also scarcer. Revocation entries might thus be analyzed with higher priority, provided they occur frequently enough to be significant.

4   Conclusion

Our work contributes toward utilizing transaction logs in access control. We formalize the notion of transaction logs in access control. We depict typical IAM infrastructures and locate access control transaction logs within them. Finally, we ground the evaluation of access control transaction logs in typical IAM processes.

We invite fellow researchers to contribute to access control transaction logs in future work: (i) Association rules based on transaction logs may help to find new rules for automated role assignment, ABAC policies, or errors in existing policies and attributes. (ii) Understanding access control policies is a challenge for their maintainers [20]. Automatically generating descriptions of policies based access control transaction logs might add comprehensibility by adding context, e.g., "This role is typically granted to recently promoted managers". (iii) A seamless record of transaction logs allows for inspecting past states. Browsing these past states can provide further insights or visualize the development of metrics not yet defined in the past. Overall, we conclude that transaction logs are a promising yet underutilized data source for improving access control.

Acknowledgments. The German Federal Ministry of Education and Research supported the research leading to these results as part of the DEVISE project.

References

1. Baumer, T., Müller, M., Pernul, G.: System for cross-domain identity management (SCIM): survey and enhancement with RBAC. IEEE Access **11**, 86872–86894 (2023)

2. Baumer, T., Reittinger, T., Kern, S., Pernul, G.: Digital nudges for access reviews: guiding deciders to revoke excessive authorizations. In: Proceedings of the Twentieth USENIX Conference on Usable Privacy and Security, SOUPS 2024. USENIX Association, USA (2024). https://doi.org/10.5555/3696899.3696912

3. Beck, R., Czepluch, J.S., Lollike, N., Malone, S.: Blockchain–the gateway to trust-free cryptographic transactions. In: Twenty-Fourth European Conference on Information Systems (ECIS), İstanbul, Turkey, pp. 1–14. Springer (2016)

4. Benedetti, M., Mori, M.: Parametric RBAC maintenance via max-SAT. In: Proceedings of the 23nd ACM on Symposium on Access Control Models and Technologies, pp. 15–25 (2018)

5. Benedetti, M., Mori, M.: On the use of max-SAT and PDDL in RBAC maintenance. Cybersecurity **2**, 1–25 (2019)

6. Benkaouz, Y., Erradi, M., Freisleben, B.: Work in progress: K-nearest neighbors techniques for ABAC policies clustering. In: Proceedings of the 2016 ACM International Workshop on Attribute Based Access Control, pp. 72–75 (2016)

7. Buffardi, K.: Assessing individual contributions to software engineering projects with git logs and user stories. In: Proceedings of the 51st ACM Technical Symposium on Computer Science Education, pp. 650–656 (2020)

8. Cao, Y., Yang, L.: A survey of identity management technology. In: 2010 IEEE International Conference on Information Theory and Information Security, pp. 287–293 (2010). https://doi.org/10.1109/ICITIS.2010.5689468

9. Davis, T., Shaw, G., Delaney, K.: SQL Server Transaction Log Management. Simple Talk Pub. (2012)

10. Fuchs, L., Kunz, M., Pernul, G.: Role model optimization for secure role-based identity management. In: European Conference on Information Systems (ECIS), pp. 1–15. AIS, Tel Aviv (2014). https://epub.uni-regensburg.de/30394/

11. Fuchs, L., Pernul, G.: Supporting compliant and secure user handling - a structured approach for in-house identity management. In: The Second International Conference on Availability, Reliability and Security (ARES 2007), pp. 374–384. IEEE, Vienna (2007). https://doi.org/10.1109/ARES.2007.145

12. Fuchs, L., Pernul, G.: Hydro–hybrid development of roles. In: Information Systems Security: 4th International Conference, ICISS 2008, Hyderabad, India, 16–20 December 2008. Proceedings 4, pp. 287–302. Springer (2008)

13. Groll, S., Kern, S., Fuchs, L., Pernul, G.: Monitoring access reviews by crowd labelling. In: Trust, Privacy and Security in Digital Business: 18th International Conference, TrustBus 2021, Virtual Event, 27–30 September 2021, Proceedings 18, pp. 3–17. Springer (2021)

14. Gunter, C.A., Liebovitz, D., Malin, B.: Experience-based access management: a life-cycle framework for identity and access management systems. IEEE Secur. Priv. **9**(5), 48 (2011)

15. Hasel Mehri, G., Wester, I.L., Paci, F., Zannone, N.: Mitigating privilege misuse in access control through anomaly detection. In: Proceedings of the 18th International Conference on Availability, Reliability and Security, ARES 2023. Association for Computing Machinery, New York (2023)

16. Hein, P., Biswas, D., Martucci, L.A., Muhlhauser, M.: Conflict detection and life-cycle management for access control in publish/subscribe systems. In: 2011 IEEE 13th International Symposium on High-Assurance Systems Engineering, pp. 104–111. IEEE (2011)

17. Hunt, P., Cam-Winget, N., Kiser, M., Schreiber, J.: SCIM profile for security event tokens. internet-draft draft-ietf-scim-events-07. Internet Engineering Task Force (2024). Work in Progress

18. Jaferian, P., Rashtian, H., Beznosov, K.: To authorize or not authorize: helping users review access policies in organizations. In: 10th Symposium On Usable Privacy and Security (SOUPS 2014), pp. 301–320 (2014)
19. Karimi, L., Aldairi, M., Joshi, J., Abdelhakim, M.: An automatic attribute-based access control policy extraction from access logs. IEEE Trans. Dependable Secure Comput. **19**(4), 2304–2317 (2021)
20. Kern, S., Baumer, T., Fuchs, L., Pernul, G.: Maintain high-quality access control policies: an academic and practice-driven approach. In: Atluri, V., Ferrara, A.L. (eds.) DBSec 2023. LNCS, vol. 13942, pp. 223–242. Springer, Cham (2023). https://doi.org/10.1007/978-3-031-37586-6_14
21. Kern, S., Baumer, T., Groll, S., Fuchs, L., Pernul, G.: Optimization of access control policies. J. Inf. Secur. Appl. **70**, 103301 (2022)
22. Leitner, M., Rinderle-Ma, S.: Anomaly detection and visualization in generative RBAC models. In: Proceedings of the 19th ACM Symposium on Access Control Models and Technologies, pp. 41–52 (2014)
23. Mitra, B., Sural, S., Vaidya, J., Atluri, V.: A survey of role mining. ACM Comput. Surv. **48**(4) (2016). https://doi.org/10.1145/2871148
24. Molloy, I., Chen, H., Li, T., Wang, Q., Li, N., Bertino, E., Calo, S., Lobo, J.: Mining roles with multiple objectives. ACM Trans. Inf. Syst. Secur. (TISSEC) **13**(4), 1–35 (2010)
25. Morisset, C., Sanchez, D.: VisABAC: a tool for visualising ABAC policies. In: ICISSP, pp. 117–126 (2018)
26. Pang, C., Hansen, D., Maeder, A.: Managing RBAC states with transitive relations. In: Proceedings of the 2nd ACM Symposium on Information, Computer and Communications Security, pp. 139–148 (2007)
27. Parkinson, S., Khan, S.: A survey on empirical security analysis of access-control systems: a real-world perspective. ACM Comput. Surv. **55**(6) (2022)
28. Schrimpf, A., Drechsler, A., Dagianis, K.: Assessing identity and access management process maturity: first insights from the German financial sector. Inf. Syst. Manag. **38**(2), 94–115 (2021)
29. Shen, B., Shan, T., Zhou, Y.: Improving logging to reduce permission over-granting mistakes. In: 32nd USENIX Security Symposium (USENIX Security 2023), pp. 409–426. USENIX Association, Anaheim (2023)
30. Skopik, F., Wurzenberger, M., Höld, G., Landauer, M., Kuhn, W.: Behavior-based anomaly detection in log data of physical access control systems. IEEE Trans. Dependable Secure Comput. **20**(4), 3158–3175 (2023)
31. Strembeck, M.: Scenario-driven role engineering. IEEE Secur. Priv. **8**(1), 28–35 (2010)
32. Van Der Aalst, W.: Process mining: overview and opportunities. ACM Trans. Manage. Inf. Syst. (TMIS) **3**(2), 1–17 (2012)
33. Xia, H., Dawande, M., Mookerjee, V.: Role refinement in access control: model and analysis. INFORMS J. Comput. **26**(4), 866–884 (2014)
34. Xiang, C., et al.: Towards continuous access control validation and forensics. In: Proceedings of the 2019 ACM SIGSAC Conference on Computer and Communications Security, pp. 113–129 (2019)

Cryptography for security and privacy

The Privacy Impact of Dash Mixing Fee Payments

Michael H. Ziegler$^{(\boxtimes)}$ ⓘ, Mariusz Nowostawski ⓘ, and Basel Katt ⓘ

NTNU, Teknologiveien 22, Gjøvik, Norway
{michael.h.ziegler,mariusz.nowostawski,basel.katt}@ntnu.no

Abstract. We have conducted a comprehensive examination of the fee payment process within the Dash CoinJoin implementation. We have discovered that the fee payment process leaks privacy information. This privacy leakage leads to the potential linking of addresses that the Coin-Join transaction design attempts to maintain private. We demonstrate that the transactions involved in the mixing process are identifiable and provide classification rules to build a transaction data set with appropriate classifications. Using this dataset, we highlight how the fee payment mechanism reveals sensitive information about users' mixing activities. We achieve this by linking the fee-payment transactions and analyzing their timestamps. Finally, our analysis reveals a significant occurrence of address reuse within the fee payment process and we provide a summary of the statistics obtained.

Keywords: Blockchain · Cryptocurrency · Privacy · Dash

1 Introduction

The emergence of blockchain technology has fundamentally transformed the financial landscape, enabling the creation of decentralized digital currencies that operate without the need for central authorities. Bitcoin, introduced in 2008 (cf. [11]), was the first cryptocurrency to leverage this innovative technology, providing a peer-to-peer electronic cash system that enabled secure and transparent peer-to-peer transactions. However, as Bitcoin gained traction, it faced significant challenges related to scalability, transaction speed, and privacy, which prompted the development of alternative cryptocurrencies designed to address these limitations.

The inherent transparency of blockchain transactions poses significant privacy risks, exposing users' financial histories and potentially revealing sensitive information through public data stored in the blockchain. This lack of privacy can deter adoption, particularly for individuals and businesses seeking to protect their financial data and financial histories from unwanted scrutiny. Privacy-enhancing technologies are therefore crucial to fostering wider acceptance and usage of cryptocurrencies.

ⓒ IFIP International Federation for Information Processing 2025
Published by Springer Nature Switzerland AG 2025
S. Katsikas and B. Shafiq (Eds.): DBSec 2025, LNCS 15722, pp. 427–438, 2025.
https://doi.org/10.1007/978-3-031-96590-6_23

One such protocol is Dash, launched in 2014, which aism to optimize transactional efficiency and augment user privacy. A core component of the Dash architecture is its integrated CoinJoin functionality, executed through `masternodes`, which aims to obfuscate the provenance of digital assets, thus strengthening transactional confidentiality. CoinJoin transactions in Dash aim to enhance privacy by mixing multiple users' inputs into a single transaction, obfuscating the source and destination of funds. Dash implements this through `masternodes`, which facilitate the mixing process, thereby disrupting the traceability of transactions on the blockchain.

Although blockchain systems employ diverse privacy-preserving techniques, such as zero-knowledge proofs in ZCash and ring signatures in Monero, this study specifically focuses on the CoinJoin method within the Dash ecosystem. CoinJoin itself is not exclusive to Dash; it is a broader privacy technology utilized in various blockchains, as exemplified by implementations like Wasabi Wallet in Bitcoin. Dash's distinctive approach to CoinJoin involves funding mixing fees through `masternode` collateral. This study investigates the intricacies of this fee payment mechanism, identifying and analyzing two potential privacy vulnerabilities.

We aim to answer the following research questions:

- **RQ1:** How can transactions involved in the Dash mixing process be identified?
- **RQ2:** Can the mixing activity of a user be observed via the mixing fee payment process of the Dash CoinJoin system?
- **RQ3:** Are addresses part of the mixing fee payment process of the Dash CoinJoin system being reused?

In Sect. 2 the necessary concepts are introduced to be able to discuss the privacy issues presented in Sect. 4 and Sect. 5. In Sect. 3 the classification rules for collateral transactions are presented, which are necessary to build the transaction dataset that is used to answer the research questions. Lastly, Sect. 6 explores potential avenues for future research based on the privacy issues discussed.

Note, this paper utilizes real-world transaction data from the public Dash blockchain to illustrate our findings. Recognizing that financial transactions constitute personal data, and to safeguard user privacy, we present anonymized examples by displaying truncated transaction hashes. Although obscured, these examples are fully reproducible using publicly available data from the Dash blockchain.

2   Background

2.1   Blockchain

A blockchain is a type of decentralized database that is distributed through replication across its network of peers. It was introduced by Nakamoto [11] in 2008 to build a decentralized digital currency called *Bitcoin*, where users can interact peer-to-peer without a central trusted coordinator. Instead of directly updating data, in blockchain systems, a collection of change records (transactions), is appended in aggregated units called blocks to its database. These transactions alter the state of the blockchain system. All participating peers can validate these state changes and must reach a consensus on the state maintained in the distributed database. Consequently, a blockchain serves as an immutable record of state changes initiated by the transactions of its peers, extending up to the most recent block.

The Bitcoin blockchain system is intended to achieve value transfers between its users. But it is not limited only to support value transfers. Any type of state can be recorded in the decentralized blockchain. The only limitations are the memory capacity and processing power of the peers in the decentralized network. As blockchain systems use cryptographic methods to provide security and data authenticity, a currency operating on blockchain systems is known as a cryptocurrency.

UTXO stands for Unspent Transaction Output. In UTXO-based blockchains, like Bitcoin or Dash, transactions are structured around these UTXOs. Each transaction consumes existing UTXOs as inputs and creates new UTXOs as outputs. Essentially, instead of account balances, the system tracks a ledger of these unspent outputs, which represent discrete amounts of cryptocurrency. When you send cryptocurrency, you are essentially spending one or more of your UTXOs and creating new ones for the recipient and, if needed, for the change amount back to yourself. Transactions in blockchain systems which use the UTXO-based model are therefore composed of inputs and outputs. A transaction spends inputs and creates new outputs. Newly created outputs can become inputs for other transactions. Each output is associated with a script that defines how it may be spent. Each output is linked to a blockchain address.

The Dash cryptocurrency is similar to the Bitcoin blockchain. However, it extends and puts the focus on user privacy by including a native implementation of a trustless CoinJoin system (see Sect. 2.4). Its native currency is DASH. It uses a forked blockchain client, as well as the UTXO account model. However, a major difference is its `masternode` system. By staking 1000 DASH, users can operate a `masternode` that provides a variety of services to the users of the blockchain system, one of which is the CoinJoin service.

2.2   Address Clustering

In blockchain systems, identities are represented by cryptographic addresses, which are derived from the public keys of cryptographic key pairs. Since transaction outputs are signed by their creators, ownership can be verified. Each user in blockchain systems owns multiple addresses, and their respective private and public keys are stored in the user wallets.

In Bitcoin, Dash and many other cryptocurrencies, all transactions are accessible in plain text to any participating peer. This transparency allows for the complete transaction history to be examined, enabling the tracing of value movements between addresses. Consequently, addresses controlled by a user serve as their pseudonyms.

Address clustering techniques are used by blockchain analysts to deduce ownership and connections between seemingly disparate addresses, thereby compromising user privacy. The motivation behind address clustering stems from the desire to trace financial flows, identify illicit activities, and gain insights into user behavior. A fundamental technique, the multi-input heuristic (cf. [9]), leverages the common assumption that non-CoinJoin transactions originate from a single entity. This heuristic operates by linking all input addresses within a given transaction, effectively clustering them under a presumed common owner. The rationale is that users consolidating funds from multiple addresses are likely controlling those addresses, facilitating the reconstruction of their transaction history and potential identification.

2.3   Address Reuse

Blockchain address reuse refers to the practice of using the same address multiple times for receiving or sending transactions. In UTXO-based blockchains, such as Bitcoin and Dash, this practice is strongly discouraged because it compromises privacy. Each address and its associated transaction history become linked, revealing the flow of funds and potentially exposing the user's financial activity. This linkage defeats the intended anonymity of the blockchain, making it easier to trace transactions and identify users.

In [1] the practice of address reuse in the Bitcoin blockchain is examined. The authors find that address reuse is widespread, from Bitcoin mining to exchanges. They calculate an average reuse of addresses of 2.15 outputs in their study at the end of 2018.

The authors of [7] also study address reuse in the Bitcoin system. They note that once an address spends all its funds, it is statistically unlikely to be used again. However, they have also found that existing addresses are used 55.25% of the time instead of newly generated ones.

Although previous studies address broader address reuse in Bitcoin, our investigation is uniquely focused on the privacy-critical context of address reuse within Dash's mixing fee payments, where it directly conflicts with the core purpose of the mixing protocol.

In [2,12] common transaction patterns within the Bitcoin blockchain are analyzed to improve address clustering methods. While these are also applicable to the Dash blockchain system, the attention in our work is on the transaction patterns of the Dash mixing fee payment process and the privacy implications of the fee payments.

2.4   CoinJoin

The inherent transparency of Bitcoin's blockchain, where all transaction data is publicly accessible, significantly limits user privacy. The visibility of value transfers enables straightforward tracking of fund movements, potentially revealing sensitive financial information. Adding to this issue, address clustering techniques, which exploit patterns in transaction data to link addresses to common ownership, further erode user privacy by facilitating the reconstruction of transaction histories and the potential identification of individuals. This combination of public data and analytical techniques underscores the need for privacy-enhancing mechanisms in blockchain systems. In the early days of Bitcoin [8] noted that a single transaction can be created by multiple users, as each user could contribute their own input and output pairs before the transaction was published. As the outputs or coins are joined, it is called a *CoinJoin* or *CoinJoin transaction*. Creating such transactions multiple times in sequence further obscures the ownership of the original funds and is referred to as mixing or a mixing process. The multi-input address clustering heuristic, which relies on the assumption that a single entity controls all inputs within a transaction, is rendered ineffective against CoinJoin transactions. This is because CoinJoin transactions deliberately aggregate inputs from multiple, distinct users, thereby violating the heuristic's foundational premise.

2.5   Dash CoinJoin

Dash offers a native CoinJoin implementation based on its master node network. As it is native, it is able to have CoinJoin transactions with a transaction fee of zero because the transaction fee is paid via a separate collateral payment system.

To participate in a Dash CoinJoin transaction, commonly referred to as *PrivateSend*, users must first structure their funds into standardized denominations. This preparatory step ensures that the mixing process can effectively obfuscate the origin of funds by creating a pool of identically valued inputs. Dash facilitates this denomination process through a specialized transaction type, the *Denomination Creation* transaction. This transaction splits user-held UTXOs into specific predefined denominations, such as 0.1 DASH, 1 DASH, or 10 DASH, which are then eligible for mixing. By standardizing the input values, Dash's CoinJoin implementation creates a more uniform and indistinguishable set of inputs, making it significantly harder for blockchain analysts to trace the flow of funds and link inputs to specific users. This denomination requirement is a crucial aspect of Dash's privacy strategy, as it directly contributes to the effectiveness of its CoinJoin mechanism.

To prevent abuse, users are randomly selected to pay collateral during the mixing process. Similarly to the *Denomination Creation* transaction, collateral outputs have to be created first. This is achieved via *Collateral Creation* transactions. *Collateral Creation* transactions are created by spending outputs of CoinJoin transactions or *Denomination Creation* transactions. If a user is selected to pay a collateral, outputs of *Collateral Creation* transactions are then used by *Collateral Payment* transactions, which pay the collateral via the transaction fee. *Collateral Payment* transactions can use either an output of a *Collateral Creation* transaction or an output of another *Collateral Payment* transaction.

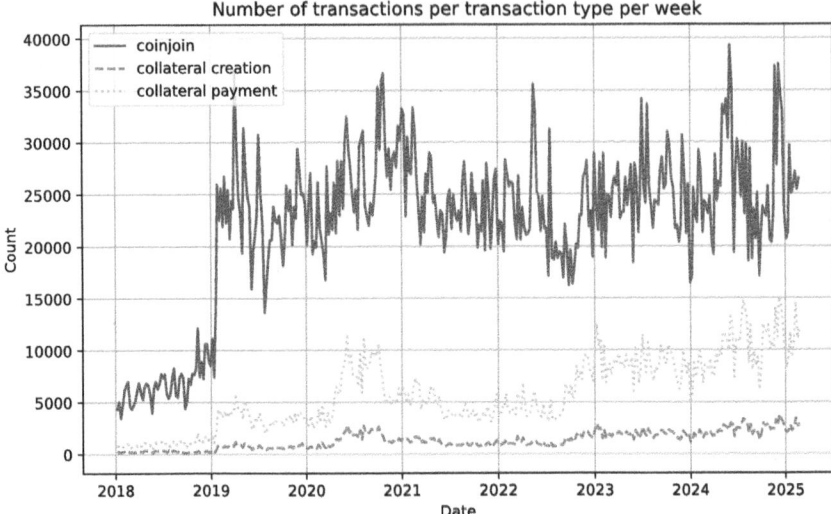

Fig. 1. Number of transactions per transaction type per week starting from 2018 until March 2025.

3   Collateral Transaction Classification (RQ1)

To identify transactions involved in the Dash mixing process, significant attributes of each transaction type must be identified. This is possible by reviewing the Dash documentation (see [5]) and by assessing the on-chain transaction data.

We determined several transaction characteristics related to the number of inputs, number of outputs, transaction fee and denominations. Appendix A contains the concrete classification rules.

After applying the classification rules, we can identify each transaction involved in the Dash mixing process. Lacking a formal validation dataset, we rely on the inherent properties of Dash CoinJoin transactions: their unique denominations and zero fees, to establish validity. The necessary relationship between these transactions and other types greatly reduces the risk of false positives. We are confident in our methodology and the reproducibility of our results, which are based on verifiable blockchain data.

Figure 1 depicts the results of the classification rules applied for the collateral and CoinJoin transactions. The steep increase in CoinJoin transactions at the beginning of 2019 is due to the release of Dash core version 0.13 (see [4]), which enabled parallel mixing sessions and added new mixing amount denominations. The number of collateral creation and collateral payment transactions follows the trend of mixing activity.

The proposed classification rules establish that transactions associated with the Dash mixing process can be effectively identified. The resulting data set,

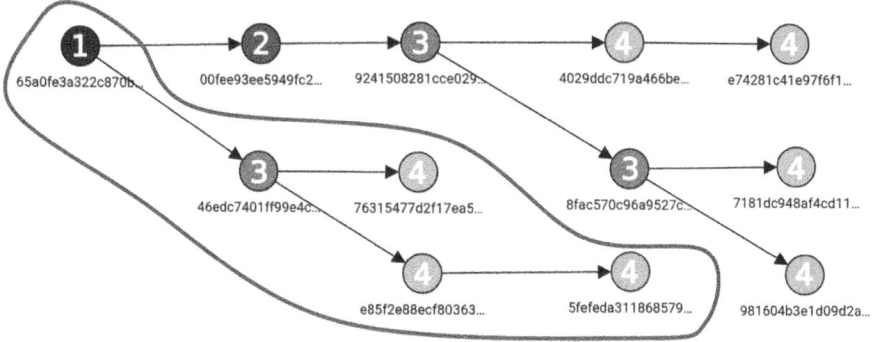

Fig. 2. Transaction graph of the start of a mixing process. The dark red node (1) on the top left is a *Denomination Creation* transactions. The red node (2) directly connected to its right a CoinJoin transaction. The dark green nodes (3) are *Collateral Creation* transactions, while the light green nodes (4) are *Collateral Payment* transactions. The nodes inside the area marked by the red lasso can be attributed to the user who started this mixing process.

derived from this identification process, serves as the foundation for addressing the remaining research questions, which are explored in detail in the subsequent sections.

4   Observability of Multiple Mixing Sessions (RQ2)

The start of a Dash mixing process can be observed by searching for *Denomination Creation* transactions. *Denomination Creation* transactions split the initial amount into Dash mixing denominations (see Appendix A.1). Outputs of *Denomination Creation* transactions are then used by CoinJoin transactions to perform the mixing. Some of the outputs are also used by *Collateral Creation* transactions to prepare funds for the collateral payment process. Note that all inputs and outputs of *Denomination Creation*, *Collateral Creation* and *Collateral Payment* transactions of a mixing process are controlled by the respective user. This is in contrast to normal blockchain transactions, where usually at least one of the transaction outputs is controlled by a different entity. By traversing the transaction graph forward in time, starting at a *Denomination Creation* transaction, the collateral transactions can be found.

Figure 2 depicts a transaction graph with two collateral payment processes. The transaction nodes inside the area marked by the red lasso can be attributed to the user who started the mixing process, while the collateral transactions outside of the area cannot be attributed to a user, as they stem from a CoinJoin transaction.

As the collateral payment process is probabilistic, the prepared collateral amounts are not always fully consumed after the mixing process. When the user starts another mixing process, the leftover collateral outputs of previous mixing processes are used for new collateral payments. The prepared collateral outputs

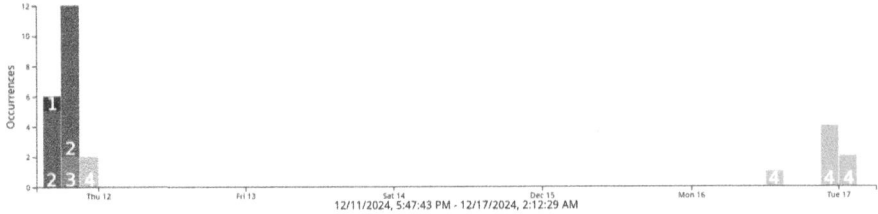

Fig. 3. Timeline of occurrences of Dash CoinJoin transactions. The start of the chart shows an accumulation of *Denomination Creation* transactions and its connected collateral transactions on the 11th of December 2024, while a few days later at the end of the chart, more *Collateral Payment* transactions appear. The gap between the transactions indicates separate mixing processes by the same user. *Denomination Creation* transactions are marked in dark red (1), CoinJoin transactions in red (2), *Create Collateral* transactions in dark green (3) and *Collateral Payment* transactions in light green (4). (Color figure online)

of a user are therefore not bound to a single mixing process and are instead shared by multiple mixing processes of a user.

This behaviour can be exploited to determine if a user is participating in secondary mixing processes after the initial mixing process has ended: If more *Collateral Creation* transactions or *Collateral Payment* transactions are created, which are connected to the start of the initial mixing process, then the same user is again mixing coins.

Figure 3 shows an example of shared collaterals between two mixing sessions. The first mixing session is determined by detecting the *Denomination Creation* transaction and following the links to the collateral transactions. The figure depicts that after a few days more *Collateral Payment* transactions are created, which are connected to the transactions of the initial mixing process start.

We want to determine wether this behavior is prevalent. We define any *Collateral Payment* transaction which uses an output that is older than 12 h compared to the creation time of the *Collateral Payment* transaction as an indicator for a separate mixing session.

We examined the Dash blockchain from the beginning of 2018 and collected all *Collateral Payment* transactions until the start of March 2025. We found that 10.36% of the collected 2196242 transactions spend outputs that are at least 12 h old and therefor indicators of secondary mixing sessions. The indicator transactions utilize outputs from transactions which are, on average, 14 days old, with a median age of 2 days and 6 h. We found a maximum output age of 1970 days. We therefore conclude that by analyzing *Collateral Payment* transaction timestamps, the mixing activity of users can be often followed.

Users use CoinJoins to increase the privacy of their on-chain activity by obscuring the ownership of the funds that they control. By being able to (partially) observe the activity of multiple mixing processes via the collateral transactions, the privacy properties of Dash CoinJoins are reduced. While this method is not enough to fully connect different mixing sessions of a single user, it leaks important information that could be used in combination with user information leaks.

To alleviate these issues, we recommend the following:

– Prefer to pay collaterals created from outputs of CoinJoin transactions. As outputs of CoinJoin transactions can not be easily linked to their owner, collaterals created from these outputs share the same property.
– Do not share collaterals which are directly linked to the *Denomination Creation* transaction between mixing sessions. Leftover collateral outputs should not be used in secondary mixing processes.

5 Reuse of Fee Payment Addresses (RQ3)

As discussed in Sect. 2.3, using an address for multiple transaction outputs constitutes a reuse of an address. Reused addresses generally decrease the privacy of their users, as on-chain activity can be easily followed, even without address clustering (see Sect. 2.2). Users participating in a mixing process aim to increase their on-chain privacy by obscuring the ownership and linkage of their funds.

Our goal is to assess whether address reuse is prevalent in the fee payment mechanism of the Dash CoinJoin system. To do this, we analyze the collected collateral transactions mentioned in Sect. 3 and examine whether any of the addresses involved in these transactions control more than one output. If an address controls multiple outputs, it is an address reuse.

Figure 4 summarizes the result of this analysis. The chart depicts the ratio of addresses that control at least two outputs. The data includes addresses used in collateral transactions from 2018 until the beginning of March 2025. *Collateral Creation* transactions use outputs with 143 323 unique addresses and *Collateral Payment* transaction use outputs with 83 234 unique addresses. Especially addresses of *Collateral Creation* transactions are often reused (13.26%) compared to the ratio of addresses of *Collateral Payment* transactions (3.77%). Address reuse in this context is especially damaging to the privacy of its users, as they directly link them to their mixing activity.

We note that the reuse of addresses is likely not due to human actions, but rather is a result of the mixing process within the Dash core wallet software. This conclusion is supported by our findings that there are numerous instances of address reuse occurring between CoinJoin transactions and collateral transactions. Note that these transactions are generated automatically by the wallet software, rather than being created manually by a user and thus leak some of the privacy guarantees potentially without the user realizing it.

In the opinion of the authors, the address reuse occurring in collateral transactions can be easily avoided by generating new addresses for new transaction outputs. There is no technical challenge to solve.

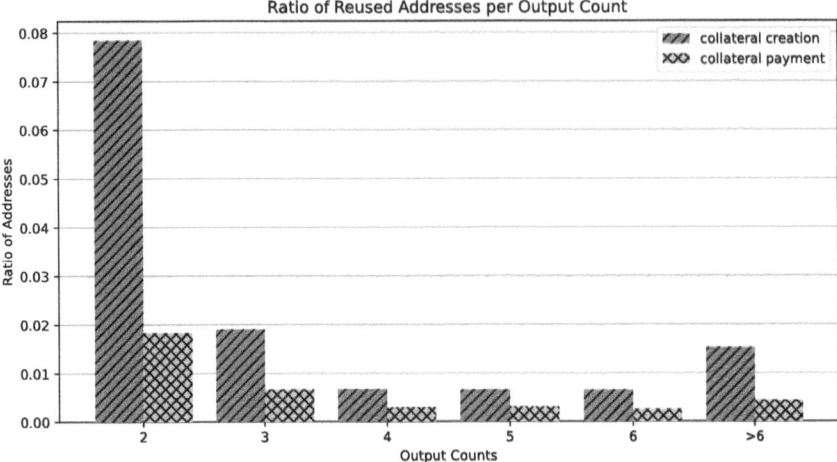

Fig. 4. Ratio of addresses used by collateral transactions which control at least two outputs. While *Collateral Creation* transactions have generally a higher ratio of address reuse compared to *Collateral Payment* transactions, the practice of address reuse for both transaction types is significant.

6   Conclusion

In this study, we conducted an in-depth analysis of the fee payment process within the Dash CoinJoin implementation to identify potential privacy vulnerabilities. Our findings reveal three critical insights: First, we demonstrated that transactions involved in the mixing process can be systematically identified. Second, using the resulting dataset, we established that the fee payment mechanism inadvertently leaks information about users' mixing activities, compromising their privacy. Third, we observed that address reuse in the fee payment process is widespread, further exacerbating privacy risks.

These findings open several avenues for future research. The insights from this work could be leveraged to develop an enhanced address clustering algorithm, as all addresses associated with the fee payment mechanism can be directly linked to their respective users. Additionally, future work could explore the development of improved privacy-preserving fee payment mechanisms for Coin-Join implementations, such as decoupling fee payments from mixing transactions or integrating zero-knowledge proofs to obscure fee-related metadata. Furthermore, a broader investigation into the prevalence and impact of address reuse across other privacy-focused cryptocurrencies could provide valuable comparative insights. Finally, the methodology employed in this work could be adapted to analyze other mixing protocols, such as CoinSwap, Wassabi (cf. [6]) or Chaumian CoinJoins [3,10] (utilizing blind signatures), to assess their privacy guarantees and identify potential vulnerabilities.

Disclosure of Interests. The authors have no competing interests to declare which are relevant to the content of this article.

A   Appendix

A.1   CoinJoin Transaction Classification Algorithm

Dash defines the following denominations: 10.0001, 1.00001, 0.100001, 0.0100001, 0.00100001 [5].

The classification criteria for CoinJoin transactions are:

- The number of inputs and outputs must be equal
- The transaction fee must be zero
- All input and output amounts must be part of the defined denominations
- All inputs and outputs must be of the same denomination

A.2   Denomination Creation Transaction Classification Algorithm

Classification criteria for *Denomination Creation* transactions depend on the classification of CoinJoin transactions and thus should be classified afterwards. The criteria are:

- Must not be CoinJoin transaction itself
- At least one of its outputs must be spent by a CoinJoin transaction

A.3   Collateral Creation Transaction Classification Algorithm

Outputs created by the *Collateral Creation* transaction are used by *Collateral Payment* transactions to pay the collateral in the Dash mixing process. The minimum collateral is 10% of the smallest denomination, which currently translates to 0.0001 DASH. In previous versions, the collateral was 0.001 DASH as the lowest denomination had a higher value.

The classification criteria for *Collateral Creation* transactions are [5]:

- The transaction must pay a transaction fee
- All transaction inputs must be owned by a single address
- The transaction must create exactly two outputs, each owned by a unique address
- One of the transaction outputs must have enough funds to pay the minimum collateral 4 times
- At least one of the transaction inputs must be an output of a CoinJoin transaction, a *Collateral Creation* transaction or a *Denomination Creation* transaction

A.4   Collateral Payment Transaction Classification Algorithm

Classification criteria for *Collateral Payment* transactions are [5]:

- The transaction must have exactly one input
- The transaction must have exactly one output
- The transaction must spend an output from either a *Collateral Creation* transaction or from a *Collateral Payment* transaction
- The transaction must pay a transaction fee of at least the minimum collateral (see Appendix A.3).

References

1. Bistarelli, S., Mercanti, I., Faloci, F., Santini, F.: Highlighting poor anonymity and security practice in the blockchain of bitcoin. In: Proceedings of the 36th Annual ACM Symposium on Applied Computing, SAC 2021, pp. 265–272. ACM (2021). https://doi.org/10.1145/3412841.3441909
2. Chang, T.H., Svetinovic, D.: Improving bitcoin ownership identification using transaction patterns analysis. IEEE Trans. Syst. Man Cybern.: Syst. **50**(1), 9–20 (2020). https://doi.org/10.1109/tsmc.2018.2867497
3. Chaum, D.: Blind signatures for untraceable payments. In: Chaum, D., Rivest, R.L., Sherman, A.T. (eds.) Advances in Cryptology, pp. 199–203. Springer, Boston (1983). https://doi.org/10.1007/978-1-4757-0602-4_18
4. Dash Core Group, I.: Dash core version 0.13.0.0 (2019). https://github.com/dashpay/dash/blob/v0.13.0.0/doc/release-notes.md#privatesend
5. Dash Core Group, I.: Dash core CoinJoin documentation (2025). https://docs.dash.org/projects/core/en/stable/docs/guide/dash-features-coinjoin.html
6. Ficsór, A., Seres, I.A., Kogman, Y., Ontivero, L.: WabiSabi: centrally coordinated coinjoins with variable amounts. Cryptoecon. Syst. (2021).https://doi.org/10.21428/58320208.29539ffd
7. Gaihre, A., Luo, Y., Liu, H.: Do bitcoin users really care about anonymity? An analysis of the bitcoin transaction graph. In: 2018 IEEE International Conference on Big Data (Big Data), pp. 1198–1207. IEEE (2018). https://doi.org/10.1109/bigdata.2018.8622442
8. Maxwell, G.: CoinJoin: bitcoin privacy for the real world (2013). https://bitcointalk.org/index.php?topic=279249
9. Meiklejohn, S., et al.: A fistful of bitcoins: characterizing payments AmongMen with no names. In: Proceedings of the 2013 conference on Internet measurement conference, IMC 2013. ACM (2013). https://doi.org/10.1145/2504730.2504747
10. Mizrahi, A.: Coin mixing using Chaum's blind signatures (2013). https://bitcointalk.org/index.php?topic=150681.0
11. Nakamoto, S.: Bitcoin: a peer-to-peer electronic cash system (2008). https://bitcoin.org/bitcoin.pdf
12. Ranshous, S., et al.: Exchange Pattern Mining in the Bitcoin Transaction Directed Hypergraph. In: Brenner, M., et al. (eds.) FC 2017. LNCS, vol. 10323, pp. 248–263. Springer, Cham (2017). https://doi.org/10.1007/978-3-319-70278-0_16

Cryptanalysis and Modification of a Variant of Matrix Operation for Randomization or Encryption (v-MORE)

Sona Alex[✉] and Bian Yang

Norwegian University of Science and Technology, Gjøvik, Norway
{sona.alex,bian.yang}@ntnu.no

Abstract. A variant of Matrix Operation for Randomization or Encryption (v-MORE) is a lightweight, real number-based, fully homomorphic encryption scheme used for outsourced secure medical data processing. This paper shows the vulnerability of v-MORE to a ciphertext-only attack when it is used in privacy-preserving applications where the data is not random. From the ciphertexts of v-MORE, the attacker can solve for its secrets based on linear algebra and predict the plaintext from a new ciphertext with 100% confidence. Hence, v-MORE can not ensure the privacy of medical data, which is not random, while processing it remotely and transmitting it over networks. Experimental analysis shows that the attack complexity is very low. v-MORE encryption is modified to mitigate the proposed ciphertext-only attack and developed additively homomorphic encryption that operates on real numbers (AHE-R). Also, experimental analysis and security analysis confirm that the modifications do not noticeably affect the computational and communication overhead while providing data security.

Keywords: Homomorphic encryption · security · cryptanalysis

1 Introduction

The homomorphic encryption schemes (HE) are a promising solution to preserve data confidentiality while allowing secure processing in an untrusted environment [1–3]. HE schemes are widely used for outsourced data processing such as cloud-based privacy-preserving disease detection (PPDD) [4–7]. Additively homomorphic encryptions (AHE) (e.g., Paillier [2,8] and Two-trapdoor cryptosystem [5]) and fully homomorphic encryption (FHE) schemes (e.g., FHMRS [4], BGV [3], v-MORE [9]) are used in machine learning (ML)-based PPDD. Also, the HE schemes should be computationally efficient as outsourced PPDD involves processing at resource-constrained devices [10,11]. Symmetric-key-based HE schemes show better computational and communication efficiency compared to public-key-based schemes [4,9,12–14]. Hence, symmetric-key-based HE schemes are suitable for PPDD [4,9,12–14].

© IFIP International Federation for Information Processing 2025
Published by Springer Nature Switzerland AG 2025
S. Katsikas and B. Shafiq (Eds.): DBSec 2025, LNCS 15722, pp. 439–455, 2025.
https://doi.org/10.1007/978-3-031-96590-6_24

Most HE schemes, including lightweight symmetric key-based schemes, operate on integers [1–7,13,14]. However, ML algorithms, such as deep neural networks, operate on real numbers. Hence, real numbers need to be converted to integers without affecting accuracy and efficiency. Moreover, an encryption scheme that operates on real numbers can mitigate the real number to integer conversion [9,12].

A variant of Matrix Operation for Randomization or Encryption (v-MORE) encryption scheme [9] is one of the lightweight symmetric-key based fully homomorphic encryption (FHE) that operates on real numbers. v-MORE is used for outsourced secure medical data processing [9,12]. v-MORE is derived from Matrix Operation for Randomization or Encryption (MORE) [15], a symmetric-key-based FHE scheme that operates on integers. The known-plaintext attacks proposed for MORE [17,18] are also applicable to the v-MORE. Hence, it is essential to analyze the attack resistance of the v-MORE when it is used in sensitive application domains [16–18] such as the healthcare domain. Moreover, in most applications, including healthcare applications, the data may not be uniformly distributed, and the attacker may have some a priori information regarding it [19].

In this paper, we have analyzed the security of v-MORE encryption scheme applied in privacy-preserving healthcare applications where health data is not uniformly distributed and found its vulnerability to a ciphertext-only attack. As an encryption scheme vulnerable to ciphertext-only attacks is considered to be non-secure, there is a need to modify v-MORE to resist ciphertext-only attacks. Hence, the following are the primary contributions of this paper,

- Revealed a low-complex method to break the v-MORE encryption scheme by knowing only the ciphertexts. The attack relies on linear algebra and reveals the plaintext with 100% confidence.
- Modified v-MORE to mitigate the proposed ciphertext-only attack and the modified scheme (Additively Homomorphic Encryption on Real Numbers (AHE-R)) is additively homomorphic and operates on real numbers. Also, the resistance of AHE-R against security threats (ciphertext-only attacks and known-plaintext attacks) and the performance efficiency are analyzed.

The structure of the paper is as follows: Sect. 2 contains the details of the v-MORE encryption scheme. Section 3 gives the related works. The fourth section covers the proposed ciphertext-only attack. In Sect. 5, the proposed modification to v-MORE is presented. Sections 6 and 7 contain the security and performance analysis of the proposed methods. Section 8 gives the concluding remarks.

2   Preliminaries

This section details the v-MORE encryption method used for privacy-preserving healthcare applications [9] and lemmas on diagonal matrices given in [18].

2.1   Variant of Matrix Operation for Randomization or Encryption (v-MORE)

Matrix Operation for Randomization or Encryption (MORE) [15] is a symmetric-key-based encryption that encrypts messages by conjugating a random invertible matrix over an RSA modulus. MORE encryption works on integers. v-MORE [9] is derived from MORE to apply encryption on the real numbers, so privacy-preserving neural networks do not require real-to-integer number conversion. The functions involved in v-MORE are detailed below.

– KeyGeneration(): The function KeyGeneration() generates a secret key matrix $\mathbf{S} \in \mathbb{R}^{2\times 2}$ such that determinant of $\mathbf{S} \neq 0$. $\mathbf{S}$ is an invertible matrix.
– Encryption($m, \mathbf{S}$): Accepts secret key ($\mathbf{S}$) and the message $m \in \mathbb{R}$ to be encrypted as inputs. Choose a random number $r \in \mathbb{R}$. Then a 2×2 input matrix is created as $\mathbf{M} = \begin{bmatrix} m & 0 \\ 0 & r \end{bmatrix}$. The ciphertext matrix $\mathbf{C}$ is computed as $\mathbf{C} = \mathbf{S} \times \mathbf{M} \times \mathbf{S}^{-1}$.
– Decryption($\mathbf{C}, \mathbf{S}$): This function takes the ciphertext matrix $\mathbf{C}$ and secret matrix $\mathbf{S}$ as inputs. The message (m) is computed as the $(0, 0)^{th}$ element of $\mathbf{S}^{-1} \times \mathbf{C} \times \mathbf{S}$.

MORE encryption supports homomorphic addition and multiplication. E.g., Assume $\mathbf{C}_1$ and $\mathbf{C}_2$ are ciphertexts corresponding to m_1 and m_2, respectively.

(1) Homomorphic addition: Addition of $\mathbf{C}_1$ and $\mathbf{C}_2$ corresponds to addition of m_1 and m_2 as given in Eq. (1).

$$\mathbf{C}_1 + \mathbf{C}_2 = \mathbf{S} \times \mathbf{M}_1 \times \mathbf{S}^{-1} + \mathbf{S} \times \mathbf{M}_2 \times \mathbf{S}^{-1} = \mathbf{S} \times (\mathbf{M}_1 + \mathbf{M}_2) \times \mathbf{S}^{-1} \quad (1)$$

(2) Homomorphic multiplication: Multiplication of $\mathbf{C}_1$ and $\mathbf{C}_2$ corresponds to multiplication of m_1 and m_2 as given in Eq. (2)

$$\mathbf{C}_1 \times \mathbf{C}_2 = \mathbf{S} \times \mathbf{M}_1 \times \mathbf{S}^{-1} \times \mathbf{S} \times \mathbf{M}_2 \times \mathbf{S}^{-1} = \mathbf{S} \times (\mathbf{M}_1 \times \mathbf{M}_2) \times \mathbf{S}^{-1} \quad (2)$$

2.2   Properties of Diagonal Matrices

The lemmas related to diagonal matrices given in [18] are as follows:

Lemma 1. *Each matrix* $\boldsymbol{A} = \begin{bmatrix} a & b \\ c & d \end{bmatrix}$ *with non-zero diagonal entries is of the form* $\begin{bmatrix} a & 0 \\ 0 & d \end{bmatrix} \times \begin{bmatrix} 1 & b/a \\ c/d & 1 \end{bmatrix}$

Lemma 2. *A 2×2 matrix commutes with all diagonal matrices if an only if it is diagonal.*

3   Related Works

Kipnis et al. proposed a lightweight symmetric key-based fully homomorphic encryption scheme based on matrix multiplication over a Rivest–Shamir–Adleman (RSA) modulus and named as MORE [15]. However, the simplicity in the MORE construction makes the scheme vulnerable to known-plaintext attacks [17,18]. Vizar et al. [17] show that MORE does not possess indistinguishability property as plaintext is always a root of the characteristic polynomial of its ciphertext. The authors proposed a key recovery attack on the MORE scheme based on the known polynomial relation between some plaintexts. This known plaintext attack is possible since the message is an eigenvalue of the ciphertext matrix.

Tsaban et al. [18] proposed a known-plaintext attack on MORE based on diagonal matrix properties. If the attacker knows the single plaintext-ciphertext pair, an equation can be derived from the ciphertext matrix to solve for a single variable. The attacker can solve for the plaintext when he gets the next ciphertext.

Even though MORE is vulnerable to known-plaintext attack, Vizitiu et al. modified MORE to incorporate plaintext as a real number for the development of privacy-preserving deep neural networks for healthcare applications and termed as v-MORE [9]. Here, the authors assumed that only ciphertext data is available to external computing services while the raw data remains private and safe on the side of the medical user. Hence, an attacker will not get ciphertext-plaintext pairs to mount a known-plaintext attack. In connection with the previous proposal, Vizitiu et al. proposed a framework for privacy-preserving wearable health data analysis based on v-MORE and considered Atrial fibrillation detection as an application [12].

It is essential to analyze the attack resistance of v-MORE as it is used in healthcare applications.

4   Cryptanalysis of v-MORE

This section details the cryptanalysis of the v-MORE encryption scheme given in Sect. 2.1 to deduce plaintext from the ciphertext.

4.1   Ciphertext-Only Attack

An attacker can mount a ciphertext-only attack on v-MORE using ciphertexts transmitted over networks or stored in the cloud for secure medical data processing. In v-MORE, ciphertext matrix, $C = S \times M \times S^{-1}$, where $M = \begin{bmatrix} m & 0 \\ 0 & r \end{bmatrix}$. Since C and M are similar matrices, they have the same eigenvalues. Also, as

$\mathbf{M}$ is a diagonal matrix, its eigenvalues are diagonal elements m and r.

$$\lambda = \frac{Tr(\mathbf{C})}{2} \pm \frac{\sqrt{(Tr(\mathbf{C}))^2 - 4 \times Det(\mathbf{C})}}{2}$$

$$= \frac{(c_{0,0} + c_{1,1})}{2} \pm \frac{\sqrt{(c_{0,0} + c_{1,1})^2 - 4 \times (c_{0,0} \times c_{1,1} - c_{0,1} \times c_{1,0})}}{2} \tag{3}$$

Hence, finding the eigenvalues of $\mathbf{C}$ (λ) by computing the roots of the characteristic polynomial of $\mathbf{C}$ as shown in Eq. (3) gives the knowledge of m and r. However, the attacker can not differentiate which eigenvalue corresponds to the exact message m. I.e. by computing only the eigenvalues of $\mathbf{C}$, the attacker can find m with 50% confidence. Hence, the next task is identifying which eigenvalue (λ_1 or λ_2) corresponds to m with 100% confidence. Assume the secret matrix and its inverse are $\mathbf{S} = \begin{bmatrix} s_{0,0} & s_{0,1} \\ s_{1,0} & s_{1,1} \end{bmatrix}$ and $\mathbf{S}^{-1} = \frac{1}{\Delta}\begin{bmatrix} s_{1,1} & -s_{0,1} \\ -s_{1,0} & s_{0,0} \end{bmatrix}$, respectively, where $\Delta = (s_{0,0} \times s_{1,1}) - (s_{0,1} \times s_{1,0})$. Let $\mathbf{C} = \begin{bmatrix} c_{0,0} & c_{0,1} \\ c_{1,0} & c_{1,1} \end{bmatrix}$ be the ciphertext matrix corresponding to the message m and input matrix $\mathbf{M} = \begin{bmatrix} m & 0 \\ 0 & r \end{bmatrix}$. Then $\mathbf{C} = \mathbf{S} \times \mathbf{M} \times \mathbf{S}^{-1}$ can be written as in Eq. (4). In Eq. (4),

$$x = \frac{s_{0,0} \times s_{1,1}}{\Delta}, y = \frac{-s_{0,1} \times s_{1,0}}{\Delta}, a = \frac{-s_{0,1} \times s_{0,0}}{\Delta} \text{ and } b = \frac{s_{1,0} \times s_{1,1}}{\Delta}$$

$$\begin{bmatrix} c_{0,0} & c_{0,1} \\ c_{1,0} & c_{1,1} \end{bmatrix} = \begin{bmatrix} s_{0,0} & s_{0,1} \\ s_{1,0} & s_{1,1} \end{bmatrix} \times \begin{bmatrix} m & 0 \\ 0 & r \end{bmatrix} \times \frac{1}{\Delta}\begin{bmatrix} s_{1,1} & -s_{0,1} \\ -s_{1,0} & s_{0,0} \end{bmatrix}$$

$$= \begin{bmatrix} x \times m + y \times r & a \times m - a \times r \\ b \times m - b \times r & y \times m + x \times r \end{bmatrix} \tag{4}$$

Since, $\Delta = (s_{0,0} \times s_{1,1}) - (s_{0,1} \times s_{1,0})$, we have

$$x + y = 1 \tag{5}$$

From Eq. (4), we have

$$x \times m + y \times r = c_{0,0} \tag{6}$$

$$y \times m + x \times r = c_{1,1} \tag{7}$$

The attacker collects more ciphertexts and solves Eq. (3) for the corresponding eigenvalues λ_1 and λ_2. Assuming λ_1 and λ_2 corresponds to m and r, respectively, find $x = \frac{s_{0,0} \times s_{1,1}}{\Delta}$ and $y = \frac{-s_{0,1} \times s_{1,0}}{\Delta}$ by solving Eq. (6) and Eq. (7). Let x' and y' denotes the solutions for x and y, respectively. The solution of the message that results in $x = x'$ and $y = y'$ is placed in Group-1.

Similarly, assuming λ_2 and λ_1 corresponds to m and r, respectively, find x and y by solving Eq. (6) and Eq. (7). Let x'' and y'' denotes the solutions for x and y, respectively. The solution of the message that results in $x = x''$ and $y = y''$ is placed in Group-2. For the n number of ciphertexts, group the solutions in Eq. (3) that corresponds to x' and y' into single group (Group-1) and other solution to Group-2. The attacker needs to find which group corresponds to health data m.

As the health data can be easily differentiated from random numbers by the nature of the data values, the attacker can find the group corresponding to the health data. E.g., medical data values may be within a range of values/medical data values may be correlated over time [20] or medical data has a normal distribution/skewed Distributions/bimodal Distributions [21–24]. In contrast, random numbers which are distributed uniformly are random in nature and will not repeat for a long period [25–27]). If the attacker possesses some a priori information on health data, such as the health data has two possibilities (e.g., Thyroid surgery status: True or False [20]), then the attacker can mount this attack with two ciphertexts. If there is no a priori information on health data, the attacker can apply the Chi-squared test [28] on Group-1 and Group-2 to check which group is uniformly distributed. The uniformly distributed group corresponds to random numbers, and the other group corresponds to health data.

Grouping messages and random values is possible as the encryption function does not randomize the message m and input matrix $\mathbf{M}$ is a diagonal matrix. After getting sufficient ciphertexts, an attacker can group the solutions into two groups and find the group corresponding to the message by analyzing the nature of the data. Then, the attacker can select one message m and corresponding ciphertext $\mathbf{C}$. After choosing the message m and corresponding ciphertext $\mathbf{C}$, the attacker needs to solve for a single unknown from a single equation so that the attacker can deduce new messages from the new ciphertexts as in [18] as follows: Assume $\mathbf{D} = \begin{bmatrix} d_{0,0} & d_{0,1} \\ d_{1,0} & d_{1,1} \end{bmatrix}$ and $\mathbf{S} = \mathbf{D}^{-1}$. From Lemma 2.1 in Sect. 2.2,

we have $\mathbf{D} = \begin{bmatrix} d_{0,0} & d_{0,1} \\ d_{1,0} & d_{1,1} \end{bmatrix} = \begin{bmatrix} d_{0,0} & 0 \\ 0 & d_{1,1} \end{bmatrix} \times \begin{bmatrix} 1 & \dfrac{d_{0,1}}{d_{0,0}} \\ \dfrac{d_{1,0}}{d_{1,1}} & 1 \end{bmatrix}$. Then, $\mathbf{C} = \mathbf{S} \times \mathbf{M} \times$

$\mathbf{S}^{-1} = \mathbf{D}^{-1} \times \mathbf{M} \times \mathbf{D}$ can be written as

$$
\begin{bmatrix} c_{0,0} & c_{0,1} \\ c_{1,0} & c_{1,1} \end{bmatrix} =
$$

$$
\begin{bmatrix} 1 & \dfrac{d_{0,1}}{d_{0,0}} \\ \dfrac{d_{1,0}}{d_{1,1}} & 1 \end{bmatrix}^{-1} \times \begin{bmatrix} d_{0,0} & 0 \\ 0 & d_{1,1} \end{bmatrix}^{-1} \times \begin{bmatrix} m & 0 \\ 0 & r \end{bmatrix}
$$

$$
\times \begin{bmatrix} d_{0,0} & 0 \\ 0 & d_{1,1} \end{bmatrix} \times \begin{bmatrix} 1 & \dfrac{d_{0,1}}{d_{0,0}} \\ \dfrac{d_{1,0}}{d_{1,1}} & 1 \end{bmatrix}
\tag{8}
$$

As diagonal matrices commute [18] (Lemma 2.2 in Sect. 2.2), Eq. (8) can be re-written as

$$
\begin{bmatrix} c_{0,0} & c_{0,1} \\ c_{1,0} & c_{1,1} \end{bmatrix} = \begin{bmatrix} 1 & \dfrac{d_{0,1}}{d_{0,0}} \\ \dfrac{d_{1,0}}{d_{1,1}} & 1 \end{bmatrix}^{-1} \times \begin{bmatrix} m & 0 \\ 0 & r \end{bmatrix} \times \begin{bmatrix} 1 & \dfrac{d_{0,1}}{d_{0,0}} \\ \dfrac{d_{1,0}}{d_{1,1}} & 1 \end{bmatrix}
\tag{9}
$$

From, Eq. (9), we have

$$
\begin{bmatrix} 1 & \dfrac{d_{0,1}}{d_{0,0}} \\ \dfrac{d_{1,0}}{d_{1,1}} & 1 \end{bmatrix} \times \begin{bmatrix} c_{0,0} & c_{0,1} \\ c_{1,0} & c_{1,1} \end{bmatrix} = \begin{bmatrix} m & 0 \\ 0 & r \end{bmatrix} \times \begin{bmatrix} 1 & \dfrac{d_{0,1}}{d_{0,0}} \\ \dfrac{d_{1,0}}{d_{1,1}} & 1 \end{bmatrix}
\tag{10}
$$

From, Eq. (10), we have

$$
m = c_{0,0} + c_{1,0} \times \frac{d_{0,1}}{d_{0,0}}
\tag{11}
$$

Since, $\mathbf{S} = \mathbf{D}^{-1}$, $\dfrac{d_{0,1}}{d_{0,0}} = -\dfrac{s_{0,1}}{s_{1,1}}$. Equation (11) can be re-written as follows

$$
m = c_{0,0} - c_{1,0} \times \frac{s_{0,1}}{s_{1,1}}
\tag{12}
$$

I.e., once the value of m is fixed from the corresponding ciphertext based on the nature of the data in Group-1 and Group-2, Eq. (10) can be solved for getting $\dfrac{s_{0,1}}{s_{1,1}}$. After getting the ratio $\dfrac{s_{0,1}}{s_{1,1}}$, the attacker can find the message from the next received ciphertext using Eq. (12). The proposed ciphertext-only attack also applies to the MORE encryption scheme, where every computation involves modular reduction by a known large integer (L). As most of the health data are small values compared to L, based on the theorem of Coppersmith in [29], it is possible to find the square root   mod L in polynomial time $(log(L))$ for $m < \sqrt{L}$, which is required for the proposed ciphertext-only attack.

Algorithm 1 elaborates on the proposed ciphertext-only attack. After getting the secret $\dfrac{s_{0,1}}{s_{1,1}}$, from the ciphertext $\begin{bmatrix} c_{0,0_{n+1}} & c_{0,1_{n+1}} \\ c_{1,0_{n+1}} & c_{1,1_{n+1}} \end{bmatrix}$ the corresponding plaintext m_{n+1} can be found as $m_{n+1} = c_{0,0_{n+1}} - c_{1,0_{n+1}} \times \dfrac{s_{0,1}}{s_{1,1}}$.

v-MORE encryption can not provide security if used in healthcare applications, as it is susceptible to a ciphertext-only attack. Therefore, the v-MORE encryption scheme needs to be modified to resist the proposed ciphertext-only attack.

Algorithm 1. Proposed Ciphertext-only Attack

1: **Input:** ciphertexts $C_i = \begin{bmatrix} c_{0,0_i} & c_{0,1_i} \\ c_{1,0_i} & c_{1,1_i} \end{bmatrix}$, where $1 \leq i \leq n$ and maximum value of n is 30.

2: **For i =1 to n do**
Solve for λ_i from characteristic equation of the ciphertext matrix C_i, $\lambda_i^2 - (c_{0,0_i} + c_{1,1_i}) \times \lambda_i + (c_{0,0_i} \times c_{1,1_i} - c_{0,1_i} \times c_{1,0_i}) = 0$, using quadratic formula. Let

$$\lambda_1 = \frac{(c_{0,0_i} + c_{1,1_i})}{2} + \frac{\sqrt{(c_{0,0_i} + c_{1,1_i})^2 - 4 \times (c_{0,0_i} \times c_{1,1_i} - c_{0,1_i} \times c_{1,0_i})}}{2}$$

and

$$\lambda_2 = \frac{(c_{0,0_i} + c_{1,1_i})}{2} - \frac{\sqrt{(c_{0,0_i} + c_{1,1_i})^2 - 4 \times (c_{0,0_i} \times c_{1,1_i} - c_{0,1_i} \times c_{1,0_i})}}{2}$$

End For

3: Solve for x and y in equations $x \times m_1 + y \times r_1 = c_{0,0_1}$ (refer Eq. (6)) and $y \times m_1 + x \times r_1 = c_{1,1_1}$ (refer Eq. (7)) by putting λ_1 as m_1 and λ_2 as r_1. Let x' and y' denotes the solutions for x and y, respectively. The solution of the message that results in $x = x'$ and $y = y'$ is placed in Group 1. Here, λ_1 goes to Group-1.

4: Solve for x and y in equations $x \times m_1 + y \times r_1 = c_{0,0_1}$ and $y \times m_1 + x \times r_1 = c_{1,1_1}$ by putting λ_2 as m_1 and λ_1 as r_1. Let x'' and y'' denotes the solutions for x and y, respectively. The solution of the message that results in $x = x''$ and $y = y''$ is placed in Group 2. Here, λ_2 goes to Group-2.

5: **For i =2 to n do**
Put the eigenvalue (λ_1 or λ_2) that gives $x = x'$ and $y = y'$ by solving the equations $x \times m_i + y \times r_i = c_{0,0_i}$ and $y \times m_i + x \times r_i = c_{1,1_i}$ to Group-1 and the other solution to Group-2.
End For

6: **If** There is no a priori information on health data, the attacker can apply the Chi-squared test [28] on Group-1 and Group-2 to check which group is uniformly distributed. The uniformly distributed group corresponds to random numbers, and the other group corresponds to plaintext messages.
Else Based on the a priori information on the health data, find the group corresponding to the plaintext messages.

7: Choose solution of m_1 from the group that corresponds to the messages and the respective $c_{0,0_1}$ and $c_{1,0_1}$, solve for $\frac{s_{0,1}}{s_{1,1}}$ from $m_1 = c_{0,0_1} - c_{1,0_1} \times \frac{s_{0,1}}{s_{1,1}}$

8: **Output:** $\frac{s_{0,1}}{s_{1,1}}$

---

5 Proposed Additively Homomorphic Encryption on Real Numbers (AHE-R)

It should be remarked that the ciphertext-only attack mentioned in Sect. 4.1 is possible since the input matrix **M** is diagonal and m is not randomized while constructing the **M**. If the construction of input matrix is modified as

$\mathbf{M} = \begin{bmatrix} (m + r_1 \times u) & r_2 \\ r_3 & r_4 \end{bmatrix}$, where r_1, r_2, r_3 and r_4 are random numbers, and u is a constant prime number, ciphertext-only-attack mentioned in Sect. 4.1 can be mitigated. The modified scheme is additively homomorphic: it can support homomorphic addition, homomorphic constant addition and homomorphic constant multiplication. Also, the decryption function involves modular operation on the $(0,0)^{th}$ element of $\mathbf{S}^{-1} \times \mathbf{C} \times \mathbf{S}$ by u to get m. Hence, the following functions are involved in the proposed Additively Homomorphic Encryption on Real Numbers (AHE-R).

- KeyGen(κ, $\mathbb{M}$): The function KeyGen() takes κ (security parameter) and $\mathbb{M}$ (message space) as inputs and generates a secret key matrix $\mathbf{S} \in \mathbb{R}^{2 \times 2}$ such that determinant of $\mathbf{S} \neq 0$. $\mathbf{S}$ is an invertible matrix. It also generates a prime number u such that $\mathbb{M} << u$. $\mathbf{S}$ and u are kept as secret.
- Enc(m, $\mathbf{S}$, u): Accepts secret keys ($\mathbf{S}$ and u) and the message $m \in \mathbb{R}$ and $\left\lfloor -\dfrac{u}{2} \right\rfloor < m < \left\lfloor \dfrac{u}{2} \right\rfloor$ to be encrypted as inputs. Choose four random numbers r_1 in $\in \mathbb{Z}$ and r_2, r_3 and r_4 in $\in \mathbb{R}$. Then an input 2×2 matrix is created as $\mathbf{M} = \begin{bmatrix} (m + r_1 \times u) & r_2 \\ r_3 & r_4 \end{bmatrix}$. The ciphertext matrix $\mathbf{C}$ is computed as $\mathbf{C} = \mathbf{S} \times \mathbf{M} \times \mathbf{S}^{-1}$.
- Dec($\mathbf{C}$, $\mathbf{S}$, u): This function takes the ciphertext matrix $\mathbf{C}$ and secret keys ($\mathbf{S}$ and u) as inputs. The message (m) is computed as $(((0,0)^{th}$ element of $\mathbf{S}^{-1} \times \mathbf{C} \times \mathbf{S}))$ $fmod\ u$.

$fmod$ is the modular operation on real numbers. $x\ fmod\ y = x - (\left\lfloor \dfrac{x}{y} \right\rfloor \times y)$.
I.e., by performing $((m + r_1 \times u))\ fmod\ u$, random number r_1 will be removed from m without storing r_1.

5.1   Homomorphic Properties

Homomorphic properties of AHE-R can be verified using matrix algebra. Assume $\mathbf{C}_1 = \mathbf{S} \times \mathbf{M}_1 \times \mathbf{S}^{-1}$ and $\mathbf{C}_2 = \mathbf{S} \times \mathbf{M}_2 \times \mathbf{S}^{-1}$ are AHE-R ciphertexts corresponding to m_1 and m_2, respectively, where $\mathbf{M}_1 = \begin{bmatrix} (m_1 + r_{11} \times u) & r_{21} \\ r_{31} & r_{41} \end{bmatrix}$ and $\mathbf{M}_2 = \begin{bmatrix} (m_2 + r_{12} \times u) & r_{22} \\ r_{32} & r_{42} \end{bmatrix}$.

- Homomorphic addition: AHE-R encryption of $m_1 + m_2$ can be computed as in Eq. (13)

$$\mathbf{C}_1 + \mathbf{C}_2 = \mathbf{S} \times \mathbf{M}_1 \times \mathbf{S}^{-1} + \mathbf{S} \times \mathbf{M}_2 \times \mathbf{S}^{-1} = \mathbf{S} \times (\mathbf{M}_1 + \mathbf{M}_2) \times \mathbf{S}^{-1} \quad (13)$$

- Homomorphic constant addition: AHE-R encryption of $a + m_1$ can be computed as addition of scalar matrix with a as diagonal elements ($\mathbf{A} = \begin{bmatrix} a & 0 \\ 0 & a \end{bmatrix}$) and $\mathbf{C}_1$ as in Eq. (14), where a is a scalar.

$$\mathbf{C}_1 + \mathbf{A} = \mathbf{S} \times \mathbf{M}_1 \times \mathbf{S}^{-1} + \mathbf{A} \quad (14)$$

- Homomorphic constant multiplication: AHE-R encryption of $a \times m_1$ can be computed as multiplication of scalar matrix with a as diagonal elements ($\mathbf{A} = \begin{bmatrix} a & 0 \\ 0 & a \end{bmatrix}$) and $\mathbf{C}_1$ as in Eq. (15), where a is a scalar.

$$\mathbf{C}_1 \times \mathbf{A} = \mathbf{S} \times \mathbf{M}_1 \times \mathbf{S}^{-1} \times \mathbf{A} \tag{15}$$

Similarly, $\mathbf{C}_1 - \mathbf{C}_2$ gives the AHE-R encryption of m_1- m_2.

6   Security Analysis of AHE-R

The security of the proposed AHE-R is determined in terms of the complexity of solving for the message (m) provided ciphertext matrix $\mathbf{C}$. Solving for m from ciphertext matrix $\mathbf{C}$ requires the computation of the secret matrix $\mathbf{S}$ and secret prime u. As a result, the security of AHE-R relies on the difficulty in solving u and $\mathbf{S}$. Let the size of elements of $\mathbf{S}$ be l_s-bits, and the size of prime numbers u be l_u-bits. The number of primes with maximum size l is approximately, $d_l = \dfrac{2^l - 1}{ln(2^l - 1)}$ [30]. The following section examines the security of the proposed AHE-R against ciphertext-only attacks and known-plaintext attacks.

6.1   Ciphertext-Only Attacks

In this attack, the proposed ciphertext-only attack in Sect. 4.1 is not possible since the eigenvalues of $\mathbf{C}$ do not correspond to the message as the input matrix ($\mathbf{M}$) is not a diagonal matrix and message m is randomized. In AHE-R, eigenvalues, trace and determinant of $\mathbf{C}$ and $\mathbf{M}$ are the same since $\mathbf{C}$ and $\mathbf{M}$ are similar matrices. The eigenvalues depend on trace and determinant, as shown in Eq. (16).

$$\lambda = \frac{Tr(\mathbf{C})}{2} \pm \frac{\sqrt{(Tr(\mathbf{C}))^2 + 4 \times Det(\mathbf{C})}}{2} = \frac{Tr(\mathbf{M})}{2} \pm \frac{\sqrt{(Tr(\mathbf{M}))^2 + 4 \times Det(\mathbf{M})}}{2} \tag{16}$$

$Tr(\mathbf{C}) = Tr(\mathbf{M})$ and $Det(\mathbf{C}) = Det(\mathbf{M})$ in Eq. (16) is given in Eq. (17) and Eq. (18), respectively.

$$Tr(\mathbf{C}) = Tr(\mathbf{M}) = (m + r_1 \times u) + r_4 \tag{17}$$

$$Det(\mathbf{C}) = Det(\mathbf{M}) = ((m + r_1 \times u) \times r_4) - (r_2 \times r_3) \tag{18}$$

With known $Tr(\mathbf{C})$ and $Det(\mathbf{C})$, the attacker has two equations with six unknowns. Hence attacker cannot solve for m from Eq. (17) and Eq. (18) as number of unknowns is more than two. Hence, the brute force method is a possible way to retrieve secrets. With the known ciphertexts, the attackers try all possible combinations of keys $\mathbf{S}$ and u until the correct key is achieved. The effective keyspace, which reflects the possibilities of $\mathbf{S}$ and u, determines the robustness of the proposed AHE-R against brute force attacks. As a result, the overall number of trials needed for discovering secrets ($\mathbf{S}$ and u) is ($p_{l_s} \times p_{l_s} \times p_{l_s} \times p_{l_s} \times d_{l_u}$) where p_{l_s} and d_{l_u} are the number of possibilities of elements of $\mathbf{S}$ with size l_s bits and u of size l_u bits, respectively. As a result, the attack complexity is 2^{139} if l_s, and l_u are 25-bits and 45-bits, respectively.

6.2 Known-Plaintext Attacks

The known-plaintext attack (KPA) mentioned in [17,18] for attacking MORE encryption, which can be applied to v-MORE, will not break the proposed AHE-R. The known-plaintext attack mentioned in [18] against v-MORE is possible since input matrix $\mathbf{M}$ is diagonal and m is a diagonal element of $\mathbf{M}$. Authors in [18] utilized Lemma 2 related to the diagonal matrix to attack MORE/v-MORE. However, KPA in [18] cannot be applied to the proposed AHE-R since the input matrix $\mathbf{M}$ is not a diagonal matrix. When we apply this KPA on AHE-R, we get (Eq. (19)), where $\mathbf{D} = \begin{bmatrix} d_{0,0} & d_{0,1} \\ d_{1,0} & d_{1,1} \end{bmatrix}$ and $\mathbf{S} = \mathbf{D}^{-1}$.

$$\begin{bmatrix} c_{0,0} & c_{0,1} \\ c_{1,0} & c_{1,1} \end{bmatrix} =$$

$$\begin{bmatrix} 1 & \frac{d_{0,1}}{d_{0,0}} \\ \frac{d_{1,0}}{d_{1,1}} & 1 \end{bmatrix}^{-1} \times \begin{bmatrix} d_{0,0} & 0 \\ 0 & d_{1,1} \end{bmatrix}^{-1} \times \begin{bmatrix} (m + r_1 \times u) & (r_2 \times u) \\ r_3 & r_4 \end{bmatrix}$$

$$\times \begin{bmatrix} d_{0,0} & 0 \\ 0 & d_{1,1} \end{bmatrix} \times \begin{bmatrix} 1 & \frac{d_{0,1}}{d_{0,0}} \\ \frac{d_{1,0}}{d_{1,1}} & 1 \end{bmatrix} \tag{19}$$

From Eq. (19), it is evident that Lemma 2 cannot be used to cancel $\begin{bmatrix} 1 & \frac{d_{0,1}}{d_{0,0}} \\ \frac{d_{1,0}}{d_{1,1}} & 1 \end{bmatrix}^{-1}$ and $\begin{bmatrix} 1 & \frac{d_{0,1}}{d_{0,0}} \\ \frac{d_{1,0}}{d_{1,1}} & 1 \end{bmatrix}$ since $\mathbf{M}$ is not a diagonal matrix.

The attack mentioned in [17] finds the eigenvector (v) of a ciphertext matrix which corresponds to encryption of zero and uses the eigenvector v to solve for m from the ciphertext matrix $\mathbf{C}$ from the following relation $\mathbf{C} \times v = m \times v$. In MORE and v-MORE, the relation $\mathbf{C} \times v = m \times v$ holds because m is an eigenvalue of $\mathbf{C}$. However, in the proposed AHE-R, m is not an eigenvalue of $\mathbf{C}$ since $\mathbf{M}$ is not a diagonal matrix in AHE-R. Hence, in the proposed AHE-R, the above relation does not hold, i.e., $\mathbf{C} \times v \neq m \times v$ and the attack proposed in [17] cannot break AHE-R.

In a KPA with known $Tr(\mathbf{C})$, $Det(\mathbf{C})$ and m in Eq. (17) and Eq. (18), the attacker cannot find the secret u since u cannot be solved from two equations with five unknowns. Even if the attacker possesses more known plaintext-ciphertext pairs, the number of equations will be lesser than the number of unknowns since each input matrix is associated with four random numbers. Also, these random numbers are different for different input matrices.

When an attacker gets AHE-R ciphertext-plaintext pairs, the attacker can perform the following KPA to get the secret keys of AHE-R. The KPA against AHE-R attempts to retrieve the secret matrix $\mathbf{S}$ and the secret prime u based on known m and $\mathbf{C}$. As given in Sect. 5, the message m corresponding to the ciphertext matrix $\mathbf{C}$ is computed as in Eq. (20)). Hence, by solving Eq. (20) for all possible values of $\mathbf{S}$ and u, the KPA may reveal true secrets from the known m and $\mathbf{C}$.

$$m_i = ((\mathbf{S}^{-1} \times \mathbf{C} \times \mathbf{S})_{0,0}) \ fmod \ u \tag{20}$$

The steps in KPA are described as follows:

1. Select a message m and its corresponding AHE-R ciphertext $\mathbf{C}$.
2. Predict a possible set of secret matrix $\mathbf{S}$ and prime number u.
3. Substitute u and $\mathbf{S}$ in the Eq. (20) and check if the right-hand side equals the message m.
4. Repeat the previous step for all possible values of u and $\mathbf{S}$ until the equation holds true.
5. The values of u and $\mathbf{S}$ that satisfy the Eq. (20) are the true secret parameters of AHE-R.

In AHE-R, u is having d_{l_u} possibilities and $\mathbf{S}$ is having $(p_{l_s} \times p_{l_s} \times p_{l_s} \times p_{l_s})$ possibilities. Therefore, the maximum trails to get true secret parameters of AHE-R ($\mathbf{S}$ and u) are $(p_{l_s} \times p_{l_s} \times p_{l_s} \times p_{l_s} * d_{l_u})$. The minimum trails to get true secret parameters $\mathbf{S}$ and u are one. Hence, on average, an attacker needs to try $(p_{l_s} \times p_{l_s} \times p_{l_s} \times p_{l_s} * d_{l_u} + 1)/2$ possibilities. Therefore, the total keyspace for KPA is approximately equal to $(p_{l_s} \times p_{l_s} \times p_{l_s} \times p_{l_s} * d_{l_u})/2$. Therefore, the KPA attack complexity is 2^{138} if l_s, and l_u are 25-bits and 45-bits, respectively.

7   Experimental Analysis

Experimental analysis is performed to evaluate the time complexity of the proposed ciphertext-only attack. Also, the computational complexity of the proposed AHE-R is compared with that of v-MORE [9,12] and additively homomorphic Paillier [8] used in privacy-preserving ML [2]. An Intel(R) Core(TM) i7-1355U with 1.7 GHz operating frequency and 16 GB memory is used for conducting experiments.

7.1   Time Complexity Analysis of Proposed Ciphertext-only Attack

The medical data sets available in the UCI [20] repository and PhysioNet [31] are used to analyze the proposed ciphertext-only attack's time complexity. The considered secret matrix sizes of v-MORE are 128 bits and 256 bits. Table 1 shows the time complexity of the proposed ciphertext-only attack with a priori information on health data. Thyroid surgery health data from [32] has two possible

Table 1. Time complexity of proposed ciphertext-only attack with a priori information on health data

Secret size	Health Data	Number of ciphertexts	Nature of data utilized for differentiating Group-1 and Group-2	Time μs
128-bits	Thyroid surgery [32]	3	Health data has two possibilities (False True)	85.5
	Resting blood pressure [33]	10	correlated and within a range	280.8
256-bits	Thyroid surgery [32]	3	Health data has possibilities (False or True)	93.72
	Resting blood pressure [33]	10	correlated and within a range	307.99

Table 2. Time complexity of proposed ciphertext-only attack without a priori information on health data

Health Data	Secret size	Number of ciphertexts	Nature of data utilized for differentiating Group-1 and Group-2	Time μs
ECG [31]	128-bits	30	Random numbers show Uniform distribution	1911
	256-bits	30	Random numbers shows Uniform distribution	1992.39

values (False or True). With this a priori information, the attacker can differentiate between messages and random numbers after solving Eq. (3) as given in Sect. 4.1 since health data has only two possibilities. Hence, if the attacker gets a minimum of two ciphertexts, he can do the proposed ciphertext-only attack. Also, ten ciphertexts corresponding to resting blood pressure health data from [33] are considered since resting blood pressure values are correlated over time and come within a range of values. After solving ten equations corresponding to ten ciphertexts, an attacker can differentiate message and random numbers and successfully mount the proposed ciphertext-only attack.

Table 2 shows the time complexity of the proposed ciphertext-only attack without a priori information on health data. For analyzing the time complexity of the proposed ciphertext-only attack without a priori information on health data, ECG data from [31] is considered. As ECG is represented using 500 data points per second instead of a priori information, the statistical property of random number, as discussed in Sect. 4.1, is considered. By applying the Chi-squared test [28] on 30 data values obtained after solving 30 equations corresponding to 30 ciphertexts, an attacker can differentiate health data and random numbers and hence break the v-MORE security.

The time required for solving Eq. (3) once is 27.9 µs and 30.61 µs for a secret size of 128-bits and 256-bits, respectively. Also, the time required for a Chi-squared test with 30 values is 1072.2 µs. Table 1 and Table 2 show that time complexity is only in µs, and variation in time complexity with increased key size is small. Hence, v-MORE can be attacked with a low-capacity computing system.

7.2   Performance Analysis of Proposed AHE-R

Table 3 shows encryption time, decryption time and ciphertext size for proposed AHE-R, v-MORE [9,12] and Paillier [8]. For 128-bit security, in AHE-R, the elements of the secret matrix S and prime number u are selected as 29-bits and 33-bits, respectively. Both AHE-R and v-MORE show low computational complexity and ciphertext size, and AHE-R shows a slight increase in the computational time and ciphertext size compared to v-MORE. AHE-R is additively homomorphic, whereas v-MORE is fully homomorphic. However, v-MORE could not provide any security as it is vulnerable to ciphertext-only attacks. Hence, v-MORE cannot be used to secure data in privacy-preserving applications. Though AHE-R is additively homomorphic and shows a slight increase in computational and communication overhead, it can support privacy-preserving applications which require additive homomorphism and data security, such as secure data aggregation and secure ML. Also, AHE-R is compared with Paillier [8], additive homomorphic encryption used in privacy-preserving ML [2]. From Table 3, it is evident that the computational time and ciphertext size of Paillier for 128-bit security are significantly greater than that of the proposed AHE-R since Pailllier is a public-key-based scheme.

Table 3. Performance comparison of the proposed AHE-R with schemes in [8,9,12]

Encryption	Security (bit)	Homomorphism	Encryption Time (µs)	Decryption	Ciphertext Size (bits)
Proposed AHE-R	128	Additive	33.5	19	404
v-MORE [9,12]	No security	Additive and multiplicative	22.1	18.5	336
Paillier [8]	128	Additive	35942.5	1218.7	6144

8   Conclusion

This paper outlines a ciphertext-only attack to break the v-MORE encryption used in outsourced privacy-preserving healthcare applications based on linear algebra. The experimental analysis shows that v-MORE can be broken even with a computing system with low computing capacity. Hence, v-MORE cannot be used in privacy-preserving outsourced medical applications where medical data can be differentiated from random numbers generated from secure random number generators. This paper also proposes a secure additively homomorphic matrix-based encryption scheme on real numbers, AHE-R, to mitigate the security vulnerabilities in v-MORE. The proposed AHE-R can resist ciphertext-only attacks and known-plaintext attacks. As AHE-R's encryption and decryption times are in the range of microseconds and the ciphertext size is a few hundred bits, it is suitable for resource-constrained devices in healthcare applications. As AHE-R supports only additive homomorphism, it may be modified to support both additive and multiplicative homomorphism by redesigning the input matrix in AHE-R without introducing security vulnerability.

References

1. Sun, X., Zhang, P., Liu, J.K., Yu, J., Xie, W.: Private machine learning classification based on fully homomorphic encryption. IEEE Trans. Emerg. Top. Comput. **8**(2), 352–364 (2018)
2. Bost, R., Popa, R.A., Tu, S., Goldwasser, S.: Machine learning classification over encrypted data. In: Network and Distributed System Security Symposium 2015, San Diego, California, pp. 1–14 (2015)
3. Brakerski, Z., Gentry, C., Vaikuntanathan, V.: (Leveled) fully homomorphic encryption without bootstrapping. In: Proceedings of the 3rd Innovations in Theoretical Computer Science Conference, pp. 309–325. ACM (2012)
4. Alex, S., Dhanaraj, K.J., Deepthi, P.P.: Privacy-preserving and energy-saving random forest-based disease detection framework for green Internet of Things in mobile healthcare networks. IEEE Trans. Dependable Secure Comput. **21**(4), 4180–4192 (2024). https://doi.org/10.1109/TDSC.2023.3347342
5. Ma, Z., et al.: Lightweight privacy-preserving medical diagnosis in edge computing. IEEE Trans. Serv. Comput. **15**(3), 1606–1618 (2022). https://doi.org/10.1109/TSC.2020.3004627
6. Ma, Z., Ma, J., Miao, Y., Liu, X.: Privacy-preserving and high-accurate outsourced disease predictor on random forest. Inf. Sci. **496**, 225–241 (2019)
7. Liu, X., Deng, R.H., Choo, K.R., Yang, Y.: Privacy-preserving outsourced clinical decision support system in the cloud. IEEE Trans. Serv. Comput. **14**(1), 222–234 (2021)
8. Paillier, P.: Public-key cryptosystems based on composite degree residuosity classes. In: Stern, J. (ed.) EUROCRYPT 1999. LNCS, vol. 1592, pp. 223–238. Springer, Heidelberg (1999). https://doi.org/10.1007/3-540-48910-X_16
9. Vizitiu, A., Nita, C.I., Puiu, A., Suciu, C., Itu, L.: Applying deep neural networks over homomorphic encrypted medical data. Comput. Math. Methods Med. (2020). https://doi.org/10.1155/2020/3910250
10. Trappe, W., Howard, R., Moore, R.S.: Low-energy security: limits and opportunities in the internet of things. IEEE Secur. Priv. **13**(1), 14–21 (2015)
11. Kaur, M., Singh, D., Kumar, V., Gupta, B.B., Abd El-Latif, A.A.: Secure and energy-efficient e-health care framework for green Internet of Things. IEEE Trans. Green Commun. Netw. **5**(3), 1223–1231 (2021). https://doi.org/10.1109/TGCN.2021.3081616

12. Vizitiu, A., Nita, C.I., Toev, R.M., Suditu, T., Suciu, C., Itu, L.M.: Framework for privacy-preserving wearable health data analysis: Proof-of-concept study for atrial fibrillation detection. Appl. Sci. **11** (2021). https://doi.org/10.3390/app11199049

13. Lakshmi, V.S., Deepthi, S., Deepthi, P.P.: Collusion-resistant secret sharing scheme for secure data storage and processing over cloud. J. Inf. Secur. Appl. **60**, 2214–2126 (2021). https://doi.org/10.1016/j.jisa.2021.102869

14. Alex, S., Dhanaraj, K.J., Deepthi, P.P.: Private and energy-efficient decision tree-based disease detection for resource-constrained medical users in mobile healthcare network. IEEE Access **10**, 17098–17112 (2022). https://doi.org/10.1109/ACCESS.2022.3149771

15. Kipnis, A., Hibshoosh, E.: Efficient methods for practical fully homomorphic symmetric-key encryption, randomization, and verification. IACR Cryptology ePrint Arch. **2012**, 637 (2012)

16. Wang, B., Zhan, Y., Zhang, Z.: Cryptanalysis of a symmetric fully homomorphic encryption scheme. IEEE Trans. Inf. Forensics Secur. **13**(6), 1460–1467 (2018)

17. Vizar, D., Vaudenay, S.: Cryptanalysis of chosen symmetric homomorphic schemes. In: Proceedings of CRYPTO 2014, Santa Barbara, CA, USA (2014)

18. Tsaban, B., Lifshitz, N.: Cryptanalysis of the more symmetric key fully homomorphic encryption scheme. J. Math. Cryptol. **9**(2), 75–78 (2014)

19. Goldreich, O.: Foundations of Cryptography, Volume II: Basic Applications. Cambridge University Press, Cambridge (2004)

20. UCI Machine Learning Repository. https://archive.ics.uci.edu/ml/index.php. Accessed 14 Jun 2024

21. Bland, M.: An Introduction to Medical Statistics. Oxford University Press (2015)

22. Altman, D.G., Bland, J.M.: Statistics notes: the normal distribution. BMJ **308** (1995)

23. Kirkwood, B.R., Sterne, J.A.C.: Essential Medical Statistics, 2nd edn. Blackwell Science (2003)

24. Campbell, M.J., Machin, D., Walters, S.J.: Medical Statistics: A Textbook for the Health Sciences. Wiley (2007)

25. Aljohani, M., Ahmad, I., Basheri, M., Alassafi, M.O.: Performance analysis of cryptographic pseudorandom number generators. IEEE Access **7**, 39794–39805 (2019). https://doi.org/10.1109/ACCESS.2019.2907079

26. Rock, A.: Pseudorandom Number Generators for Cryptographic Applications. Master's thesis, Paris-Lodron University, Salzburg (2005)

27. Ankur, Divyanjali, Pareek, V.: A new approach to pseudorandom number generation. In: 2014 Fourth International Conference on Advanced Computing & Communication Technologies, pp. 290–295. IEEE (2014). https://doi.org/10.1109/ACCT.2014.26

28. Pearson, K.X.: On the criterion that a given system of deviations from the probable in the case of a correlated system of variables is such that it can be reasonably supposed to have arisen from random sampling. Lond. Edinb. Dublin Philos. Mag. J. Sci. **50**, 157–175 (2009). https://doi.org/10.1080/14786440009463897

29. Don, C.: Small solutions to polynomial equations, and low exponent RSA vulnerabilities. J. Cryptol. **10**(4), 233–260 (1997)

30. How Many Primes are There? https://primes.utm.edu/howmany.html. Accessed 10 June 2024

31. Goldberger, A.L., Amaral, L.A., Glass, L., et al.: PhysioBank, PhysioToolkit, and PhysioNet: components of a new research resource for complex physiologic signals. Circulation **101**, E215–E220 (2000)
32. UCI Machine Learning Repository-Thyroid Disease. https://archive.ics.uci.edu/dataset/102/thyroid+disease. Accessed 14 June 2024
33. UCI Machine Learning Repository-Heart Disease. https://archive.ics.uci.edu/dataset/45/heart+disease. Accessed 14 June 2024

Author Index

© IFIP International Federation for Information Processing 2025
Published by Springer Nature Switzerland AG 2025
S. Katsikas and B. Shafiq (Eds.): DBSec 2025, LNCS 15722, pp. 457–458, 2025.
https://doi.org/10.1007/978-3-031-96590-6

The manufacturer's authorised representative in the EU is Springer
Nature Customer Service Centre GmbH, Europaplatz 3, 69115 Heidelberg,
Germany. If you have any concerns regarding our products, please
contact ProductSafety@springernature.com

Printed and bound by CPI Group (UK) Ltd, Croydon, CR0 4YY

28/04/2026

02098515-0008